GUIDE TO LIBRARIES IN LONDON

Compiled by
VALERIE McBURNEY
and PAUL WILSON

THE BRITISH LIBRARY

Guide to Libraries in London

ISBN 0-7123-0852-0

Published by:
The British Library
96 Euston Road
London NW1 2DB

2nd edition published 2004

British Library Cataloguing-in-Publication Data
A catalogue record for this book is available from The British Library

Typeset by Concerto, Leighton Buzzard, Bedfordshire.
Tel: 01525 378757

Printed in Great Britain by Antony Rowe Ltd

CONTENTS

LIST OF PHOTOGRAPHS

PREFACE

This is the second edition of *Guide to Libraries in London* published by the British Library. The *Guide* lists all types of library: public, academic and 'special' (i.e. libraries in companies, professional organisations, government departments, charities, pressure groups, etc.) located in 33 London boroughs.

List of boroughs covered by the *Guide*

Barking	Hackney	Lewisham
Barnet	Hammersmith and Fulham	Merton
Bexley	Haringey	Newham
Brent	Harrow	Redbridge
Bromley	Havering	Richmond upon Thames
Camden	Hillingdon	Southwark
Corporation of London	Hounslow	Sutton
Croydon	Islington	Tower Hamlets
Ealing	Kensington and Chelsea	Waltham Forest
Enfield	Kingston upon Thames	Wandsworth
Greenwich	Lambeth	City of Westminster

Inclusions policy

The *Guide* does not claim to be exhaustive in its coverage. The main emphasis is on libraries and information services offering some access to serious enquirers, although a number of libraries have been included which serve the needs of specific large user groups (such as members of a particular profession). Libraries which offer no 'outside' access or exist only to serve staff within an organisation have been excluded.

The directory focuses primarily on non-commercial information services although exceptions have been made for a few commercial libraries with particularly good collections in their subject area. Most of the libraries listed in this directory are not strictly commercial, but researchers should be aware that many libraries charge for access and/or for providing specialist information services. If in doubt, researchers should consult the library in advance to find out whether a charge will be made.

Although a few photographic collections are included, the *Guide*'s main emphasis is on book collections. The task of identifying potential entries was carried out by the compilers. The entries were compiled from information provided by the libraries themselves or from other published sources. Inevitably a number of organisations failed to reply, declined to be included or indicated that they were unable to accept any outside enquiries. However, a good proportion of those approached did supply the required details and their entries appear in the following pages.

How the *Guide* is arranged

A–Z List of Entries

The main body of the *Guide* consists of a single alphabetical* sequence of entries for the various organisations.

The entries are filed in word-by-word rather than letter-by-letter, thus Institut Français du Royaume Uni appears before Institute and Guild of Brewing. The *Guide* also includes three other sections to aid retrieval, these are: a listing of libraries by borough, an organisation index and a subject index. All the indexes refer to entry numbers **not** page numbers.

*See note on public library sub-entries under 'Understanding the entries' below.

Libraries Listed by Borough

The listing of libraries by borough helps the researcher to check which libraries are most conveniently located for home or work. The section includes a map of the 33 boroughs included in the *Guide* and separate maps for each of the boroughs to illustrate the area covered.

Organisation Index

Users looking for a specific organisation may need to refer to the Organisation Index to check the form of name used in the main alphabetic listing. This index makes extensive use of *see* references as many of the organisations listed are commonly known by more than one name or by an acronym. Entries in the *Guide* are listed under the name that has been indicated as the preferred name by the organisation concerned. Researchers who are unable to find an organisation under one form of name are advised to consult the Organisation Index to check they are looking for the entry under its preferred name.

Subject Index

The Subject Index provides a quick way for researchers to pinpoint entries relevant to their subject of interest. As with the other indexes it lists individual entry numbers and not page numbers.

Understanding the entries

Some libraries (most notably those in colleges of further education, government departments and other complex organisations) have a number of branch or sub-libraries. Where the organisation has provided detailed information on these libraries they have been listed as sub-entries numbered [a], [b], [c], etc. Where less detailed information has been given the entry simply refers to the branch libraries.

Libraries in the University of London have been listed separately rather than as sub-entries under one heading. An entry under 'University of London' lists the libraries included in the *Guide* and leads the researcher to the individual entries.

Users will note that not all entries have the same level of detail. Public libraries were asked to submit detailed information for their larger reference libraries and briefer entries for branch libraries. *In the public library entries the main libraries in each borough are listed first. Depending on the structure of library services in the borough, this entry may be followed by: other major libraries in the borough, then the smaller branch libraries in alphabetical order; or a more straightforward listing of all the branch libraries in alphabetic order.

The following example shows a typical 'ordinary' entry and explains the type of information listed under each heading.

Sample entry

---

[347]
Kenneth Ritchie Wimbledon Library
Wimbledon Lawn Tennis Museum
Church Road
Wimbledon
London SW19 5AE
Borough: Merton
Telephone: 020 8946 6131
Fax: 020 8944 6497
Constitution: Independent non-profit distributing   ←———— Type of organisation
    organisation and private venture
Objectives/purposes: To provide research facilities on the
    subject of lawn tennis
Key staff: Honorary Librarian: JA Little; Assistant
    Librarian: Miss Audrey Snell
Stock and subject coverage: Materials from around the
    world on lawn tennis. Stock includes: books, annuals,
    programmes, newspaper cuttings, journals,
    photographs and specialist papers
Services: Photocopies
Availability: Open to the public free of charge, by   ←———— Information on who can use the
    appointment, for reference only   library and whether charges are made
Hours: 10.30-13.00, 14.00-17.00 Tuesday to Friday
Transport: Tube: Southfields, Wimbledon; Rail: ←———— Nearest public transport to the library
    Wimbledon
Special facilities: Refreshment and toilet facilities available;   ←— Information on whether refreshment and
    access for users with disabilities with prior notice   toilet facilities are available and on facilities
                                          for users with disabilities

Linked organisations ←————————— Related bodies, including subordinate and
Wimbledon Lawn Tennis Museum   higher level bodies, and links to outside
    The Library is part of the Museum which is based at   organisations
    the All England Lawn Tennis Club, Wimbledon

ALPHABETICAL LIST

[1]
Action for Blind People
14–16 Verney Road
London SE16 3DZ
Borough: Southwark
Telephone: 020 7635 4800
Fax: 020 7635 4900
E-mail: central@afbp.org
World Wide Web: www.afbp.org
Constitution: Registered charity
Objectives/purposes: Support for people with visual impairments and those with an interest in visual impairment
Key staff: Information and Advice Services Manager: Ida Forster
Stock and subject coverage: Visual impairment service provision
Services: Photocopies, CCTV magnifier
Availability: Reference facilities only. Free leaflets and audio tapes. Open to anyone by appointment
Hours: Information service open 09.30-13.00, 14.00-17.00 Monday to Friday
Transport: Tube: Elephant and Castle; Rail: South Bermondsey; Bus: 21, 53, 172
Special facilities: Toilet facilities available on site. Wheelchair access
Publications: Annual Report

[2]
Action for Sick Children
300 Kingston Road
Wimbledon
London SW20 8LX
Borough: Merton
Telephone: 020 8542 4848
Fax: 020 8542 2424
E-mail: enquiries@actionforsickchildren.org
World Wide Web: www.actionforsickchildren.org
Constitution: Registered charity
Objectives/purposes: Supporting sick children and their families, and promoting the best possible health care for them at home and in hospital
Key staff: Librarian: Polly Moreton
Stock and subject coverage: The collection covers the psycho-social needs of children undergoing medical treatment, either in hospital or at home. Stock consists of books, journals, articles and theses. It is the only library in Britain solely collecting material on this subject. The library also contains archive material on the organisation, and on the development of nursing care for children in hospital
Services: Photocopies; fax and internet access
Availability: Reference only. Free access, by appointment, to all. Search fee for non-members applying by post. Charges for photocopying
Hours: Librarian available 09.00-17.00 Wednesday and Thursday

Transport: Rail: Wimbledon Chase (Thameslink)
Special facilities: Access for readers with disabilities
Publications: Annual Report; factsheets on various aspects of child health care; reading lists, quarterly magazine – Cascade; current awareness bulletin; student pack; family information leaflets; quality standards

Linked organisations
Local branches in England. Affiliated associations in Scotland, Wales, Isle of Man and Eire

[3]
Action on Smoking and Health ASH
102 Clifton Street
London EC2A 4HW
Borough: Hackney
Telephone: 020 7739 5902
Fax: 020 7613 0531
E-mail: action.smoking.health@dial.pipex.com
World Wide Web: www.ash.org.uk
Constitution: Registered charity
Objectives/purposes: To alert the public to the dangers of smoking; to promote policies to discourage it and so reduce the appalling toll of disease, death and disability it causes
Key staff: Amanda Sandford
Stock and subject coverage: Books, grey literature, press cuttings and journals on tobacco, smoking and health and all aspects of tobacco smoking
Services: Limited access to photocopier (charges made)
Availability: Access to bona fide researchers by written or telephone enquiry. Some material available for loan but mostly reference
Hours: 09.30-17.00 Monday to Friday
Transport: Tube: Liverpool Street, Old Street; Rail: Liverpool Street
Special facilities: Toilet facilities available on site; access for users with disabilities (ground floor location but one step makes wheelchair access difficult)
Publications: Burning Views – ASH information journal (6 p.a.); factsheets and other briefings available on ASH website

[4]
Active Birth Centre
25 Bickerton Road
London N19 5JT
Borough: Islington
Telephone: 020 7482 5554
Fax: 020 7267 9683
E-mail: mail@activebirthcentre.com
World Wide Web: www.activebirthcentre.com
Constitution: Private venture

Objectives/purposes: The Centre aims to provide a
context in which expectant mothers and their
partners can empower themselves for birth and
parenthood
Key staff: Janet Balaskas, Keith Braining, Diane
McDonald
Stock and subject coverage: Information service involved in
training active birth teachers, conducting midwife
workshops, international and national programmes
Services: Photocopies, telephone, fax machine, website
Other services: Waterbirth pool suppliers, for hire and
permanent installation; mail order of own products
Availability: Available for midwives, hospitals, doctors and
expectant parents
Hours: Official office opening hours 09.00-18.30
Monday to Friday
Transport: Tube: Tufnell Park; Rail: Gospel Oak; Bus: C2,
C11, 4, 10, 19, 134, 135, 214; easy car parking
Special facilities: Refreshment and toilet facilities available
Publications: Range of books, tapes and videos

[5]
Advertising Association
Information Centre
AA

Abford House
15 Wilton Road
London SW1V 1NJ
Borough: Westminster
Telephone: Business enquiries: 020 7828 2771; General
public enquiries: 020 7828 4831
Fax: 020 7931 0376
E-mail: aa@adassoc.org.uk
World Wide Web: www.adassoc.org.uk
Constitution: Association with subscribing membership
Key staff: Head of Information Services: P Spink BA
ALA; Information Officer: Anna Rutstein
Stock and subject coverage: Over 2,000 volumes including
current works on advertising, marketing, sales
promotion, media and public relations; reference
section (mainly on the UK); over 150 English
language journal titles on advertising, marketing and
related subjects; statistics, notably on advertising and
economics; over 300 files of press cuttings
Services: Enquiries by post, telephone or e-mail;
photocopies of material required solely for research
or private study; internet access for research; some
Advertising Association publications on sale in the
Information Centre; some publications and
information available only on the AA website
Availability: Open to all bona fide enquirers. Visitors
must make an appointment, as space is limited
Hours: 09.30-13.00 and 14.00-17.00 Monday to Friday
for members; non-members 14.00-16.00 Tuesday to
Thursday only. See website for details
Transport: Tube, Rail and coach: Victoria
Special facilities: Toilet facilities available

Linked organisations

Federation of 24 trade organisations

[6]
Advertising Standards Authority
ASA

2 Torrington Place
London WC1E 7HW
Borough: Camden
Telephone: 020 7580 5555
Fax: 020 7631 3051
E-mail: info@asa.org.uk
World Wide Web: www.asa.org.uk
Objectives/purposes: Regulator of non-broadcast
advertising in the UK
Key staff: Communications Team: Zoe Kalu
Stock and subject coverage: British codes of advertising and
sales promotion, and information relating to self-
regulation of advertising in non-broadcast media.
Covers advertisements in print, direct mail, sales
promotions, cinema, posters and non-broadcast
electronic media
Services: Bi-monthly report of complaint adjudications;
general informational literature
Availability: Telephone, fax, e-mail or postal information
only
Hours: 09.30-17.30 Monday to Friday

[7]
Advisory, Conciliation and
Arbitration Service
ACAS

Library and Information Service
Brandon House
180 Borough High Street
London SE1 1LW
Borough: Southwark
Telephone: 020 7210 3911
Fax: 020 7210 3615
E-mail: library@acas.org.uk
World Wide Web: www.acas.org.uk
Constitution: Government funded body
Key staff: Acting Librarian: Mr R Wilsher BA DipLib,
ext 3917; Temporary Assistant Librarian: Ms L Jane,
ext 3671
Stock and subject coverage: Ca. 10,000 books and
pamphlets; 150 current journals. Covers industrial
relations; employment law; trade unions; personnel
management; job design; the quality of working life;
employee involvement; new work patterns; total
quality management; management of change;
organisational behaviour; work stress
Services: Loans to government departments and
reciprocating libraries. Enquiry service. Range of
publications
Availability: Stock available for reference only
Hours: 10.00-16.00 Monday to Friday
Transport: Tube: Borough; Rail: London Bridge; Bus: 35,
40
Special facilities: Access for disabled persons - with lifts
and toilet facilities. Wheelchair access through rear
entrance - telephone in advance

Linked organisations

ACAS has a head office and a regional office
structure

[8]
Africa Centre
38 King Street
London WC2E 8JT
Borough: Westminster
Telephone: 020 7836 1973
Fax: 020 7836 1975
E-mail: info@africacentre.org.uk
World Wide Web: www.africacentre.org.uk
Key staff: Resource and Information Officer: David Harris
Constitution: Registered charity
Objectives/purposes: The Centre aims to be a flagship for Africa in Europe: a high profile Centre promoting the best of African art, culture and opinion. Aims to build a bridge to a new era of relations between Africa and Europe
Stock and subject coverage: Over 170 contemporary journals and newspapers published in the UK, Africa and elsewhere. United Nations publications; files containing information on each African country; wealth of African magazines covering gender issues, political, economic and environmental issues. Other subjects covered include: feminism, work, education, health, the arts, science and technology
Services: Photocopies (charged); Centre for African Language Learning; Africa Book Centre, Africa Education Trust
Availability: Access is open to all. Material is available for reference only
Hours: 09.30-17.30 Monday, Wednesday, Thursday and Friday; 09.00-15.00 Tuesday
Transport: Tube: Covent Garden, Charing Cross; Rail: Charing Cross
Special facilities: Basement bar and calabash restaurant; toilet facilities; limited access for users with disabilities (redevelopment plans include full access)
Special features: The Africa Centre was incorporated and registered as a charity in 1961 to inform and educate the British public about Africa. It was officially opened in 1964 by Kenneth Kaunda, the President of Zambia. The Centre has for more than 30 years served as a focus on Africa in Britain.
The building is listed and has some unusual features such as the gallery
Publications: Quarterly Africa Centre Events Sheet; Habari online arts magazine

[9]
Age Concern England
ACE
Astral House
1268 London Road
London SW16 4ER
Borough: Croydon
Telephone: 020 8765 7200
Fax: 020 8765 7211
E-mail: ace@ace.org.uk
World Wide Web: www.ageconcern.org.uk
Constitution: Registered charity
Objectives/purposes: Age Concern exists to promote the well-being of all older people and to help make later life a fulfilling and enjoyable experience
Key staff: Librarians: Marian Chinn, Elizabeth Johnston;
Library Resources Unit Manager: Cherry-Ann Dowling
Stock and subject coverage: Collections on social policy and older people. The stock includes books, ca. 10,000 reports, 150 current journal titles, videos, annual reports, government materials, press releases and subject files of ephemeral material
Services: Internet access; literature searches on request; photocopies (charged)
Availability: Loan service to staff only; open by appointment, for reference only, to outside enquirers
Hours: 09.30-17.00 Monday to Friday
Transport: Rail: Norbury
Special facilities: Refreshments (drinks only) available; disabled toilet facilities; parking available by prior arrangement for visitors with disabilities
Publications: Monthly current awareness Information Bulletin; monthly accessions list; quarterly journal articles list; library leaflet and guide; reading lists

Linked organisations
Age Concern Scotland
Age Concern Northern Ireland
Age Concern Cymru

[10]
Akina Mama wa Afrika
AMWA
334-336 Goswell Road
London EC1V 7LQ
Borough: Islington
Telephone: 020 7713 5166
Fax: 020 7713 1959
E-mail: thoko@akinamama.org
World Wide Web: www.akinamama.org
Constitution: Independent non-profit distributing organisation
Objectives/purposes: To provide a platform for African women to participate in policy and decision making. AMWA's programmes fall under four key areas: community development; human rights; education and research; international development
Key staff:
Stock and subject coverage: Materials on development, health, human rights, African literature; conference reports (aid and development), refugee women
Services: Photocopies; translation service
Availability: Access to all bona fide researchers. Material is not available for loan. Some charges are made for reproduction of material and consultancy
Hours: 10.00-16.00 Monday to Friday
Transport: Tube: Angel, Old Street, Barbican
Special features: Only resource centre in London dedicated to issues about African women

[11]
Al-Anon Family Groups UK & Eire
Al-Anon
61 Great Dover Street
London SE1 4YF
Borough: Southwark
Telephone: 020 7403 0888 (confidential helpline available 10.00-22.00)

Fax: 020 7378 9910
E-mail: alanonuk@aol.com
World Wide Web: www.hexnet.co.uk/alanon/
*Constitution:*Registered charity and company limited by
  guarantee (Family Groups Ltd)
Objectives/purposes: Al-Anon offers help and support for
  families and friends of problem drinkers. Alateen, a
  part of Al-Anon, is for teenagers aged 12-20 whose
  lives are, or have been, affected by someone else's
  drinking
Key staff: Public Information Secretary
Stock and subject coverage: Books, leaflets and pamphlets
  for families and friends of alcoholics
Availability: Service for researchers in the field of
  alcoholism; not available for loan or for reference
Hours: 10.00-16.00 Monday to Friday
Transport: Tube: Borough, London Bridge; Rail: London
  Bridge; Bus: 21
Special facilities: Toilet facilities available; access for users
  with disabilities

Linked organisations

Part of a fellowship with over 30,000 Al-Anon and
Alateen groups meeting worldwide

[12]
Alcohol Concern

Waterbridge House
32-6 Loman Street
London SE1 0EE
Borough: Southwark
Telephone: 020 7922 8667
Fax: 020 7928 4644
E-mail: info@alcoholconcern.org.uk
World Wide Web: www.alcoholconcern.org.uk
Constitution: Company limited by guarantee; registered
  charity
Objectives/purposes: Alcohol Concern aims to reduce the
  incidence and costs of alcohol related harm and to
  increase the range and quality of the services available
  to people with alcohol-related problems
Key staff: Librarian: Roy Johnson; Information Assistant:
  Gemma Cantelo
Stock and subject coverage: Ca. 2,000 books, 130 journal
  titles (ca. 65 current), newspaper cuttings. Subject
  coverage of all aspects of alcohol use: treatments;
  regional and government policy; effects on health,
  family and society; history; drink/driving; community
  care. Coverage is mainly UK, with some American
  journals and books and some European journals
Services: Photocopies; database covering about 5,000
  items (since 1990); bookshop selling selected titles
  published by Alcohol Concern and by other
  publishers
Availability: Open to all (telephone for appointment).
  No loan facilities
Hours: 09.30-16.30 Monday to Friday, telephone or e-
  mail in advance for an appointment
Transport: Tube: Borough, Waterloo, Southwark; Rail:
  Waterloo; Bus: P3, 21, 35, 40, 45, 59, 63, 133, 172
Special facilities: Toilet facilities available; wheelchair
  accessible lift to 2nd floor Information Unit

Publications: Alcohol Concern (quarterly magazine);
  Acquire (quarterly research summaries); Annual
  Report; reading lists; publications list available on
  request

[13]
Alpine Club Library

55 Charlotte Road
London EC2A 3QF
Borough: Hackney
Telephone: 020 7613 0755
Fax: 020 7613 0755
E-mail: library@alpine-club.org.uk
World Wide Web: www.alpine-club.org.uk
Constitution: Registered charity and company limited by
  guarantee
Objectives/purposes: Wide ranging resource on
  mountaineering, past and present, and related subjects
  for mountaineers, geographers, historians and others
Key staff: Librarian: Margaret Ecclestone
Stock and subject coverage: Founded in 1858, the Alpine
  Club Library is one of the most comprehensive
  collections of mountaineering literature in the world
  with over 25,000 books as well as journals,
  pamphlets, guidebooks and expedition reports. The
  library includes novels, poetry, biographies, high
  altitude medicine and art as well as books on the
  mountain areas of the UK, rest of Europe and the
  greater ranges of the world and polar regions. There
  is a limited selection of maps and a collection of
  historical photographs. The archives of the Alpine
  Club include newspaper cuttings from 1891, diaries
  and correpondence. The collection includes 10 16th
  century titles, 21 17th century titles and 196 18th
  century titles. The library maintains a computerised
  database: the Himalayan Index of records of
  expeditions to Himalayan and Karakoram peaks over
  6,000m
Services: Photocopies
Availability: Reserved for Alpine Club members on
  Tuesday afternoons. Open to the public for reference
  use Wednesdays to Fridays, 14.00-17.00, by prior
  appointment. Brief enquiries may be answered by
  post. Borrowing is restricted to Alpine Club members
  only
Hours: 14.00-17.00 Wednesday to Friday, by
  appointment
Transport: Tube: Old Street; Rail: Old Street, Liverpool
  Street; Bus: 26, 35, 48, 55, 67, 149, 242, 243, 505
Special facilities: Toilet facilities available on site
Publications: Alpine Club Library catalogue: books and
  journals, Vol. 1 (Heinemann, 1982. ISBN
  043586050X); Index to the Ladies' Alpine Club Year-
  Books, 1910-1975

Linked organisations

The Alpine Club UK based mountaineering club
catering specifically for those who climb in the Alps
and the greater ranges of the world

[14]
Alzheimer's Society, Ann Brown Memorial Library
AS
Gordon House
10 Greencoat Place
London SW1P 1PH
Borough: Westminster
Telephone: 020 7306 0606
Fax: 020 7306 0808
E-mail: info@alzheimers.org.uk
World Wide Web: www.alzheimers.org.uk
Constitution: Registered charity
Objectives/purposes: The Alzheimer's Society is the leading care and research charity for people with dementia and their carers. It provides information and education, support for carers, and quality day and home care. AS provides support in England, Wales and Northern Ireland through a network of branches, support groups and contacts
Key staff: Librarian: Lesley Mackinnon; Director Information and Education: Clive Evers
Stock and subject coverage: Database of approximately 6,000 book and journal articles relating to health and social care of dementia. Holdings include 70 journals, videos, international newsletters. The Library is primarily for national and regional staff and for Council members.
Services: Reference service; photocopies subject to Copyright Act; subject searches of database
Availability: 09.00-17.00 by appointment
Hours: 09.00-17.00 Monday to Friday, by appointment
Transport: Tube: St James's Park; Rail: Victoria; Bus: 11, 24, 211, 507; Coach: Victoria Coach Station
Special facilities: Toilet facilities available on site. Access for users with disabilities
Publications: AS Newsletter (monthly); AS information and advice sheets; range of AS publications

[15]
Amateur Rowing Association
ARA
6 Lower Mall
Hammersmith
London W6 9DJ
Borough: Hammersmith and Fulham
Telephone: 020 8237 6700
Fax: 020 8237 6749
E-mail: info@ara-rowing.org
World Wide Web: www.ara-rowing.org
Constitution: Association with voluntary subscribing membership
Objectives/purposes: Governing body for the sport of rowing
Key staff: National Manager: Rosemary Napp
Stock and subject coverage: Historic and current books about rowing, including technique and the social history of rowing. Collections of British Rowing Almanack from 1864 to present and Regatta magazine from 1987 onwards
Services: Photocopies
Availability: By appointment only. Open for research and reference, no loans
Hours: 09.00-16.00 Monday to Friday
Transport: Tube: Hammersmith; Bus: buses to Hammersmith Bus Station
Special facilities: Toilet facilities available
Publications: British Rowing Almanack (contains Yearbook, Annual Report, results of domestic and international contests and of Henley Royal Regatta)

Linked organisations
Regional rowing councils for Thames, South East, East, East Midlands, West Midlands, Yorkshire and Humberside, North, North West, Wiltshire, Avon Gloucestershire and Somerset

[16]
American Embassy
The Information Resource Center
United States Embassy
24 Grosvenor Square
London W1A 1AE
Borough: Westminster
Telephone: 020 7499 9000, ext 2638/2643
Fax: 020 7629 8288
E-mail: reflond@pd.state.gov
World Wide Web: www.usembassy.org.uk/
Key staff: Center Director: Kate Bateman
Stock and subject coverage: Ca. 2,000 reference books and 40 journals covering US current affairs; security/defence issues; foreign and domestic policies; legislative developments; government, politics and society. Special collections include CIS microfiche library (1976-2000), which contains all Congressional documents; basic documents of US foreign policy, e.g. Foreign Relations of the United States series, Department of State Bulletin, (1939-1989); legislative materials such as United States Statutes at Large (1789) and the United States Code Annotated. (NB The Center does not provide tourist information). Certain other types of enquiries, such as commercial, visa, tax and customs questions are handled by the appropriate Embassy sections
Services: Telephone enquiries accepted from the public 10.00-12.00 on 020 7894 0925. Photocopies
Availability: By appointment only, at the discretion of the Center Director, to accredited researchers, representatives of the media, UK government employees and academics. Appointments should be arranged by telephoning a day or so in advance
Hours: 08.30-17.30, British and American public holidays excepted
Transport: Tube: Bond Street

[17]
Anti-Slavery International
Thomas Clarkson House
The Stableyard
Broomgrove Road
London SW9 9TL
Borough: Lambeth
Telephone: 020 7501 8939
Fax: 020 7738 4110
E-mail: j.howarth@antislavery.org
World Wide Web: www.antislavery.org
Constitution: Registered charity and association with voluntary subscribing membership

Objectives/purposes: Anti-Slavery promotes the
eradication of slavery and slavery-like practices and
freedom for everyone who is subjected to them. The
abuses which Anti-Slavery opposes include: slavery
and the buying and selling of people as objects;
trafficking of women and the predicament of migrant
workers who are trapped into servitude; debt
bondage and other traditions which force people into
low status work; forced labour; forced prostitution;
abusive forms of child labour; and early or forced
marriage and other forms of servile marriage. Anti-
Slavery focuses on the rights of people who are
particularly vulnerable to exploitation of their labour;
notably women, children, migrant workers and
indigenous peoples

Key staff: Director: Mike Dottridge: Librarian: Jeff
Howarth

Stock and subject coverage: Research library for Anti-
Slavery; 150 years of abolitionist campaign literature,
films, photographs and videos. Current collections
include issues such as: child labour, child prostitution,
bonded labour, forced prostitution and trafficking of
women, and codes of conduct relating to these issues.
Historical material includes a collection of over 600
pamphlets on the Trans-Atlantic slave trade, books,
journals and images of slavery and indigenous rights
in the Americas, Africa and Asia

Services: Photocopies

Availability: Researchers should confirm by phone
before paying a visit

Hours: 10.00-17.00 Monday to Friday

Transport: Tube: Brixton, Stockwell

Special facilities: Toilet facilities available; access for users
with disabilities (limited wheelchair access)

Publications: Anti-Slavery Reporter (4 p.a.); various
publications on contemporary slavery

Linked organisations

**Rhodes House Library, part of the Bodlian
Library, Oxford** Rhodes House Library contains
the Anti-Slavery archives

---

[18]
Arab-British Centre
ABC

21 Collingham Road
London SW5 0NU

Borough: Kensington and Chelsea

Telephone: 020 7373 8414

Fax: 020 7835 2088

Constitution: Independent non-profit organisation and
registered charity

Objectives/purposes: To encourage learning about the
Arab world

Key staff: Director: William Fullerton

Stock and subject coverage: Ca. 2,000 books, plus journals
and papers on Arab countries (recent history and
political affairs) and the Arab-Israeli conflict

Services: Photocopies (charges made); rooms available for
lectures and meetings

Availability: Reference facilities only. Open to bona fide
researchers, students and private individuals

Hours: 09.30-17.00 Monday to Friday

Transport: Tube: Gloucester Road, Earls Court

Special facilities: Toilet facilities available; limited access

for people with disabilities – Victorian building with
eight steps at entrance

Linked organisations

**Council for the Advancement of Arab-British
Understanding
Middle East International
Friends of Bir Zeit University
Labor Middle East Council**
Housed in the same building

---

[19]
Architectural Association
AA

36 Bedford Square
London WC1B 3ES

Borough: Camden

World Wide Web: www.arch-assoc.org.uk

Constitution: Independent non-profit organisation with
voluntary subscribing membership, registered charity

Transport: Tube: Tottenham Court Road, Russell Square;
Bus: 10, 24, 73

Special facilities: Refreshment and toilet facilities; access
for people with disabilities by prior arrangement

[19][a]
Architectural Association Library

as above

Telephone: 020 7887 4036

Fax: 020 7414 0782

E-mail: hsklar@aaschool.ac.uk

World Wide Web: www.aaschool.ac.uk/library/

Key staff: Librarian: Hinda F Sklar; Deputy Librarian:
Aileen Smith

Stock and subject coverage: 30,000 volumes; 110 current
journals. Covers architecture; urban and regional
design; building construction; art; design; landscape
architecture. Special collections: Rare books; AA
Collection; International Exhibitions

Services: Loan and reference collection: 50,000 classified
journal articles; card index to journals; interlibrary
loans; small collection of CD-ROMs; limited internet
access; photocopier; cumulative index to AA journal
1887-1982; index to AA membership records 1846-
1905; SIRSI computerised library system

Availability: Members only; 5-day research only
membership available (charged)

Hours: Term-time: 10.00-20.00 Monday to Friday;
11.00-15.00 Saturday

Transport: See above

Special facilities: See above

[19][b]
Architectural Association Photo Library
AA Slide Library

Address as above

Telephone: 020 7887 4086/66/78

Fax: 020 7414 0782

Key staff: Photo Librarian: Valerie Bennett; Assistants:
Anna Jury, Sarah Farmer

Stock and subject coverage: 120,000 slides. In addition:
20,000 4.5 inch slides and 20,000 negatives. The
collection is mainly of architecture but now includes
other allied subject areas. Architecture of all countries

and periods from the earliest times to the present day is broadly covered. Additional subjects include town planning; roads and traffic; parks, gardens and landscape; painting and applied arts; natural and man-made forms; design

Availability: AA school, staff and students; AA membership in Great Britain (hire charge); others (hire charge). By appointment only

Hours: 10.00-13.00 and 14.00-17.00 Monday to Friday

Transport: See above

Special facilities: See above

[20]
Archway Healthcare Library
AHL

    Holborn Union Building
    The Archway Campus
    Highgate Hill
    London N19 5ND

Borough: Islington

Telephone: 020 7288 3580

Fax: 020 7288 3571

E-mail: AHL@mdx.ac.uk

World Wide Web: www.archway.ac.uk/AHL

Constitution: Funded by Middlesex University, University College London, The Whittington Hospital NHS Trust, Camden and Islington Community Health Services NHS Trust and Camden and Islington Mental Health Services Trust

Objectives/purposes: To provide library and information services to support research, clinical practice, education and training for staff and students of Middlesex University, Royal Free and UCL Medical School, the Whittington Hospital, Camden and Islington Mental Health and Community Trusts and local primary care groups

Key staff: Library and Information Manager: Ms BJ Chapman

Stock and subject coverage: General medicine, health-related subjects and nursing

Services: Internet access to main medical and health-related databases and full-text electronic journals; photocopying; access to Microsoft Office software; printing; IT training room (bookable) for groups of up to 16

Availability: Open to staff and students of the partners (listed under constitution), including members of the Central London Confederation. Charges for photocopying and interlibrary loans for certain user groups

Hours: 10.00-17.00 Monday, 09.00-20.00 Tuesday to Thursday; 09.00-17.00 Friday; 10.00-14.30 Saturday

Transport: Tube: Archway; Rail: Upper Holloway; Bus: W5, 41, 43, 134, 210, 271

Special facilities: Users with disabilities should telephone in advance

Linked organisations

    Run on behalf of a number of partner organisations listed under constitution

[21]
Arthur Sanderson and Sons Ltd, Archive

    Sanderson Archive
    Oxford Road
    Denham UB9 4DX

Borough: Hounslow

Telephone: 01895 830079

Fax: 01895 830068

World Wide Web: www.sanderson-uk.com

Constitution: Private limited company

Key staff: Archivist: Frederika Launert

Stock and subject coverage: Predominantly a design archive, the collection includes: approximately 11,000 wallpapers, ca.1850 to date, including designs by well known 19th and 20th century designers; ca. 2,500 French figured velvets, brocades and damasks 18th-20th century; ca. 2,500 19th and 20th century chintzes; approximately 5,000 woven and printed textiles ca. 1915 to date, including all designs manufactured by Sanderson; several thousand wallpaper and textile designs on paper; wallpaper printing logs of Jeffrey and Co., Morris and Co., Charles Knowles and Sanderson; log and pattern books of Sanderson fancy papers 1920-1970s; wallpaper and textile pattern books from 1852 to date including several from the later years of Morris and Co.; miscellaneous photographs of the Sanderson family, premises and staff; small collection of company records e.g. minute books, account and wages books and designers' logs

Availability: Predominantly a design resource used by the company's inhouse designers. Access for specialist researchers at the company's discretion. Material for reference only. Application should be made to the Archivist

Hours: Visits by appointment only

Transport: Tube: Uxbridge

Special facilities: Limited refreshment facilities; toilet facilities

Special features: Arthur Sanderson and Sons was established in 1860

Publications: Sanderson 1860-1985, exhibition catalogue, edited by Christine Woods, published by Arthur Sanderson and Sons Ltd, 1985

[22]
Arts Council of England Library and Enquiry Service

    14 Great Peter Street
    London SW1P 3NQ

Borough: Westminster

Telephone: 020 7973 6517

Fax: 020 7973 6590

Minicom: 020 7973 6517

E-mail: enquiries@artscouncil.org.uk

World Wide Web: www.artscouncil.org.uk

Constitution: Registered charity and independent non-profit distributing organisation. The Arts Council of England (formerly the Arts Council of Great Britain) is the main channel for distributing government aid to the performing arts

Key staff: Acting Information Manager: Virginia
   Hennessy
Stock and subject coverage: Cultural policy; arts economy;
   management; marketing and market research
Services: Internet access and photocopying
Availability: Staff of the Arts Council and organisations
   and artists funded by the Council; partner arts
   funding agencies; serious arts researchers (by prior
   arrangement only)
Hours: 14.00-17.00 Monday to Friday. Appointment
   required
Transport: Tube: Westminster, St James Park; Bus: 3, 11,
   24, 77A, 159, 507, 511
Special facilities: Refreshment and toilet facilities available;
   access for people with disabilities; CCTV for users
   with visual impairments
Publications: Occasional bibliographies and factsheets

Linked organisations

Department for Culture, Media and Sport
Channels government funds to the Arts Council for
distribution

---

[23]
Aslib, The Association for Information Management

Temple Chambers
3–7 Temple Avenue
London EC4Y 0HP
Borough: Westminster
Telephone: 020 7583 8900
Fax: 020 7583 8401
E-mail: aslib@aslib.com
World Wide Web: www.aslib.co.uk
Constitution: Company limited by guarantee; registered
   charity
Key staff: IRC Manager: Alison Ross
Services: Photocopying
Availability: Charges for non-members
Hours: 09.15-17.15 Monday to Friday
Transport: Tube: Temple; Rail: Waterloo
Special facilities: Toilet facilities available

Linked organisations

Brussels office, 29 Avenue Gribaumont, B-1150
Brussels, tel: +(32) 2 77 94 601, fax: +(32) 2 77 94
603

Information Resource Centre

A complete information service available to Aslib
corporate members and non-members (who may be
charged) providing information solutions, from
immediate enquiry response to value-added services.
A CD-ROM Test Drive facility offers impartial
advice to guide the enquirer through the full range
of CD-ROM products available in the marketplace
Stock and subject coverage: 5,000 books and 150 periodical
   titles covering online information retrieval;
   automation; library information and knowledge
   management
Key staff: Enquiries: Information Resource Centre

Aslib Professional Development

Offers a combination of short courses and seminars
for all levels of employee, as well as in-house training

to suit specific requirements. Courses on offer
include training in information handling techniques,
information sources, management and
communication skills
Key staff: Enquiries: Professional Development Group
   Manager

Aslib Professional Recruitment Ltd

A subsidiary company, helps organisations select
suitable staff for their information departments and
libraries
Key staff: Enquiries: Aslib Professonal Recruitment Ltd.

Aslib Publications

Booklist (monthly); Managing Information
(monthly); Aslib Proceedings (monthly); Current
Awareness Abstracts (monthly); Forthcoming
International Scientific and Technical Conferences
(quarterly); Journal of Documentation (quarterly);
Program (quarterly); Online Notes (monthly);
Records Management Journal (bi-annual). Also a
range of research reports, surveys, bibliographies,
directories, hardbacks and monographs
Key staff: Enquiries: Publications Manager, Sarah Blair

---

[24]
Association of Anaesthetists of Great Britain and Ireland

BJA Library
British Journal of Anaesthesia Library
9 Bedford Square
London WC1B 3RE
Borough: Camden
Telephone: 020 7631 8806
Fax: 020 7631 4352
E-mail: trishwillis@aagbi.org
World Wide Web: www.aagbi.org
Constitution: Registered charity
Objectives/purposes: To manage a unique specialist
   collection relating to the history of anaesthesia
Key staff: Patricia Willis
Stock and subject coverage: In association with the Charles
   King Collection of Historic Anaesthetic Apparatus –
   which is housed in the BOC (British Oxygen
   Company) Museum in the same building – and the
   archives of the Association of Anaesthetists, the
   Library and the museum collection form a national
   archive of the history of anaesthesia. The material
   includes a collection of historic audiovisual material
Services: Photocopies
Availability: Access to the reference collection of books,
   archives and the museum exhibit, which is changed
   every year, is open to bona fide researchers into the
   history of anaesthesia by appointment only
Hours: 09.30-17.00 Monday to Friday
Transport: Tube: Tottenham Court Road, Euston, Russell
   Square; Bus: (serving Gower Street and Bloomsbury
   Street) 10, 24, 29, 73, 134
Special facilities: Toilet facilities available; restricted access
   for users with disabilities
Special features: The Association of Anaesthetists of Great
   Britain and Ireland was founded in 1932. Anaesthesia
   is the largest clinical specialty in the hospital service
   of the National Health Service

---

[25]
Association of Certified Book-Keepers
ACB

Akhtar House
2 Shepherd's Bush Road
London W6 7PJ
Borough: Hammersmith and Fulham
Telephone: 020 8749 7126
Fax: 020 8749 7127
E-mail: icea@enta.net
World Wide Web: www.icea.enta.net
Constitution: Independent non-profit organisation and company limited by guarantee
Objectives/purposes: Professional examining body for book-keeping and accounting
Key staff: Administration: Susana Ercilla
Stock and subject coverage: Material on book-keeping; accounting; taxation; computerised book-keeping; and small business administration
Services: Photocopying
Availability: Restricted to members, students and Diploma holders
Transport: Tube: Shepherd's Bush
Publications: Certified Book Keeper

Linked organisations
Institute of Cost and Executive Accountants
Association of Financial Controllers and Administrators

[26]
Association of Commonwealth Universities Reference Library
ACU

36 Gordon Square
London WC1H 0PF
Borough: Camden
Telephone: 020 7380 6700
Fax: 020 7387 2655
E-mail: info@acu.ac.uk
World Wide Web: www.acu.ac.uk
Constitution: Registered charity and association with voluntary subscribing membership
Key staff: Librarian: Nick Mulhern
Stock and subject coverage: 18,000 volumes on higher education in the Commonwealth, including university prospectuses, calendars and reports, and awards guides
Services: Photocopies
Availability: Freely available to all
Hours: 10.00-13.00 and 14.00-17.00 Monday to Friday
Transport: Tube: Euston, Euston Square, Russell Square; Rail: Euston; Bus: 91, 188, 168, (Tavistock Square); 10, 24, 73, 134 (Gower Street)
Special facilities: Toilet facilities available
Publications: Accessions List

[27]
Association of Financial Controllers and Administrators
AFCA

Tower House
139 Fonthill Road
London N4 3HF
Borough: Islington
Telephone: 020 7272 3925
Fax: 020 7281 5723
E-mail: lcea@enta.net
World Wide Web: www.icea.enta.net
Constitution: Independent non-profit organisation and company limited by guarantee
Key staff: Information Officer: Miss S Cutillo
Stock and subject coverage: Material on accounting; finance; management; business law; company law; and taxation
Services: Photocopies
Availability: Restricted to members, students and diploma holders
Hours: 10.00-15.00 Monday to Friday
Transport: Tube and Rail: Finsbury Park
Special facilities: Toilet facilities available

Linked organisations
Institute of Cost and Executive Accountants

[28]
Association of the British Pharmaceutical Industry
ABPI

12 Whitehall
London SW1A 2DY
Borough: Westminster
Telephone: 020 7930 3477
Fax: 020 7747 1447
E-mail: ccoomber@abpi.org.uk
World Wide Web: www.abpi.org.uk
Constitution: Trade association for manufacturers of prescription medicines in the UK
Key staff: Librarian: Caroline Coomber
Stock and subject coverage: Joint library between the Office of Health Economics and ABPI. Contains approximately 600 books and 200 journals covering economics, health, general medicine and pharmacy
Services: Interlibrary loans and photocopies
Availability: Not usually open to external users. Enquiries from other libraries welcome. Loans only through libraries
Hours: 10.00-16.00 Monday to Friday
Transport: Tube and Rail: Charing Cross; Bus: 3, 11, 12, 24, 53, X53, 77A, 88, 91, 109, 139, 159
Special facilities: Toilet facilities available
Publications: Details of OHE publications available from the OHE Secretary and ABPI publications from the Publications Officer

Linked organisations
Office of Health Economics Funded by ABPI

[29]
Astrological Lodge of London
ALL
50 Gloucester Place
London W1H 3HJ
Borough: Westminster
Telephone: 01787 224701
Constitution: Registered charity; independent non-profit organisation
Objectives/purposes: The study of astrology in all its branches with an emphasis upon the philosophical, historical and symbolic aspects of astrological studies
Key staff: President: Wanda Sellar; Librarian: Gill Larner
Stock and subject coverage: Astrology books and magazines, some foreign
Availability: Restricted to members. The library is housed with the library books of the AA
Hours: Monday 18.15-21.30
Transport: Tube: Baker Street, Marble Arch; Bus: 2, 13, 30, 74, 82, 113, 139, 159, 274
Special facilities: Toilet facilities available
Publications: Astrology Quarterly (free to members)

[30]
The Athenaeum
107 Pall Mall
London SW1Y 5ER
Borough: Westminster
Telephone: 020 7930 9843
Fax: 020 7839 4114
E-mail: library@hellenist.org.uk
Constitution: Private, independent non-profit distributing organisation with a voluntary subscribing membership
Objectives/purposes: Private club
Key staff: Librarian: Miss S J Dodgson
Stock and subject coverage: Approximately 60,000 volumes of general reference material relating to the members, their interests and collections; 19th and 20th century pamphlets and ephemera. Basil Hall, Morton-Pitt, Gibbon and Dreyfus Collections; Boer War and Tractarian Controversy Collections.
Services: Photocopies (20 pence per sheet)
Availability: Bona fide researchers should apply, in writing, to the Librarian one month in advance of their intended visit to obtain a written appointment agreement. Reference only for non-members
Hours: 09.30-17.30 Monday to Friday
Transport: Tube: Piccadilly Circus, Charing Cross; Rail: Charing Cross; Bus: 9, 12, 13, 14, 15, 22, 23, 38, 139
Special facilities: Toilet facilities available on site

[31]
Australia and New Zealand Chamber of Commerce UK
ANZCC
393 Strand
London WC2R 0JQ
Borough: Westminster
Telephone: 020 7379 0720
Fax: 020 7379 0721
E-mail: enquiries@anzcc.org.uk
World Wide Web: www.anzcc.org.uk

Constitution: Independent non-profit organisation
Key staff: Kelly Madden
Stock and subject coverage: Collection of books and directories divided into three sections: Australia, New Zealand and UK. Includes Kompass products and services; local telephone directories; serials; trade journals, etc.
Services: Paid research facilities for Australia, New Zealand and UK company information; information on trade fairs, exhibitions, etc. Collection available for reference by appointment, or lists compiled for a charge
Availability: Telephone and written enquiries; library is available for research by appointment (charges may apply)
Hours: 09.30-17.30 Monday to Friday
Transport: Tube: Charing Cross, Embankment; Rail: Charing Cross
Special facilities: Refreshment and toilet facilities; access for users with disabilities
Publications: British Australasian Business Directory; ANZCC Up and Under Updates (bi-monthly)

[32]
Aviation Environment Federation
AEF
Sir John Lyon House
5 High Timber Street
London EC4V 3NS
Borough: Corporation of London
Telephone: 020 7248 2223
Fax: 020 7329 8160
E-mail: info@aef.org.uk
World Wide Web: www.aef.org.uk
Constitution: Non-profit making environmental association with voluntary subscribing membership
Objectives/purposes: Concerned with the environmental impact of aviation including commercial, business and general/light aviation
Key staff: Director: Mr Tim Johnson BA; Information Officer: Ed Wright; Administrator: Mr P Fairhurst
Stock and subject coverage: Materials on most aspects of aviation and the environment including: noise, air and water pollution; aircraft and airports; and planning. Stock includes journals; reference books; industry and government reports; public enquiry documents and evidence; and environmental impact statements
Services: Photocopies; extract service; fax machine (charges made for services)
Availability: Library available to all members, low membership fee for students
Hours: 09.00-17.00 Monday to Friday, closed for two weeks at Christmas
Transport: Tube and Rail: Mansion House, Blackfriars, Cannon Street
Special facilities: Refreshment and toilet facilities available; access for users with disabilities – some steps, please telephone in advance
Publications: Flying Green newsletter (6-8p.a.); reports on current topics (approximately 3 p.a.); Members Briefings (2 p.a.); Annual Report and/or Directors' Report; In the Air, On the Ground, a classroom pack to stimulate discussion and debate on aviation and the environment

Linked organisations

Airfields Environment Trust Charitable Trust with related objectives but operating in research and educational fields

[33]
Bank of England Archive

Archive Section HO-SV
Bank of England
Threadneedle Street
London EC2R 8AH
Borough: Corporation of London
Telephone: 020 7601 5096/4889
Fax: 020 7601 4356
E-mail: archive@bankofengland.co.uk
World Wide Web: www.bankofengland.co.uk
Objectives/purposes: Central bank of the UK
Key staff: Archivist
Stock and subject coverage: Ca. 65,000 separate items. Records reflecting the principal activities of the Bank: advice to Government; market operations; management of government, Bank and private accounts; management of stock issues; economic intelligence; industrial liaison; banknote design and printing; exchange control; relations with central banks and other institutions abroad
Services: Limited photocopying
Availability: Access to all bona fide researchers for reference. The 30-Year Rule applies but some records are closed for longer. Telephone for appointment
Hours: 10.00-16.30 Monday to Friday
Transport: Tube: Bank
Special facilities: Toilet facilities available on site
Special features: The Archive and a Museum are housed within the Bank of England, which was established by Royal Charter in 1694
Publications: Guide to the Archive

[34]
Bank of England Information Centre

Threadneedle Street
London EC2R 8AH
Borough: Corporation of London
Telephone: 020 7601 4715/4846; Enquiries: exts 4846/4715; Public Information Enquiries: 020 7601 4878
Fax: 020 7601 4356
E-mail: informationcentre@bankofengland.co.uk
World Wide Web: www.bankofengland.co.uk
Objectives/purposes: Central bank of the UK
Key staff: Librarian: Ms PA Hope
Stock and subject coverage: About 75,000 volumes of books and journals; 1,500 journals taken. UK and overseas coverage in banking and financial economics. Special collections of central bank reports, UK 17th to 19th century economic tracts and government reports in the field of banking and finance
Availability: Free advice and information to enquirers; photocopies (priced)
Hours: 09.30-17.30 Monday to Friday
Transport: Tube: Bank

Special facilities: Toilet facilities available on site; limited access for people with disabilities

[35]
Barking and Dagenham (London Borough of Barking and Dagenham)

Barking and Dagenham Libraries

World Wide Web: www.bardaglea.org.uk/4-libraries/libraries-menu.html
Constitution: Public library, funded by local government. Part of the Department of Education, Arts and Libraries
Key staff: Head of Library Service: Trevor Brown
Availability: Free public access for reference, book borrowing and internet access. Charges are made for the loan of music cassettes, CDs, videos and pictures
Special facilities: The Borough's main library is Barking Central Library. The main local history collection is at Valence Library (and Valence House Museum) with some material at Barking Central Library

[35][a]
Barking Central Library

Barking
Essex IG11 7NB
Telephone: 020 8227 3604
Fax: 020 8227 3699
Key staff: Librarian in Charge: Sylvia Currie; Lending Librarian: Ann Hall; Audio-visual Librarian: Colin Clare
Stock and subject coverage: Comprehensive reference and loan collections in the following subjects: arts, languages, music, science and technology, social science, business and local history. The local history collection includes maps and an extensive photographic archive as well as printed materials. The business collection covers current financial and business data, including newspapers and journals; current UK and overseas trade directories; and market research reports. There is also a collection of books for children and a collection of books in Asian languages
Services: Photocopying service for printed materials and microforms; multimedia; internet access; fax
Hours: 09.30-19.00 Monday, Tuesday, Thursday and Friday; 09.30-17.00 Wednesday and Saturday
Transport: Tube and Rail: Barking; Bus: 5, 62, 87, 287
Special facilities: Access for users with disabilities

[35][b]
Fanshawe Library

Barnmead Road
Dagenham
Essex RM9 5DX
Telephone: 020 8270 4244
Key staff: Branch Librarian: Freda Price
Stock and subject coverage: Reference collection; local information; children's collection; internet access and multimedia; fax
Hours: 09.30-19.00 Tuesday; 09.30-17.00 Thursday

Transport: Tube: Dagenham Heathway; Bus: 173, 174, 175, 364
Special facilities: Access for users with disabilities

[35][c]
Marks Gate Library
Marks Gate Community Centre
Rose Lane
Chadwell Heath
Romford
Essex RM6 5NJ
Telephone: 020 8270 4165
Key staff: Branch Librarian: Jean Sibley
Reference facilities: Reference collection; local information; children's collections; internet access; multimedia; fax
Hours: 09.30-12.30, 13.30-17.00 Tuesday; 15.15-19.00 Thursday; 09.30-13.00 Saturday
Transport: Rail: Chadwell Heath; Bus: 62, 296, 362
Special facilities: Access for users with disabilities

[35][d]
Markyate Library
Markyate Road
Dagenham
Essex RM8 2LD
Telephone: 020 8270 4137
Key staff: Branch Librarian: Jennifer Murphy
Reference facilities: Reference collection; local information; children's collection; internet access; multimedia; fax
Hours: 09.30-19.00 Monday, Friday; 09.30-13.00 Saturday
Transport: Tube: Becontree; Bus: 62, 145, 368
Special facilities: Access for users with disabilities

[35][e]
Rectory Library
Rectory Road
Dagenham
Essex RM10 9SA
Telephone: 020 8270 6233
Key staff: Branch Librarian: Freda Price
Reference facilities: Reference collection; local information; children's collection; internet access; multimedia; fax
Hours: 09.30-19.00 Monday, Tuesday and Thursday: 09.30-17.00 Friday; 09.30-13.00 Wednesday and Saturday
Transport: Tube: Dagenham East, Dagenham Heathway; Bus: 129, 145, 173, 174, 175
Special facilities: Access for users with disabilities

[35][f]
Rush Green Library
Dagenham Road
Rush Green
Romford
Essex RM7 0TL
Telephone: 020 8270 4304
Key staff: Branch Librarian: Anne Long
Reference facilities: Reference collection; local information; children's collection; internet access; multimedia; fax

Hours: 14.00-17.00 Monday; 09.30-17.00 Tuesday and Thursday; 09.30-13.00 Saturday
Transport: Tube: Dagenham East; Bus: 174
Special facilities: Access for users with disabilities

[35][g]
Thames View Library
2A Farr Avenue
Barking
Essex IG11 0NZ
Telephone: 020 8270 4164
Key staff: Branch Librarian: Christine Pereira
Reference facilities: Reference collection; local information; children's collection; internet access; multimedia; fax
Hours: 09.30-12.30, 13.30-19.00 Tuesday; 09.30-17.00 Friday; 09.30-13.00 Saturday
Transport: Tube and Rail: Barking; Bus: 369
Special facilities: Access for users with disabilities

[35][h]
Valence Library
Becontree Avenue
Dagenham
Essex RM8 3HT
Telephone: 020 8227 5292
Key staff: Branch Librarian: Jennifer Murphy
Reference facilities: Reference collection; local information; children's collection; internet access; multimedia; fax. Valence Library houses the main local history collection for the Borough. Local history archive material is housed in the attached Valence House Museum
Hours: 09.30-19.00 Monday, Tuesday, Thursday and Friday; 09.30-13.00 Wednesday and Saturday
Transport: Tube: Dagenham Heathway; Rail: Chadwell Heath; Bus: 62
Special facilities: Access for users with disabilities

[35][i]
Wantz Library
Rainham Road
North Dagenham
Essex RM10 7DX
Telephone: 020 8270 4169
Key staff: Branch Librarian: Ann Long
Reference facilities: Reference collection; local information; children's collection; internet access; multimedia; fax
Hours: 09.30-19.00 Monday, Tuesday and Thursday; 09.30-17.00 Friday; 09.30-13.00 Saturday
Transport: Tube: Dagenham East; Bus: 103, 129, 174
Special facilities: Access for users with disabilities

[35][j]
Whalebone Library
High Road
Chadwell Heath
Romford
Essex RM6 6AS
Telephone: 020 8270 4305
Key staff: Branch Librarian: Jean Sibley
Reference facilities: Reference collection; local information; children's collection; internet access; multimedia; fax

Hours: 09.30-19.00 Monday, Tuesday, Thursday and
   Friday; 09.30-13.00 Wednesday and Saturday
Transport: Rail: Chadwell Heath; Bus: 62, 86, 173, 362
Special facilities: Access for users with disabilities

[35][k]
Woodward Library
   Woodward Road
   Dagenham
   Essex RM9 4SP
Telephone: 020 8270 4166
Key staff: Branch Librarian: Christine Pereira
Reference facilities: Reference collection; local
   information; children's collection; internet access;
   multimedia; fax
Hours: 09.30-19.00 Monday, Tuesday and Thursday;
   09.30-17.00 Friday; 09.30-13.00 Wednesday and
   Saturday
Transport: Tube: Becontree; Bus: 62, 145
Special facilities: Access for users with disabilities

[36]
Barnardo's
   Tanners Lane
   Barkingside
   Ilford
   Essex IG6 1QG
Borough: Redbridge
Telephone: 020 8498 7146
Fax: 020 8551 6870
E-mail: library@barnardos.org.uk
World Wide Web: www.barnardos.org.uk
Constitution: Registered charity
Key staff: Librarian: Mr Christopher Reeve
Stock and subject coverage: 15,000 books, reports, etc. and
   190 current journals, covering social welfare (care of
   children; young persons and families; social work;
   social services; adoption and foster care; delinquency);
   education (preschool education; special education);
   psychology (child development; psychotherapies);
   law; management (human resources; organisational
   behaviour); history of Barnardo's
Services: Internet access, photocopies, faxing facilities
Availability: Interlibrary loans; reference services available
   if the Librarian is contacted in advance to make an
   appointment. Charges are made for some services
Hours: 09.30-16.30 Monday to Friday
Transport: Tube: Barkingside
Special facilities: Refreshment and toilet facilities available;
   access for readers with disabilities

[37]
Barnet Libraries (London Borough of Barnet)
   Cultural Services
   The Old Town Hall
   Friern Barnet Lane
   London N11 3DL
Telephone: 020 8359 3164
Fax: 020 8359 3171
World Wide Web: www.barnet.gov.uk
Constitution: Public library, funded by local authority
Availability: Free public access for reference; borrowing

facilities for those who live, work or study in Barnet.
Barnet Libraries also operate a mobile library service
and a housebound readers' service, for more
information telephone 020 8458 1139. An Action
Point service provides the first point on contact for
residents who want information and advice about the
council and its services. Action Points are located at
four major sites in the borough: Hendon Town Hall,
Chipping Barnet Library, Edgware Library and
Golders Green Library

[37][a]
Barnet Local Studies and Archives Centre
   Hendon Catholic Social Centre
   Chapel Walk, Egerton Gardens
   London NW4
   (for visitors)

   c/o Hendon Library
   The Burroughs
   London NW4 4BQ
   (for correspondence)
Telephone: 020 8359 2876
Fax: 020 8359 2885
Email: hendon.library@barnet.gov.uk
Objectives/purposes: Archive repository and research
   centre for the Borough of Barnet
Key staff: Borough Archivist
Stock and subject coverage: Official records of the London
   Borough of Barnet and its administrative predecessors
   including parish and manor. Privately deposited
   records of people, institutions, estates and societies
   with the Borough. Printed information of all kinds
   relating to the Borough, including maps and
   illustrations
Services: Photocopies; microfilm reader-printer
Availability: Free access to members of the public, by
   appointment. Visitors should bring identification with
   them on their first visit
Hours: 09.30-12.30, 13.30-17.00 Tuesday, Wednesday and
   Saturday; 12.30-19.30 Thursday
Transport: Tube: Hendon; Bus: 143
Special facilities: Toilet facilities available
Publications: Finchley and Friern Barnet, by S Gillies and
   P Taylor; Hendon, Childs Hill, Golders Green, by S
   Gillies and P Taylor; Barnet, Edgware, Hadley and
   Totteridge, by J Corden and P Taylor (all published
   by Phillimore, £11.95 each). Full list of publications
   available on request

[37][b]
Burnt Oak Library
   Watling Avenue
   Edgware
   Middlesex HA8 0UB
Telephone: 020 8959 3112
Key staff: Branch Administrator
Stock and subject coverage: Adult and children's collections;
   open learning centre; local and community
   information; learning packs available to borrow
Services: Photocopies; PCs with internet access;
   room/hall for hire
Hours: 09.30-17.00 Tuesday, Wednesday and Friday;
   09.30-20.00 Thursday; 09.30-13.00, 14.00-17.00
   Saturday

Transport: Tube: Burnt Oak; Bus: 114, 204, 251, 302, 305
Special facilities: OPAC; access for users with disabilities

[37][c]
Childs Hill Library
320 Cricklewood Lane
London NW2 2QE
Telephone: 020 8455 5390
Key staff: Branch Administrator
Stock and subject coverage: Adult and children's collections; local and community information
Services: Photocopies; PCs with internet access; room/hall for hire
Hours: 09.30-17.00 Tuesday and Saturday; 09.30-20.00 Thursday and Friday
Transport: Tube: Golders Green; Bus: 113, 245, 260

[37][d]
Chipping Barnet Library
3 Stapylton Road
Barnet
Hertfordshire EN5 4QT
Telephone: 020 8539 4040
Minicom: 020 8539 4039
Key staff: Librarian
Stock and subject coverage: Adult and children's collections; reference collection; local and community information
Services: OPAC; b&w and colour photocopies (coin-operated); microfilm reader-printer; telephone and fax; PCs with internet access
Hours: 09.00-20.00 Monday, Wednesday and Friday; 09.00-17.00 Tuesday, Thursday and Saturday; 14.00-17.00 Sunday
Transport: Tube: High Barnet; Bus: X43, 84, 234, 326, 389, 399; small car park
Special facilities: Public toilets with baby changing facilities; access for users with disabilities

[37][e]
Church End Library
24 Hendon Lane
Finchley
London N3 1TR
Telephone, fax and Minicom: 020 8346 5711
Key staff: Librarian
Stock and subject coverage: Adult and children's collections; reference collection; local and community information
Services: OPAC; b&w and colour photocopies (coin-operated); PCs with internet access
Hours: 09.30-20.00 Monday and Wednesday; 09.30-17.00 Tuesday, Thursday, Friday and Saturday
Transport: Tube: Finchley Central; Bus: 82, 125, 143, 260, 326
Special facilities: Limited access for users with disabilities - access to ground floor only; CCTV magnifier and Minicom available

[37][f]
East Barnet Library
85 Brookhill Road
East Barnet
Hertfordshire EN4 8SG
Telephone: 020 8440 4376
Fax: 020 8449 1883
Key staff: Librarian
Stock and subject coverage: Adult and children's collections
Services: OPAC; b&w and colour photocopies (coin-operated); fax
Hours: 09.00-20.00 Tuesday and Thursday; 09.00-17.00 Monday, Wednesday, Friday and Saturday
Transport: Tube: Cockfosters (20 minute walk); Rail: Oakleigh Park (20 minute walk); Bus: 184, 307, 326, 384
Special facilities: Limited disabled access to ground floor only

[37][g]
East Finchley Library
226 High Road
Finchley
London N2 9BB
Telephone: 020 8883 2664
Key staff: Branch Administrator
Stock and subject coverage: Adult and children's collections; local and community information
Services: Photocopies; PCs with internet access; room for hire
Hours: 09.30-17.00 Tuesday, Friday and Saturday; 09.30-20.00 Wednesday and Thursday
Transport: Tube: East Finchley (15 minute walk); Bus: 263; small car park on premises
Special facilities: Access for users with disabilities – ramp to entrance with handrail

[37][h]
Edgware Library
Hale Lane
Edgware
Middlesex HA8 8NN
Telephone: 020 8359 2626
Fax: 020 8359 2139
Key staff: Librarian
Stock and subject coverage: Adult and children's collections; reference collection; local and community information
Services: OPAC; b&w and colour photocopies; CCTV magnifier; microfiche reader; PCs with internet access
Hours: 09.30-17.00 Monday, Wednesday, Friday and Saturday; 09.30-20.00 Tuesday and Thursday
Transport: Tube: Edgware; Bus: 220, 240, 288; small car park
Special facilities: Access for users with disabilities

[37][i]
Friern Barnet Library
Friern Barnet Road
Friern Barnet
London N11 3DS
Telephone: 020 8368 2680
Key staff: Branch Administrator

Stock and subject coverage: Adult and children's collections; reference collection; local and community information

Services: Photocopies; room for hire

Hours: 09.30-13.00, 14.00-20.00 Tuesday; 09.30-13.00, 14.00-17.00 Wednesday, Thursday and Friday; 09.30-17.00 Saturday

Transport: Tube: Arnos Grove (15 minute walk); Bus: 221; car park

Special facilities: Access for users with disabilities – ramp to entrance

[37][j]
Golders Green Library

156 Golders Green Road
London NW11 8HE

Telephone: 020 8359 2060
Fax: 020 8359 2066
Key staff: Branch Administrator
Stock and subject coverage: Adult and children's collections
Services: Photocopies; CCTV magnifier; room for hire; PCs with internet access
Hours: 09.30-20.00 Tuesday and Thursday; 09.30-17.00 Wednesday, Friday and Saturday; 14.00-17.00 Sunday
Transport: Tube: Golders Green; Bus: 83, 183, 240

[37][k]
Grahame Park Library

The Concourse
Grahame Park
London NW9 5XL

Telephone: 020 8200 0470
Key staff: Branch Administrator
Stock and subject coverage: Adult and children's collections; local and community information
Services: Photocopies; PCs with internet access
Hours: 09.30-13.00, 14.00-20.00 Tuesday; 09.30-13.00, 14.00-17.00 Wednesday, Thursday and Saturday; 09.30-13.00 Friday
Transport: Tube: Colindale (10 minute walk); Bus: 32, 204, 303; car park
Special facilities: Access for users with disabilities

[37][l]
Hampstead Garden Suburb Library

15 Market Place
Hampstead Garden Suburb
London NW11 6LB

Telephone: 020 8455 1235
Key staff: Branch Administrator
Stock and subject coverage: Adult and children's collections; local and community information
Services: Photocopies; PCs with internet access
Hours: 09.30-13.00, 14.00-18.00 Tuesday; 09.30-13.00 Wednesday; 09.30-13.00, 14.00-20.00 Thursday; 09.30-13.00, 14.00-17.00 Friday; 09.30-17.00 Saturday
Transport: Bus: H2, 102
Special facilities: Access for users with disabilities – slope to entrance with one step

[37][m]
Hendon Library

The Burroughs
Hendon
London NW4 4BQ

Telephone: 020 8359 2629 (enquiries)
  020 8359 2883 (reference)
Minicom: 020 8359 2879
Fax: 020 8359 2885
Key staff: Librarian
Stock and subject coverage: Comprehensive reference and loan collections on all subjects for adults and children. Music library with tapes, CDs and sheet music for loan. Large collection of business information and special collection of books on Alzheimer's disease
Services: B&w and colour photocopies; microfilm reader; CD-ROMs; PCs with internet access; computer courses; fax
Hours: 09.30-20.00 Monday, Wednesday and Thursday; 09.30-17.00 Tuesday, Friday and Saturday; 14.00-17.00 Sunday
Transport: Tube: Hendon Central (10 minute walk); Rail: Hendon, Thameslink (15 minute walk); Bus: 113, 143, 183, 186, 326
Special facilities: Toilet facilities; coffee lounge; access for users with disabilities to the ground floor only – reference and music libraries are on the first floor; CCTV magnifier and Minicom available

[37][n]
Mill Hill Library

Hartley Avenue
London NW7 2HX

Telephone: 020 8959 5066
Key staff: Branch Administrator
Stock and Subject coverage: Adult and children's collections; local and community information
Services: Photocopies; PCs with internet access; rooms for hire
Hours: 09.30-20.00 Tuesday and Thursday; 09.30-17.00 Wednesday, Friday and Saturday
Transport: Tube: Mill Hill Broadway; Bus: 114, 186, 221, 240, 302, 303
Special facilities: Access for users with disabilities – ramp entrance

[37][o]
North Finchley Library

Ravensdale Avenue
North Finchley
London N12 9HP

Telephone: 020 8445 4081
Key staff: Branch Administrator
Stock and subject coverage: Adult and children's collections; local and community information
Services: Photocopies; PCs with Internet access
Hours: 09.30-20.00 Tuesday and Friday; 09.30-17.00 Wednesday, Thursday and Saturday
Transport: Tube: Woodside Park (15 minutes walk); Bus: 125, 134, 263
Special facilities: Access for users with disabilities – ramp to entrance; two steps to adult and children's library and study facilities

[37][p]
Osidge Library
Brunswick Park Road
London N11 1EY
Telephone: 020 8368 0532
Key staff: Branch Administrator
Stock and subject coverage: Adult and children's collections; local and community information
Services: Photocopies; PCs with internet access; room/hall for hire
Hours: 09.30-20.00 Tuesday; 09.30-17.00 Wednesday, Thursday and Friday; 09.30-13.00, 14.00-17.00 Saturday
Transport: Bus: 125, 184; car park
Special facilities: Access for users with disabilities – wheelchair access to rear entrance

[37][q]
South Friern Library
Colney Hatch Lane
Muswell Hill
London N10 1HD
Telephone: 020 8883 6513
Key staff: Branch Administrator
Stock and subject coverage: Adult and children's collections; local and community information; special collection of vocal score sets
Services: Photocopies; microfiche reader; PCs with internet access
Hours: 09.30-13.00, 14.00-17.00 Tuesday; 09.30-13.00, 14.00-20.00 Wednesday; 09.30-13.00 Thursday; 09.30-13.00, 14.00-18.00 Friday; 09.30-17.00 Saturday
Transport: Bus: 43, X43, 134; car park
Special facilities: Access for users with disabilities – 16 steps from car park to entrance

[37][r]
Totteridge Library
109 Totteridge Lane
London N20 8DZ
Telephone: 020 8445 5288
Key staff: Branch Administrator
Stock and subject coverage: Adult and children's collections; local and community information
Services: Photocopies; PCs with internet access; room/hall for hire
Hours: 09.30-13.00, 14.00-20.00 Tuesday; 09.30-13.00, 14.00-18.00 Wednesday; 09.30-13.00, 14.00-17.00 Friday and Saturday
Transport: Tube: Totteridge and Whetstone; Bus: 251, 326
Special facilities: Access for users with disabilities – 12 steps to entrance with handrail; 18 steps to library on first floor

[38]
Barnet Hospital Library
Barnet and Chase Farm Hospitals NHS Trust
Postgraduate Medical Centre
Barnet Hospital
Wellhouse Lane
Barnet
Hertfordshire EN5 3DJ
Borough: Barnet

Telephone: 020 8216 4834
Fax: 020 8216 4678
E-mail: guy@barnet2.demon.co.uk
Constitution: NHS library
Key staff: Librarian: Guy Robinson; Library Assistant: Des Mogg
Stock and subject coverage: Medicine and health care
Services: Photocopies (priced), literature searching
Availability: Open to all NHS staff within the Hospital Trust
Hours: 09.00-17.00 Monday to Friday
Transport: Tube: High Barnet
Special facilities: Refreshment and toilet facilities available on site
Publications: Library list; Annual Report; special lists on individual topics, e.g. paediatrics

Linked organisations
Chase Healthcare Information Centre There is a separate Library at the Chase Farm Hospital, the Trust's other site

[39]
Barnet Museum
31 Wood Street
Barnet
Hertfordshire EN5 4BE
Borough: Barnet
Telephone: 020 8440 8066
Constitution: Registered charity
Key staff: Secretary: Dr Gillian Gear
Stock and subject coverage: Local history ephemera, books, photographs and costume collections
Availability: Reference only, by appointment
Hours: 14.30-16.30 Tuesday to Thursday; 10.30-12.30, 14.00-16.00 Saturday
Transport: Tube: Barnet; Bus: 84A
Special facilities: Toilet facilities available on site
Publications: Bulletins (annual); intermittent publications on local history
Note: The Museum acts as an agency for the Borough which owns the building but not the collections

[40]
The Basic Skills Agency Resource Centre
Information Services
Institute of Education
University of London
20 Bedford Way
London WC1H 0AL
Borough: Camden
Telephone: 020 7612 6069
Fax: 020 7612 6093
E-mail: b.sakarya@ioe.ac.uk
World Wide Web: www.ioe.ac.uk/library/bsa.html
Constitution: Established and funded by The Basic Skills Agency (formerly ALBSU), a registered charity. Situated in, and administered by, the Institute of Education, University of London
Objectives/purposes: Updating basic skills material
Key staff: Institute Librarian; Resource Centre Librarian
Stock and subject coverage: Opened in November 1993, the Resource Centre is relevant for anyone involved

or interested in basic skills. It holds all Basic Skills Agency material as well as substantial collections from other publishers

Services: Photocopies; CD-ROM PC, limited internet access; audio facilities and video viewing facilities

Availability: Reference facilities open to all who specify they wish to visit the Resource Centre at the Institute library membership desk

Hours: Full service as follows. Term-time: 09.30-21.00 Monday to Thursday, 10.30-17.00 Friday, 09.30-17.00 Saturday
Summer: 09.30-18.00 Monday to Thursday, 10.30-18.00 Friday

Transport: Tube: Russell Square, Holborn, Euston; Rail: Euston

Special facilities: Access for disabled users from Woburn Square or Bedford Way. Wheelchair access to all floors of the library. Toilet facilities available on site

Special features: The Institute of Education holds the largest collection of books and other materials on education in the UK

Publications: Basic Skills Agency Annual Report; Basic Skills (quarterly); BSA publications catalogue

Linked organisations

Institute of Education, London University The Resource Centre is based and run within the University of London

[41]
BBC Information and Archives

Telephone: 020 7557 2452
E-mail: commercial.unit@bbc.co.uk
For licensing agreements:
  Telephone: 020 8433 2861/2
  Fax: 020 8433 2939
  E-mail: ukls@bbcfootage.com
World Wide Web: www.bbcfootage.com/

Stock and subject coverage: BBC Information and Archives comprises the BBC's regional and national libraries, programme archives and research centres, and have a wealth of resources which stretch back over 70 years. Collections cover programme archive, photographs, music (both sheet and recorded), sound material and effects and document archives. BBC I&A has several research centres where its services and resources can be accessed. It is the largest service of its kind in the UK and the most extensive in the world. In addition to programme archives, the BBC has guardianship of the documents which are part of the Corporation's history and these holdings date back to the BBC's inception. External access to the collections and services is available and is subject to copyright or contractual restrictions. Licensing of material is dealt with through BBC Worldwide Library Sales (see contact details above)

Services: BBC Information and Archives accept payment by Visa, Delta, Mastercard and Switch. Under appropriate circumstances account can be set up for regular users

Availability: Commercial services available to all

[42]
The Benesh Institute

36 Battersea Square
London SW12 8EN
Borough: Wandsworth
Telephone: 020 7326 8031
Fax: 020 7326 8033
E-mail: beneshinstitute@rad.org.uk
World Wide Web: www.rad.org.uk
Constitution: Registered charity with voluntary subscribing membership
Objectives/purposes: International centre for Benesh Movement notation
Key staff: Senior Librarian (RAD): Eleanor Jack, Director: Liz Cunliffe
Stock and subject coverage: Main holding consists of a collection of Benesh Movement notation scores, including records of choreographic works, anthropological and medical research and teaching syllabuses. The Library takes all major dance publications and offers a range of dance, movement, notation and arts related books
Services: Internet access; photocopies (20 pence per copy)
Availability: Open to the public, by appointment only. Members of the Academy have full access on presentation of a membership card. Members of the Society for Dance Research are able to use the Library facilities free of charge, otherwise visiting fees will be charged. Details are available from Library staff
Hours: 10.00-18.00 Monday to Thursday; Fridays 10.00-17.30 excluding Bank holidays)
Transport: Tube: South Kensington; Rail: Clapham Junction; Bus: 48, 345
Special facilities: Refreshment and toilet facilities available; access for users with disabilities
Publications: Benesh News newsletter (annual, to Benesh members only), articles and Benesh News in Dance Gazette (3p.a.)

Linked organisations

Royal Academy of Dance The Benesh Institute is incorporated within the Royal Academy of Dance (since 1997)

[43]
Bexley (London Borough of Bexley)

World Wide Web: www.bexley.gov.uk/service/library.html
Constitution: Public library, funded by local authority
Key staff: Project Development Librarian: Peter Marshall
Special features: There are 13 libraries, divided into three areas: Contract Areas East; North West and South. The Administrative Headquarters is at the Libraries and Cultural Services Division of Leisure Services (Hill View, Hill View Drive, Welling, Kent DA16 3RY)
Contract Area East: Area Library: Central Library. Branch libraries: Barnehurst, Erith, North Heath and Slade Green

Contract Area North West: Area Library: Welling Library.
Branch libraries: Bostall, Thamesmead, Upper
Belvedere
Contract Area South: Area Library: Sidcup Library.
Branch libraries: Bexley Village Library, Blackfen
Library, Crayford Library
The three main Area Libraries are listed first followed by
the branch libraries in alphabetical order

[43][a]
Central Library
Townley Road
Bexleyheath
Kent DA6 7HJ
Telephone: 020 8301 1066
020 8301 5151 (information line)
020 8301 1545 (local studies)
020 8303 2393 (Education Information, Advice and
Guidance Centre)
Stock and subject coverage: Substantial lending and
reference departments; Local Studies and Archive
Centre; Education Information, Advice and Guidance
Centre, operated jointly with Prospects Careers
Services; community information; CD-ROMs for
loan; talking books; tourist information
Services: Photocopying and fax services; study facilities
Hours: 09.30-17.30 Monday to Wednesday, Friday;
09.30-20.00 Thursday; 09.30-17.00 Saturday; 10.00-
14.00 Sunday
Transport: Bus: B13, 229, routes to adjacent Broadway
Shopping Centre; on-street meter parking; adjacent
off-street parking
Special facilities: Access for users with disabilities to both
floors

[43][b]
Sidcup Library
Hadlow Road
Sidcup
Kent DA14 4AQ
Telephone: 020 8300 2958
Key staff: Customer Services Manager
Reference facilities: Adult and children's library;
community information; CDs; talking books; videos;
Council local information point
Services: Photocopying; study facilities
Hours: 09.30-20.00 Monday, Wednesday and Friday;
09.30-17.30 Tuesday; 09.30-17.00 Saturday
Transport: Rail: Sidcup; Bus: B14, R11, 51, 233, 321, 492,
854, 855, mobility buses pass along the adjacent High
Street; restricted street parking; nearby off-street car
parks
Special facilities: Access for users with disabilities

[43][c]
Welling Library
Bellegrove Road
Welling
Kent DA16 3PA
Telephone: 020 8303 2788
Key staff: Customer Services Manager
Reference facilities: Adult and children's library; reference
collection; community information; CDs; talking
books; videos; Council local information point
Services: Photocopying

Hours: 09.30-17.30 Monday, Thursday and Friday;
09.30-20.00 Tuesday; 09.30-13.00 Wednesday; 09.30-
17.00 Saturday
Transport: Rail: Welling; Bus: B16, 51, 89, 96; off-street
car parks nearby
Special facilities: Access for users with disabilities; lift to
separate children's library

[43][d]
Barnehurst Library
168 Mayplace Road East
Bexleyheath DA7 6EJ
Telephone: 01322 521663
Key staff: Customer Services Manager
Reference facilities: Adult and children's libraries;
community information; talking books; audio-visual
materials; photocopier
Hours: 14.15-17.30 Tuesday and Friday; 09.30-17.30
Thursday; 09.30-17.00 Saturday; closed 13.00-14.15
Transport: Rail: Barnhurst; Bus: 469, 492; some street
parking at Midfield Parade
Special facilities: Access for users with disabilities

[43][e]
Bexley Village Library
Bourne Road
Bexley
Kent DA5 1LU
Telephone: 01322 522168
Key staff: Customer Services Manager
Reference facilities: Adult and children's collections; small
reference collection; community information; talking
books; audio-visual materials; photocopier
Hours: 14.15-17.30 Monday, Tuesday and Thursday;
09.30-17.30 Friday; 09.30-13.00 Saturday; closed
13.00-14.15
Transport: Rail: Bexley; Bus: B15, 132, 229, 492; nearby
off-street parking
Special facilities: Access for users with disabilities

[43][f]
Blackfen Library
Cedar Avenue
Sidcup
Kent DA15 8NJ
Telephone: 020 8300 3010
Key staff: Customer Services Manager
Reference facilities: Separate adult and children's
departments; community information; study facilities;
CDs, talking books; videos; photocopier
Hours: 09.30-20.00 Tuesday; 09.30-13.00 Wednesday;
09.30-17.30 Thursday and Friday; 09.30-17.00
Saturday; closed 13.00-14.15
Transport: Bus: B13, 51, 429; on-street parking
Special facilities: Access for users with disabilities

[43][g]
Bostall Library
King Harold's Way
Bexleyheath
Kent DA7 5RE
Telephone: 020 8310 1779
Key staff: Customer Services Manager
Reference facilities: Adult and children's collections;

community information; talking books; audio-visual materials; photocopier
Hours: 09.30-13.00 Monday; 09.30-17.30 Tuesday and Thursday; 09.30-20.00 Friday; 09.30-17.00 Saturday; closed 13.00-14.15
Transport: Bus: 422; on-street parking
Special facilities: Access for users with disabilities

[43][h]
Crayford Library
Crayford Road
Crayford
Kent DA1 4ER
Telephone: 01322 526050
Key staff: Customer Services Manager
Reference facilities: Adult and children's library; small reference stock; community information; study facilities; talking books; Council local information point
Hours: 09.30-17.30 Monday, Tuesday and Thursday; 09.30-13.00 Wednesday; 09.30-17.00 Saturday
Transport: Rail: Crayford; Bus: 96, 428, 492
Special facilities: Access for users with disabilities

[43][i]
Erith Library
Walnut Tree Road
Erith
Kent DA8 1RS
Telephone: 01322 336582
Key staff: Customer Services Manager
Reference facilities: Adult and children's collections; small reference collection; community information; Council library information point; study facilities; Indic language section; videos, CDs and talking books; ten-workstation IT Suite jointly operated with Bexley Youth Services (available to library customers 09.30-17.30 Monday and Wednesday; 09.30-17.30 Tuesday and Friday and 09.30-12.30 Saturday); photocopier
Hours: 09.30-17.30 Monday and Wednesday; 09.30-20.00 Tuesday and Friday; 09.30-17.00 Saturday; closed 13.00-14.15
Transport: Train: Erith; Bus: 229, 469, 858 (mobility bus stop outside); restricted street parking, nearby off-street parking
Special facilities: Access for users with disabilities to library
Special features: Grade II listed building, newly refurbished and relaunched in September 2000. Erith Museum is located on the first floor

[43][j]
North Heath Library
Northumberland Heath
Erith
Kent DA8 1HG
Telephone: 01322 333663
Key staff: Readers' adviser
Reference facilities: Adult and children's library; small reference collection; community information; photocopier
Hours: 14.15-17.30 Monday; 09.30-20.00 Tuesday; 09.30-17.30 Thursday and Friday; 09.30-17.00 Saturday; closed 13.00-14.15

Transport: Bus: 229, 469; parking in adjacent pay-and-display car park
Special facilities: Access for users with disabilities

[43][k]
Slade Green Library
Bridge Road
Slade Green
Kent DA8 2HS
Telephone: 01322 335027
Key staff: Customer Services Manager
Reference facilities: Adult and children's library; community information; audio-visual collections; talking books; playsets for loan; photocopier
Hours: 14.15-17.30 Monday, Wednesday and Friday; 14.15-20.00 Tuesday; 09.30-17.00 Saturday; closed 13.00-14.15
Transport: Rail: Slade Green; Bus: 89, 469; small car park
Special facilities: Access for users with disabilities

[43][l]
Thamesmead Library
Binsey Walk
Thamesmead
London SE2 9TS
Telephone: 020 8310 9944
Key staff: Customer Services Manager
Reference facilities: Adult and children's library; community information; study facilities; Vietnamese and Chinese language collections; CDs, talking books, videos; Council local information point, photocopier
Hours: 09.30-17.30 Monday and Tuesday; 09.30-13.00 Wednesday; 09.30-20.00 Friday; 09.30-17.00 Saturday; closed 13.00-14.15
Transport: Rail: Abbey Wood; Bus: 229, 272, 401; parking at Binsey Walk
Special facilities: Access for users with disabilities to each floor (no internal lift)

[43][m]
Upper Belvedere Library
Upper Belvedere
Kent DA17 5EQ
Telephone: 01322 439760
Key staff: Customer Services Manager
Reference facilities: Adult and children's library; community information; talking books; videos; photocopier
Hours: 09.30-13.00 Monday; 09.30-20.00 Tuesday; 09.30-17.30 Wednesday and Friday; 09.30-17.00 Saturday; closed 13.0-14.15
Transport: Bus: 99, 401; small car park
Special facilities: Access for users with disabilities

[44]
Bharatiya Vidya Bhavan (Institute of Indian Art and Culture)
The Bhavan Centre
4A Castletown Road
West Kensington
London W14 9HQ
Borough: Hammersmith and Fulham

Telephone: 020 7381 4608
Fax: 020 7381 8758
E-mail: info@bhavan.net
World Wide Web: www.bhavan.net
Constitution: Registered charity and company limited by guarantee
Objectives/purposes: Promotion of Indian art and culture through classes in Indian music, dance, drama, languages, and complementary events
Key staff: Director: Dr MN Nandakumara
Stock and subject coverage: Titles on Indian philosophy, religion, art and culture
Availability: Open to all, by appointment, for reference only
Hours: 11.00–19.30 Monday to Friday
Transport: Tube: West Kensington, Barons Court
Special facilities: Vending machine; toilet facilities
Publications: Monthly newsletters

Linked organisations

Branch of parent organisation based in Bombay

[45]
Birkbeck College Library

Malet Street Library
Malet Street
London WC1E 7HX
The Library operates from three sites:

(i) Malet Street Library

(ii) Gresse Street Library
7-15 Gresse Street
London W1P 1PA
(economics, geography)

(iii) Continuing Education Library
(supplies by book-box to teaching centres only – no public access)
Borough: Camden
Telephone: 020 7631 6239
Fax: 020 7631 6066
E-mail: library-help@bbk.ac.uk
World Wide Web: www.bbk.ac.uk
Constitution: Department of a university
Key staff: Librarian: Philippa Dolphin; Deputy Librarian: Nick Bevan; Continuing Education Librarian: Elizabeth Charles
Stock and subject coverage: General university library covering all subjects except medicine, engineering and music. Research collections in: organisational psychology; English Victorian literature; macroeconomics; geographical information systems (GIS). Trevelyan Collection (library of RC Trevelyan, poet and classical scholar). College Archives (access by prior written appointment) containing: administrative records of the College and its predecessors 1823 onwards (London Mechanics' Institution 1823-1866; Birkbeck Literary and Scientific Institution 1866-1903; Birkbeck College 1903 onwards); papers of Sir John Lockwood (educational administrator), referring to the development of East African universities; papers of David Bohm, physicist. The papers of JD Bernal are on permanent loan to Cambridge University Library
Services: Self-service photocopies (Main Library and Gresse Street); self-service microform reader-printers;

video playback facilities; use of portable PCs permitted in certain parts of the Library; online searching restricted to use by College members only, for contractual and copyright reasons
Availability: Reciprocal reference access agreement for all current members of London University, members of UK Libraries Plus, the M25 Access Scheme and the SCONUL Vacation Scheme. Borrowing permitted for London University research postgraduates and academic staff. For external membership arrangements see website. All journals are for reference use only. Online and CD-ROM information services restricted to College members only
Hours: Term-time: 10.00-22.30 Monday to Thursday; 11.00-22.30 Friday; 10.00-20.00 Saturday and Sunday (Gresse Street: 10.00-21.30 Monday to Thursday; 11.00-21.30 Friday; 10.00-17.00 Saturday) Easter, Christmas and Summer vacation opening times: see Library website for details
Closed public holidays, between Christmas and New Year and for four days at Easter
Transport: Tube: Russell Square, Goodge Street, Warren Street, Euston Square; Bus: 10, 14, 24, 29, 68, 73, 91, 134, 168
Special facilities: Refreshment facilities; toilet facilities. Access for users with disabilities – direct wheelchair access available on the flat to most of Main Library (a ramp permits access up one low step at College entrance). The entrance to Gresse Street has a short flight of steps but assistance can be given. Access can be arranged locally to aids for partially-sighted and blind users
Publications: Series of paper and web-based user guides to library and information services and databases

Linked organisations

University of London Autonomous School of the federal University of London

[46]
Bishopsgate Institute

230 Bishopsgate
London EC2M 4QH
Borough: Corporation of London
Telephone: 020 7247 6198
Fax: 020 7247 6318
E-mail: amackay@bishopsgatelib.freeserve.co.uk
Constitution: Registered charity; independent non-profit distributing organisation
Objectives/purposes: General reference library and local history centre, with several special collections
Key staff: Chief Librarian: Alice Mackay; Acting Deputy: Jeff Abbott
Stock and subject coverage: General reference materials covering all subjects plus special collections including: London Collection on local history and family history covering inner London. Howell Collection on early trade unionism and labour history 1830-1914. Holyoake Collection on the Cooperative Movement 1840-1900. National Secular Society Library, including the Charles Bradlaugh Collection of manuscripts. Cooperative Societies Archive 1928 to present, largely London and the Home Counties, including some Cooperative

Women's Guild minute books. Freedom Press Library on the anarchist movement 1870 to present day (much on the Spanish Civil War). Raphael Samuel Working Papers (limited access)

Services: Photocopies; microfiche reader-printer

Availability: Access to all at no charge; charges made for services (photocopies, etc)

Hours: 09.30–17.30 Monday to Wednesday, Friday; 11.00–17.30 Thursday

Transport: Situated opposite Liverpool Street Station; Tube and Rail: Liverpool Street; Bus: 8, 26, 35, 47, 48, 149, 242

Special facilities: Toilet facilities; access for readers with disabilities

Special features: Grade II listed building designed by Art Nouveau architect Charles Harrison Townsend (opened 1894)

[47]
Bloomsbury Healthcare Library

52 Gower Street
London WC1E 6EB

Borough: Camden
Telephone: 020 7380 9097
Fax: 020 7436 5111
E-mail: ILL@bhlib.demon.co.uk
World Wide Web: www.bhllib.demon.co.uk
Constitution: NHS funded library
Key staff: Michael Larkin
Stock and subject coverage: Total stock 20,000 volumes, plus 200 journal titles and audiovisual materials. Subject coverage includes: all aspects of nursing; midwifery; some physiotherapy; psychology; sociology; education and management. Collection of local material relating to population, health, employment, etc.
Services: Photocopies; CD-ROM searching facilities
Availability: Available to staff and students of the local trust hospitals
Hours: 09.00–17.00 Monday, Wednesday and Friday; 09.00–19.00 Tuesday and Thursday. Closed weekends and public holidays
Transport: Tube: Goodge Street; Bus: 24, 29, 73
Special facilities: Toilet facilities available

Linked organisations
UCLH NHS Trust

[48]
BMI Health Services

Library and Information Services
Murray House
5 Vandon Street
London SW1H 0AL

Borough: Westminster
Telephone: 020 7593 5369
Fax: 020 7593 5351
E-mail: icameron@bmihs.co.uk
World Wide Web: www.bmihs.co.uk
Constitution: Private venture; company limited by guarantee
Key staff: Librarian/Information Officer: Isabel Cameron MA ALA
Stock and subject coverage: Ca. 1,000 books and pamphlets

and 100 journals covering occupational health, and health and safety
Services: Enquiries; photocopies; loans. Charges on application
Availability: To staff and others at the discretion of the Librarian
Hours: 09.00–17.00 Monday to Friday
Transport: Tube: St James's Park, Victoria; Rail: Victoria
Special facilities: Toilet facilities available

[49]
Boldero Library

Royal Free and University College Medical School
48 Riding House Street
London W1W 7EY

Borough: Camden
Telephone: 020 7679 9454
E-mail: bolderolib@ucl.ac.uk
Constitution: The Boldero Library is part of University College London
Key staff: Site Librarian: Patricia Campbell
Stock and subject coverage: Collections on clinical medicine
Services: Photocopiers; networked databases (available to members only)
Availability: Open to all bona fide researchers for reference only
Hours: Term-time: 09.00–21.00 Monday to Thursday: 09.30–17.00 Friday
Vacations: 09.00–19.00 Monday to Thursday; 09.30–17.00 Friday
Transport: Tube: Euston, Goodge Street, Oxford Circus; Rail: Euston
Special facilities: Toilet facilities available; access for users with disabilities by appointment only

Linked organisations
University College London Member of the College

[50]
Booktrust
(formerly Young Book Trust)

Book House
45 East Hill
London SW11 5PA

Borough: Wandsworth
Telephone: 020 8516 2977
Fax: 020 8516 2978
E-mail: info@booktrust.org.uk
World Wide Web: www.booktrust.org.uk and www.booktrusted.org
Constitution: Registered charity
Objectives/purposes: Booktrust is an educational charity which promotes books and reading
Key staff: Edgardo Zaghini
Stock and subject coverage: The children's library holds the majority of books for children published in the last two years. Those books are put onto a database from which age and subject related book lists are produced
Services: General research; photocopies
Availability: Free access to anybody interested in children's books. Reference only
Hours: 09.30–17.00 Monday to Friday

Transport: Rail: Clapham Junction, Wandsworth; Bus: 37, 39, 77A, 77C, 156, 170, 337

Special facilities: Toilet facilities available; access for users with disabilities including lift

Publications: Children's Book Handbook (annual); Children's Book News (3 p.a.); 100 Best Books (annual); Looking for an Author (biannual)

---

[51]
Brent Libraries (London Borough of Brent)

World Wide Web: www2.brent.gov.uk/library.nsf

Constitution: Public library, funded by local authority

Availability: Membership open to anyone living, working or studying in Brent. Reference, reading room facilities open to anyone

Special features: Main reference and information points at Willesden Green Library and Town Hall Library (listed first). The local history collections are housed at Cricklewood Library and Archive

[51][a]
Brent Library Service (Administrative Headquarters)

Room 410
Chesterfield House
9 Park Lane
Wembley
Middlesex HA9 7RW

Telephone: 020 8937 3144

Fax: 020 8937 3008

E-mail: karen.tyerman@brent.gov.uk

Key staff: Head of Libraries and Lifelong Learning: Karen Tyerman; Deputy Head of Libraries: John Readman

Hours: 09.00–17.00 Monday to Friday

[51][b]
Town Hall Library

Brent Town Hall
Forty Lane
Wembley Lane
Wembley
Middlesex HA9 9HV

Telephone: 020 8937 3500

Fax: 020 8937 3504

Key staff: Principal Librarian: Kevin Batchelor; Customer Services Officer: Christine Simpson

Stock and subject coverage: Comprehensive fiction and non-fiction collections; music library; reference library; European Information Point

Services: Photocopies (colour); CD-ROM searches and printouts; fax facilities; minicom; study area; free events

Availability: Open to the public

Hours: 11.00–20.00 Monday; 09.30–18.00 Tuesday and Friday; 09.30–20.00 Thursday; 09.30–1700 Saturday

Transport: Tube: Wembley Park; Bus: 83, 182, 245, 297

Special facilities: Toilet facilities available; access for users with disabilities

[51][c]
Willesden Green Library

95 High Road
Willesden NW10 2ST

Telephone: 020 8937 3400

Fax: 020 8937 3401

Key staff: Principal Librarian: John Verstraete; Customer Services Manager: Joan Jordan

Stock and subject coverage: Comprehensive fiction and non-fiction collections. Reference and business information, toy library, music library. Free events, advice sessions

Services: Colour photocopier; CD-ROM searches and printouts; fax facility; large study area

Hours: 11.00–20.00 Monday; 09.30–20.00 Tuesday and Thursday; 09.30–18.00 Wednesday and Saturday; 11.00–18.00 Sunday

Transport: Tube: Willesden Green; Bus: 6, 52, 98, 266, 302

Special facilities: Refreshment and toilet facilities available; access for users with disabilities – wheelchair access, toilet and lift

[51][d]
Barham Park Library

Harrow Road
Sudbury
Middlesex HA0 2HB

Telephone: 020 8937 3550

Fax: 020 8937 3553

Key staff: Principal Librarian: Kevin Batchelor; Customer Services Manager: Yamuna Tharmendiran

Reference facilities: Reference collection; local information; children's collection

Hours: 09.30–20.00 Wednesday; 11.00–18.00 Friday; 09.30–17.00 Saturday

Transport: Tube: Sudbury Town; Bus: 182, 18, 92

Special facilities: Access for users with disabilities; wheelchair access

[51][e]
Cricklewood Library and Archive

Olive Road
Cricklewood
London NW2 8UV

Telephone: 020 8937 3540

Fax: 020 8450 5211

Key staff: Principal Librarian: Mike Perry; Customer Services Manager: Daksha Vara

Reference facilities: Reference collection; local information

Hours: 13.00–17.00 Monday; 10.00–17.00 Tuesday and Saturday; 13.00–20.00 Thursday

Transport: Tube: Willesden Green, Dollis Hill; Bus: 16, 245, 226, 32

Special facilities: Access for users with disabilities

[51][f]
Ealing Road Library

Ealing Road
Wembley
Middlesex HA0 4BR

Telephone: 020 8937 3560

Fax: 020 8795 3425

Key staff: Principal Librarian: Kevin Batchelor;
Customer Services Officer: Sofiah Khan
Reference facilities: Reference collection; local
information; children's collection
Hours: 11.00-18.00 Monday; 09.30-18.00 Tuesday;
09.30-20.00 Thursday; 09.30-17.00 Saturday
Transport: Tube: Wembley Central, Alperton; Bus: 18, 79,
83, 92, 182, 224, 297
Special facilities: Access for users with disabilities

[51][g]
Harlesden Library
Craven Park Road
Harlesden
London NW10 1QJ
Telephone: 020 8965 7132
Fax: 020 8838 2199
Key staff: Principal Librarian: Mike Perry; Customer
Services Officer: John Sharkey
Reference facilities: Reference collection; local
information; children's collection
Hours: 11.00-18.00 Monday; 09.30-20.00 Thursday;
09.30-18.00 Friday; 09.30-17.00 Saturday
Transport: Tube: Willesden Junction; Bus: 18, 260, 266
Special facilities: Access for users with disabilities;
wheelchair access

[51][h]
Kensal Rise Library
Bathurst Gardens
Kensal Rise
London NW10 5JA
Telephone: 020 8969 0942
Fax: 020 8960 8399
E-mail: kensalriselibrary@brent.gov.uk
Key staff: Customer Services Officer: Robert Barker;
Librarian: Christie Ikeogu
Reference facilities: Reference collection; local
information; children's collection
Hours: 11.00-18.00 Monday; 13.00-19.00 Tuesday and
Thursday; 09.30-17.00 Saturday
Transport: Tube: Kensal Green; Rail: Kensal Rise; Bus: 6,
46, 52, 187, 302
Special facilities: Access for users with disabilities –
wheelchair access

[51][i]
Kilburn Library
Salusbury Road
Kilburn
London NW6 6NN
Telephone: 020 8937 3530
Fax: 020 7625 6387
E-mail: kilburnlibrary@brent.gov.uk
Key staff: Customer Services Officer: Pat Inkpin;
Librarian: Christie Ikeogu
Reference facilities: Reference collection; local
information; children's collection
Hours: 11.00 -18.00 Monday; 13.00-20.00 Tuesday;
09.30-18.00 Thursday; 09.30-17.00 Saturday
Transport: Tube: Queens Park; Bus: 6, 36, 46, 187, 206
Special facilities: Access for users with disabilities – access
for wheelchairs

[51][j]
Kingsbury Library
Stag Lane
Kingsbury
London NW9 9AE
Telephone: 020 8937 3520
Fax: 020 8905 0264
E-mail: kinsburylibrary@brent.gov.uk
Key staff: Customer Services Officer: Ann Doman;
Librarian: Janice Neil
Reference facilities: Reference collection; local
information; children's collection
Hours: 11.00-18.00 Monday; 09.30-20.00 Thursday;
09.30-17.00 Saturday
Transport: Tube: Kingsbury; Bus: 183, 204, 302
Special facilities: Access for users with disabilities –
wheelchair access

[51][k]
Neasden Library
277 Neasden Lane
London NW10 1QJ
Telephone: 020 8937 3580
Fax: 020 8208 3909
E-mail: neasdenlibrary@brent.gov.uk
Key staff: Customer Services Officer: Joy Ssendagire;
Librarian: Keith Hinton
Reference facilities: Local information
Hours: 13.00-18.00 Monday and Tuesday; 11.00-18.00
Thursday; 09.30-17.00 Saturday
Transport: Tube: Neasden; Bus: 297, 116
Special facilities: Access for users with disabilities – lift
provided

[51][l]
Preston Library
Carlton Avenue East
Wembley
Middlesex HA9 8PL
Telephone: 020 8937 3510
Fax: 020 8908 6220
E-mail: prestonlibrary@brent.gov.uk
Key staff: Customer Services Officer: Ann Doman;
Librarian: Janice Neil
Reference facilities: Reference collection; local
information; children's collection
Hours: 09.30-20.00 Tuesday; 11.00-18.00 Friday; 09.30-
17.00 Saturday
Transport: Tube: Preston Road; Bus: 79, 204, 224
Special facilities: Access for users with disabilities –
wheelchair access

[51][m]
Tokyngton Library
Monks Park
Wembley
Middlesex HA9 6JE
Telephone: 020 8937 3590
Fax: 020 8795 3440
E-mail: tokyngtonlibrary@brent.gov.uk
Key staff: Customer Services Officer: Yamuna
Tharmendiran; Librarian: Dave Lee
Reference facilities: Reference collection; local
information; children's collection
Hours: 13.00-18.00 Monday and Tuesday; 11.00-18.00
Thursday; 09.30-17.00 Saturday

Transport: Tube and Rail: Stonebridge Park; Bus: 18
Special facilities: Access for users with disabilities –
   wheelchair access

[52]
The Bridgeman Art Library
17-19 Garway Road
London W2 4PH
Borough: Westminster
Telephone: 020 7727 4065
Fax: 020 7792 8509
E-mail: info@bridgeman.co.uk
World Wide Web: www.bridgeman.co.uk
Constitution: Company limited by guarantee
Objectives/purposes: Fine art image archive for
   reproduction, representing thousands of museums,
   galleries and private collections around the world
Key staff: Picture Research Manager: Jenny Page; Rights
   Manager: Vivien Wheeler
Stock and subject coverage: Fine art, painting, sculpture,
   antiquities, architecture and design
Services: Online catalogue: fully searchable archive of
   over 100,000 images. In house database available for
   personal research by appointment
Availability: Transparencies are available on six week loan
   for consideration. Reproduction fees are charged for
   use – please apply to the library for a price list
Hours: 09.30-17.30 Monday to Friday
Transport: Tube: Bayswater, Queensway; Bus: 7, 27, 28,
   36, 70
Special facilities: Toilet facilities available; restricted access
   for users with disabilities
Publications: Quarterly newsletter for clients; book with
   800 captioned images; fully-searchable online archive

[53]
British Association for the Advancement of Science
BA
23 Savile Row
London W1S 2EZ
Borough: Westminster
Telephone: 020 7973 3500
Fax: 020 7973 3051
E-mail: help@the-ba.net
World Wide Web: www.the-ba.net
Constitution: Registered charity with subscribing
   membership
Objectives/purposes: Scientific society that exists to
   promote understanding of science, engineering and
   technology and their contribution to economic,
   cultural and social life
Key staff: PA to the Chief Executive: Lucy Johnson
Stock and subject coverage: Information on science and
   technology
Availability: Telephone and postal enquiries only
Publications: Science and Public Affairs (bi-monthly); The
   Banter (monthly)

Linked organisations
   Member organisation of COPUS – Committee on
   the Public Understanding of Science, along with the
   Royal Society and the Royal Institution

[54]
British Association of Psychotherapists
BAP
37 Mapesbury Road
London NW2 4HJ
Borough: Brent
Telephone: 020 8452 9823
Fax: 020 8452 5182
E-mail: library@bap-psychotherapy.org
World Wide Web: www.bap-psychotherapy.org
Constitution: Company limited by guarantee; registered
   charity; chartered professional body and training
   organisation
Key staff: Librarian (part time): Lucia Asnaghi
Stock and subject coverage: Ca. 4,000 books and 19 journal
   titles on child and adult psychoanalytic
   psychotherapy
Services: Photocopies; fax; some literature searches
Availability: Open to bona fide researchers upon
   application to the Librarian. Reference only. In some
   cases it may be possible for outside professionals to
   become subscribing members of the Library
Hours: Librarian present 18 hours per week
Transport: Tube: Kilburn; Rail: Brondesbury

Linked organisations
   The British Confederation of Psychotherapists
   BAP is a member of the British Confederation of
   Psychotherapists

[55]
The British Autogenic Society
BAS
Royal London Homoeopathic Hospital
Great Ormond Street
London WC1N 3HR
Borough: Camden
Telephone: 020 7713 6336
Fax: 020 7713 6336
World Wide Web: www.autogenic-therapy.org.uk
Constitution: Registered charity; association with
   voluntary subscribing membership; company limited
   by guarantee
Objectives/purposes: To promote, teach and further
   research into autogenic training and ensure proper
   guidance for training and practice
Key staff: Diana Altman
Stock and subject coverage: The Luthe Memorial Library.
   Includes reference works on autogenic therapy and
   the personal library and biographical material on the
   late Dr Wolfgang Luthe (founder of autogenic
   therapy in the UK, 1978)
Availability: By telephone appointment with Dr Alice
   Greene (020 7580 4188)
Transport: Tube: Russell Square
Special facilities: Toilet facilities available; access for users
   with disabilities
Publications: BAS Newsletter (bi-annual, available free to
   Members, Associate Members and Friends of BAS)
Special features: Library will move to the Royal
   Homoeopathic Hospital in 2003, after refurbishment
   has taken place

[56]
British Clothing Industry Association
BCIA
5 Portland Place
London W1N 3AA
Borough: Westminster
Telephone: 020 7636 7788
Fax: 020 7636 7515
E-mail: bcia@dial.pipex.com
Constitution: Association with voluntary subscribing
  membership
Services: Information, statistics and advice concerning the
  British clothing industry
Transport: Tube: Oxford Circus
Publications: Statistics; market surveys; health and safety
  briefing papers

---

[57]
The British College of Naturopathy and Osteopathy
BCNO
Frazer House
6 Netherhall Gardens
London NW3 5RR
Borough: Camden
Telephone: 020 7431 8859
Fax: 020 7431 3630
Constitution: Company limited by guarantee and
  registered charity
Key staff: Pete Folly BA DipLib
Stock and subject coverage: Ca. 3,000 books, 30 journals,
  dissertations and other materials on naturopathic and
  osteopathic subjects: dietetics; podiatry; orthopaedics;
  sports medicine; rheumatism; herbal medicine and
  special therapies. The Library includes historical
  collections of books on naturopathy and osteopathy
  dating from 1865, plus collections of videotapes,
  slides and slide tape sets
Services: Photocopier; CD-ROM Medline; Dietplan
  database and videos
Availability: Free access to College members. Reference
  access, by written application only, to genuine
  researchers and osteopaths
Hours: 08.30-18.30 Monday to Thursday; 08.30-17.30
  Friday
Transport: Tube: Finchley Road, Frognal
Special facilities: Refreshment and toilet facilities available
Special features: The main building, completed in 1883,
  was commissioned by the artist Thomas Davidson
  RA. The main library room was his studio with tall
  north facing mullioned windows
Publications: Free library guide leaflets

Linked organisations
General Osteopathic Council
General Council and Register of Naturopaths
University of Westminster
The College is professionally linked to both of the
Councils

[58]
British Council Education Information Service
10 Spring Gardens
London SW1A 2BN
Borough: Westminster
Telephone: 020 7389 4383 (answering machine)
Fax: 020 7389 4292
E-mail: education.enquiries@britishcouncil.org
World Wide Web: www.britishcouncil.org
Constitution: Registered charity
Services: The EIS is the London public enquiry point for
  the British Council, providing an enquiry service for
  overseas students in Britain and for British enquirers
  wishing to teach English as a foreign language
  (TEFL). The Information Centre provides a
  photocopying service, internet access and many CD-
  ROMs for information on educational opportunities
  in the UK. EIS also provides UK equivalents of
  international qualifications
Availability: Material available for reference only. Free
  information sheets, some priced publications
Hours: Personal callers 13.00-16.00 Tuesday to Thursday
Transport: Tube and Rail: Charing Cross; Bus: any bus to
  Trafalgar Square
Special facilities: Access for readers with disabilities; toilet
  facilities (including disabled toilet) on site
Publications: Hard copy education reference material
  available

---

[59]
British Dental Association Information Centre
BDA
64 Wimpole Street
London W1G 8YS
Borough: Westminster
Telephone: 020 7563 4545
Fax: 020 7935 6492
E-mail: infocentre@bda-dentistry.org.uk
World Wide Web: www.bda-dentistry.org.uk
Constitution: Association with voluntary subscribing
  membership
Key staff: Librarian: Mr RA Farbey BA ALA MIInfSc,
  ext 4193
Stock and subject coverage: Over 13,000 books, including
  600 in the Rare Books Collection; 250 current
  journals and several hundred no longer current;
  pamphlets; reprints; over 500 Packages (collections of
  reprints and photocopies on individual subjects).
  Main subject dentistry and oral health
Services: Loans (members only); online searching and
  CD-ROM MEDLINE service; photocopying
  (subject to copyright)
Availability: By appointment only to bona fide
  researchers. Loans to members only; telephone and
  written enquiries accepted, time permitting
Hours: 09.00-18.00 Monday to Friday
Transport: Tube: Oxford Circus, Bond Street
Special facilities: Toilet facilities available
Publications: Information Centre guide

[60]
British Energy Association
BEA

Second Floor
65 Buckingham Gate
London SW1E 6AP
Borough: Westminster
Telephone: 020 7222 9717
Fax: 020 7222 1935
E-mail: robbie.r.huston@bnfl.com
Constitution: Registered charity and independent non-profit making organisation
Key staff: Chairman: Neville Chamberlain; Vice Chairman: Graham Ward; Secretary: Colin Duncan; Administration Secretary: Robbie Huston (tel: 01925 834877; fax: 01925 835302)
Stock and subject coverage: Variety of books ranging from World Energy Council study reports to books covering energy published by other companies
Availability: Telephone, fax and email enquiries accepted
Hours: 09.00–17.00 Monday to Friday
Transport: Tube and Rail: Victoria

Linked organisations

World Energy Council The British Member of the Committee of the World Energy Council. The Association represents almost all the main UK energy companies, many smaller companies, institutions and consultancies interested in British energy and related issues in a global context, and communicates worldwide with those of similar interests and professional backgrounds through the network of the World Energy Council

[61]
British Film Institute National Library

21 Stephen Street
London W1P 2LN
Borough: Camden
Telephone: 020 7255 1444
Fax: 020 7436 2338
E-mail: library@bfi.org.uk
Key staff: Head of BFI National Library: Ray Templeton; Deputy Head (User Services): David Sharp; Deputy Head (Technical Services): Stephen Pearson
Stock and subject coverage: The Library holds the largest collection of information and documentation available on cinema; cinematography; television broadcasting; video; and related subjects.
The online database, SIFT (Summary of Information on Film and Television), includes information on the details of films, TV programmes and journal references. The database contains information about 500,000 titles, 750,000 personalities, 115,000 organisations, 6,000 events (festivals, awards, etc.) and 900,000 journal references.
The stock includes 41,000 books and pamphlets; 500 current journals (5,000 titles in stock, including old runs); 1.5 million newspaper clippings and press releases; 20,000 scripts; 250 personal collections, memorabilia, etc.; 22,000 press books and files on 3,000 festivals (1935 to date)

Services: Photocopies; SIFT database; CD-ROMs; microfilm reader-printer; printing from SIFT and CD-ROMs. Separate search room for access to special collections, scripts, etc. Advice to other libraries about film and TV literature. Staff in the Information Services Unit are available to undertake research and compile bibliographies on a fee paying basis. Telephone enquiries are free to occasional users. Commercial subscription service available
Availability: Access to the Reading Room is available to Annual Pass holders (£33 full, £20 discount) for reference only. Telephone, fax and written enquiries from individuals and other libraries are handled
Hours: 10.30–17.30 Monday, Friday; 13.00–20.00 Wednesday; 10.30–20.00 Tuesday, Thursday. Please phone to check opening times before calling in person. Special Collections Unit by appointment
Transport: Tube: Tottenham Court Road, Goodge Street
Special facilities: Toilet facilities; access for users with disabilities
Publications: Quarterly Accessions; bibliographies; Current Journals List; information packs (for A level students); BFI Film and Television Handbook

Linked organisations

British Film Institute The BFI National Library is part of the Education Department of the British Film Institute (BFI). The BFI Collections Department includes the National Film and Television Archive (NFTVA). For information about the holdings of the NFTVA, contact Olwyn Terris, Chief Cataloguer; for the Stills, Posters and Designs Unit (SPD), available by appointment only, contact SPD. For other access services, e.g. footage sales, viewing services, films for distribution, etc., contact BFI Collections Access. All services can be reached through the same telephone number

[62]
British Geological Survey, London Information Office
BGS

Natural History Museum Earth Galleries
Exhibition Road
London SW7 2DE
Borough: Kensington and Chelsea
Telephone: 020 7589 4090, 020 7942 5344
Fax: 020 7584 8270
E-mail: bgslondon@bgs.ac.uk
World Wide Web: www.bgs.ac.uk
Constitution: Government funded body
Key staff: Officer-in-Charge: Miss SJ Brackell
Stock and subject coverage: The material covers the geology of the British Isles and overseas countries. Stock includes British Geological Survey publications, including detailed geological maps, memoirs, formal reports, technical reports, well catalogues and photographs. Some textbooks and overseas maps. Holiday geology guides, Earthwise publications, BGS popular publications and some non BGS materials
Services: Geological information and advisory service. Affords public access to a reference and sale collection of BGS, and some non-BGS materials. Over the counter, telephone and mail-order sales of

Survey publications, including maps. Orders may also be placed for out-of-print and unpublished material. Online access to databases and indexes to collections, records and archives held by the National Geoscience Information Service at BGS Headquarters. Photocopying and facsimile transmission are available at standard charges

Availability: Open to the public for reference purposes. No appointment necessary. Bona fide visitors to the Office are exempt from museum entrance charges provided a BGS Visitor's Pass is collected at the Exhibition Road entrance to the museum

Hours: 10.00-17.00 Monday to Friday

Transport: Tube: South Kensington; Bus: C1, 9, 10, 14, 52, 74

Special facilities: Refreshment and toilet facilities available on site; access for users with disabilities

Publications: Guide to the London Information Office, Annual Reports, Earthwise (official magazine of BGS) and numerous lists and catalogues of Survey publications. Copies available on request

Linked organisations

Natural Environment Research Council (Swindon) The British Geological Survey is a component body of the Council

[63]
British Homeopathic Association
BHA

The Burford Loan Library
27A Devonshire Street
London W1G 6PN
Borough: Westminster
Telephone: 020 7486 2957
Fax: 020 7486 2957
E-mail: brithom@talk21.com
World Wide Web: www.trusthomeopathy.org
Constitution: Registered charity; association with voluntary subscribing membership
Objectives/purposes: An association which promotes homoeopathy and provides information on homoeopathic treatment availability
Key staff: Chief Executive: Sally Penrose
Stock and subject coverage: Collection of approximately 1,500 books and a number of journals, both historical and contemporary, on the subject of homeopathy. Listing of homeopathic doctors and homeopathic hospitals available
Services: Photocopies (at cost); free information on availability of homeopathy and explanatory leaflets
Availability: Open to friends of the Association for loan and reference services. Annual subscription £15. Researchers who apply in advance may be admitted, in which case a £5 day fee applies.
Hours: 09.30-17.00 Monday to Wednesday
Transport: Tube: Baker Street, Regent's Park
Publications: Health and Homeopathy (quarterly) and a selection of books

[64]
British Institute of International and Comparative Law
BIICL

Charles Clore House
17 Russell Square
London WC1B 5JP
Borough: Camden
Telephone: 020 7862 5168/5151
Fax: 020 7862 5152
E-mail: e.wintle@biicl.org
info@biicl.org
World Wide Web: www.biicl.org
Constitution: Registered charity; independent non-profit organisation and association with a voluntary subscribing membership
Objectives/purposes: Founded in 1958 to provide a centre for research, discussion and publication on the practical application of public and private international law and comparative and EC law
Key staff: Librarian: Elaine Wintle
Stock and subject coverage: Books, reports, journals, newsletters, press releases and treatises on the following subjects: public international law; private international law; foreign national law; European Communities and comparative law. Human rights depositary (European Convention on Human Rights)
Services: Photocopies; online searches of human rights database
Availability: The Library is open to members only, but at the discretion of the Librarian the public and researchers are allowed access. The material is available for reference only
Hours: 09.30-17.30 Monday to Friday
Transport: Tube: Russell Square
Special facilities: Refreshment and toilet facilities available on site; access for readers with disabilities
Publications: International and Comparative Law Quarterly; Bulletin of Legal Developments (fortnightly); Newsletter (quarterly). Wide range of publications on public international law; comparative law; private international law, European law and human rights

[65]
British Institute of Radiology
BIR

36 Portland Place
London W1B 1AT
Borough: Westminster
Telephone: 020 7307 1405
Fax: 020 7307 1414
E-mail: infocentre@bir.org.uk
World Wide Web: www.bir.org.uk
Constitution: Registered charity and independent non-profit organisation
Key staff: Librarian: Mrs Kate Sanders
Stock and subject coverage: Over 7,500 current books; approximately 80 current journals; unique historical and archive collections. Subject coverage includes: radiology, radiotherapy, radiography, MRI, ultrasound, radiation physics; nuclear medicine, computed tomography
Services: Online searching; photocopies. Members room

Guide to Libraries in London

available for BIR members only
Availability: Access to non-members by appointment
only. Library is for reference only and charges are
made for all services
Hours: 09.00-17.00 Monday, Wednesday and Friday;
10.00-18.00 Tuesday and Thursday
Transport: Tube: Oxford Circus, Great Portland Street,
Regent's Park
Special facilities: Free refreshments available for members;
meeting rooms and lecture theatre for hire
Special features: Prestigious location in Central London.
The Library is welcoming and offers a beautiful place
to work in
Publications: Annual report; British Journal of Radiology
(monthly); Imaging (quarterly); list of other BIR
publications available on request

Linked organisations

The Society and College of Radiographers
The Royal College of Radiologists
The British Medical Ultrasound Society
BIR maintains links with all these organisations

[66]
The British Knitting and Clothing Export Council
UK Fashion Exports
5 Portland Place
London W1N 3AA
Borough: Westminster
Telephone: 020 7636 5577
Fax: 020 7636 7848
E-mail: bkcec@bkcec.org.uk
Constitution: Independent non-profit distributing
organisation; company limited by guarantee and
association with voluntary subscribing membership
Objectives/purposes: Dedicated to helping manufacturers,
wholesalers and designers of clothing in the UK to
export
Key staff: Alison Ledgerwood, Laurian Davies, Maria
Alvarez
Stock and subject coverage: Small library of books, journals,
magazines and directories. Although small, all material
is gathered to be of use to the apparel exporter and is
regularly updated making it a practical and
commercially useful resource
Services: Photocopies
Availability: Access only to members of UK Fashion
Exports, BCIA, KIF or RATD (see sister
organisations). Access by appointment only. Material
is not available for loan
Hours: 09.00-17.30 Monday to Friday, by appointment
Transport: Tube: Oxford Circus
Special facilities: Refreshment and toilet facilities available;
access for users with disabilities
Publications: Fashion Buyer's Guide to Britain (annual);
British Apparel Export Awards Book (annual); British
Clothing Industry Yearbook (annual, published by
Kemps)

Linked organisations

British Apparel and Textile Confederation
Umbrella organisation

British Clothing Industry Association (BCIA)
Sister company
**Register of Apparel and Textile Designers
(RATD)** Sister company
British Fashion Council (BFC) Sister company
Knitting Industry Federation (KIF) Sister
company

[67]
The British Library
96 Euston Road
London NW1 2DB
Borough: Camden
Telephone: 020 7412 7332
World Wide Web: www.bl.uk

The British Library is the national library for the
United Kingdom, formed in 1973 from several major
national institutions. The Library is organised into five
directorates: Scholarship and Collections, Operations
and Services, Strategic Marketing and Communications,
e-Strategy, and Finance and Corporate Resources.
Contact information on the Library's London sites at St
Pancras and Colindale is provided here. The Library
also includes the **Document Supply Centre** and the
National Bibliographic Service, located at Boston
Spa, Wetherby, West Yorkshire LS23 7BQ, telephone
01937 546000
Contacting the British Library: Library users should
contact the Admissions Office (for enquiries about
acquiring a reader's pass); or the appropriate reading
room. Visitors to the St Pancras building should contact
Visitor Services. Enquiries from the media should be
directed to the British Library's Press Office.
For remote users the Library offers a number of
photocopy and reprographic services (subject to
copyright restrictions). Contact details for these are
listed under the reading room entries. For general
enquiries about reproductions, including the Picture
Library, telephone 020 7412 7614, fax: 020 7412 7771,
e-mail: reproductions@bl.uk
Transport: Tube and Rail: King's Cross/St Pancras,
Euston; Buses: SL1, SL2, 10, 30, 73, 91; there is a
covered area in the piazza for bicycles and street
parking in Midland Road and Ossulston Street
(metered until 18.30 Monday to Friday)
Special facilities: The British Library welcomes visitors
with disabilities and all parts of the building are
wheelchair-accessible. Induction loops are installed in
many areas, including the Conference Centre
auditorium. A Reader's Adviser is available to help
answer enquiries about assistance for readers with
disabilities, telephone 020 7412 7666, fax: 020 7412
7789
Publications: The British Library Bookshop stocks a wide
range of titles published by the BL, and other
publishers, on all aspects of the history and making of
books. For enquiries, or to request a catalogue,
telephone 020 7412 7735, e-mail bl-
bookshop@bl.uk. British Library titles can also be
purchased from Turpin Distribution Services Ltd.,
Blackhorse Road, Letchworth, Hertfordshire SG6
1HN, telephone: 01462 672555 (callers should ask
for 'The British Library Section'), fax: 01462 480947,
e-mail: turpin@turpinltd.com

The British Library

Note: The Library's entry is organised into two main sections. The first provides details of sections serving specific user communities – The National Bibliographic Service, The National Preservation Office, Press and Public Relations; Reader Admissions and Visitor Services. The second section focuses on specialist reading rooms or collection areas of the Library

[67][a]
National Bibliographic Service
NBS, London Unit

The British Library National Bibliographic Service is based primarily in Boston Spa, Yorkshire (Tel: 01937 546585, fax: 01937 546586, e-mail: nbs-info@bl.uk) and provides a range of services to the library and information community. The principal aim of NBS is to make available information both on UK publications and the British Library's collections to support customers' selection, acquisition, cataloguing, reference and information retrieval functions. To this end it is both a publisher and a database host. Its primary resource is the bibliographic records created for books, new journal titles and other materials deposited with the UK Legal Deposit Office or otherwise acquired by the British Library. These are supplemented by advance details of books from publishers who participate in the UK Cataloguing in Publication Programme and by the US Library of Congress database and other bibliographic databases. The main publication is the British National Bibliography, which is available in print, online and on CD-ROM. The NBS is responsible for replacing and developing the Catalogue Bridge database system by which records created by the British Library are distributed for use under licence by online database hosts and library suppliers worldwide.

[67][b]
National Preservation Office
NPO

Telephone: 020 7412 7612
Fax: 020 7412 7796
E-mail: npo@bl.uk
World Wide Web: www.bl.uk/services/preservation
Objectives: The aim of the National Preservation Office is to provide an independent focus for ensuring the preservation and continued accessibility of library and archive material held in the United Kingdom and Ireland.
  The NPO is supported by the British Library, with additional financial support provided by The Public Record Office, The National Library of Scotland, Trinity College Library Dublin, The consortium of University Research Libraries, Cambridge University Library, The National Library of Wales, The Bodleian Library, Oxford University, The National Library of Ireland, The Public Record Office of Northern Ireland and The Consortium of National and University Libraries.
Services: The NPO provides enquirers with information relating to preservation issues. Enquiry, information and referral services aim to promote best practice in print and digital preservation

Publications: NPO Journal (2 p.a.); range of free and priced publications, for further information contact the NPO or consult the website

[67][c]
Press and Public Relations

Telephone: 020 7412 7111
Fax: 020 7412 7168
E-mail: press-and-pr@bl.uk
Key staff: Head of Public Affairs: Greg Hayman; Head of PR: Valerie McBurney; Senior Press Officer: Catriona Finlayson; Press Officers: Bart Smith, Colin Beesley
Services: Press and Public Relations handles enquiries from the media on all aspects of the Library's work
Hours: 09.00-18.00 Monday to Friday

[67][d]
Reader Admissions Office

Telephone: 020 7412 7677
Fax: 020 7412 7794
E-mail: reader-admissions@bl.uk
Availability: Access to the British Library's London reading rooms is by pass only, which is issued through the Reader Admissions Office. The British Library is a research library and not a public reference library. Access to the reading rooms is provided to those who have reached a point in their research where no other library can adequately supply all the information required, or who can demonstrate a legitimate need to use items in the collection to further their research. The Admissions staff interview each applicant to confirm whether the Library can provide access to the national collection. If the criteria are met applicants are asked to complete a registration form and provide proof of identity bearing a signature (cheque card, driving license or passport)
Hours: 10.00-18.00 Monday; 09.30-18.00 Tuesday to Thursday; 09.30-16.30 Friday and Saturday

[67][e]
Visitor Services

Telephone: 020 7412 7332
E-mail: visitor-services@bl.uk (general visitor enquiries) boxoffice@bl.uk (Box Office and ticketing enquiries)
Attractions: The Library's St Pancras building is open seven days a week for visitors. Attractions include: a lively events programme, a range of exhibitions, services for schools and colleges, works of art by contemporary artists displayed inside and outside the building, a bookshop and catering facilities
Exhibitions: The Library's exhibition galleries are open to the public seven days a week. Free or charged temporary exhibitions are held in the Pearson Gallery on the Library's lower-ground floor, other permanent exhibitions are open to the public free of charge.
  The John Ritblat Gallery: Treasures of the British Library displays over 200 beautiful and fascinating items, including the Codex Sinaiticus (ca.350); the Lindisfarne Gospels (ca. 698), Magna Carta (1215), the Gutenberg Bible (1455); and Shakespeare's First Folio (1623). The displays include a wide range of

religious, literary, historical and musical works in the handwriting of Leonardo da Vinci, Lord Nelson, Jane Austen, Handel, Sir Paul McCartney and many others. 'Turning the Pages' – a unique interactive system also enables visitors to browse through a number of the Library's treasures.

The Workshop of Words, Sounds and Images is a hands-on interactive gallery that helps visitors to understand the people and the processes behind the creation of the manuscripts, printed books, sound recordings and other items on display in the exhibition galleries.

The Philatelic Exhibition provides the best permanent display of diverse, classic stamps in the world: approximately 80,000 items in 1000 display frames, including the Great Britain one penny black and the Chand Collection of Classic Mauritius Postage Stamps and Postal History, lent by Singapore philatelist Vikram Chand.

Guided tours: There are guided tours of the public areas of the building on Monday, Wednesday, and Friday at 15.00, and on Saturday at 10.30 and 15.00. These cost £5 per person (£3.50 concessions) and last approximately one hour. Tours, which include a visit to one of the Library's reading rooms, take place on Tuesday at 18.30 and on Sunday at 11.30 and 15.00. These cost £6 per person (£4.50 concessions). Bookings can be made up to two weeks in advance and are limited to a maximum of five tickets per transaction.

Hours: The St Pancras building is open to visitors at the following times: 09.30-18.00 Monday, Wednesday, Thursday and Friday; 09.30-20.00 Tuesday; 09.30-17.00 Saturday; 11.00-17.00 Sunday and Bank Holidays. Events in the Conference Centre, which has a separate entrance from the Piazza, often take place outside these hours

[67][f]
Humanities Reading Rooms

Telephone: 020 7412 7000 (switchboard)
020 7412 7676 (Enquiries, holdings, etc.)
Fax: 020 7412 7609
E-mail: reader-services-enquiries@bl.uk
Key staff: Head of British Collections: John Tuck; Head of European and American Collections: Stephen Bury
Stock and subject coverage: The collection contains over 9 million printed books and journals on humanities and social sciences
Services: Reference help and bibliographical advice are given by post and telephone on all subjects covered by the main library and on special materials as indicated below. However, extended research on enquiries cannot be undertaken. Photocopy and photographic services for onsite and remote users, telephone: 020 7412 7613, fax: 020 7412 7596
A full photographic and reprographic service is provided
Hours: 10.00-20.00 Monday; 09.30-20.00 Tuesday to Thursday; 09.30-17.00 Friday and Saturday

[67][g]
Librarianship and Information Sciences Service
LIS

Telephone: 020 7412 7676
Fax: 020 7412 7691
E-mail: lis@bl.uk
Key staff: Head of British Collections: John Tuck
Stock and subject coverage: Extensive collection of material on librarianship and information science, which covers both current practice and the history of libraries internationally. Information retrieval, computer applications, library management and archives management are covered in depth. Publishing, new information storage techniques and traditional and modern printing practices are examples of related subjects collected more selectively
Services: The British Library Public Catalogue (BLPC) is available free of charge on the web. Both Library and Information Science Abstracts and Library Literature and Information Science Full Text are available online (onsite only). Searches are free, but there is a charge for printouts. Self-service photocopies; photocopy and photographic services for onsite and remote users, telephone: 020 7412 7613, fax: 020 7412 7596
Hours: 10.00-20.00 Monday; 09.30-20.00 Tuesday to Thursday; 09.30-17.00 Friday and Saturday

[67][h]
Manuscripts Reading Room

Telephone: 020 7412 7513
Fax: 020 7412 7745
E-mail: mss@bl.uk
Key staff: Head of British Collections: John Tuck; Curator and Reading Room Manager: Brett Dolman
Stock and subject coverage: An extensive collection of manuscripts (ca. 100,000 volumes), including books and documents of all kinds, in all European languages, ranging from Greek papyri to modern material, illuminated mss, charters, rolls, detached seals, manuscript music, maps, plans, topographical drawings and many literary and historic archives. Facilities for readers are provided in the Manuscripts Reading Room. The Department provides a full range of information and photographic services
Services: The Manuscripts catalogue (molcat.bl.uk) on the web offers access to the mainstream catalogues of the Department of Manuscripts and covers accessions from 1753 to the present day. Photocopy and photographic services for onsite and remote users, telephone: 020 7412 7512, fax: 020 7412 7511, e-mail: reproductions-mss@bl.uk
Publications: The best source for detailed information on the Manuscripts Collection is The British Library: Guide to the Catalogues and Indexes of the Department of Manuscripts, 3rd ed., Margaret Nickson

[67][i]
Maps Reading Room
Telephone: 020 7412 7702
Fax: 020 7412 7780
E-mail: maps@bl.uk
Key staff: Head of European and American Collections: Stephen Bury; Map Librarian and Curator of Manuscript Maps: Peter Barber
Stock and subject coverage: Over 4 million cartographic items including atlases, maps, charts, globes and topographical views in both manuscript and printed form. In particular the collection covers British cartography past and present, including legal deposit holdings of Ordnance Survey and other British map publications, Colonial and Revolutionary maps of America, Renaissance cartography and thematic maps. The special collections are King George III's Maritime and Topographical Collections, the Crace Collection of maps and plans of London, the Beudeker Collection of Dutch maps and views (1600-1750). The Map Library also holds current topographic map series for all parts of the world at scales 1:50,000 and smaller. An archive of Landsat imagery of the British Isles is held, with catalogues and browse film of satellite imagery worldwide
Services: Enquiry service by correspondence, personal visit and telephone. The catalogue of most of the Library's map collections is not on the main online catalogue but available in the reading room on CD-ROM and in printed form. Photocopy and photographic services for onsite and remote users, telephone: 020 7412 7892, fax: 020 7412 7511
Hours: 10.00-17.00 Monday; 09.30-17.00 Tuesday to Saturday
Publications: Range of catalogues and books on the Map Library exhibitions and collections available from the British Library bookshop

[67][j]
Newspaper Library
Colindale Avenue
London NW9 5HE
Borough: Barnet
Telephone: 020 7412 7353
Fax: 020 7412 7379
Key staff: Head of British Collections: John Tuck; Head of Newspaper Library: Ed King; Information Officer: Jill Allbrooke
Stock and subject coverage: The British Library Newspaper Library holds London newspapers from 1801 onwards; English provincial, Welsh, Scottish, Irish, Commonwealth and foreign newspapers from about 1700 onwards and British weekly and fortnightly popular journals. Holdings include over 52,000 separate newspaper, journal, and periodical titles – including over 664,000 volumes and parcels of newspapers and 330,000 reels of microfilm.
Services: Photocopies; photographs and microfilm copies may be ordered. There is normally no same-day service, but self-service microfilm reader-printers are available. CD-ROMs of British national newspapers are available on open access
Availability: Admission is granted for the purposes of research and reference not readily available in other public libraries. Persons under 18 require written

permission to use the Library. Readers must provide proof of identity. Holders of the main British Library pass are admitted without formality. Material is not available for loan
Hours: 10.00-16.45 Monday to Saturday
Transport: Tube: Colindale; Bus: 32, 204, 292, 303
Special facilities: Refreshment and toilet facilities available on site; readers can use their own laptop computers in the reading rooms and there are facilities for users who wish to use their own typewriters or tape-recorders. Disabled readers are advised to telephone in advance so that any special arrangements for access can be made. Some signage in public areas of the Library incorporates braille for visually impaired users and an induction loop is in operation at the entrance to the reading rooms
Publications: Newsletter (2 p.a.); Bibliography of British Newspapers (ongoing); NEWSPLAN reports (ongoing)
Special features: The only large integrated newspaper library service in the world

[67][k]
Oriental and India Office Collections Reading Room
Telephone: 020 7412 7873/7883
Fax: 020 7412 7641
Key staff: Head of Asian, Pacific and African Collections: Graham Shaw; Reading Room Manager, Oriental and India Office Collections: Hedley Sutton
Stock and subject coverage: Oriental and India Office Collections provides the focus within the British Library for collecting and providing access to material relating to all the cultures of Asia and North Africa and the European interaction with them.
Oriental language collections: The collection includes 65,000 oriental manuscripts (plus thousands more fragments in the Stein, Genizah and other collections), some 900,000 printed books in oriental languages and about 120,000 volumes of oriental periodicals and newspapers. Oriental Collections covers over 350 languages or language groups, ranging from Chinese, spoken by one-third of the world's population, to languages of the New Guinea group spoken by only a few hundred people. It is particularly rich in Hebrew, Arabic, Turkish, Persian, Indian and Chinese manuscripts, and there are important collections of Chinese, Japanese and Tibetan blockprinted books. Contemporary material on the countries and peoples of Asia is also well represented
India Office collections: The India Office Records are the documentary archives of the administration in London of the pre-1947 government of India. They comprise the archives of the East India Company (1600-1858), of the Board of Control or Board of Commissioners for the Affairs of India (1784-1858), of the India Office (1858-1947), of the Burma Office (1937-1948), and of a number of related British agencies overseas. The India Office Records are administered by the British Library as part of the public records of the United Kingdom. The collection includes 11,700 volumes and unbound manuscripts relating to Indian and British-Indian history, 70,200 volumes of Indian Official Publications and the relevant UK Official

Publications from 1800 plus 41,000 printed and manuscript maps, charts and plans.

The Prints, Drawings and Photographs Section of the Oriental and India Office Collections comprises the majority of the British Library's holdings of visual material relating to South Asia. The collections now comprise about 12,000 Indian paintings, 16,000 British drawings, and 250,000 photographs, as well as smaller collections in other media

Hours: 10.00-17.00 Monday; 09.30-17.00 Tuesday to Saturday

The Print Room is open by appointment: 10.00-12.00, 14.00-17.00 Monday to Friday

Services: Microfilm, photocopying and reprographic services

Publications: Guide to the India Office Library, by SC Sutton (1967); Guide to the India Office Records, 1600-1858, by W Foster; various guides to the records and catalogues of printed books, manuscripts, and prints and drawings

[67][l]
Philatelic Collections

Telephone: 020 7412 7635
Fax: 020 7412 7745
E-mail: philatelic@bl.uk
Key staff: Head of European and American Collections: Stephen Bury; Head of the Philatelic Collections: DR Beech

Stock and subject coverage: The British Library Philatelic Collections are the National Philatelic Collections of the United Kingdom. The Collections were established in 1891, with the bequest of the Tapling Collection, and consist of over eight million items, including postage and revenue stamps, postal stationery, artwork, essays, proofs, covers and entires, 'cinderella' material, specimen issues, airmails, some postal history materials, official and private posts, etc. for almost all countries and periods. This range of material, together with philatelic books, photographs, general reference material, maps, newspapers and official publications elsewhere in the Library, make the British Library one of the world's prime philatelic research centres

Services: Photographic and reprographic services available

Hours: By appointment only: 10.00-16.00 Monday; 09.30-16.00 Tuesday to Friday

[67][m]
Rare Books and Music Reading Room

Telephone: 020 7412 7676 (Rare Books)
E-mail: rare-books@bl.uk
Telephone: 020 7412 7772 (Music)
E-mail: music-collections@bl.uk
Key staff: Head of British Collections: John Tuck; Reading Room Manager and Early Printed Collections Support: John Goldfinch

Stock and subject coverage: The Rare Books and Music reading room provides access to: reference collections of early (printed before 1851) and rare printed material in Western languages; printed and manuscript music, and manuscript papers relating to music and musicians; and to the Listening and Viewing Service of the National Sound Archive. The Library's music collection comprises over

1,500,000 individual items of printed music from all periods from the 16th century to the present, from all countries, with an emphasis on Western art music. Holdings of pre-1800 music are particularly strong. Over 100,000 single items of manuscript music are held. The collection aims to be as complete an archive as possible of British music and contains many primary sources for the history of music in England, especially for the 20th century. One copy of every current British publication (including popular and ephemeral music) is received by copyright deposit. Current and antiquarian foreign publications are bought more selectively, but still extensively. Special collections include the Royal Music Library (noted for its Handel autographs), the Paul Hirsch Music Library, which is particularly strong in first and early editions of the Viennese classics, and the Stefan Zweig collection, which includes autographs of Mozart and many other major composers

Services: Photocopy and photographic services for onsite and remote users

Hours: 10.00-20.00 Monday; 09.30-20.00 Tuesday to Thursday; 09.30-17.00 Friday and Saturday

Publications: Catalogues and books on the music collections available from the BL Bookshop

[67][n]
Sound Archive

Telephone: 020 7412 7418 (Listening and Viewing Service)
020 7412 7440 (Recorded Sound Information Service)
Fax: 020 7412 7441
E-mail: nsa@bl.uk
Key staff: Head of British Collections: John Tuck; Director, Sound Archive: Crispin Jewitt

Stock and subject coverage: The British Library Sound Archive holds about 1,178,000 discs and over 195,000 tape recordings. It aims to be comprehensive with special responsibility to British recording. The collection includes music of all kinds (western art music, pop, international and jazz), oral history, sound effects and documentary material, wildlife sounds, drama and spoken literature; selective recordings from BBC broadcasts, BBC transcription discs and duplicate copies of BBC Sound Archives material. Through voluntary deposit it attempts to acquire copies of every disc commercially issued in the UK, and it also makes its own recordings at outside venues and encourages deposit of private collections. The printed material relating to sound recordings includes books and periodicals from around the world, an extensive collection of discographies, and one of the largest collections of commercial record catalogues dating back to the early 1900s

Services: Catalogue of sound recordings available free online and in the reading rooms (cadensa.bl.uk), Listening and Viewing Service and Library and Information Service

The Archive's catalogue of sound recordings includes information on 2.5 million published and unpublished recordings and allows users to search for artists, composers, musical works, interviews, recordings of plays and poetry, wildlife sounds, oral history, sound effects, record companies and radio broadcasts.

The Listening and Viewing Service is based in the Rare Books and Music reading room of the British Library. It operates by appointment, to ensure the availability of equipment and of recordings, which may need essential preservation work prior to playback. Both individual and group listening and viewing facilities are available. There is also a Northern Listening Service at the British Library's premises at Boston Spa in Yorkshire. To use the Listening and Viewing Service users should select recordings using the catalogue and note down the 'Call Number', which is given on the screen, to help staff deal with the request more quickly. A Recorded Sound Information Service is also available for those who are unable to find a particular recording (some recordings held in the Archive's collections are not yet included in the catalogue). Having located the recordings they want, users should make an appointment (by phone, fax, post or e-mail).
The Recorded Sound Information Service is based in the Humanities 2 reading room. Reference collections include a wide range of CD-ROMs such as the RED catalogue and 'Gramofile'. BBC Sound Archive and EMI Archive catalogues are held on microfiche and in printed form. Expert subject curators can offer further advice and assistance

Hours: Listening and Viewing Service: 10.00-18.00 Monday and Thursday; 10.0-20.00 Tuesday and Wednesday; 10.00-17.00 Friday and Saturday
Northern Listening Service at British Library Document Supply Centre, Boston Spa, West Yorkshire (tel: 020 7412 7418) 09.15-16.30 Monday to Friday
Recorded Sound Information Service: 10.00-20.00 Monday; 09.30-20.00 Tuesday and Thursday; 09.30-17.00 Friday and Saturday

Publications: The Sound Archive produces a range of print and audio publications available from the BL Bookshop

[67][o]
Science Technology and Business Reading Rooms

Since June 1999 all five of the British Library Science, Technology and Business reading rooms have been brought together at the St Pancras site. The Library has the most comprehensive reference collection in Western Europe of modern science, technology and commerce and patents information. There are special services providing business, patent, health care, scientific, technical and environmental information, and online searching of computerised databases. A charge is made for some services: further details on request

Telephone: 020 7412 7494/7496 (General enquiries)
020 7412 7454/7977 (The British Library Business Line)
020 7412 7919 (British and EPO patent enquiries)
020 7412 7902 (Foreign patents)
020 7412 7536 (Social Policy Information Service enquiries)

Fax: 020 7412 7217/7495 (General enquiries)

E-mail: scitech@bl.uk (General enquiries)
business-information@bl.uk
social-policy@bl.uk
patents-information@bl.uk

Key staff: Head of Science, Technology and Innovation Information Services: position vacant

Stock and subject coverage: Physical sciences and technologies; engineering; business information on companies, markets and products; British, European and Patent Co-operation Treaty patents. Life sciences and technologies, including biotechnology, medicine and agriculture; earth sciences, mathematics and astronomy. Current and historical government publications of all countries and intergovernmental bodies, and for social science subjects

Services: Self-help and while-you-wait photocopy services available

Hours: 10.00-20.00 Monday; 09.30-20.00 Tuesday to Thursday; 09.30-17.00 Friday and Saturday

[68]
British Library of Political and Economic Science
BLPES

Lionel Robbins Building
10 Portugal Street
London WC2A 2HD

Borough: Westminster

Telephone: 020 7955 7229

Fax: 020 7955 7454

E-mail: library@lse.ac.uk

World Wide Web: www.library.lse.ac.uk

Key staff: Librarian and Director of Information Services: Jean Sykes; Deputy Librarian: Maureen Wade; Information Services Manager: Kate Sloss; Archivist: Sue Donnelly

Stock and subject coverage: Ca. 1 million bound volumes and 28,000 journals. Perhaps the largest single collection in the world covering the social sciences as a whole. Over 12,000 non-government journals, 4,600 of which are taken currently. Over 13,000 government serials, of which 8,700 are received currently. Extensive manuscript and archival collections

Services: Self service photocopies

Availability: Reference access to non-LSE members if linked to an academic institution. Charges made to most other categories. For admission enquiries contact 020 7955 6733, e-mail: library.admissions@lse.ac.uk

Hours: Term-time and Easter vacation: 09.00-21.20; 10.00-17.00 Saturday
Summer vacation: 09.00-20.00 Monday to Thursday; 09.00-17.00 Friday

Transport: Tube: Holborn, Aldwych, Charing Cross, Temple; Rail: Charing Cross

Special facilities: Refreshment and toilet facilities available on site; access for users with disabilities

Publications: International Bibliography of the Social Sciences (IBSS); IBSS On-line (and CD version)

Linked organisations

University of London   Part of the University

[69]
British Maritime Technology
BMT

Orlando House
1 Waldegrave Road
Teddington
Middlesex TW11 8LZ
Borough: Richmond on Thames
Telephone: 020 8943 5544
Fax: 020 8943 5347
E-mail: davidg@bmtlib.demon.co.uk
World Wide Web: www.bmt.org
Constitution: As of June 1998, BMT is owned by an
 employee benefit trust
Objectives/purposes: Maritime and related research,
 consultancy and technology transfer
Key staff: Chief Executive: Mr D Goodrich; Managing
 Director: Mr R Swann; Librarian: Mr DJ Griffiths
Stock and subject coverage: Textbooks, technical reports,
 journals, conference proceedings and transactions of
 specialised institutions. Subject coverage includes:
 naval architecture; maritime technology; offshore
 engineering; wind engineering and fluid mechanics.
 Special holdings include: report material of former
 ship, aero and maritime science divisions of the
 National Physical Laboratory; report material of the
 former National Maritime Institute; transactions of
 the Royal Institution of Naval Architects, the Society
 of Naval Architects and Marine Engineers, the North
 East Coast Institution of Engineers and Shipbuilders
 and the Institution of Engineers and Shipbuilders in
 Scotland
Services: Photocopying and fax machines not normally
 available to visitors. Online searching by Librarian
 (charges are made). BMT Abstracts, publicly available
 database available online at
 www.marinescienceandtechnology.com Also
 available as part of Marine Technology Abstracts
 (CD-ROM and web versions), see www.imare.org.uk
 jointly produced with the Institute of Marine
 Engineers
Availability: Access limited to special cases (by
 arrangement only). Material available for loan
 through inter-library loan system. Charges are made
 for research/subject enquiries
Hours: 08.30-17.00 Monday to Thursday; 08.30-16.30
 Friday
Transport: Rail: Teddington; Bus: 33, R68, 281, 285
Special facilities: Toilet facilities; access for users with
 disabilities
Publications: BMT Abstracts summaries of worldwide
 literature on maritime technology (monthly); BMT
 News (quarterly - free); Report and Profile (annual -
 free)

Linked organisations

BMT was formed in 1985 by a merger of NMI Ltd
(formerly the National Maritime Institute) and the
British Ship Research Association. It has a group of
wholly owned subsidiary companies

[70]
British Medical Association
BMA

BMA Library
BMA House
Tavistock Square
London WC1H 9JP
Borough: Camden
Telephone: 020 7383 6625 (general enquiries)
 020 7383 6060 (reference desk)
Fax: 020 7388 2544
E-mail: bma-library@bma.org.uk
World Wide Web: www.bma.org.uk
Constitution: Independent non-profit organisation
Key staff: Librarian: Tony McSean
Stock and subject coverage: 50,000 monographs, 3,200
 journals (1,250 currently received), 3,000 videos and
 films, specialising in clinical medicine and allied
 sciences, and the social aspects of medicine.
 Comprehensive reference collection
Services: Photocopying; book, video and film loans;
 footage and film research; bibliographic research and
 consultancy. Free, unlimited access to Medline for
 BMA members. Some priced services available to
 non-members
Availability: All members of the BMA; any library or
 information service with institutional membership of
 the Library; others at the Librarian's discretion
Hours: 09.00-18.00 Monday to Friday
Transport: Tube: Russell Square, Euston; Rail: Euston;
 Bus: 68
Special facilities: Refreshment and toilet facilities available
 on site; access for readers with disabilities

[71]
The British Museum
World Wide Web: www.thebritishmuseum.ac.uk
Constitution: Government funded body

[71][a]
Anthropology Library, British Museum
Department of Ethnography

6 Burlington Gardens
London W1S 3EX
The Museum of Mankind closed to the public on 31
December 1997 but the Library remains open
Telephone: 020 7323 8031 (direct to Reading Room)
Fax: 020 7323 8013
E-mail: s.mackie@british-museum.ac.uk
Key staff: Senior Librarian: Mrs Sheila Mackie
Stock and subject coverage: Comprises the stock of the
 Department of Ethnography Library, British Museum
 and the former Royal Anthropological Institute
 Library. About 120,000 books and monographs and
 4,000 journal titles (1,400 current). The collection
 covers social and cultural anthropology; material
 culture and traditional art; archaeology (mainly of the
 Americas); some biological anthropology and
 linguistics. Special Collections include: Sir Eric
 Thompson Library (Mesoamerican archaeology with
 emphasis on the Maya); Christy Library (19th
 century antiquarian and travel)

Services: Enquiry service (telephone enquiries should be made direct to the Reading Room, not to the Librarian); loans to Fellows of the Royal Anthropological Institute; photocopies

Availability: Limited places available: researchers and readers may apply for entry in writing or by telephoning the Reading Room for an appointment

Hours: 10.00-16.45; closed Bank Holidays and last two weeks in September

Transport: Tube: Piccadilly Circus, Green Park; Bus: any bus to Regent Street or Piccadilly

Special facilities: Toilet facilities available on site; access for users with disabilities (lift)

Publications: The Anthropological Index, formerly published from 1964-1994, is now available on the internet at http://lucy.ukc.ac.uk/AIO.html

[71][b]
Central Library, The British Museum

Great Russell Street
London WC1B 3DG
Borough: Camden
Telephone: 020 7323 8491
Fax: 020 7323 8118
E-mail: jbowring@thebritishmuseum.ac.uk
Objectives: Staff reference library of the British Musuem
Key staff: Central Librarian: Joanna Bowring
Stock and subject coverage: Archaeology, museology, art history and general reference collections. Especially strong on museums and the history of the British Museum
Services: Photocopying; British Museum archive also available on microfiche
Availability: All material is for reference only. Access open to readers who cannot easily obtain material elsewhere, by arrangement with the Librarian
Hours: 10.00-16.45 Monday to Friday
Transport: Tube: Tottenham Court Road, Holborn, Russell Square; Rail: Euston, King's Cross, St Pancras; Bus: 1, 7, 8, 10, 14, 19, 22, 24, 25, 29, 38, 55, 68, 73, 91, 168, 176, 188
Special facilities: Refreshment and toilet facilities available on site
Special features: The Central Library is in an early iron library built in 1850 by Sir Robert Smirke. The Library retains its innovative cast iron fittings, galleries and staircases

[71][c]
Department of Prints and Drawings

Great Russell Street
London WC1B 3DG
Access is via the British Museum's Montague Place entrance and Room 90 (Prints and Drawings gallery) on the fourth floor
Telephone: 020 7636 1555
Fax: 020 7323 8480
E-mail: ???
Key staff: ???
Stock and subject coverage: The Department of Prints and Drawings holds one of the most representative and distinguished collections of Western prints and drawings. The collection contains ca. three million works on paper from the 15th century to present day.

The strengths of the collection lie in the fields of Old Master prints and drawings from all schools, satires of the 18th and 19th centuries, and British material of all periods. The Department also holds the most extensive reference library in the UK of books, journals and sale catalogues relevant to the history of prints and drawings
Services: *[photocopies, fax, etc???]*
Availability: Open to bona fide researchers, visitors are required to show evidence of identification on arrival
Hours: 10.00-13.00, 14.15-16.00 Monday to Friday; 10.00-13.00 Saturday
Transport: Tube: Tottenham Court Road, Holborn, Russell Square; Rail: Euston, King's Cross, St Pancras; Bus: 1, 7, 8, 10, 14, 19, 22, 24, 25, 29, 38, 55, 68, 73, 91, 168, 176, 188
Special facilities: Refreshment and toilet facilities available on site; access for users with disabilities
Publications: ???

[71][d]
The Paul Hamlyn Library

The British Museum
Great Russell Street
London WC1B 3DG
Telephone: 020 7323 8838 (Admission enquiries)
020 7323 8907 (Library enquiries)
E-mail: psmith@thebritishmuseum.ac.uk
Objectives: The Library and the Walter and Leonore Annenberg Centre, within the reading room, together aim to bridge the gap between the general enquiry services offered by the Museum's information desks and the specialist research facilities of the Department of Prints and Drawings Student's Rooms
Key staff: The Fleming Librarian: Pam Smith
Stock and subject coverage: Over 13,000 books and 16 current journals on subjects relating to the Museum's collections, including ancient history, archaeology, art, anthropology, museum studies and travel
Services: Photocopying facilities; COMPASS interactive multimedia system of ca. 5,000 objects from the Museum's collections (also available on the web at www.thebritishmuseum.ac.uk/compass)
Availability: Open access public reference library – open to all without prior appointment
Hours: 10.00-17.30 Saturday to Wednesday; 10.00-20.30 Thursday and Friday; check website for up-to-date information
Transport: Tube: Tottenham Court Road, Holborn, Russell Square; Rail: Euston, King's Cross, St Pancras; Bus: 1, 7, 8, 10, 14, 19, 22, 24, 25, 29, 38, 55, 68, 73, 91, 168, 176, 188
Special facilities: Refreshment and toilet facilities available on site; access for users with disabilities including wheelchair access, accessible desks, book reader and scanner, screen magnifier and screen reader
Special features: The Paul Hamlyn Library is housed in the famous Round Reading Room previously occupied by The British Library

Linked organisations

The Paul Hamlyn Foundation The purchase of books and journals for the Library is funded by the Foundation

[72]
British Music Information Centre
BMIC

10 Stratford Place
London W1C 1BA
Borough: Westminster
Telephone: 020 7499 8567
Fax: 020 7499 4795
E-mail: info@bmic.co.uk
World Wide Web: www.bmic.co.uk
Constitution: Registered charity and company limited by guarantee
Objectives/purposes: Resource centre for contemporary British classical music including a collection of over 40,000 scores and recordings
Key staff: Director: Matthew Greenall; Information Manager: Daniel Goren
Stock and subject coverage: Over 40,000 scores and recordings of 20th century British classical music as well as an archive of press cuttings and articles/reviews of contemporary composers and their works
Services: Internet access; photocopies; score copying and binding facilities; Sibelius music setting software on permanent demonstration; small concert venue available for hire
Availability: Open to the public free of charge; no appointment necessary. Reference only, with listening facilities on the premises. Some scores, from ca. 200 of the composers represented, are available for sale
Hours: 12.00-17.00 Monday to Friday
Transport: Tube: Bond Street
Special facilities: Toilet facilities available; access for people with disabilities – two steps at entrance, help is available for wheelchair users (telephone in advance), no disabled toilet
Special features: Situated in Stratford Place, a cul-de-sac of Georgian townhouses off Oxford Street
Publications: Counterpoints, the BMIC newsletter (6 p.a)

Linked organisations

International Association of Music Information Centres (IAMIC) The Centre is a member of the Association

[73]
British National Space Centre Library
BNSC

151 Buckingham Palace Road
London SW1W 9SS
Borough: Westminster
Telephone: 020 7215 0901
Fax: 020 7215 0936
E-mail: bnscinfo@dti.gsi.gov.uk
World Wide Web: www.bnsc.gov.uk
Constitution: Government funded body
Key staff: Librarian: Stuart Grayson
Stock and subject coverage: European Space Agency Documentation; information on space projects, programmes and companies; satellites and remote sensing
Services: Photocopier
Availability: Open to the public by appointment only

Hours: 09.00-17.00 Monday to Friday
Transport: Tube and Rail: Victoria
Special facilities: Toilet facilities available; access for users with disabilities
Publications: Range of materials available via the BNSC website

Linked organisations

This Library operates as part of the Department of Trade and Industry Library Services

[74]
British Nutrition Foundation
BNF

High Holborn House
52-4 High Holborn
London WC1V 6RQ
Borough: Camden
Telephone: 020 7404 6504
Fax: 020 7404 6747
E-mail: postbox@nutrition.org.uk
World Wide Web: www.nutrition.org.uk
Constitution: Independent non-profit organisation and registered charity; company limited by guarantee; association with voluntary subscribing membership
Objectives/purposes: To help individuals understand how they may best match their diet with their lifestyle
Key staff: Library: June Schultes
Stock and subject coverage: Small collection of journals and books on nutrition and related health matters
Availability: By arrangement only; no loan facility; no charges
Hours: 09.00-17.00 Monday to Friday, by appointment only
Transport: Tube: Holborn, Chancery Lane; Bus: 8, 22B, 501, 521; limited on-street metered parking at the rear in Bedford Row
Special facilities: Toilet facilities; access for people with disabilities
Publications: Annual Report; BNF News; BNF Bulletin; Task Force reports; briefing papers, occasional books, publications list

[75]
British Olympic Association

1 Wandsworth Plain
London SW18 1EH
Borough: Wandsworth
Telephone: 020 8871 2677
Fax: 020 8871 9104
E-mail: boa@boa.org.uk
World Wide Web: www.olympics.org.uk
Constitution: Registered charity; company limited by guarantee
Objectives/purposes: To organise and coordinate Great Britain and Northern Ireland's participation in the Olympic Games and to promote the values of the Olympic Movement
Key staff: Director of Olympic Foundation: Jan Paterson
Stock and subject coverage: Official Olympic Games Reports 1900 onwards. General information about Olympic sports and competitors, International Olympic Committee reports, host city bidding documents. Political and other issues associated with

the Games, e.g. drugs, historical matters (Ancient Games), and women and the Olympics
Services: Photocopies (10 pence per sheet)
Availability: Open to all bona fide researchers, for reference only
Hours: 09.00-17.00 Monday to Friday
Transport: Tube: East Putney; Rail: Wandsworth Town
Special facilities: Refreshment and toilet facilities on site
Publications: Annual Reports; BOA handbooks produced before each Games; BOA report and official report produced after each Games for sale

Linked organisations
International Olympic Committee (IOC)

[76]
British Psychoanalytical Society
112A-114 Shirland Road
London W9 2EQ
Borough: Westminster
Telephone: 020 7563 5008
Fax: 020 7563 5001
E-mail: ipa_library@compuserve.com
World Wide Web: psychoanalysis.org.uk
Constitution: Registered charity
Objectives/purposes: Professional society and postgraduate training institute
Key staff: Executive Officer, Library: Andrea Chandler
Stock and subject coverage: Psychoanalysis and peripheral subject areas
Services: Photocopies
Availability: Access for reference only is available to all – a sliding-scale of fees applies. Applicants must show proof of their identity and status. Undergraduates should also provide an introductory letter from their academic librarian or head of department
Hours: 12.00-21.00 Monday to Thursday
Transport: Tube: Maida Vale; Bus: 6, 28, 36
Special facilities: Laptop points; toilet facilities; access for readers with disabilities

[77]
British Psychological Society
BPS
University of London Library
Senate House
Malet Street
London WC1E 7HU
Borough: Camden
Telephone: 020 7862 8461
Fax: 020 7862 8480
E-mail: ull@ull.ac.uk
World Wide Web: www.ull.ac.uk; www.bps.org.uk
Constitution: Professional and learned organisation
Key staff: Psychology Librarian, University of London Library: Mrs Susan Tarrant
Stock and subject coverage: Extensive collection of psychology journals
Services: Internet access; photocopies
Availability: Access to members of BPS and the University of London with readers tickets. Other users admitted by day tickets (£7 per day)
Hours: Term-time and Easter vacation: 09.00-21.00 Monday to Thursday; 09.00-18.30 Friday; 09.30-

17.30 Saturday. Other vacations: 09.00-18.00 Monday to Friday; 09.30-17.30 Saturday
Transport: Tube: Russell Square, Tottenham Court Road; Bus: 7, 10, 73, 68, 91, 168, 188
Special facilities: Refreshment and toilet facilities on site; lift access for readers with disabilities

Linked organisations
University of London Library The BPS Library is housed in the University of London Library

[78]
British Records Association
BRA
c/o LMA
40 Northampton Road
London EC1R OHB
Borough: Tower Hamlets
Telephone: 020 7833 0428
Fax: 020 7833 0416
E-mail: britrecassoc@hotmail.com
World Wide Web: www.hmc.gov.uk/bra/
Constitution: Registered charity with voluntary subscribing membership. Grant-in-aid received annually via the Royal Commission on Historical Manuscripts
Key staff: Jean Harper
Stock and subject coverage: Books and other publications on archives and records management; manuscript collections
Services: Photocopies
Availability: By appointment only
Hours: By appointment only
Transport: Tube: Bethnal Green, Liverpool Street; Rail: Liverpool Street; Bus: 8, 35, 47, 78
Special facilities: Toilet facilities available
Publications: Archives the journal of the BRA (2 p.a.); Archives and the User (series 1-8); Newsletter and Annual Report

Linked organisations
Records Preservation Section The Section acts as a clearing house for archives (principally from London solicitors), and distributes them to libraries and record offices as appropriate
Record Editors Group

[79]
British Red Cross
BRCS
National Headquarters
9 Grosvenor Crescent
London SW1X 7EJ
Borough: Westminster
Constitution: Registered charity
Telephone: 020 7235 5454
Fax: 020 7235 0876
E-mail: information@redcross.org.uk
World Wide Web: www.redcross.org.uk
Key staff: Librarian: Hazel Lee; Information Assistant: Naeem Khan
Stock and subject coverage: Books and reports on the Red Cross and its work in the UK and overseas. Specialised collection on International Humanitarian

Law and the Geneva Conventions. Also holds videos and slides

Services: Enquiry service; photocopying service (charges apply)

Hours: 10.00–16.00 Monday to Friday

Availability: By appointment; reference only for members of the public

Transport: Tube: Hyde Park Corner

Special facilities: Toilet facilities available; access for users with disabilities

Special features: The British Red Cross also has a museum on site – please telephone for details

Publications: Annual Report; first aid manuals; promotional literature about the work of the British Red Cross

Linked organisations

International Committee of the Red Cross (www.icrc.org)

International Federation of Red Cross and Red Crescent Societies (www.ifrc.org)
Member of both the above

[80]
The (British) Refugee Council

3 Bondway
London SW8 1SJ
Borough: Lambeth
Telephone: 020 7820 3110
Fax: 020 7820 3107
E-mail: info@refugeecouncil.demon.co.uk
World Wide Web: www.refugeecouncil.org.uk
Constitution: Registered charity
Objectives/purposes: National library on refugees, in Britain and overseas
Key staff: Internal Communications Manager: Matti Ojanen
Stock and subject coverage: Over 12,500 documents on refugees, including books, reports, journals, off-prints, press cuttings
Services: Photocopies (charges made); computerised bibliographic and subject catalogue
Availability: Open to the public for reference only. No lending except to staff and member agencies
Hours: 10.00–17.00 Monday to Friday
Transport: Tube and Rail: Vauxhall
Special facilities: Access for people with disabilities, including lift and accessible toilets
Publications: List available on request from the Publications Officer

Linked organisations

The BRC is an 'umbrella' organisation with some 50 full or associate members working for refugees in Britain and overseas

European Council for Refugees and Exiles International Refugee Documentation Network
The BRC is a member of both organisations

[81]
British Retail Consortium
BRC

2nd floor
21 Dartmouth Street
London SW1H 9BP
Borough: Westminster
Telephone: 020 7854 8900
Fax: 020 7854 8901
E-mail: info@brc.org.uk
World Wide Web: www.brc.org.uk
Constitution: Association with voluntary subscribing membership
Key staff: Researcher: Nuong Trieu
Stock and subject coverage: Retail books, research reports, trade journals and press cuttings
Services: Reference facilities; enquiries; programme of events, see website for details
Hours: 10.30–16.30 Monday to Friday
Availability: Members of the Consortium by prior arrangement
Transport: Tube: St James Park
Special facilities: Toilet facilities available

Linked organisations

Eurocommerce (Brussels based) BRC is a member organisation of Eurocommerce

[82]
British School of Osteopathy
BSO

275 Borough High Street
London SE1 1JE
Borough: Southwark
Telephone: 020 7407 0222 ext 215
Fax: 020 7839 1098
E-mail: library@bso.ac.uk
World Wide Web: www.bso.ac.uk
Constitution: Registered charity
Objectives/purposes: Higher education institution, awarding a BSc (Honours) in Osteopathy
Key staff: Librarian
Stock and subject coverage: Comprehensive coverage of osteopathy, plus collections on medicine and complementary medicine. Approximately 10,000 books, 40 current journals and 200 videos
Services: Photocopies; internet access to all sites, including Medline; CATS databases on complementary medicine, physiotherapy and rehabilitation. Charges are made for searches
Availability: Open to the public. Loans only to BSO students, staff and graduates
Hours: Term-time: 09.00–19.30 Mondays and Tuesdays; 09.00–21.30 Wednesdays and Thursdays; 09.00–17.00 Fridays
Holidays: 09.00–17.00
Transport: Tube: Borough
Special facilities: Refreshment and toilet facilities on site, access for users with disabilities
Publications: Study methods and research methods; Index to British Osteopathic Journal; bibliographies on palpation, the osteopathic profession and cranial osteopathy

[83]
British Schools Exploring Society
BSES

at, The Royal Geographical Society
1 Kensington Gore
London SW7 2AR
Borough: Kensington and Chelsea
Telephone: 020 7591 3141
Fax: 020 7591 3140
E-mail: bses@rgs.org
World Wide Web: www.bses.org.uk
Constitution: Charity with voluntary subscribing
   membership; company limited by guarantee
Objectives/purposes: To develop the characters and
   leadership skills of young people aged 16–20 through
   overseas expeditions involving adventures and
   scientific field work in wilderness areas
Key staff: Executive Director: Alexander Matheson;
   Expeditions Officer: Ben Boddy; Administrative
   Secretary: Clare Furnival
Stock and subject coverage: Books about early exploration
   mainly to Arctic regions, Newfoundland and
   Labrador. Expedition reports, annual reports and
   science reports of BSES Expeditions from 1932 to
   the present day
Availability: Available to all bona fide researchers, for
   reference only, at no charge
Hours: 09.30–17.30 Monday to Friday (except bank
   holidays and normal seasonal breaks)
Transport: Tube: South Kensington; Bus: 9, 10, 52
Special facilities: Tea room available in the Royal
   Geographical Society; toilet facilities available; access
   for users with disabilities (lift available)
Publications: Annual reports of expeditions, science
   reports of expeditions; newsletter to members (3 p.a.)

Linked organisations

Royal Geographical Society BSES is a tenant of
the RGS and shares the same aims with regard to
youth exploration, but it is an entirely independent
organisation

[84]
British Stammering Association
BSA

15 Old Ford Road
Bethnal Green
London E2 9PJ
Borough: Tower Hamlets
Telephone: 020 8983 1003, 020 8981 8818, Helpline:
   0845 6032001 (charged at local rate)
Fax: 020 8983 3591
E-mail: mail@stammering.org
World Wide Web: www.stammering.org
Constitution: Registered charity
Objectives/purposes: To provide information about
   stammering and the problems faced by stammerers,
   and encourage self-help and research into
   stammering
Key staff: Director: Norbert Lieckfeldt
Stock and subject coverage: Books, videos and tapes on
   stammering and self-help related subjects
Availability: Open to members of BSA
Hours: Postal lending library only

Publications: Speaking Out magazine (quarterly); Annual
   Report

[85]
British Standards Institution
BSI

389 Chiswick High Road
London W4 4AL
Borough: Hounslow
Telephone: 020 8996 7004
Fax: 020 8996 7005
E-mail: library@bsi-global.com
World Wide Web: www.bsi-global.com
Constitution: Independent non-profit organisation with
   voluntary subscribing membership
Objectives/purposes: To facilitate the production of
   standards in the UK and to represent UK interests in
   European and international standardisation activities.
   Also: quality assurance testing, product certification,
   information provision on standards and related
   technical requirements
Key staff: Library Manager: Mary Yates
Stock and subject coverage: National and international
   standards from countries around the world (not
   military or company standards); foreign technical
   regulations and legislation, books on quality and
   environmental management
Services: Perinorm CD-ROM database available for use
   by visitors; small specialist bookshop
Availability: Library is open to BSI subscribing members
   and committee members. British standards available
   for reference only, other standards may be borrowed
   by members (a charge is made). Various information
   services available
Hours: 09.00–17.00 Monday to Friday
Transport: Tube: Gunnersbury, Chiswick Park; Rail:
   Gunnersbury
Special facilities: Refreshment and toilet facilities available;
   access for readers with disabilities
Publications: BSI Catalogue, paper or CD-ROM (annual
   plus monthly supplement); Business Standards
   monthly magazine; Standards Update list of new
   standards; catalogue of BSI publications

[86]
British Tourist Authority
BTA

Thames Tower
Black's Road
Hammersmith
London W6 9EL
Borough: Hammersmith and Fulham
Telephone: 020 8846 9000
Fax: 020 8846 0302
World Wide Web: www.britishtouristauthority.org
Constitution: Government funded bodies
Objectives/purposes: BTA was set up to encourage people
   to visit Britain
Key staff: Information Resources Manager: Gaynor
   Evans
Stock and subject coverage: Collection of books, files and
   research reports covering all aspects of the tourism
   industry and the British tourism product

Availability: Primarily for internal use

Transport: Tube: Hammersmith

Publications: For a list of relevant publications see the official website of the UK Research Liaison Group at www.staruk.org.uk. The group is made up of representatives of the national tourist boards for England, Scotland, Northern Ireland, Wales, Britain and the Department for Culture, Media and Sport

Linked organisations

The 1969 Development of Tourism Act established four statutory tourist boards – the British Tourist Authority, the English Tourism Council (formerly the English Tourist Board), the Scottish Tourist Board and the Wales Tourist Board. The Northern Ireland Tourist Board was set up in 1948

[87]
British Universities Film and Video Council
BUFVC

77 Wells Street

London W1T 3QJ

Borough: Westminster

Telephone: 020 7393 1500

Fax: 020 7393 1555

E-mail: ask@bufvc.ac.uk

World Wide Web: www.bufvc.ac.uk

Constitution: Registered charity; company limited by guarantee; association with voluntary subscribing membership

Key staff: Head of Information: Luke McKernan; Library and Database Manager: Sergio Angelini

Stock and subject coverage: Books, journals, catalogues, videos, CD-ROMs and original papers. Subject coverage includes film, television, video and news media. Specialist collections include: Slade Film History Register collection of documentation relating to newsreels; BKSTS book collection on cinematography; and records of the Scientific Film Association

Services: Film and video viewing facilities; photocopies; fax machines and internet access available to members

Availability: Access to BUFVC members, for reference only. Charges are generally made to non-members for enquiries and research access

Hours: 09.30-17.30 Monday to Friday

Transport: Tube: Oxford Circus; Bus: 8, 25, 38, 73

Special facilities: Toilet facilities available on site (first floor)

Publications: Viewfinder (4 issues p.a.); BUFVC Handbook; Researcher's Guide: Film, Television, Radio and Related Documentation Collections in the UK; Researcher's Guide to British Newsreels (3 vols); British Universities Newsreel Project Database CD-ROM

Databases: AVANCE; Television Index; Researcher's Guide Online; Moving Image Gateway; British Universities Newsreel Database

[88]
British Water Ski Federation
BWSF

390 City Road

London EC1V 2QA

Borough: Islington

Telephone: 020 7833 2855

Fax: 020 7837 5879

E-mail: info@bwsf.co.uk

World Wide Web: www.britishwaterski.co.uk

Constitution: Company limited by guarantee; organisation funded by the Sports Council

Objectives/purposes: Governing body for water skiing within Great Britain

Key staff: Assistant Executive Officer and Magazine Editor: Harriet Owen

Stock and subject coverage: Various instruction books, hundreds of water ski magazines dating back to the 1960s, competition results from national through to world championships dating from the 1950s to the present. Probably the most complete record of results within Europe, if not the world. The magazine collection is believed to be the most complete collection of British water ski magazines (some US, French, German and Dutch magazines are also held). Note: resources are not held in library format

Services: Photocopies

Availability: Open to the general public for reference only by prior appointment

Hours: 09.00-17.00 Monday to Friday

Transport: Tube: Angel; Bus: 4, 19, 30, 38, 43, 56, 73, 171

Special facilities: Refreshment and toilet facilities available

Publications: British Waterskier magazine (5 p.a. to members)

Linked organisations

International Water Ski Federation BWSF is affiliated to the Federation

European Water Ski Federation (EAME)

[89]
British Wind Energy Association

26 Spring Street

London W2 1JA

Borough: Westminster

Telephone: 020 7402 7102/3

Fax: 020 7402 7107

E-mail: info@bwea.com

World Wide Web: www.bwea.com

Constitution: Company limited by guarantee

Key staff: Chief Executive: Nick Goodall; Administrator: Theresa Moses; Communications Manager: Alison Hill

Stock and subject coverage: Newsletter/magazine of the BWEA; proceedings of conferences, workshops and seminars on wind energy topics

Services: Lists of consultants, developers, etc.; policy documents; various guides and factsheets; Wind Farm Guide – all available from website

Availability: Postal or telephone enquiries only

[90]
Bromley Libraries (London Borough of Bromley)
World Wide Web: www.bromley.gov.uk
Constitution: Public library funded by local authority
Key staff: Chief Librarian: Barry Walkinshaw;
   Operations – Library Operations Manager: Leo Favret;
   Central Manager: John Wilkins; West Area Manager:
   Tina Alabaster; East Area manager: Tim Woolgar
   Development – Library Development Manager: David
   Brockhurst; Stock and Services Manager (Adult):
   John Levett; Stock and Services Manager (Children
   and Young People): Pat Jones; Partnerships and
   Commercial Manager: Chris Upton
   Electronic Library Manager: Diana Moulding; Arts
   Development Manager: Liz Dart
Availability: Free public access for reference and book
   borrowing. Charges are made for the loan of non-
   book materials and for some specialist services
Special features: The Borough's main library is Bromley
   Central Library

[90][a]
Bromley Central Library
   High Street
   Bromley
   Kent BR1 1EX
Telephone: 020 8460 9955
Fax: 020 8313 9975
E-mail: reference.library@bromley.gov.uk
Stock and subject coverage: Comprehensive reference and
   loans collection. Special collection within subject
   areas covered by Dewey 915-919 and 950-999.
   Information service includes 'Business Information
   Service' a feature collection of information on careers
   and education, including open learning material for
   loan; 'Health Point' health information, including
   Helpbox database; 'Upfront' a specialised collection of
   teenage material including Faxfile (GCSE revision)
   but mainly recreational.
   A comprehensive local studies and archives centre
   includes special collections about the Crystal Palace,
   HG Wells and Walter De La Mare.
   Community Services offers the loan and delivery of
   library materials to housebound readers and old
   people's homes in the borough
Services: Photocopies; online searching; fax machines;
   word processing facilities; CD-ROMs; binding
Availability: Free public access for reference and book
   borrowing. Charges are made for borrowing cassettes,
   CDs, videos, open learning packs, DvDs, language
   courses and some specialist services, e.g. Business
   Information Service, computer hire, study carrel hire
Hours: All departments: 09.30-18.00 Monday, Wednesday
   and Friday, 09.30-20.00 Tuesday and Thursday;
   09.30-17.00 Saturday. Business Information Service
   09.30-17.00 Monday to Friday
Transport: Rail: Bromley South, Bromley North; Bus: 61,
   119, 126, 138, 146, 162, 208, 227, 261, 269, 314, 320,
   336, 354, 367, 402, 351, 352, 358, 726, 746
Special facilities: No refreshment or toilet facilities; access
   for users with disabilities (lifts available to all floors
   from ground level, with tactile lift buttons, induction
   loop available in Large Hall, video loan service
   includes 'closed caption' videos)

Publications: Free guide to library services in the
   borough; User Survey Report (annual); Recent
   Additions booklist (monthly); Palace of the People
   (history of Crystal Palace) by Graham Reeves;
   Undaunted (story of Bromley in WW2) by Graham
   Reeves

[90][b]
Anerley Branch Library
   Anerley Town Hall
   Anerley Road
   Anerley
   London SE20 8BD
Telephone: 020 8778 7457
Key staff: Group Manager: Tina Alabaster
Reference facilities: Reference collection; local
   information; children's collection
Hours: 09.30-20.00 Monday; 09.30-18.00 Tuesday,
   Wednesday and Friday; 09.30-17.00 Saturday
Transport: Rail: Anerley; Bus: 75, 157, 312, 351, 352, 358
Special facilities: Limited access for users with disabilities
   (ramp but heavy fire doors), contact staff in advance

[90][c]
Beckenham Branch Library
   Beckenham Road
   Beckenham
   Kent BR3 4PE
Telephone: 020 8650 7292
Key staff: Group Manager: Tina Alabaster
Reference facilities: Reference collection; local
   information; children's collection
Hours: 09.30-18.00 Monday and Tuesday; 09.30-20.00
   Wednesday and Friday; 09.30-17.00 Saturday
Transport: Rail: Clockhouse; Bus: 54, 194, 227, 351, 358
Special facilities: Access for users with disabilities (ramp at
   rear – advise staff before visiting; forecourt parking
   restricted)

[90][d]
Biggin Hill Branch Library
   Church Road
   Biggin Hill
   Kent TN16 3LB
Telephone: 0959 574468
Key staff: Group Manager: Tim Woolgar
Reference facilities: Reference collection; local
   information; children's collection
Hours: 09.30-18.00 Monday, Thursday and Friday;
   09.30-20.00 Tuesday; 09.30-17.00 Saturday
Transport: Bus: 146, 320, 356, R2
Special facilities: Access for users with disabilities

[90][e]
Burnt Ash Branch Library
   Burnt Ash Lane
   Bromley
   Kent BR1 5AF
Telephone: 020 8460 3405
Key staff: Group Manager: Tina Alabaster
Reference facilities: Reference collection; local
   information; children's collection
Hours: 09.30-18.00 Monday and Thursday; 09.30-17.00
   Saturday
Transport: Rail: Sundridge Park; Bus: 126, 138, 261, 338

[90][f]
Chislehurst Branch Library
Red Hill
Chislehurst
Kent BR7 6DA
Telephone: 020 8467 1318
Key staff: Group Manager: Tim Woolgar
Reference facilities: Reference collection; local
   information; children's collection
Hours: 09.30-18.00 Tuesday and Friday; 09.30-20.00
   Monday and Thursday; 09.30-17.00 Saturday
Transport: Rail: Chislehurst; Bus: 61, 161, 162, 228, 328,
   338
Special facilities: Access for users with disabilities

[90][g]
Hayes Branch Library
Hayes Street
Hayes
Kent BR2 7LH
Telephone: 020 8462 2445
Key staff: Group Manager: Tina Alabaster
Reference facilities: Reference collection; local
   information; children's collection
Hours: 09.30-18.00 Tuesday and Friday; 14.00-20.00
   Thursday; 09.30-17.00 Saturday
Transport: Rail: Hayes; Bus: 119, 146, 356
Special facilities: Limited access for users with disabilities,
   ask staff for assistance

[90][h]
Mottingham Branch Library
31 Mottingham Road
Mottingham
London SE9 4QZ
Telephone: 020 8857 5406
Key staff: Group Manager: Tim Woolgar
Reference facilities: Reference collection; local
   information; children's collection
Hours: 09.30-18.00 Monday, Tuesday and Wednesday;
   09.30-20.00 Friday; 09.30-17.00 Saturday
Transport: Rail: Mottingham; Bus: 124, 126, 161, 338,
   424
Special facilities: Access for users with disabilities

[90][i]
Orpington Branch Library
The Priory
Church Hill
Orpington
Kent BR6 0HH
Telephone: 0689 831551
Key staff: Group Manager: Tim Woolgar
Reference facilities: Reference collection; local
   information; children's collection
Hours: 09.30-18.00 Monday; 09.00-20.00 Tuesday and
   Friday; 09.00-18.00 Wednesday; 09.00-17.00 Saturday
Transport: Rail: Orpington; Bus: 51, 61, 208, 476, 477,
   478, R1, R2, R3, R4, R7, R8, R11 (also 358, 493)
Special facilities: Access for users with disabilities (ramp
   provided, but not near car park – advise staff)

[90][j]
Penge Branch Library
186 Maple Road
Penge
London SE20 8HT
Telephone: 020 8778 8772
Key staff: Group Manager: Tina Alabaster
Reference facilities: Reference collection; local
   information; children's collection
Hours: 09.30-18.00 Monday, Tuesday, Thursday, Friday;
   09.30-17.00 Saturday
Transport: Bus: 75, 176, 194, 227, 312, 351, 358
Special facilities: Access for users with disabilities (level
   entrance, but limited space)

[90][k]
Petts Wood Branch Library
Frankswood Avenue
Petts Wood
Kent BR5 1BP
Telephone: 0689 821607
Key staff: Group Manager: Tim Woolgar
Reference facilities: Reference collection; local
   information; children's collection
Hours: 09.30-18.00 Tuesday and Friday; 09.30-20.00
   Monday and Thursday; 09.00-17.00 Saturday
Transport: Rail: Petts Wood; Bus: 208, R7 (also 162, 661,
   R2, R3)
Special facilities: Access for users with disabilities

[90][l]
St Pauls Cray Branch Library
Mickleham Road
St Pauls Cray
Kent BR5 2RW
Telephone: 020 8300 5454
Key staff: Group Manager: Tim Woolgar
Reference facilities: Reference collection; local
   information; children's collection
Hours: 09.30-18.00 Monday, Thursday and Friday:
   09.30-20.00 Tuesday; 09.30-17.00 Saturday
Transport: Rail: St Mary Cray; Bus: R1, R11
Special facilities: Access for people with disabilities

[90][m]
Shortlands Branch Library
110 Shortlands Road
Bromley
Kent BR2 0HP
Telephone: 020 8460 9692
Key staff: Group Manager: Tina Alabaster
Reference facilities: Reference collection; local
   information; children's collection
Hours: 09.30-18.00 Tuesday, Wednesday and Friday;
   09.30-20.00 Monday; 09.30-17.00 Saturday
Transport: Rail: Shortlands; Bus: 162, 358
Special facilities: Access for users with disabilities

[90][n]
Southborough Branch Library
Southborough Lane
Bromley
Kent BR2 8HP
Telephone: 020 8467 0355

Key staff: Group Manager: Tim Woolgar
Reference facilities: Reference collection; local
information; children's collection
Hours: 09.30-18.00 Monday, Tuesday and Thursday;
09.30-20.00 Friday; 09.30-17.00 Saturday
Transport: Bus: 208, 336
Special facilities: Limited access for users with disabilities
(limited wheelchair access advise the Library before
visiting)

[90][o]
West Wickham Branch Library
Glebe Way
West Wickham
Kent BR4 0SH
Telephone: 020 8777 4139
Key staff: Group Manager: Tina Alabaster
Reference facilities: Reference collection; local
information; children's collection
Hours: 09.30-18.00 Tuesday and Thursday; 09.30-20.00
Monday and Friday; 09.30-17.00 Saturday
Transport: Rail: West Wickham; Bus: 119, 194, 356
Special facilities: Access for users with disabilities (ramp
and wide doors)

[91]
Brunel University Library
Uxbridge
Middlesex UB8 3PH
Telephone: 01895 274000 ext 2787
Fax: 01895 203264
E-mail: library@brunel.ac.uk
World Wide Web: www.brunel.ac.uk/depts/lib/
Constitution: Department of a university
Key staff: Head of Library Services: Beryl-Anne
Thompson
Stock and subject coverage: Material on science, technology,
social sciences, law, arts, humanities. Special transport
history collection of over 10,000 items, mainly the
bequests of Charles Clinker and David Garnett.
Collection of working class autobiographies – over
230 photocopies of unpublished autobiographies
available for consultation
Services: Self-service photocopiers; telephone
Availability: Free for university staff and students. Open
to the public for reference. Members of the public
who wish to borrow will need to pay a registration
fee and annual subscription
Hours: Term-time: 09.00-21.00 Monday to Thursday;
09.00-19.00 Friday; 09.30-13.00 Saturday, 14.00-
19.00 Sunday
Vacations: 09.00-17.00, closed Saturday and Sunday
Transport: see www.brunel.ac.uk/campus/where.html
Special facilities: Refreshment and toilet facilities; access
for users with disabilities (lift)
Publications: A Student's Guide to Writing, John
Aanonson

[91][a]
Osterley Campus Library
Borough Road
Isleworth TW7 5DU

Borough: Hillingdon
Telephone: 020 8891 0121 ext 2815
Fax: 020 8891 8251
E-mail: library@brunel.ac.uk
Stock and subject coverage: Materials on sports science,
health science and business
Hours: Term-time: 09.00-21.00 Monday to Thursday;
09.00-17.00 Friday; 09.30-13.00 Saturday
Vacations: 09.00-12.30, 13.30-17.00 Monday to
Friday
Transport: Rail: Isleworth
Special facilities: Lending materials and issue desk on the
ground floor; access to the first floor by stairs only;
CCTV and large text networked PC for users with
visual impairments

[91][b]
Runnymede Campus Library
Englefield Green
Surrey TW20 0JZ
Telephone: 01784 431341
Fax: 01784 470342
E-mail: library@brunel.ac.uk
Stock and subject coverage: The library holds materials on
design and technology and part of the transport
history collection. Special collections include the
Shoreditch College and Institute of Craft Education
archives
Hours: Term-time: 09.00-17.00 Monday and Friday;
09.00-21.00 Tuesday and Wednesday; 09.00-19.00
Thursday; 09.30-13.00 on selected Saturdays
Vacations: 09.00-12.30, 13.30-17.00 Monday to
Friday
Special facilities: Limited lift facilities for access to upper
floor levels

[91][c]
Twickenham Campus Library
300 St Margaret's Road
Twickenham TW1 1PT
Borough: Hounslow
Telephone: 020 8891 0121 ext 2205
Fax: 020 8891 8240
E-mail: library@brunel.ac.uk
Stock and subject coverage: Materials on education and
applied social science, including a collection of
children's literature. Special collections include a
teaching practice collection and the Elsie Riach
Murray collection of 19th and 20th century childrens
books (this collection may be consulted by
appointment)
Hours: Term-time: 09.00-21.00 Monday to Thursday;
09.00-17.00 Friday; 09.30-13.00 Saturday
Vacations: 09.00-12.30, 13.30-17.00 Monday to
Friday
Transport: Rail: St Margarets
Special facilities: All materials and issue desk are on the
ground floor; CCTV screen for visually impaired
users

[92]
BT Archives
Third floor
Holborn Telephone Exchange
268-270 High Holborn
London WC1V 7EE
Borough: Camden
Telephone: 020 7492 8792
Fax: 020 7242 1967
E-mail: archives@bt.com
World Wide Web: www.bt.com/archives/
Constitution: Company archive and information resource
Objectives/purposes: Responsible, on behalf of the Public Record Office, for historical telecommunications records up to plc, and on behalf of BT since plc. First point of contact for information on the history of telecommunications
Key staff: Head of Group Archives: David Hay; Group Archivist: Lucy Jones
Stock and subject coverage: Archives of British Telecommunications plc and its predecessors, including private telegraph and telephone companies, Post Office telecommunications and BT (public corporation). Historical phone book collection, 1880 to date (on microfilm); photographic, film and video library from the 19th century to date. Telecommunications library of printed sources, including several hundred publications, 1769 to date and numerous in-house and external journals
Services: Photocopies; microfilm reader-printer (for phone books); microfiche readers; image scanning; online searching of archives catalogues; photography
Availability: Free access for researchers and BT staff by appointment only. First four photocopies free of charge
Hours: 10.00-16.00 Monday to Friday, by appointment
Transport: Tube: Chancery Lane, Holborn; Rail: City Thameslink; Bus: 8, 25, 242, 501, 521
Special facilities: Toilet facilities; lift access for users with disabilities
Publications: Guide to Events in Telecommunications History; introductory leaflet

[93]
Building Societies Association
BSA
3 Savile Row
London W1 3BP
Borough: Westminster
Telephone: 020 7437 0655
Fax: 020 7734 6416
E-mail: simon.rex@bsa.org.uk
World Wide Web: www.bsa.org.uk
Constitution: Registered charity; association with voluntary subscribing membership
Objectives/purposes: Trade association for the building society industry
Key staff: Simon Rex; Theresa Monk
Stock and subject coverage: Information on building societies and mortgage lenders; the housing finance and savings market
Services: Photocopies
Availability: Access to the Library by appointment only, enquiries to the Information Officer
Hours: 09.00-17.00 Monday to Friday

Transport: Tube: Oxford Circus, Piccadilly Circus; Bus: any bus to Regent Street
Publications: Annual report; Building Societies Yearbook; Building Society News

[94]
Bureau Veritas
BV
2nd Floor
Tower Bridge Court
224-6 Tower Bridge Road
London SE1 2TX
Borough: Southwark
Telephone: 020 7403 8900
Fax: 020 7403 1590
World Wide Web: www.bureauveritas.com
Constitution: Company limited by guarantee
Objectives/purposes: International classification society
Key staff: Publications Manager
Stock and subject coverage: Rules for the Construction and Classification of Steel Vessels, Marine Register, Associated Guidance Notes, Annual Report, Bulletin Techniques, Rules for the Classification-Certification of Yachts, Rules and Regulations for the Classification of Steel Ships and Offshore Units, Rules and Regulations for the Construction and Classification of Inland Navigation Vessels
Services: Photocopies; fax machine (charges made for use of both)
Availability: Material available for reference only
Hours: 09.00-17.00 Monday to Friday (closed weekends and public holidays)
Transport: Tube and Rail: London Bridge
Special facilities: Refreshment and toilet facilities available on site
Publications: Rules for the Construction and Classification of Steel Vessels; Marine Registers; associated guidance notes; Bulletin Techniques; Annual Reports

[95]
Business Archives Council
BAC
Floors 3-4
101 Whitechapel High Street
London E1 7RE
Borough: Tower Hamlets
Telephone: 020 7247 0024
Fax: 020 7422 0026
E-mail: businessarchives.council.sqr@virgin.net
Constitution: Registered charity
Objectives/purposes: To rescue and encourage the use of business records
Key staff: Office Manager: Sharon Quinn-Robinson
Stock and subject coverage: Business history library with approximately 4,500 books and pamphlets dating from the 1850s to the present day. The collections focus on individual company histories (British owned companies only), many were privately produced, often for commemorative purposes and are not available in other libraries (including the British Library)
Services: Photocopies; catalogue available on microfiche and disc

Availability: Access to bona fide researchers by appointment only. Materials are for reference only, not for loan; charges are made for photocopies

Hours: 10.00–17.00 Monday, Tuesday, Wednesday and Friday by appointment

Transport: Tube: Aldgate East; Bus: 25, 253

Special facilities: Toilet facilities available

Publications: Business Archives Sources and History (annual), Business Archives Principles and Practice (annual); 4 newsletters (quarterly); annual conference proceedings and yearbook; microfiche catalogue of holdings

Linked organisations

Business Archives Council of Scotland

[96]
The Calnan Library, St John's Institute of Dermatology

St Thomas' Hospital
Lambeth Palace Road
London SE1 7EH
Borough: Lambeth
Telephone: 020 7928 9292 ext 1313
Fax: 020 7928 1428
E-mail: patricia.tharratt@kcl.ac.uk
Constitution: Department of a university
Objectives/purposes: The Calnan Library, named after the first holder of a Chair of Dermatology in London, specialises in books and journals on skin diseases and related disorders
Key staff: Librarian: Pat Tharratt
Stock and subject coverage: Approximately 2,700 books and 88 current journal titles plus a small historical collection of books dating back to the 1700s with some journals from the late 1800s. The collection of American journals to 1955 and the European titles held also cover venereology. The Library also holds a small collection of moulages (wax models) dating from the 1940s and 50s for use in teaching.
The slide collection is separate from the Library, contact Mr Stuart Robertson 020 7928 9292 ext 1305 regarding access
Services: Photocopies (charges made); Medline, PubMed and other databases
Availability: Open to all bona fide researchers by appointment (visitors are advised to telephone first). Journals are for reference only; some books are available to borrowers through interlibrary loan services
Hours: 09.30–17.30 Monday to Friday, except for public holidays
Transport: Tube: Lambeth North, Waterloo, Westminster; Rail: Waterloo; Bus: 3, 12, 53, 77, 159, 184, 344, 507, C10
Special facilities: Refreshment and toilet facilities available; access for users with disabilities – wheelchair access possible but difficult

Linked organisations

Guy's, King's and **St Thomas' Schools of Medicine, Dentistry and the Biomedical Sciences** Parent body

[97]
Camberwell College of Arts

Peckham Road
London SE5 8UF
Borough: Southwark
Telephone: 020 7514 6349
Fax: 020 7514 6324
World Wide Web: www.linst.ac.uk/library/intranet
Constitution: Higher education corporation
Key staff: Head of Learning Resources: Liz Kerr DipLib ALA
Stock and subject coverage: Subject coverage includes: fine art and design, ceramics, textiles, photography, printing, bookbinding, papermaking, conservation of works of art, paper and artefacts, printmaking and cinema. Special collections include: the Walter Crane Collection, the Thorold Dickinson Cinema Collection and literature on the history and design of poster art
Services: Photocopies; electronic resources; video and computer facilities (not available to outside users)
Availability: Access for reference and lending to all staff and students of The London Institute. Applications for access (for reference only), by bona fide enquirers outside the Institute, should be made in writing to the Head of Learning Resources
Hours: Term-time only: 10.00–17.00 Monday and Friday; 10.00–20.00 Tuesday and Thursday; 10.00–19.30 Wednesday
Transport: Tube: Oval, Elephant and Castle; Rail: Denmark Hill, Peckham Rye, Vauxhall, Elephant and Castle; Bus: 12, 36, 45A, 171
Special facilities: Refreshment and toilet facilities available; hearing loop system; wheelchair access

Linked organisations

The London Institute Part of the Institute

[98]
Camden (London Borough of Camden)
Camden Libraries and Information Service

World Wide Web: www.camden.gov.uk/learn/libraries/libs_fr.htm
Constitution: Public library service funded by local authority
Availability: Free public access for reference. Free access for borrowing to anyone who lives, works or studies in Camden, and to others via interavailability arrangements. Charges for loan of CDs, videos, DvDs and talking books. Free internet access
Key staff: Head of Libraries: Neal Hounsell; Head of Operations: Stella Richards; Head of Quality and Development: Jim Moulson
Special features: The library service is arranged in tiers as follows
Central Library: Swiss Cottage
Town Libraries: Holborn, St Pancras, Kentish Town
Neighbourhood Libraries: Heath, Camden Town, Queen's Crescent, West Hampstead
Community Libraries: Belsize, Kilburn, Highgate, Chalk Farm, Regents Park

[98][a]
Swiss Cottage Central Library
88 Avenue Road
London NW3 3HA
Telephone: 020 7974 6522
Fax: 020 7974 6532
Key staff: Library Manager: Mark Osterfield; Assistant Library Managers: Chris Arscott, Caroline Spencer, Sue Moulson
Stock and subject coverage: Swiss Cottage is the central library for Camden, with a large Lending Library incorporating a separate philosophy and psychology collection. The Reference Library has a substantial stock, including a broad range of newspapers and journals, directories and annuals, government publications, British Standards and a map collection. The Audiovisual Library has a collection of music books, scores, CDs, cassettes and videos. The Children's Library includes a toy library for use by children resident in Camden. The Schools Library Service provides a loan service of books and other learning resources to primary and special schools throughout the borough
Services: Photocopying and computer printing (charges made), microfilm/fiche reader-printers; PCs with printers and word processing facilities (bookable and charged per hour); teletext; video telephone for use by users with hearing impairments (limited hours)
Hours: 10.00-19.00 Monday and Thursday; 10.00-18.00 Tuesday and Friday; 10.00-17.00 Saturday
Transport: Tube: Swiss Cottage; Bus: C11, C12, 13, 31, 46, 82, 113
Special facilities: Toilet facilities; access for users with disabilities (level entrance, automatic entrance doors, lift to all floors)
Special features: The Library opened in 1964 and was designed by Sir Basil Spence
Publications: Camden Libraries and Information Service Annual Report

[98][b]
Belsize Library
Antrim Road
London NW3 4XN
Telephone: 020 7974 6518
Fax: 020 7974 6518
E-mail: belsizelibrary@camden.gov.uk
Key staff: Library Manager: Marion Hill, Gloria Keys; Assistant Library Manager: Sue Moulson
Reference facilities: General branch library stock; Key Stage books, internet access; CDs and videos for loan; audio-visual loans; talking books; photocopying and computer printing
Hours: 10.00-19.00 Tuesday; 10.00-17.00 Wednesday; 10.00-17.00 Saturday
Transport: Tube: Belsize Park; Bus: C11, C12, 268
Special facilities: Access for users with disabilities - entrance ramp

[98][c]
Camden Town Library
Crowndale Centre
218 Eversholt Street
London NW1 1BD
Telephone: 020 7974 1560
Fax: 020 7974 1582
E-mail: camdentownlibrary@camden.gov.uk
Key staff: Library Manager: Shirley Jacobs; Assistant Library Manager: Sonia Evelyn
Reference facilities: General branch library stock; small reference collection; children's library with Key Stage books; CDs and videos for loan; audio-visual loans and talking books; photocopiers and computer printing; computers with internet access
Hours: 10.00-19.00 Monday and Thursday; 10.00-18.00 Tuesday, Wednesday and Friday; 10.00-17.00 Saturday
Transport: Tube: Camden Town, Mornington Crescent; Bus: 24, 29, 32, 46, 134, 135, 168, 214
Special facilities: Access for users with disabilities

[98][d]
Chalk Farm Library
Sharpleshall Street
London NW1 8YN
Telephone: 020 7974 6526
Fax: 020 7974 6502
E-mail: chalkfarmlibrary@camden.gov.uk
Key staff: Library Manager: Roberto Cioccari; Assistant Library Manager: Mary Anyanwu
Reference facilities: General branch library stock; children's library; Key Stage books; computers with Internet access; CDs and videos for loan; audio-visual loans; talking books; photocopying and computer printing
Hours: 10.00-19.00 Monday; 10.00-18.00 Friday; 10.00-17.00 Saturday
Transport: Tube: Chalk Farm; Bus: 31
Special facilities: Access for users with disabilities – wheelchair accessible (shallow step)

[98][e]
Heath Library
Keats Grove
London NW3 2RR
Telephone: 020 7974 6520
Fax: 020 7974 6618
E-mail: heathlibrary@camden.gov.uk
Key staff: Library Manager: Gloria Keys/Marion Hill; Assistant Library Manager: Katharine Chasey
Reference facilities: Small reference collection; children's library; general branch library stock; self-help collection; Key stage books; CDs and videos for loan; computers with internet access
Hours: 10.00-19.00 Thursday; 10.00-18.00 Friday; 10.00-17.00 Saturday
Transport: Tube: Hampstead, Belsize Park; Rail: Hampstead Heath; Bus: C11, C12, 24, 46, 168, 268
Special facilities: Access for users with disabilities

[98][f]
Highgate Library
Chester Road
London N19 5DH
Telephone: 020 7974 5752
Fax: 020 7974 5555
E-mail: highgatelibrary@camden.gov.uk
Key staff: Library Manager: Pamela Butler
Reference facilities: Local information; children's collection; learning centre with 12 PCs for free individual and group use; photocopier

Hours: 10.00–18.00 Tuesday and Wednesday; 10.00–19.00
   Thursday; 10.00–17.00 Saturday
Transport: Tube: Archway, Tufnell Park; Bus: C12, 43, 271
Special facilities: Access for users with disabilities –
   entrance ramped

[98][g]
Holborn Library
32–38 Theobalds Road
London WC1X 8PA
Telephone: 020 7413 6345/6
Fax: 020 7974 6556
E-mail: holbornlibrary@camden.gov.uk
Key staff: Library Manager: Bob Gryspeerdt; Principal
   Librarian Local History: Richard Knight; Assistant
   Library Managers: Maureen Nicholls, Jill Marpole
Stock and subject coverage: Adult and children's lending
   libraries including a small amount of reference
   material and a loan collection of CDs and DVDs.
   Separate collection of English law which includes
   files of major series of law reports. Special collection
   of Beethoven recordings on CD, cassette and record.
   Self-help collection and Key Stage books. Camden
   Local Studies and Archive Centre
Services: Photocopying and computer printing,
   computers with internet access and word processing
   software
Hours: 10.00–19.00 Monday and Thursday; 10.00–18.00
   Tuesday and Friday; 10.00–17.00 Saturday
Transport: Tube: Holborn, Chancery Lane; Bus: 19, 38,
   55, 68, 77A, 168, 171, 188
Special facilities: Toilet facilties available; access for people
   with disabilities (entrance ramp, automatic doors, lift
   access to all floors, one reserved parking space for
   drivers with Camden Disabled Disc)

[98][h]
Kentish Town Library
262–6 Kentish Town Road
London NW5 2AA
Telephone: 020 7974 6253
Fax: 020 7482 5650
E-mail: kentishtownlibrary@camden.gov.uk
Key staff: Library Manager: Dennis Chase; Assistant
   Library Manager: Tony Adams, Yasmin Hounsell
Reference facilities: Small reference collection; local
   information and children's collection; CDs and
   videos for loan; coin operated photocopier; internet
   and PC access; computer printing
Hours: 10.00–19.00 Monday and Thursday; 10.00–18.00
   Tuesday, Wednesday and Friday; 10.00–18.00 Saturday
Transport: Tube: Kentish Town; Bus: C2, 27, 134, 135,
   214
Special facilities: Access for users with disabilities –
   wheelchair lift access to Library

[98][i]
Kilburn Library
Cotleigh Road
London NW6 2NP
Telephone: 020 7974 1965
Fax: 020 7974 6524
E-mail: kilburnlibrary@camden.gov.uk
Key staff: Library Manager: Karen Egbunike; Assistant
   Library Manager: Mary Anyanwu

Reference facilities: General branch library stock; children's
   library; homework collection; Key Stage books; small
   reference collection; self-help collection; computers
   with internet access; CDs and videos for loan; audiovisual loans; talking books; photocopying and
   computer printing
Hours: 10.00–18.00 Tuesday; 10.00–19.00 Thursday;
   10.00–17.00 Saturday
Transport: Tube and Rail: West Hampstead; Bus: C11 16,
   32, 98, 139, 189, 316, 328
Special facilities: Access for users with disabilities –
   ramped entrance, toilet facilities

[98][j]
Queen's Crescent Library
165 Queen's Crescent
London NW5 4HH
Telephone: 020 7974 6243
Fax: 020 7974 6252
E-mail: queenscrescentlibrary@camden.gov.uk
Key staff: Library Manager: Roberto Cioccari; Assistant
   Library Manager: Damian Mansi
Reference facilities: General branch library stock; small
   reference collection; children's library with Key Stage
   books; Learning Centre with 14 PCs with
   Learndirect online computer courses; internet access;
   tutorial/study room for up to 12 people; CDs and
   videos for loan; audio-visual loans; talking books;
   photocopying and computer printing
Hours: 10.00–19.00 Monday and Thursday; 10.00–18.00
   Tuesday, Wednesday and Friday; 10.00–17.00 Saturday
Transport: Tube: Chalk Farm; Kentish Town; Rail: Gospel
   Oak; Bus: C2, 4, C11, C12, 27, 46, 134, 135
Special facilities: Toilet facilities and access for users with
   disabilities

[98][k]
Regent's Park Library
Compton Close
Robert Street
London NW1 3QT
Telephone: 020 7974 1530
Fax: 020 7974 1531
E-mail: regentsparklibrary@camden.gov.uk
Key staff: Library Manager: Shirley Jacobs; Assistant
   Library Manager: Jill Marpole
Reference facilities: Local information and children's
   collection; learning centre; internet access; small
   collection of CDs and videos for loan; coin operated
   photocopier
Hours: 10.00–19.00 Tuesday and Thursday; 10.00–18.00
   Wednesday; 10.00–17.00 Saturday
Transport: Tube: Warren Street, Euston Square, Great
   Portland Street; Bus: C2, 24, 27, 29, 134
Special facilities: Access for users with disabilities –
   ramped entrance

[98][l]
St Pancras Library
Town Hall Extension
Argyle Extension
Argyle Street
London WC1H 8NN
Telephone: 020 7974 5833
Fax: 020 7974 5963

E-mail: stpancraslibrary@camden.gov.uk

Key staff: Library Manager: Glyn Hughes; Assistant Library Managers: Michael Dempsey, Charlotte Copus-Hayes

Reference facilities: Small reference collection; children's library; Key Stage books, self-help collection including education guides and career information. Camden Direct information point. Large branch library stock and special Chinese collection; CDs and videos for loan; photocopying and computer printing; internet access

Hours: 10.00-19.00 Monday and Thursday; 10.00-18.00 Tuesday, Wednesday and Friday; 10.00-17.00 Saturday

Transport: Tube and Rail: King's Cross, Euston; Bus: 10,30, 46, 73, 91, 214

Special facilities: Toilets; access for users with disabilities – ramp to automatic doors, disabled toilet

[98][m]
West Hampstead Library

Dennington Park Road
London NW6 1AU

Telephone: 020 7974 6610

Fax: 020 7974 6539

E-mail: westhampsteadlibrary@camden.gov.uk

Key staff: Library Manager: Karen Egbunike; Assistant Library Manager: Joanna Birch

Reference facilities: General branch library stock; small reference collection; self-help collection; children's collection; Key Stage books and homework collection; CDs and videos for loan; photocopying and computer printing; internet access

Hours: 10.00-19.00 Monday and Tuesday; 10.00-20.00 Thursday; 10.00-18.00 Friday; 10.00-17.00 Saturday; 11.00-16.00 Sunday

Transport: Tube and Rail: West Hampstead; Bus: C11, 139, 328

Special facilities: Toilet facilities; access for users with disabilities – ramped access to Adult Library and lift to children's library

[99]
Campaign Against Arms Trade
CAAT

11 Goodwin Street
Finsbury Park
London N4 3HQ

Borough: Islington

Telephone: 020 7281 0297

Fax: 020 7281 4369

E-mail: enquiries@caat.demon.co.uk

World Wide Web: www.caat.org.uk

Constitution: Independent non-profit distributing organisation

Objectives/purposes: CAAT is a broad coalition of groups and individuals working for the reduction and ultimate abolition of the international arms trade and the re-orientation of the UK economy away from military industry towards civil production

Key staff: Research Co-ordinator: Ian Prichard

Stock and subject coverage: Founded in 1974, CAAT has built up a considerable information library on the arms trade, especially with reference to the UK. The library includes: comprehensive files on the international arms trade categorised by country, company and topic; a range of standard reference works; company brochures advertising the equipment of the major arms manufacturers; exhibition catalogues from the major military exhibitions; and books, magazines and pamphlets covering aspects of the arms trade and related issues

Services: Photocopies

Availability: Available for anyone to use by appointment. Reference only.

Hours: 10.30-17.30 Mondays to Fridays

Transport: Tube and Rail: Finsbury Park; Bus: 4,19, 29, 106, 153, 221, 236, 253, 259, 279, W2, W3, W7

Special facilities: Refreshment and toilet facilities available on site; access for users with disabilities – office on ground floor but no special facilities

Publications: CAAT publishes a newsletter every two months covering arms trade news and campaigning. Factsheets and briefings are published on issues such as the arms trade and development and on particular countries and areas such as Indonesia and Turkey

[100]
Cancer BACUP

3 Bath Place
Rivington Street
London EC2A 3JR

Borough: Hackney

Telephone: 020 7613 2121
0808 800 1234 (Freephone)

Fax: 020 7696 9002

E-mail: info@cancerbacup.org

World Wide Web: www.cancerbacup.org.uk

Constitution: Registered charity

Objectives/purposes: Information and support on all aspects of cancer through a telephone information service, a counselling service and a variety of publications

Stock and subject coverage: Computerised directory and a library of resources are used by specially trained cancer nurses to provide information to anyone who enquires about treatment, research, support groups, therapists, counsellors, financial assistance, insurance, home nursing services and more. The nurse can also provide BACUP's booklets on cancer

Availability: Access only to people with cancer, their families and friends

Hours: 09.00-19.00 Monday to Friday (telephone services)

Publications: Annual Report; BACUP News (3 p.a.); booklets on different cancers and aspects of living with cancer

Linked organisations

Network of eight drop-in centres across the UK, including three in London at
St Bartholemew's Hospital
Charing Cross Hospital
Homerton Hospital

[101]
Cancer Research UK
(formerly Imperial Cancer Research Fund)

PO Box 123
Lincoln's Inn Fields
London WC2A 3PX
Borough: Camden
Telephone: 020 7269 3206
Fax: 020 7269 3084
E-mail: lib.info@cancer.org.uk
World Wide Web: www.cancerresearchuk.org
Constitution: Registered charity
Key staff: Head of Library and Information Services:
  Julia Chester
Stock and subject coverage: Specialist medical research
  collection; ca. 10,000 books and 300 current
  periodicals
Services: Enquiry service; loans and photocopies
Availability: Bona fide researchers admitted on
  application to the Library Committee, for reference
  only. Serious enquiries accepted
Hours: 08.30–17.30 Monday to Friday
Transport: Tube: Holborn; Bus: 4, 68, 168
Special facilities: Refreshment and toilet facilities; access
  for users with disabilities
Publications: Current journals/periodicals holdings list;
  library bulletin; annual scientific report

[102]
Catholic Central Library
CCL

Lancing Street
London NW1 1ND
Borough: Camden
Telephone: 020 7383 4333
Fax: 020 7388 6675
E-mail: librarian@catholic-library.org.uk
World Wide Web: www.catholic-library.org.uk
Constitution: Registered charity and company limited by
  guarantee
Key staff: Librarian: Mrs Joan Bond
Stock and subject coverage: 55,000 volumes; ca. 150 journal
  titles; collection of pamphlets. Covers scripture;
  theology; spiritual life; Catholic social teaching;
  Catholic faith; church history (worldwide); religious
  orders; ecumenism; education; and biography.
  Collection of parish registers from the Library of the
  Thomas Merton Society
Services: Photocopying. Subscription for borrowing
  books is £25 for five tickets
Availability: Open to the public. Reader's ticket required
  for loans; reference facilities freely available
Hours: 10.30–17.00 Monday, Tuesday, Thursday and
  Friday; 10.30–19.00 Wednesday
Transport: Tube and Rail: Euston; Bus: 30, 59, 68, 73, 91,
  168, 263
Special facilities: Toilet facilities available; wheelchair
  access
Publications: List of journals held; new book lists
  (3 times p.a.)

[103]
Catholic Fund for Overseas Development
CAFOD

Romero Close
Stockwell Road
London SW9 9TY
Borough: Lambeth
Telephone: 020 7326 5600
Fax: 020 7274 9630
E-mail: ismith@cafod.org.uk
World Wide Web: www.cafod.org.uk
Constitution: Registered charity
Objectives/purposes: The promotion of human
  development and social justice in witness to Christian
  faith and gospel values
Key staff: Information Services Manager: Ian Smith
Stock and subject coverage: Books, journals, non-book
  information and newspaper material on the following
  subjects: Africa, Asia, Pacific and Middle East, Latin
  America, Eastern Europe, theology, spirituality,
  environment, development education, international
  economics, conflict, health, AIDS, etc.
Services: Photocopies (charges made); computerised
  OPAC linking library, archive and record store; CD-
  ROM system. The Library has contacts with other
  libraries in charity sectors and provides some current
  awareness services
Availability: Access is open to all bona fide researchers.
  An appointment must be made with the Librarian.
  Material is available for use within the Library only.
  It is helpful to inform the Librarian in advance about
  the intended area of research
Hours: 10.00–16.30 Monday to Friday
Transport: Tube: Brixton, Stockwell; Rail: Brixton
Special facilities: Toilet facilities available; access for users
  with disabilities to the Library but not to the Archive
Publications: CAFOD Magazine (quarterly); CAFOD
  Bulletin (monthly); CAFOD Annual Review

[104]
Central Middlesex Hospital Library

Avery Jones Postgraduate Centre
Central Middlesex Hospital
North West London Hospital NHS Trust
Acton Lane
London NW10 7NS
Borough: Brent
Telephone: 020 8453 2504
Fax: 020 8453 2503
E-mail: library@cmhlib.demon.co.uk
World Wide Web: www.cmhlib.demon.co.uk
Constitution: NHS Trust hospital library
Key staff: Barbara Cumbers
Objectives/purposes: Provides a service to Central
  Middlesex Hospital NHS Trust and NW London
  Mental Health Trust, operating in conjunction with
  St Mary's Hospital Medical School Library and
  within London Regional Library and Information
  Service
Key staff: Library Manager: Ms BJ Cumbers
Stock and subject coverage: Ca. 3,000 books and 140
  current journal titles in the fields of medicine,
  psychiatry, nursing and allied subjects

Services: Photocopies; CD-ROM databases; internet access

Availability: Open to all members of North West London Hospitals NHS Trust and Brent, Kensington, Chelsea and Westminster Mental Health Trust; GP's, dentists and other primary care staff in Brent and Harrow; nurses and professions allied to medicine from Parkside NHS Trust; students on placement at the hospital. Others on application

Hours: 09.00-17.00 Monday, Thursday and Friday; 09.00-19.00 Tuesday and Wednesday; keycard access at other times

Transport: Tube: Park Royal, North Acton, Harlesden; Rail: Harlesden; Bus: PR1, PR2, 187, 226, 260

Special facilities: Toilet facilities available

Publications: Quarterly Newsletter

Linked organisations
London Library and Information Development Unit

[105]
Central Saint Martins College of Art and Design

World Wide Web: www.linst.ac.uk/library/intranet

Constitution: Higher education corporation

Availability: Written application should be made for access. Reference access may be granted to those whose needs can not be met elsewhere. Students and staff of the London Institute can use and borrow materials from any of the libraries of the Institute

Special features: Central Saint Martins libraries are located on three sites at Southampton Row (including Slide library), Charing Cross Road and Chalk Farm (Drama Centre library)

Linked organisations
The London Institute   Part of the Institute

[105][a]
Charing Cross Road Library
107 Charing Cross Road
London WC2H 0DU
Borough: Westminster
Telephone: 020 7514 7191
Fax: 020 7514 7189
E-mail: a.huxstep@csm.linst.ac.uk
Key staff: Site Librarian: Arja Huxstep
Stock and subject coverage: Materials on fine art, photography and fashion. Special file collection covering designers and other specific areas of fashion; Fashion Look books
Services: Photocopying and IT facilities
Hours: Term-time only: 09.30-20.00 Monday to Thursday; 10.00-19.00 Friday
See website for details of vacation opening hours
Transport: Tube: Tottenham Court Road; Bus: 1, 14, 19, 24, 38, 176
Special facilities: Wheelchair access by special arrangement

[105][b]
Drama Centre London
176 Prince of Wales Road
Chalk Farm
London NW5 3PT
Borough: Camden
Telephone: 020 7267 1177
Fax: 020 7514 7129
E-mail: c.barontini@csm.linst.ac.uk
Key staff: Drama Centre London Librarian: Chiara Barontini
Stock and subject coverage: Specialist drama school to prepare students for the professional stage, cinema and television. The Library stock covers all aspects of the performing arts
Hours: Term-time only: 11.00-16.00 Monday, Tuesday and Thursday; 13.00-16.00 Friday
Closed during vacations
Transport: Tube: Chalk Farm

[105][c]
Southampton Row Library
London WC1B 4AP
Borough: Camden
Telephone: 020 7514 7037
Fax: 020 7514 7033
E-mail: j.holt@csm.linst.ac.uk
Key staff: Site Librarian: Jane Holt
Stock and subject coverage: Materials on product and industrial design, ceramics, film, animation, graphics, illustration, metalwork, photography, printmaking, jewellery and textiles. Reference collection of manufacturers' catalogues and samples of products and materials. Slide library
Services: Photocopying and IT facilities
Hours: Term-time: 09.30-20.00 Monday to Thursday; 10.00-19.00 Friday
Slide Library: 10.00-13.00, 14.00-18.00 Monday to Friday
See website for details of vacation opening hours
Transport: Tube: Holborn; Bus: 8, 19, 38, 55, 68, 77, 172, 188, 501, 505
Special facilities: Wheelchair access by special arrangement

[106]
Central School of Speech and Drama
CSSD
Embassy Theatre
64 Eton Avenue
London NW3 3HY
Borough: Camden
Telephone: 020 7559 3942
Fax: 020 7722 4132
E-mail: a.edwards@cssd.ac.uk
World Wide Web: www.cssd.ac.uk
Constitution: Registered charity and company limited by guarantee
Key staff: Head of Learning and Information Services: Adam Edwards; Library Services Manager: Peter Collett

Stock and subject coverage: Materials on art and design; education and theatre

Services: Photocopies

Availability: Open free of charge to bona fide researchers. Borrowing rights available to members on payment of annual membership fee of £100 plus VAT

Hours: 09.30–20.00 Monday to Thursday; 09.30–17.00 Friday; 13.00–17.00 Saturday during Term-time. Telephone for details of vacation opening hours

Transport: Tube: Swiss Cottage

Special facilities: Photocopiers

Special features: Refreshment facilities available on site (term-time only); toilet facilities; access for users with disabilities

Linked organisations

The Circus Space The CSSD's BA in Theatre Practice (Circus) is taught jointly with The Circus Space

[107]
Centre for Accessible Environments
CAE

Nutmeg House
60 Gainsford Road
London SE1 2NY

Borough: Islington

Telephone/minicom: 020 7357 8182

Fax: 020 7357 8183

E-mail: info@cae.org.uk

World Wide Web: www.cae.org.uk

Constitution: Registered charity; association with voluntary subscribing membership

Objectives/purposes: Information and training resource on accessibility for the construction industry, care professions and disabled people. The Centre is committed to the provision of buildings and environments that are accessible to all people, including disabled and older people. Services include information and advice on technical matters, design guidance, a journal and a training programme

Key staff: Information Officer

Stock and subject coverage: Wide range of books and journals covering access to the built environment. Current awareness files

Services: Architectural Advisory Service – register of architects experienced in designing accessible buildings

Availability: Open to researchers, students and interested people. Queries can be answered in person, by telephone, e-mail and by letter. Library material is for reference only

Hours: 09.00–17.00 Monday to Friday

Transport: Tube: Angel

Publications: Access by Design (3 p.a.). Other recent publications include: Reading and Using Plans; Access Audits - A Guide and Checklist; Designing for Accessibility - An Introductory Guide

[108]
Centre for Armenian Information and Advice
CAIA

105A Mill Hill Road
Acton
London W3 8JF

Borough: Ealing

Telephone: 020 8992 4621

Fax: 020 8993 8953

E-mail: library@caia.org.uk

World Wide Web: www.caia.org.uk

Constitution: Independent registered charity

Objectives/purposes: To further the education of the Armenian Community in London

Key staff: General Secretary

Stock and subject coverage: Extensive book collections on Armenian affairs, culture, history, etc. in English and Armenian. The Library receives and stores publications, maps, CDs, records, audio-visual and other resources from around the world and holds a database on Armenians in the UK and abroad. A press cuttings and photographic library on Armenian communities and on genocide is being developed

Services: Photocopies; translations from Armenian to English or vice versa; fax machine and searches also available

Availability: Access open to bona fide researchers, students and groups by appointment only. No loan service. Phone or write in advance to the General Secretary

Hours: By arrangement

Transport: Tube: Acton Town

Special facilities: Refreshment and toilet facilities available; access for users with disabilities

Publications: Annual report of CAIA activities; Armenian Voice, bi-lingual newsletter (quarterly)

Linked organisations

CAIA has extensive links with Armenian newspapers, institutions and libraries throughout the world

[109]
The Centre for Independent Transport Research in London
CILT

207 The Colourworks
2 Abbot Street
London E8 3DP

Borough: Hackney

Telephone: 020 7275 9900

Fax: 020 7254 6777 (mark 'CILT')

E-mail: cilt@dial.pipex.com

World Wide Web: www.cilt.dial.pipex.com

Constitution: Registered charity with voluntary subscribing membership (affiliates); company limited by guarantee; independent non-profit distributing organisation largely funded by the ALG (Association of London Government)

Objectives/purposes: Research and resource unit which explores ways of making public transport more accessible, efficient and safe for all who want to use it

Key staff: Chris Wood, David Hurdle, Alix Stredwick, Jocelyn Lomax
Stock and subject coverage: Books, journals, reports, press cuttings, etc. on: transport, land use planning, accessibility and related issues
Services: Photocopies (charged)
Availability: Access to all by appointment. Material available for reference only
Hours: Variable, core opening hours 11.00–15.00 Monday to Friday. Appointment necessary
Transport: Rail: Dalston Kingsland; Bus: 38, 242, 277
Special facilities: Toilet facilities available; lift to all floors (users with disabilities are advised to discuss access needs when making an appointment so that special arrangements, e.g. parking and opening the gate for wheelchair users, can be ensured)
Publications: Transition Journal (quarterly); Annual Report; range of publications and seminar papers on topics such as: environment, rail investment, transport policy, women and transport, and community transport

[110]
Centre for Information on Language Teaching and Research, Resources Library
CILT
20 Bedfordbury
London WC2N 4LB
Borough: Westminster
Telephone: 020 7379 5110
Fax: 020 7379 5082
E-mail: library@cilt.org.uk
World Wide Web: www.cilt.org.uk
Constitution: Registered charity, national government funded organisation
Key staff: Librarian: John Hawkins
Stock and subject coverage: Applied linguistics, language teaching principles and methods with special reference to the languages taught in schools. Includes linguistic studies and a teaching materials collection for each language. Stock includes 14,000 book titles (including textbooks), 260 current journals, and a collection of audio-visual resources and language learning software
Services: Information service provided for teachers, libraries and individuals. Listening and viewing facilities for teachers inspecting audio-visual language courses and computer software. Self-service photocopying available on-site (10p/A4 copy)
Availability: Books may be consulted on a reference basis by anyone concerned with language teaching
Hours: 10.30–17.00 (extended opening on Wednesday evenings and Saturday mornings during school term-times)
Transport: Tube: Charing Cross, Embankment, Covent Garden, Leicester Square; Rail: Charing Cross
Special facilities: Wheelchair lift at entrance; lift to library and wheelchair accessible toilet
Publications: List of priced publications available on request. Information sheets free

Linked organisations
CILT is part of a national network which includes Scottish CILT, Northern Ireland CILT and Comenius Centres in England and Wales. (The Comenius Centres provide a regional focus for information, resources and in-service training for language teachers.) CILT also houses the Languages NTO and BLIS, the Business Language Information Service, as well as the National Advisory Centre on Early Language Learning (NACELL)

[111]
Centre for Micro-Assisted Communication
CENMAC
Charlton Park School
Charlton Park Road
London SE7 8HX
Borough: Greenwich
Telephone: 020 8316 7589
Fax: 020 8317 3843
Constitution: Supported by funds from subscribing inner London Local Education Authorities
Objectives/purposes: To promote the use of information technology to support learners with a physical disability
Key staff: Director: Myra Tingle; Rehab. Engineer: John Hillsdon; Advisors: Lesley Rahamim, Trish Davidson
Stock and subject coverage: Journals relating to: physical disability and social communication, and physical disability and written communication. Books on attitudes towards disability and disability issues. IT and curriculum access, aids and adaptations for learners with physical disabilities
Services: Photocopies (charged)
Availability: Open to bona fide researchers by appointment only; material may be borrowed or copied
Hours: Term-time only
Transport: Rail: Woolwich Arsenal then bus 53, 54, 75; bus 53 from Central London
Special facilities: Toilet facilities available; access for users with disabilities (Charlton Park is a school for pupils with physical disabilities, therefore all areas have disabled access)

[112]
Centre for Policy on Ageing
CPA
19-23 Ironmonger Row
London EC1V 3QP
Borough: Hackney
Telephone: 020 7553 6500
Fax: 020 7553 6501
E-mail: cpa@cpa.org.uk
World Wide Web: www.cpa.org.uk
Constitution: Independent non-profit distributing organisation; company limited by guarantee; registered charity
Objectives/purposes: Works to influence public policy affecting the lives of older people, to develop and promote policies that enable people to lead fulfilled lives and maintain independence for as long as possible

Key staff: Deputy Director and Head of Information:
   Gillian Crosby
Stock and subject coverage: Collection of materials on the
   social and behavioural aspects of older age (social
   gerontology). Ca. 350 journals plus 22,000
   bibliographic entries on CPA's computer databases
   (books, reports, legislation, theses, dissertations, grey
   literature, etc.)
Services: Photocopies (charges made); fax; online
   searching; internet access
Availability: Open to the public by appointment for
   reference only
Hours: 14.00-17.00 Monday; 10.00-17.00 Tuesday to
   Friday
Transport: Tube: Barbican, Old Street; Rail: Old Street
Special facilities: Refreshment and toilet facilities available;
   limited wheelchair access, visitors should advise the
   library in advance
Publications: AGEINFO CD-ROM (updated quarterly);
   New Literature on Old Age (6 p.a.); bibliographies
   and reading lists

[113]
Centre of Construction Law and Management
CCLM
   King's College London
   Old Watch House
   Strand
   London WC2R 2LS
Borough: Westminster
Telephone: 020 7848 2643
Fax: 020 7872 0210
E-mail: susan.bart@kcl.ac.uk
Constitution: Department of a university; self-financing
   centre
Key staff: Manager: Linda Jones; Assistant: Sue Hart
Stock and subject coverage: Journals and law reports in the
   following areas: arbitration (domestic and
   international); building and construction law;
   construction technology; CIRIA publications; the
   English legal system; international construction law
   and practice; MSc dissertations and doctoral theses
Services: Photocopies (self-service)
Availability: Free access for students and members of staff
   of KCL and Society of Construction Law members.
   Other university students may have free access by
   arrangement. Open to members of the public on
   payment of a day fee (for research only)
Hours: Term-time and vacation: 10.00-17.00 Monday to
   Friday. Please telephone before paying a visit
Transport: Tube: Temple, Holborn, Covent Garden; Rail:
   Charing Cross, Blackfriars; Bus: 4, 9, 11, 15, 23, 26,
   68, 76, 77, 77A, 91, 168, 171, 304, 501, 505, 520, 521
Special facilities: Refreshment facilities available during
   term-time; toilet facilities; access for users with
   disabilities
Publications: Conference papers and books

Linked organisations
   King's College London, School of Physical
   Sciences and Engineering CCLM is part of King's
   College London

[114]
Centre of Medical Law and Ethics Library Collection
   Chancery Lane Library and Information Services
   Centre
   King's College London
   Chancery Lane
   London WC2A 1LR
Borough: Corporation of London
Telephone: 020 7848 2424
Fax: 020 7848 2277
E-mail: vivien.robertson@kcl.ac.uk
World Wide Web: www.kcl.ac.uk
Constitution: Department of King's College London
Key staff: Information Services Centre Manager: Vivien
   Robertson
Stock and subject coverage: Medical law and medical ethics
   in the UK, with material from the USA and the
   Commonwealth also represented. Wide collection of
   journals. The collection was started in 1980
Services: Photocopies, self-service
Availability: Once only reference use free of charge with
   proof of identity. More frequent use apply for
   reference ticket in writing by post. Annual fee for
   borrowing if privilege granted
Hours: Term-time: 08.30-22.00 (reference only after
   20.30); 09.30-17.30 Saturday; 11.00-19.00 Sunday.
   Vacations: 09.30-17.30
Transport: Tube: Holborn, Chancery Lane, Blackfriars;
   Rail: Blackfriars; Bus: 6, 11, 68, 171, 176, 188
Special facilities: Refreshment and toilet facilities available
   on site; limited wheelchair access, disabled visitors
   should telephone in advance of visiting
Publications: Information sheet on the medical law and
   ethics collection

Linked organisations
   King's College London Library The Centre is
   part of the Library

[115]
Charity Commission
   Harmsworth House
   13-15 Bouverie Street
   London EC4Y 8DP
Borough: Corporation of London
Telephone: 020 7674 2409
Fax: 020 7674 2300
E-mail: feedback@charity-commission.gov.uk
World Wide Web: www.charity-commission.gov.uk
Constitution: Government department
Key staff: Librarian (post vacant)
Stock and subject coverage: Books and serials on law,
   particularly charity law; charity administration,
   management and history
Availability: Departmental staff and government
   departments only
Transport: Tube: Blackfriars, Temple; Rail: Blackfriars,
   City Thameslink; Bus: any bus stopping in Fleet
   Street
Special facilities: Toilet facilities
Publications: Annual Report; guidance leaflets (see
   website for details)

[116]
Charles Williams Society Reference Library

Room 9E
Chesham Building
King's College
London WC2R 2LS
Borough: Westminster
Telephone: 020 7848 1797
E-mail: brian.horne@kcl.ac.uk
Constitution: Registered charity and association with voluntary subscribing membership
Key staff: BL Horne
Stock and subject coverage: Complete collection of all Charles Williams's published works, some of his manuscripts and typescripts and books and articles about him
Availability: Free access to bona fide students and members of the Charles Williams Society. No material available for loan
Hours: By arrangement with the Society's Librarian
Transport: Tube: Temple; Bus: 9, 11, 13, 15
Special facilities: Refreshment and toilet facilities available
Publications: Charles Williams Society Newsletter (4 p.a.)

[117]
Chartered Institute of Management Accountants

CIMA
63 Portland Place
London W1N 4AB
Borough: Westminster
Telephone: 020 7917 9259
Fax: 020 7323 0587
E-mail: tas@cimaglobal.com
World Wide Web: www.cimaglobal.com
Constitution: Association with voluntary subscribing membership
Key staff: Technical Advisory Service Information Manager: Denise Metcalf
Stock and subject coverage: Ca. 3,000 volumes of books and pamphlets and ca. 120 current periodical titles. Covers cost and management accountancy; financial accounting; corporate planning; quantitative techniques; financial management; and company law and taxation
Services: Enquiry service; loans through the British Library; photocopy service (all primarily for members)
Availability: Reference use for CIMA members by appointment
Hours: 10.00-16.00 Monday to Friday
Transport: Tube: Regent's Park, Oxford Circus
Special facilities: Toilet facilities available
Special features: Adam building, inhabited by Frances Hodgson Burnett between 1849-1924
Publications: Periodicals – current titles list; subject bibliographies

[118]
Chartered Institute of Personnel and Development

CIPD
35 Camp Road
London SW19 4UX
Borough: Merton
Telephone: 020 8971 9000
Fax: 020 8263 3400
E-mail: cipd@cipd.co.uk
World Wide Web: www.cipd.co.uk
Constitution: Registered charity and association with voluntary subscribing membership
Key staff: Barbara Salmon
Stock and subject coverage: Subject coverage includes: personnel management; industrial relations; pay and employment conditions; occupational health and safety; equal opportunities; occupational psychology; employment law; manpower planning; training and development. Special collections of: company documentation; European pay and conditions materials and training manuals
Services: Information service; loans; photocopying; specialist advisory service (all aspects of employment, including advice on legislation relating to personnel management)
Availability: For members; non-members admitted on a day ticket at £50 per day or part of a day
Hours: 09.15-17.00 Monday to Friday
Transport: Tube: Wimbledon (1 mile); CIPD minibus available to shuttle staff and visitors to and from Wimbledon station, contact Library for schedule
Special facilities: Coffee machine; toilet facilities; access for users with disabilities

Linked organisations

European Association of Personnel Management

[119]
Chartered Institute of Public Finance and Accountancy

CIPFA
3 Robert Street
London WC2N 6RL
Borough: Westminster
Telephone: 020 7543 5600
Fax: 020 7543 5700
Key staff: Information Centre/Help Desk Manager: Nigel Cook
Constitution: Registered charity with voluntary subscribing membership; independent non-profit distributing organisation
Objectives/purposes: CIPFA is the leading professional accountancy body for public services, whether in the public or private sectors. It provides education and training in accountancy and financial management, and sets and monitors professional standards
Stock and subject coverage: Books, including CIPFA publications, journals, official publications, statistics and CIPFA archives. Subject coverage includes: aspects of public finance, including public expenditure, and the management and administration of public services; accountancy, including audit,

financial management and financial reporting in central and local government; health care services, higher and further education; housing and the regulated utilities

Services: Photocopies; faxed information service; some online services; bibliographies

Availability: Available to all CIPFA members and students free of charge. Available to corporate users and other for a fee. Serious academic researchers may have access free at the Librarian's discretion

Hours: 09.00–17.00 Monday to Friday

Transport: Tube: Embankment, Charing Cross; Rail: Charing Cross; Bus: any bus along the Strand

Special facilities: Toilet facilities; access for users with disabilities (restricted access to upper part of library)

Special features: Located in Georgian building designed by Robert Adam

Publications: CIPFA has a large programme of publishing in its core areas (see stock and subject coverage)

[120]
Chartered Institute of Taxation
CIOT

Chancery Lane Library and ISC
King's College, London
Chancery Lane
London WC2A 1LR
Borough: Camden
Telephone: 020 7235 9381
Fax: 020 7235 2562
E-mail: post@tax.org.uk
World Wide Web: www.tax.org.uk
Constitution: Registered charity; chartered professional body
Objectives/purposes: Leading professional body in the UK devoted solely to taxation
Key staff: Secretary General of the Institute: RA Dommett, BA FCIS FCIB MCIPD FRSA. Contact the Head of Membership Department: Peter Harrington
Stock and subject coverage: Comprehensive coverage of UK; some information on international taxation
Services: Photocopies and fax facilities
Availability: To members; others by appointment
Hours: 09.00–17.00 Monday to Friday
Transport: Tube: Chancery Lane
Special facilities: Refreshment and toilet facilities available; limited access for users with disabilities
Publications: Tax Adviser (monthly); Annual Directory of Chartered Tax Advisers; Annotated Finance Act, Annual Report and Accounts
Note: The Library moved, in September 2001, to King's College London's Chancery Lane Library. It retains its separate identity as The Tony Arnold Library of CIOT, and continues to belong to the Institute

Linked organisations
Association of Taxation Technicians (ATT)

[121]
Chartered Institution of Water and Environmental Management
CIWEM

15 John Street
London WC1N 2EB
Borough: Camden
Telephone: 020 7831 3110
Fax: 020 7405 4967
E-mail: admin@ciwem.org.uk
World Wide Web: www.ciwem.org.uk
Constitution: Registered charity
Key staff: Volunteer member of CIWEM acts as Honorary Librarian
Objectives/purposes: To advance the science and practice of water and environmental management and to promote education and research
Stock and subject coverage: Subject coverage includes: water resources; river management; pollution control; sea defence and flood alleviation; water supply and distribution; sewerage; sewage and industrial wastewater; navigation; fisheries and water recreation; building services; waste management; land reclamation; noise abatement; air pollution and environmental conservation. Collection includes archive material related with water and wastewater in the UK
Services: Photocopies, online searches, fax machines (charges apply), internet access for water/environment
Availability: Open to members of the public for reference (charges apply). Loans to members of CIWEM only
Hours: 09.00–17.00 Monday to Friday, by appointment
Transport: Tube: Chancery Lane; BR: King's Cross
Special facilities: Toilet facilities available
Publications: Journal (6 p.a.); Yearbook; Newsletter and Magazine (WEM) (monthly to members); symposium/conference papers, manuals and handbooks

[122]
Chartered Insurance Institute
CII

The Hall
20 Aldermanbury
London EC2V 7HY
Borough: Corporation of London
Telephone: 020 7417 4415/4416
Fax: 020 7972 0110
E-mail: library@cii.co.uk
World Wide Web: www.ciilo.org
Constitution: Chartered professional body
Key staff: Librarian: RL Cunnew BA FLA
Stock and subject coverage: About 20,000 books and pamphlets, 2,600 journal titles and other material on microfiche, video and CD-ROM, covering insurance and related subjects worldwide. The Library maintains a directory of other sites on its website, together with a digital archive of journal articles

Services: Internet access, computer based training, photocopying, online services, fax machine. Catalogue and index to journal articles available on the Library website

Availability: Open to non-members on a fee basis

Hours: 09.00-17.00 Monday, Tuesday, Thursday; 10.00-17.00 Wednesday; 09.00-16.45 Friday

Transport: Tube: Moorgate, Mansion House, St Pauls, Bank

Special facilities: Toilet facilities available

Publications: Institute publications: The Journal (6 times p.a.); Occasional Papers; textbooks; Insurance Research and Practice (2 p.a.); careers literature; computer-based training packages; miscellaneous papers. Library publication on Sources of Insurance History

Subordinate societies

Society of Fellows
Society of Technicians in Insurance
Society of Financial Advisers
Local insurance institutes throughout the UK (ca. 80) act as quasi-autonomous branches. CII has many affiliated insurance institutes worldwide

[123]
Chartered Society of Designers
CSD

5 Bermondsey Exchange
London SE1 3UW
Borough: Southwark
Telephone: 020 7357 8088
Fax: 020 7407 9878
E-mail: csd@csd.org.uk
World Wide Web: www.csd.org.uk
Constitution: Registered charity with voluntary subscribing membership; independent non-profit distributing organisation
Key staff: Head of Membership
Stock and subject coverage: Contemporary design magazines and journals from the UK and worldwide (2,500). Design books, directories and general reference works (400). Collection of 350 brochures of UK design consultancies, and 200 from overseas
Services: Information service; listings; publications
Hours: 09.30-17.30 Monday to Friday
Availability: To members of the Society only
Transport: Tube: London Bridge
Special facilities: Toilet facilities available
Publications: CSD magazine (quarterly)

[124]
Chase Healthcare Information Centre
CHIC

Chase Farm Hospital
The Ridgeway
Enfield
Middlesex EN2 8JL
Borough: Enfield
Telephone: 020 8967 5982
Fax: 020 8367 4561
E-mail: libcfl1@mdx.ac.uk

World Wide Web: www.ilrs.mdx.ac.uk/hc/chic.htm
Constitution: Department of a university (Middlesex)
Key staff: Library Manager: Linda Farley
Stock and subject coverage: Books, videos and CDs on health care, medicine and nursing
Services: Photocopies; online searching; internet access; computing facilities
Availability: Available to all employees of the NHS Trusts and staff and students of Middlesex University
Hours: Term-time: 09.30-17.00 Monday and Friday; 09.30-18.00 Tuesday to Thursday
Vacations: 09.30-17.00 Monday, Tuesday, Thursday and Friday; 09.30-18.00 Wednesday
Transport: Rail: Gordon Hill; Bus: W8, W9, 313
Special facilities: Toilet facilities available

Linked organisations

CHIC is a multidisciplinary centre run by Middlesex University on behalf of Barnet and Chase Farm Hospitals NHS Trusts, Enfield Community Care Trust and the University

[125]
Chelsea College of Art and Design

World Wide Web: www.linst.ac.uk/library
Constitution: Department of an educational organisation
Availability: By appointment, for reference only. Researchers should apply in writing; admittance at the discretion of the librarian
The College's library collections are located on three sites at Manresa Road (main library), Hugon Road and Lime Grove

Linked organisations

London Institute   Part of the Institute

[125][a]
Manresa Road Library

London SW3 6LS
Borough: Kensington and Chelsea
Telephone: 020 7514 7773
Fax: 020 7514 7785
Key staff: Librarian: Liz Ward
Stock and subject coverage: Modern art 1850–; contemporary art; art journals; exhibition catalogues; artists' books; artists' multiples
Services: Photocopies (charged)
Hours: Term-time: 09.00-18.00 Monday, Tuesday and Thursday; 09.00-19.00 Wednesday; 09.00-17.00 Friday
See website for vacation opening hours
Transport: Tube: South Kensington, Sloane Square; Bus: 11, 19, 22, 49, 219, 249, 349
Special facilities: Refreshment and toilet facilities available; access for users with disabilities including wheelchair access

[125][b]
Hugon Road Library

London SW6 3ES
Borough: Hammersmith and Fulham
Telephone: 020 7514 7901
Stock and subject coverage: Collections on architecture and interior design

Services: Photocopies (charged)
Hours: Term-time: 09.00-17.00 Monday to Friday.
  See website for vacation opening hours
Transport: Tube: Parsons Green; Train: Wandsworth Town;
  Bus: C3, C4, 28, 295 from Wandsworth Bridge Road,
  11, 22 from New King's Road
Special facilities: Refreshment and toilet facilities available;
  access for users with disabilities including wheelchair
  access

[125][c]
Lime Grove Library
  Lime Grove
  London W12 8EA
Borough: Hammersmith and Fulham
Telephone: 020 7514 7833
Stock and subject coverage: Collections on design history,
  public art and textiles
Services: Photocopies (charged)
Hours: Term-time: 10.00-18.00 Monday to Thursday;
  09.00-17.00 Friday.
  See website for vacation opening hours
Transport: Tube: Shepherd's Bush, Goldhawk Road; Bus:
  12, 49, 72, 94, 95, 105, 207, 220, 237, 260, 283, 295
Special facilities: Refreshment and toilet facilities available;
  access for users with disabilities including wheelchair
  access

[126]
Chelsea Physic Garden
  66 Royal Hospital Road
  London SW3 4HS
Borough: Kensington and Chelsea
Telephone: 020 7352 5646, ext 3
Fax: 020 7376 3910
E-mail: enquiries@cpgarden.demon.co.uk
World Wide Web: www.cpgarden.demon.co.uk
Constitution: Registered charity
Objectives/purposes: Botanic garden with several
  specialised collections including medicinal plants
Key staff: Curator: Sue Minter
Stock and subject coverage: Original 18th century working
  library of the Society of Apothecaries. In addition
  there is a modern library specialising in works on
  herbal medicines, medicinal plants, etc.; plant
  collecting; botanical history (especially the history of
  the Garden); and a good working collection covering
  the particular interests of the Garden
Services: Photocopies (charges made)
Availability: Open to bona fide researchers by
  appointment only. Reference only, no loans
Transport: Tube: Sloane Square; Bus: 11, 19, 22 to Kings
  Road, 239
Special facilities: Toilet facilities available; users with
  disabilities can be accommodated in a study room

[127]
Child Accident Prevention Trust
CAPT
  18-20 Farringdon Lane
  London EC1R 3HA
Borough: Islington
Telephone: 020 8608 3828

Fax: 020 8608 3674
E-mail: safe@capt.org.uk
World Wide Web: www.capt.org.uk and
  www.childsafetyweek.org.uk
Constitution: Registered charity
Objectives/purposes: Research into, and reduction of
  preventable childhood accidents
Key staff: Information Manager
Stock and subject coverage: Reports, articles, journals and
  conference proceedings on the following subjects:
  child accidents; historical background information;
  statistics and statistical studies; data collection; the
  child (background, development and rights); the
  child's environment; road traffic and other transport
  accidents; home, farm, school, sports and leisure
  accidents; play areas; poisoning; burns and scalds;
  drowning; accidents by injury; accident prevention;
  consumer product safety and accident management
Services: Photocopies; fax machine (charges made for use
  of both)
Availability: Access by appointment
Hours: 09.30-16.30 Monday to Friday
Transport: Tube: Farringdon
Publications: Annual Report; range of subject related
  priced publications, leaflets

[128]
The Children's Society
TCS
  Edward Rudolf House
  Margery Street
  London WC1X 0JL
Borough: Islington
Telephone: 020 7841 4400
E-mail: info@childrenssociety.org.uk
World Wide Web: www.childrenssociety.org.uk
Constitution: Registered charity
Key staff: Librarian: Denise Tinant, Sue Peisley
Stock and subject coverage: Ca. 10,000 books, reports,
  papers, and 100 journals covering childcare, social
  work, the voluntary sector, fundraising and other
  topics relevant to a large childcare charity
Services: Interlibrary loans
Availability: Public enquiry service answers enquiries
  about the work of the Society from the general
  public, schoolchildren and others. Enquiries by e-
  mail, letter or telephone
Hours: 10.00-12.00, 14.00-16.00 Monday to Friday
Transport: Bus: 341; Tube and bus: Angel then bus 19, 38,
  King's Cross then bus 63, Farringdon then bus 63
Special facilities: Refreshment facilities (drinks only);
  toilet facilities; access for users with disabilities
Publications: Annual review; promotional leaflets about
  the work of TCS; publications catalogue

Linked organisations

Records and Archives Management Section,
Block A, Floor 2, Tower Bridge Business Complex,
100 Clements Road, London SE16 4DG, tel: 020
7232 2966, fax: 020 7252 302
Based at Bermondsey the Section contains historic
and modern records reflecting every aspect of the
Society's work, from administrative functions to
fundraising and social work practice, policy and case
files. Includes a photographic collection dating from

the 1880s to the present day. Enquiries from bona fide researchers welcome. Access to some archival records is restricted. Open from 09.30-17.00 Monday to Friday

[129]
Christian Aid Information Resources Centre

PO Box 100
35-41 Lower Marsh
London SE1 7RT
Borough: Lambeth
Telephone: 020 7523 2187
Fax: 020 7620 0719
E-mail: irc@christian-aid.org.uk
World Wide Web: www.christian-aid.org.uk
Constitution: Registered charity
Objectives/purposes: Development aid agency
Key staff: Information Resources Manager: Sarah Heery; Information Resources Officer: Margaret Gilbane
Stock and subject coverage: Approximately 5,000 books and documents; 90 current journal titles. Subject coverage includes: charities and non-governmental organisations (including annual reports); economics; development issues; human rights; aid and poverty; education; women; health; agriculture; country information on developing countries in Africa, Asia, Caribbean, Latin America, Middle East, Eastern Europe and Central Asia
Services: Photocopies (charges made)
Availability: Free access to bona fide researchers, for reference only. Telephone first for appointment
Hours: 10.00-17.00 Monday to Friday
Transport: Tube and Rail: Waterloo; Bus: 4, 12, 26, 52, 68, 76, 168, 176, 188, 211, 501, 505, 507
Special facilities: Toilet facilities (and toilet for users with disabilities) available; access for users with disabilities
Publications: Press reports (daily)

[130]
Christian Social Order
CSO

157 Vicarage Road
London E10 5DU
Borough: Waltham Forest
Telephone: 020 8539 3876
Fax: 020 8539 3876
E-mail: social@smartgroups.com
World Wide Web: www.smartgroups.com/vault/social
Constitution: Independent non-profit distributing organisation
Objectives/purposes: To foster a Christian social order
Key staff: Librarian: Ronald King
Stock and subject coverage: Books, journals, CD-ROMs and newspaper cuttings on political and social questions
Availability: At the discretion of the Librarian
Hours: By appointment only
Transport: Tube: Leyton, Walthamstow Central; Rail: Leyton Midland; Walthamstow Central; Bus: 48, 69, 97, 256
Special facilities: Refreshment and toilet facilities available on site

Publications: The Keys of Peter (bi-monthly); The Laity (quarterly); Centrepoint (quarterly); Viewpoint (quarterly)

Linked organisations
Christian Centre Party

[131]
Church of England Record Centre

15 Galleywall Road
South Bermondsey
London SE16 3PB
Borough: Southwark
Telephone: 020 7898 1033
Fax: 020 7898 7018
E-mail: sarah.duffield@c-of-e.org.uk
Key staff: Archivist: Sarah Duffield
Stock and subject coverage: Archive of correspondence on individual Church schools, including grant applications, reports, plans and information about the schools. For the family historian the Archive contains an index of schoolteachers from 1812-1855. Other records include Trust Deeds, minute books of the National Society and the archives of some Church schools
Availability: Contact the Archivist for information on availability
Transport: Tube: Surrey Quays; Rail: South Bermondsey

Linked organisations

The National Society The Archive contains the archives of the National Society, founded in 1811 to promote Church schools

[132]
Cinema Theatre Association
CTA

Brian Oakaby (Archivist)
c/o 17 Marten Road
Walthamstow
London E17 4NL
(Archive housed in other premises)
Borough: Waltham Forest
Telephone: 020 8531 2127
World Wide Web: www.cinema-theatre.org.uk
Constitution: Association with voluntary subscribing membership
Objectives/purposes: Study of all aspects of cinema buildings; visits to cinemas and theatres; campaigning for the preservation of cinemas and theatres of interest
Key staff: Chairman: Richard Gray; Secretary: Adam Unger; Archivist: Brian Oakaby
Stock and subject coverage: Large holdings of historical photographs of cinemas in the UK; pre-war opening programmes of cinemas; newspaper cuttings; kine year books; photographs of publicity campaigns; technical survey books on certain cinema properties. Special collections: George Coles (cinema architect) collection of photographs, plans and drawings; Maurice Cheepen (cinema manager) collection of film publicity campaigns
Availability: Free access to all bona fide researchers. Material available for reference and some for loan.

Charges made to commercial organisations and
others at the discretion of the Archivist
Hours: By arrangement with the Archivist
Transport: Tube and rail: Stratford
Special facilities: Toilet facilities available (Archive only)
Publications: CTA Bulletin (6 p.a to members); Picture
House magazine (annual); ABC-The First Name in
Entertainment by Allen Eyles, published jointly by
CTA and the British Film Institute

Linked organisations
Theatres' Trust

[133]
City University
World Wide Web: www.city.ac.uk
Constitution: University
Key staff: Director of Library Information Services:
Brendan Casey
Library Information Services manages libraries at
Northampton Square, City University Business School,
the two sites of the St Bartholemew School of Nursing
and Midwifery (SONAM) at West Smithfield and
Whitechapel, the Department of Arts Policy
Management and the Department of Radiography

[133][a]
University Library
Northampton Square
London EC1V 0HB
Borough: Islington
Telephone: 020 7040 8191
Fax: 020 7477 8194
E-mail: library@city.ac.uk
Key staff: Head of Operations: Liz Harris
Stock and subject coverage: Social sciences, engineering,
optometry, journalism, music, mathematics, law,
computing and information science
Services: Photocopiers, online public access catalogue,
range of databases, access to internet
Availability: Students and staff of City University,
members of M25 Access Scheme
Hours: 09.00-21.00 Monday to Thursday; 09.00-20.00
Friday; 12.00-18.00 Saturday (during term-time
only). First Saturday opening of term 12 October, last
Saturday opening of term 8 December 2002
Transport: Tube: Angel, Farringdon; Buses: 4, 56, 153

[133][b]
Arts Policy Resource Centre
City University
Frobisher Crescent
Barbican Centre
London EC2Y 8HB
Borough: Corporation of London
Telephone: 020 7040 8752
Fax: 020 7040 8887
Key staff: To be appointed
Stock and subject coverage: Grey literature in cultural
management
Services: Photocopies; study space
Availability: By appointment only
Hours: 09.00-17.00 Monday to Friday
Transport: Tube: Barbican

[133][c]
Cass Business School Learning Resource Centre
City University
Bunhill Row
London EC1Y 8TZ
Borough: Hackney
Telephone: 020 7040 8787
Fax: 020 7638 1080
Key staff: Cass Librarian: Leslie Baldwin
Stock and subject coverage: Business, management and
finance at postgraduate level
Services: Photocopies; study space
Availability: Access under co-operative schemes
(SCONUL, M25, LLiL) and by payment of external
membership fees only
Hours: 09.00-17.00 Monday to Friday for enquiries
from other librarians
Transport: Tube and Rail: Old Street

[133][d]
Department of Radiography Library
Rutland Place
Charterhouse Square
London EC1M 6PA
Borough: Corporation of London
Telephone: 020 7040 5653
Fax: 020 7505 5691
Key staff: Radiography Librarian: Endang Scanlon
Stock and subject coverage: Specialist academic material on
radiography
Services: Photocopies, study space
Availability: By appointment only
Hours: 09.00-17.30 Monday to Friday
Transport: Tube: Barbican, Farringdon

[133][e]
West Smithfield Library, City University
St Bartholemew School of Nursing and Midwifery
20 Bartholemew Close
London EC1A 7QN
Borough: Corporation of London
Telephone: 020 7505 5979
Fax: 020 7040 5762
E-mail: sonmlibraries@city.ac.uk
World Wide Web: www.city.ac.uk/library/sonm
Stock and subject coverage: Nursing and midwifery, some
sociology, psychology, biological sciences (especially
physiology)
Services: Photocopies; online public access catalogue,
range of databases available on CD-ROM including
Cinahl, Medline and the Cochrane database; access to
the internet
Availability: Comprehensive information service
available to all City University students on full-time
and part-time courses, to University employees, and
to qualified nursing staff at the Barts and the London,
City and Hackney Community Trust and Tower
Hamlets Health Care Trust
Hours: 08.30-20.00 Monday; 08.30-18.00 Tuesday to
Friday
Transport: Tube: Farringdon

[133][f]
Whitechapel Library, City University
St Bartholemew School of Nursing and Midwifery
Philpot Street
Whitechapel
London E1 2EA
Borough: Tower Hamlets
Telephone: 020 7505 5979
Fax: 020 7505 5858
E-mail: d.m.beckett@city.ac.uk
World Wide Web: www.city.ac.uk/library/sonm
Stock and subject coverage: Nursing and midwifery, some sociology, psychology, biological sciences (especially physiology)
Services: Photocopies; online public access catalogue, range of databases available on CD-ROM including Cinahl, Medline and the Cochrane database; access to the internet
Availability: Comprehensive information service available to all City University students on full-time and part-time courses, to University employees, and to qualified nursing staff at the Barts and the London, City and Hackney Community Trust and Tower Hamlets Health Care Trust
Hours: 08.30-20.00 Monday ; 08.30-18.00 Tuesday to Friday
Transport: Tube: Whitechapel; DLR: Shadwell
Special facilities: Toilet facilities available
Publications: Annual report

[134]
The Civic Trust
17 Carlton House Terrace
London SW1Y 5AW
Borough: City of Westminster
Telephone: 020 7930 0914
Fax: 020 7321 0180
E-mail: pride@civictrust.org.uk
World Wide Web: www.civictrust.org.uk
Constitution: Registered charity; association with voluntary subscribing membership
Objectives/purposes: Improving the built environment
Key staff: Librarian: S Hallam
Stock and subject coverage: Comprehensive reference library covering all aspects of the built environment. National archive of Local Civic Society publications
Services: Photocopies
Availability: Free access for reference only
Hours: 09.00-17.00 Monday to Friday
Transport: Tube and Rail: Charing Cross
Special facilities: Toilet facilities available
Publications: Publications list available

[135]
Clarinet Heritage Society
47 Hambalt Road
Clapham
London SW4 9EQ
Borough: Lambeth
Telephone: 020 8675 3877
E-mail: chs@chello.se
World Wide Web: website in production
Constitution: Private venture, association with voluntary subscribing membership, independent non-profit distributing organisation
Key staff: Stephen Bennett
Stock and subject coverage: Rare contemporary recordings of first performances; sheet music, books and music in production
Availability: Open to all bona fide researchers, charges made
Hours: 10.30-18.00 weekdays and Saturday by appointment. Visitors should contact the Society before visiting
Transport: Tube: Clapham Common, Clapham South; Rail: Clapham Junction, Balham
Special facilities: Refreshment facilities by arrangement, toilet facilities available, access for users with disabilities – disabled visitors should advise the Society in advance
Publications: Drama documentary film series Winds of Change in production

[136]
College of Arms
Queen Victoria Street
London EC4V 4BT
Borough: Corporation of London
Telephone: 020 7248 2762
Fax: 020 7248 6448
E-mail: enquiries@college-of-arms.gov.uk
World Wide Web: www.college-of-arms.gov.uk
Constitution: Independent corporation of the English heralds operating under royal charter
Key staff: Enquiries: The Officer in Waiting
Stock and subject coverage: Over 30,000 volumes on heraldry, genealogy and related subjects; extensive manuscript holdings; the official records of the College, plus the collections of individual heralds and others
Services: Fees may be charged; photocopying facilities; photographs may be arranged; N.B. Official records may not be photocopied, high quality artwork and calligraphy available
Availability: Outside enquiries accepted, but fees may be charged; inspection of particular manuscripts allowed by special arrangement; all searches are carried out by the Officer in Waiting
Hours: 10.00-16.00 Monday to Friday
Transport: Tube: Blackfriars, Mansion House, St Paul's; Rail: Blackfriars
Special features: The present College building dates from ca. 1670-1690
Publications: A Catalogue of Manuscripts in the College of Arms: Collections, Vol 1 (Campbell & Steer, 1988); Catalogue of Welsh Manuscripts in the College of Arms (Francis Jones, Harleian Society, N.S. Vol 7, 1988)

[137]
College of Occupational Therapists Library
106-114 Borough High Street
London SE1 1LB
Borough: Southwark

Telephone: 020 7450 2316
Fax: 020 7450 2364
E-mail: library@cot.co.uk
World Wide Web: www.cot.org.uk
Constitution: Registered charity with voluntary
  subscribing membership
Objectives/purposes: Collect and promote knowledge base
  of occupational therapy
Key staff: Assistant Librarian
Stock and subject coverage: Specialist occupational therapy
  literature collection
Services: Photocopy and search service available to
  members. Self-service photocopying, database and
  internet access available to visitors
Availability: Reference library for bona fide members of
  the British Association of Occupational Therapists
  (BAOT) and those with a legitimate interest in
  ocuupational therapy
Hours: 09.00–17.00 Monday to Friday
Transport: Tube and rail: London Bridge
Special facilities: Refreshment and toilet facilities available;
  access for users with disabilities (ground floor toilet
  for users with disabilities, lift, wheelchair access)
Publications: Range of in-house publications including
  COT standards guidelines and reports

Linked organisations

British Association of Occupational Therapists
Parent body

[138]
College of Optometrists
42 Craven Street
London WC2N 5NG
Borough: Westminster
Telephone: 020 7839 6000
Fax: 020 7839 6800
E-mail: librarian@college-optometrists.org.uk
World Wide Web: www.college-optometrists.org
Constitution: Independent non-profit distributing
  organisation; company limited by guarantee;
  registered charity; part of the British College of
  Optometrists
Objectives/purposes: The College is the main professional
  body and examining body for optometrists in the
  UK. Its aims are the improvement and conservation
  of human vision, the promotion of research, the
  promotion and maintenance of high standards in
  optometry for the public benefit
Key staff: Librarian: Mrs Jan Ayres
Stock and subject coverage: Collection of 10,000 books and
  100 journals covering optics, vision science,
  optometry and ophthalmology. Additional collections
  of rare books and theses
Services: Photocopies (charged); interlibrary loans;
  enquiry service
Availability: Open to members of the College for loans
  and reference. Non-members may use the library for
  reference by appointment. Subscription membership
  available for members of the public wishing to
  borrow books. Reference facilities and loans to
  members free of charge

Hours: 09.30–13.00, 14.00–17.00 Monday to Friday
Transport: Rail: Charing Cross; Tube: Charing Cross and
  Embankment
Special facilities: Toilet facilities available, access for users
  with disabilities

[139]
Commission for Local Administration in England (Local Government Ombudsmen)
21 Queen Anne's Gate
London SW1H 9BU
Borough: Westminster
Telephone: 020 7915 3210
Fax: 020 7233 0396
World Wide Web: www.lgo.org.uk
Constitution: Government funded body
Key staff: Assistant Secretary: Hilary Pook
Stock and subject coverage: Ca. 6,000 reports on individual
  complaints made to the local government
  ombudsmen, issued since the Commission was set up
  in 1974
Services: Reports on particular topics or against
  particular authorities can be traced by CLAE staff.
  These can be copied and posted for a small charge.
  Recent report summaries are available on the
  Commission's website at www.lgo.org.uk
Availability: Personal visits by researchers (by prior
  appointment). Material available for reference only
  but photocopies can be made for a small charge.
  Charges also made for extensive research
Hours: 09.00–17.00 Monday to Friday
Transport: Tube: St James's Park
Special facilities: Toilet facilities available

[140]
Commission for Racial Equality CRE
St Dunstan's House
201–211 Borough High Street
London SE1 1EZ
Borough: Southwark
Telephone: 020 7939 0091
Fax: 020 7939 0001
World Wide Web: www.cre.gov.uk
Key staff: Librarian: P Pinto
Stock and subject coverage: Small library with unique
  collection on race relations. Ca. 17,000 books and
  over 17,000 journals plus press cuttings, dating back
  to 1970, on microfilm
Services: Coin-operated self-service photocopier (10p
  per sheet, visitors should bring sufficient change with
  them)
Availability: Open to the public by appointment only
Hours: 10.00–16.00 Monday to Friday
Transport: Tube: Borough

[141]
Committee on Standards in Public Life

35 Great Smith Street
London SW1P 3BQ
Borough: Westminster
Telephone: 020 7276 2595
Fax: 020 7276 2585
E-mail: nigel.wicks@gtnet.gov.uk
World Wide Web: www.public-standards.gov.uk
Key staff: Press Secretary: Fiona Dick
Services: Summaries of reports; copies of complete
    reports can be purchased from the Stationery Office
Hours: 09.30-17.30 Monday to Friday

[142]
Commonwealth Institute

Commonwealth Resource Centre
Kensington High Street
London W8 6NQ
Borough: Kensington and Chelsea
Telephone: 020 7603 4535, ext. 210 (Information);
    ext 292 (Loans)
Fax: 020 7602 7374
E-mail: crc@commonwealth.org.uk
World Wide Web: www.commonwealth.org.uk
Constitution: Registered charity, independent pan-
    Commonwealth agency
Key staff: Head of Library and Information Services:
    Marie Bastiampillai
Stock and subject coverage: Reference and general books,
    pamphlets, journals, newspaper cuttings, information
    files, slides, audio and video cassettes, maps and
    wallcharts. Subject coverage includes: a collection of
    publications aimed especially at teachers and young
    people, but with information also of interest to the
    general public, on the geographical, historical and
    cultural background of Commonwealth countries
    and people; comprehensive stock of Commonwealth
    literature in English; related subjects such as
    development, multicultural education, world
    religions, race awareness, etc.
Services: Public enquiries service, photocopying facilities
Availability: Loan facilities available to members
Hours: 10.00-16.00 Monday to Saturday
Transport: Tube: High Street Kensington
Special facilities: Toilet facilities available on site; access for
    users with disabilities (report to reception for
    assistance)
Publications: Annual Review; CI publications for sale

[143]
Commonwealth Secretariat
COMSEC

Marlborough House
Pall Mall
London SW1Y 5HX
Borough: Westminster
Telephone: 020 7747 6164
Fax: 020 7747 6168
E-mail: library@commonwealth.inst
World Wide Web: www.thecommonwealth.org
Constitution: Inter-governmental organisation

Key staff: Librarian: David Blake; Deputy Librarian and
    Archivist: Jay Gilbert
Stock and subject coverage: Over 4,000 serials currently
    received, including official statistical publications,
    development plans and publications from
    international organisations. Emphasis is on current
    Commonwealth development. Subjects include trade;
    statistics; economics; industry; agriculture; politics;
    education; women and development; youth and
    health. Archives of the Commonwealth Secretariat
    from 1965
Services: Photocopies
Availability: Access for bona fide researchers for
    reference only
Hours: 09.30-17.00 Monday to Friday
Transport: Tube: Green Park, Charing Cross; Rail:
    Charing Cross
Special facilities: Toilet facilities available; access for users
    with disabilities – includes lift
Publications: Various reports on aspects of the
    Commonwealth

[144]
Communications Workers Union
CWU

150 The Broadway
Wimbledon
London SW19 1RX
Borough: Merton
Telephone: 020 8971 7200
Fax: 020 8971 7300
World Wide Web: www.cwu.org
Constitution: Trade union
Objectives/purposes: Trade union representing the
    communications industry
Key staff: Information Managers: Ian Cook, Jane Taylor
Stock and subject coverage: Wide range of employment
    related material plus a specialist collection relating to
    telecommunications, postal services and trade unions.
    Archives are held at the Modern Records Centre
Services: Photocopies
Availability: Open to bona fide researchers. There are no
    charges and materials are for reference only, not for
    loan
Hours: By appointment, 09.00-17.00 Monday to Friday
Transport: Tube and rail: Wimbledon
Special facilities: Refreshment and toilet facilities available;
    lift access to all floors
Publications: Voice, monthly magazine

Linked organisations
    The National Communications Union (NCU)
    merged with the Union of Communication Workers
    (UCW) in December 1994 to form the
    Communications Workers Union (CWU)

[145]
Competition Commission

New Court
48 Carey Street
London WC2A 2JT
Borough: Westminster
Telephone: 020 7271 0243
Fax: 020 7271 0367

E-mail: info@competition-commission.org.uk
World Wide Web: www.competition-commission.gov.uk
Constitution: Independent public body
Key staff: Linda Fisher, ext 0240; Cilla Mitchell, ext 0243
Stock and subject coverage: Books and serials in the fields of monopolies, competition and industrial economics
Services: Enquiry service. Information pack on the Commission sent on request
Availability: Normally restricted to CC staff and members. Staff of government departments admitted by appointment
Hours: 09.00-17.15 Monday to Friday (closes 17.00 on Friday)
Transport: Tube: Holborn, Temple
Publications: Various lists of Commission reports and enquiries

Linked organisations

Department of Trade and Industry Information and Library Services This library operates as part of the Departmental network

---

[146]
Confederation of British Industry
CBI
Information Centre
Centre Point
103 New Oxford Street
London WC1A 1DU
Borough: Westminster
Telephone: 020 7379 7400
Fax: 020 7240 0988
E-mail: enquiry.desk@cbi.org.uk
World Wide Web: www.cbi.org.uk
Key staff: Information Centre Manager: Emma Hollingsworth; Information Officers: Laura Doran, James Dowling
Stock and subject coverage: Industry and government relations; parliamentary affairs; economic policy; statistics; manufacturing policy; environmental policy; industrial relations; wages and conditions of employment; industrial and company law; energy policy; education and training; technology and innovation policy; e-business policy; European affairs. Archives: CBI and predecessor organisations; papers held on permanent loan by the Modern Records Centre, University of Warwick Library, Coventry CV4 7AL (Telephone: 024 7652 4219)
Services: Enquiries; loans
Availability: By arrangement to Members and to co-operating libraries
Hours: 09.00-17.30 Monday to Friday
Transport: Tube: Tottenham Court Road; Bus: 10, 25, 73
Publications: Economic and Business Outlook; Industrial Trends; Distributive Trades; Regional Trends; Service Sector survey; Financial Services survey; Business Voice; Annual Report; various monographs; Innovation Trends survey; SME Trends survey

[147]
Confraternity of St James
CSJ
Stephen Badger Library of Pilgrimage
27 Blackfriars Road
London SE1 8NY
Borough: Southwark
Telephone: 020 7928 9988
Fax: 020 7928 2844
E-mail: office@csj.org.uk
World Wide Web: www.csj.org.uk
Constitution: Registered charity; company limited by guarantee
Objectives/purposes: To act as a focus for interest in the medieval pilgrim routes through France and Spain
Key staff: CSJ Secretary: Marion Marples
Stock and subject coverage: Ca. 2,000 books, articles and guides covering: the pilgrimage to Saint James of Compostela in North West Spain; the routes thereto through France and Spain; the associated heritage of art, architecture and music; related aspects of medieval history; and the general history and practice of pilgrimage worldwide. Slide library with ca. 2,600 slides
Services: Fax machine; translations can be provided (off site)
Availability: Access and loans available to members of CSJ (annual subscription £10). Facilities could be made available to other bona fide researchers for a small charge
Hours: Office open 11.00-15.00 Tuesday; other times possible by prior arrangement
Transport: Tube and rail: London Bridge
Special facilities: Refreshment and toilet facilities on site; no access for users with disabilities to the library but books can be provided for reading on the ground floor
Publications: Library catalogue available from the Confraternity's online bookshop

Linked organisations

There are similar associations in most countries of Western Europe and in the USA. These have informal links with the CSJ

---

[148]
The Congregational Library
14 Gordon Square
London WC1H 0AR
Borough: Camden
Telephone: 020 7387 3727
Stock and subject coverage: Founded in 1831, the Library contains printed and manuscript material on Congregationalism and earlier Puritan tradition
Services: Photocopies
Availability: All queries should be directed to Dr Williams's Library
Hours: 10.00-17.00 Monday, Wednesday and Friday; 10.00-18.30 Tuesday and Thursday
Transport: Tube: Euston, Goodge Street, Warren Street, Euston Square, Russell Square; Rail: Euston
Special facilities: Toilet facilities available

Linked organisations

Dr Williams's Library Managed by Dr Williams's Library and housed in the same building

[149]
Conservative and Unionist Central Office

Conservative Research Department Library
32 Smith Square
London SW1P 3HH
Borough: Westminster
Telephone: 020 7222 9000 ext 8203
E-mail: library@conservatives.com
World Wide Web: www.conservative-party.org.uk
Key staff: Head of Library
Stock and subject coverage: Agriculture; economics; industry; finance; communications; biography; history; current affairs; law; justice; government; politics; Party archives; social questions'. Conservative Party publications since 1945; HMSO publications; current journals; pamphlets; Candidates' general election addresses since 1974. Pre-1945 Conservative publications, election posters and pre-1974 election addresses are housed at the Party archive in the Bodleian Library, Oxford
Services: Photocopier
Availability: Not open to the public, but co-operation and assistance can sometimes be offered concerning material not readily available elsewhere
Hours: 10.00-17.00 Monday to Friday
Transport: Tube: Westminster

[150]
Consumers in Europe Group
CEG

European Parliament UK Office
2 Queen Anne's Gate
London SW1H 9AA
Borough: Westminster
Fax: 020 7227 4301
E-mail: eplondon@europarl.eu.int
World Wide Web: www.europarl.org.uk
Constitution: Independent voluntary organisation, funded mainly by the Department of Trade and Industry with its grant paid via the National Consumer Council
Objectives/purposes: CEG is an umbrella body for UK voluntary, statutory and professional organisations concerned with the effects of European Union policies and proposals on UK consumers
Key staff: Senior Research Officer: Samantha Mitchell; Information/Research Officer: Jennie Pugh
Stock and subject coverage: Small library with files of European Parliament reports, minutes and debates from January 1973 to the most recent plenary session; Written Questions from 1980 to present date. Reports, debates and minutes from July 1994 are available on the Europarl website
Services: Photocopies (charged); EPOQUE database searches undertaken on request
Availability: Access for member organisations. Other researchers may be allowed access on request. Materials available for reference only. By appointment only

Hours: 10.00-13.00, 14.00-17.00 Monday to Friday
Transport: Tube: Victoria, Westminster; Rail: Victoria
Special facilities: Toilet facilities available; wheelchair access
Publications: Consumers and Europe (quarterly newsletter); Annual Report; free publications list available on request; most of CEG's reports on individual subjects are free

[151]
Copyright Tribunal

Harmsworth House
13-15 Bouverie Street
London EC4Y 8DP
Borough: Corporation of London
Telephone: 020 7596 6510
Fax: 020 7596 6526
E-mail: copyright.tribunal@patent.gov.uk
World Wide Web: www.patent.gov.uk (information available on the Patent Office website) Government Telecommunications Network: 3555 6510
Minicom: 0845 9222250
Constitution: Government funded tribunal
Key staff: Secretary: Jill Durdin; Chairman: Christopher Tootal
Stock and subject coverage: Copies of decisions and orders made by the Copyright Tribunal and its predecessor, the Performing Right Tribunal. Evidence brought forward by the parties (in completed cases) and transcripts of hearings
Services: Photocopies provided (15p per sheet); decisions and orders can be sent by post
Availability: Open to all. Appointments should be made to view evidence as it may need to be brought from remote storage
Hours: 10.00-16.00 Monday to Friday
Transport: Tube and Rail: Blackfriars
Special facilities: Toilet facilities available; access for users with disabilities – ramps and lifts, loop for hearing impaired people, wheelchairs available
Publications: Annual entry in The Patent Office Annual Report; factsheet on the Copyright Tribunal

[152]
Corporation of London Library Services

World Wide Web: www.cityoflondon.gov.uk
Constitution: Local authority public reference library
Special features: Corporation of London library services are provided for those who live, work or study in the Square Mile. Libraries include: Barbican, Camomile Street and Shoe Lane lending libraries; City Business Library, Guildhall Library and St Bride Printing Library

[152][a]
Barbican Library

Barbican Centre
Silk Street
London EC2Y 8DS
Telephone: 020 7638 0569
020 7638 0568 (renewals line)

Fax: 020 7638 2249

E-mail: barbicanlib@corpoflondon.gov.uk

Key staff: Librarian: John Lake; Deputy Librarian: Mary Lupton; Music Librarian: Robert Tucker; Systems Librarian: Vincent Keedle; Children's Librarian: Mary Ann Stevens

Stock and subject coverage: General public lending library including large music library, plus arts and children's sections and crime novel collection. Special collections on: finance, conservation, Marxism, and the history of London

Services: Black and white and colour photocopies (self-service); listening booths including Music Performance Research Centre Studio of Live Recordings

Availability: Membership open to all who live, work or study within the City of London, plus members of other UK public libraries. Lending library with quick reference facilities, except in music and the arts. Charges for borrowing videos, music sound recordings and CD-ROMs

Hours: 09.30-17.30 Monday, Wednesday, Thursday and Friday; 09.30-19.30 Tuesday; 09.30-12.30 Saturday

Transport: Tube: Moorgate, Barbican; Rail: Farringdon; Liverpool Street; Bus: 8, 11, 26, 35, 42, 43, 47, 48, 55, 56, 76, 78, 100, 133, 141, 214, 242, 271 (also, 243 Monday to Saturday and 21, 23, 25, 172, 501, 505, 521 Monday to Friday)

Special facilities: Refreshment and toilet facilities available nearby within Barbican Centre; access for users with disabilities; chairlift to music library; CCTV magnifier for print and illustrated material; induction loops at all enquiry desks

[152][b]
Camomile Street Library

12-20 Camomile Street

London EC3A 7EX

(Formerly Bishopsgate Library)

Telephone: 020 7247 8895

Fax: 020 7377 2972

E-mail: camomile@corpoflondon.gov.uk

Key staff: Librarian: Malcolm Key

Stock and subject coverage: General public lending library including children's books, videos and music CDs; small quick-reference collection

Services: Photocopies (self-service); internet access

Availability: Open to all who live, work or study within the City of London, plus members of other UK public libraries. Charges for loans of videos and music sound recordings

Hours: 09.30-17.30 Monday to Friday

Transport: Tube: Aldgate; Rail: Liverpool Street, Fenchurch Street; Bus: 8, 11, 26, 35, 42, 47, 48, 78, 133, 149, 214, 242

Special facilities: Access for users with disabilities (ramped entrance); induction loop system

[152][c]
City Business Library

1 Brewers' Hall Garden

London EC2V 5BX

Telephone: 020 7332 1812

Fax: 020 7332 1847

World Wide Web: www.cityoflondon.gov.uk

Constitution: Local authority public library

Key staff: Business Librarian: GP Humphreys; Deputy Business Librarian: JMG Considine; Information Technology Librarian: LA Smith

Stock and subject coverage: Current information about companies, products and industries, markets and the economy. Collection of several hundred titles, printed directories and CD-ROMs

Services: Business Information Focus (fee-based service offering online, research and photocopying services - Telephone: 020 7600 1461, fax: 020 7600 1185); self-service photocopying; CD-ROMs

Availability: Open to the public for reference use only. This is a very busy library, so priority is given to personal visitors. Prospective users from outside the City of London should try their own local libraries first

Hours: 09.30-17.00 Monday to Friday

Transport: Tube and Rail: Moorgate, Liverpool Street; Tube: Bank

Special facilities: Refreshment and toilet facilities available; access for users with disabilities (ramps or lifts to all levels); induction loop system at enquiry desk

Publications: List of newspaper and journal holdings (also available at www.earl.org.uk/magnet); single sheet guides describing services, stock and suggested search strategies

Special features: Established in 1874 as the commercial reference room of Guildhall Library

[152][d]
Corporation of London Records Office CLRO

PO Box 270

Guildhall

London EC2P 2EJ

Telephone: 020 7332 1251

Fax: 020 7710 8682

E-mail: clro@corpoflondon.gov.uk

World Wide Web: www.cityoflondon.gov.uk/archives/clro

Constitution: Local authority record office

Objectives/purposes: Custody of the official archives of the Corporation of the City of London. Responsible to the Town Clerk (and Chief Executive)

Key staff: City Archivist: James Sewell; Deputy City Archivist: Juliet Bankes

Stock and subject coverage: Official archives of the Corporation of London, including: Royal Charters, 1067-1957; custumals or collections of grants, customs, precedents, etc. for the medieval and Tudor period (including several illuminated manuscripts); administrative records, including proceedings of City government, 1275 to date; judicial records, including City sessions and magistrates' court records from the 17th century; records of civic courts from the medieval period onwards, e.g. Husting, Mayor's Sheriff's, Coroner's and Orphans'; financial records, including Bridge House accounts, 1381-1942, City's cash accounts 1632-1942; City freedom records, recording admissions, 1681-1940; and architectural plans and drawings from the 18th century to date

Services: Photocopies; photography by arrangement; microfiche reader and printer; microfilm readers

Availability: Access open to all without charge, for reference only. Appointments are not generally necessary (except to see rate books) but advance warning of a visit may help both readers and staff

Hours: 09.30-16.45 Monday to Friday

Transport: Tube: Moorgate, Bank, Mansion House, St Paul's; Rail: Liverpool Street, Fenchurch Street, Blackfriars, Cannon Street, Moorgate, City Thameslink; Bank (Docklands Light Railway)

Special facilities: Toilet facilities available; access for users with disabilities but prior notice is advisable (limited wheelchair access). A special leaflet on access for people with disabilities within the City of London (and covering Guildhall) is available

Special features: Guildhall has been the centre of civic government in the City of London for nearly 900 years. The Great Hall and Crypt are medieval

Publications: Lists of free publications and publications for sale; Annual Report from the Libraries, Art Gallery and Archives Committee

Linked organisations

Guildhall Library MSS Section Another of the Corporation of the City of London's archives is located in the Manuscripts Section of Guildhall Library. It acts as the local record office for the City of London apart from the official archives of the Corporation located in the CLRO

London Metropolitan Archives Administred by the Corporation, London Metropolitan Archives looks after the official records of the Greater London Council and its predecessors; receives by gift, deposit or purchase collections of original records relating to the Greater London area, including records of official London-wide bodies; and maintains a specialist library relating to collections of source material in the office and to the history of the Greater London area and local government

[152][e]
Guildhall Library
Aldermanbury
London EC2P 2EJ

Telephone: 020 7332 1868/1870 (printed books)
020 7332 1839 (prints and maps)
020 7332 1862 (manuscripts)

Fax: 020 7600 3384

E-mail: printedbooks.guildhall@corpoflondon.gov.uk

World Wide Web: www.cityoflondon.gov.uk

Key staff: Principal Reference Librarian: Irene Gilchrist

Stock and subject coverage: Collections on London past and present; good coverage of general English historical subjects and topography; genealogy; business history; maritime history; legal and parliamentary publications; food and wine; and clockmaking

Services: Fee-based service offering in-depth research (telephone 020 7332 1854; fax: 020 7600 3384; e-mail: search.guildhall@corpoflondon.gov.uk; website: www.cityoflondon.gov.uk/searchguildhall)

Availability: Open to all for reference use only. No charges for enquiry services

Hours: 09.30-17.00 Monday to Saturday

Transport: Tube: Moorgate, St Pauls, Bank, Mansion House; Rail: Liverpool Street, Fenchurch Street, Blackfriars, Cannon Street, St Pauls Thameslink; Moorgate; Bus: 8, 21, 22B, 25, 43, 76, 133, 141, 501

Special facilities: Toilet facilities available; ramp access and toilet facilities for users with disabilities

Publications: Wide range of publications, details from the Library bookshop 020 7332 1858

Linked organisations

Charles Lamb Society The Library of the Charles Lamb Society is housed at the Guildhall Library (tel: 020 7606 3030 to make an appointment)

[152][f]
St Bride Printing Library
Bride Lane
London EC4Y 8EQ

Telephone: 020 7353 4660

Fax: 020 7583 7073

Key staff: Librarian

Stock and subject coverage: One of the world's largest reference collections on printing, papermaking and bookbinding, publishing and bookselling, newspapers and journals, illustration, graphic design, calligraphy and type. Over 40,000 books and pamphlets, 2,000 journals (200 current titles), extensive collections of prints, drawings, manuscripts, prospectuses, patents and materials for printing and type-founding. Large collection of photographs and slide loan collection

Services: Photocopy and photography facilities

Availability: Reference only. Readers wanting to use materials in special collections are advised to make an appointment

Hours: 09.30-17.30 Monday to Friday

Transport: Tube: Blackfriars, St Paul's; Rail: City Thameslink, Blackfriars; Bus: 4, 11, 15, 23, 26, 45, 63, 76

[152][g]
Shoe Lane Library
Hill House
Little New Street
London EC4A 3JR

Telephone: 020 7583 7178

Fax: 020 7353 0884

E-mail: shoelane@corpoflondon.gov.uk

Constitution: Public library, funded by local authority

Key staff: Acting Librarian: Leslie King

Stock and subject coverage: General public library. Fiction and non-fiction collections; Cds and videos. Small reference collection

Services: Photocopies

Availability: Open to all who live in, work or study within the City of London

Hours: 09.30-17.30 Monday, Wednesday, Thursday and Friday; 09.30-18.30 Tuesday

Transport: Rail: City Thameslink

Special facilities: Full access for users with disabilities

[153]
The Corporation of Trinity House
Trinity House
Tower Hill
London EC3N 4DH

Borough: Tower Hamlets

Telephone: 020 7481 6900

Fax: 020 7480 7662

E-mail: butlera@thcorp.co.uk

World Wide Web: www.trinityhouse.co.uk

Constitution: Registered charity

Objectives/purposes: General lighthouse authority for England, Wales and the Channel Islands; deep-sea pilotage authority; marine charitable organisation

Key staff: Librarian: Miss Adele Butler

Stock and subject coverage: Corporation of Trinity House, General lighthouse and maritime books

Services: Photocopies

Availability: Library open to bona fide researchers for reference only, by appointment

Hours: Strictly by appointment only from 09.00–17.00 Monday to Friday

Transport: Tube: Tower Hill; Rail: Fenchurch Street

Special facilities: Toilet facilities available; access for users with disabilities

Publications: Annual Review (annual – September); Annual Yearbook (December)

[154]
Council for Education in World Citizenship
CEWC

Sir John Lyon House
5 High Timber Street
London EC4V 3NS

Borough: Corporation of London
Telephone: 020 7329 1500
Fax: 020 7329 8160
E-mail: info@cewc.org.uk
World Wide Web: www.cewc.org.uk
Constitution: Registered charity with a voluntary subscribing membership
Objectives/purposes: To promote education for international understanding
Key staff: Gaby Rowberry
Stock and subject coverage: Materials on: international issues; organisations working on international issues; specific geographical areas; the UN, EU and Council of Europe. The Library also holds teachers' support material, classroom and background materials on education for international understanding. The Archives include early UNESCO (originally proposed at a CEWC conference) and UNA material
Services: Photocopies; fax machine
Availability: Access to all researchers; preference given to members of CEWC
Hours: 09.30–17.00 Monday to Friday, telephone in advance to make an appointment
Transport: Tube and Rail: Blackfriars
Special facilities: Refreshment and toilet facilities available on site; access for users with disabilities
Publications: Global Education News newsletter; bi-monthly broadsheets (papers, digests and activities sheets for teachers)

[155]
Council for Science and Technology
CST
Office of Science and Technology

Bay 482
1 Victoria Street
London SW1H 0ET

Borough: Westminster
Telephone: 020 7215 5671
Fax: 020 7215 0394
E-mail: www.cstinfo@dti.gsi.gov.uk
World Wide Web: www.cst.gov.uk
Constitution: The CST is the government's top level advisory body on science and technology issues of strategic importance to the UK
Key staff: Secretary: Lynne Edwards; Deputy Secretary: Maurice Potts
Stock and subject coverage: Materials on science and technology issues, the work of the Council for Science and Technology
Availability: Enquiries by letter, e-mail or telephone accepted

[156]
Council for the Advancement of Arab-British Understanding
CAABU

21 Collingham Road
London SW5 0NU

Borough: Kensington and Chelsea
Telephone: 020 7373 8414
Fax: 020 7835 2088
E-mail: caabu@caabu.org
World Wide Web: www.caabu.org
Constitution: Independent non-profit distributing organisation with voluntary subscribing membership
Objectives/purposes: To advance Arab-British understanding and foster a wider awareness of Middle East issues
Key staff: Director: Sir Cyril Townsend; Information Officers: Chris Doyle and Gillian Watt
Stock and subject coverage: Extensive collection of books, press cuttings, magazine articles and journals on all areas of the Arab World, and on Middle East issues. The collections are primarily in English
Services: Photocopier available. CAABU gives lectures to schools and holds public meetings. Staff are willing to assist with information, advice and contacts.
Availability: Open to all bona fide researchers. Materials are available for reference and for photocopying
Hours: 09.30–17.30 Monday to Thursday, 09.30–16.30 Fridays
Transport: Tube: Gloucester Road, Earls Court; Rail: Victoria; Bus: 74 (Cromwell Road)
Special facilities: Refreshment and toilet facilities
Publications: Annual Report, newsletter and occasional briefings

Linked organisations

Arab British Centre (ABC) Housed in the ABC building

[157]
Council for the Care of Churches

Church House
Great Smith Street
London SW1P 3NZ

Borough: Westminster
Telephone: 020 7898 1866
Fax: 020 7898 1881

*Constitution:*Permanent commission of the General Synod of the Church of England

Objectives/purposes: Permanent Commission of the General Synod of the Church of England. Concerned with church architecture and furnishings

Key staff: Librarian: Miss Janet Seeley

Stock and subject coverage: About 12,000 volumes, a collection of 6,000 slides, survey files for about 15,000 churches (the majority with photographs, and many with guide books), 120 current journals (including annual reports of Cathedral Friends). The subject coverage includes: ecclesiastical art and architecture, with special reference to the buildings and furnishings of Anglican places of Worship; the conservation of churches and their furnishings; ecclesiology; liturgy; ecclesiastical history and law insofar as they concern church fabric or fittings. The Library holds a number of special collections including: the Canon BFL Clarke Collection on church building and restoration; the Clarke postcard collection (20,000 items); the Canon JL Cartwright collection on ecclesiastical heraldry and the Gordon Barnes Bequest of photographic and manuscript material. The Council also maintains illustrated records of the work of artists and craftsmen who are interested in ecclesiastical commissions

Services: Photocopies

Availability: The library is available to the general public for reference. Prospective readers are asked to telephone in advance to make an appointment

Hours: 09.30-16.30 Monday to Friday, by appointment only

Transport: Tube: Westminster, St James's Park; Rail: Charing Cross, Victoria, Waterloo

Special facilities: Toilet facilities available

Publications: Churchscape journal (annual), wide range of publications on the care of churches and their furnishings

Linked organisations

Cathedrals Fabric Commission for England Related body

[158]
Courtauld Institute of Art

Somerset House
Strand
London WC2R 0RN

Borough: Westminster

Telephone: 020 7848 2701

Fax: 020 7848 2887

E-mail: booklib@courtauld.ac.uk

World Wide Web: www.courtauld.ac.uk

Constitution: Part of a university

Key staff: Librarian: Dr Sue Price; Deputy Librarian: Timothy Davies

Stock and subject coverage: Over 140,000 items covering the history of the fine arts and architecture in Europe and in the European tradition, from Classical antiquity to the present day. Large numbers of journals, pamphlets and exhibition catalogues. Author and subject index to journals (up to end of 1983)

Services: Photocopies; microfiche and film reader-printer

Availability: Specialist library within the University of London, which is a last resort reference library for research in the field of art history. It is not a public library, but exists primarily to provide a service to the Institute's undergraduate and postgraduate students and academic staff, and to visiting scholars and researchers from within and outside the University who can not obtain the material they require elsewhere

Hours: Term-time: 09.30-19.00 Monday to Friday Vacations: 10.30-17.00 (closed for four weeks in the summer vacation)

Transport: Tube: Temple, Covent Garden: Rail: Waterloo, Charing Cross, Blackfriars

Linked organisations

University of London Part of the University

[159]
CPRE (Council for the Protection of Rural England)

Warwick House
25 Buckingham Palace Road
London SW1W 0PP

Borough: Westminster

Telephone: 020 7976 6433

Fax: 020 7976 6373

E-mail: info@cpre.org.uk

World Wide Web: www.cpre.org.uk

Constitution: Registered charity

Key staff: Head of Library and Records: Hilary Morris

Stock and subject coverage: Planning and environmental information; CPRE publications; government publications; annual reports; periodicals

Services: Interlibrary loans

Availability: Reference only, by prior appointment

Hours: 09.30-17.30 Monday to Friday

Transport: Tube and Rail: Victoria

Special facilities: Toilet facilities available

Linked organisations

Branch in every English county and regional groups

[160]
Crafts Council

44a Pentonville Road
London N1 9BY

Borough: Islington

Telephone: 020 7278 7700

Fax: 020 7837 6891

World Wide Web: www.craftscouncil.org.uk

Constitution: Registered charity, independent non-profit distributing organisation that promotes British contemporary craft. Funded mostly by the Arts Council of England

Hours: 11.00-18.00 Tuesday to Saturday; 14.00-18.00 Sunday

Transport: Tube: Angel; Bus: X43, 4, 19, 30, 38, 43, 56, 73, 153, 171, 214, 314

Special facilities: Wheelchair access; toilet facilities (when gallery is open)

[160][a]
Photostore

E-mail: photostore@craftscouncil.org.uk

Key staff: Photostore Officer: Mary Myers

Stock and subject coverage: Photostore is the Crafts Council's visual database that features over 900 selected craftspeople (makers) and 40,000 images of their work. It also includes a record of the 2,000 objects in the Crafts Council collection. It documents crafts over the last 30 years and covers all craft disciplines

Services: Colour images and biographies can be printed (for a fee), a slide loan service is available (for a fee) and some images are available for reproduction by special arrangement with the Photostore Officer. Terminals are located at the Crafts Council and in regional venues (check www.craftscouncil.org.uk/photostore for details)

Availability: Open to the public

Hours: 11.00-17.45 Tuesday to Saturday; 14.00-17.45 Sunday

[160][b]
Reference Library
Telephone: 020 7806 2501
E-mail: reference@craftscouncil.org.uk
Key staff: Ursula Everett
Stock and subject coverage: Over 5,000 books and catalogues as well as 160 journals from the UK and overseas, covering the contemporary crafts from the 1970s to present day. The Library includes directories, reports and technical information in relation to the contemporary crafts, training in the crafts and setting up a crafts business
Services: Photocopies
Availability: Open to the public for reference only
Hours: 11.00-17.45 Tuesday to Saturday; 14.00-17.45 Sunday

[161]
The Cricket Society
(library is based, unmanned, at:)
Royal Over-Seas League
Park Place
London SW1A 1LR

(mailing address)
c/o 48 Mortimer Court
Abbey Road
London NW8 9AB
Borough: Westminster
Telephone: 020 7286 2136 (evenings only)
E-mail: csoc@cricket.org (for the Society)
howard.milton@ukgateway.net (for the Library)
World Wide Web: www.cricsoc.cricket.org/
Constitution: Association with voluntary subscribing membership
Objectives/purposes: Library for Cricket Society members
Key staff: Honorary Librarian: Howard Milton
Stock and subject coverage: Largest collection of loanable cricket books and journals – around 6,000 items. Stock includes complete runs of Wisden, The Cricketer, extensive collection of biographies, club and county histories and tour books
Availability: Access and loans to members only. Non-members and members may send postal queries
Hours: 18.00-19.15 one evening per month (January-April, September-December)

Transport: Tube: Green Park
Special facilities: Refreshment and toilet facilities on site for members
Publications: Printed catalogue available for consultation in Library, also available on disk for a charge

[162]
Crown Prosecution Service
CPS
Library Information Services
6th floor
50 Ludgate Hill
London EC4M 7EX
Borough: Corporation of London
Constitution: Government funded body
Telephone: 020 7796 8364
Fax: 020 7796 8366
E-mail: library@cps.gov.uk
World Wide Web: www.cps.gov.uk
Key staff: Head Librarian: Robert Brall BA ALA
Stock and subject coverage: Books and serials principally on the criminal law of England and Wales. Government publications and limited stock of other legal and management subjects
Services: Information service; limited lending to other Government libraries; internet access; photocopying facilities
Availability: Departmental staff and government departments only
Hours: 09.00-17.00 Monday to Friday
Transport: Tube: St Paul's, Farringdon, Blackfriars; Rail: Blackfriars
Special facilities: Refreshment and toilet facilities on site

[163]
Croydon (London Borough of Croydon)
Croydon Libraries, Museum and Arts
World Wide Web: www.croydon.gov.uk
Constitution: Public library, funded by local authority
Key staff: Borough Libraries and Museum Officer: Chris Batt BA FLA MIInfSC; Principal Librarian: Adie Scott BA ALA
Special features: The main library is Croydon Central Library with links to 12 branch libraries, mobile library and housebound library services

[163][a]
Croydon Central Library
Katharine Street
Croydon CR9 1ET
Telephone: 020 8760 5400
Fax: 020 8253 1004
E-mail: controldesk@croydononline.org;
childrens@croydononline.org;
level1@croydononline.org;
level2@croydononline.org; level3@croydononline.org
Key staff: Assistant Director, Libraries: Adie Scott; Libraries Operations Manager: Brenda Constable; Reference and Information Services Manager: Heather Kirby; Childrens Services Manager: Margaret Fraser and Grace McElwee

Stock and subject coverage: General stock for loan and reference, integrated and arranged in subject groupings on three levels of the library for adult stock. A large children's library is on the ground level, near the entrance. Specialisation subject was economics and is now computers. Special areas include local studies library, business information, information technology and arts

Services: Photocopier; colour photocopier; fax; CD-ROMs, free internet use (Net Corner); community information pack; Information for Business in Croydon; Tourist Information Centre; archives; local studies; open learning; PCs for hire

Availability: Free to anyone living, working or visiting Croydon. There are no restrictions or charges for users from anywhere outside Croydon. Hire charges for the loan of music cassettes, CDs and videos. IBC, Information for Business in Croydon, is a charged service, but a wide range of current directories and CD-ROMs is available on public access, free of charge

Hours: 09.00-19.00 Monday; 09.00-18.00 Tuesday and Wednesday; 09.30-18.00 Thursday; 09.00-17.00 Saturday; 14.00-17.00 Sunday

Transport: Rail: East Croydon, West Croydon; Bus: 50, 109, 250, 468; Tramlink: George Street

Special facilities: Refreshment and toilet facilities available; access for users with disabilities – large public lift to all floors open to the public, entrance ramp, automatic doors; access for users with disabilities to toilet and refreshment facilities

Special features: The Library is part of the Clocktower Cultural Centre, home to the David Lean Cinema, museum, gallery, shop, cafe, Braithwaite Hall and Tourist Information Centre

Publications: Community Information Pack (updated quarterly)

[163][b]
Ashburton Library

Lower Addiscombe Road
Croydon CR0 6RX
Telephone: 020 8656 4148
E-mail: ashburton@croydononline.org
Key staff: Library Manager: Sharon Knox
Reference facilities: Reference facilities; small reference collection; local information; children's collection; ICT facilities; talking books; videos; CD-ROMs; ; photocopier (charges made)
Hours: 09.00-13.00, 14.00-18.00 Monday, Tuesday and Thursday; 09.30-13.00, 14.00-18.00 Friday; 09.00-17.00 Saturday. Children's library closed Friday am during term-time
Transport: Rail: Woodside; Bus: 54, 289, 312, 726; Tramlink: Blackhorse Lane, Woodside
Special facilities: Limited access for users with disabilities to children's library

[163][c]
Bradmore Green Library

Bradmore Way
Coulsdon CR5 1PE
Telephone: 01737 553267
E-mail: bradmoregreen@croydononline.org
Key staff: Library Manager: Linda Wilkins

Reference facilities: Small reference collection; local information; children's collection; ICT facilities; videos; talking books; photocopier (charges made)
Hours: 09.30-13.00, 14.00-18.00 Monday; 09.00-13.00, 14.00-19.00 Tuesday; 09.00-13.00, 14.00-18.00 Wednesday and Friday; 09.00-17.00 Saturday
Transport: Rail: Coulsdon South; Bus: 166, 301, 304, 363, 400, 405, 498; street parking and car park
Special facilities: Access for users with disabilities – ramp access to library, toilet facilities

[163][d]
Broad Green Library

89 Canterbury Road
Croydon CR0 3HH
Telephone: 020 8684 4829
E-mail: broadgreen@croydononline.org
Key staff: Library Manager: Colin Williamson
Reference facilities: Reference collection; local information; children's section; ICT facilities; videos; talking books; photocopier (charges made)
Hours: 09.30-13.00, 14.00-18.00 Monday; 09.00-13.00, 14.00-18.00 Tuesday; 09.00-13.00, 14.00-19.00 Friday; 09.00-17.00 Saturday
Transport: Bus: 264, 289; Tramlink: Therapia Lane
Special facilities: Full access for users with disabilities – including automatic doors; toilet facilities

[163][e]
Coulsdon Library

Brighton Road
Coulsdon CR5 2NH
Telephone: 020 8660 1548
E-mail: coulsdon@croydononline.org
Key staff: Library Manager: Richard Roberts
Stock and subject coverage: Small reference collection; local information; children's collection; videos; talking books
Services: ICT facilities; photocopier (charges made)
Hours: 09.00-18.00 Monday and Tuesday; 09.30-18.00 Thursday; 09.00-19.00 Friday; 09.00-17.00 Saturday
Transport: Rail: Coulsdon South; Bus: 166, 301, 304, 363, 400, 405, 498
Special facilities: Full access for users with disabilities; ramp

[163][f]
New Addington Library

Central Parade
New Addington CR0 0JB
Telephone: 01689 841248
E-mail: newaddington@croydononline.org
Key staff: Library Manager: Giles Cordwell
Reference facilities: Small reference collection; local information; children's collection; homework help club (contact library for times); ICT facilities; videos; talking books; photocopier (charges made)
Hours: 09.00-18.00 Monday, Tuesday and Friday; 09.30-18.00 Thursday; 09.00-17.00 Saturday
Transport: Bus: X30, 64, 130, 314; Tramlink: New Addington
Special facilities: Full access for users with disabilities to all areas of Library; toilet facilities

[163][g]
Norbury Library
Beatrice Avenue
Norbury SW16 4UW
Telephone: 020 8679 1597
E-mail: norbury@croydononline.org
Key staff: Library Manager: Penelope Long
Reference facilities: Small reference collection; local
information; children's collection; homework help
club (contact library for times); ICT facilities; videos;
talking books; photocopier (charges made)
Hours: 09.00-19.00 Monday; 09.00-18.00 Tuesday and
Friday; 09.30-18.00 Thursday; 09.00-17.00 Saturday
Transport: Rail: Norbury; Bus 109
Special facilities: Full access for users with disabilities –
includes ramp and toilet facilities

[163][h]
Purley Library
Banstead Road
Purley CR8 3YH
Telephone: 020 8660 1171
E-mail: purley@croydononline.org
Key staff: Library Manager: Mr J Rimmer
Reference facilities: Small reference collection; local
information; children's collection; ICT facilities;
videos; talking books; photocopier (charges made)
Hours: 09.00-19.00 Monday; 09.00-18.00 Tuesday and
Friday; 09.30-18.00 Thursday; 09.00-17.00 Saturday
Transport: Rail: Purley; Bus: 50, 109, 127, 166, 289, 301,
304, 400, 405, 407, 409, 412, 450, 490
Special facilities: Full access for users with disabilities –
ramp to front door; toilet facilities

[163][i]
Sanderstead Library
Farm Fields
South Croydon CR2 0HL
Telephone: 020 8657 2882
E-mail: sanderstead@croydononline.org
Key staff: Library Manager: Felicity Cudworth, Sue
Springbett
Reference facilities: Small reference collection; local
information; children's collection; ICT facilities;
videos; talking books; photocopier (charges made)
Hours: 09.00-13.00, 14.00-19.00 Monday; 09.00-13.00,
14.00-18.00 Tuesday and Friday; 09.30-13.00, 14.00-
18.00 Wednesday; 09.00-17.00 Saturday
Transport: Rail: Sanderstead; Bus: 403
Special facilities: Access for users with disabilities – ramp
to front door, automatic doors

[163][j]
Selsdon Library
Addington Road
Selsdon CR2 8LA
Telephone: 020 8657 7210
E-mail: selsdon@croydononline.org
Key staff: Library Manager: Pat Lemans
Reference facilities: Small reference collection; local
information; children's collection; ICT facilities;
videos; talking books; photocopier (charges made)
Hours: 09.00-18.00 Monday and Tuesday; 09.30-18.00
Thursday; 09.00-19.00 Friday; 09.00-17.00 Saturday

Transport: Bus: 64, 354, 412
Special facilities: Full access for users with disabilities –
ramp; free disabled parking for badge holders

[163][k]
Shirley Library
Wickham Road/Hartland Way
Shirley CR0 8BH
Telephone: 020 8777 7650
E-mail: shirley@croydononline.org
Key staff: Library Manager: J Hierons
Reference facilities: Small reference collection; local
information; children's collection; ICT facilities;
videos; talking books; photocopier (charges made)
Hours: 09.00-13.00, 14.00-18.00 Monday, Tuesday and
Friday; 09.30-13.00, 14.00-19.00 Thursday; 09.00-
17.00 Saturday
Transport: Bus: 119, 166, 194, 198, 356, 367
Special facilities: Access for users with disabilities – ramp
for wheelchair access; handrail at entrance

[163][l]
South Norwood Library
Lawrence Road
South Norwood SE25 5AA
Telephone: 020 8653 4545
E-mail: southnorwood@croydononline.org
Key staff: Library Manager: Kaye Nightingale
Reference facilities: Small reference collection; local
information; children's collection; ICT facilities;
videos; talking books; photocopier (charges made)
Hours: 09.00-18.00 Monday and Tuesday; 09.30-18.00
Wednesday; 09.00-19.00 Friday; 09.00-17.00
Saturday
Transport: Rail: Norwood Junction; Bus: 75, 157, 196,
352
Special facilities: Access for users with disabilities – lift to
all levels; wheelchair ramp

[163][m]
Thornton Heath Library
Brigstock Road
Thornton Heath CR7 7JB
Telephone: 020 8684 4432
E-mail: thorntonheath@croydononline.org
Key staff: Library Manager: Sharon Clark
Reference facilities: Small reference collection; local
information; children's collection; ICT facilities;
videos; talking books; photocopier (charges made)
Hours: 09.00-18.00 Monday to Wednesday; 09.30-19.00
Friday; 09.00-17.00 Saturday
Transport: Rail: Thornton Heath; Bus: 198, 250, 450
Special facilities: Access for users with disabilities to all
areas of the library

---

[164]
Croydon College Library
Croydon College
College Road
Fairfield
Croydon CR9 1DX
Borough: Croydon
Telephone: 020 8760 5843
World Wide Web: www.croydon.ac.uk

Constitution: College of further education

Key staff: Library Operations Manager: Kathy Treagus; Resources Team Leader: Hilda Elsmere; Information Services Team Leader: Christopher Babcock; Technical and Systems Team Leader: Louisa York

Stock and subject coverage: Books, journals, videos, audiotapes, resource based learning (RBL) materials to support courses in art and design; health; community care; social studies; management; education; business, law; accounting; service industry studies; information technology; construction; engineering; marketing; 'A' levels and GCSEs. Small collection on the history of the college

Services: Multi-media area with CD-ROM and internet machines; black and white and colour photocopies; microfiche reader-printer; IT area offering word processing facilities and a wide range of software packages

Availability: Mainly restricted to staff and students of the college. Some materials for use in the Library only. Certain groups such as Open University students are allowed reference/study access on payment of a fee

Hours: Term-time: 09.30-20.30 Monday, Tuesday and Thursday; 10.00-20.30 Wednesday; 09.00-17.00 Friday; 09.30-13.00 Saturday
Vacations: 09.30-16.30 (varies) Monday to Friday, not open on Saturdays

Transport: Rail: East Croydon; Bus: all routes into Central Croydon

Special facilities: Refreshment and toilet facilities available on site; access for users with disablties, Kurzweil scanners in IT area

Special features: Newly designed, purpose-built library (opened in September 1998)

Publications: Series of leaflets giving details of all services on offer in the Library

[165]
Croydon Natural History and Scientific Society Ltd
CNHSS

96A Brighton Road
South Croydon
Surrey CR2 6AD
Borough: Croydon
Telephone: 020 8681 6293
Constitution: Registered charity with voluntary subscribing membership; company limited by guarantee
Objectives/purposes: Local studies in and around Croydon, especially archaeology, local history, geology and natural history
Key staff: Librarian: Paul W Sowan
Stock and subject coverage: Good collection of books, survey publications, maps and journals on the geology and natural history of South East England. Also, good collection of books, journals, etc. on the archaeology and local history of Surrey and Kent (including the London boroughs of Croydon, Bromley, Sutton, etc.). One of the Library's particular strengths is its holdings of material related to economic (extractive) geology and water supply.
Availability: By arrangement only, requests to be made in writing in the first instance
Hours: By arrangement

Transport: Rail: South Croydon, Purley Oaks; Bus: 60, 166, 312, 405, 407, 466, 468 along Brighton Road
Special facilities: Toilet facilities available on site
Publications: Proceedings of the Society have been published continuously since 1871; Bulletin for members (2 p.a.)

[166]
Cruciform Library

Cruciform Building
Gower Street
London WC1E 6AU
Borough: Camden
Telephone: 020 7679 6079
Fax: 020 7209 6981
E-mail: clinscilib@ucl.ac.uk
Constitution: The Cruciform Library is part of University College London
Key staff: Site Librarian: Kate Cheney
Stock and subject coverage: Materials on clinical medicine
Services: Photocopiers
Availability: Open to all bona fide researchers for reference only
Hours: Term-time: 09.00-21.00 Monday to Friday; 09.30-16.30 Saturday
Vacations: 09.00-19.00 Monday to Friday
Transport: Tube: Euston, Euston Square, Warren Street, Goodge Street; Bus: 10, 24, 134
Special facilities: Toilet facilities available; access for users with disabilities

Linked organisations
University College London Member of the College

[167]
Cystic Fibrosis Trust
CF Trust

11 London Road
Bromley
Kent BR1 1BY
Borough: Bromley
Telephone: 020 8464 7211
Fax: 020 8313 0472
E-mail: enquiries@cftrust.org.uk
World Wide Web: www.cftrust.org.uk
Constitution: Registered charity
Objectives/purposes: To fund medical research into treating and curing Cystic Fibrosis as well as providing support for families affected by the disease. CF Trust also aims to ensure that children and adults with CF receive the best possible clinical care and support
Key staff: Chief Executive: Rosie Barnes
Stock and subject coverage: Booklets, factsheets, videos and tapes covering all aspects of Cystic Fibrosis
Availability: Materials available on request – donations in lieu of charges (for large orders postage and packing is invoiced)
Hours: 09.00-17.00 Monday to Friday
Transport: Rail: Bromley South, Shortlands, Bromley North
Special facilities: Toilet facilities available
Publications: CF News (3 p.a.); Annual Report

[168]
The Dairy Council
5-7 John Princes Street
London W1G 0JN
Borough: Westminster
Telephone: 020 7499 7822
Fax: 020 7408 1353
E-mail: info@dairycouncil.org.uk
World Wide Web: www.milk.co.uk
Objectives/purposes: The Dairy Council, founded in
1920, is the coordinating body for the dairy
industry's generic information and promotion
activities in Great Britain. Dairy farmers fund it via
the Milk Development Council and milk processors
and manufacturers via the Diary Industry Federation
Stock and subject coverage: Materials to promote the
positive image of milk, its products and the industry
Transport: Tube: Oxford Circus

Linked organisations:
  Milk Development Council
  The Dairy Industry Federation

[169]
Daiwa Anglo-Japanese Foundation, Library and Information Centre
Daiwa Foundation Japan House
13-14 Cornwall Terrace
London NW1 4QP
Borough: Westminster
Telephone: 020 7486 3054
Fax: 020 7486 2914
E-mail: office@daiwa-foundation.org.uk
World Wide Web: www.daiwa-foundation.org.uk
Constitution: Registered charity
Objectives/purposes: To promote Anglo-Japanese relations
by supporting British/Japanese students and
academics in their further education and research
fields
Stock and subject coverage: Directories, reference books
and standard works. Covers wide range of Japan-
related fields
Services: Enquiries on non-commercial aspects of
information on Japan; photocopies, no loans
Availability: Open to the public
Hours: 09.30-16.30 Monday to Friday
Transport: Tube: Baker Street
Special facilities: Toilet facilities; access for users with
disabilities; lift available
Publications: Daiwa Foundation Seminar publication;
Guide to Japanese Degree Courses in the UK

[170]
Daycare Trust/National Childcare Campaign
21 St George's Road
London SE1 6ES
Borough: Southwark
Telephone: 020 7840 3350
Fax: 020 7840 3355
E-mail: info@daycaretrust.org.uk
World Wide Web: www.daycaretrust.org.uk

Constitution: Registered charity; independent non-profit
organisation and association with voluntary
subscribing membership
Objectives/purposes: To promote quality, affordable
childcare for all and advise parents, providers,
employers, trade unions and policy makers on
childcare issues
Key staff: Director: Stephen Burke
Stock and subject coverage: Reports, research and briefing
papers on a range of childcare issues for parents,
providers and policymakers
Availability: Premises can be visited by appointment; no
loan service available
Hours: 09.00-17.30 Monday to Friday
Transport: Tube and rail: Elephant and Castle
Special facilities: Access for users with disabilities
Publications: Childwise (4 p.a.); Childcare Now (4 p.a.);
Policy Briefing Papers (6 p.a.); Policy Papers (3 p.a.)

[171]
Department for Culture, Media and Sport
DCMS
Information Centre
2-4 Cockspur Street
London SW1Y 5DH
Borough: Westminster
Telephone: 020 7211 6200
Fax: 020 7211 6032
E-mail: enquiries@culture.gov.uk
World Wide Web: www.culture.gov.uk
Constitution: Government department
Key staff: Manager: Felicitas Montgomery; Deputy:
Abigail Humber
Stock and subject coverage: Reference stock; parliamentary
papers; journals; statistics; annual reports; archive of
DCMS publications; books for loan. Covers the
architecture, archives, arts, broadcasting, and the
creative industries; export licensing of cultural goods;
film; gambling; Golden Jubilee; Government Art
Collection; libraries; licensing; museums and galleries;
National Lottery; press freedom and regulation; the
Royal Parks; sport and tourism
Information and Library services: Research, supply of
publications and translations, online, internet and
CD-ROM searching and training, networked
electronic services, advice on copyright, legal deposit
and IAR (Information Asset Register) issues, website
and intranet projects
Availability: Primarily to DCMS staff, other government
departments, agencies and NDPBs. Open to
members of the public as a library of last resort and
by advance appointment only
Hours: 09.00-17.30 Monday to Friday. Public enquiries:
09.30-12.30 and 14.00-16.30
Transport: Tube: Charing Cross, Piccadilly Circus; Rail:
Charing Cross; Bus: , X15, X53, 3, 6, 9, 11, 12, 13,
15, 23, 24, 29, 53, 77a, 88, 91, 94, 109, 139, 159, 176,
184
Special facilities: Toilet facilities; access for users with
disabilities including lift access and wide doors

[172]
Department for Education and Skills
DFES
Sanctuary Buildings
Great Smith Street
London SW1P 3BT
Borough: Westminster
Telephone: 020 7925 5040
Fax: 020 7925 5085
E-mail: enquiries.library@dfes.gsi.gov.uk
World Wide Web: www.dfes.gov.uk
Constitution: Government department
Key staff: Chief Librarian: vacant; Deputy Librarian: Julia
    Reid, 0114 259 3339; Information Services
    (London): 020 7925 5040; Historical Enquiries:
    Arabella Wood, 020 7925 5040
    General Enquiries, London: 020 7925 5040;
    Sheffield: 0114 259 3338
Stock and subject coverage: Collection of material relating
    to the organisation and history of education;
    educational psychology; methods of teaching
Availability: Available for reference, by appointment only
Hours: 10.00-12.00 and 14.00-16.00 Monday to Friday
    for visitors; 09.30-18.00 for staff
Transport: Tube: St James's Park
Special facilities: Refreshment and toilet facilities available
    on site; access for users with disabilities including
    wheelchair access and induction loop

[173]
Department for Environment, Food and Rural Affairs
DEFRA
Borough: Westminster
Telephone: 020 7270 plus extension
Government Telecommunications Network: 270
Fax: 020 7270 8419
World Wide Web: www.defra.gov.uk
Key staff: Chief Librarian: Peter McShane BA MA ALA,
    ext 8448; Senior Librarian, Library Services: Kevin
    Jackson BSc ALA, ext 8428; Senior
    Librarian/Electronic Publishing Manager: Martin
    Bennett BA MA ALA, ext 8401

[173][a]
Whitehall Place Library
Room 11
3 Whitehall Place
London SW1A 2HH
Telephone: 020 7270 8000/8421
Fax: 020 7270 8419
E-mail: w.library@defra.gsi.gov.uk
Key staff: Librarian-in-Charge: Christine Smith BA
    ALA, ext 8429; Website Manager: Rosanna Salbashian
    MA DipLib, ext 8583
Stock and subject coverage: Some 160,000 volumes; 2,000
    current periodicals and serials. Subjects covered:
    temperate agriculture and horticulture, environment
    protection and wildlife conservation
Services: Enquiry service; DEFRA Helpline (08459
    335577), a general contact point providing
    information on the work of DEFRA either directly

or by referring callers to appropriate Ministry staff;
    loans to other UK government libraries on direct
    application by telephone, e-mail or post
Availability: For reference by prior appointment only to
    bona fide research workers
Hours: 09.00-17.00 Monday to Friday
Transport: Tube: Charing Cross, Embankment; Rail:
    Charing Cross; Bus: 11, 12, 24, 53, X53, 77A, 109,
    139, 159
Special facilities: Toilet facilities available; access for users
    with disabilities – wheelchair lift to building

[173][b]
Nobel House Library
Room 320
17 Smith Square
London SW1P 3JR
Telephone: 020 7238 plus extension
    020 7238 6575 (enquiries)
Fax: 020 7238 6609
E-mail: nobel.library@defra.gsi.gov.uk
Key staff: Librarian-in-Charge: Jenny Carpenter BA
    DipLib DipBIT ALA, ext 6571
Stock and subject coverage: 20,000 books and pamphlets;
    350 current serials on food and nutrition
Hours: 09.00-17.00 Monday to Friday
Note: For details of availability, loans and publications
    see Whitehall Place Library entry above
Transport: Tube: Westminster; Rail: Charing Cross,
    Victoria, Waterloo; Bus: 3, 77A, 507
Special facilities: Toilet facilities available; access for users
    with disabilities

[174]
Department for International Development
DFID
Information Department
Information Centre and Library V424
94 Victoria Street
London SW1E 5JL
Borough: Westminster
Telephone: 020 7917 0005
Fax: 020 7917 0523
E-mail: enquiry@dfid.gov.uk
World Wide Web: www.dfid.gov.uk
Constitution: Government department
Key staff: Librarian: Julia Chandler
Stock and subject coverage: Books, journals and electronic
    sources on development assistance; economic and
    geographic descriptions of developing countries; aid
    giving bodies; aid aspects of scientific and technical
    disciplines such as agriculture and medicine; primary
    statistics publications from national and international
    organisations
Services: Interlibrary loans; enquiries; photocopies (at
    cost); sale of DFID publications
Availability: Visits by appointment; telephone and
    written enquiries accepted; loans only via the British
    Library
Hours: 09.30-17.00 Monday to Friday
Transport: Tube and Rail: Victoria; Bus: 11, 24

[175]
Department for Work and Pensions Information Services
Room 114
Adelphi
1-11 John Adam Street
London WC2N 6HT
Borough: Westminster
Telephone: 020 7712 2500
Fax: 020 7962 8491
E-mail: library@ms41.dss.gov.uk
Key staff: Head of Information Services: Graham Monk
(020 7962 8322); Information Services Team Leader:
Melanie Harris (020 7962 9487); Information
Services Manager: Angela Tailby (020 7962 8911);
Legal Librarian: Liz Murray (020 7412 1333)
Stock and subject coverage: About 45,000 books and
pamphlets, and 200 current journals dealing with
social security and matters affecting the claiming of
benefits. Also covers social welfare; social policy in
general; pension provision; disability; industrial
injuries and poverty
Services: Enquiries, loans, interlibrary loans, current
awareness and abstracting services, online searches
and photocopying
Availability: Primarily to staff. Research workers and
other accredited persons by appointment, for material
not readily available elsewhere
Hours: 09.00-17.00 Monday to Friday
Transport: Tube: Embankment and Charing Cross; Rail:
Charing Cross
Special facilities: Toilet facilities; access for users with
disabilities – lift to all floors, disabled toilet facilities

[176]
Department of Health
DH
Skipton House
80 London Road
London SE1 6LW
Borough: Southwark
Constitution: Government department
Telephone: 020 797 plus extension
World Wide Web: www.doh.gov.uk
Key staff: Head, Library and Information Services: Pek
Lan Bower BA DipLib ALA, ext 25927; Senior
Librarian: John Scott Cree MA ALA (Customer
Services London, ext 25928)
Availability: To staff; other government libraries for
borrowing. Not open to the public. Written requests
for access should be addressed to the Customer
Services Librarian

Linked organisations
There are eight regional offices with their own library
facilities. DH executive agencies with library facilities
are the Medicines Control Agency, Medical Devices
Agency and the National Health Services Estates Agency

[176][a]
Skipton House Library
Room G17C
Skipton House
80 London Road
London SE1 6LW

Telephone: 020 797 plus extension 26541
Fax: 020 7972 5976
Key staff: Customer Services Librarian: Melanie Peffer
BA PGDipLib
Stock and subject coverage: Ca. 200,000 books and 2,000
journals on health services; public health; medicine
hospitals and social care
Hours: 09.00-17.00 Monday to Friday
Transport: Tube and Rail: Elephant and Castle; Bus: C10,
P3, 1, 12, 35, 40, 45, 53, 63, 68, 133, 168, 171, 172,
176, 188, 199, 322, 344
Special facilities: Refreshment facilities; access for users
with disabilities
Publications: Health Services Abstracts (for details e-mail:
health-service-abstracts@doh.gis.gov.uk); Health CD
(from The Stationery Office); HMIC CD (from
SilverPlatter); DH-Data (from Dialog)

Department of Trade and Industry
Organisation declined to be included in this
directory

[177]
Diabetes UK
(Formerly called the British Diabetic Association)
10 Queen Anne Street
London W1G 9LH
Borough: Westminster
Telephone: 020 7462 2601
Fax: 020 7637 5444
E-mail: infoscience@diabetes.org.uk
World Wide Web: www.diabetes.org.uk
Constitution: Registered charity
Key staff: Mairi Benson
Stock and subject coverage: All aspects of diabetes care and
research
Services: Literature searching of biomedical, nursing,
psychology, social sciences and clinical evidence
databases
Availability: Enquiries are dealt with principally by letter
or telephone – no personal visits or loans
Hours: 09.00-17.00 Monday to Friday
Publications: Diabetes Update – newsletter for health
professionals (quarterly to health care professional
members); Balance – magazine for members (people
with diabetes and their carers). Diabetes International
publishes a wide range of patient information leaflets
plus a report for health care professionals. For a
catalogue call 080 585 088

[178]
DIALOG
Diversity in Action in Local Government
Layden House
76-86 Turnmill Street
London EC1M 5LG
Borough: Islington
Telephone: 020 7296 6737
Fax: 020 7296 6666
World Wide Web: www.lg-employers.gov.uk/dialog/
Constitution: Government organisation
Objectives/purposes: Employers' organisation for local
government. DIALOG addresses diversity in all areas

The Dickens House Museum

– in service delivery, in employment practice and the diverse needs of local government arising from the modernising agenda

Key staff: Information Manager: Michael Macauley

Stock and subject coverage: Latest information on race, age, lesbian and gay, disability and gender issues together with best value, procurement and the Equalities Standard

Availability: Through website only

Publications: Dialogue (quarterly)

Linked organisations

DIALOG was formed through the merging of LARRIE (the Local Authorities Race Relations Information Exchange) and the Equalities Issues team

[179]
The Dickens House Museum
48 Doughty Street
London WC1N 2LF

Borough: Camden

Telephone: 020 7405 2127

Fax: 020 7831 5175

E-mail: dhmuseum@rmplc.co.uk

World Wide Web: www.dickensmuseum.com

Constitution: Registered charity

Objectives/purposes: Research library for Dickens studies

Key staff: Curator: Andrew Xavier

Stock and subject coverage: The Library of the Dickens House holds about 7,000 books by and relating to Charles Dickens, 4 journals (3 current) devoted to Dickens, and large quantities of ephemera, scrapbooks, etc. There is also a manuscript collection, including over 700 autograph Dickens letters, other contemporary material, and more modern collections of scholarly papers. The photographic collection, chiefly portraits of Dickens and his contemporaries and topographical material, totals about 4,000 images

Services: Photocopies

Availability: The Library is available to all bona fide Dickensians, free of charge. A charge is made for photocopying

Hours: By appointment between 09.00–17.00. Though the Museum may be open, the Library is not available for use at weekends, on public holidays, or between 24 December and 1 January

Transport: Tube: Russell Square, Chancery Lane, King's Cross; Bus: 17, 18, 19, 45, 46, 171, 171A, 196, 243, 259, 503, 505

Special facilities: Toilet facilities available

Special features: The Library is housed in the Dicken's House Museum, Charles Dicken's home from April 1837 to December 1839. Here he worked on Pickwick Papers, Oliver Twist and Nicholas Nickleby. Books, manuscripts, pictures, furniture and personalia are on display

Publications: Reports about the Dickens House Library are published from time to time in The Dickensian, journal of the Dickens Fellowship

[180]
Docklands Library and Archive

No 1 Warehouse
West India Quay
Hertsmere Road
London E14 4AL
Borough: Tower Hamlets
Telephone: 020 7515 1162
Fax: 020 7538 0209
E-mail: docklands@museum-london.org.uk
Constitution: Department of a museum
Objectives/purposes: To maintain and consolidate the collections relating to the Port of London and London's Docklands
Key staff: Librarian: Bob Aspinall
Stock and subject coverage: Material on the history of the Port of London, 1770 to date, including the regeneration of London's Docklands 1981 to date. Specialist collection relating to the history of the Port of London from 1770 to date. Secondary material includes a large section on the regeneration of Docklands. The Library includes a unique collection of photographic images and engineering and architectural drawings plus a good map collection of Docklands
Services: Photocopies (charges made); photographic transparencies for hire/reproduction (fees charged); photographic prints for sale and for reproduction (fees charged); VHS video cassettes of historic films available for hire (extracts for screening available)
Availability: Free access for students and members of the general public wishing to research some aspect of the history and development of the Port of London and London's Docklands. No loans, reference only. Visitors must telephone first for an appointment and directions
Hours: Severely restricted, by appointment only
Transport: Tube: Canary Wharf; DLR: West India Quay

Special facilities: Refreshment and toilet facilities available; access for users with disabilities – wide doors, lift, no stairs
Publications: Docklands Life – A Pictorial History of London's Docks 1860-1970, by Ellmers and Werner, Mainstream, 1991

Linked organisations

Museum of the Port of London and Docklands

[181]
Dr Johnson's House

17 Gough Square
London EC4A 3DE
Borough: Corporation of London
Telephone: 020 7353 3745
E-mail: curator@www.drjohnsonshouse.org
World Wide Web: www.drjohnsonshouse.org
Constitution: Private venture; registered charity
Objectives/purposes: Museum of Johnsoniana
Key staff: Curator: Natasha McEnroe
Stock and subject coverage: Paintings and engravings of Dr Samuel Johnson and his circle; a few Johnson relics and some simple furniture of the period. First and other editions of Johnson's Dictionary; some first editions of his works; various editions of Boswell's Life of Johnson; works on many of Johnson's friends including Reynolds, Goldsmith, the Thrales; copy of the Isham collection of Boswell's papers; books on 18th century England, and numerous modern works on Johnson
Availability: Application to use the Library must be in writing. No books may be taken from the Library. No charge made for minor services
Hours: Monday to Saturday (closed Sundays and Bank holidays): May to September 11.00-17.30, October to April 11.00-17.00
Transport: Tube: Blackfriars, Temple, Chancery Lane; Rail: Blackfriars; Bus: 4, 11, 15, 23, 75
Special facilities: Toilet facilities available

[182]
Dr Williams's Library

14 Gordon Square
London WC1H 0AR
Borough: Camden
Telephone: 020 7387 3727
Fax: 020 7388 1142
E-mail: 101340.2541@compuserve.com
Key staff: Director: Dr D Wykes
Stock and subject coverage: Primarily a theological library intended for the use of ministers, students and other persons engaged in the study of theology, religion and ecclesiastical history. Also contains materials on philosopy, history, literature and kindred subjects. Pre-eminent research collections on pre-19th century English Nonconformity
Services: Photocopies
Availability: Reference use of the Library is free. Regular users are asked to apply for a reader's ticket. An annual fee is payable for borrowing books
Hours: 10.00-17.00 Monday, Wednesday and Friday; 10.00-18.30 Tuesday and Thursday
Transport: Tube: Euston, Goodge Street, Warren Street, Euston Square, Russell Square; Rail: Euston

Special facilities: Toilet facilities for users with disabilities
Publications: Annual Bulletin, Friends of Dr Williams's Library Annual Lectures, Occasional Papers

Linked organisations

Dr Williams's Trust The Library is part of the Trust
Congregational Library The Congregational Library is housed in the same building and managed by Dr Williams's Library on behalf of the Congregation Manorial Hall Trust

[183]
Down's Syndrome Association
DSA

155 Mitcham Road
Tooting
London SW17 9PG
Borough: Wandsworth
Telephone: 020 8682 4001
Fax: 020 8682 4012
E-mail: info@downs-syndrome.org.uk
World Wide Web: www.downs-syndrome.org.uk
Constitution: Registered charity
Objectives/purposes: Support and information for people with Down's Syndrome and their parents, carers and professionals working in the field
Key staff: Information office
Stock and subject coverage: Leaflets and books on all aspects of Down's Syndrome
Availability: Open to bona fide researchers for reference only. Charges made for some services
Hours: 09.00–17.00 Monday to Friday
Transport: Tube: Tooting Broadway; Bus: 44, 57, 77, 133, 264, 280, 355
Special facilities: Toilet facilities available
Publications: Annual Review; Newsletter (4 p.a.)

[184]
The Drapers' Company

Drapers' Hall
Throgmorton Avenue
London EC2N 2DQ
Borough: Corporation of London
Telephone: 020 7448 1308
Fax: 020 7628 1988
E-mail: heritage@thedrapers.co.uk
World Wide Web: www.thedrapers.co.uk
Constitution: One of the 12 Great Livery Companies of the City of London
Key staff: The Archivist
Stock and subject coverage: Archives of the Company (dating from the 13th century) and covering City history, pageantry and hospitality, charity (education and poor relief), and the English settlement in County Londonderry
Services: Photocopying
Availability: Open to the public for research, by appointment, at the discretion of the Company Archivist
Hours: 09.30–16.30 Monday to Friday
Transport: Tube: Bank, Cannon Street, Liverpool Street, Mansion House, Moorgate; Rail: Cannon Street, Liverpool Street, Moorgate

[185]
DrugScope
(formerly Institute for the Study of Drug Dependence)

36 Loman Street
London SE1 0EE
Borough: Southwark
Telephone: 020 7928 1211
Fax: 020 7928 1771
E-mail: enquiries@drugscope.org.uk
World Wide Web: www.drugscope.org.uk
Objectives/purposes: DrugScope is the UK's leading drugs charity and centre of expertise on drugs. It aims to provide balanced and up-to-date drug information to professionals and the public; conduct research and develop policies on drugs and drug-related issues; promote humane and effective ways of responding to drugs and drug use; encourage informed debate and provide a voice for over 800 member bodies working on the ground
Key staff: Director: Roger Howard; Head of Information and Customer Services: Janice Field
Stock and subject coverage: Over 8,000 books, 80,000 reprints and research reports, and nearly 70,000 press cuttings on all aspects of drug abuse. DrugScope also has a video library
Services: Enquiry service; conferences and meetings; catalogue available on the web; document delivery service
Availability: Open by appointment to any enquirer for reference. No loans
Hours: 10.00–16.30 Monday to Friday
Transport: Tube: Borough; Rail: London Bridge, Waterloo, Blackfriars
Special facilities: Toilet facilities available; access for users with disabilities
Publications: Druglink

[186]
Duchy of Cornwall Library and Archives

10 Buckingham Gate
London SW1E 6LA
Borough: Westminster
Telephone: 020 7931 9541
Fax: 020 7931 9541
Constitution: The Duchy of Cornwall is a landed estate providing an income for the heir to the throne
Key staff: Archivist and Records Manager: Miss EA Stuart
Stock and subject coverage: The Duchy of Cornwall has existed since 1337 to provide an income for the heir to the throne. As such, its archives span a spectrum of over six and a half centuries and range from agricultural estate to modern business records. The Archives include: an extensive series of medieval account rolls of the Receivers, Ministers and court officials of the Duchy; household receipts and vouchers for Frederick and subsequently Augusta, Prince and Princess of Wales respectively (1728–1772); 19th-early 20th century estate correspondence. Non-manuscript materials include: the Duchy photograph collection, prints and engravings including 18th century Vauxhall Gardens prints

Services: Photocopies; photography by arrangement. The collection is in the process of being catalogued

Availability: On written application. Record Agency service available (Staff are not available to undertake research on behalf of members of the public but can recommend a number of record agents with access to the Duchy collection). In order to protect the privacy of lessees, material less than 100 years old is available for inspection only with the specific permission of the Secretary

Hours: 14.00-17.00 Wednesdays only, by prior appointment

Transport: Tube: St James's Park, Victoria; Rail: Victoria; Bus: any bus to Victoria Street; Coach: Victoria Coach Station

Publications: On the Historical Documents in the Duchy of Cornwall Office, Royal Cornwall Polytechnic Society Annual Report, RL Clowes (1930)

[187]
Dulwich College, Wodehouse Library

Dulwich Common
London SE21 7LD
Borough: Southwark
Telephone: 020 8299 9201
Fax: 020 8299 9245
E-mail: fletcherpj@dulwich.org.uk
World Wide Web: www.dulwich.org.uk
Constitution: Independent school; registered charity and independent non-profit distributing organisation
Objectives/purposes: Collections and research connected with every aspect of Dulwich College
Key staff: Keeper of Archives: Dr JR Piggott; Archivist: Mr PJ Fletcher
Stock and subject coverage: The Archive at the College contains rare printed books and diverse collections of manuscripts. The most important are probably the Henslowe and Alleyn papers relating to the Stuart and Elizabethan theatres; the Reading collection of manuscript music of the 18th century; Court Rolls from 1314; the papers of the Dulwich College Estate from 1619 until recent times; manuscripts and letters of PG Wodehouse; and materials connected with Shackleton and other famous Old Alleynians
Services: Photocopier available in the adjacent boys' library; photography available, but must be prepaid; fees are charged for searched information
Availability: Access to all bona fide researchers by appointment; reference only
Hours: Open during school term only; hours vary from year to year
Transport: Rail: West Dulwich; Bus: P4, P13, 3
Special facilities: Toilet facilities available
Special features: Building designed by Charles Barry Junior
Publications: History of Dulwich College and Architectural Guide to the buildings

Linked organisations

Dulwich Picture Gallery The College and Gallery are from the same Foundation

Dulwich College Library Connected with the College Library, a department of Dulwich College

[188]
Ealing (London Borough of Ealing)
Ealing Library and Information Service
E-mail: libuser@elaing.gov.uk
World Wide Web: www.ealing.gov.uk/libraries
Constitution: Public library, funded by local authority
Key staff: Head of Library and Information Service: BE Cope
Availability: Open to the general public for lending and reference. Charges made for audio and video loans
Special features: The Borough's main library is Ealing Central Library

[188][a]
Ealing Central Library
103 Ealing Broadway Centre
Ealing
London W5 5JY
Telephone: 020 8567 3670 (lending)
020 8567 3656 (reference)
020 8840 2351 (fax)
Key staff: Library Manager: Mr LP Bowen; Reference Librarian: John Gauss; Archivist: Jonathan Oates
Stock and subject coverage: General public library including reference, children's and local history collections. Subject specialisations include: general, electrical and electronic engineering; automatic control engineering, including robotics; telecommunications; Hindi, Gujerati, Punjabi and Urdu literatures. Collections of audio CDs, audio cassettes, videos and DVDs for loan
Services: Microfiche and microfilm reader-printers; photocopies (b&w and colour); Ealing Local Information Service (ELIS) online terminal; photobooth
Availability: Open to the general public for lending and reference. Charges made for audio and video loans
Hours: 09.30-19.45 Tuesday to Thursday; 09.30-17.00 Friday and Saturday
Transport: Tube and Rail: Ealing Broadway; Bus: E1, E2, E7, E8, E9, 65, 83, N89, 112, 207, 297, 607, 879, 983, 987, 989
Special facilities: Access for users with disabilities – full wheelchair access
Special features: Building opened in 1984
Publications: Various publications relating to Ealing local history

[188][b]
Acton Library
High Street
London W3 6NA
Telephone: 020 8752 0999
Fax: 020 8992 6086
Reference facilities: Reference collection; local information and children's collection
Hours: 09.30-19.45 Tuesday to Thursday; 09.30-17.00 Friday and Saturday
Transport: Tube: Acton Town; Rail: North Acton; Bus: E3, H40, 7, 70, 207, 266, 607, 879, 943, 989
Special facilities: Access for users with disabilities – full wheelchair access

[188][c]
Greenford Library
25 Oldfield Lane South
Greenford UB6 9LG
Telephone: 020 8578 1466
Fax: 020 8575 7800
Reference facilities: Reference collection; local information and children's collection
Hours: 09.30-19.45 Tuesday, Thursday and Friday; 09.30-17.00 Wednesday and Saturday
Transport: Bus: E1, E2, E3, E6, E7, E9, 92, 95, 105, 282, 983, 986
Special facilities: Access for users with disabilities – full wheelchair access

[188][d]
Hanwell Library
Cherington Road
London W7 3HL
Telephone: 020 8567 5041
Reference facilities: Reference collection; local information and children's collection
Hours: 09.30-13.00, 14.00-19.45 Tuesday and Thursday; 09.30-13.00, 14.00-17.00 Friday and Saturday
Transport: Rail: Hanwell; Bus: E3, E8, 83, 207, 607, 983, 987
Special facilities: Part wheelchair access

[188][e]
Jubilee Gardens Library
Jubilee Gardens
Southall UB1 2TJ
Telephone: 020 8578 1067
Reference facilities: Reference collection; local information and children's collection
Hours: 09.30-13.00, 14.00-19.45 Tuesday and Thursday; 09.30-13.00, 14.00-17.00 Thursday to Saturday
Transport: Rail: Southall then bus 105; Bus: E5, 95, 105
Special facilities: Access for users with disabilities – full wheelchair access

[188][f]
Northfields Library
Northfield Avenue
Ealing
London W5 4UA
Telephone: 020 8567 5700
Fax: 020 8567 5572
Reference facilities: Reference collection; local information and children's collection
Hours: 09.30-13.00, 14.00-19.45 Tuesday and Thursday; 09.30-13.00, 14.00-17.00 Friday and Saturday
Transport: Tube: Northfields; Bus: E2, E3
Special facilities: Access for users with disabilities – full wheelchair access

[188][g]
Northolt Library
Church Road
Northolt UB5 5AS
Telephone: 020 8845 3380
Reference facilities: Reference collection; local information and children's collection
Hours: 09.30-13.00, 14.00-19.45 Tuesday and Thursday; 09.30-13.00, 14.00-17.00 Friday and Saturday

Transport: Tube: Northolt; Bus: 92, 120, 140, 282
Special facilities: Access for users with disabilities – full wheelchair access

[188][h]
Perivale Library
Horsenden Lane South
Perivale
Greenford UB6 7NT
Telephone: 020 8997 2830
Reference facilities: Reference collection; local information and children's collection
Hours: 09.30-13.00, 14.00-19.45 Tuesday and Thursday; 09.30-13.00, 14.00-17.00 Friday
Transport: Tube: Perivale; Bus: 95, 297
Special facilities: Access for users with disabilities – full wheelchair access

[188][i]
Pitshanger Library
143-5 Pitshanger Lane
London W5 1RH
Telephone: 020 8997 0230
Key staff: Gill Laws
Reference facilities: Reference collection; local information and children's collection
Hours: 09.30-13.00, 14.00-19.45 Tuesday and Thursday; 09.30-13.00, 14.00-17.00 Friday and Saturday
Transport: Tube: Ealing Broadway; Bus: E2, E9
Special facilities: Wheelchair access

[188][j]
Southall Library
Osterley Park Road
Southall UB2 4BL
Telephone: 020 8574 3412
Fax: 020 8571 7629
Reference facilities: Reference collection; local information and children's collection
Hours: 09.30-19.45 Tuesday to Thursday; 09.30-17.00 Friday and Saturday
Transport: Rail: Southall; Bus: E5, 95, 120, 195
Special facilities: Part wheelchair access

[188][k]
West Ealing Library
Melbourne Avenue
London W13 9BT
Telephone: 020 8567 2812
Fax: 020 8567 1736
Reference facilities: Reference collection; local information and children's collection
Hours: 09.30-19.45 Tuesday to Thursday; 09.30-17.00 Friday and Saturday
Transport: Rail: West Ealing; Bus: E3, E8, 83, 207, 607, 983, 987, 989
Special facilities: Access for users with disabilities – full wheelchair access

[188][l]
Wood End Library
Whitton Avenue West
Greenford UB6 0EE

Telephone: 020 8422 3965
Reference facilities: Reference collection; local information and children's collection
Hours: 09.30-13.00, 14.00-19.45 Tuesday and Thursday; 09.30-13.00, 14.00-17.00 Friday and Saturday
Transport: Tube: Sudbury Hill, Northolt; Bus: 187
Special facilities: Access for users with disabilities – full wheelchair access

[189]
Ealing, Hammersmith and West London College

World Wide Web: www.hwlc.ac.uk
Constitution: Further education college
Objectives/purposes: The college provides courses such as A level, GNVQ, Access and other vocational courses
Availability: The learning resource centres offer free access to all staff and students. Members of the local community may use the facilities for reference only. The College is located on four sites each with its own Learning Centre.
*During 2004 the College will relocate all its construction education and training courses to Acton and West London College from its current home at Lime Grove (Shepherd's Bush, London W12 8EA) to a new purpose built department within the Acton site.

[189][a]
Acton and West London College

Mill Hill Road
Acton
London W3 8UX
Borough: Ealing
Telephone: 020 8231 6000
Fax: 020 8993 2725
Key staff: Learning Resource Manager: Mr S Stirling; Learning Resource Coordinators: Ms A Ray and Mr D McGrath
Stock and subject coverage: Collections to support adult and general vocational courses in construction; English for speakers of other languages; motor vehicle engineering; engineering and computing technologies
Services: Photocopies; CD-ROM services; computing facilities with various network databases
Hours: Term-time: 09.00-19.30 Monday to Thursday; 09.00-16.00 Friday. Vacation: 09.30-16.00
Transport: Tube: Acton Town; Rail: Acton Central; Bus: E3, H40, 70, 207, 266, 607
Special facilities: Refreshment facilities available during term time; toilet facilities available; access for users with disabilities – disabled chair lift

[189][b]
Ealing and West London College

The Green
Ealing
London W5 5EW
Borough: Ealing
Telephone: 0800 980 2175
Fax: 020 8231 6013

Stock and subject coverage: Collections to support adult and general vocational courses in the humanities; business; languages; science, maths and computing; and English for speakers of other languages
Services: Photocopies; CD-ROM services; computing facilities with various network databases
Transport: Tube and rail: Ealing Broadway; Bus: E1, E7, E8, E9, 65, 83, 112, 207, 297, 607

[189][c]
Hammersmith and West London College

Gliddon Road
Barons Court
London W14 9BL
Borough: Hammersmith and Fulham
Telephone: 020 8741 1688
Fax: 020 8563 8247
E-mail: cic@hwlc.ac.uk
Stock and subject coverage: Books, magazines and newspapers to support courses on business; English for speakers of other languages; hair and beauty; hospitality and catering; health, early years and care; humanities and art; ICT; performing arts and media; science and maths; travel, leisure and tourism
Services: Photocopying and printing facilities in b&w and colour; CD-ROM services; computing facilities with various network databases
Transport: Tube: Barons Court, Hammersmith; Bus: H91, 9, 10, 27, 33, 190, 208, 211, 220, 266, 267, 391

[189][d]
Southall and West London College

Beaconsfield Road
Southall
Middlesex UB1 1DP
Borough: Ealing
Telephone: 0800 980 2175
Fax: 020 8574 2460
Stock and subject coverage: Materials to support adult and vocational courses on a range of topics; English for speakers of foreign languages
Services: Photocopies; CD-ROM services; computing facilities with various network databases
Transport: Rail: Southall; Bus: H32, 105, 120, 207

[190]
Eastman Dental Institute for Oral Health Care Sciences
EDI

Eastman Dental Hospital
256 Gray's Inn Road
London WC1X 8LD
Borough: Camden
Telephone: 020 7915 1045
Fax: 020 7915 1147
E-mail: ic@eastman.ucl.ac.uk
World Wide Web: www.eastman.ucl.ac.uk
Constitution: University department
Key staff: Librarian: Heather Lodge

Stock and subject coverage: Journals, books and online resources on dentistry, oral medicine and oral health care sciences

Services: Internet access; photocopies

Availability: Staff and all members of the Eastman Institute and Hospital. Visitors charged £10 per visit

Hours: 08.00-20.00 Monday to Thursday; 08.00-17.30 Friday

Transport: Tube and Rail: King's Cross

Special facilities: Refreshment and toilet facilities available on site; access for users with disabilities including wheelchair access

Publications: Annual Report; Library and Information Centre Handbook

Linked organisations

University College London The Institute is affiliated to UCL

---

[191]
Ecclesiological Society

c/o Society of Antiquaries of London
Burlington House
Piccadilly
London W1V 0HS
Borough: Westminster
Fax: 020 7213 3181
E-mail: trevcooper@aol.com
World Wide Web: www.ecclsoc.org
Constitution: Registered charity with voluntary subscribing membership
Objectives/purposes: Study of architecture, arts and liturgy of the Christian Church
Key staff: Honorary Chairman of Council; Honorary Secretary
Stock and subject coverage: Books, pamphlets, photographs, prints and postcards on church architecture, arts and liturgy
Availability: Access restricted to the Society's own membership (subscription rates from £12 to £50 p.a., £10 concessions). Material available for reference only, normally without charge
Hours: By appointment only
Publications: Ecclesiology Today newsletter (3 p.a. to members). Monographs published irregularly, most recent title: Martin Travers 1886-1948, a Handlist of His Work (1997)

---

[192]
Edexcel Foundation

Stewart House
32 Russell Square
London WC1B 5DN
Borough: Camden
Telephone: 020 7758 5503
Fax: 020 7758 6996
E-mail: library@edexcel.org.uk
World Wide Web: www.edexcel.org.uk
Constitution: Registered charity and company limited by guarantee
Key staff: Corporate Information Resource Centre Manager: Katie Peddlesden
Stock and subject coverage: 4,000 documents and 160 journals on academic and vocational education and training in the secondary and tertiary sectors. Archive of BTEC and Edexcel reports

Services: Enquiry service

Availability: Telephone and email enquiries welcome. Enquiries about Edexcel's awards or programmes of study should be directed to the Customer Response Centre on 0870 240 9800

Hours: 09.00-17.30 Monday to Friday

Transport: Tube: Euston, Russell Square, Warren Street; Rail: Euston, Kings Cross; Bus: 24, 68, 73, 188

Linked organisations

Business and Technology Education Council (BTEC)

London Examinations (ULEAC) Edexcel was formed following the merger of the Business and Technology Education Council (BTEC) and London Examinations (ULEAC)

---

[193]
Edgware Community Hospital
Information and Knowledge Services

Postgraduate Centre
Burnt Oak Broadway
Edgware
Middlesex HA8 0AD
Borough: Barnet
Telephone: 020 8732 6603
Fax: 020 8951 1692
E-mail: library@barnet-pct.nhs.uk
Constitution: NHS Hospital
Key staff: Library, Information and Knowledge Manager: Gill Terry; Assistant Librarian: Delia Wilkinson; Clinical Librarians: Liz Rigby and Lucy Reid
Stock and subject coverage: Medical library
Availability: Open to employees of Barnet Primary Care NHS Trust, employees of Barnet, Enfield and Haringey Mental Health NHS Trust and Barnet, Enfield and Haringey Health Authority who work in the Barnet area. Also open to Barnet and Chase Farm NHS Trust staff who are based at Edgware Community Hospital and to GPs and other health care personnel and their staff working within Barnet. Students on placement with these organisations are offered reference access to the collections. Visitors should bring their Trust identification card or other ID when visiting the Library
Hours: 08.30-16.30, Monday to Friday
Transport: Tube: Burnt Oak, Edgware; Bus: 32, 107, 142, 251, 292, 708

---

[194]
Educational and Television Films Ltd
ETV Films Ltd

247A Upper Street
London N1 1RU
Borough: Islington
Telephone: 020 7226 2298
Fax: 020 7226 8016
E-mail: zoe@etvltd.demon.co.uk
World Wide Web: www.etvltd.demon.co.uk

Constitution: Company limited by guarantee
Key staff: Manager: Stanley Forman; Director: Betty
  Baker; Librarian: Zoe Moore; Archival Consultant:
  Jack Amos
Stock and subject coverage: Film archive stock shot library.
  16mm and 35mm film on: Eastern Europe, former
  Soviet Union, China, Vietnam, Cuba, Chile plus film
  material on the history of the British Labour
  Movement of the 1930s, the Spanish Civil War and
  Afghanistan
Availability: Commercial library with limited viewing
  facilities. Material can be loaned to bona fide film
  researchers
Hours: 09.30-17.30 Monday to Friday
Transport: Tube: Highbury and Islington; Bus: 4, 19, 30,
  43, 271
Special facilities: Toilet facilities available
Publications: Catalogue available on request

Linked organisations
  Plato Films Ltd Associate company

[195]
The Egyptian Exploration Society
EES
  3 Doughty Mews
  London WC1N 2PG
Borough: Camden
Telephone: 020 7242 2266
Fax: 020 7404 6118
E-mail: eeslibrary@talk21.com
World Wide Web: www.ees.ac.uk
Constitution: Registered charity with voluntary
  subscribing membership, company limited by
  guarantee
Objectives/purposes: Excavation and research in Egypt and
  publication of the results. Dissemination of
  information concerning ancient Egypt
Key staff: Librarian: Chris Naunton; Secretary: Patricia
  Spencer; Financial Administration: David Butcher
Stock and subject coverage: The Society's Library covers all
  aspects of the study of the ancient Egyptian
  civilisation, including Egypt in the Greek, Roman
  and Coptic periods. Related subjects, such as Islamic
  Egypt and the ancient Near East are also represented,
  though not as fully. The Library contains
  approximately 20,000 volumes (including journals)
Services: Photocopies
Availability: The Library is open to members of the
  Egypt Exploration Society only. Other students or
  researchers may use the Library (but not borrow
  books) with permission, for which a fee may be
  charged
Hours: 10.30-12.45, 14.15-16.30 Monday to Friday
Transport: Tube: Russell Square, Holborn, Chancery
  Lane; Bus: 17, 19, 38, 45, 46, 55, 171
Publications: Annual Report; Journal of Egyptian
  Archaeology; Egyptian Archaeology Graeco-Roman
  Memoirs and publications of excavations and research

[196]
Electricity Association, Business Information Centre
EA
  30 Millbank
  London SW1P 4RD
Borough: Westminster
Telephone: 020 7963 5700 (switchboard)
E-mail: enquiries@electricity.org.uk
World Wide Web: www.electricity.org.uk
Constitution: Association with voluntary subscribing
  membership
Objectives/purposes: Trade association for electricity
  generators and suppliers
Key staff: Mrs ML Deighton
Stock and subject coverage: Collection on the
  administrative, commercial and economic aspects of
  electricity supply in the UK and overseas. 15,000
  books, reports and pamphlets, including a substantial
  proportion of statistical works. 200 current journals
  plus collection of annual reports of electricity supply
  undertakings worldwide (half in foreign languages)
Availability: To staff of Electricity Association member
  companies
Publications: Electricity Industry Review (annual);
  International Electricity Prices (annual); UK
  Electricity Prices; UK Electricity Supply Rates,
  Distribution Use of System Charges

[197]
Elimination of Leukaemia Fund
ELF
  Regent House
  291 Kirkdale
  London SE26 4QD
Borough: Lewisham
Telephone: 020 8778 5353
Fax: 020 8778 7117
E-mail: elffund@ukonline.co.uk
Constitution: Registered charity
Objectives/purposes: To raise funds and to improve
  facilities for the care and treatment of leukaemia
  sufferers
Key staff: Director: Martyn Hall
Stock and subject coverage: Materials on leukaemia and
  related blood disorders
Services: Photocopies; fax machine
Availability: Open to all without charge, material can be
  loaned
Hours: 10.00-18.00 Monday to Friday
Transport: Rail: Sydenham; Bus: 75, 194, 122, 202, 312,
  450
Special facilities: Refreshment and toilet facilities available
  on site
Publications: ELFLINE (2 p.a.)

[198]
Employment Appeal Tribunal Library
  58 Victoria Embankment
  London EC4Y 0DS
Borough: Westminster
Telephone: 071-273 1049

Librarian-in-Charge: Tony Bunting
Stock and Subject Coverage: Employment Appeal Tribunal judgments
Availability: Priced copies of EAT judgments available on request, or for inspection by appointment
Hours: 10.00-16.30 Monday to Friday

---

[199]
Enfield Libraries (London Borough of Enfield)

Leisure Services
Civic Centre
Silver Street
Enfield EN1 3XJ
Telephone: 020 8379 3710
Fax: 020 8379 3753
E-mail: claire.lewis@enfield.gov.uk
World Wide Web: www.enfield.gov.uk/libs.htm
Constitution: Local authority library service
Key staff: Assistant Director Libraries and Culture: Claire Lewis; Libraries Resources and Development Manager: Heather Wills
Availability: Open to all

[199][a]
Central Library

Cecil Road
Enfield
Middlesex EN2 6TW
Telephone: 020 8366 2244
Fax: 020 8379 8401
Key staff: Area Library Manager: Sheila Barford
Stock and subject coverage: General library lending stock; children's library; music and video library collections. Reference library subject specialisation in the humanities arts, literature, history. Reference book stock of ca. 11,000 volumes. Special collection of art exhibition catalogues
Services: Photocopies (b&w and colour); fax service; microfilm-fiche reader-printer; CD-ROMs; First Stop information point; wordprocessing; internet access
Hours: 09.00-20.00 Monday, Tuesday and Thursday; 09.00-17.00 Wednesday (Reference library and First Stop only); 09.00-17.30 Friday; 09.00-17.00 Saturday
Transport: Rail: Enfield Chase, Enfield Town; Bus: W8, W9, W10, 121, 191, 192, 231, 307, 310, 311, 313, 317, 329, 517, 610
Special facilities: Access for users with disabilities to lending library (but not to reference library); Open Book machine and electronic newspaper

[199][b]
Bowes Road Library

Bowes Road
London N11 1BD
Telephone: 020 8379 1707
Fax: 020 8368 6025
Key staff: Library Administrator
Reference facilities: Small quick reference collection; local information and children's collection
Hours: 14.00-19.00 Tuesday; 14.00-19.00 Thursday; 09.00-17.00 Saturday
Transport: Tube: Arnos Grove; Bus: 34, 232

[199][c]
Bullsmoor Library

Kempe Road
Enfield
London EN1 4QS
Telephone: 020 8379 1723
Fax: 01992 788761
Key staff: Library Administrator
Reference facilities: Small quick reference collection; local information and children's collection
Hours: 09.30-12.30, 15.00-19.00 Tuesday and Thursday; 09.30-12.30 Saturday
Transport: Tube: Kensal Green; Rail: Kensal Rise
Special facilities: Toilet facilities; access for users with disabilities including wheelchair access

[199][d]
Bush Hill Park Library

Agricola Place
Enfield
Middlesex EN1 1DW
Telephone: 020 8367 1709
Fax: 020 8367 2213
Key staff: Library Administrator
Reference facilities: Small quick reference collection; local information and children's collection
Hours: 14.00-19.00 Tuesday and Thursday; 09.00-17.00 Friday; 09.00-17.00 Saturday
Transport: Rail: Bush Hill Park; Bus: 192, 517
Special facilities: Limited access for users with disabilities

[199][e]
Edmonton Green Library

36-44 South Mall
Edmonton Green
London N9 0TN
Telephone: 020 8807 3618
Fax: 020 8379 2615
Key staff: Area Library Manager: Peter Brown
Stock and subject coverage: Reference library stock of ca. 6,000 volumes with subject specialisation in the social sciences. The collection includes official statistical publications and Command papers. Lending library; children's library; music and video library
Services: Microfilm-fiche reader-printer; photocopies (black and white and colour copier); fax service; CD-ROM; word processor and internet access available for a fee. First Stop information service providing information on council services. Community room available for hire. Open Learning Centre and Homework Centre
Hours: 09.00-19.00 Monday to Thursday; 09.00-17.30 Friday; 09.00-17.00 Saturday
Transport: Rail: Edmonton Green; Bus: W6, W8, 102, 144, 149, 191, 192, 259, 279
Special facilities: Access for users with disabilities; CC-TV machine; toilet facilities (including facilities for users with disabilities); baby changing facilities

[199][f]
Enfield Business Library

Enfield Business Centre
201 Hertford Road
Enfield
Middlesex EN3 5JH

Telephone: 020 8443 1701
Key staff: Business Information Officer: Tony Eves
Stock and subject coverage: Dedicated business library
Services: Online searching service and fee-based research.
  Word processing and internet hire
Hours: 09.00-17.00 Monday to Friday
Transport: Rail: Southbury, Brimsdown; Bus: 121, 191,
  279, 307
Special facilities: Access for users with disabilities

[199][g]
Enfield Highway Library
  258 Hertford Road
  Enfield
  Middlesex EN3 5BA
Telephone: 020 8379 1710
Fax: 020 8443 5034
Key staff: Library Administrator
Reference facilities: Small quick reference collection; local
  information and children's collection
Hours: 09.00-19.00 Monday and Thursday; 09.00-17.00
  Tuesday and Saturday
Transport: Rail: Brimsdown; Bus: 121, 191, 279, 307,
  310A, 310B, 363
Special facilities: Access for users with disabilities

[199][h]
Enfield Local History Unit
  Southgate Town Hall
  Green Lanes
  London N13 4XD
Telephone: 020 8379 2724
Fax: 020 8379 2761
Objectives/purposes: To collect material relevant to the
  history of Enfield and its immediate environs
Key staff: Local History Officer: Graham Dalling
Stock and subject coverage: The bookstock covers all
  aspects of Enfield's history. The collection is
  particularly strong in the fields of religion, education,
  transport history and industry. There is a substantial
  collection of pre-current O.S. maps and extensive
  local newspaper files
Services: Photocopies
Availability: Reference only, access by prior appointment
  only
Hours: 10.00-17.00 Monday, Tuesday, Thursday and
  Friday
Transport: Tube: Wood Green, Arnos Grove; Rail:
  Palmers Green; Bus: 121, 329
Special facilities: Toilet facilities available

Linked organisations
> **London Borough of Enfield Library Service**
> The Local History Unit is part of Enfield Library
> Service

[199][i]
Merryhills Library
  Enfield Road
  Enfield
  Middlesex EN2 7HL
Telephone: 020 8379 1711
Fax: 020 8367 4715
Key staff: Library Administrator

Reference facilities: Small quick reference collection; local
  information and children's collection
Hours: 14.00-19.00 Tuesday and Thursday; 09.00-13.00
  Friday; 09.00-17.00 Saturday
Transport: Tube: Oakwood; Rail: Enfield Chase; Bus:
  121, 307
Special facilities: Access for users with disabilities

[199][j]
Ordnance Road Library
  645 Hertford Road
  Enfield
  Middlesex EN3 6ND
Telephone: 01992 710588
Fax: 01992 788763
Key staff: Senior Branch Librarian
Stock and subject coverage: Small general reference
  collection (no subject specialisation); lending library
  with general stock; children's library; music and video
  library. Sir Jules Thorn multi-media centre for people
  with sensory impairment
Services: Microfiche reader; photocopies (b&w and
  colour); fax service; CD-ROMs; First Stop
  information service providing information on
  council services
Hours: 09.00-20.00 Monday, Tuesday and Thursday;
  09.00-17.30 Friday; 09.00-17.00 Saturday
Transport: Rail: Enfield Lock, Turkey Street; Bus: 121,
  279, 310A, 310B, 327, 363, 517
Special facilities: Access for users with disabilities

[199][k]
Palmers Green Library
  Broomfield Lane
  London N13 4EY
Telephone: 020 8886 3728
Fax: 020 8982 2712
Key staff: Area Library Manager
Stock and subject coverage: Reference library with subject
  specialisation in science and technology; education
  and British Standards, stock of ca. 10,000 volumes.
  General lending library; children's library; music and
  video library
Services: Microfiche reader; photocopies (b&w and
  colour); fax service; CD-ROM; First Stop
  information point; open learning service
Hours: 09.00-20.00 Monday, Tuesday and Thursday;
  09.00-17.30 Friday; 09.00-17.00 Saturday
Transport: Rail: Palmers Green; Bus: 121, 329
Special facilities: Access for users with disabilities

[199][l]
Ponders End Library
  College Court
  High Street
  Enfield
  Middlesex EN3 4EY
Telephone: 020 8379 1712
Fax: 020 8443 5035
Key staff: Library Administrator
Reference facilities: Small quick reference collection; local
  information and children's collection; homework
  centre
Hours: 09.00-19.00 Tuesday and Wednesday; 09.00-17.00
  Friday and Saturday

Transport: Rail: Ponders End, Southbury; Bus: 149, 279, 363, 517
Special facilities: Access for users with disabilities

[199][m]
Ridge Avenue Library
Ridge Avenue
London N21 2RH
Telephone: 020 8379 1714
Fax: 020 8364 1352
Key staff: Branch Librarian
Reference facilities: Main reserve book store for London Borough of Enfield libraries: ca. 70,000 volumes. Quick reference collection; local information and children's collection
Hours: 09.00-20.00 Monday, Tuesday and Thursday; 09.00-17.30 Friday; 09.00-17.00 Saturday
Transport: Rail: Bush Hill Park; Bus: W8, 329
Special facilities: Access for users with disabilities

[199][n]
Southgate Circus Library
High Street
London N14 6BP
Telephone: 020 8882 8849
Fax: 020 8886 3669
Key staff: Branch Librarian
Reference facilities: Quick reference collection; local information and children's collection
Hours: 09.00-19.00 Monday and Thursday; 09.00-17.30 Friday; 09.00-17.00 Tuesday and Saturday
Transport: Tube: Southgate; Bus: W6, W9, 121, 299
Special facilities: Access for users with disabilities

[199][o]
Weir Hall Library
Millfield Arts Complex
Silver Street
London N18 1PJ
Telephone: 020 8884 2420
Fax: 020 8807 3193
Key staff: Library Administrator
Reference facilities: Quick reference collection; local information and children's collection
Hours: 09.00-19.00 Monday and Wednesday; 09.00-17.00 Friday and Saturday
Transport: Rail: Silver Street; Bus: W6, 34, 102, 144, 217, 231, 444
Special facilities: Access for users with disabilities

[199]p]
Winchmore Hill Library
Green Lanes
London N21 3AP
Telephone: 020 8360 8344
Fax: 020 8364 1060
Key staff: Library Administrator
Reference facilities: Small quick reference collection; local information and children's collection
Hours: 09.00-19.00 Tuesday and Thursday; 09.00-17.00 Wednesday and Saturday
Transport: Rail: Winchmore Hill; Bus: 329
Special facilities: Access for users with disabilities

[200]
Engineering Employers' Federation
EEF
Broadway House
Tothill Street
London SW1H 9NQ
Borough: Westminster
Telephone: 020 7222 7777
Fax: 020 7222 2782
E-mail: eef-fed@org.uk
World Wide Web: www.eef.org.uk
Constitution: Association with voluntary subscribing membership
Key staff: Jean Bennett; Catherine Rochester
Stock and subject coverage: 15,000 books, reports and pamphlets, 250 journals, covering industrial relations and the engineering industry and related subjects
Services: Enquiries; photocopies (all at the discretion of the staff)
Availability: Primarily for use by the EEF and its member firms, but requests/enquiries from outside the organisation will be answered at the staff's discretion
Hours: 09.00-17.00 Monday to Friday
Transport: Tube: St James's Park
Special facilities: Toilet facilities available
Publications: Engineering Outlook

Linked organisations
Engineering and Marine Training Authority (EMTA)
Engineering Construction Industry Association (ECIA) The Federation collaborates with both EMTA and ECIA
CBI Member organisation of the CBI

[201]
English Folk Dance and Song Society
EFDSS
Vaughan Williams Memorial Library
Cecil Sharp House
2 Regent's Park Road
London NW1 7AY
Borough: Camden
Telephone: 020 7485 2206 ext 19/18
Fax: 020 7284 0523
E-mail: library@efdss.org
World Wide Web: www.efdss.org
Constitution: Registered charity
Objectives/purposes: Collection and dissemination of information on the folk arts
Key staff: MH Taylor, BA(Hons)Lib ALA
Stock and subject coverage: Unique multi-media archive (films, videos, photographs, sound recordings and printed materials) on British folk culture and similar elements of British based cultures in other lands, particularly North America and Ireland. The collection dates back to the 17th and 18th centuries and also includes information from and about other world cultures and some foreign language material. The archive is based around Cecil Sharp's extensive collections of books, manuscripts and papers on traditional songs and dances

English-Speaking Union of the Commonwealth, Page Memorial Library

Availability: Free to members of the EFDSS, who may borrow some of the literature. Non-members are charged a daily fee and do not have borrowing facilities. This system also applies to postal and telephone enquiries, which are welcomed

Hours: 09.30-17.30 Tuesday to Friday; 10.00-16.00 first and third Saturday each month (sometimes closed between 11.00-14.00)

Transport: Tube: Camden; Bus: C2, 274

Special facilities: Refreshment facilities available in term time; toilet facilities

Publications: Folk Music Journal; English Dance and Song journal; range of books, study guides, audio cassettes and videos

[202]
English National Board for Nursing, Midwifery and Health Visiting
ENB

Victory House
170 Tottenham Court Road
London W1T 7HA

Borough: Camden
Telephone: 020 7391 6206
Fax: 020 7391 6248
E-mail: library@enb.org.uk
World Wide Web: www.enb.org.uk
Constitution: Government funded body
Key staff: Information Officer/Librarian: Betty Fox
Stock and subject coverage: Small collection of nursing and midwifery reports to meet the needs of staff. Range of UK nursing journals

Availability: Library for staff only. The Health Care Database, and much more information, is available via the website and on CD-ROM. The database covers 90 UK nursing journals (with abstracts), organisations and open learning suppliers

Publications: Contact the Publications Department on 020 7391 6314

[203]
English-Speaking Union of the Commonwealth
ESU

Page Memorial Library
Dartmouth House
37 Charles Street
London W1J 5ED

Borough: Westminster
Telephone: 020 74529 1550
Fax: 020 7495 6108
E-mail: library@esu.org
World Wide Web: www.esu.org
Constitution: Registered charity
Key staff: Andrea K Wathern BA(Hons) DipLib
Stock and subject coverage: Ca. 15,000 volumes and 35 journal titles. Specialist collection on the USA (politics, sociology, literature and history), with ca. 10% of the stock on Commonwealth countries (chiefly Australia, Canada and New Zealand). Information about studying in these countries, and some US university prospectuses
Services: Telephone enquiry service, freely available; loans to ESU members only; interlibrary loans; special loans service to schools; photocopies

Availability: Open to the public for reference

Hours: 10.00–16.00. Library open, but not always staffed, at lunchtime

Transport: Tube: Green Park, Bond Street; Bus: 8

Special facilities: Refreshment and toilet facilities available; access for users with disabilities. Mews entrance at street level may be suitable for wheelchairs, please check with Librarian before visit

Special features: Library situated in refurbished mews property, adjacent to a Georgian mansion in Mayfair. The main building includes such features as Louis XIV walnut panelling and an ornate marble staircase

Publications: Quarterly accessions list; series of annotated reading guides to the Library stock (normally prepared in response to requests from schools and colleges, but available to anyone)

[204]
The Environment Council

212 High Holborn
London WC1V 7BF
Borough: Camden
Telephone: 020 7836 2626
Fax: 020 7242 1180
E-mail: info@envcouncil.org.uk
World Wide Web: www.the-environment-council.org.uk
Constitution: Registered charity
Objectives/purpose: To help people from all sectors of business and society to make decisions to improve the environment and their lives
Stock and subject coverage: Directories and leaflets available free of charge (on receipt of SAE), signposting environmental organisations and resources
Services: No Library service, the Council provides free publications on request and operates a referral service
Publications: Who's Who in the Environment (available on computer disk for £15); leaflet listing full range of publications available

[205]
Environmental Studies Library

University College London
Faculty of Environmental Studies
Wates House
22 Gordon Street
London WC1H 0QB
Borough: Camden
Telephone: 020 7679 4900
E-mail: library@ucl.ac.uk
Constitution: The Environmental Studies Library is part of University College London
Key staff: Site Librarian: Suzanne Page
Stock and subject coverage: Materials on architecture, construction management and town planning
Services: Photocopiers; networked databases
Availability: Open to all bona fide researchers for reference only
Hours: Term-time: 09.30–20.00 Monday and Thursday: 09.30–19.00 Tuesday and Wednesday; 09.30–19.00 Friday; 09.30–16.30 Saturday
Christmas and Easter vacations: closes at 18.45 Monday to Friday; Saturday opening hours apply during Easter vacations only and the Library is shut

between 13.00–14.00
Summer vacation: 09.30–17.00 Monday to Friday
Transport: Tube and Rail: Euston
Special facilities: Toilet facilities available; access for users with disabilities

Linked organisations

University College London Member of the College

[206]
European Bank for Reconstruction and Development, Business Information Centre
EBRD

One Exchange Square
London EC2A 2EH
Borough: Corporation of London
Telephone: 020 7338 6361
Fax: 020 7338 6155
E-mail: kroonr@ebrd.com
Key staff: Promotion and Marketing Executive: Rosemarie Kroon
Stock and subject coverage: Extensive collection of information sources in the form of databases, books, grey literature, reports, journals, newspapers. Covers business information in central and eastern Europe, including the CIS
Services: Business information retrieval
Availability: Staff and students free; others on a subscription basis
Hours: 09.00–17.00 Monday to Friday
Transport: Tube and Rail: Liverpool Street

[207]
European Commission Representation in the UK

8 Storey's Gate
London SW1P 3AT
Borough: Westminster
Telephone: 020 7973 1992
Fax: 020 7973 1900
World Wide Web: www.europe.olf.uk
Constitution: Government department
Key staff: Mrs Marguerite-Marie Brenchley
Stock and subject coverage: All European Union official publications except European Parliament materials, which can be found in their own library at 2 Queen Anne's Gate, London SW1
Services: National network of information 'relays' available through European Documentation Centres
Availability: Enquiries may only be referred to the Library via a recognized European Public Information Centre (EPIC). For details of your nearest EPIC Centre please contact your local library
Hours: By appointment
Transport: Tube: St James's Park

Linked organisations

European Commission (Brussels)

European Documentation Centres

There is a comprehensive network of European Documentation Centres (EDCs) around the United Kingdom. They receive, or are entitled to claim, one free copy of every EC publication. This is intended to ensure adequate resources for the study of European integration. The documents received by the EDCs fall into three broad categories: a) legislation and documents connected with the legislative process; b) research reports, books and journals; c) background reports and explanatory documents.

In return for receiving these free publications, the Host Libraries are obliged to designate a professional librarian to manage the colllection, and to maintain the collection as a self-contained entity, which is readily identifiable and adequately signposted and guided. Within the London area there is one host library:

[208]
European Documentation Centre
EDC
London School of Economics
British Library of Political and Economic Science
10 Portugal Street
London WC2A 2HD
Borough: Westminster
Telephone: 020 7955 7273
Fax: 020 7955 7454
E-mail: library.information.desk@lse.ac.uk
World Wide Web:
www.blpec.lse.ac.uk/collections/govpubls/ev.html
Constitution: Department of a university
Key staff: Maria Bell
Stock and subject coverage: EC publications
Transport: Tube: Holborn, Temple; Rail: Charing Cross
Special facilities: Toilet facilities available

Linked organisations
British Library of Political and Economic Science Part of the Library

[209]
The Evangelical Library
EL
78A Chiltern Street
London W1U 5HB
Borough: Westminster
Telephone: 020 7935 6997
E-mail: stlibrary@aol.com
World Wide Web: www.evangelical-library.org.uk
Constitution: Registered charity
Objectives/purposes: To promote the study and general knowledge of those truths of holy scripture traditionally known as evangelical
Key staff: Librarian: Stephen Taylor; Other Libraries Contact: Rosemary Prentice
Stock and subject coverage: The Evangelical Library is distinguished from most general religious libraries by its concentration on specifically evangelical literature. The stock of about 80,000 volumes, ranges from the Puritans to today's writers and covers subjects such as bible commentaries, bible study, theology, devotional literature, sermons, hymnology, church work, ethics, church history, cults, missions, revivals, biographies and childrens literature. The stock includes books, pamphlets, magazines and slides as well as a collection of manuscripts, including a large number of original letters
Services: Photocopies
Availability: Open to members paying the annual subscription fee. Reference and lending facilities available to members – postal service available following pre-payment of postage. Hourly rate charged for research carried out by staff
Hours: 10.00-17.00 Monday to Saturday. Closed for an extended period at Easter and Christmas and over all bank holiday weekends. Visitors should check if in doubt
Transport: Tube: Baker Street; Bus: 2, 13, 18, 27, 30, 74, 82, 113, 139, 159, 274
Special facilities: Toilet facilities available
Publications: The Evangelical Library Bulletin (2 p.a.), annual lecture, various catalogues, history of the Evangelical Library
Special features: The Library was started in about 1924 as the personal collection of Geoffrey Williams (1886-1975), whose aim was to build up a worldwide evangelical library. Towards the end of World War II, it was moved from Surrey into Central London, largely due to the influence of the preacher Dr D Martyn Lloyd-Jones (1899-1981). The main library is housed in the hall of a school built in 1859 and has an interesting beamed roof

Linked organisations
Linked with other Christian libraries worldwide. The Evangelical Library supplies them with books if postal costs are met

[210]
Export Credits Guarantee Department
ECGD
PO Box 2200
2 Exchange Tower
Harbour Exchange Square
London E14 9GS
Borough: Tower Hamlets
Telephone: 020 7512 7421
Fax: 020 7512 7021
E-mail: rogleby@ecgd.gov.uk
World Wide Web: www.ecgd.gov.uk
Constitution: Government body
Key staff: Robin Ogleby
Stock and subject coverage: ECGD is a separate government department responsible to the Secretary of State for Trade and Industry, which aims to assist the export of capital and project-related goods from the UK by providing insurance against non-payment and guarantees for financing. Supporting relevant material is held
Services: Range of reports, handbooks, brochures, etc
Hours: 09.00-17.00 Monday to Friday
Transport: DLR: Crossharbour

[211]
Family Records Centre
FRC

1 Myddelton Street
London EC1R 1UW
Borough: Islington
Telephone: 020 8392 5300
E-mail: enquiry@pro.gov.uk
World Wide Web: www.familyrecords.gov.uk/frc
Objectives/purposes: Run jointly by the General Register Office and the Public Record Office to bring together some of the most important sources for family history
Stock and subject coverage: Information to aid genealogical research, including Census records (note 1901 Census information on fiche is housed at the Public Record Office); information on wills and probate materials
Services: Online service provider for the 1901 Census
Availability: Open to the public for reference use
Hours: 09.00-17.00 Monday, Wednesday and Friday; 10.00-19.00 Tuesday; 09.00-19.00 Thursday; 09.30-17.00 Saturday
Transport: Tube: Angel, Farringdon, King's Cross; Rail: King's Cross; Bus: 19, 38, 341 along Rosebery Avenue, 63 along Farringdon Road
Special facilities: Reserved parking for visitors with disabilities but spaces must be booked in advance
Publications: Shop selling a wide range of family history publications

Linked organisations
General Register Office
Public Record Office

[212]
The Fan Museum

12 Crooms Hill
Greenwich
London SE10 8ER
Borough: Greenwich
Telephone: 020 8305 1441
Fax: 020 8293 1889
World Wide Web: www.fan.museum.org.uk
Constitution: Registered charity
Objectives/purposes: Promoting the study and research of fans as well as fan making and conservation
Key staff: Curator and Director: Mrs Hélène Alexander
Stock and subject coverage: Books and journals on the history of the fan, collecting fans and associated topics: costume, chinoiserie, lace, the china trade, general, etc. Journals include: Journal of the Costume Society; Fan Circle International Bulletin 'Fans'; RSA Journals; Fan Association of North America Journals; Collectors Guide and Royal Academy Magazine; sale catalogues from Sotheby's, and Bonhams; Benezit dictionaries
Services: Photocopies (black and white and colour – charge per copy); fax machine
Availability: Access by appointment only for individuals who are bona fide researchers or students; reference only, no loans
Hours: 11.00-17.00 Tuesday to Saturday, 12.00-17.00 Sunday
Transport: Rail: Greenwich; Bus: 177, 180, 185, 188, 286, 386

Special facilities: Refreshments available on Sundays and Tuesdays; toilet facilities; access for users with disabilities – including ramp and lift

[213]
Federation of Master Builders
FMB

14-15 Great James Street
London WC1N 3DP
Borough: Camden
Telephone: 020 7242 7583
Fax: 020 7404 0296
E-mail: central@fmb.org.uk
World Wide Web: www.fmb.org.uk
Constitution: Association with voluntary subscribing membership
Objectives/purposes: To assist small and medium sized companies in the construction industry in running their businesses and representing their interests to Government and the EC
Key staff: Librarian/Information Officer: Betty Green; Information Officer: Pauline Borland
Stock and subject coverage: Information on: government legislation, employment law, health and safety, planning, environmental matters of relevance to construction, education and training, housing, technical data, statistics, contract law, etc.
Availability: Assistance to bona fide researchers and FMB members by telephone, letter or fax, no visits. Materials are for reference only
Hours: 09.00-17.00 Monday to Friday
Publications: FMB State of Trade Survey (quarterly – free); Annual Yearbook for each of FMB's 11 regions (free to government departments and public libraries); Master Builder Journal (monthly available by subscription)

Linked organisations
Head office plus 11 regional offices

[214]
Feminist Library and Information Centre

5A Westminster Bridge Road
London SE1 7XW
Borough: Southwark
Telephone: 020 7928 7789
Constitution: Registered charity and independent non-profit organisation. Supported by the London Borough of Southwark since 1993
Objectives/purposes: Research library and information centre on contemporary feminism worldwide; training organisation for volunteers
Key staff: Administered by a voluntary collective; no paid staff
Stock and subject coverage: Approximately 10,000 books, 1,500 journals on feminism worldwide since 1968. The collections include newsletters, ephemera and fiction. Special sections on working class women, women of colour, Jewish women, women with disabilities, lesbians and Irish women
Services: Photocopies
Availability: No charge for use of reference facilities; charges for borrowing material (sliding membership

scale); most material (excluding journals) is available
for loan

Hours: 11.00–20.00 Tuesday; 15.00–20.00 Wednesday;
14.00–17.00 Saturday

Transport: Tube: Lambeth North, Elephant and Castle,
Waterloo; Rail: Elephant and Castle, Waterloo; Bus: 1,
12, 44, 53, 59, 63, 68, 141, 171, 176, 184, 188 (bus
stop is St George's Circus)

Special facilities: Refreshment and toilet facilities; access
for users with disabilities (lift from ground floor, full
access details available)

Special features: Founded in 1975, feminist discussion
group meets fortnightly

Publications: Feminist Library Newsletter (4 p.a.);
Feminist Library publicity leaflet

[215]
Ferriman Information and Library Service

North Middlesex University Hospital Trust
Sterling Way
Edmonton
London N18 1QX

Borough: Edmonton
Telephone: 020 8887 2223
Fax: 020 8887 2714
E-mail: libnm1@mdx.ac.uk
World Wide Web: www.nthames-
health.tpmde.ac.uk/libraries/northmiddx/

Constitution: Multidisciplinary hospital and college,
medical and nursing library; part of an NHS hospital

Objectives/purposes: Contributes to the quality of patient
care by supporting education, training, practice and
research of health care personnel, students and related
staff via the provision of a multi-disciplinary library
and information service

Key staff: Librarian: Linda Farley; Assistant Librarian:
John Buchanan

Stock and subject coverage: Books and journals on
medicine, nursing, midwifery, and the professions
allied to medicine

Services: Photocopies; interlibrary loans; health care
databases

Availability: Reference facilities available to bona fide
researchers (identification required). Full services for
funded user groups only

Hours: Term-time: 09.00–19.00 Monday, Tuesday and
Thursday; 08.00–18.00 Wednesday; 09.00–18.00
Friday; 09.00–12.00 Saturday
Vacations: 09.00–18.00 Monday to Friday

Transport: Rail: Silver Street; Bus: W6, W8, 34, 102, 144,
149, 191, 192, 259, 279, 333, 444

Special facilities: Toilet facilities available; access for users
with disabilities

Publications: Annual Report; List of Journal Holdings

Linked organisations

Middlesex University The Service provides library
facilities to the University's staff and students

[216]
Fire Protection Association
FPA

Bastille Court
2 Paris Garden
London SE1 8ND

Borough: Southwark
Telephone: 020 7902 5300
Fax: 020 7902 5301
E-mail: fpa@thefpa.co.uk
World Wide Web: www.thefpa.co.uk

Constitution: Company limited by guarantee

Key staff: Librarian: Judith Rebbeck BA(Hons) ALA, ext
202

Stock and subject coverage: 15,000 documents on fire and
loss prevention; chemical hazards; security; building
design; and risk management. Various journals are
held

Services: Information service; audit services; consultancy
and training; no loans

Availability: Use of library, information service and
journal are all part of the membership package

Hours: 09.30–17.00 Monday to Friday (10.00–16.30 for
visitors)

Transport: Tube: Southwark; Rail: Waterloo, Blackfriars,
London Bridge

Special facilities: Toilet facilities available

Publications: Fire Prevention (journal – 10 p.a.); full list of
publications available on request

Linked organisations

Loss Prevention Council (LPC) The FPA is
under the aegis of the LPC and based at the same
address

[217]
The Florence Nightingale Museum

2 Lambeth Palace Road
London SE1 7EW

Borough: Lambeth
E-mail: alex@florence-nightingale.co.uk
World Wide Web: www.florence-nightingale.co.uk

Constitution: Registered charity

Objectives/purposes: The Museum aims to grow as the
international centre for preserving Florence
Nightingale's heritage and interpreting the relevance
of her life and work for the benefit of present and
future generations

Key staff: Resource Centre Curator: Alex Attewell

Stock and subject coverage: Collections include a collection
of 63 letters from Florence Nightingale; books
written, owned, given and inscribed by Florence
Nightingale; histories of subjects relevant to
Nightingale, the Crimean War, hospitals and nursing;
and biographies. The collection also includes portraits
of Florence Nightingale and of nurses and hospitals
associated with her

Services: Photocopies

Availability: Open to bona fide researchers by
appointment, for reference use. On a first visit visitors
will require a 30 minute consultation with the
Curator for orientation and advice about further
sources of information

Transport: Tube: Lambeth North
Special facilities: Toilet facilities available; access for users with disabilities

Linked organisations

The British Library
London Metropolitan Archives
Both organisations hold substantial collections on Florence Nightingale

[218]
The Food Commission

94 White Lion Street
London N1 9PF
Borough: Islington
Telephone: 020 7837 2250
Fax: 020 7837 1141
E-mail: enquiries@foodcomm.org.uk
World Wide Web: www.foodcomm.org.uk
Constitution: Independent non-profit organisation and registered charity
Objectives/purposes: The Commission campaigns for better food by reporting on topics such as food labelling, additives, pesticides, BSE, BST, baby foods, animal welfare, nutrition, hygiene, irradiation, etc
Stock and subject coverage: Reference library of books, magazines and press cuttings. Material on food issues such as food labelling, additives, pesticides, BSE, BST, irradiation, animal welfare, hygiene, nutrition, genetic engineering, children's food, supermarkets and food policy
Services: Photocopies (charges per page)
Availability: Open to bona fide researchers by appointment, for reference use
Hours: 11.00–18.00 Monday to Friday
Transport: Tube: Angel; Bus: 19, 30, 43, 73, 74
Special facilities: Toilet facilities available; access for users with disabilities – including ramp, lift and toilet facilities
Publications: The Food Magazine (4 p.a. by subscription); books and reports

[219]
Foreign and Commonwealth Office
FCO

World Wide Web: www.fco.gov.uk
Borough: Westminster
Constitution: Government department
Transport: Tube: Westminster, Waterloo, Charing Cross; Rail: Waterloo; Bus: 3, 11, 12, 24, 53, 77A, 88, 109

[219][a]
Foreign and Commonwealth Office Library

King Charles Street
London SW1A 2AH
Telephone: Enquiries: 020 7270 3925; Loans: 020 7270 3025
Fax: 020 7270 3270; 020 7270 3682
Key staff: Chief Librarian: Joy Herring; Senior Librarians: Carole Edwards; Stephen Latham
Stock and subject coverage: The FCO Library embodies the libraries of the former Foreign Office, Colonial Office and Commonwealth Relations Office. Large collection, mainly in European languages, on international relations, international law, diplomacy and the politics, history, administration, economies and law of overseas countries
Services: Photocopies (self-service)
Availability: Public access by appointment only
Hours: 09.30–17.00 Monday to Friday
Special facilities: Toilet facilities available; access for users with disabilities – please contact the Library in advance
Special features: Housed in the historic former Colonial Office library

[219][b]
Legal Library

Room K168
King Charles Street
London SW1A 2AH
Telephone: Enquiries 020 7270 3082
Fax: 020 7270 4259
E-mail: legal@lrdln.mail.fco.gov.uk
Key staff: Librarian: Susan Halls
Stock and subject coverage: Material on International law; European Community law; English law and the law of the UK Overseas Territories. Also contains treaty collections and some Council of Europe cases and treaties
Availability: By appointment only
Hours: 09.30–17.30 Monday to Friday

[219][c]
United Nations Information Resources

King Charles Street
London SW1A 2AH
Telephone: 029 7270 2503/4
Fax: 020 7270 1473
E-mail: docs.und.fco@gtnet.gov.uk
Key staff: Head of Section: Jane Crellin
Stock and subject coverage: United Nations documents from 1946 onwards - Security Council, General Assembly, Economic and Social Council and other bodies. UN yearbooks and handbooks
Hours: 09.30–17.30 Monday to Friday

[220]
Forensic Science Service
FSS

Metropolitan Laboratory
109 Lambeth Road
London SE1 7LP
Borough: Lambeth
Telephone: 020 7230 6255
Fax: 020 7230 6003
E-mail: isged@fss.org.uk
World Wide Web: www.forensic.gov.uk
Constitution: Government funded body
Key staff: Library Services Manager
Stock and subject coverage: About 5,000 books and 250 current scientific journals, in the subject area of forensic science (this covers aspects of serology, immunology, drugs and toxicology, trace element analysis, fibre analysis, fingerprints and firearms)

Services: Enquiry and literature service provide for UK forensic science laboratories and Home Office pathologists. Loans and photocopies supplied on request to UK forensic science laboratories. Computerised literature retrieval system for forensic science. Monthly current awareness bulletin

Availability: To authorised law enforcement agencies; not open to personnel from outside the forensic science service, but serious outside enquiries accepted (charges may apply)

Hours: 08.00-17.30 Monday to Friday

Transport: Tube: Waterloo, Lambeth North; Rail: Waterloo

Special facilities: Refreshment and toilet facilities available

Publications: FORS - scientific literature CD-ROM; Forsight - FSS current awareness bulletin

[221]
Fostering Network
formerly National Foster Care Association

87 Blackfriars Road
London SE1 8HA

Borough: Southwark

Telephone: 020 7620 6400

Fax: 020 7620 6401

E-mail: info@fostering.net

Constitution: Registered charity

Objectives/purposes: National watchdog for standards in foster care

Key staff: Information Officer and Librarians

Stock and subject coverage: Materials on foster care and state child care

Services: Photocopies (charges made); database searches

Availability: Access open to all bona fide researchers for reference only

Hours: By appointment, telephone in advance

Transport: Tube: Southwark; Rail: Waterloo; Bus: 45, 63

Special facilities: Refreshment and toilet facilities available

Publications: Foster Care (4 p.a.); Annual Report; National Standards for Foster Care (published on behalf of UK Joint Working Party on Foster Care)

[222]
FPA
(formerly Family Planning Association)

2-12 Pentonville Road
London N1 9FP

Borough: Islington

Telephone: 020 7923 5228

Fax: 020 7837 3034

E-mail: libraryandinformation@fpa.org.uk

World Wide Web: www.fpa.org.uk

Constitution: Registered charity with voluntary subscribing membership

Key staff: Information and Library Officer: Margaret McGovern

Stock and subject coverage: 3,000 books and publications, 70 journals, and files. Material on all aspects of birth control, fertility, sexuality and reproductive health

Services: Reference only; no loans; photocopying service; enquiries

Availability: Open to all by appointment

Hours: 09.00-17.00 Monday to Thursday; 09.00-16.30 Friday

Transport: Tube: Angel; Bus: 4, 19, 30, 38, 43, 56, 73

Special facilities: Toilet facilities available; access for users with disabilities

Publications: Annual Review; Contraceptive Education Bulletin (4 p.a.); Sexual Health Agenda (members newsletter); factsheets

[223]
Garrick Club

15 Garrick Street
London WC2E 9AY

Borough: Westminster

Telephone: 020 7379 6478

Constitution: Private club

Key staff: Librarian: Enid Foster MBE

Stock and subject coverage: Material related to British drama and the theatre. The collection is far from comprehensive, but it is particularly strong in the theatrical history of the late 18th and early 19th centuries and includes letters, prints, playbills and theatre programmes, as well as books and pamphlets

Services: No photocopies or microfilming of Library material. Photographic copies can be made by arrangement with the Librarian but material may not be published in any form without permission in writing from the Library Committee

Availability: Members of the Club and other bona fide researchers by arrangement. Visiting scholars are asked to write to the Librarian stating the subject of their research. If material on that subject is available, an appointment can be made. The Club asks a fee of £5 from visiting scholars and reserves the right to request a further fee should use of the Library be extensive

Hours: 10.00-13.00, 14.00-17.00 Wednesday only

Transport: Tube: Leicester Square; Rail: Charing Cross

Special facilities: Toilet facilities available

Special features: Theatre Library started in 1831

[224]
Geffrye Museum

Kingsland Road
Shoreditch
London E2 8EA

Borough: Hackney

Telephone: 020 7739 9893 (main switchboard)
020 7739 8543 (recorded information)

Fax: 020 7729 5647

E-mail: info@geffrye-museum.org.uk

World Wide Web: www.geffrye-museum.org.uk

Constitution: Registered charity; company limited by guarantee; and independent non-profit distributing organisation. The Geffrye is an independent trust, grant-aided by the Government

Objectives/purposes: Museum of English domestic interiors also period gardens relating to interior roomsets. Special interest in English furniture and history of London furniture trades

Key staff: Director: David Dewing; Keeper of Collections: Eleanor John

Stock and subject coverage: English domestic interiors, furniture and decorative arts from 1600 to present day. Archive material on the East End furniture trade and English domestic interiors

Services: Photocopier (limited availability, by arrangement, charges made)

Availability: Access open to all bona fide researchers. Some material on open shelves for the general public, some for access by appointment only. All items for reference only. Service is generally free

Hours: 10.00-17.00 Tuesday to Saturday; 12.00-17.00 Sundays and Bank Holiday Mondays; closed Mondays (except Bank holidays), Good Friday, Christmas Eve and Christmas Day, Boxing Day and New Year's Day

Transport: Tube: Liverpool Street (Bishopsgate exit), then bus 149 or 242, Old Street (exit 2) then bus 243 or 15 minute walk; Rail: Liverpool Street; buses: 67, 149, 242, 243

Special facilities: Refreshment and toilet facilities available on site; access for users with disabilities – wheelchair access, disabled toilet facility

Special features: The museum is housed in Grade I listed 18th century former almshouses and has an extension designed by Branson Coates Architects, which opened in November 1998. The Museum's gardens, which are open from April to October, include an award-winning herb garden and a series of period gardens laid out to show London town house gardens from 1600-1910

[225]
General Optical Council
41 Harley Street
London W1G 8DT
Borough: Westminster
Telephone: 020 7580 3898
Fax: 020 7436 3525
E-mail: goc@optical.org
Constitution: Independent non-profit organisation
Key staff: Registrar: Peter Coe
Stock and subject coverage: Annual register of registered optometrists and dispensing opticians, and list of enrolled bodies corporate
Services: Registers and lists can be supplied in computer media
Availability: Open to anyone, but an appointment is advisable
Hours: 09.00-17.00 Monday to Thursday; 09.00-16.45 Friday
Transport: Tube: Oxford Circus, Bond Street

[226]
The Geological Society of London
Burlington House
Piccadilly
London W1J 0BG
Borough: Westminster
Telephone: 020 7734 5673
Fax: 020 7439 3470
E-mail: library@geolsoc.org.uk
World Wide Web: www.geolsoc.org.uk
Constitution: Learned society; registered charity and association with voluntary subscribing membership
Key staff: Librarian: Miss S Meredith; Assistant Librarian: Miss WA Cawthorne

Stock and subject coverage: 300,000 volumes; 35,000 geological maps; 800 current journals; 3,500 rare books; Murchison manuscript collection. Covers earth sciences and palaeontology

Services: Photocopies, microfiche reader, online catalogue (also available via website)

Availability: Open to bona fide researchers by appointment only. Material is for reference use only and some restrictions on services apply. There is a daily charge for use of the Library. The Archive Collection can be consulted by appointment with the Archivist

Hours: 09.30-17.30 Monday to Friday
Transport: Tube: Green Park, Piccadilly
Special facilities: Refreshment and toilet facilities available
Publications: A Brief Guide to the Geological Society Library; Recent Additions list

[227]
German-British Chamber of Industry and Commerce
Mecklenburg House
16 Buckingham Gate
London SW1E 6LB
Borough: Westminster
Telephone: 020 7976 4100
Fax: 020 7976 4101
E-mail: mail@ahk-london.co.uk
World Wide Web: www.ahk-london.co.uk
www.germanbritishchamber.co.uk
Constitution: Company limited by guarantee; association with voluntary subscribing membership
Key staff: Marketing Manager: Sven Riemann
Stock and subject coverage: Details of UK companies: size, turnover, main activities and contact details; details of German companies: size, turnover, main activities and contact details; information about UK and German associations; magazines and newspapers
Services: CD-ROM of German subsidiary companies in the UK; specialist publications on British-German trade (list available)
Availability: No reading room available. Telephone and written enquiries accepted (written enquiries preferred); charges to non-members
Hours: 10.00-17.00 Monday to Friday
Transport: Tube: Victoria, St James's Park, Green Park; Rail: Victoria
Special facilities: Access for users with disabilities

[228]
German Historical Institute Library/Deutsches Historisches Institut
GHIL
17 Bloomsbury Square
London WC1A 2LP
Borough: Camden
Telephone: 020 7404 5486
Fax: 020 7404 5573
E-mail: library-ghil@ghil.co.uk
World Wide Web: www.ghil.co.uk
Constitution: Independent non-profit organisation

Key staff: Ms Anna Hamá Klauk, Mr Christoph Schönberger

Stock and subject coverage: Ca. 64,000 books (mainly in German) on the history of Germany, Britain, and Anglo-German relations. Special attention to the Third Reich and post-war Germany. Ca. 220 journals on German and English history, current English and German newspapers and weekly journals

Services: Microfilm and microfiche reader-printer; photocopies; catalogue available via internet

Availability: Open to the general public free of charge for reference only. Readers' tickets are issued - passport photograph required on first visit

Hours: 10.00-20.00 Monday and Thursday; 10.00-17.00 Tuesday, Wednesday and Friday

Transport: Tube: Holborn, Tottenham Court Road

Special facilities: Refreshment and toilet facilities; access for users with disabilities – lift to all floors but steps to front door

Special features: House designed by John Nash in the late 17th century, with impressive original ceilings and bookshelves installed by The Pharmaceutical Society of Great Britain, which occupied the building for over 130 years

Publications: Bulletin (2 p.a.); Annual lecture series - Veröffentlichungen des Deutschen Historischen Instituts London

[229]
Glass and Glazing Federation
GGF

44-48 Borough High Street
London SE1 1XB
Borough: Southwark
Telephone: 020 7403 7177
Fax: 020 7357 7458
World Wide Web: www.ggf.org.uk
Constitution: Trade association
Key staff: Head of Public Relations: Catherine Hogan; PR Assistant: Lis Chapelhow
Stock and subject coverage: A range of leaflets, booklets and technical data sheets on glass-related topics from double glazing and home extensions to conservatories and mirrors. Also videos
Services: Advice on all matters to do with the industry (especially if a member company is involved); experienced technical team available; no market information or statistics
Availability: Written requests only
Hours: 09.00-17.00
Publications: Booklets; leaflets; guide books; videos. List available on request

[230]
Goethe-Institut Library

50 Princes Gate
London SW7 2PH
Borough: Westminster
Telephone: 020 7596 4040
Fax: 020 7594 0230
E-mail: library@london.goethe.org
World Wide Web: www.goethe.de/gr/lon/enibib.htm
Constitution: Registered society, funded by the German government

Objectives/purposes: The Library provides information about Germany and German culture

Key staff: Head Librarian: Gerlinde Buck; Deputy Librarian: Simone Mühlen; Deputy Librarian and Teachers' Centre: Rachel Kirkwood; Information Officer: Gunhild Muschenheim; Lending Service: Clare Muddyman; Teachers' Centre: Silvia Grieser

Stock and subject coverage: The Library holds 25,000 volumes (5,000 in English), 131 journals, 15 newspapers, 3,300 AV-media (including 1,700 videos). All fields of the humanities are covered with an emphasis on German literature and language, history, social sciences and the arts

Services: Two video screens, CD player and cassette players; photocopies (10 pence per sheet)

Availability: Open to the public; membership fees for 3, 6 or 12 months, contact the Library for details

Hours: 12.00-20.00 Monday to Thursday; 11.00-17.00 Saturday; closed Friday

Transport: Tube: South Kensington

Special facilities: Refreshment and toilet facilities available; access for users with disabilities by arrangement

Publications: Catalogues of selected material held in the library (mainly media); German Plays in English Translation

[231]
Goldsmiths College Library

New Cross
London SE14 6NW
Borough: Lewisham
Telephone: 020 7919 7150
Fax: 020 7919 7165
E-mail: library@gold.ac.uk
World Wide Web: www.goldsmiths.ac.uk
Constitution: Department of a university
Key staff: Director of Information Services: Joan Pateman; Deputy Librarian: Sacha Shaw
Stock and subject coverage: Arts, humanities, social sciences, education, mathematical and computing sciences
Services: Self service photocopiers
Availability: Reference access to books and journals, but not audiovisual materials, for all bona fide researchers. Vacation readers tickets available on application. Day tickets to a maximum of three per term available in term-time. Proof of identity must be shown when applying for a visitor's ticket
Hours: Term-time and Easter vacation: 09.15-20.45 Monday to Friday; 09.30-17.00 Saturday Other vacations: 09.15-16.45
Transport: Tube and Rail: New Cross, New Cross Gate; Bus: 21, 36, 53, 171, 172
Special facilities: Toilet facilities available; access for users with disabilities
Linked organisations
University of London School of the University

[232]
The Goldsmiths' Company

Goldsmiths' Hall
Foster Lane
London EC2V 6BN
Borough: Corporation of London
Telephone: 020 7606 7010

Fax: 020 7606 1511
E-mail: the.library@thegoldsmiths.co.uk
World Wide Web: www.thegoldsmiths.co.uk
Constitution: One of the 12 Great Livery Companies of the City of London
Key staff: The Librarian
Stock and subject coverage: Archives (dating from the 14th century), books, journals, negatives and slides on silver, jewellery, regalia, assaying and hallmarking. Photographic collection of 5,000 slides and over 10,000 photographs on named modern jewellers and silversmiths and their works, and on antique British and foreign silver and jewellery.
Services: Photocopying
Availability: Available, by appointment, to members of the Company and the general public
Hours: 10.00-16.45 Monday to Friday
Transport: Tube: Barbican, St Paul's, Bank, Cannon Street, Mansion House; Rail: Cannon Street, Blackfriars
Publications: Goldsmiths' Company Review (annual); list of publications available on request

[233]
Gray's Inn Library
The Library
5 South Square
Gray's Inn
London WC1R 5ET
Borough: Camden
Telephone: 020 7458 7822
Fax: 020 7458 7850
E-mail: library@graysinn.org.uk
World Wide Web: www.graysinn.org.uk
Constitution: Independent non-profit distributing organisation
Key staff: Librarian: Theresa Thom
Stock and subject coverage: Current law collection, primarily on English law; specialist collection of public international law; Archives of Gray's Inn; Records of Barnard's Inn and Staple Inn
Services: Photocopies; microform reader-printer; CD-ROMs; online facilities; access to the computerised catalogues of other Inns; internet document delivery for barrister members and for student members on a trial basis (contact library or see website to check if this facility is available)
Availability: Legal reference collection open to Gray's Inn members, both students and barristers. Barrister members of other Inns also admitted. Others may be admitted by arrangment. Researchers seeking access to the Inn Archives should apply in advance (references are required)
Hours: 09.00-20.00. Reduced hours during legal vacations (check website for details)
Transport: Tube: Chancery Lane
Special facilities: Refreshment facilities for members only; toilet facilities
Publications: In-house library guides

[234]
Great Britain-China Centre
GBCC
15 Belgrave Square
London SW1X 8PS
Borough: Westminster
Telephone: 020 7235 6696
Fax: 020 7245 6885
E-mail: contact@gbcc.org.uk
World Wide Web: www.gbcc.org.uk
Constitution: Non-departmental public body (NDPB) of the Foreign Office. Non-profit distributing organisation with voluntary subscribing membership
Objectives/purposes: To promote cultural relations between Britain and the People's Republic of China
Key staff: Director: Katie Lee; Chairperson: David Brewer; President: Lord Howe of Aberavon; Head of Information Services: Laura Rivkin
Stock and subject coverage: English language collection covering all subjects concerning China, except trade and applied science. The collection is particularly strong in contemporary subjects and the Cultural Revolution. Audiovisual holdings include cassette tapes, slides, videos and Chinese arts and crafts for loan to schools
Services: Photocopies; careers and other briefing advice available for a fee, or free to members
Availability: Public reference. Materials are circulated to members only (exceptions may be made for schools); deposits required for AV materials. Visitors are advised to telephone in advance
Hours: 10.00-17.30 Monday to Friday; librarian available Wednesday to Friday
Transport: Tube: Hyde Park Corner, Victoria; Rail: Victoria; Bus: C1, 2, 8, 9, 10, 14, 16, 19, 22, 36, 38, 52, 73, 74, 82, 137
Special facilities: Refreshment facilities (drinks only); toilet facilities available
Special features: The Library was started by the Society for Anglo-Chinese Understanding in the 1960s. The GBCC took over its management in 1990 and continues to expand the collection
Publications: China Review (3 p.a.); Annual Report; Directory of British Organisations with a China Interest, 4th ed., 1999; information and reading lists
Linked organisations

Great Britain-China Educational Trust (GBCET) Registered charity administered by the GB-China Centre

[235]
Greater London Association of Disabled People
GLAD
336 Brixton Road
London SW9 7AA
Borough: Lambeth
Telephone: 020 7346 5800
020 7346 5819 (information line)
020 7326 4554 (minicom)
Fax: 020 7346 8844
E-mail: info@glad.org.uk
World Wide Web: www.glad.org.uk
Constitution: Registered charity and company limited by guarantee
Objectives/purposes: To gain equality for all disabled people in London and promote the positive contribution that disabled people make to society
Key staff: Information Officer: Poppy Hasted

Stock and subject coverage: Coverage of all non-medical disability issues with particular emphasis on discrimination. Newspaper cuttings service (Disability Update)

Services: Photocopies (charges made)

Availability: Material is available for reference only. Visitors must contact GLAD in advance to arrange a time and date to visit the library

Hours: 09.00-12.30, 13.30-17.00 Monday to Friday

Transport: Tube and Rail: Brixton; Bus: 3, 109, 133, 159

Special facilities: Refreshment facilities (limited hours); toilet facilities available.
Building fully accessible for users with disabilities, minicom available for people unable to use voice telephones. Information (including GLAD publications) are available on audio tape and some in braille. Induction loop available on request

Publications: London Disability News (10 p.a.); Disability Update (fortnightly current awareness bulletin); Boadicea, newsletter for disabled women (6 p.a.)

Linked organisations
British Council of Disabled People (BCODP)
London Voluntary Service Council (LVSC)
Rights Now! Campaign
Royal Association for Disability and Rehabilitation (RADAR)

GLAD is a member of all the above organisations

[236]
Greater London Authority
GLA
City Hall
The Queens Walk
London SE1 2AA
Borough: Southwark
Telephone: 020 7983 4666
020 7983 4458 (minicom)
E-mail: rlenquiry@london.gov.uk
World Wide Web: www.london.gov.uk
Constitution: Part of the Greater London Authority – the Library is the successor to the former London Research Centre Research Library. The London Research Centre was absorbed into the GLA in 2000
Key staff: Head of Research Library: Annabel Davies
Stock and subject coverage: Extensive collection of books and reports, including grey literature, journals, statistics and other material. Collections on urban and social policy, including planning, transport, social and community issues, environment, economic development, education and training, housing, police, fire and emergency planning, health and public health, culture
Services: Enquiry services; online databases, including Acompline and Urbaline; Urbadisc CD-ROM; interlibrary loans and current awareness services
Availability: The GLA Research Library provides library and information services to the GLA. Selected services are available to other organisations – some on a charged basis. Enquirers should telephone or e-mail for further information
Hours: 09.00-17.00 Monday to Friday

[237]
Greenwich (London Borough of Greenwich)
Greenwich Library and Information Service
Support Services
c/o Plumstead Library
Plumstead High Street
London SE18 1JL
Telephone: 020 8317 4466
Fax: 020 8317 4868
E-mail: libraries@greenwich.gov.uk
World Wide Web: www.greenwich.gov.uk
Constitution: Public library funded by local authority
Key staff: Head of Community Services: Margaret Snook; Group Library Managers: Paul Clarke, Martin Stone, Steve Woods
Special features: The library service is part of the Directorate of Public Services, Greenwich Council. London Borough of Greenwich does not have a main central library. There are three district libraries (Blackheath, Eltham and Woolwich – listed first) and ten model libraries. Additional services are provided by the Local History Library, Mobile and Home Service, Ethnic Library Service, Project Loans (service to schools) and the library service to Belmarsh Prison

[237][a]
Blackheath Library
Old Dover Road
London SE3 7BT
Telephone: 020 8858 1131
Fax: 020 8853 3615
Key staff: Senior Library Manager
Stock and subject coverage: Reference and children's collections
Services: Internet access; photocopies (black and white and colour); CD-ROMs for children
Hours: 10.00-19.00 Monday and Thursday; 10.00-17.30 Tuesday and Friday; 10.00-17.00 Saturday
Transport: Rail: Westcombe Park Station; Bus: 53, 54, 108, 202, 286, 380, 386, 422
Special facilities: Access for users with disabilities – wheelchair access, low level shelving, disabled parking bay, disabled toilet; induction loop

[237][b]
Eltham Library
Eltham High Street
London SE9 1TS
Telephone: 020 8850 2268
Fax: 020 8850 1368
Key staff: Senior Library Manager
Stock and subject coverage: Reference and children's collection
Services: Internet access; photocopies (black and white and colour); CD-ROMs for children; small dyslexia collection for adults and children
Hours: 10.00-19.00 Monday and Thursday; 10.00-17.30 Tuesday and Friday; 10.00-17.00 Saturday
Transport: Rail: Eltham (one mile); Bus: B16, 124, 126, 132, 160, 161, 233, 286, 321

Special facilities: Access for users with disabilities –
wheelchair access (side door, ring bell for attention),
low level shelving, induction loop

[237][c]
Woolwich Library and Woolwich Reference Library
Calderwood Street
Woolwich SE18 6QZ
Telephone: 020 8921 5750
020 8316 6663 (Reference Library only)
Fax: 020 8316 1645
Key staff: Senior Library Manager
Stock and subject coverage: General public library stock and
Borough's main reference collection
Services: Internet access; photocopies (black and white
and colour); CD-ROMs, microfilm/fiche reader
Hours: 10.00-19.00 Monday and Thursday; 10.00-17.30
Tuesday and Friday; 10.00-17.30 Wednesday
(Lending Library only); 10.00-17.00 Saturday
Transport: Rail: Woolwich Arsenal; Bus: 51, 53, 54, 96, 99,
122, 161, 177, 178, 180, 244, 291, 380, 422, 469, 472
Special facilities: Access for users with disabilities –
wheelchair access (not to first floor reference library),
low level shelving, induction loop system

[237][d]
Abbey Wood Library
Eynsham Drive
London SE2 9PT
Telephone: 020 7130 4185
Key staff: Library Manager
Stock and subject coverage: Adult and children's collections;
videos and CD-ROMs
Services: Photocopies
Hours: 14.00-19.00 Monday and Thursday; 10.00-13.00,
14.00-17.30 Tuesday and Friday; 10.00-13.00, 14.00-
17.00 Saturday
Transport: Rail: Abbey Wood
Special facilities: Access for users with disabilities – street
level entrance, induction loop, low level shelving

[237][e]
Charlton Library
Charlton House
Charlton Road
London SE7 8RE
Telephone: 020 8319 2525
Key staff: Library Manager
Stock and subject coverage: Adult and children's collections;
videos and CDs
Services: Photocopies
Hours: 14.00-19.00 Monday and Thursday; 10.00-12.30,
13.30-17.30 Tuesday and Friday; 10.00-12.30, 13.30-
17.00 Saturday
Transport: Rail: Charlton
Special facilities: Access for users with disabilities – ramp
access

[237][f]
Claude Ramsey Library
Thamesmere Leisure Centre
London SE28 8DT
Telephone: 020 8310 4246

Key staff: Library Manager
Stock and subject coverage: Adult and children's collections;
videos, CD-ROMs and CDs
Services: Photocopies
Hours: 14.00-19.00 Monday and Thursday; 10.00-12.30,
13.30-17.30 Wednesday and Friday; 10.00-12.30,
13.30-17.00 Saturday
Special facilities: Access for users with disabilities – street
level entrance, low level shelving

[237][g]
Coldharbour Library
William Barefoot Drive
London SE9 3AY
Telephone: 020 8857 7346
Key staff: Library Manager
Stock and subject coverage: Adult and children's collections;
videos and CD-ROMs
Services: Photocopies
Hours: 14.00-17.30 Monday; 10.00-13.00, 14.00-17.30
Tuesday and Friday; 14.00-19.00, Thursday
Transport: Rail: Elmstead Woods
Special facilities: Access for users with disabilities – ramp
access, low level shelving, disabled parking bay

[237][h]
East Greenwich Library
Woolwich Road
London SE10 0RL
Telephone: 020 8858 6656
Key staff: Library Manager
Stock and subject coverage: Adult and children's collections;
videos and CDs
Services: Photocopies
Hours: 14.00-19.00 Monday; 10.00-13.00, 14.00-17.30
Tuesday; 10.00-13.00, 14.00-19.00 Thursday; 14.00-
17.30 Friday; 10.00-13.00, 14.00-17.00 Saturday
Transport: Rail: Westcombe Park
Special facilities: Access for users with disabilities – ramp
access, low level shelving, disabled parking bay

[237][i]
Ferrier Library
Telemann Square
London SE3 9YR
Telephone: 020 8856 5149
Key staff: Library Manager
Stock and subject coverage: Adult and children's collections;
videos
Services: Photocopies
Hours: 09.00-13.00 Monday to Saturday
Transport: Rail: Kidbrooke
Special facilities: Access for users with disabilities – street
level entrance, induction loop, low level shelving

[237][j]
Greenwich Local History Library
Woodlands
90 Mycenae Road
Blackheath
London SE3 7SE
Telephone: 020 8858 4631
Fax: 020 8293 4721
E-mail: local.history@greenwich.gov.uk

Objectives/purposes: Collecting, preserving and making available for study records relating to the communities within the London Borough of Greenwich

Key staff: Senior Library Manager: Julian Watson; Librarian: Caroline Warhurst; Library Assistants: Frances Ward, Jenny O'Keefe, Gwyn Roberts

Stock and subject coverage: Documents relating to the history, topography, and people of Deptford, Greenwich, Charlton, Woolwich, Plumstead, Shooters Hill, Eltham, Kidbrooke and Blackheath. Books, pamphlets, maps, illustrations, local authority archives, manuscripts, microfilms and fiche, audiotapes and video tapes. The illustration collection includes ca. 900 watercolours and drawings of the Borough from the 18th century onwards. The Library houses the Martin Collection of ca. 10,000 items relating to the history of Blackheath, Greenwich, Kidbrooke, Charlton and Lewisham. It is the official repository for the records of the London Borough of Greenwich and its predecessors

Services: Photocopies and photography (charged); fax machine

Availability: Free access for reference only. Prior notice is required for use of microfilm or fiche readers and for some categories of archives

Hours: 09.00-17.30 Monday and Tuesday; 09.00-20.00 Thursday; 09.00-17.00 Saturday

Transport: Tube: North Greenwich (then bus 108 or 422); Rail: Westcombe Park Station; Bus: 53, 54, 286, 380

Special facilities: Toilet facilities available; limited access for users with disabilities – ramp to ground floor only – but staff will assist as much as possible

Special features: Woodlands is a Georgian villa designed in 1774 by George Gibson, for John Julius Angerstein, a Lloyds underwriter and collector of old master paintings. On his death in 1823 the Government bought his London House, 100 Pall Mall, and his collection of pictures. The house was opened as the first National Gallery

Publications: Family History in Greenwich: a Guide to Sources by Len Reilly, 1991 (revised guide on website, access via A-Z index); Woolwich Reviewed by Julian Watson, 1986; Free for All by Julian Watson and Wendy Gregory, 1993; In the Meantime: a Book on Greenwich by Julian Watson and Kit Gregory, 1988; The Twentieth Century: Greenwich by Barbara Ludlow and Julian Watson, 1999; Sugar, Spices and Human Cargo: an Early Black History of Greenwich by Joan Anim-Addo, 1996

[237][k]
New Eltham Library

Southwood Road
London SE9 3QT
Telephone: 020 8850 2322
Key staff: Library Manager
Stock and subject coverage: Adult and children's collections; videos
Services: Photocopies; internet access
Hours: 14.00-19.00 Monday and Thursday; 10.00-13.00, 14.00-17.30 Tuesday and Friday; 10,00-13.00, 14.00-17.00 Saturday
Transport: Rail: New Eltham
Special facilities: Access for users with disabilities – ramp

access, low level shelving, induction loop

[237][l]
Plumstead Library

Plumstead High Street
London SE18 1JL
Telephone: 020 8854 1728
Key staff: Library Manager
Stock and subject coverage: Adult and children's collections; videos; music cassettes; DVDs and CD-ROMs
Services: Photocopies
Hours: 10.00-13.00, 14.00-19.00 Monday and Thursday; 10.00-13.00, 14.00-17.30 Tuesday and Friday; 10.00-13.00, 14.00-17.00 Saturday
Transport: Rail: Plumstead
Special facilities: Access for users with disabilities – low level shelving, induction loop

[237][m]
Slade Library

Erindale
London SE18 2QQ
Telephone: 020 8854 7900
Key staff: Library Manager
Stock and subject coverage: Adult and children's collections; videos
Services: Photocopies
Hours: 14.00-19.00 Monday and Thursday; 10.00-13.00, 14.00-17.30 Tuesday and Friday; 10.00-13.00, 14.00-17.00 Saturday
Transport: Rail: Plumstead
Special facilities: Access for users with disabilities – ramp access, low level shelving, induction loop

[237][n]
West Greenwich Library

Greenwich High Road
London SE10 8NN
Telephone: 020 8858 4289
Key staff: Library Manager
Stock and subject coverage: Adult and children's collections; videos and CDs
Services: Photocopies
Hours: 14.00-19.00 Monday; 10.00-13.00, 14.00-17.30 Tuesday; 10,00-13.00, 14.00-19.00 Thursday; 14.00-17.30 Friday; 10.00-13.00, 14.00-17.00 Saturday
Transport: Rail: Greenwich
Special facilities: Access for users with disabilities – induction loop

[238]
The Guide Association

Commonwealth Headquarters
17-19 Buckingham Palace Road
London SW1W 0PT
Borough: Westminster
Telephone: 020 7834 6242
Fax: 020 7828 8317
World Wide Web: www.guides.org.uk
Constitution: Registered charity with voluntary subscribing membership
Objectives/purposes: Part of a worldwide movement, the Guide Association helps girls and young women to fulfil their potential to take an active and responsible

role in society through its distinctive, stimulating and enjoyable programme of activities delivered by trained volunteer leaders. Guiding for girls takes place in four sections: Rainbow Guides; Brownie Guides; Guides and the Senior Section

Key staff: Archivist: Margaret Courtney

Stock and subject coverage: The Archive holds all records and publications from 1910. Stock includes ca. 5,000 books; registrations; photographic collection 1908 to date; letters relating to the Baden Powell family; training material; uniforms; badges; exhibits; film; videos and press cuttings

Services: Photocopies; microfiche reader; collection on computer

Availability: Available to all bona fide researchers by appointment (references required). No research charge

Hours: 10.00–16.00 Monday to Friday

Transport: Tube, Rail and Coach: Victoria

Special facilities: Toilet facilities; access for users with disabilities

Special features: Contact the Guide Heritage Centre, The Guide Association, 17-19 Buckingham Palace Road, London SW1W 0PT (tel: 020 7834 6242)

Publications: Fact sheets on the history and founders of the Guide Association; Annual Report; magazines include Guiding (monthly) and Brownie (monthly)

[239]
Guy's and St Thomas' NHS Trust, Medical Toxicology Unit

Avonley Road
New Cross
London SE14 5ER
Borough: Lewisham
Telephone: 020 7771 5364
Fax: 020 7771 5363
E-mail: helaina.checketts@gstt.sthames.nhs.uk
World Wide Web: www.medtox.org.uk
Constitution: Government funded body
Key staff: Librarian: Helaina Checketts BA MLib BSc
Stock and subject coverage: Clinical toxicology; pharmacology; and analytical chemistry
Services: Photocopying; librarian mediated literature searches, both charged; internet access; access to Medline and Toxline
Availability: Open to bona fide researchers, strictly by appointment only
Hours: 09.00–17.00
Transport: Tube: New Cross Gate; Bus: 21, 53, 172
Special facilities: Toilet facilities; access for users with disabilities – but no wheelchair accessible toilet

Linked organisations

Guy's and St Thomas' NHS Trust, Clinical Services Group Part of the Group

[240]
Hackney (London Borough of Hackney)

Hackney Library Services
World Wide Web: www.hackney.gov.uk
Constitution: Public library funded by local authority

Key staff: Head of Library Services: Heather Newham; Principal Librarians: John Pateman, Angela Fletcher, Bethan Williams

Availability: Open to residents and individuals working in the borough. Free reference and lending services, charges for loan of CDs, cassettes and videos

Note: A new Technology and Learning Centre is being constructed in Mare Street and will be a major learning resource for the borough

[240][a]
Hackney Central Library and Reference Library

Technology and Learning Centre
1 Reading Lane
London E8 1GP
Telephone: 020 8356 4359
Fax: 020 8356 2531
E-mail: hackref@gw.hackney.gov.uk
Key staff: Reference Librarian: Frank Merrigan; Reference Librarian: Jill Keeling
Stock and subject coverage: General reference and loan collections, music and children's libraries. The Library also houses the Three Continents Liberation Collection including books reflecting the liberation struggles in Africa, Asia and Latin America as well as in the Caribbean and Britain. Materials are available in a range of languages including Urdu, Punjabi, Gujarati, Turkish, Greek, Chinese and Vietnamese. The reference library has a European Information Collection and a London and local history collection. Also holds law reports and Halsbury's Statutes. Large selection of newspapers, magazines and journals
Services: PCs for free public use with internet access (booking necessary); photocopies (b&w and colour); CD-ROMs; online database searching, Black writers reading group, homework club, under 5's storytime sessions, toy library
Hours: 09.30–20.00 Monday, Tuesday and Thursday; 10.00–20.00 Friday; 09.00–17.00 Saturday
Toy Library: 10.30–12.00 Tuesday; Under 5's storytime sessions: 11.00–12.00 Friday
Transport: Rail: Hackney Central, Hackney Downs
Special facilities: Fully accessible for users with disabilities

[240][b]
Clapton Library

Northwold Road
London E5 8RA
Telephone: 020 8356 2570
Fax: 020 8806 7849
Key staff: Site Supervisor
Stock and subject coverage: Adult and children's library collections. Stock includes books, newspapers, periodicals and audiovisual recorded materials for loan and reference plus an Islamic collection
Services: Internet access, photocopier and fax service; monthly readers' group called 'Teen Scene'
Hours: 09.30–20.00 Monday, Tuesday and Thursday; 10.00–20.00 Friday; 09.00–17.00 Saturday
Transport: Rail: Clapton; Bus: 106, 253
Special facilities: Limited access for users with disabilities. Building has many unavoidable steps and no wheelchair access
Publications: Range of local history publications available

[240][c]
Clr James Library
24–30 Dalston Lane
London E8 3AZ
Telephone: 020 8356 1665
Fax: 020 8254 4655
Key staff: Site Supervisor
Stock and subject coverage: Quick reference collection, local information, adult and children's collections; videos and audio materials
Services: Internet access, photocopier; hall for hire; homework club; under 5's storytime sessions
Hours: 09.30–20.00 Monday, Tuesday and Thursday; 10.00–20.00 Friday: 09.00–17.00 Saturday
Homework club: 16.00–18.00 Tuesday (term-time only); Under 5's storytime with toy library: 10.30–12.30 Friday
Transport: Tube: Old Street; Rail: Dalston, Kingsland; Bus: 22A, 22B, 30, 38, 56, 67, 76, 149, 236, 243, 243A, 277
Special facilities: Limited access for users with disabilities – ramp available; toilet with access for users with disabilities; parking for blue badge holders nearby

[240][d]
Homerton Library
Homerton High Street
London E9 6AS
Telephone: 020 8356 1690
Fax: 020 8525 7945
Key staff: Site Supervisor
Stock and subject coverage: Quick reference collection, local information and adult and children's collections
Services: Photocopier and fax service; internet access; adult literacy advice; homework club; under 5's storytime; hall for hire
Hours: 09.30–20.00 Monday, Tuesday and Thursday; 10.00–20.00 Friday; 09.00–17.00 Saturday
Under 5's storytime: 11.00–12.00 Tuesday
Transport: Rail: Homerton; Bus: S2, W15, 220, 236, 276
Special facilities: Access for users with disabilities – car parking nearby, lift available, level or ramped access via the main or side door

[240][e]
Shoreditch Library
80 Hoxton Street
London N1 6LP
Telephone: 020 8356 4350
Fax: 020 8356 4353
Key staff: Site Supervisor
Stock and subject coverage: Open learning, quick reference, local information and children's collections, books in community languages
Services: Internet access; colour photocopier and fax service; word processing and desktop publishing facilities; music practice room for hire
Hours: 09.30–20.00 Monday, Tuesday and Thursday; 10.00–20.00 Friday; 09.00–17.00 Saturday
Under 5's storytime with toy library: 11.00–12.00 Thursday
Transport: Tube and Rail: Liverpool Street, Old Street; Bus: 5, 22A, 22B, 26, 35, 43, 47, 55, 67, 78, 149, 243, 243A, 505
Special facilities: Access for users with disabilities – parking for blue badge holders nearby, lift available, level or ramped access via the main or side door

[240][f]
Stamford Hill Library
Portland Avenue
London N16 6SB
Telephone: 020 8356 2573
Fax: 020 8809 5986
Key staff: Site Supervisor
Stock and subject coverage: Torah collection for the Jewish community; quick reference, local information, and adult and children's collections
Services: Internet access; photocopier and fax service; homework club; under 5's storytime sessions; readers group; study area; hall for hire
Hours: 09.30–20.00 Monday, Tuesday and Thursday; 10.00–20.00 Friday; 09.00–17.00 Saturday; 13.00–17.00 Sunday
Homework club: 16.00–18.00 Tuesday (term-time only); Under 5's storytime 10.30–12.00 Friday; Readers group: 14.00–15.30 first Tuesday of each month
Transport: Tube: Manor House; Rail: Stamford Hill; Bus: 24, 67, 73, 76, 149, 243, 243A, 253
Special facilities: Access for users with disabilities – including adapted toilet, ramps

[240][g]
Stoke Newington Library
Stoke Newington Church Street
Hackney
London N16 0JS
Telephone: 020 8356 5230/5231
Fax: 020 8356 5237/5233
Key staff: Site Supervisor
Stock and subject coverage: Disabilities information; HIV resource centre; local history collection; reference collection; adults and children's collections
Services: Internet access; photocopier and fax facilities; gallery and small meeting room for hire
Hours: 09.30–20.00 Monday, Tuesday and Thursday: 09.30–17.00 Wednesday; 10.00–20.00 Friday; 09.00–17.00 Saturday
Under 5's storytime sessions: 11.00–12.00 Saturday
Transport: Tube: Seven Sisters; Rail: Stoke Newington, Rectory Road; Bus: 67, 73, 76, 106, 149, 243
Special facilities: Building converted to give access to users with disabilities, automatic press button doors, parking for blue badge holders nearby

---

[241]
Hackney Archives Department, London Borough of Hackney
HAD
43 De Beauvoir Road
London N1 5SQ
Borough: Hackney
Telephone: 020 7241 2886
Fax: 020 7241 6688
E-mail: archives@hackney.gov.uk
World Wide Web: www.hackney.gov.uk
Constitution: Record office and local history library funded by local authority (not part of main Borough library service)
Objectives/purposes: Collects and maintains collections of archives, local history materials, visual, audio and other information forms

Key staff: Borough Archivist: David Mander

Stock and subject coverage: Archives of Hackney – the administrative records of the Borough Council and its predecessors back to 1700, and of organisations within the Borough. The main categories of material are: local authority records; business and industry records; land and estate records (mostly deeds); and institution, club and society records.

Materials available on microfilm include: early ratebooks; the Abney Park Cemetery Burial Registers; local newspapers and census returns for the area.

HAD's local history library contains a large and growing collection of books and local publications (parish magazines, tenants association newsletters, etc.) on: the history of the Borough, areas within Hackney, biographies, and subjects which had an impact on the Borough's history. A special collection of local directories for the 19th and early 20th centuries (covering mainly the north of the Borough) lists householders and local trades people alphabetically or by street, or both

The photographic collection has over 21,000 images (including significant numbers of watercolours, drawings and prints). The collection is much richer for Stoke Newington and Hackney (especially northern Hackney), than for Shoreditch, which was always poorer and therefore considered less picturesque.

The map collection dates back to 1745, with Ordnance Survey Maps providing comprehensive coverage from 1870 onwards

Services: Photocopies; search service; digital reprographic service (includes illustrations); Hackney on Disk - a database of ca. 12,000 digital images accessed by map and subject/keyword. Some catalogues available on the Access to Archives website at www.a2a.pro.gov.uk

Availability: Reference only. Visitors should telephone to make an appointment before visiting the Department

Hours: 09.30-13.00, 14.00-17.00 Monday, Tuesday and Thursday; 09.30-13.00 Friday

Transport: Tube: Liverpool Street; Rail: Liverpool Street, Dalston Kingsland; Bus: 38, 56, 67, 76, 141, 149, 242, 243; Road: on the A10, car parking nearby

Special facilities: Toilet facilities; access for users with disabilities – external ramp access, internal doors allow passage of wheelchairs, adapted toilet

Publications: Guide to London Local History Resources (Hackney); Annual Report. For a full list of publications contact HAD on 020 7241 2886

Linked organisations

London Borough of Hackney, Learning and Leisure Directorate Service within the Directorate
Friends of Hackney Archives Independent user group

---

[242]
Hammersmith and Fulham (London Borough of Hammersmith and Fulham)
Hammersmith and Fulham Libraries
World Wide Web: www.lbhf.gov.uk
Key staff: Head of Libraries and Archives: Nigel Bouttell;

Principal Librarian Public Services: David Herbert; Support Services Manager: John Aquilina; Research and Development Officer: Stephen Riethmüller

Constitution: Public library funded by local authority

Availability: Free public access for reference and book loan. Charges made for loan of audio cassettes, videos and compact discs

[242][a]
Hammersmith Library
Shepherd's Bush Road
London W6 7AT
Telephone: 020 8753 3813
Fax: 020 8753 3815
Key staff: Senior Librarian: Linda Hardman; Senior Librarian: Gaynor Lynch

Stock and subject coverage: Adult and children's books, videos, audio-cassettes, compact discs. Reference library includes comprehensive collection of law reports, acts, bills and legal practitioners' material. Special subject collection on religion is housed at Fulham Library

Services: Enquiry, loan and photocopy services; fax machine; online searches (charged at cost)

Hours: 09.30-20.00 Monday, Tuesday and Thursday; 09.30-17.00 Wednesday, Friday and Saturday; 13.15-17.00 Sunday

Transport: Tube: Hammersmith; Bus: 9, 9A, 10, 27, 33, R69, 72, H91, 190, 211, 220, 266, 267, 283, 290, 295, 391

Special facilities: Limited access for users with disabilities – two steps at main entrance, stairs to reference library, ramped side entrance. Kurzweil reader and CCTV scanner in reference library

[242][b]
Askew Road Library
87-91 Askew Road
London W12 9AS
Telephone: 020 8753 3863
Reference facilities: Reference collection; local information and children's collection
Hours: 09.30-13.00, 14.00-20.00 Monday and Thursday; 09.30-13.00, 14.00-17.00 Tuesday, Friday and Saturday
Transport: Tube: Ravenscourt Park; Bus: 266
Special facilities: Access for users with disabilities

[242][c]
Barons Court Library
North End Crescent
London W14 8TG
Telephone: 020 8753 3888
Reference facilities: Reference collection; local information and children's collection
Hours: 09.30-13.00, 14.00-20.00 Monday and Thursday; 09.30-13.00, 14.00-17.00 Tuesday, Friday and Saturday
Transport: Tube: West Kensington, Bus: 28, 391
Special facilities: Access for users with disabilities

[242][d]
Fulham Library
598 Fulham Road
London SW6 5NX

Hammersmith and Fulham Archives and Local History Centre

Telephone: 020 8753 3879
Fax: 020 7736 3741
Key staff: Senior Librarian: Jenny Samuels
Reference facilities: Reference collection; local information and children's collection. Special subject collection on religion
Hours: 09.30-20.00 Monday, Tuesday and Thursday; 09.30-17.00 Wednesday, Friday and Saturday; 13.15-17.00 Sunday
Transport: Tube: Parsons Green; Bus: C4, 14

[242][e]
Sands End Library
The Community Centre
59-61 Broughton Road
London SW6 2LA
Telephone: 020 8753 3885
Reference facilities: Reference collection; local information and children's collection
Hours: 09.30-13.00, 14.00-20.00 Monday and Thursday; 09.30-13.00, 14.00-17.00 Tuesday, Friday and Saturday
Transport: Tube: Parsons Green; Bus: C4
Special facilities: Access for users with disabilities

[242][f]
Shepherd's Bush Library
7 Uxbridge Road
London W12 8LJ
Telephone: 020 8753 3842
Fax: 020 8740 1712
Reference facilities: Reference collection; local information and children's collection

Hours: 09.30-20.00 Monday, Tuesday and Thursday; 09.30-17.00 Friday and Saturday
Transport: Tube: Shepherd's Bush; Bus: 12, 49, 72, 94, 95, 105, 207, 220, 237, 260, 283, 295, 607
Special facilities: Limited access for users with disabilities – ramp to side door

[243]
Hammersmith and Fulham Archives and Local History Centre
The Lilla Huset
191 Talgarth Road
London W6 8BJ
Borough: Hammersmith and Fulham
Telephone: 020 8741 5159
Fax: 020 8741 4882
World Wide Web: www.lbhf.gov.uk/Council_Services/ education/libraries_and_archives/archives/ archives.htm
Constitution: Local authority funded body
Objectives/purposes: Centre for studying all aspects of the history of the area covered by the present London Borough of Hammersmith and Fulham
Key staff: Borough Archivist: Jane Kimber; Archivist (Public Service): Anne Wheeldon; Conservator: Sandra Knight; Records Manager: James Lappin
Stock and subject coverage: Borough archive and local history centre, opened in new purpose-built premises in 1992. Holds around 2 miles of records; earliest original document dates from 1484. Holdings include the usual local authority records, 1623 to date, plus deposited records of local churches, schools,

businesses, etc., from the 17th to 20th century.
Extensive local history collections and some 60,000
photographs, plus maps, directories, electoral registers
and local newspapers (1855 to date). Approved as a
Place of Deposit for Public, Manorial and Tithe
records

Services: Photocopying can be done (subject to state of
the original) by staff; microfilm and fiche readers
available. Staff can assist in deciphering old
handwriting and documents in Latin

Availability: Access, by appointment only, is free to all.
There is a donations box in the search room and
donations are welcome. All material is for reference
only and cannot be borrowed

Hours: 09.30–20.00 Monday; 09.30–13.00 Tuesday;
09.30–16.30 Thursday; closed Wednesday and Friday.
Open 09.30–13.00 on one Saturday in each month,
usually the first. Telephone in advance to make an
appointment

Transport: Tube: Hammersmith; Bus: 9, 9A, 10, 11, 27,
33, 72, 190, 211, 220, 266, 267, 283, 290, 295, 391,
415

Special facilities: Toilet facilities; access for users with
disabilities – lift, toilets all designed for wheelchair
users, one parking space for drivers with disabilities,
with prior notice

Special features: The Lilla Huset forms part of the
prestigious London Ark development designed by
Ralph Erskine

Publications: Numerous local history publications,
including Life in Fulham: Old Fulham in Pictures;
The Instant Past: Old Hammersmith in Pictures;
Hammersmith and Shepherds Bush in Old
Photographs; Fulham in Old Photographs; also
various postcards and publications of the Ethnic
Communities Oral History Project

Linked organisations

**London Borough of Hammersmith and
Fulham, Education Department** The Centre is
part of the Education Department

[244]
Haringey (London Borough of Haringey)
Haringey Library Services
World Wide Web: www.haringey.gov.uk
Constitution: Public library funded by local authority
Availability: Open access for reference; identification
required for loan facilities; no charges for reference
and most lending; charges for loan of CDs and
cassettes
Note: Until December 2002 Instant Library Ltd is
providing interim management of Haringey libraries.
Haringey has nine libraries, with the main library
located at Wood Green. There are also five special
library services: Baby Bus Service; Housebound
Library; Mobile Library; Schools Library Service and
Sure Start Book and Toy Bus (see website for details)

[244][a]
Central Library
High Road
Wood Green
London N22 6XD

Telephone: 020 8489 2700
Stock and subject coverage: Adult and junior general
lending collections; main reference collection for
Haringey. Stock includes: books, journals, records,
cassettes, CDs, language courses and local community
languages collections
Services: Photocopier and fax services; internet and e-
mail facilities
Hours: 09.00–19.00 Monday to Thursday; 09.00–17.00
Saturday
Transport: Tube: Wood Green; Rail: Alexandra Palace;
Bus: W3, W4, 29, 67, 84A, 112, 121, 123, 141, 144,
221, 230, 243, 329
Special facilities: Toilet facilities available; access for users
with disabilities – wheelchair access, Kurzweil reading
machine, minicom service

[244][b]
Alexandra Park Library
Alexandra Park Road
London N22 4UJ
Telephone: 020 8883 8553
Key staff: Senior Librarian
Stock and subject coverage: Reference collection; local
information and children's collection; newspapers and
magazines in community languages
Services: Photocopier; study area
Hours: 09.00–13.00, 14.00–19.00 Monday and
Wednesday; 09.00–13.00, 14.00–17.00 Saturday
Transport: Bus: 84A, 102, 299
Special facilities: Access for users with disabilities
including wheelchair access

[244][c]
Coombes Croft Library
Tottenham High Road
Tottenham
London N17 8AG
Telephone: 020 8808 0022
Key staff: Senior Librarian: Hazel Green
Stock and subject coverage: Reference collection; local
information and children's collection; newspapers and
magazines in community languages
Hours: 09.00–13.00, 14.00–19.00 Monday, Tuesday and
Thursday, 09.00–13.00, 14.00–17.00 Friday; 09.00–
13.00, 14.00–17.00 Saturday (except for Spurs home
games - Library located opposite White Hart Lane
football stadium)
Transport: Rail: White Hart Lane; Bus: 149, 259, 279, 359
Special facilities: Access for users with disabilities
including wheelchair access

[244][d]
Highgate Library
Shepherd's Hill
Highgate
London N6 5QT
Telephone: 020 8348 3443
Key staff: Senior Librarian
Stock and subject coverage: Reference collection; local
information; children's collection; newspapers and
magazines in community languages

Hours: 09.00-13.00, 14.00-17.00 Monday, Friday and
Saturday; 09.00-13.00, 14.00-19.00 Tuesday and
Thursday
Transport: Tube: Highgate; Bus: 43, 134, 234, 263
Special facilities: Access for users with disabilities
including wheelchair access

[244][e]
Hornsey Library
Haringey Park
London N8 9JA
Telephone: 020 8489 1427
Key staff: Neighbourhood Librarian
Stock and subject coverage: Reference collection; local
information and children's collection. Audiovisual
collections and newspapers and magazines in
community languages
Services: Photocopier and fax service; open learning
facility
Hours: 09.00-19.00 Monday and Wednesday; 09.00-
17.00 Tuesday, Thursday and Saturday
Transport: Bus: W2, W3, W5, W7
Special facilities: Access for users with disabilities
including wheelchair access

[244][f]
Marcus Garvey Library
Tottenham Green Centre
1 Philip Lane
London N15 4JA
Telephone: 020 8489 5309
020 8489 5360 (Children's Library)
Key staff: Principal Librarian, Tottenham Area;
Neighbourhood Librarian
Stock and subject coverage: Reference collection; local
information and children's collection; materials in
community languages
Services: Photocopier and fax service; open learning
facility
Hours: 09.00-19.00 Monday and Thursday; 09.00-17.00
Tuesday, Friday and Saturday
Transport: Tube and Rail: Seven Sisters; Bus: W4, 41, 73,
76, 123, 149, 230, 243, 259, 279, 359
Special facilities: Access for users with disabilities
including wheelchair access

[244][g]
Muswell Hill Library
Queens Avenue
Muswell Hill
London N10 3PE
Telephone: 020 8883 6734
Key staff: Senior Librarian
Stock and subject coverage: Reference collection; local
information and children's collection; materials in
community languages
Services: Photocopier and fax services; storytime sessions;
toy library (subscription £6 p.a.)
Hours: 09.00-19.00 Monday to Wednesday, Friday;
09.00-17.00 Thursday and Saturday
Toy Library: 14.00-15.30 Monday; 09.30-12.00
Wednesday and Thursday
Storytime sessions: 14.45-15.15 Monday; 11.00-11.30
Thursday

Transport: Bus: W3, W7, 43, 102, 134, 144, 234
Special facilities: Limited access for users with disabilities

[244][h]
St Anns Library
Cissbury Road
Tottenham
London N15 5PU
Telephone: 020 8800 4390
Key staff: Senior Librarian
Stock and subject coverage: Reference collection; local
information and children's collection
Services: Photocopier; open learning facility
Hours: 09.00-19.00 Monday to Thursday; 09.00-17.00
Friday and Saturday
Transport: Bus: 67, 171
Special facilities: Access for users with disabilities
including wheelchair access

[244][i]
Stroud Green Library
Quernmore Road
London N4 4QR
Telephone: 020 8348 4363
Stock and subject coverage: Reference collection; local
information and children's collection
Hours: 09.00-13.00, 14.00-19.00 Tuesday; 09.00-13.00,
14.00-17.00 Friday and Saturday
Transport: Rail: Haringey West; Bus: W5

---

[245]
Haringey Archive Service
Bruce Castle Museum
Lordship Lane
London N17 8NU
Borough: Haringey
Telephone: 020 8808 8772
Fax: 020 8808 4118
Constitution: Local authority library
Objectives/purposes: The Service holds the archive and
local history collection for the borough of Haringey
Key staff: Local History Officer: Rita Read
Stock and subject coverage: The collection covers the
modern London Borough of Haringey which
consists of the three former boroughs of Tottenham,
Wood Green and Hornsey. All aspects of local life in
the past are covered including housing, streets,
agricultural life, industry, transport, people, social and
sports activities, services and institutions
Services: Photocopies (charges made); microfilm reader-
printer
Availability: Free access to the search room by
appointment only
Hours: Search room days vary between Wednesday and
Saturday. Held twice a week from 13.00-16.45. By
appointment only
Transport: Tube: Wood Green then 243 bus; Rail: Bruce
Grove; Bus: 123, 243
Special facilities: Toilet facilities available
Special features: Bruce Castle, which was the manor
house of Tottenham, was built in the 16th century.
The Coleraine family made substantial alterations to
the building in the 1680s. Rowland Hill, the inventor
of the Penny Post, came to live at Bruce Castle in

1827, and he and other members of his family ran a boys' school in the house. Bruce Castle opened as a museum in 1906

---

[246]
Harrow (London Borough of Harrow)
Harrow Library Services
World Wide Web: www.harrow.gov.uk
Constitution: Public library funded by local authority
Special features: The London Borough of Harrow has two central libraries with complementary collections at the Civic Centre (including the reference library) and Gayton Library (the main lending library and music library)

[246][a]
Civic Centre Library (Harrow Central Reference Library)
PO Box 4
Civic Centre
Harrow
Middlesex HA1 2UU
Telephone: 020 8424 1055/1056
Fax: 020 8424 1971
E-mail: civiccentre.library@harrow.gov.uk
Key staff: Senior Reference Librarian: Sarah Edis; Local History Librarian: Bob Thomson
Stock and subject coverage: General reference stock and lending stock for students with an emphasis on management and law. Loan collections in architecture, building and town planning (LASER specialisation). TSO, genealogical and business collections for reference. Local history collection of books, newspapers, journals, maps, prints, photographs, census records and archives on Harrow, Middlesex and the Greater London area
Services: Colour and black and white photocopiers; microfilm and fiche readers and reader-printers, CD-ROMs; internet access; word processing facilities and 100 study spaces
Availability: Open to all for reference. 60% of the stock is reference only (integrated shelf arrangement). Loan stock available on production of satisfactory identification documents
Hours: 09.30-20.00 Monday, Tuesday and Thursday; 09.30-13.00 Friday; 09.00-17.00 Saturday
Transport: Tube: Harrow on the Hill; Rail: Harrow and Wealdstone; Bus: 140, 182, 186, 258, 340
Special facilities: Refreshment facilities (cold drinks machine); toilet facilities; access for users with disabilities and adapted toilet
Special features: 120 study spaces available
Publications: Guide to Local History Resources

[246][b]
Gayton Library (Central Lending Library)
Gayton Road
Harrow
Middlesex HA1 2HL
Telephone: 020 8427 6012/8986
Fax: 020 8424 1971

E-mail: gayton.library@harrow.gov.uk
Key staff: Principal Librarian (Lending Services): John Pennells; Music Librarian: John Roche
Stock and subject coverage: General lending stock covering in particular the humanities and arts, complementing the Civic Centre Library stock. Special collections: books in Chinese and on Chinese music; music and art reference materials; central music library with orchestral and choral performance sets available for loan
Services: Photocopies (black and white and colour); internet access; 25 study spaces
Availability: Reference facilities open to all. Borrowing facilities open to all on production of appropriate identification documents. Charges for music and spoken word loans
Hours: 09.30-20.00 Monday, Tuesday and Thursday; 09.30-13.00 Friday; 09.00-17.00 Saturday
Transport: Tube: Harrow on the Hill; Bus: H10, H11, H14, H17, H18, 114, 140, 182, 183 , 186, 223, 258, 340, 350
Special facilities: Toilet facilities available; access for users with disabilities – mezzanine study area not wheelchair accessible
Special features: Exhibition area available

[246][c]
Bob Lawrence Library
6-8 North Parade
Mollison Way
Edgware
Middlesex HA8 5QH
Telephone: 020 8952 4140
E-mail: boblawrence.library@harrow.gov.uk
Key staff: Librarian: John Clifford; Senior Assistant Librarian: Karen Galber
Reference facilities: Quick reference collection; local information and children's collection
Hours: 10.00-13.00, 14.00-18.00 Monday and Thursday; 15.30-19.00 Tuesday; 09.00-17.00 Saturday
Transport: Tube: Queensbury; Bus: 114
Special facilities: Access for users with disabilities – entrance ramp; toilet facilities; induction loop

[246][d]
Hatch End Library
Uxbridge Road
Hatch End
Pinner
Middlesex HA5 4EA
Telephone: 020 8428 2636
E-mail: hatchend.library@harrow.gov.uk
Key staff: Librarian: John Clifford; Senior Assistant Librarian: Lilian Stark
Reference facilities: Quick reference collection; local information and children's collection
Hours: 15.30-19.00 Monday; 10.00-13.00, 14.00-18.00 Tuesday and Thursday; 09.00-17.00 Saturday
Transport: Rail: Hatch End; Bus: H12, H14
Special facilities: Access for users with disabilities – entrance ramp

[246][e]
Kenton Library
Kenton Lane
Kenton
Middlesex HA3 8UJ
Telephone: 020 8907 2463
E-mail: kenton.library@harrow.gov.uk
Key staff: Librarian: Maggie Timms; Senior Assistant
Librarian: Ann Chesney
Reference facilities: Reference collection; local information
and children's collection
Services: Photocopies; spoken word materials; internet
access
Hours: 09.30–13.00, 14.00–20.00 Monday, Tuesday and
Thursday; 09.30–13.00 Friday; 09.00–17.00 Saturday
Transport: Bus: H10, H18, 114
Special facilities: Access for users with disabilities

[246][f]
North Harrow Library
429–433 Pinner Road
Harrow
Middlesex HA1 4HN
Telephone: 020 8427 0611
E-mail: northharrow.library@harrow.gov.uk
Key staff: Librarian: Stella Davies; Senior Assistant
Librarian: Margaret Eamon
Reference facilities: Quick reference collection; local
information and children's collection
Services: Photocopies; spoken word materials; internet
access
Hours: 10.00–13.00, 14.00–18.00 Monday and Thursday;
15.30–19.00 Tuesday; 09.00–17.00 Saturday
Transport: Tube: North Harrow; Bus: H10, 183, 350
Special facilities: Access for users with disabilities – ramp
to front door; adapted toilet available

[246][g]
Pinner Library
Marsh Road
Pinner
Middlesex HA2 0HT
Telephone: 020 8866 7827
E-mail: pinner.library@harrow.gov.uk
Key staff: Librarian: Patricia Watts; Senior Assistant
Librarian: Marian Heneghan
Reference facilities: Quick reference collection; local
information and children's collection
Services: Photocopies; spoken word materials; internet
access
Hours: 09.30–13.00, 14.00–20.00 Monday, Tuesday and
Thursday; 09.30–13.00 Friday; 09.00–17.00 Saturday
Transport: Tube: Pinner; Bus: H11, H12, H13, 183
Special facilities: Access for users with disabilities – ramp
access to front door, disabled toilet. No access for
wheelchairs to first floor quick reference section and
study area

[246][h]
Rayners Lane Library
Imperial Drive
Harrow
Middlesex HA2 7HJ

Telephone: 020 8866 9185
E-mail: raynerslane.library@harrow.gov.uk
Key staff: Librarian: Carol Manson; Senior Assistant
Librarian: Stephen Emerson
Reference facilities: Quick reference collection; local
information and children's collection
Services: Photocopies; spoken word materials; internet
access
Hours: 15.30–19.00 Monday; 10.00–13.00, 14.00–18.00
Tuesday and Thursday; 09.00–17.00 Saturday
Transport: Tube: Rayners Lane: Bus: H10, H12, 398
Special facilities: Limited access for users with disabilities
– split levels and stairs throughout the library and
children's and reference collection on the first floor

[246][i]
Roxeth Library
Northolt Road
South Harrow
Middlesex HA2 8EQ
Telephone: 020 8422 0809
E-mail: roxeth.library@harrow.gov.uk
Key staff: Librarian: Carol Manson; Senior Assistant
Librarian: Shobhna Trivedi
Reference facilities: Quick reference collection; local
information and children's collection
Services: Photocopies; spoken word materials; internet
access
Hours: 10.00–13.00, 14.00–18.00 Monday and Thursday;
15.30–19.00 Tuesday; 09.00–17.00 Saturday
Transport: Tube: South Harrow; Bus: H10, H12, 114,
140, 187, 258, 398
Special facilities: Access for users with disabilities – ramp
to front door

[246][j]
Stanmore Library
8 Stanmore Hill
Stanmore
Middlesex HA7 3BQ
Telephone: 020 8954 9955
E-mail: stanmore.library@harrow.gov.uk
Key staff: Librarian: Richard Young; Senior Assistant
Librarian: Helen Physick
Reference facilities: Quick reference collection; local
information; children's collection and music CD
lending collection
Services: Photocopies; music and spoken word materials;
internet access
Hours: 09.30–13.00, 14.00–20.00 Monday, Tuesday and
Thursday; 09.30–13.00 Friday; 09.00–17.00 Saturday
Transport: Tube: Stanmore; Bus: H12, 142, 340
Special facilities: Access for users with disabilities – good
wheelchair access throughout the library

[246][k]
Wealdstone Library
Grant Road
Wealdstone
Harrow
Middlesex HA3 7SD
Telephone: 020 8427 8670
E-mail: wealdstone.library@harrow.gov.uk
Key staff: Librarian: Stella Davies; Senior Assistant
Librarian: Christine Crowther

Reference facilities: Quick reference collection; local information and children's collection

Services: Photocopies; spoken word materials; internet access

Hours: 15.30-19.00 Monday; 10.00-13.00, 14.00-18.00 Tuesday and Thursday; 09.00-17.00 Saturday

Transport: Tube and Rail: Harrow and Wealdstone; Bus: H10, 140, 182, 186, 258, 340

Special facilities: Access for users with disabilities – no wheelchair access to first floor or children's collection; public toilet but without wheelchair access

[247]
Harrow School Vaughan Library
High Street
Harrow on the Hill
London HA1 3HT
Borough: Harrow
Telephone: 020 8872 8278
Fax: 020 8872 8313
E-mail: mek@harrowschool.org.uk
World Wide Web: www.harrowschool.org.uk
Constitution: Registered charity
Key staff: Librarian: ME Knight ALA MIInfSc
Stock and subject coverage: School library with general collections. Special collections: incunabula; Aldine Press; Byron, Sheridan and Churchill Collections
Services: Photocopies; online searching, internet access; fax; word-processing; CD-ROM; computerised catalogue
Availability: Open to researchers for reference use by appointment only
Hours: 08.30-18.30 Monday to Friday; 14.00-17.00 Saturday and Sunday
Transport: Tube: Harrow on the Hill; Rail: Harrow and Wealdstone, Harrow on the Hill
Special facilities: Toilet facilities available
Special features: Designed by George Gilbert Scott in 1861, refurbished in 1999

[248]
Harry Simpson Memorial Library
at the University of Westminster
35 Marylebone Road
London NW1 5LS
Borough: Westminster
Telephone: 020 7911 5816
Fax: 020 7911 5856
E-mail: librarian@hsml.co.uk
World Wide Web: www.hsml.co.uk
Constitution: Registered charity
Objectives/purposes: Specialist library for housing, urban regeneration and related subjects
Key staff: Librarian: Christine Pittman
Stock and subject coverage: Ca. 10,000 titles on all aspects of housing in the social rented, owner-occupied and private rented sectors; housing and planning journals
Services: Photocopies; study area; fax; meeting space for community and professional groups; exhibition space
Availability: Open to anyone with a personal or professional interest in housing and related subjects, for reference use only. No user fee but a donation is appreciated; corporate and group membership available

Hours: 09.00-17.00 Monday to Friday; flexible lunch-hour closing
Transport: Tube and Rail: Baker Street; Bus: 2, 36, 73, 82
Special facilities: Refreshment and toilet facilities within the University; access for users with disabilities including wheelchair ramp

Linked organisations
Chartered Institute of Housing
Ulster Garden Villages Trust The Library is a charitable trust which receives support from these organisations
The Joseph Rowntree Foundation The Foundation regularly donates publications to the Library

[249]
Havering Libraries (London Borough of Havering)
World Wide Web: www.havering.gov.uk
Constitution: Public library, funded by local authority
Availability: Free public access for reference and borrowing books, charges for audio and video material; photocopies and internet use

[249][a]
Central Library
St Edward's Way
Romford
Essex RM1 3AR
Telephone: 01708 432389
Fax: 01708 432391
E-mail: romfordlib2@rmplc.co.uk
Key staff: Central Lending Librarian: S Wolstenholme ALA; Central Reference Librarian: J Johns BA FLA
Stock and subject coverage: General public library book stock on a wide range of subjects. Adult and children's books for lending and reference; large print books; music and spoken word collections; DVDs; videos; open learning materials; local history collection and family history collection
Services: Photocopies (b&w and colour); microfilm and fiche readers and printers; internet access; open learning (computer training) facility; Kurzweil reading machine; minicom
Hours: 10.00-20.00 Monday; 09.00-20.00 Tuesday to Friday; 09.00-16.00 Saturday
Transport: Tube: Hornchurch, Elm Park, Dagenham East; Rail: Romford; Bus: 2A, 66, 86, 87, 103, 128, 151, 165, 174, 175, 193, 247, 248, 251, 252, 265, 294, 296, 324, 348, 350, 351, 365, 370, 373, 499
Special facilities: Access for users with disabilities – automatic doors, induction loop
Publications: Reading lists; audio and video lists; guide to library services in the Borough

[249][b]
Collier Row Library
45 Collier Row Road
Collier Row
Romford
Essex RM5 5NR
Telephone: 01708 760063
Key staff: Branch Librarian: Rose Houghton

Reference facilities: Adult and junior books and videos
Services: Photocopies; fees charged for video loans
Hours: 10.00-20.00 Monday; 09.00-20.00 Tuesday and
    Thursday; 09.00-17.00 Friday; 09.00-16.00 Saturday
Transport: Bus: 175, 247, 252, 294, 365
Special facilities: Access for users with disabilities –
    wheelchair access; induction loop; minicom

[249][c]
Elm Park Library
St Nicholas Avenue
Elm Park
Hornchurch
Essex RM12 4PT
Telephone: 01708 451270
Key staff: Branch Librarian: Christine Hipperson ALA
Reference facilities: General adult and junior book stock
    and videos
Hours: 10.00-20.00 Monday; 09.00-13.00 Tuesday;
    09.00-20.00 Wednesday and Friday; 09.00-16.00
    Saturday
Transport: Tube: Elm Park; Bus: 165, 252, 324, 365, 952,
    961
Special facilities: Access for users with disabilities –
    wheelchair accessible, induction loop and minicom

[249][d]
Gidea Park Library
Balgores Lane
Gidea Park
Romford
Essex RM2 6BS
Telephone: 01708 441856
Key staff: Branch Librarian: P Pilkington ALA
Reference facilities: General adult and junior books, music
    CDs and videos
Hours: 10.00-20.00 Monday; 09.00-20.00 Tuesday and
    Thursday; 09.00-13.00 Friday; 09.00-16.00 Saturday
Transport: Rail: Gidea Park; Bus: 265, 294, 296
Special facilities: Access for users with disabilities –
    wheelchair access; induction loop; minicom

[249][e]
Harold Hill Library
Hilldene Avenue
Harold Hill
Romford
Essex RM3 8DJ
Telephone: 01708 342749
Key staff: Branch Librarian: D Mahoney ALA
Reference facilities: General adult and junior books and
    videos
Hours: 10.00-20.00 Monday; 09.00-20.00 Tuesday and
    Thursday; 09.00-17.00 Friday; 09.00-16.00 Saturday
Transport: Bus: 151, 174, 256, 374, 294
Special facilities: Access for users with disabilities –
    wheelchair acess, induction loop and minicom

[249][f]
Harold Wood Library
Arundel Road
Harold Wood
Romford
Essex RM3 0RX

Telephone: 01708 342071
Key staff: Branch Librarian: S Donoghue BA
Reference facilities: General adult and junior books and
    videos
Hours: 10.00-12.30, 13.30-20.00 Monday; 09.00-12.30,
    13.30-17.00 Tuesday; 09.00-12.30, 13.30-20.00
    Thursday; 09.00-13.00 Friday; 09.30-12.30, 13.30-
    16.00 Saturday
Transport: Rail: Harold Wood; Bus: 256, 294, 296
Special facilities: Access for users with disabilities –
    wheelchair access, induction loop and minicom

[249][g]
Hornchurch Library
44 North Street
Hornchurch
Essex RM11 1LW
Telephone: 01708 452248
Key staff: Branch Librarian: M Campbell BA ALA
Reference facilities: General adult and junior books, videos
    and music CDs
Hours: 10.00-20.00 Monday; 09.00-20.00 Tuesday,
    Thursday and Friday; 09.00-16.00 Saturday
Transport: Tube: Hornchurch; Bus: 256, 324, 370, 373
Special facilities: Access for users with disabilities –
    wheelchair access, minicom and induction loop

[249][h]
Rainham Library
7-11 The Broadway
Rainham
Essex RM13 9YW
Telephone: 01708 551905
Key staff: Branch Librarian: R Gedalovitch BA ALA
Reference facilities: General adult and junior books and
    videos
Hours: 10.00-12.30, 13.30-20.00 Monday; 09.00-12.30,
    13.30-17.00 Tuesday; 09.00-13.00 Wednesday; 09.00-
    12.30, 13.30-20.00 Friday; 09.00-12.30, 13.30-16.00
Transport: Rail: Rainham; Bus: 103, 165, 324
Special facilities: Access for users with disabilities –
    wheelchair access, minicom and induction loop

[249][i]
South Hornchurch Library
Rainham Road
Rainham
Essex RM13 7RD
Telephone: 01708 554126
Key staff: Branch Librarian: M Ashton
Reference facilities: Reference collection; local information
    and children's collection
Hours: 09.30-12.30, 13.30-17.00 Monday; 09.00-12.30,
    13.30-20.00 Tuesday and Thursday; 09.00-13.00
    Friday; 09.00-16.00 Saturday
Transport: Bus: 103, 165
Special facilities: Access for users with disabilities –
    wheelchair access, minicom and induction loop

[249][j]
Upminster Library
26 Corbets Tey Road
Upminster
Essex RM14 2BB

Telephone: 01708 222864/221578
Key staff: Branch Librarian: DE Hitchings ALA
Reference facilities: General adult and junior collections, videos and music CDs
Hours: 09.30-20.00 Monday, Tuesday, Wednesday and Friday; 09.30-16.00 Saturday
Transport: Tube and Rail: Upminster; Bus: 346, 348, 370, 373
Special facilities: Access for users with disabilities – wheelchair access, minicom and induction loop

[250]
Health and Safety Executive
HSE
Information Centre
Rose Court
2 Southwark Bridge
London SE1 9HS
Borough: Southwark
Telephone: 020 7717 6104
Fax: 020 7717 6134
World Wide Web: www.hse.gov.uk
Constitution: Government department
Key staff: Manager, Site Services: Mrs Avril Heaney; Information Manager: vacant
Stock and subject coverage: All aspects of occupational health and safety policy
Services: Enquiry service; photocopies (charges apply)
Availability: Open to the general public; prior appointment preferred. Material available for reference purposes – with the exception of free leaflet documentation
Hours: 09.00-17.00 Monday to Friday
Transport: Tube: Mansion House, Bank; Rail: Waterloo, London Bridge
Special facilities: Access for users with disabilities
Publications: Free leaflets; publications catalogue

Linked organisations

Department of Transport, Local Government and the Regions (DTLR) HSE is part of DTLR

[251]
Health Development Agency
Holborn Gate
330 High Holborn
London WC1V 7BA
Borough: Westminster
Telephone: 020 7430 0850
Fax: 020 7061 3390
E-mail: hda.enquirydesk@hda-online.org.uk
World Wide Web: www.hda-online.org.uk
Constitution: Registered charity
Objectives/purposes: The Health Development Agency (HDA) is a special health authority, working to improve the health of people and communities in England, in particular, to reduce health inequalities. In partnership with others, it gathers evidence of what works, advises on standards and develops the skills of all those working to improve people's health. The HDA opened its doors for business on 3 April 2000
Stock and subject coverage: Library stock: about 10,000 volumes, 400 current periodicals (books are available

on loan). The Resources section is a reference collection comprising a range of audiovisual formats. The stock of both covers all aspects of health education, and the Library also holds a reference collection of dissertations and theses on health education and evaluation studies
Services: Enquiry service and provision of bibliographies based on book stock and journal holdings. Photocopies (self-service)
The HAD maintains an online public health information service comprising nine websites: (www. artsncommunities.hda-online.org.uk) (food.poverty.hda-online.org.uk) (www.hda-online.org.uk/evidence/) (www.hawnhs.hda-online.org.uk) (www.healthpromis.hda-online.org.uk/) (www.hda-online.org.uk/nhpis/) a Quality Information Checklist to helps children and young people assess the quality of the information they find on the internet (www.quick.org.uk) (www.hda-online.org.uk/yphn/)
Availability: Open to health professionals, teachers and students of relevant courses by appointment
Hours: 09.00-17.00 Monday to Friday, by appointment
Transport: Tube: St James Park, Westminster, Victoria; Rail: Victoria
Special facilities: Toilet facilities available; limited access for users with disabilities
Publications: Health Development Today magazine (bimonthly); range of publications

[252]
Heythrop College Library
Kensington Square
London W8 5HQ
Borough: Kensington and Chelsea
Telephone: 020 7795 4250
Fax: 020 7795 4253
E-mail: library@heythrop.ac.uk
World Wide Web: www.heythrop.ac.uk
Constitution: Department of a university
Key staff: Librarian: CJ Pedley; Deputy Librarian: MG Morgan
Stock and subject coverage: Collection of material on philosophy and theology together with related disciplines, e.g. history. The collection is biased towards continental philosophy and medieval philosophy, and to Roman Catholic authors in theology. The Library was founded in 1614 and includes a large number of early printed books, as well as 17th and 18th century works of Roman Catholic interest
Services: Photocopies, fax and online searching (charges made for online searching)
Availability: Access open to all members of the University of London and to all bona fide students and researchers. Material loaned through interlibrary loan
Hours: Term-time: 09.00-19.00. Vacations: 09.00-17.00
Transport: Tube: High Street Kensington
Special facilities: Refreshment and toilet facilities available

Linked organisations
University of London The College is part of the University

[253]
Highgate Literary and Scientific Institution
HLSI

11 South Grove
London N6 6BS
Borough: Camden
Telephone: 020 8340 3343
Fax: 020 8340 5632
E-mail: admin@hlsi.demon.co.uk
Constitution: Registered charity
Objectives/purposes: To stimulate and satisfy the educational, intellectual and social needs of members
Key staff: Administrator: Rosalind Erskine; Librarian: Robert Walker; Honary Archivist: Gwynydd Gosling
Stock and subject coverage: HLSI was founded in 1838 and the Library was, and is, at its centre. There is a general collection, though fiction and biography predominate. Special collections on London (particularly on Highgate) and on local writers of note: Samuel Taylor Coleridge and John Betjeman. The archive room contains documents, maps and pictures relating to Highgate and its residents since the early 17th century
Services: Photocopies
Availability: Free access to members; open to others by arrangement for reference only. Charges may be made for prolonged use
Hours: 10.00-17.00 Tuesday to Friday; 10.00-16.00 Saturday
Transport: Tube: Archway, Highgate; Rail: Gospel Oak; Bus: 143, 210, 214, 271
Special facilities: Refreshment and toilet facilities available
Special features: Grade II listed building occupied by HLSI since 1840
Publications: Newsletter (2 p.a.); Heart of a London Village - HLSI 1839-1990; occasional papers by Archive Group

[254]
Highways Agency
HA

Library and Information Centre
Room AG16B
43 Marsham Street
London SW1P 3HW
Borough: Southwark
Telephone: 020 7081 7773
Fax: 020 7081 7005
E-mail: paulalewis@highways.gsi.gov.uk
World Wide Web: www.highways.gov.uk
Constitution: Executive agency
Key staff: Information Manager/Librarian: Mrs P Lewis; Assistant Librarian: Alan Pratt
Stock and subject coverage: Books, reports and journals covering all aspects of the work of the Agency including roads and bridges, civil and structural engineering, traffic engineering and management
Availability: Limited access to researchers, by appointment, for reference only. Loans to other Government Departments
Hours: 09.00-17.00 Monday to Friday
Transport: Tube: St James's Park
Special facilities: Toilet facilities available

Linked organisations

Department for Transport The Agency is an executive agency of the Department for Transport

[255]
Hillingdon (London Borough of Hillingdon)
Hillingdon Libraries

World Wide Web:
www.hillingdon.gov.uk/library/index.htm
Constitution: Public library, funded by local authority
Special features: Part of London Borough of Hillingdon Local Services, Cultural Activities and Libraries Unit. Library services are currently organised into four areas with separate heads for each area. This structure is under review

[255][a]
Uxbridge Library (Central Library)

14-15 High Street
Uxbridge
Middlesex UB8 1HD
Telephone: 01895 250600
Fax: 01895 239794
Constitution: Public library funded by local authority
Key staff: Area Head: Linda Ash; Information Services: Alison Scannell; Local Studies: Carolynne Cotton
Stock and subject coverage: Comprehensive reference and loan collections; HMSO SSS documents; range of CD-ROMs including newspapers, EC information; ECCTIS and UKOP; local history collection
Services: Photocopies; online searching; CD-ROM; fax bureau service; tourist information centre; council information service; internet access
Availability: Free public access for reference and borrowing; charges made for loan of AV material and online searches
Hours: 09.30-20.00 Monday, Tuesday and Thursday; 09.30-17.30 Wednesday; 09.30-17.30 Friday; 09.30-16.00 Saturday
Transport: Tube: Uxbridge
Special facilities: Toilet facilities for users with disabilities
Publications: List of newspaper and journal holdings; list of standing order directories and yearbooks; guide to the library service

[255][b]
Eastcote Library

Field End Road
Eastcote
Middlesex HA5 1RL
Telephone: 020 8866 3668
Key staff: Head of Area: Mrs Josie Mitchell; Community Librarian: Miss Marianne Hallett; Community Library Manager: Miss Fiona Smith
Reference facilities: Local information; talking books collection; children's collection
Hours: 09.30-19.00 Tuesday and Thursday; 09.30-17.30 Friday; 09.30-16.00 Saturday
Transport: Tube: Eastcote; Bus: 282
Special facilities: Partial access for users with disabilities

[255][c]
Harefield Library
Park Lane
Harefield UB9 6BJ
Telephone: 01895 822171
Key staff: Head of Area: Mrs Josie Mitchell; Community Librarian: Catherine Kelter; Community Branch Manager: Mrs C Jordan; Uxbridge Area Co-ordinator: Mrs S Wilkie
Reference facilities: Local information; children's collection
Hours: 13.30-17.30 Monday; 10.00-19.00 Tuesday and Thursday; 10.00-17.30 Friday; 09.30-16.00 Saturday
Transport: Bus: U1, U9, 348
Special facilities: Access for users with disabilities

[255][d]
Harlington Library
Pinkwell Lane
Harlington
Middlesex UB3 1PB
Telephone: 020 8569 1612
Fax: 020 8569 1625
Key staff: Area Head: Linda Ash; Area Co-ordinator: Julie Fairburn; Community Librarian: Pam Pollicott; Branch Manager: Brenda O'Rourke
Reference facilities: Local information collection; children's collection
Hours: 09.00-17.00 Monday; 09.00-19.00 Tuesday; 09.00-13.30 Wednesday; 09.00-19.00 Thursday; 09.00-17.00 Friday; 09.30-16.00 Saturday
Transport: Bus: U4, 90, H98, 140
Special facilities: Access for users with disabilities

[255][e]
Hayes End Library
1346 Uxbridge Road
Hayes UB4 8JQ
Telephone: 020 8573 4209
Key staff: Head of Area: Linda Ash; Adult Community Librarian: Helen Wood; Children's Community Librarian: Maggie Roche; Community Library Manager: Judith Chennells
Reference facilities: Local information; children's collection
Hours: 10.00-19.00 Tuesday and Thursday; 09.30-16.00 Saturday
Transport: Bus: 98, 207, 207A, 607
Special facilities: Partial access for users with disabilities

[255][f]
Hayes Library
Golden Crescent
Hayes UB3 1AQ
Telephone: 020 8573 2855
Fax: 020 8848 0269
Key staff: Area Head: Linda Ash; Area Co-ordinator: Julie Fairburn; Community Librarian: Pam Pollicott; Branch Manager: Brenda O'Rourke
Reference facilities: Reference collection; local information; children's collection
Hours: 10.00-20.00 Monday and Thursday; 10.00-17.30 Tuesday and Friday; 09.30-16.00 Saturday
Transport: Rail: Hayes and Harlington; Bus: U4, U6, 90, H98, 195
Special facilities: Access for users with disabilities

[255][g]
Ickenham Library
Long Lane
Ickenham
Middlesex UB10 8RE
Telephone: 01895 635945
Key staff: Head of Area: Mrs Josie Mitchell; Community Librarian: Mrs V Rogerson; Community Library Manager: Mrs A Fleming
Reference facilities: Local information collection; children's collection
Hours: 09.30-19.00 Tuesday and Thursday; 09.30-17.30 Friday; 09.30-16.00 Saturday
Transport: Bus: U1
Special facilities: Access for users with disabilities

[255][h]
Kingshill Library
Bury Avenue
Hayes
Middlesex UB4 8LF
Telephone: 020 8845 3773
Key staff: Head of Area: Linda Ash; Adult Community Librarian: Helen Wood; Children's Community Librarian: Maggie Roche; Community Library Manager: Judith Chennells
Reference facilities: Local information collection; children's collection
Hours: 10.00-19.00 Monday and Thursday; 10.00-17.30 Friday; 09.30-16.00 Saturday
Transport: Bus: 195, 207A
Special facilities: Access for users with disabilities

[255][i]
Manor Farm Library
Bury Street
Ruislip
Middlesex HA4 7SU
Telephone: 01895 633651
Fax: 01895 677555
Key staff: Head of Area: Mrs Josie Mitchell; Community Librarian: Miss Marianne Hallett; Community Library Manager: Miss Fiona Smith
Reference facilities: Reference collection; local information; talking books collection; children's collection
Hours: 10.00-20.00 Monday and Thursday; 10.00-17.30 Tuesday and Friday; 09.30-16.00 Saturday
Transport: Tube: Ruislip; Bus: U1, E7, H13, 114
Special facilities: Partial access for users with disabilities

[255][j]
Northwood Hills Library
Potter Street
Northwood HA6 1QQ
Telephone: 01923 824595
Key staff: Head of Area: Mrs Josie Mitchell; Community Librarian: Lynn Farrow
Reference facilities: Small local information collection; talking books collection; children's collection
Hours: 09.30-19.00 Monday and Thursday; 09.30-17.30 Tuesday; 09.30-16.00 Saturday
Transport: Tube: Northwood Hills; Bus: H11, H13, 183, 282
Special facilities: Partial access for users with disabilities

[255][k]
Oak Farm Library
Sutton Court Road
Hillingdon
Middlesex UB10 9PB
Telephone: 01895 234690
Key staff: Head of Area: Linda Ash; Community
    Librarian: Mrs V Rogerson; Community Library
    Manager: Mrs A Fleming
Reference facilities: Local information collection; children's
    collection
Hours: 09.30-19.00 Monday and Thursday; 09.30-17.30
    Tuesday; 09.30-16.00 Saturday
Transport: Bus: U2, 98
Special facilities: Access for users with disabilities

[255][l]
Oaklands Gate Library
Green Lane
Northwood HA6 3AB
Telephone: 01923 826690
Key staff: Head of Area: Trisha Grimshaw; Community
    Librarian: Jo Hutton; Community Branch Manager:
    Katy Foot
Reference facilities: Small local information collection,
    talking books collection; children's collection
Hours: 09.30-19.00 Tuesday and Thursday; 09.30-17.30
    Friday; 09.30-16.00 Saturday
Transport: Tube: Northwood; Bus: U1, H11, 282, 348
Special facilities: Partial access for users with disabilities

[255][m]
Ruislip Manor Library
Victoria Road
Ruislip Manor
Middlesex HA4 9BW
Telephone: 01895 633668
Key staff: Adult Community Librarian: Frances Tracey;
    Children's Community Librarian: Hilary Collins;
    Community Library Manager: Mike Brown
Reference facilities: Local information collection; children's
    collection
Hours: 09.30-19.00 Monday and Thursday; 09.30-17.30
    Tuesday; 09.30-16.00 Saturday
Transport: Tube: Ruislip Manor; Bus: 114
Special facilities: Limited access for users with disabilities,
    ramp for wheelchairs but no access to first floor

[255][n]
South Ruislip Library
Victoria Road
South Ruislip
Middlesex HA4 0JE
Telephone: 020 8845 0188
Key staff: Adult Community Librarian: Frances Tracey;
    Children's Community Librarian: Hilary Collins;
    Community Library Manager: Mike Brown
Reference facilities: Local information collection; children's
    collection
Hours: 09.30-19.00 Tuesday and Thursday; 09.30-17.30
    Friday; 09.30-16.00 Saturday
Transport: Tube: South Ruislip; Bus: 114
Special facilities: Access for users with disabilities

[255][o]
West Drayton Library
124A Station Road
West Drayton
Middlesex UB7 7JS
Telephone: 01895 443238
Key staff: Head of Area: Linda Ash; Adult Community
    Librarian: Janet Quilter; Children's Community
    Librarian: Elizabeth McMillan; Community Library
    Manager: Mandy Layzell
Reference facilities: Reference collection; local
    information; children's collection
Hours: 09.30-19.00 Tuesday and Thursday; 09.30-17.30
    Friday; 09.30-16.00 Saturday
Transport: Tube: Uxbridge; Rail: West Drayton; Bus: U5,
    222
Special facilities: Access for users with disabilities

[255][p]
Yeading Library
Yeading Gardens
Hayes UB4 0DJ
Telephone: 020 8573 0261
Key staff: Head of Area: Linda Ash; Adult Community
    Librarian: Helen Wood; Children's Community
    Librarian: Maggie Roche; Community Library
    Manager: Judith Chennells
Reference facilities: Local information and children's
    collection
Hours: 10.00-20.00 Tuesday and Thursday; 10.00-17.30
    Friday; 09.30-16.00 Saturday
Transport: Bus: E6, 140
Special facilities: Partial access for users with disabilities

[255][q]
Yiewsley Library
192 High Street
Yiewsley
West Drayton
Middlesex UB7 7BE
Telephone: 01895 442539
Key staff: Head of Area: Linda Ash; Adult Community
    Librarian: Janet Quilter; Children's Community
    Librarian: Elizabeth McMillan; Community Library
    Manager: Mandy Layzell
Reference facilities: Reference collection; local
    information; children's collection
Hours: 09.30-19.00 Monday and Thursday; 09.30-17.30
    Tuesday; 09.30-16.00 Saturday
Transport: Tube: Uxbridge; Rail: West Drayton; Bus: U3,
    U5, 222
Special facilities: Access for users with disabilities

---

[256]
Hillingdon Hospital Medical Library
Postgraduate Centre
The Hillingdon Hospital
Uxbridge
Middlesex UB8 3NN
Borough: Hillingdon
Telephone: 01895 279250
Fax: 01895 234150

E-mail: peter@hil21.demon.co.uk
Constitution: Department within the Hillingdon
Hospital Trust
Key staff: Librarian: Peter Lovegrove
Stock and subject coverage: 3,500 books, ca. 150 journal
titles. Medicine, nursing and closely related subjects
only, catalogued according to NLM
Services: Study areas; photocopies; inter-library loans;
internet access; word processing facilities
Availability: Restricted to registered membership: staff of
the Hillingdon Hospital Trust and other agreed trusts
and authorities, local general practitioners and GP
staff
Hours: Library staffed 09.00-17.00, entry 24 hours, 7
days a week for registered members
Transport: Tube: Uxbridge; Bus: U2, U3, U4, U5
Special facilities: Toilet facilities; limited wheelchair access,
advise the Library before visiting
Publications: Annual Report

Linked organisations

**North West Thames Regional Library and
Information Service** The Library is a member of
the NW Thames Regional Library and Information
Service

[257]
Hispanic and Luso-Brazilian Council

Canning House Library
2 Belgrave Square
London SW1X 8PJ
Borough: Westminster
Telephone: 020 7235 2303
Fax: 020 7235 3587
E-mail: enquiries.library@canninghouse.com
World Wide Web: www.canninghouse.com
Constitution: Registered charity
Objectives/purposes: To foster relations between the UK
and Latin America, the Caribbean, Portugal and
Spain
Key staff: Head Librarian: Carmen Suarez; Assistant
Librarian: Frances Lee
Stock and subject coverage: Subject coverage: history;
economics; politics; art; literature; culture of Latin
America, the Caribbean, Portugal and Spain.
Approximately 60,000 volumes in English, Spanish,
Portuguese, Catalan, Basque and Ameridian
languages. Special economics collection (reference)
for businessmen, exporters, etc. About 100 current
journal titles held plus video and CD-ROM
collections
Services: Reference and lending; photocopies; interlibrary
loans. The Canning House Centre (subscription
£25-35 p.a., including half price British Bulletin)
organises lectures, recitals, film shows, etc. to stimulate
interest in these countries
Availability: Open to all for reference purposes. Loans
only to members of Canning House Centre.
Membership £25-£60
Hours: 14.00-18.30 Monday; 09.30-13.00, 14.00-17.30
Tuesday to Friday
Transport: Tube: Hyde Park Corner
Special facilities: Toilet facilities available
Publications: British Bulletin of Publications on Latin

America, The Caribbean, Portugal and Spain (2 p.a.);
Canning House Newsletter (3 p.a); Annual Report;
reading lists and information leaflets

[258]
Historical Manuscripts Commission
The National Archives (HMC)

Quality House
Quality Court
Chancery Lane
London WC2A 1HP
Borough: Corporation of London
Telephone: 020 7242 1198
Fax: 020 7831 3550
E-mail: nra@hmc.gov.uk
World Wide Web: www.hmc.gov.uk
Constitution: Independent body, funded by Government
Key staff: Secretary: CJ Kitching PhD
Stock and subject coverage: The Commission collects and
disseminates information about the nature and
location of historical manuscripts and papers outside
the Public Records, and acts as an independent
advisory body on matters connected with their care.
The Commission maintains the National Register of
Archives (NRA), consisting of over 43,000
unpublished reports. Its computerised indexes are
available for consultation in the Search Room and on
the internet. The Commission also maintains the
Manorial Documents Register, which provides
locations of surviving manorial documents
Services: Limited and specific enquiries can be made by
post, fax or e-mail. Those using fax or e-mail should
include a postal address to which a reply may be sent.
Wide range of publications; list available on request.
Internet access to the Commission's own website and
others of related interest provided in the search room
Availability: Open to all for reference. No reader's ticket
necessary
Hours: 09.30-17.00 Monday to Friday
Transport: Tube: Chancery Lane, Temple, Holborn
Special facilities: Toilet facilities available
Publications: Annual Review; Guides to Sources for
British History series; Reports to the Crown. For a
full list of publications contact the HMC or consult
the website

Linked organisations

The National Archives Launched in April 2003,
the National Archives brings together the HMC and
the Public Record Office. The two organisations will
merge more fully by Spring 2004

[259]
HM Customs and Excise Library, London
C&E

2nd Floor Central
New Kings Beam House
22 Upper Ground
London SE1 2PJ
Borough: Southwark
Telephone: 020 7865 5668

Fax: 020 7865 5720
Telex: 886231 CE HO LNG
Government Telecommunications Network: 3913
Constitution: Government department
Key staff: Information and Library Resources Manager
Stock and subject coverage: Customs and excise
Services: Internet access; photocopies; online searching and fax machines
Availability: Staff at HMCE and other government departments; open to authenticated researchers at the Librarian's discretion
Hours: 08.30–17.00 Monday to Friday
Transport: Tube: Blackfriars, Waterloo, Southwark; Rail: Blackfriars, Waterloo
Special facilities: Refreshment and toilet facilities; access for users with disabilities

Linked organisations
Libraries in Manchester, Southend and Liverpool

---

[260]
HM Land Registry
Land Registry
32 Lincoln's Inn Fields
London WC2A 3PH
Borough: Camden
Telephone: 020 7917 8888
Fax: 020 7955 0110
E-mail: hmlr@landreg.gov.uk
World Wide Web: www.landreg.gov.uk
Key staff: Chief Land Registrar: Peter Collis; Head of Communications: Michèle Bennett
Constitution: Government executive agency
Objectives/purposes: The Land Registry was set up in 1862 to facilitate conveyancing by the registration of title to land. By 1990 this system of compulsory registration had been extended to the whole of England and Wales. Some 18 million of the estimated 20 million possible titles have already been registered. Since 1990 the register has been open to public inspection
Stock and subject coverage: All aspects of land registration in England and Wales
Availability: Public Enquiry Office open 09.00–17.00 Monday to Friday
Transport: Tube: Holborn, Chancery Lane; Bus: 1, 8, 22B, 25, 68, 168, 188
Publications: The 'Open Register' – a guide to information held by the Land Registry and how to obtain it – can be obtained from any of the 24 District Land Registries. Addresses and telephone numbers can be obtained from local telephone directories, CABs and some local libraries. The Registry also produces an annual report and a number of explanatory leaflets on various aspects of land registration

---

[261]
HM Treasury and Cabinet Office Library and Information Service
Treasury Chambers
Parliament Street
London SW1P 3AG
Borough: Westminster

Telephone: 020 7270 5290
Fax: 020 7270 5681
World Wide Web: www.cabinet-office.gov.uk
www.hm-treasury.gov.uk
Constitution: Government department
Key staff: Chief Librarian: Jean Clayton BA ALA, ext 5259; Acquisitions Librarian: Sarah Plank BA MA, ext 5270; Reader Services Librarian: Anne Furness BSC DipLib, ext 5309; Systems and Cataloguing Librarian: Nichola Last BA (Hons), ext 4927
Stock and subject coverage: Over 40,000 books and ca. 600 journals taken. Main subjects are economics; official statistics; management; public administration; and law. Also, a large collection of Parliamentary Papers dating back to the 18th century; the Northcote-Trevelyan Collection on Civil Service Management and Reform, are all maintained
Services: Information can be supplied on Cabinet Office publications not published through the Stationery Office. All other external enquiries should be directed to the Treasury Public Enquiry Unit on 020 7270 4558
Availability: Primarily for staff in HM Treasury and the Cabinet Office. Interlibrary loans to other government libraries
Hours: 09.00–18.00 Monday to Friday
Transport: Tube: Westminster
Special facilities: Refreshment and toilet facilities; access for users with disabilities

[261][a]
Treasury Public Enquiry Unit
Room 88/2
Treasury Chambers
Parliament Street
London SW1P 3AG
Borough: Westminster
Telephone: 020 7270 4558
Fax: 020 7270 4574
E-mail: public.enquiries@hm-treasury.gov.uk
World Wide Web: www.hm-treasury.gov.uk
Key staff: PEU Manager: Miss Claire T Coast-Smith BA ALA
Services: Information service for all aspects of Treasury business. Sale and distribution of Treasury publications
Availability: Enquiries from anyone, except for the press
Hours: 09.00–17.00 Monday to Friday (answering machine at other times)
Transport: Tube: Westminster
Special facilities: Refreshment and toilet facilities; access for users with disabilities

---

[262]
Home Office Commission for Racial Equality
CRE
Elliot House
10-12 Allington Street
London SW1E 5EH
Borough: Westminster
Telephone: 020 7932 5296
Fax: 020 7931 0429
Constitution: Government funded body

Key staff: Librarian: Philip Pinto

Stock and subject coverage: 200 journals and 5,000 books and pamphlets, covering race relations; immigration; and ethnic minorities. Includes government reports and press cuttings on the above subjects

Services: Help and guidance on race relations issues; general information relating to race relations

Availability: Reference library available to the public by appointment

Hours: 10.00-16.00 Monday to Friday

Transport: Tube and Rail: Victoria

Special facilities: Refreshment and toilet facilities available on site; access for users with disabilities

Publications: Various publications available from CRE in London. Alternatively, CRE publications are available by mail order from: Central Books, 99 Wallis Road, London E9 5LN, telephone: 020 8986 5488, web: www.cre.gov.uk/publs/crepubs.html

Linked organisations

Racial Equality Councils

[263]
Home Office Information Services Group

[263][a]
Main Library

50 Queen Anne's Gate
London SW1H 9AT

Borough: Westminster

Telephone: 020 7273 plus extension

Fax: 020 7273 3957

E-mail: holibrary@homeoffice.gsi.gov.uk

World Wide Web: www.homeoffice.gov.uk

Constitution: Government department

Key staff: Deputy Chief Librarian: Karen George, ext 3080; Librarian: Louise Stemp, ext 2763; Library Enquiries, ext 3398; Loans, ext 2152/3496; Home Office Publications, ext 3072

Stock and subject coverage: About 53,000 volumes of monographs and around 150 current journals. Covers social sciences, especially Parliamentary Affairs publications; criminal law; administration of justice; immigration; community relations; police; penology; civil defence; probation services. Archival collection of Home Office publications

Services: Information service; limited lending to other libraries

Availability: Home Office staff. Other Government staff by appointment

Hours: 09.15-17.30 Monday to Friday

Transport: Tube: St James' Park; Rail: Victoria; Bus: 11, 24, 211, 507

Special facilities: Toilet facilities; access for users with disabilities

[263][b]
Prison Service Headquarters Library

Room 224
Abell House
John Islip Street
London SW1P 4LH

Borough: Westminster

Telephone: 020 7217 5253/5452

Fax: 020 7217 5209

World Wide Web: www.hmprisonservice.gov.uk

Key staff: Librarian: Gareth Hazzelby

Stock and subject coverage: Material on Prisons administration and penology; penal legislation; Prison Service Orders and instructions; prison design, building and construction

Services: Enquiry service; limited lending to other libraries; reading lists; free Prison Service publications. Home Office contact point for prisons and the provision of information under the code of practice on open government. Archival collection of Prison Service Publications

Availability: Prison Service and Home Office staff. Other Government staff by appointment

Hours: 09.30-17.00 Monday to Friday

Transport: Tube: Pimlico

[264]
Homerton Hospital NHS Trust

Newcomb Library
Homerton Row
London E9 6SR

Borough: Hackney

Telephone: 020 8510 7751

Fax: 020 8510 7281

E-mail: newcomb.library@homerton.nhs.uk

World Wide Web: www.newcolib.demon.co.uk

Constitution: NHS Hospital

Key staff: Isabel Cantwell

Objectives/purposes: The Newcomb Library at Homerton Hospital aims to contribute to the delivery of high quality health care by all staff and students eligible to use its services by supporting their clinical effectiveness, education, training, professional development and research needs

Key staff: Library Manager: Isabel Cantwell; Assistant Librarians: Heather Mills; Sophie Robinson; Evening Library Assistant: Ambreen Yaqoob

Stock and subject coverage: Clinical medicine, midwifery, nursing, general practice, paramedical and management subjects. Ca. 5,000 books and 150 current journals

Services: Interlibrary loans; access to Medline and CINAHL and 173 full-text journals via the internet. Access to PsycINFO and 10 full-text journals via the internet; access to BinleysOnline via the internet; access to Medline, CINAHL, PsycINFO, Cochrane Library, Best Evidence, BookFind, National Research Register, RCOG Dialog via CD-ROM plus various textbooks and multimedia programmes on CD-ROM. Word processing, spreadsheet and graphics packages plus internet connectivity on all public access machines plus printing facilities

Availability: Open to all staff of the Homerton Hospital NHS Trust, East London and the City Mental Health Trust, City and Hackney Primary Care Trust plus City University nursing students, students of St Bartholomew's and the Royal London School of Medicine and Dentistry (QMW), and other students on placement at the Homerton Hospital. Materials available for loan and reference only. Other users wishing to use the facilities may be granted reader only status on application

Hours: 11.00-20.00 Monday; 09.00-18.00 Tuesday to Friday

Transport: Tube: Bethnal Green; Rail: Homerton; Bus: S2, W15, 236, 242, 276

Special facilities: Refreshment and toilet facilities available; access for users with disabilities

Publications: Annual Report; Newcomb Library and Information Services Guide; new books lists

[265]
The Honourable Company of Master Mariners
HCMM

HQS 'Wellington'
Temple Stairs
Victoria Embankment
London WC2R 2PN
Borough: Westminster
Telephone: 020 7836 8179
Fax: 020 7240 3082
E-mail: info@hcmm.org.uk
World Wide Web: www.hcmm.org.uk
Constitution: Livery company
Objectives/purposes: Reference library for members
Key staff: Clerk to the Company: Mr JAV Maddock
Stock and subject coverage: Library built up, chiefly by donation, since the foundation of the Company in 1932. Stock of about 2,500 books and journals covering: maritime history, voyages, navigation, naval architecture, maritime law, maritime biography, nautical fiction and related subjects. There is also a small collection of books on the City of London and Livery companies. The catalogue is held on the Company's computer and a printout is available for consultation in the library
Services: Photocopies (charges made)
Availability: Open to bona fide researchers for reference only; members may borrow books
Hours: By appointment only
Transport: Tube: Temple; Rail: Charing Cross, Blackfriars
Special facilities: Toilet facilities available
Special features: The library is on the lower deck of the ship, and also houses a small collection of artefacts
Publications: Journal of the Honourable Company of Master Mariners (4 p.a.)

[266]
The Horniman Library

The Horniman Museum and Gardens
100 London Road
Forest Hill
London SE23 3PQ
Borough: Lewisham
Telephone: 020 8291 8681
Fax: 020 8291 5506
E-mail: enquiry@horniman.ac.uk
World Wide Web: www.horniman.ac.uk
Constitution: Registered charity; department of an independent non-profit distributing organisation, funded by central government

Objectives/purposes: To support the parent organisation in its objective of encouraging a wider appreciation of the world, its peoples and their cultures, and its environments
Key staff: Librarian: David Allen
Stock and subject coverage: The Horniman Library is a specialist library which is open to the public for reference use. It provides information on the three subject areas of the museum: ethnography, natural history and musical instruments. Materials are selected to help people understand the objects in the museum, to enable a greater understanding of other cultures and the natural world we inhabit. The collections consist of over 20,000 books; 100 serial titles; audiovisual materials: videos; tapes; records; compact discs; photographs and slides
Services: Photocopies
Availability: The Library is open to the public, free, by appointment for reference only
Hours: 10.30-17.30 Tuesday to Saturday; 14.00-17.30 Sunday
Transport: Rail: Forest Hill; Bus: P4, 176, 185, 312, 352
Special facilities: Refreshment and toilet facilities
Publications: Regular reading lists and accessions lists

[267]
The Hospice Information Service

St Christopher's Hospice
51 Lawrie Park Road
London SE26 6DZ
Borough: Bromley
Telephone: 020 8778 9252
Fax: 020 8776 9345
World Wide Web: www.hospiceinformation.co.uk
Constitution: Independent non-profit distributing organisation; registered charity and association with voluntary subscribing membership. The Hospice Information Service raises a proportion of its income through subscriptions from its membership, publications and services. It is also sponsored by Macmillan Cancer Relief, Help the Hospices and subsidised by St Christopher's
Objectives/purposes: To provide a worldwide network and resource for those working in hospice or palliative care
Key staff: Information Officers: Avril Jackson and Ann Eve
Stock and subject coverage: Information on the nature and location of hospice and palliative care services in the UK and overseas
Services: Photocopies; enquiry service
Availability: Open access, visits by appointment only. Material available for reference or purchase. An annual membership fee enables members to receive regular mailings and free fact sheets
Hours: 09.00-17.00 Monday to Friday by appointment
Transport: Rail: Penge East, Sydenham
Special facilities: Refreshment and toilet facilities available; access for users with disabilities
Publications: 2001 Directory of Hospice and Palliative Care Services in the UK and Ireland (annual); Hospice Bulletin (quarterly newsletter); Job Opportunities, listing of employment vacancies in palliative care; Choices, listing of education and

training opportunities; fact sheets on the planning and development of palliative care services

Linked organisations
St Christopher's Hospice Part of the Hospice

---

[268]
Hounslow (London Borough of Hounslow)
Hounslow Library Network (Community Initiative Partnerships)
Centrespace
Treaty Centre
High Street
Hounslow
Middlesex TW3 1ES
Telephone: 020 8583 4545
World Wide Web: www.cip.org.uk
Constitution: Public library funded by local authority
Key staff: Borough Librarian: Linda Simpson
Publications: Annual Report (for whole library service)
Special features: The London Borough of Hounslow has three main libraries: Chiswick, Feltham and Hounslow (listed first) and eight branch libraries. Libraries contain general public library stock focused on leisure and study. LASER subject specialisation scheme: non fiction - Dewey: 550-559; fiction - author: T-TH; Classical music: Debussy and Wagner; jazz artists: CHAM-COL; American literature; folk music of Turkey

[268][a]
Chiswick Library
Dukes Avenue
Chiswick
London W4 2AB
Telephone: 020 8994 1008
Fax: 020 8995 0016
Key staff: Library Manager
Stock and subject coverage: General collection of material with separate lending and reference sections. Stock includes CDs, videos and spoken word CDs as well as books. Adult and children's collections. Local history collection of books, newspapers, maps and prints relevant to the Chiswick area. Stationery Office selective subscription
Services: Photocopies; fax machine
Availability: Free public access for reference and borrowing. Charges for audio and video materials and for local studies research
Hours: 09.30-20.00 Monday and Thursday; 09.30-17.30 Tuesday, Friday and Saturday
Transport: Tube: Chiswick Park, Turnham Green; Bus: E3, H40, H91, 27, 237, 267, 391
Special facilities: Access for users with disabilities – wheelchair access restricted to the ground floor

[268][b]
Feltham Library
210 The Centre
High Street
Feltham TW13 4BX
Telephone: 020 8890 3506

Fax: 020 8893 2748
Key staff: Library Manager
Stock and subject coverage: General collection of integrated lending and reference material. Stock includes books, CDs and videos. Material for adults and children, including videos and journals in Asian languages. Small local history collection relevant to the Feltham area
Services: Photocopies; fax machine, OPACs
Availability: Free public access for reference and borrowing. Charges for audio and video materials
Hours: 09.30-20.00 Monday and Thursday; 09.30-17.30 Tuesday, Friday and Saturday
Transport: Rail: Feltham; Bus: H24, H25, H26, N90, 117, 235, 400
Special facilities: Refreshment facilities available; access for users with disabilities plus adapted toilet

[268][c]
Hounslow Library
Centrespace
Treaty Centre
Hounslow TW3 1ES
Telephone: 020 8583 4545
Fax: 020 8583 4595
Key staff: Customer Services Managers: Ann Greene, Indra Bhadhal, Deirdre Lewis
Stock and subject coverage: General collection of integrated lending and reference material. Stock includes books, CDs and videos. Material for adults and children, including works in Asian languages. Local history collection of books, newspapers, maps and prints relevant to the local authority area
Services: Photocopies; fax machine; OPAC
Availability: Free public access for reference and borrowing. Charges for audio and video material and for local studies research
Hours: 09.30-17.30 Monday, Wednesday, Friday and Saturday; 09.30-20.00 Tuesday and Thursday
Transport: Tube: Hounslow Central; Rail: Hounslow; Bus: H20, H22, H23, H28, H32, H98, 81, N97, H98, 110, 111, 116, 117, 120, 203, 222, 232, 235, 237, 281
Special facilities: Refreshment and toilet facilities available in café bar; access for users with disabilities, Kurzweil machine for the visually impaired

[268][d]
Beavers Library
103 Salisbury Road
Hounslow TW4 7NW
Telephone: 020 8572 6995
Fax: 020 8570 5066
Key staff: Library Manager
Reference facilities: Reference collection and children's collection
Hours: 12.30-20.00 Monday and Thursday; 12.30-17.30 Tuesday; 09.30-13.00 Saturday
Transport: Bus: H23
Special facilities: Access for users with disabilities and wheelchair users

[268][e]
Bedfont Library
Staines Road
Bedfont TW14 8BD

Telephone: 020 8890 6173
Fax: 020 8893 2287
Key staff: Library Manager
Reference facilities: Reference collection and children's collection
Hours: 10.00-20.00 Monday and Thursday; 10.00-17.30 Tuesday; 09.30-17.30 Saturday
Transport: Bus: 116
Special facilities: Access for users with disabilities and wheelchair users

[268][f]
Brentford Library
Boston Manor Road
Brentford TW8 8DW
Telephone: 020 8560 8801
Fax: 020 8560 2150
Key staff: Library Manager
Reference facilities: Reference collection and children's collection
Hours: 10.00-20.00 Monday and Thursday; 10.00-17.30 Tuesday; 09.30-17.30 Saturday
Transport: Rail: Brentford; Bus: E2, E8
Special facilities: Access for users with disabilities and wheelchair users

[268][g]
Cranford Library
Bath Road
Cranford TW5 9TL
Telephone: 020 8759 0641
Fax: 020 8564 8335
Key staff: Library Manager
Reference facilities: Reference collection and children's collection
Hours: 10.00-20.00 Monday and Thursday; 10.00-17.30 Tuesday; 09.30-17.30 Saturday
Transport: Bus: 81, 98, 111, 222
Special facilities: Access for users with disabilities and wheelchair users

[268][h]
Hanworth Library
2-12 Hampton Road West
Hanworth TW13 6AW
Telephone: 020 8898 0256
Fax: 020 8893 3967
Key staff: Library Manager
Reference facilities: Reference collection and children's collection
Hours: 10.00-20.00 Monday and Thursday; 10.00-17.30 Tuesday; 09.30-17.30 Saturday
Transport: Bus: H25, 90, 111, 285
Special facilities: Access for users with disabilities and wheelchair users

[268][i]
Heston Library
New Heston Road
Heston TW5 0LW
Telephone: 020 8570 1028
Fax: 020 8570 5206
Key staff: Library Manager
Reference facilities: Reference collection and children's collection

Hours: 10.00-20.00 Monday and Thursday; 10.00-17.30 Tuesday; 09.30-17.30 Saturday
Transport: Bus: 111, 120
Special facilities: Access for users with disabilities and wheelchair users

[268][j]
Isleworth Library
Twickenham Road
Isleworth TW7 7EU
Telephone: 020 8560 2934
Fax: 020 8560 9986
Key staff: Library Manager
Reference facilities: Reference collection and children's collection; cybercentre for study support
Hours: 10.00-20.00 Monday and Thursday; 10.00-17.30 Tuesday; 09.30-17.30 Saturday
Transport: Bus: Hounslow Hoppa, 37, 267
Special facilities: Access for users with disabilities and wheelchair users

[268][k]
Osterley Library
St Mary's Crescent
Osterley TW7 4NB
Telephone: 020 8560 4295
Fax: 020 8560 9871
Key staff: Library Manager
Reference facilities: Reference collection and children's collection
Hours: 10.00-20.00 Monday and Thursday; 10.00-17.30 Tuesday; 09.30-17.30 Saturday
Transport: Tube: Osterley; Bus: H91
Special facilities: Access for users with disabilities and wheelchair users

[269]
House of Commons
House of Commons Library
Westminster
London SW1A 0AA
Note: For most sections the postal address is:
1 Derby Gate, Westminster SW1A 2DG
Borough: Westminster
Telephone: 020 7219 plus extension
Government Telecommunications Network: 219
World Wide Web: www.parliament.uk
Constitution: Special library primarily for Members of Parliament
Key staff: Librarian: Miss PJ Baines: Enquiries: Ext 4272 (all enquiries except interlibrary loans): Interlibrary Loans: Ext 3396
Stock and subject coverage: 180,000 bound volumes, plus British official publications; European Communities and United Nations publications; 3,000 journals. Special subjects: Parliament and politics
Availability: Enquiries from the public, organisations and other libraries about the work, composition and history of the House of Commons are dealt with by letter or telephone by the House of Commons Information Office, (Head of Office, Mr Bryn Morgan). The telephone enquiry service is available 09.00-18.00 (closes 16.30 on Friday; open 10.00-17.00 in recesses). Readers can be accommodated

only rarely and by special request. There is an Education Unit (Education Officer, Ms C Weeds) to supply information on educational aids to schools and colleges. To deal with enquiries from Members of Parliament there are specialist research sections, all based at 1 Derby Gate, dealing with international affairs and defence, home affairs, science and the environment, economic and statistical, business and transport, social policy, parliament and constitution matters. There is also a specialist section, based in the Palace of Westminster (the Reference & Reader Services Section) which provides a quick over-the-counter enquiry service for MPs. Approaches to these sections should not be made directly; in the first instance, contact the House of Commons Information Office. Interlibrary loans generally to other national/government departmental libraries only
Transport: Tube: Westminster
Publications: House of Commons Library Documents; Sessional Information Digest★; House of Commons Weekly Information Bulletin★; Research Papers★; Factsheets★; Education Sheets★ (★indicates available on website at www.parliament.uk). Generates the Parliamentary Online Indexing Service (www.polis.parliament.uk)

[270]
House of Lords Library
Westminster
London SW1A 0PW
Borough: Westminster
Telephone: 020 7219 5242
Fax: 020 7219 6396
Government Telecommunications Network: 219
Constitution: Government body
Key staff: Librarian: DL Jones; Deputy Librarian: PG Davis
Stock and subject coverage: Ca. 120,000 volumes, mainly on law and Parliament, with smaller collections on history and the peerage
Availability: May be used, on application to the Librarian, by researchers for material not readily available elsewhere
Transport: Tube: Westminster
Special facilities: Refreshment and toilet facilities available; access for users with disabilities

[271]
Howard League for Penal Reform
1 Ardleigh Road
London N1 4HS
Borough: Hackney
Telephone: 020 7249 7373
Fax: 020 7249 7788
E-mail: howardleague@ukonline.co.uk
World Wide Web: www.howardleague@ukonline.co.uk
Constitution: The Howard League is the oldest penal reform charity in the UK. It was established in 1866 and is named after John Howard, one of the first prison reformers. The Howard League is entirely independent of government and is wholly funded by voluntary donations
Objectives/purposes: The Howard League works for humane and rational reform of the penal system. It

researches and comments on criminal justice policy and practice, holds conferences and debates, and publishes books and reports as well as running projects in schools and prisons
Key staff: Director: Frances Crook
Stock and subject coverage: Material on penology and criminology – limited access, on request only
Availability: To members of the Howard League; others by arrangement
Hours: 10.00–16.30 Monday to Friday
Transport: Tube: Angel, Highbury and Islington

[272]
Human Communication Science Library
National Information Centre for Speech and Language Therapy
NICEST
Department of Human Communication Science
Chandler House
2 Wakefield Street
London WC1N 1PG
Borough: Camden
Telephone: 020 7679 4207
Fax: 020 7713 0861
E-mail: hcs.library@ucl.ac.uk
World Wide Web: http://library.hcs.ucl.ac.uk
Constitution: Department of a university
Objectives/purposes: The Department of Human Communication Science runs undergraduate, postgraduate and research programmes in human communication and speech sciences
Key staff: Site Librarian: Stevie Russell
Stock and subject coverage: Ca. 6,000 books and over 2,000 journals on: speech sciences; voice, psychology; linguistics; hearing sciences; neurology and special education. TEST Collection on voice, speech and language; over 100 videos
Services: Photocopies; audiovisual resources rooom; online catalogue
Availability: Free to members of UCL. External membership scheme and other services available to non-members on payment of fees (membership only available to members of the Royal College of Speech and Language Therapists)
Hours: Term-time: 09.15–18.00 Monday; 09.15–19.00 Tuesday, Wednesday and Thursday; 10.00–18.00 Friday. No access to building after 17.00 Vacations: 09.30–17.00. Telephone before visiting the Library to check opening hours
Transport: Tube: Russell Square, King's Cross; Rail: King's Cross; Bus: 10, C11, 14, 14A, 17, 18, 30, 45, 46, 63, 73, 77A, 214, 221, 259
Special facilities: Refreshment and toilet facilities available on site; access for users with disabilities – including lift, ramps and toilet facilities
Publications: Library guides

Linked organisations
University College London Library Services
Branch of UCL Library Services
Royal College of Speech and Language Therapists

[273]
Imperial College Library

World Wide Web: www.lib.ic.ac.uk/

Constitution: Imperial College of Science, Technology and Medicine is an independent constituent part of the University of London. Founded in 1907, the College teaches a full range of science, engineering, medical and management disciplines at the highest level.

Key staff: Director of Library Services: Clare Jenkins

Availability: The Imperial College and Science Museum Libraries are open to the public for reference without charge, for consultation of printed material in the fields of science, technology and medicine. The Humanities, Management and Social Sciences collections are for support of College taught courses only and are not included in the general access arrangements. Electronic databases and journals can only be made available to visitors on designated machines where licences allow. For a single visit, visitors need to show personal identification and sign the Visitors' Book at the Reception Desk to be issued with a Day Ticket. Visitors intending to visit more often must apply for a Library Admission Card. The College is the largest applied science and technology university institution inthe UK, with one of the largest annual turnovers and research incomes. There are four main groups of libraries in Imperial College: the Imperial College and Science Museum Libraries building; the Departmental Libraries on the South Kensington campus; the Medical libraries on the Faculty of Medicine campuses; the Kempe Centre at Wye and the Michael Way Library at Ascot

Linked organisations

The Michael Way Library (Silwood Park, Buckhurst Road, Ascot, Berkshire SL5 7TA) incorporates the former libraries of The International Institute of Entomology and Imperial College's Biology field stations. It specialises in ecology, applied entomology, pest management and environmental science

Imperial College at Wye In August 2000 Wye College, Kent, merged with Imperial College to form the Imperial College at Wye campus (Wye, Ashford, Kent TN25 5AH, tel: 020 759 42915). Wye College is internationally renowned for research-led teaching in biological sciences, the environment, agricultural economics and business management, agriculture and horticulture

[273][a]
Imperial College and Science Museum Libraries

Imperial College Road
South Kensington
London SW7 2AZ

Borough: Kensington and Chelsea
Telephone: 020 7594 8820
Fax: 020 7594 8876

Constitution: In 1992 the Science Museum Library linked its building with the adjacent Central Libraries of Imperial College of Science, Technology and Medicine to form the Imperial College and Science Museum Libraries

E-mail: libhelp@ic.ac.uk

Key staff: Director of Library Services: Clare Jenkins

Stock and subject coverage: The Central Library shares its building with the Science Museum Library and together they provide many amalgamated services and collections. They hold some 750,000 volumes (about two thirds of the total printed holdings), and have seats for over 900 readers. There are special facilities for users with disabilitites. The Central Library has information on all subjects taught by the College, although it specialises in undergraduate, interdisciplinary and electronic material. It holds special collections on computing, the Haldane Collection (humanities); life sciences and medicine; and management and social sciences. The Science Museum Library is a national reference library for the history and biography of science and technology (including engineering and transport) and the public understanding of science and technology, as well as a working library for the staff of the Science Museum. The Science and Technology Studies Collection contains ca. 65,000 volumes including ca. 1,500 periodical titles, on the above specialist subjects. The primary science and technology collections contain ca. 7,000 pre-1800 volumes, including 85 periodical titles; ca. 350,000 19th and 20th century volumes, including ca. 20,000 periodical titles; and ca. 100,000 microfiche technical reports.
Comben Collection of historic books on veterinary science and animal husbandry. Archive Collection of material with special relevance to the Museum's collections in physical sciences and engineering. Trade Literature Collection. Archive for the History of Quantum Physics (microfilm)

Services: Photocopies; electronic journals and CD-ROMs; online catalogue

Hours: Term-time: 08.30–22.00 Monday to Friday; 09.30–17.30 Saturday; 13.00–19.00 Sunday (for IC members and Science Museum staff only)
Summer vacation: 08.30–17.30 Monday to Friday; 09.30–17.30 Saturday

Transport: Tube: South Kensington; Bus: C1, 9, 10, 14, 345, 49, 52, 70, 74

Special facilities: College coffee bar in nearby building (not available weekends); toilet facilities; access and toilet for users with disabilities and fetching service available

Publications: Pictorial Histories of the College available from the College Archives, www.lib.ic.ac.uk/archives/publications.htm

Linked organisations

National Museum of Science and Industry The Science Museum is part of the National Museum which also includes the National Railway Museum, York, and the National Museum of Photography, Film and Television, Bradford

South Kensington Campus

[273][b]
Aeronautics Department Library

Roderic Hill Building
London SW7 2BY

Borough: Kensington and Chelsea
Telephone: 020 7594 5069

Fax: 020 7584 8120
Stock and subject coverage: Materials relating to aeronautics, including over 4,000 books and 7,000 journals plus theses and reports
Opening hours: Term-time: 09.30-13.00, 14.00-17.30 Monday to Friday; Vacations: 09.30-13.00, 14.00-17.30 Monday to Friday. An appointment should be made prior to visiting

[273][c]
Chemical Engineering and Chemical Technology Department Library
Roderic Hill Building
London SW7 2BY
Borough: Kensington and Chelsea
Telephone: 020 7594 5598
Fax: 020 7594 5604
Stock and subject coverage: Over 6,000 books and 6,000 journals relating to chemical engineering and chemical technology
Opening hours: Term-time and vacations: 09.30-13.00, 14.00-17.30 Monday to Friday
An appointment should be made prior to visiting

[273][d]
Chemistry Department Library
Chemistry Department
London SW7 2AY
Borough: Kensington and Chelsea
Telephone: 020 7594 5736
Fax: 020 7594 5804
Stock and subject coverage: Over 4,000 books and 10,000 journals on chemistry
Opening hours: Term-time: 09.00-18.00 Monday to Friday
Christmas and Easter vacations: 09.30-17.30 Monday to Friday
Summer vacation: 09.00-17.00 Monday to Friday
An appointment should be made prior to visiting

[273][e]
Civil and Environmental Engineering Department Library
Room 402
4th Floor
Civil Engineering Building
London, SW7 2BU
Borough: Kensington and Chelsea
Telephone: 020 7594 6007
Fax: 020 7225 2716
Stock and subject coverage: Over 10,000 books and 5,500 journals on civil engineering
Opening hours: Term-time: 09.30-18.00 Monday to Friday
Vacations: 10.00-17.30 Monday to Friday
An appointment should be made prior to visiting

[273][f]
Electrical and Electronic Engineering Department Library
Rooms 607 & 601
Level 6
Electrical and Electronic Engineering Building
London SW7 2BT
Borough: Kensington and Chelsea
Telephone: 020 7594 6182
Fax: 020 7823 8125
Stock and subject coverage: 7,000 books, 3,000 journals (257 new titles) on electrical and electronic engineering
Opening hours: Term-time: 09.30 - 17.30 Monday to Friday; vacations: 09.30 - 17.30 Monday to Friday; an appointment should be made prior to visiting

[273][g]
Materials Department Library
Rooms B436 & B434
Level 4
Bessemer Building
Materials Department
London SW7 2BP
Borough: Kensington and Chelsea
Telephone: 020 7594 6751
Fax: 020 7584 3194
Stock and subject coverage: 6,000 books and 5,000 journals relating to materials
Opening hours: Term-time: 09.30-17.30 Monday to Friday; vacations: 09.30-17.30 Monday to Friday; an appointment should be made prior to visiting

[273][h]
Mathematics Department Library
Huxley Building
Queen's Gate
London SW7 2BZ
Borough: Kensington and Chelsea
Telephone: 020 7594 8542
Fax: 020 7589 9463
Stock and subject coverage: 19,000 books and over 9,000 journals relating to mathematics
Opening hours: Term-time: 09.30-18.00 Monday to Friday
Vacations: 09.30-18.00 Monday to Friday
An appointment should be made prior to visiting

[273][i]
Mechanical Engineering Department Library
Level 3
Mechanical Engineering Building
London SW7 2BX
Borough: Kensington and Chelsea
Telephone: 020 7594 7166
Fax: 020 7594 8517
Stock and subject coverage: Over 16,000 books and 11,500 journals relating to mechanical engineering
Opening hours: Term-time: 09.30-18.00 Monday to Friday; vacations: 09.30-17.30 Monday to Friday; an appointment should be made prior to visiting

[273][j]
Physics Department Library
Blackett Laboratory, Level 2
Prince Consort Road, London
SW7 2BW
Borough: Kensington and Chelsea
Telephone: 0207 594 7871
Stock and subject coverage: Ca. 10,000 books and 6,000

journals. Subject strengths include astrophysics, condensed matter theory, high energy physics, optics, plasma physics, space and atmospheric physics and theoretical physics

Opening hours: 09.30-18.00 Monday to Friday; vacations: 9.30-17.30 Monday to Friday; an appointment should be made prior to visiting

Faculty of Medicine

[273][k]
Charing Cross Campus
The Library
Charing Cross Campus
The Reynolds Building
St Dunstan's Road
London W6 8RP

Borough: Hammersmith and Fulham
Telephone: 020 7594 0755
Fax: 020 7594 0851
E-mail: librarycx@ic.ac.uk
Stock and subject coverage: Over 20,000 books and 400 current medical journals (plus older issues of ca. 450 other titles) on medical, nursing, allied health and mental health topics and biomedicine
Opening hours: Term-time: 09:00- 21.00 Monday to Thursday; 09:00-20:00 Friday, 09:00-12:00 Saturday; Christmas and Easter vacation: 9:00-19.00 Monday to Friday; summer vacation: 9:00-18.00 Monday to Friday; an appointment should be made prior to visiting

[273][l]
Chelsea and Westminster Campus
Medical Library
Lower Ground Floor
Chelsea and Westminster Hospital
369 Fulham Road
London SW10 9NH

Borough: Hammersmith and Fulham
Telephone: 020 8746 8107
Fax: 020 8746 8215
E-mail: librarycw@ic.ac.uk
Stock and subject coverage: The library holds over 20,000 books and 400 current journals (plus older issues of ca. 450 other titles) covering nursing and allied health, mental health and biomedicine
Opening hours: Term-time: 09:00-21.00 Monday to Thursday; 09.00-20.00 Friday: 09:00-17.00 Saturday Christmas and Easter vacation: 09.00-19.00; summer vacation: 09.00-18.00; an appointment should be made prior to visiting

[273][m]
The Hammersmith Campus (Wellcome Library)
Du Cane Road
London W12 0NN

Borough: Hammersmith and Fulham
Telephone: 020 8383 3246
Fax: 020 8383 2195
E-mail: lib.hamm@ic.ac.uk

Stock and subject coverage: Primarily a research library with a collection of almost 1,000 current medical and scientific periodicals and over 60,000 bound volumes. It has about 8,000 books and a small collection of audiovisual programmes.
Opening hours: 09.00-21.00 Monday to Friday: 09.30-12.30 Saturday; an appointment should be made prior to visiting

[273][n]
Royal Brompton Campus
Dovehouse Street
London SW3 6LY

Borough: Kensington and Chelsea
Telephone: 020 7351 8150
Fax: 020 7351 8117
E-mail: nhli.library@ic.ac.uk
Stock and subject coverage: Ca. 280 current journals in heart and lung disease; biochemistry, pharmacology, surgery, social medicine, nursing and allied health topics. Ca. 6,000 in the current textbook collection, plus rare book material and a historical collection
Services: Photocopies (self-service, charges made)
Availability: Access to bona fide researchers where material is unavailable elsewhere (charges may be made). An appointment should be made prior to visiting
Hours: Term-time and vacations: 09.00-21.00 Monday to Friday
Transport: Tube: South Kensington; Bus: 11, 14, 19, 22, 49, 211, 345

[273][o]
St Mary's Campus
Norfolk Place
Paddington
London W2 1PG

Borough: Kensington and Chelsea
Telephone: 020 7594 3692
Fax: 020 7402 3971
World Wide Web: www.lib.ic.ac.uk
Constitution: Part of Imperial College of Science, Technology and Medicine
Objectives/Purposes: The Library aims to provide a library and information service for undergraduates, post-graduates and academic staff of Imperial College and the staff of St Mary's NHS Trust and its associated health district (KCWHA)
Stock and subject coverage: Ca. 30,000 bound journals, 300 current journals, 5,000 books on pre-clinical and clinical medicine
Services: See www.lib.ic.ac.uk
Hours: Pre-clinical term-time: 09.00-21.00; 09.00-13.00 Saturday; August: 09.00-19.00
Transport: Tube and rail: Paddington; Bus: 7, 15, 23, 27, 36
Publications: Annual Report and Bibliography of Sir Alexander Fleming 1881-1955 (all published by St Mary's Hospital Medical School); St Mary's Hospital Medical School: An Historical Anthology, 1990 (published by Imperial College and St Mary's Hospital and Medical School Archives)

[274]
Imperial War Museum
IWM
Lambeth Road
London SE1 6HZ
Borough: Southwark
Telephone: 020 7416 5000
Fax: 020 7416 5374
E-mail: mail@iwm.org.uk
World Wide Web: www.iwm.org.uk
Constitution: National Museum part-funded by
   Government; registered charity
Key staff: Information Officer: Ruth Findlay
Stock and subject coverage: The museum houses reference
   departments covering all aspects of war in the 20th
   century which have affected Britain and other
   members of the Commonwealth. The reference
   collections may be viewed by appointment only
Hours: Reference departments:10.00-17.00; museum
   hours: 10.00-18.00 daily
Services: Microfilms; photocopies
Transport: Tube: Lambeth North, Elephant and Castle;
   Rail: Waterloo, Elephant and Castle; Bus: 1, 3, C10,
   12, 53, 63, 68, 109, 159, 168, 171, 172, 176, 188, 344
Special facilities: Refreshment and toilet facilities available;
   access for users with disabilities but please advise in
   advance of visiting
Publications: Corporate Plan (annual); IWM Review
   (annual)
Special features: The IWM building was Royal Bethlem
   Hospital ('Bedlam') until 1930

[274][a]
Department of Art
Key staff: Keeper: Ms AH Weight BA, ext 5210
   Enquiries and Appointments: ext 5211
Stock and subject coverage: The Art Collection contains
   about 16,000 paintings, drawings, prints and
   sculptures, mainly the results of official government
   commissions during the two World Wars. Since 1972
   the Artistic Records Committee has continued the
   tradition of commissioning artists to cover recent
   conflicts in which British forces have been involved.
   The Department itself purchases contemporary art
   on themes relevant to the Museum's terms of
   reference. The Department also has a very large
   collection of British, European and American posters,
   of which about 4,000 are available for study. The War
   Artists Archive, available on microfilm, contains
   extensive correspondence between the
   commissioning bodies and artists in the two World
   Wars
Availability: Open to bona fide researchers, at least 48
   hours notice required
Hours: 10.00-17.00 Monday to Friday by appointment
Services: Electronic access to over 3,000 images with
   colour printout facility. Hire of 5x4 transparencies
   from stock (allow 4 weeks for new photography).
   Black and white photographic prints and 35mm
   slides produced to order. Copyright reproduction fees
   payable. Exhibition catalogues and leaflets relating to
   the Department's art exhbition programme

[274][b]
Department of Documents
Key staff: Keeper: RWA Suddaby MA, ext 5220
   Enquiries and Appointments: exts 5222/5223
E-mail: docs@iwm.org.uk
World Wide Web: www.iwm.org.uk/docs_hp.htm
Stock and subject coverage: The Department holds
   collections of German World War II records, mostly
   in copy form; the records of the major War Crimes
   Trials; and extensive private papers of servicemen,
   women and civilians, principally from the two World
   Wars. The Department also provides information on
   the holdings of other British, American and
   European archives in the field of contemporary
   history. Photostat copies of documents in the
   Department's collections can normally be purchased

[274][c]
Department of Exhibits and Firearms
Telephone: 020 7416 5272
Fax: 020 7416 5374
E-mail: exfire@iwm.org.uk
Key staff: The Keeper
Stock and subject coverage: The Department is responsible
   for all three dimensional material held by the
   Museum. The collections cover such fields as
   uniforms, badges, personal equipment, medals, edged
   weapons, flags, artillery, aircraft, ship models, tanks
   and armoured fighting vehicles. It also administers
   the national collection of modern firearms, which
   includes examples of almost all firearms issued on a
   significant scale by the major powers in both World
   Wars. In addition to material on public display there
   are extensive reserve collections, which may be
   viewed by appointment. Allowance should be made
   for the circumstance that over half of the collections
   are stored outside London
Services: Enquiry service; two loan services, one to
   schools, the other for displays or exhibitions in
   museums, galleries or institutions
Hours: Researchers should apply, by written application,
   to the Keeper

[274][d]
Department of Printed Books
Key staff: Keeper: Richard Golland BA DipLib ALA
   MIInfSc; Head of Acquisitions, Cataloguing and
   Computing: Mary Wilkinson; Head of Public
   Services: Christopher Hunt
   General Enquiries, ext 5342
   Reading Room Appointments: ext 5344
E-mail: books@iwm.org.uk
Stock and subject coverage: The Department has a
   collection of over 100,000 books covering the
   political, economic and social implications of war, as
   well as its military, naval and air aspects. It houses a
   comprehensive range of journals, pamphlets and maps
   and receives over 400 current journals. Several
   bibliographies and short booklists are published by
   the Department
Availability: Open to all, for reference only, but under
   15s must be accompanied by an adult
Hours: Reading Room: 10.00-17.00 Monday to
   Saturday; appointment required; telephone enquiries:
   09.00-17.00 Monday to Friday

Special facilities: Refreshment and toilet facilities available; access for users with disabilities – no wheelchair access to main reading room but services provided in nearby room; equipment to assist people with visual impairments

Special features: The Reading Room is housed under the Museum's Dome, former chapel of the Bethlem ('Bedlam') Hospital

[274][e]
Film and Video Archive
IWMFVA

Key staff: Keeper: ext 5290; General Enquiries: exts 5291/5292

Fax: 020 7416 5379

E-mail: film@iwn.org.uk

Stock and subject coverage: The collection comprises 50 million feet of film, mainly from the two World Wars. Apart from material shot by Service cameramen, and films sponsored by the war ministries and Ministry of Information, there are also extensive holdings from Allied and enemy sources as well as many important documentaries, television compilations and feature films. There is also a growing collection of material on the major post-war conflicts, drawn from both official and commercial sources. Amateur film records play an increasingly important part in the collection

Services: Public film shows screened in the Museum Cinema at weekends and in school holidays

Availability: Collection open to the general public; one week's notice required from visitors

Hours: Film may be viewed by appointment, 10.00–16.45 Monday to Friday

Publications: Film and Video Archive Handbook

[274][f]
Photographic Archive

Key staff: Keeper: Miss Bridget Kinally, ext 5287

Enquiries and Appointments: exts 5333/5338

E-mail: photos@iwm.org.uk

Stock and subject coverage: The Library contains some six million photographs, mostly taken by official photographers, illustrating all theatres of operation in the two World Wars, including the home front. There are large collections relating to the ships, aircraft and military equipment of many countries. Donations from private sources are also an important part of the collection. Copies of these photographs may be purchased from the Department. Enquiries about their reproduction should be addressed to the Commercial Assistant

Services: Copy prints may be purchased, reproduction fees are payable if prints are required for publication

Hours: Visitors' Room open by appointment, 10.00–17.00

[274][g]
Sound Archive

Key staff: Keeper: Margaret Brooks MA ext: 5360 Enquiries and Appointments: ext 5363

E-mail: sound@iwm.org.uk

Stock and subject coverage: The collection comprises more than 33,000 hours of recordings. This material falls into three main categories: oral history interviews recorded by Museum staff in various service and

civilian fields bearing on conflict and war in the 20th century; broadcast recordings acquired from television and radio organisations; a miscellany of other sound documents including lectures, contemporary topical recordings, poetry readings, sound effects, etc. There is a searchable database and the collection is available for reference at the Museum; copies of many recordings may be purchased by the public. A number of printed catalogues and listings are also available

Hours: 10.00–17.00 Monday to Friday, by appointment

[275]
Independent Healthcare Association
IHA

9th Floor
Westminster Tower
3 Albert Embankment
London SE1 7SP

Borough: Camden

Telephone: 020 7793 4620

Fax: 020 7820 3738

E-mail: tim.evans@iha.org.uk

World Wide Web: www.iha.org.uk

Constitution: Registered charity

Key staff: Executive Director of Public Affairs: Dr Tim Evans

Stock and subject coverage: Publications concerning the independent health and social care sector

Availability: Reference facilities available, but written enquiries preferred. Information service mainly for government, MPs, the media and IHA members

Hours: 09.00–17.00 Monday to Friday

Transport: Tube: Westminster; Bus: 3, 11, 77, 344, 507

Publications: List available on request

[276]
Independent Housing Ombudsman Ltd
IHO

Norman House
105–9 Strand
London WC2R 0AA

Borough: Westminster

Telephone: 020 7836 3630

Fax: 020 7836 3900

E-mail: ombudsman@ihos.org.uk

World Wide Web: www.ihos.org.uk

Key staff: General Manager: Lawrence Greenberg

Stock and subject coverage: Materials on resolving complaints by tenants against member landlords. Publications include annual reports, research reports, reports of formal enquiries, standard statistics

Availability: Services offered to bona fide researchers

Hours: 09.15–17.15 Monday to Friday

Transport: Tube: Charing Cross, Embankment

[277]
Independent Schools Council Information Service
ISCis
35-37 Grosvenor Gardens
London SW1W 0BS
Borough: Westminster
Telephone: 020 7798 1500
Fax: 020 7798 1501
E-mail: info@iscis.uk.net
World Wide Web: www.iscis.uk.net
Constitution: Company limited by guarantee
Key staff: National Director: David J Woodhead
Stock and subject coverage: Information on independent schools in the UK; extensive range of publications on independent schools including an annual census of schools, market research and other surveys. Information services, material not available for loan but can be available for reference with prior warning
Services: Telephone and written enquiries dealt with as time permits
Availability: Information service open to enquirers
Hours: 09.00-17.30 Monday to Friday
Transport: Tube and Rail: Victoria
Publications: ISC Guide to Accredited Schools (annual guide available free of charge); Annual Guide to Independent Schools; Annual Census

Linked organisations
Independent Schools Council Part of the Council

[278]
Independent Television Commission
ITC
33 Foley Street
London W1W 2TL
Borough: Westminster
Telephone: 020 7306 7763
Fax: 020 7306 7750
Constitution: Licensing and regulatory body for commercial television
Key staff: Information Centre Manager: Jan Kacperek BA DipLib
Stock and subject coverage: Books; journals; research reports; government and parliamentary publications; press cuttings; television company and programme publicity. Covers broadcasting; television programmes; cable and satellite broadcasting; mass media; advertising; telecommunications. Primarily UK but also overseas
Services: Photocopies (coin-operated machine); microfiche reader-printer; internet access (to ITC website only)
Availability: Open to the public for reference use only
Hours: 12.00-16.00 Tuesday to Friday
Transport: Tube: Oxford Circus; Bus: C2, 3, 7, 10, 19, 23, 25, 53, 73, 88, 98, 159, 176
Special facilities: Toilet facilities available; access for users with disabilities – entrance ramp, special toilets
Publications: Library guide; selected subject bibliographies; Update (quarterly Library bulletin); list of journal holdings

[279]
Index on Censorship
33 Islington High Street
London N1 9LH
Borough: Islington
Telephone: 020 7278 2313
Fax: 020 7278 1878
E-mail: contact@indexoncensorship.org
World Wide Web: www.indexoncensorship.org
Constitution: Registered charity
Objectives/purposes: Promotion, defence and study of freedom of expression and access to information
Key staff: Editor and Chief Executive: Ursula Owen; Publisher: Henderson Mullin
Stock and subject coverage: Small reference collection of books about censorship, freedom of expression. Back issues of Index on Censorship, reports by human rights organisations. Index to Index on Censorship
Services: Self-service photocopies (charges made); fax; internet access; Reuters listing
Availability: Free access by appointment for reference only
Hours: 09.30-18.00 Monday to Friday
Transport: Tube: Angel; Bus: 4, 19, 30, 38, 43, X43, 56, 73, 171A, 214, 279, 921
Special facilities: Refreshment and toilet facilities available; access for users with disabilities – lift available
Publications: Index on Censorship magazine (bimonthly magazine); anthologies of Index material

Linked organisations
Writers and Scholars International
Writers and Scholars Educational Trust

[280]
India Welfare Society
11 Middle Row
North Kensington
London W10 5AT
Borough: Kensington and Chelsea
Telephone: 020 8969 9493
Fax: 020 8960 2637
E-mail: iwslondon@hotmail.com
Key staff: Volunteers only
Constitution: Registered charity
Objectives/purposes: To assist the distressed and needy
Stock and subject coverage: Collections on subjects connected with India
Availability: Open to all by appointment for reference only. Researchers should book an appointment by telephone
Hours: By appointment
Transport: Tube: Ladbroke Grove
Special facilities: Refreshment and toilet facilities available; access for users with disabilities
Publications: 18th, 25th and 30th anniversary brochures; Nehru Centenary Brochure, various leaflets

[281]
The Industrial Society
Robert Hyde House
48 Bryanston Square
London W1H 7LN
Borough: Westminster
Telephone: 020 7479 2323
Fax: 020 7479 2121
E-mail: infoserv@indsoc.co.uk
World Wide Web: www.indsoc.co.uk
Constitution: Independent non-profit organisation,
registered charity with voluntary subscribing
membership
Key staff: Head of Information Service: Brendan
McDonagh
Stock and subject coverage: Books, journals, company
policies about people at work. Covers human
resources, leadership, internal communication, people
development issues
Services: Photocopies
Availability: Open to bona fide researchers, by
appointment. Loans only available to corporate
members. A charge is levied for non-members
Hours: 09.15–17.15 Monday to Friday
Transport: Tube: Marble Arch
Special facilities: Refreshment and toilet facilities available

[282]
Information Network Focus on Religious Movements
INFORM
Houghton Street
London WC2A 2AE
Borough: Westminster
Telephone: 020 7955 7654
Fax: 020 7955 7679
E-mail: inform@lse.ac.uk
World Wide Web: www.inform.ac
Constitution: Company limited by guarantee; registered
charity
Objectives/purposes: To help the public by providing
unbiased, accurate, up-to-date information on
unfamilar religious or spiritual groups
Key staff: Amanda van Eck, San Kim, Sarah Porey
Stock and subject coverage: Books, journals, video tapes and
audio tapes on new religious movements (NRMs).
Hard files containing information on more than
1,400 NRMs from a variety of sources. Computer
database containing a summary of information on
NRMs
Services: Photocopies (charges made)
Availability: Available to all bona fide researchers, by
appointment, for reference only
Hours: 10.00–16.30 Monday to Friday
Special facilities: Refreshment and toilet facilities available
Publications: Annual Report

Linked organisations
London School of Economics (LSE) Affiliated
to the LSE

[283]
Inland Revenue Library
Room 28
New Wing
Somerset House
Strand
London WC2R 1LB
Borough: Westminster
Telephone: 020 7438 6726
Fax: 020 7438 7562
Government Telecommunications Network: 3541
E-mail: library.ir.sh@gtnet.gov.uk
World Wide Web: www.inlandrevenue.gov.uk
Constitution: Government department
Key staff: Senior Librarian: Paul Woods
Stock and subject coverage: Ca. 60,000 volumes, 800
journals. Specialises in taxation management, politics
and government
Services: Reference service; sale of consultative and
policy documents; photocopies
Availability: Open to the public on written application,
to the Librarian
Hours: 09.00–17.00 Monday to Friday
Transport: Tube: Covent Garden; Tube and Rail: Charing
Cross, Waterloo; Bus: 68, 178
Special facilities: Toilet facilities and access for users with
disabilities
Publications: Selected List of Accessions

[284]
Inner Temple Library
Inner Temple
London EC4Y 7DA
Borough: Corporation of London
Telephone: 020 7797 8217
Fax: 020 7583 6030
E-mail: library@innertemple.org.uk
World Wide Web: www.innertemplelibrary.org.uk
Constitution: Independent non-profit organisation
Key staff: Librarian: Margaret Clay; Deputy Librarian:
Adrian Blunt
Stock and subject coverage: Ca. 75,000 volumes on the law
of the UK and Commmonwealth; 9,000 manuscripts;
ca. 2,000 pamphlets
Services: Photocopies; document supply service
(members only, charges made); internet access
(members only)
Availability: A private library serving the members of the
Inns of Court. Other bona fide researchers admitted
at the Librarian's discretion, upon written application.
Reference only, no loans
Hours: 09.00–20.00 Monday to Thursday; 09.00–19.00
Friday. Shorter hours operate outside term
Transport: Tube: Temple; Rail: City Thameslink
Special facilities: Toilet facilities; access for users with
disabilities (ramp access to main entrance; lift to main
Library level on 2nd floor, no access to Gallery level
on 3rd floor; toilet facilities on ground floor)
Special features: Library founded ca. 1500
Publications: Catalogue of Manuscripts in Inner Temple
Library, JC Davies, Oxford 1972; various library
guides

Linked organisations

Honourable Society of the Inner Temple Parent body

[285]
Institut Français du Royaume Uni

La Médiathèque
17 Queensberry Place
London SW7 2DT
Borough: Kensington and Chelsea
Telephone: 020 7073 1354
Fax: 020 7073 1355
E-mail: library@ambafrance.org.uk
World Wide Web: www.institut.francais.org.uk
Constitution: French Government funded body
Key staff: Head Librarian: Isabel Fernandez
Stock and subject coverage: 50,000 books; 2,500 videos and DVDs, 3,000 CDs and 100 journals; children's library with ca. 10,000 documents. Resource centre about contemporary France (society, economics, politics, literature, cinema, music, etc) plus collection on French literature and cinema and France Libre collection
Services: Photocopying; press-cutting files; library online catalogue; inter-library loan; free access to the internet for members. Activities include reading group and 'café littéraire' once a month, events including youth festival in November and celebration of reading in October
Availability: Free access to the reading room. Loans to members (membership £40 p.a., £30 per semestre. Concessions £30 p.a., £20 per semestre)
Hours: Médiathèque: 12.00-19.00 Tuesday to Friday; 12.00-18.00 Saturday
Children's Library: 12.00-18.00 Tuesday to Saturday
Transport: Tube: South Kensington; Bus: 14, 74
Special facilities: Refreshment and toilet facilities available
Special features: Listed building and reading room from the 1930s
Publications: Bibliographies on selected topics

Linked organisations

Institut Français d'Edinbourg
Alliance Française de Glasgow
Maison Française d'Oxford
Other affiliated French libraries

[286]
Institute and Guild of Brewing

33 Clarges Street
London W1J 7EE
Borough: Westminster
Telephone: 020 7499 8144
Fax: 020 7499 1156
E-mail: enquiries@igb.org.uk
World Wide Web: www.igb.org.uk
Constitution: Association with voluntary subscribing membership
Objectives/Purposes: To provide education, training and examinations for the brewing and distilling industry
Key staff: Chief Executive: BEA Pegnall
Stock and subject coverage: Materials on brewing
Availability: Available on request

Hours: 09.00-17.00 Monday to Friday
Transport: Tube: Green Park; Rail: Victoria
Publications: The Brewer International (monthly); The Journal of The Institute of Brewing (quarterly)

[287]
The Institute for Optimum Nutrition
ION

13 Blades Court
Deodar Road
Putney
London SW15 2NU
Borough: Wandsworth
Telephone: 020 8877 9993
Fax: 020 8877 9980
E-mail: education@ion.ac.uk
info@ion.ac.uk
World Wide Web: www.ion.ac.uk
Constitution: Independent, non-profit making charity – educational trust
Objectives/purposes: To advance education of the public and health professionals in all matters relating to health. ION seeks to bridge the gap between orthodox and complementary/alternative practitioners and, through credible professional information and education, to raise the standards of health awareness to the nation
Key staff: Administration: Dennis Andrews; Head of Marketing Communications: Sarah Lumley; Information: Yara D'Avella, Caroline Garrett
Stock and subject coverage: Materials (books, leaflets, research papers and articles) covering the discipline of nutrition and health. Comprehensive information on impact of nutrition upon illness (physical, mental and emotional) and the effects of nutrients – vitamins, minerals, amino acids, etc.
Services: Photocopies (charges made)
Availability: Reference library open free of charge to members and students of ION; open to others by appointment. Charges for some enquiries and searches – details available by telephone or e-mail
Hours: 10.00-16.30 Monday to Friday
Transport: Tube: Putney Bridge, East Putney; Rail: Putney; Bus: 14
Special facilities: Toilet facilities available
Publications: Optimum Nutrition Magazine (3 p.a.)

[288]
Institute for Social Inventions
ISI

20 Heber Road
London NW2 6AA
Borough: Brent
Telephone: 020 8208 2853
Fax: 020 8452 6434
E-mail: rhino@dial.pipex.com
World Wide Web: www.globalideasbank.org
Constitution: Project of registered charity, The Nicholas Albery Foundation
Objectives/purposes: The Institute aims to gather and promote socially innovative ideas and projects. Social inventions are new social services, or new and

imaginative solutions to social problems including new laws, electoral systems, projects, organisations and ways for people to relate

Key staff: Stephanie Wienrich, Nick Temple, Retta Bowen

Stock and subject coverage: Collections on social innovations: ideas sent to the Institute since 1985; newspaper cuttings and books

Availability: Restricted access; researchers should apply by telephone or in writing

Hours: 09.30-17.30 Monday to Friday

Transport: Tube: Willesden Green; Rail: Cricklewood; Bus: 260

Special facilities: Toilet facilities available

Publications: Social Innovations (annual, £15)

Linked organisations

Natural Death Centre
Apprentice Master Alliance
Global Ideas Bank
Poetry Challenge

Projects started by the Institute.
The Institute runs the Global Ideas Bank on the internet (www.globalideasbank.org) as an international suggestion box for social innovations

[289]
Institute of Advanced Legal Studies
IALS

17 Russell Square
London WC1B 5DR

Borough: Camden
Telephone: 020 7862 5790
Fax: 020 7862 5770
E-mail: ials@sas.ac.uk
World Wide Web: ials.sas.ac.uk
Constitution: Department of a university
Key staff: Librarian: Jules Winterton; Deputy Librarian: Jennifer Jones; Reader Services Manager: David Gee; Admissions Enquiries: Joyce Quelch
Stock and subject coverage: The Library is the postgraduate legal research library of the University of London. The collection of ca. 250,000 volumes is particularly strong in the areas of Commonwealth law, Western European law, US law and public and private international law, as well as UK law. It includes material in Western European languages for all jurisdictions, for comparative and general reference purposes, and records of Legal Education Archives. IALS incorporates the Commonwealth Law Library of the Foreign and Commonwealth Office. It is one of the world's leading legal research libraries. More information on the collections is available on the IALS website and at www.lon.ac.uk/garside. The catalogue is available at http://library.sas.ac.uk
Services: Self-service photocopiers and microform reader-printer; online and CD-ROM databases; word-processing facilities; internet access
Availability: Open to academic staff and postgraduate research students from all universities worldwide. Non-university researchers admitted at the discretion of the Director on payment of a fee. Premium information services available to legal practitioners and corporate clients. Undergraduate students and students for the professional legal examinations not

admitted. The Library is primarily a reference library with limited lending

Hours: 09.00-20.00; 10.00-17.30 Saturday. Closed at public holiday weekends and for extra days at Christmas and Easter; also for the last two weeks of September

Transport: Tube: Russell Square; Rail: Euston; Bus: 7, 68, 91, 168, 188

Special facilities: Refreshment and toilet facilities; access for users with disabilities (wheelchair access; lift access to all floors; wheelchair accessible toilets)

Publications: Annual Report; Amicus Curiae journal of the Society of Advanced Legal Studies (10 p.a.); series of guides to the library, its collections and services

Linked organisations

University of London, School of Advanced Study The Institute is a member of the School of Advanced Study

[290]
Institute of Alcohol Studies
IAS

Alliance House
12 Caxton Street
London SW1H 0QS

Borough: Westminster
Telephone: 020 7222 4001/5880
Fax: 020 7799 2510
E-mail: librarian@ias.org.uk
World Wide Web: www.ias.org.uk
Constitution: Registered charity
Objectives/purposes: Promotion of knowledge and understanding of beverage alcohol and the prevention of problems associated with alcohol consumption
Key staff: Judith Crowe
Stock and subject coverage: Information on the medical harm aspects of alcohol; epidemiology and social surveys; social problems associated with alcohol. Historical temperance collection covering the 1850s-1930s
Services: Photocopies (charges made)
Availability: Open to all for reference only by prior arrangement
Hours: 09.30-16.30 Monday to Friday
Transport: Tube: St James' Park; Rail: Victoria
Special facilities: Toilet facilities available
Publications: UK Alcohol Alert (quarterly); The Globe magazine (quarterly); series of occasional papers

Linked organisations

Eurocare IAS provides the Secretariat for Eurocare, an association of agencies dealing with alcohol problems mainly within the European Union

[291]
Institute of Archaeology Library

University of London
31-4 Gordon Square
London WC1H 0PY

Borough: Camden
Telephone: 020 7679 7495
Fax: 020 7383 2572

World Wide Web: www.ucl.ac.uk/archaeology
Constitution: The Institute of Archaeology is part of University College London
Key staff: Supervisor: Katie Meheux
Stock and subject coverage: One of the finest archaeological collections in the world with ca. 80,000 books, 10,000 pamphlets and 1,000 current journals. The collection is particularly strong on prehistoric Europe, the archaeology of Western Asia, the Classical world, Egypt, Sub-Saharan Africa and Latin America. Environmental archaeology, ancient archaeology, the conservation of artefacts and museum and heritage studies are also well represented. Specialised collections include the JM de Navarro and RF Tylecote collections and the African archeological collection of Professor Thurstan Shaw. The Yates Library of Classical Archaeology and the Edwards Library of Egyptology were recently incorporated into the collections
Services: Photocopies; networked databases
Availability: Open to all bona fide researchers for reference only
Hours:
Transport: Tube: Euston, Googe Street; Rail: Euston
Special facilities: Toilet facilities available; access for users with disabilities
Publications:

Linked organisations

University College London Member of the College

[292]
Institute of Biomedical Science Library
IBMS

12 Coldbath Square
London EC1R 5HL
Borough: Islington
Telephone: 020 7713 0214
Fax: 020 7436 4946
E-mail: mail@ibms.org
World Wide Web: www.ibms.org
Constitution: The Institute of Biomedical Science is the professional body for biomedical scientists in all fields of work, including medical laboratory scientific officers in the National Health Service and related services in the United Kingdom. The Institute was founded in 1912 and is registered as a charity. It changed its name from the Institute of Medical Laboratory Sciences in January 1994.
Objectives/purposes: To promote and develop biomedical science and its practitioners and to establish and maintain professional standards.
Objectives/purposes: Professional body, founded in 1912, for biomedical scientists
Key staff: Librarian: John R Mercer
Stock and subject coverage: Ca. 1,250 books, 25 current journals, 540 bound Fellowship theses on the following subjects: cellular pathology, microscopy, haematology, blood transfusion science, cytology, clinical chemistry, microbiology, virology, immunology, serology, laboratory administration and safety. Emphasis on the history of biomedical science
Services: Photocopies

Availability: Open to all bona fide researchers. Stock mostly reference only; loan of Fellowship theses and post 1950 books loaned to other accredited libraries
Hours: 09.00-17.00 Monday to Friday by arrangement
Transport: Tube: Farringdon; Bus: 19, 38, 63
Special facilities: Toilet facilities available; access for users with disabilities
Publications: List of current periodicals received by the library; Annual Report. The IBMS publishes: British Journal of Biomedical Science (quarterly); Biomedical Scientist (monthly)

[293]
Institute of Cancer Research

Chester Beatty Laboratories
237 Fulham Road
London SW3 6JB
Borough: Kensington and Chelsea
Telephone: 020 7352 5946
Fax: 020 7352 6283
E-mail: fullib@icr.ac.uk
World Wide Web: www.icr.ac.uk
Constitution: Registered charity and department of a university
Key staff: Acting Librarian: Neroli Wolland
Stock and subject coverage: Over 500 current journals in oncology, biology and chemistry
Services: Photocopies
Availability: Free access for all staff of the Institute of Cancer Research and the Royal Marsden Hospital. Reference only access, by appointment, for University of London members
Hours: 09.00-17.30 Monday to Friday
Transport: Tube: South Kensington
Special facilities: Toilet facilities available

Linked organisations

University of London The Institute is affiliated to the University through the British Postgraduate Medical Federation
Institute of Cancer Research, 15 Cotswold Road, Belmont, Sutton, Surrey SN2 5NG. Tel: 020 8643 8901, ext 4230
The Library is located on two sites in Fulham and Sutton

[294]
Institute of Chartered Accountants in England and Wales
ICAEW

Chartered Accountants' Hall
Moorgate Place
London EC2P 2BJ
Borough: Corporation of London
Telephone: 020 7920 8620
Fax: 020 7920 8621
E-mail: library@icaew.co.uk
World Wide Web: www.icaew.co.uk/library
Constitution: Independent non-profit distributing organisation; chartered professional body
Key staff: Librarian: Ms SP Moore BA ALA, 020 7920 8441
Deputy Librarian: Ms AJ Dennis BA ALA, 020 7920 8415

Stock and subject coverage: 42,000 volumes and 27,000 abstracts of jouanl articles; 300 current journals. Company information services; files of comments on exposure drafts of UK Accounting Standards and International Accounting Standards; Comments on UK Auditing Standards. Stock and enquiry service covers: UK and international accounting and auditing, company law, finance, management, IT, taxation. Special collection of historical accounting literature from 1494

Services: Photocopies; fax; microfiche/film reader-printer; OPACs

Availability: Visitors may use the Library for reference with a letter of introduction from a Member of the Institute

Hours: 09.00–17.30 Monday to Thursday; 10.00–17.30 Friday; 24-hour answerphone 020 7920 8622

Transport: Tube: Moorgate, Bank, Liverpool Street; Rail: Liverpool Street, Cannon Street, Fenchurch Street

Special facilities: Refreshment and toilet facilities; access for users with disabilities by arrangement – stairs to Library

Publications: Publications catalogue available from Accountancy Books (020 7920 8991)

Linked organisations
Consultative Committee of Accountancy Bodies (CCAB) Member of CCAB

---

[295]
Institute of Chartered Secretaries and Administrators
ICSA
16 Park Crescent
London W1N 4AH
Borough: Westminster
Telephone: 020 7580 4741
Fax: 020 7612 7034
Telex: 268350 ICSA G
E-mail: informationcentre@icsa.co.uk
World Wide Web: www.icsa.org.uk
Constitution: Independent, self-regulating body operating under Royal Charter
Key staff: Information Centre Manager: Andrew Tillbrook; Information Officer: J Andrews
Stock and subject coverage: Practioners manuals and textbooks on company secretarial practice, company law and corporate governance. International corporate governance collection
Services: Technical enquiry service in the area of company secretarial practice, company law and corporate governance. Bibliographies on the same topics
Availability: Members only; reference and information service
Hours: 09.30–17.00 Monday to Friday
Transport: Tube: Regent's Park, Great Portland Street
Special facilities: Toilet facilities available
Publications: Chartered Secretary (monthly); The Company Secretary (monthly); ICSA Best Practice guides

---

[296]
Institute of Child Health
ICH
30 Guilford Street
London WC1E 1EH
Borough: Camden
World Wide Web: www.ich.ucl.ac.uk/library
Constitution: ICH is part of University College London
Transport: Tube: Russell Square; Bus: 59, 68, 188 (to Russell Square)

[296][a]
The Friends of the Children of Great Ormond Street Library
Telephone: 020 7242 9789 ext 2424
Fax: 020 7831 0499
E-mail: library@ich.ucl.ac.uk
Key staff: Librarian: John Clarke; Deputy Librarian and Nursing and Allied Health Liaison: Sue Holloway; Assistant Librarian: Marina Waddington; Library Assistants: Sui Jing Ly, Teresa Wood
Stock and subject coverage: Materials on medicine, nursing and child health. The Library includes the SOURCE collection (see below) and Teaching Aids at Low Cost (TALC) materials available for purchase
Services: Photocopiers; databases and internet access (registered users only); microfiche reader
Availability: Available to ICH and Great Ormond Street Hospital staff, and to students and visitors attached to either institution for a period of not less than one month. Visitors for shorter periods will be issued with reference only cards
Hours: 09.00–18.00 Monday to Friday

[296][b]
The SOURCE Collection
(housed within the ICH Library)
Telephone: 020 7242 9789 ext 8698
Fax: 020 7404 2062
E-mail: source@ich.ucl.ac.uk
World Wide Web: www.asksource.info
Key staff: Source Coordinator (Information Systems): Victoria Richardson; Assistant Librarian: Marina Waddington; Disability Information Officer: Kerstin Schaefer
Constitution: Source is a collaborative venture between ICH, Healthlink Worldwide and Handicap International
Stock and subject coverage: Unique collection of over 20,000 information resources focusing on primary health care, disability, mother and child health, HIV/AIDS, poverty and health. These include published and unpublished materials, many of which are from developing countries and are not readily available elsewhere in the UK. In 2002 Source plans to make its contacts database of organisations working in health and disability available from its website and to promote access to its collection of electronic materials
Availability: The collection is open to visitors for reference only; telephone in advance to make an appointment
Hours: 09.00–18.00 Monday to Friday. Currently Source is only fully staffed on Mondays and Tuesdays from 09.00–17.00

Linked organisations

Centre for International Child Health (at ICH)
Handicap International
Healthlink Worldwide
Source is a collaborative venture of all three
organisations

[297]
Institute of Classical Studies Library and Joint Library of the Hellenic and Roman Societies
ICS / JL
3rd Floor
Senate House
Malet Street
London WC1E 7HU
Borough: Camden
Telephone: 020 7862 8709
Fax: 020 7862 8735
E-mail: swillett@sas.ac.uk
World Wide Web: www.sas.ac.uk/icls
Constitution: Department of a university; registered
charity; association with voluntary subscribing
membership
Key staff: Librarian: Colin Annis; Deputy Librarian: Paul
Jackson; Senior Library Assistant: Sue Willetts
Stock and subject coverage: The whole of the Classical
world, covering Greek and Roman language,
literature, history, philosophy, art and archaeology.
Special collections include the Wood Donation of the
diaries of Robert Wood and his companions on the
Grand Tour in 1750/51; the Leaf Collection of
Homerica and Greek philology; the Winnington-
Ingram collection of works on ancient music and
metre; the Scullard collection of works on Roman
history and politics. The Institute of Classical Studies
Library is responsible for collecting primary material
such as standard editions of texts, the corpora of
papyri and inscriptions, dictionaries, lexica and
encyclopaedias, excavation reports and the like. The
Joint Library, which is shelved together with the
Institute Library is responsible for secondary works
Services: Photocopying available on Library's own book-
friendly machine; slide hire and filmstrip sale service
available to members; electronic resources in classics
subjects available to members
Availability: Access to members of the Institute and/or
Societies only. Membership of the Institute is open to
postgraduates and university lecturers in a classics-
related subject and is free of charge. It entitles
members to reference use of the Library only.
Membership of the Hellenic and Roman Societies is
open to all, for an annual subscription (there is a
reduced student rate). Members of the Societies can
borrow books and journals from the Library, but
material belonging to the Institute of Classical
Studies Library cannot be borrowed. Non-members
are allowed two visits to consult material not easily
available elsewhere
Hours: Term-time: 09.30-18.00 Monday, Wednesday and
Friday; 09.30-20.00 Tuesday and Thursday; 10.00-
16.30 Saturday (closed all day Saturday in August, for
a week at Christmas and Easter and two weeks at the
end of August)
Transport: Tube: Euston, Euston Square, Warren Street,
Russell Square: Rail: Euston, King's Cross; Bus: 10,
24, 29, 30, 68, 73, 91, 134, 168, 253
Special facilities: Refreshment facilities available (times:
09.30-11.30; 12.00-14.10; 15.30-16.55); toilet
facilities; access for users with disabilities
Publications: Library Guide, 4th ed.; slides catalogues
(Greek and Roman); Bulletin of the Institute of
Classical Studies (annual, published by the Institute);
Journal of Hellenic Studies and Archaeological
Reports (published by the Hellenic Society); Journal
of Roman Studies and Britannia (published by the
Roman Society)

Linked organisations

**University of London, School of Advanced
Study** The Institute is a member of the School of
Advanced Study
Society for the Promotion of Roman Studies
Society for the Promotion of Hellenic Studies
Joint Library is both Societies' library

[298]
Institute of Commonwealth Studies
ICS
28 Russell Square
London WC1B 5DS
Borough: Camden
Telephone: 020 7862 8844 (switchboard)
020 7862 8842 (Library reading room)
Fax: 020 7862 8820
E-mail: icommlib@sas.ac.uk
World Wide Web: www.sas.ac.uk/commonwealthstudies
Constitution: Department of a university
Key staff: Information Resources Manager: Erika
Gwynnett; Deputy Information Resources Manager:
Julie Evans
Stock and subject coverage: The ICS Library is a major
resource for those working on the Commonwealth as
a whole or on any of its member states, in the fields
of history, economics, politics and international
relations and other subjects such as agriculture,
education, the environment and social questions.
More than 70% of material is obtained from non-UK
Commonwealth member countries and specialises in
providing material unavailable elsewhere in the UK
or, in some cases, even in the country of origin. The
total stock contains ca. 170,000 items plus 200
archive collections, 14,000 items of political
ephemera and a run of 9,000 journals. Areas of
particular strength include the Caribbean region,
Southern Africa, Australia and Canada
Services: Photocopies; internet access; growing collection
of specialist online resources
Availability: Free access to all bona fide researchers
connected to a university. Charges for those not
working in higher education
Hours: Term-time: 09.30-18.30; vacations: 09.30-17.30
Transport: Tube: Russell Square, Goodge Street, Euston;
Rail: Euston; Bus: 7, 68, 91, 188
Special facilities: Refreshment and toilet facilities available;
access for users with disabilities (library on ground
floor)

Publications: Guides to the collections by region and subject lists of new books

Linked organisations

University of London, School of Advanced Study The Institute is a member of the School of Advanced Study

[299]
Institute of Cost and Executive Accountants
ICEA

Akhtar House
2 Shepherd's Bush Road
London W6 7PJ
Borough: Hammersmith and Fulham
Telephone: 020 8749 7126
Fax: 020 8749 7127
E-mail: icea@enta.net
World Wide Web: www.icea.enta.net
Constitution: Registered charity and company limited by guarantee
Objectives/purposes: Modern professional accounting body producing tomorrow's accountant
Key staff: Dr Sushil K Das Gupta BCom LLD ACIS FCEA
Stock and subject coverage: Accounting, business, finance, auditing and commercial law
Availability: Open to members only
Hours: 10.00-13.00
Transport: Tube: Shepherd's Bush, Hammersmith
Special facilities: Toilet facilities available
Publications: Executive Accountant magazine

Linked organisations

Association of Certified Book-Keepers
Association of Financial Controllers and Administrators

[300]
Institute of Directors
IoD

116 Pall Mall
London SW1Y 5ED
Borough: Westminster
Telephone: 020 7451 3100
Fax: 020 7321 0145
E-mail: businessinfo@iod.com
World Wide Web: www.iod.com
Constitution: Chartered professional body
Key staff: Librarian: Ms Pamela Bater
Stock and subject coverage: 6,000 items (books, reports, pamphlets, etc.); specialist collection on company directors and corporate governance; general business coverage; company law, etc.
Services: Information service, including online and CD-ROM searches; specialist advisory service for members only
Availability: By appointment for non-members
Hours: 08.30-18.30 Monday to Friday
Transport: Tube: Piccadilly Circus; Charing Cross; Rail: Charing Cross

Special facilities: Refreshment facilities (for members only); toilet facilities available; access for users with disabilities is difficult but can be arranged

[301]
Institute of Education, Information Services

20 Bedford Way
London WC1H 0AL
Borough: Camden
Telephone: 020 7612 6080
E-mail: lib.enquiries@ioe.ac.uk
World Wide Web: www.ioe.ac.uk
Constitution: Department of a university
Key staff: Head of Information Services and Librarian: Anne Peters
Stock and subject coverage: The Institute's library has Europe's largest collection of learned books and periodicals on educational studies. It contains over 300,000 volumes, including several special collections, and has files of nearly 2,000 periodicals from all over the world. There are also collections of archival material from organisations including the School's Council and an Official Publications Archive which contains central government publications on education from the early 19th century.
The largest special collection is Curriculum Resources, which has a vast selection of current books, pamphlets and other materials for use in schools. Some of these are for reference only; others can be borrowed. Books in particularly heavy demand can be borrowed on short loan.
Supplementing these major physical collections is a wide range of electronic journals, other full-text documents and research databases, many of which are available on the internet
Services: Reference, enquiry, interlibrary loan, postal loan services; postal photocopy delivery and self-service photocopying. The media section also provides a range of audiovisual and reprographic facilities as well as dedicated working space in which learning and teaching resources can be prepared in a variety of media formats. An equipment loan service is also operated, supplying audiovisual equipment suitable for project and presentation work. A specialist media suite includes video editing, audio recording and photographic equipment
Availability: Two types of visitors' membership available: associate and reference. See the website (www.ioe.ac.uk) for details
Hours: Full service and 'access' hours differ (see the website for details). Please note that library loan, enquiry and membership services are only available during full service hours. Library full service available during term-time: 09.30-21.00 Monday to Thursday; 10.30-17.00 Friday; 09.30-17.00 Saturday
Transport: Tube: Russell Square; Bus: N1, N2, N9, 10, 14, 14A, N21, 24, 29, N29, 30, N56, 68, 73, N73, N90, 134, 168, 188
Special facilities: Toilet facilities; access for users with disabilities

Linked organisations

University of London The Institute of Education is a School of the University

[302]
Institute of Financial Services Information Service
IFS

90 Bishopsgate
London EC2N 4DQ
Borough: Corporation of London
Telephone: 020 7444 7100
Fax: 020 7444 7109
E-mail: library@ifslearning.com
World Wide Web: www.ifsis.org.uk
Constitution: Registered charity; part of Chartered Institute of Bankers
Objectives/purposes: Provision of education, information and research to the financial services sector
Key staff: Manager: Susana Vazquez; Manager, Business Research and Information Service: Sarah Watts; Acquisitions Manager: Janet Scott; Systems Librarian: Lise Foster
Stock and subject coverage: Books, journals, CD-ROMs, archives and online databases on financial services. Comprehensive subject coverage of banking, monetary policy, banking law, bank history and investment
Services: Fee based business research and information service; photocopying; free internet for members; fax machines; payphone
Availability: Open to members of the Institute of Financial Services, the Association of Corporate Treasurers and the Securities Institute; discounted rates available for members of the Institute of Management Consultancy; individual and corporate subscriptions available; day fee use also available (£15 plus VAT for students, £50 plus VAT for non-students), no appointment necessary
Hours: 09.00-17.00 Monday, Wednesday and Friday; 09.00-18.00 Tuesday and Thursday
Transport: Tube and Rail: Liverpool Street
Special facilities: Toilet facilities available; access for users with disabilities – wheelchair users should advise staff in advance
Publications: City Contact Directory, Private Banks list, Banks in London list, Investment Banks list

[303]
Institute of Germanic Studies
IGS

The Library
29 Russell Square
London WC1B 5DP
Borough: Camden
Telephone: 020 7862 8967
Fax: 020 7862 8970
E-mail: igslib@ sas.ac.uk
World Wide Web: www.sas.ac.uk/igs
Constitution: Research institute within the University of London, School of Advanced Study
Key staff: Librarian: William Abbey
Stock and subject coverage: The Institute collects material (almost exclusively books and journals) in the field of German language and literature, from the beginnings to the present day. There are ca. 90,000 volumes in stock and the Library subscribes to 400 journals. Emphasis is placed on the acquisition of primary literature, Festschriften and reference books (including language dictionaries). Areas of strength include lexicography, orthography, East German literature, contemporary Swiss literature and many individual authors. The principal special collection is the Priebsch-Closs Collection which centres on the 18th and early 19th centuries but reaches back to 1475 and forward to the present. The Institute also houses the Friedrich Gundolf Archive and the papers of many important scholars in its field. Its manuscript holdings are extensive, the earliest document dating from the mid 9th century
Services: Self-service photocopies
Availability: The Library is open, free, to all bona fide researchers on application. No books or journals are loaned; the whole stock is reference only
Hours: 09.45-18.00 Monday to Friday
Transport: Tube: Russell Square, Goodge Street; Bus: 7, 10, 24, 29, 68, 73, 91, 168, 188
Special facilities: Limited refreshment facilities; toilet facilities
Publications: Research in Germanic Studies (annual); Annual Report; Bithell Series of Dissertations (monographic series published by MHRA); publications of the Institute of Germanic Studies (monographic series)

Linked organisations

University of London, School of Advanced Study The Institute is a member of the School of Advanced Study

[304]
Institute of Historical Research
IHR

University of London
Senate House
London WC1E 7HU
Borough: Camden
Telephone: 020 7862 8760
Fax: 020 7862 8762
E-mail: ihrlib@sas.ac.uk
World Wide Web: www.history.ac.uk/cwis/library.html
Constitution: Department of the University of London
Key staff: Librarian: Robert Lyons
Stock and subject coverage: The Library has a total stock of ca. 160,000 volumes. It collects printed sources, bibliographies, guides to archives, journals and reference works covering the history of Western Europe and its expansion overseas from the fall of the Roman Empire. It does not normally collect secondary monographs
Services: Self-service photocopies; microform readers and printer; computing facilities (available to members); CD-ROM service
Availability: Membership of the Institute is available free of charge to staff and postgraduate students of EU universities and other universities which subscribe to its Annual Payments Scheme. A fee is payable by other individuals. Temporary tickets are issued to members of the public who wish to consult material not otherwise available in London. No borrowing is allowed. Charges are made for copying and inter-library loans

Hours: 09.00–20.45 (last admission 20.30) Monday to Friday; 09.00–16.45 Saturday (last admission 16.30); the Library is open from 09.00–16.45 on some bank holidays
Transport: Tube: Russell Square, Goodge Street; Bus: 7, 10, 14, 24, 29, 68, 73, 77, 77A, 134
Special facilities: Refreshment and toilet facilities available; access for users with disabilities but because of the height of the bookstacks disabled readers should bring a companion
Publications: Guide to the Library (free)

Linked organisations
University of London, School of Advanced Study The Institute is a member of the School of Advanced Study

[305]
Institute of International Visual Arts Library
6–8 Standard Place
Rivington Street
London EC2A 3BE
Borough: Hackney
Telephone: 020 7729 9616
Fax: 020 7729 9509
E-mail: library@iniva.org
World Wide Web: www.iniva.org/library
Stock and subject coverage: Collection focuses on contemporary art from Africa, Asia, Latin America and the work of British artists from different cultural backgrounds. Over 4,000 exhibition catalogues, 1,000 monographs – covering cultural, political, gender and media studies – and over 150 periodicals, including titles not readily available in the UK
The Collection also includes ca. 4,500 slides (plus ephemera) stored in a collection of active artists' files
Services: Computerised catalogue; photocopier; magnifying lenses; wheelchair
Availability: Open to bona fide researchers by appointment, fees are payable (contact the website for details)
Transport: Tube: Old Street

[306]
Institute of Laryngology and Otology Library
ILO Library
Royal National Throat, Nose and Ear Hospital
330 Gray's Inn Road
London WC1X 8EE
Borough: Camden
Telephone: 020 7915 1445
E-mail: ilolib@ucl.ac.uk
World Wide Web: www.ucl.ac.uk/library/ilo
Constitution: Department of a university; postgraduate medical institute, part of UCL
Key staff: Librarian: Alex Stagg
Stock and subject coverage: Collections on laryngology, otology, rhinology, head and neck surgery and facial plastic surgery
Services: Photocopies (charges made); online searching facilities for users; videos

Availability: Reference access available to all; loans to registered users
Hours: 09.30–19.00 Monday and Tuesday; 09.30–17.30 Wednesday to Friday; 09.30–17.00 summer vacations
Transport: Tube and Rail: King's Cross; Bus: 10, 63, 73, 214
Special facilities: Refreshment and toilet facilities; limited access for users with disabilities (stairs, no lift available)

Linked organisations
University College London Part of University College

[307]
Institute of Latin American Studies Library
Library address:
35 Tavistock Square
London WC1

Postal address:
31 Tavistock Square
London WC1H 9HA
Borough: Camden
Telephone: 020 7862 8501
Fax: 020 7862 8971
E-mail: ilas.lib@sas.ac.uk
World Wide Web: www.sas.ac.uk/ilas
Constitution: Department of a university
Key staff: Information Resources Manager: Erika Gwynnett BA DipLib; Bibliographer: Alan Biggins, Bsc DipLib ALA
Stock and subject coverage: Over 6,000 bibliographies, encyclopaedias, guides to research and other reference works on Latin America (humanities and social sciences). Over 260 current journals and over 1,500 non-current titles. Academic journals are mainly in the social sciences and there is a substantial collection of news sources on and from Latin America. Ca. 3,000 papers from research centres in Latin America, Europe, the United States and elsewhere.
The Nissa Torrents Video Collection of feature films and documentaries on Latin America. The British Union Catalogue of Latin Americana. Author catalogue of the Latin American holdings of all the important UK collections in the field. Closed to new accessions in September 1988. Over 3,000 essential monographs, primarily for the use of the Institute's Master's students and selected from reading lists
Services: Self-service photocopies; internet access; self-service CD-ROM player – 14 CD-ROMs currently held. Video recordings of feature films and documentaries on Latin America may be viewed by prior appointment
Availability: Open for reference purposes to all academic staff and postgraduate students within the University of London, and to all other bona fide researchers from outside the University. Undergraduate students may only be admitted under special circumstances
Hours: 09.30–17.30 Monday, Thursday and Friday; 09.30–19.00 Tuesday and Wednesday

Transport: Tube: Euston, Euston Square, Russell Square;
Rail: Euston; Bus: 59, 68, 91, 168, 188 (Tavistock
Square), 10, 18, 30, 73 (Friends House, Euston Road)
Special facilities: Toilet facilities available
Publications: Latin American and Caribbean Library
Resources in the British Isles: a Directory compiled
by Alan Biggins and Valerie Cooper, 2002 (published
on behalf of the Advisory Council on Latin
American and Iberian Information Resources,
ACLAIIR); Latin American and Caribbean Library
Resources in London: a Guide, 7th ed. 1997
(published on behalf of the Latin American Subject
Sub-Committee of the University of London).
List of Booksellers Dealing in Latin Americana and
Caribbeana by Carole Travis, 2nd ed. 1987. Leaflet
detailing the collections and services of the Library
(annual)

Linked organisations

**University of London, School of Advanced
Study** The Institute is a member of the School of
Advanced Study

[308]
Institute of Logistics and Transport
ILT

Members' Reading Room
11-12 Buckingham Gate
London SW1E 6LB
Borough: City of Westminster
Telephone: 01536 740100
Fax: 020 7592 3111
E-mail: enquiry@iolt.org.uk
World Wide Web: www.iolt.org.uk
Constitution: Registered charity and chartered
professional body
Key staff: Librarian: Peter Huggins
Stock and subject coverage: Ca. 35 current journals, key
reference books, complete run of the Chartered
Institute of Transport journals from 1920 and the
Institute's holding of Modern Transport
Services: The Reading Room is a reference only facility
that provides members and visitors with electronic
access to the library catalogue and the means to
request book loans and photocopies
Availability: Free entry for members of ILT, charges
made for non-members (charges for library visits
must be prepaid)
Hours: 09.00-16.45 Monday to Friday
Transport: Tube: Victoria, Hyde Park Corner; Rail:
Victoria
Special facilities: Toilet facilities available
Publications: Logistics and Transport Focus (10 p.a.);
International Journal of Logistics, Research and
Applications (3 p.a.)

Linked organisations

Main library housed at the Institute's Corby office
(Earlstrees Court, Earlstrees Road, Corby, Northants
NN17 4AX, tel: 01536 740112, e-mail:
phuggins@iolt.org.uk) with a Member's Reading
Room provided in the London office

[309]
Institute of Marine Engineering, Science and Technology
IMarEST

80 Coleman Street
London EC2R 5BJ
Borough: Corporation of London
Telephone: 020 7382 2600
Fax: 020 7382 2670
E-mail: mic@imare.org.uk
World Wide Web: www.imare.org.uk
Constitution: Registered charity; chartered professional
body
Key staff: Manager: David Bartle
Stock and subject coverage: 4,000 bound volumes of
periodicals; 6,000 books and 1,000 conference
volumes; 700 reference books; 250 current periodicals
and journals. Covers marine engineering; ship
construction; general engineering; business
management; maritime law; navigation; ports and
harbours; naval architecture and offshore engineering
Services: Enquiry service; loans to members; searches on
large inhouse databases; photocopies; electronic
publications
Availability: Services are available free, or at cost price, to
members, and to non-members on a fee-paying basis
Hours: 09.00-17.00 Monday to Friday
Special facilities: Toilet facilities available; access for users
with disabilities
Transport: Tube: Bank, Moorgate, Liverpool Street; Rail:
Liverpool Street
Publications: Marine Technology Abstracts (CD-ROM
and web); International Directory of Consultants and
Technical Services (CD-ROM); Transactions
(Conferences, etc.; irregular, about 3 p.a.); Marine
Engineers Review (monthly); Journal of Offshore
Technology (quarterly)

[310]
Institute of Materials
IoM

1 Carlton House Terrace
London SW1Y 5DB
Borough: Westminster
Telephone: 020 7451 7300 (Institute line)
020 7451 7360 (Library line)
Fax: 020 7839 1702 / 020 7451 7406
E-mail: hilda_kaune@materials.org.uk
World Wide Web: www.materials.org.uk
Constitution: Registered charity and chartered
professional body
Key staff: Information Officer: Hilda Kaune
Stock and subject coverage: Materials science and
engineering including around 5,000 volumes, 14
current journal titles and back issues of the Institute's
predecessor organisations. Historical collection of
antiquarian books, biographies, technical drawings,
artefacts, portraits and photographs
Services: Photocopies and literature searches (charges
apply)
Availability: The Library is open to members of the
Institute and members of the public. Loan facilities
are available to members only
Hours: 09.30-12.30, 14.30-17.30 Monday to Friday

Transport: Tube: Piccadilly Circus, Charing Cross, St
    James' Park; Rail: Charing Cross; Bus: 6, 15, 19, 23,
    24, 29, 38

[311]
Institute of Neurology, Rockefeller Medical Library

National Hospital for Neurology and Neurosurgery
Queen Square
London WC1N 3BG
Borough: Camden
Telephone: 020 7829 8709 (Direct line)
Fax: 020 7278 1371
E-mail: library@ion.ucl.ac.uk
World Wide Web: www.ion.ucl.ac.uk/library/
Constitution: The Rockefeller Medical Library is the
    recognised Library for Neurology in the University
    of London and is a shared resource between the
    Institute of Neurology and the National Hospital for
    Neurology and Neurosurgery
Objectives/purposes: The Institute provides teaching and
    research of the highest quality in neurology,
    neurosurgery and the neurosciences, plus professional
    training for clinical careers in neurology,
    neurosurgery, neuroradiology, neuropathology and
    clinical neurophysiology in conjunction with the
    National Hospital
Key staff: Librarian: Louise Shepherd; Deputy Librarian:
    Ingrid Aubry
Stock and subject coverage: The collection covers
    neurology, neurosurgery, the neurosciences and allied
    fields. It comprises over 30,000 bound journals, 180
    current journal subscriptions, 13,700 books and
    monographs, and a unique historical collection of
    over 3,000 volumes. Consult the journal holdings list
    and library catalogue on the web for further details
    and locations
Services: Photocopier; video player, internet patient
    information
Availability: Access to all bona fide researchers, upon
    production of proof of identity, for reference only.
    Charges made for photocopies and for access by
    commercial organisations. Charges also made for
    reproduction of photographs, illustrations, etc.
    Mediated searching not available to visitors
Hours: 09.00–19.00 Monday to Friday (access to the
    building is restricted after 18.00, please phone 020
    7829 8709 for details)
Transport: Tube: Russell Square, Holborn
Publications: Annual Report

Linked organisations
University College London Part of the College
University College London Hospitals (UCLH) NHS Trust

[312]
Institute of Opthalmology and Moorfields Eye Hospital

11–43 Bath Street
London EC1V 9EL
Borough: Islington
Telephone: 020 7608 6814
Fax: 020 7608 6814
E-mail: ophthlib@ucl.ac.uk
Constitution: Department of a university, registered
    charity and specialist hospital
Key staff: Librarian: Deborah Heatlie; Assistant Librarian:
    Kay Gwyther
Stock and subject coverage: UK's largest research library in
    the field of opthalmology and visual science with
    ca.10,000 book titles and 160 journals currently
    received. Book coverage is historical and
    contemporary but generally at postgraduate level
    (general works on vision, optics, the blind, etc. aimed
    at the general public or undergraduate students are
    not collected). Journal coverage is similar and both
    historical and contemporary materials are held in a
    range of languages. There is an extensive collection of
    reprints, offprints and pamphlets dating back to the
    early 1800s. There is a small historical collection on
    opthalmology and visual science and long runs of
    many German opthalmological journals
Services: Photocopies (charges made)
Availability: Open to all bona fide researchers on
    application for reference use only (charges made for
    visits)
Hours: 09.00–17.00 Monday; 09.00–18.00 Tuesday to
    Friday
Transport: Tube: Old Street
Special facilities: Refreshment and toilet facilities available

Linked organisations
University of London Postgraduate research
Institute of the University
University College London Member of the
College
**International Resource Centre/International
Centre for Eye Health** Based in the same building
Moorfields Eye Hospital NHS Trust

[313]
Institute of Orthopaedics Library

Sir Herbert Seddon Teaching Centre
Brockley Hill
Stanmore
Middlesex HA7 4LP
Borough: Harrow
Telephone: 020 8909 5351
Fax: 020 8954 1213
E-mail: orthlib@ucl.ac.uk
World Wide Web: www.ucl.ac.uk/library/iorth.htm
Constitution: The Institute is part of University College
    London
Key staff: Site Librarian: Bethan Adams
Stock and subject coverage: Collections on orthopaedics
Services: Photocopiers
Availability: Access to students at the Institute, to others
    under the M25 Access Scheme and to bona fide
    researchers, upon production of proof of identity.
    Reference only
Hours: 09.00–17.00 Monday to Friday
Transport: Tube: Stanmore, Edgware

Linked organisations
University College London Part of the College

[314]
Institute of Petroleum
IP

61 New Cavendish Street
London W1G 7AR
Borough: Westminster
Telephone: 020 7467 7100 (Main switchboard)
Fax: 020 7255 1472
E-mail: ip@petroleum.co.uk
World Wide Web: www.petroleum.co.uk
Constitution: Registered charity; association with
  voluntary subscribing membership
Key staff: Information Service: ext 7111/3/4/5
Stock and subject coverage: Covers all aspects of petroleum,
  both technical and business aspects, dating from 19th
  century to present day
Services: Photocopies; online and internet searches
  (charges made)
Availability: Free access to all members. Non members
  charged a daily rate. Loans to members only
Hours: 09.30-17.00 Monday to Friday; Telephone
  enquiries 10.00-17.00
Transport: Tube: Oxford Circus, Great Portland Street,
  Bond Street, Regents Park; Bus: C2, 135
Special facilities: Toilet facilities available; access for users
  with disabilities (stairs to front door but lift to
  library)
Special features: Grade I listed building with painted
  ceilings
Publications: Petroleum Review (monthly); IP Standard
  Methods for Petroleum and its Products (annual); UK
  Petroleum Industry Association Statistics. Also a series
  of booklets about the petroleum industry, and a series
  of Oil Data Sheets. Conference proceedings and
  safety codes

[315]
Institute of Psychiatry

De Crespigny Park
London SE5 8AF
Borough: Southwark
Telephone: 020 7848 0204
Fax: 020 7703 4515
E-mail: spyllib@iop.kcl.ac.uk
World Wide Web:
  www.iop.kcl.ac.uk/home/depts/library.htm
Constitution: Department of a university
Key staff: Librarian: Martin Guha BA ALA; Deputy:
  Clare Martin BA ALA
Stock and subject coverage: The largest library in the UK in
  the fields of psychiatry and clinical psychology.
  Special collections include: the Henry Maudsley
  collection of historic books in psychiatry, the Mayer-
  Gross collection of rare European texts in psychiatry;
  the Guttmann-MacLay collection on art and
  psychiatry
Availability: Limited access on written application (a
  donation to the Psychiatry Research Trust will be
  requested). Full membership for Institute members
  only
Hours: 09.00-20.00 Monday to Friday; 09.00-13.00
  Saturday
Transport: Rail: Denmark Hill; Bus: 68, 176, 185, 484
Special facilities: Refreshment and toilet facilities available

Ceiling – Library, Institute of Petroleum

Publications: Institute of Psychiatry Annual Report; Maudsley Monographs; Bethlem & Maudsley Gazette

Linked organisations

Bethlem Royal Hospital Library, Monks Orchard Road, Beckenham BR3 3BX. The Institute has a small branch library at Bethlem Royal Hospital The Institute has clinical links with the Bethlem and Maudsley Hospitals and academic links with King's College and the British Postgraduate Medical Federation

[316]
Institute of Psycho-Analysis
Byron House
112a Shirland Road
Maida Vale
London W9 2EQ
Borough: Westminster
Telephone: 020 7563 5008
Fax: 020 7563 5001
E-mail: ipa_library@compuserve.com
World Wide Web: www.psychoanalysis.org.uk
Constitution: Registered charity
Key staff: Librarian: Ms A Chandler
Stock and subject coverage: 30,000 books; 30 current journals. Covers psychoanalysis and related subjects
Availability: Access to all, with charges for entrance, for reference only
Hours: 12.00–21.00 Monday to Thursday
Transport: Tube: Maida Vale; Bus: 6, 16, 46, 98
Special facilities: Toilet facilities available; access for users with disabilities

Linked organisations

International Psychoanalytical Association
Component Society of the IPA

[317]
The Institute of Public Relations
IPR
The Old Trading House
15 Northburgh Street
London EC1V 0PR
Borough: Islington
Telephone: 020 7253 5151
Fax: 020 7250 3556
E-mail: info@ipr.org.uk
World Wide Web: www.ipr.org.uk
Constitution: Company limited by guarantee; a professional body and association with voluntary subscribing membership
Objectives/purposes: Professional body for individual practitioners and students within the public relations industry
Key staff: Director General: Colin Farrington; Assistant Director, Head of Marketing and Public Relations: Ann Mealor; Assistant Director, Head of Office Services: Richard George
Stock and subject coverage: Ca. 700 books, periodicals, journals and directories covering the theory, practice and management of public relations, marketing communications, journalism and business
Services: Photocopies, PC and internet access

Availability: Open to members for reference only
Hours: 10.00–17.00 Monday to Friday
Transport: Tube: Barbican, Farringdon; Rail: Farringdon; Bus: 55
Special facilities: Toilet facilities available
Publications: Profile magazine (10 p.a.); PR in Practice series of text books; PR Evaluation Toolkit; Annual Report and Accounts

[318]
Institute of Race Relations
IRR
2-6 Leeke Street
London WC1X 9HS
Borough: Camden
Telephone: 020 7837 0041
Fax: 020 7278 0623
World Wide Web: www.homebeats.co.uk
Constitution: Registered charity and company limited by guarantee
Objectives/purposes: Educational charity concerned with race relations
Key staff: Librarian: Hazel Waters
Stock and subject coverage: Books, pamphlets and journals on race relations, racism, imperialism, Third World liberation movements and minority groups. The material is arranged on a country by country basis
Services: Photocopies
Availability: Access, for reference only, at Librarian's discretion, otherwise only for affiliated organisations. Research fees payable in certain circumstances
Hours: 10.00–13.00, 14.00–17.00 Monday to Thursday; visitors should telephone first
Transport: Tube and Rail: King's Cross; Bus: 18, 30, 63, 73, 91
Special facilities: Toilet facilities available
Publications: Catalogue of IRR publications on Britain and Europe; also Third World issues

[319]
Institution of Civil Engineers
ICE
1 Great George Street
London SW1P 3AA
Borough: Westminster
Telephone: 020 7222 7722
Fax: 020 7976 7610
E-mail: library@ice.org.uk
World Wide Web: www.ice.org.uk
Key staff: Librarian: MM Chrimes BA MLS ALA; Deputy Librarian: Rose Marney BA ALA; Archivist: Carol Morgan
Stock and subject coverage: Books, pamphlets and periodicals covering all branches of engineering and applied sciences; since 1900 civil engineering only, i.e. structural, geotechnical, public health engineering, building, transport engineering (roads, rail, ports and harbours, river and canal engineering, airport design, public transport) hydraulics, water resources and associated sciences, e.g. geology, hydrology, seismology.
Special collections: Telford, Smeaton and Rennie manuscripts; Vulliamy collection on horology; MacKenzie Collection, JG James Collection,

Fairhurst Collection, Concrete Archive, Council of Engineering Institutes and Institution of Municipal Engineering and Society of Civil Engineers records

Services: Photocopies; fax machine; online searches; online catalogue; CD-ROM databases; photographic reproductions; digitised publications on website

Availability: To ICE, ICES and IMechE members and members of other Engineering Council institutions; bona fide researchers are normally admitted when material is not readily available elsewhere. Loan services for ICE members

Hours: 09.15-17.30 Monday to Friday

Transport: Tube: St James Park, Westminster, Charing Cross, Victoria; Bus: 3, 11, 12, 24, 77, 88, 159, 501

Special facilities: Refreshment and toilet facilities; access for users with disabilities

Special features: The main library has a grade II listed late Victorian interior

Publications: Geotechnique (quarterly), Ground Engineering (monthly); Proceedings – 'Structures and Buildings', 'Transport', 'Municipal Engineering', 'Geotechnical Engineering', 'Water, Maritime and Energy', and 'Civil Engineering' (all quarterly); Conference Proceedings; reports; monographs Library Publications: Recent Additions to the Library (monthly); current awareness (monthly); bibliographies; lists and exhibition catalogues

[320]
Institution of Contemporary History and Wiener Library

4 Devonshire Street
London W1W 5BH
Borough: Westminster
Telephone: 020 7636 7247
Fax: 020 7436 6428
E-mail: info@wienerlibrary.co.uk
World Wide Web: www.wienerlibrary.co.uk
Constitution: Non-profit making company; registered charity
Objectives/purposes: Private research Library and Institute specialising in contemporary European and Jewish history and the Holocaust
Key staff: Acting Director: Ben Barkow; Senior Librarian: Colin Clarke
Stock and subject coverage: 60,000 volumes; 15,000 documents; periodicals, press archives, etc. on German/Jewish history; the Third Reich; and Fascism
Services: Enquiry services (fee may be charged); enquiries to be addressed to the Librarian. Loans to members; photocopying; microfilm reader-printers
Availability: Open to all bona fide researchers on production of a letter of introduction
Hours: 10.00-17.30 Monday to Friday
Transport: Tube: Regent's Park, Great Portland Street
Publications: Wiener Library Newsletter

[321]
Institution of Electrical Engineers
IEE

Savoy Place
London WC2R 0BL
Borough: Westminster
Telephone: 020 7344 5461
Fax: 020 7497 3557
Telex: 261 176 IEELDN G
E-mail: libdesk@iee.org.uk
World Wide Web: www.iee.org.uk
Constitution: Registered charity and chartered professional body
Key staff: Library Manager: John Coupland, tel: 020 7344 5451; Deputy Librarian: Helen Sparks, tel: 020 7344 5705; Information Enquiries: 020 7344 8429; Library Enquiries: 020 7344 5461
Stock and subject coverage: Ca. 75,000 books, pamphlets, reports, standards and conference proceedings and 1,000 current journals. Main subjects covered include: electronic, electrical, control and manufacturing engineering; computers and IT. Educational, economic, management, historical and market aspects as well as technical information are covered. The Library also contains the British Computer Society Library and as such covers computing in detail. Two special historical collections: Thompson and Ronalds; plus other archival material. Also includes the Learning Resource Service, and the Library of the Institution of Manufacturing Engineers
Services: Loans and photocopying (self-service); CD-ROMs and electronic journals. Online searching (charges made) and internet access for members only. Loans are restricted to members or interlibrary lending
Hours: 09.00-17.00 Monday to Friday
Transport: Tube: Embankment, Charing Cross; Rail: Charing Cross; Bus: 11, 23
Special facilities: Refreshment facilities (for members only); toilet facilities available; access for users with disabilities
Publications: Annual Report; IEE Proceedings (12 parts, available as an electronic journal); Power Engineering Journal; Electronics Letters (also available as an electronic journal); IEE Review; Electronics and Communication Engineering Journal; IEE News; Engineering Science and Education Journal; Computing & Control Engineering Journal; Engineering Management Journal; Manufacturing Engineer; conference proceedings and colloquium digests; monographs; technical regulations.
INSPEC Publications: Science Abstracts, Section A: Physics; Section B: Electrical and Electronics; Section C: Computers and Control; Current papers Section A, B and C; INSPEC database and Key Abstracts

Linked organisations

INSPEC INSPEC is a division of the Institution

[322]
Institution of Gas Engineers
IGasE

21 Portland Place
London W1B 1PY
Borough: Westminster
E-mail: anita@igaseng.demon.co.uk
World Wide Web: www.igaseng.com
Telephone: 020 7927 9917
Fax: 020 7636 6602
Constitution: Registered charity and chartered professional body
Objectives/purposes: Learned society for engineers, scientists, technologists and technicians connected with the gas industry
Key staff: Librarian: Anita Witten BA MLS ALA MIInfSci
Stock and subject coverage: Information on fuel gases and associated engineering, from the beginnings of the industry in the early 19th century. Journals, books, standards and some archive material
Services: Loans; photocopies; online searching; internet access
Availability: Non-members may use the Library by appointment, and borrow some material by inter-library loan. Some services (photocopies, tailor-made bibliographies, research, etc.) are charged
Hours: 09.00-17.00 Monday to Friday except bank holidays
Transport: Tube: Oxford Circus, Regent's Park
Special facilities: Refreshment and toilet facilities available; access for users with disabilities (no wheelchair lift access)
Special features: Grade II listed building, built ca. 1776-1780 by the Adam brothers
Publications: International Gas Engineering and Management (10 p.a.); Recommendations on: Transmission and Distribution Practice; Safety; Gas Measurement; Utilisation Procedures; Environment; and Gas Legislation Guidance; Directory of Consultants on Fuel Gases

[323]
Institution of Mining and Metallurgy
IMM

77 Hallam Street
London W1W 5BS
Borough: Westminster
Telephone: 020 7580 3802
Fax: 020 7436 5388
E-mail: lis@imm.org.uk
World Wide Web: www.imm.org.uk
Constitution: Registered charity
Objectives/purposes: The Institution's main activities as a professional/learned society are in education and training, the upholding of professional standards of conduct and scientific and technical expertise, the holding of meetings and conferences, publishing and the supply of library and information services in the fields of economic geology, mining technology, mineral processing and extractive metallurgy
Key staff: Head, Library and Information Services: Michael McGarr

Stock and subject coverage: 50,000 volumes; 1,100 current periodicals
Services: A comprehensive information service is provided for members and others. Detailed indexes are maintained and a computerised database (IMMAGE) is available in the library and is also available online and on CD
Availability: To members and others for reference purposes
Hours: 10.00-17.00 Monday to Friday
Transport: Tube: Regent's Park
Publications: Transactions: A. Mining Industry; B. Applied Earth Science; C. Mineral Processing and Extractive Metallurgy; International Mining and Minerals (monthly); IMM Abstracts and Index; Proceedings of Symposia and Congresses (irregular)

[324]
Institution of Structural Engineers
IStructE

11 Upper Belgrave Street
London SW1X 8BH
Borough: Westminster
Telephone: 020 7235 4535
020 7201 9105 (direct line for loans/photocopies)
Fax: 020 7201 9118
E-mail: library@istructe.org.uk
World Wide Web: www.istructe.org.uk
Constitution: Registered charity; association with voluntary subscribing membership; chartered professional body
Key staff: Manager: Information and Library Service: Sue Claxton
Stock and subject coverage: Ca. 21,000 books, reports and pamphlets, and 150 current journals on structural engineering. The Institution was founded in 1908, but a considerable quantity of older journals and books is held
Services: Loans to members and to libraries. Enquiry service; online searches; photocopies and bibliographies available to all (at a small charge); small video collection; web catalogue at www.istructe.org.uk/library
Availability: Primarily for members, but available to the public by prior appointment
Hours: 09.30-17.30 Tuesday to Friday
Transport: Tube: Hyde Park Corner, Victoria; Rail: Victoria
Special facilities: Refreshment and toilet facilities available; access for users with disabilities (steps to entrance, contact in advance)
Publications: The Structural Engineer (2 per month); Sessional Yearbook and Directory of Members; Annual Report of the Council and Accounts; wide range of reports and conference proceedings; list of journal holdings; list of video films (available on request)

Linked organisations

IABSE (International Association for Bridge and Structural Engineering), British Group
The Institution of Structural Engineers is also the administrative office for IABSE

SCOSS (Standing Committee for Structural Safety)

Both organisations' publications are held in the IStructE Library, but the bodies themselves have no library or information service

[325]
Instituto Cervantes
102 Eaton Square
London SW1W 9AN
Borough: Westminster
Telephone: 020 7201 0757
Fax: 020 7235 4115
E-mail: biblon@cervantes.es
World Wide Web: www.cervantes.es
Constitution: Worldwide non-profit public institution; government funded body
Objectives/purposes: To promote the teaching, study and use of Spanish as a second language and to contribute to the advancement of the Spanish and Hispanic-American cultures throughout the non-Spanish speaking nations
Key staff: Librarian: Matilde Javaloyes, Consuelo Alvarez
Stock and subject coverage: 30,000 volumes on Spanish literature, history, art and philosophy. Slides, tapes, records and films
Services: The Institute runs a number of courses and cultural activities; details available on request. There is also an information service concerning Spanish courses for foreigners in Spain
Availability: To members for lending and reference. Membership £20 p.a. Non-members may use the Library for reference. Loans to non-members on payment of a deposit. A reading room is open to the general public
Hours: 12.00-18.30 Mondays to Thursdays; closed Friday; 09.30-13.30 Saturday
Transport: Tube: Victoria, Sloane Square, Hyde Park Corner
Special facilities: Refreshment and toilet facilities available
Linked organisations
Network of Instituto Cervantes centres in 20 countries

[326]
International Cargo Handling Co-Ordination Association
ICHCA
Suite 2
Great Western Road
Romford
Essex RM1 3LS
Borough: Havering
Telephone: 01708 734787
Fax: 01708 734877
E-mail: postmaster@ichca.org.uk
World Wide Web: www.ichca.org.uk
Constitution: Association with voluntary subscribing membership
Objectives/purposes: To promote efficiency in cargo handling in all modes
Key staff: The Librarian
Stock and subject coverage: Collections on cargo handling in all its forms

Services: Photocopying available for small articles, at a charge
Availability: Access restricted to members; charges made to non-members. Non-members are not encouraged to visit, staff will try to answer enquiries by telephone or fax initially
Hours: 09.30-17.30 Monday to Friday
Special facilities: Toilet facilities available
Publications: Who's Who in Cargo Handling (annual, membership directory); ICHCA Annual Review

Linked organisations
The London office is the international secretariat of a trade association with members worldwide and national sections in 11 countries

[327]
International Coffee Organization
ICO
22 Berners Street
London W1T 3DD
Borough: Westminster
Telephone: 020 7580 8591
Fax: 020 7580 6129
E-mail: library@ico.org
World Wide Web: www.ico.org
Constitution: Intergovernmental organisation
Objectives/purposes: To ensure enhanced international cooperation in connection with world coffee matters
Key staff: Library Adminstrator: Martin Wattam; Library Assistant: Rebecca Hagen
Stock and subject coverage: Unique reference collection of 12,000 monographs (books, reports, theses, pamphlets) and 250 journal titles covering all aspects of coffee, as well as wider commodity trade and development issues. The library also houses the comprehensive economic and statistical data on coffee published by the ICO and a range of journal and other statistical publications of the United nations, its specialised agencies and other international organisations. In addition to printed material the Library holds a major collection of colour slides and videotapes
Services: Photocopies (charges made); internet access; online searches
Availability: Reference only. Use of the Library is by appointment only
Hours: 09.00-17.00 Monday to Friday
Transport: Tube: Oxford Circus, Goodge Street
Special facilities: Toilet facilities available; access for users with disabilities (lift available)
Publications: ICO Library Monthly Entries Bulletin

Linked organisations
Part of the United Nations system

[328]
International Institute for Strategic Studies
IISS
Arundel House
13-15 Arundel Street
London WC2R 3DX

Borough: Westminster
Telephone: 020 7395 9122
Fax: 020 7836 3108
E-mail: library@iiss.org
Constitution: Research organisation and registered
    charity; independent non-profit organisation with
    elected membership
Key staff: Chief Librarian: Ellen Peacock; Deputy
    Librarian: Emma Sullivan
Stock and subject coverage: Security, arms control and
    international relations. The Library holds a range of
    CD-ROMs and offers access to Lexis-Nexis and the
    internet
Services: Reference facilities include 10,000 books,
    11,000 pamphlets and a large collection of newspaper
    and journal clippings covering the period 1958
    onwards (online catalogue available). Loans to
    members only. Charges for photocopies, print-outs,
    Lexis-Nexis and online searches
Availability: Access is free to members, £2 entry fee for
    students, £5 entry fee for all other non-members
Hours: 10.00-17.00 Monday to Friday
Transport: Tube: Temple; Rail: Blackfriars
Publications: The Military Balance (annual); Strategic
    Survey (annual); Survival (4 p.a.); Strategic
    Comments (online publication, 10 p.a.); Adelphi
    Papers (monograph series, 8-10 p.a.); World Directory
    of Strategic Studies

[329]
International Labour Office
ILO

(A specialised agency of the United Nations)
Millbank Tower
21-24 Millbank
London SW1P 4QP
Borough: Westminster
Telephone: 020 7828 6401
Fax: 020 7233 5925
E-mail: ipu@ilo-london.org.uk
World Wide Web: ww.ilo.org/london
Key staff: Ligia Teixeira
Stock and subject coverage: All major ILO documentation
    in English. ILO publications concerning labour
    issues, health and safety, child labour, international
    regulations and human rights
Services: An enquiry service and photocopying available;
    high proportion of recent publications available for
    purchase
Availability: Access, for reference only, by appointment.
    All members of the public welcome
Hours: 10.00-13.00 and 14.00-16.00 Monday to Friday
Transport: Tube: Pimlico; Bus: 77A
Special facilities: Toilet facilities available; access for users
    with disabilities, wheelchair access is possible with
    prior notice
Publications: ILO Yearbook of Labour Statistics; World
    Labour Report; Key Indicators of the Labour Market
    (KILM) – all yearly and published by ILO Geneva

Linked organisations

London branch office of ILO (headquarters in
    Geneva), responsible for the UK and Eire

[330]
International Maritime Organization
IMO

4 Albert Embankment
London SE1 7SR
Borough: Lambeth
Telephone: 020 7735 7611
Fax: 020 7587 3210
E-mail: info@imo.org
World Wide Web: www.imo.org
Constitution: Specialised agency of the United Nations
    for maritime affairs
Key staff: Librarian: Mrs Marianne Harvey
Stock and subject coverage: Covers maritime safety;
    prevention of pollution from ships; international
    maritime law; maritime training; navigation; technical
    co-operation
Services: Information services; current awareness services;
    databases: (i) catalogue database, (ii) current awareness
    database of articles from journals. The Library is
    unable to lend material other than to Libraries or to
    provide articles for copyright reasons; however it can
    carry out searches on its bibliographic databases and
    post the results to enquirers
Availability: Open to all bona fide enquirers (by
    appointment only)
Hours: 10.00-17.00 Monday to Thursday; closed on
    Fridays and the whole of August
Transport: Tube: Waterloo, Vauxhall, Westminster; Rail:
    Waterloo, Vauxhall; Bus: 3, 77, 107, 344
Special facilities: Refreshment and toilet facilities available;
    access for users with disabilities and disabled toilet
    available
Publications: IMO Library Current Awareness Bulletin
    (twice per month); bibliographies; website

Linked organisations

World Maritime University, Malmo, Sweden
International Maritime Law Institute, Msida,
Malta

[331]
International Planned Parenthood Federation
IPPF

Regent's College
Inner Circle
Regent's Park
London NW1 4NS
Borough: Westminster
Telephone: 020 7487 7900
Fax: 020 7487 7950
E-mail: info@ippf.org
World Wide Web: www.ippf.org
Constitution: Registered charity
Objectives/purposes: The IPPF is a federation of
    autonomous national family planning associations
    (FPAs) in over 140 countries worldwide. It is the
    largest voluntary organisation in the world concerned
    with family planning and sexual and reproductive
    health
Key staff: Librarian: Rita Ward

Stock and subject coverage: Collection of ca. 6,000 books, 100 journals and newsletters, 400 videos covering the following subjects: demography, family planning, sex education, status of women and reproductive rights
Services: Telephone and postal enquiry service
Availability: Open to bona fide researchers, by appointment, for reference only
Hours: 10.00-17.00 Monday to Friday
Transport: Tube: Baker Street
Publications: People and the Planet (quarterly); Medical Bulletin (6 p.a.); Annual Report and other occasional publications (list on request)

Linked organisations

Regent's College Located on the Regent's College site

[332]
International Resource Centre/International Centre for Eye Health
IRC/ICEH

Institute of Opthalmology
11-43 Bath Street
London EC1V 9EL
Borough: Islington
Telephone: 020 7608 6923
Fax: 020 7250 3207
E-mail: eyeresource@ucl.ac.uk
World Wide Web: www.jceh.co.uk
Constitution: Registered charity; university department
Objectives/purposes: Publication of teaching and educational materials in community eye health; information resource on worldwide opthalmology with an emphasis on developing countries
Key staff: Director of ICEH: Prof Gordon Johnson; Editor of Journal of Community Eye Health and Medical Director: Dr Murray McGavin; Opthalmic Resource Co-ordinator: Sue Stevens
Stock and subject coverage: Small library of teaching and educational materials on eye health and disease worldwide (including bulletins, newsletters, journals, tapes, videos and colour slide sets); information on eye care in individual countries; research files on blindness prevention in developing countries
Services: Photocopies (charges are made)
Availability: The IRC is open to bona fide visitors; most material is for reference only
Hours: 09.30-17.00 Monday to Friday
Transport: Tube: Old Street; Bus: 43, 55, 76, 141, 214, 271
Special facilities: Toilet facilities available in next door building; refreshment facilities available nearby
Publications: Journal of Community Eye Health (4 p.a., circulation 15,000 to 175 countries); colour slide sets for teaching on eye disease and management

Linked organisations

ICEH is a World Health Organization Collaborating Centre for the prevention of blindness
Institute of Opthalmology Based in the same building as the Institute

[333]
International Rubber Study Group
IRSG

Heron House
109-115 Wembley Hill Road
Wembley HA9 8DA
Borough: Brent
Telephone: 020 8903 7727
Fax: 020 8903 2848
E-mail: irsg@compuserve.com
World Wide Web: www.rubberstudy.com
Constitution: Intergovernmental organisation
Objectives/purposes: The Study Group is the authoritative source of statistical data on production, consumption and trade in rubber and rubber products. It prepares current estimates, forecasts future trends and undertakes statistical, economic and techno-economic studies on specific aspects of the industry
Key staff: Secretary-General: Dr AFS Budiman
Stock and subject coverage: Small stock of books, journals and reports on synthetic and natural rubbers and their uses. Comprehensive economic and statistical data from founding in 1944
Services: Enquiry service on economic and statistical aspects of the world rubber industry
Availability: By appointment
Hours: 09.00-17.00 Monay to Friday
Transport: Tube: Wembley Park, Wembley Central; Rail: Wembley Stadium; Bus: 83, 182
Special facilities: Refreshment and toilet facilities available
Publications: Rubber Statistical Bulletin (monthly); Rubber Industry Report (monthly); Rubber Statistics Yearbook; Rubber Economics Yearbook; Outlook for Elastomers (annual); World Rubber Statistics Handbook (quinquennial); Key Rubber Indicators, 1996; occasional papers

[334]
International Tin Research Institute
ITRI

Kingston Lane
Uxbridge
Middlesex UB8 3PJ
Borough: Hillingdon
Telephone: 01895 272406
Fax: 01895 251841/230721
E-mail: jeremy.pearce@tintechnology.com
World Wide Web: www.tintechnology.com
Constitution: Multi-government funded, non-profit making body
Key staff: Jeremy Pearce
Stock and subject coverage: The Technology Information and Forecasting unit houses an indexed collection of more than 40,000 scientific papers on tin and its uses, as well as an extensive specialist archive of in-house journals, unpublished research results and market information. The unit makes extensive use of database, intranet and web-based technology to collate and publish information for research staff and the worldwide scientific community
Services: Photocopies, online searches, fax machine, e-mail. Charges are made for online searching, photocopies, etc.

Availability: Access open to all bona fide researchers by appointment. Access charges to commercial and industrial users. Material is available for reference only

Hours: 09.00-16.45 Monday to Friday

Transport: Tube: Uxbridge; Rail: West Drayton, Hayes; Bus: U4, U5, 207, 607, 724 (Greenline)

Special facilities: Refreshment and toilet facilities available; access for users with disabilities

Publications: Annual Report; Focus on Tin (quarterly newsletter)

Linked organisations

Association of Tin Producing Countries (ATPC) ITRI is the research and development arm of ATPC

---

[335]
Invest UK
1 Victoria St
London SW1H 0ET
Borough: Westminster
Telephone: 020 7215 2501
Fax: 020 7215 5651
E-mail: invest.uk@dti.gsi.gov.uk
World Wide Web: www.invest.uk.com
Constitution: Government funded body
Services: Invest UK provides a free and confidential service to potential overseas investors covering all aspects of locating in the UK, including advice on workforce, suppliers and sub-contractors; guidance on local and national incentives; advice on European trading conditions; and a UK-wide site-finding service. It operates overseas through British Embassies, High Commissions and Consulates, and in the UK through Regional Development Organisations
Availability: Freely available
Hours: By appointment only
Transport: Tube: Victoria, St James's Park; Rail: Victoria
Publications: Various brochures relating to information required by potential inward investors, and other promotional material

Linked organisations

Department of Trade and Industry (DTI)

Foreign and Commonwealth Office (FCO)
Invest UK is a joint DTI/FCO department

---

[336]
Islington (London Borough of Islington)
E-mail: library.information@islington.gov.uk
World Wide Web: www.islington.go.uk/learning
Telephone: 020 7527 6900
Constitution: Public library, funded by local authority
Special features: Islington Library Resources has 10 public libraries including reference library facilities at the main Central Library and at Finsbury Reference Library (listed first)

[336][a]
Central Library
2 Fieldway Crescent
London N5 1PF

Telephone: 020 7527 6900
Fax: 020 7527 6937
Key staff: Head of Library and Information Service: Val Dawson, Brendan Redmond; Information Manager: John Smith: Principal Librarian Learning: Brendan Redmond; Principal Customer Services Manager: Marilyn Gibson; Public Services Managers: Teresa Gibson, Maureen Black; ICT Development Librarian: John Usher; Local History Librarian, tel: 020 7527 6931/6933
Stock and subject coverage: Sickert collection of books, cuttings, photographs and some graphic material including pictures relating to Walter Sickert and Therese Lessore. Joe Orton collection of books, cuttings and reproductions of book jackets defaced by Orton and Halliwell. Local history collections are held in both the Central and Finsbury libraries
Services: Photocopier (card-operated); fax service (operated by staff); microfilm reader printer; microfilm and microfiche readers; lifelong learning centre; 95 study seats
Hours: 09.30-20.00 Monday, Wednesday and Thursday: 09.30-17.00 Tuesday, Friday and Saturday; 13.00-17.00 Sunday
Transport: Tube: Highbury and Islington; Rail: Drayton Park; Bus: 43, 279, 271
Special facilities: Access for users with disabilities – lift available

[336][b]
Finsbury Reference Library
245 St John Street
London EC1V 4NB
Telephone: 020 7527 7960
Fax: 020 7527 7998
E-mail: finsbury.library@islington.gov.uk
Key staff: Person in Charge: Pamela Quantrill; Assistant Local History Librarian: Martin Banham
Stock and subject coverage: Books, journals and photographic collections. Local history collections are split between the Central and Finsbury libraries. Sadlers Wells Theatre collection of playbills, theatre prints, cuttings, books and some archival material. Penton family and estate collection of papers.
Services: Photocopier (coin-operated); fax service (operated by staff); 60 study seats; microfilm and microfiche readers; lifelong learning centre; local history searches by appointment only
Hours: 09.30-20.00 Monday and Thursday; 09.30-17.00 Tuesday and Saturday; 09.00-13.00 Friday
Transport: Tube: Angel; Train: Farringdon; Bus: 153, 279
Special facilities: Access for users with disabilities to ground floor only – no access to 1st floor local history collections (consultation by arrangement); toilet facilities for users with disabilities

[336][c]
Archway Library
Hamlyn House
Highgate Hill
London N19 5PH
Telephone: 020 7527 7820
Fax: 020 7527 7833
E-mail: archway.library@islington.gov.uk
Key staff: Persons in Charge: Kate Tribe, Nicki Mullen

Stock and subject coverage: Adult and children's collections
Services: Photocopier
Hours: 09.30-20.00 Monday and Thursday; 09.30-17.00 Tuesday and Saturday; 09.30-13.00 Friday
Transport: Tube: Archway; Train: Upper Holloway; Bus: 4, W5, C11, 17, 41, 43, 135, 143, 210, 234, 263, 271
Special facilities: Wheelchair access to all services

[336][d]
Arthur Simpson Library
Hanley Road
London N4 3DL
Telephone: 020 7527 7800
Fax: 020 7527 7808
E-mail: arthursimpson.library@islington.gov.uk
Key staff: Person in Charge: Tracey Clark-Edwards
Stock and subject coverage: Adult and children's collections
Services: Photocopier
Hours: 09.30-20.00 Monday and Thursday; 09.30-17.00 Wednesday and Saturday
Transport: Tube: Finsbury Park; Train: Crouch Hill; Bus: W2, W3, W7, 210
Special facilities: Wheelchair access to the children's library on the ground floor; access to the adult library is up many steps

[336][e]
John Barnes Library
275 Camden Road
London N7 0JN
Telephone: 020 7527 7900
Fax: 020 7527 7907
E-mail: johnbarnes.library@islington.gov.uk
Key staff: Person in Charge: Yasmine Webb
Stock and subject coverage: Adult and children's collections
Services: Photocopier
Hours: 09.30-20.00 Tuesday and Thursday; 09.30-17.00 Wednesday and Saturday
Transport: Tube: Caledonian Road; Train: Caledonian Road and Barnsbury; Bus: 17, 29, 91, 253, 259
Special facilities: Wheelchair access to all services

[336][f]
Lewis Carroll Children's Library
Copenhagen Street
London N1 0ST
Telephone: 020 7527 7936
Fax: 020 7527 7935
E-mail: lewiscarroll.library@islington.gov.uk
Key staff: Person in Charge: Sharon Goldson
Stock and subject coverage: Adult and children's collections
Services: Photocopier
Hours: 09.30-20.00 Monday and Thursday; 09.30-17.00 Tuesday; 09.30-13.00 Friday
Transport: Tube and rail: King's Cross; Bus: 10, C11, 17
Special facilities: Wheelchair access to all services

[336][g]
Mildmay Library
21-23 Mildmay Park
London N1 4NA
Telephone: 020 7527 7880
Fax: 020 7527 7898
E-mail: mildmay.library@islington.gov.uk

Key staff: Person in Charge: Carol Roberts
Stock and subject coverage: Adult and children's collections
Services: Photocopier; lifelong learning centre;
Hours: 09.30-17.00 Monday and Saturday; 09.30-21.00 Tuesday and Thursday
Transport: Tube: Highbury and Islington; Train: Canonbury; Bus: 30, 38, 56, 73, 141, 171, 277
Special facilities: Wheelchair access to all services; toilet for users with disabilities

[336][h]
North Library
Manor Gardens
London N7 6JX
Telephone: 020 7527 7840
Fax: 020 7527 7854
E-mail: north.library@islington.gov.uk
Key staff: Person in Charge: Carole Levy
Stock and subject coverage: Adult and children's collections
Services: Photocopier; lifelong learning centre; PC with MS Word and Excel
Hours: 09.30-17.00 Monday and Saturday; 09.30-20.00 Tuesday and Thursday; 09.30-13.00 Friday
Transport: Tube: Holloway Road; Train: Upper Holloway; Bus: 43, 271
Special facilities: Wheelchair access to the adult library on the ground floor; access to the children's library is up several steps

[336][i]
South Library
115-17 Essex Road
London N1 2SL
Telephone: 020 7527 7860
Fax: 020 7527 7869
E-mail: south.library@islington.gov.uk
Key staff: Person in Charge: Chris Millington
Stock and subject coverage: Adult and children's collections
Services: Photocopier
Hours: 09.30-20.00 Monday and Thursday; 09.30-17.00 Tuesday and Saturday; 09.30-13.00 Friday
Transport: Tube: Highbury and Islington; Train: Essex Road; Bus: 38, 56, 73, 171A
Special facilities: Some steps to the adult library, children's library and reading room

[336][j]
West Library
Bridgeman Road
London N1 1BD
Telephone: 020 7527 7920
Fax: 020 7527 7929
E-mail: west.library@islington.gov.uk
Key staff: Person in Charge: Lucy Matheson
Stock and subject coverage: Adult and children's collections
Services: Photocopier
Hours: 09.30-20.00 Tuesday and Thursday; 09.30-17.00 Wednesday and Saturday
Transport: Tube: Caledonian Road; Train: Caledonian Road and Barnsbury; Bus: 17, 91
Special facilities: No wheelchair access – entrance is up many steps

[337]
Italian Cultural Institute
39 Belgrave Square
London SW1X 8NX
Borough: Westminster
Telephone: 020 7396 4406
Fax: 020 7235 4618
E-mail: ici@italcultur.org.uk
World Wide Web: www.italcutur.org.uk
Constitution: Government funded body
Key staff: Librarian: Mrs Reidy
Stock and subject coverage: Ca. 26,000 books on Italian literature, history, fine arts, travel and geography and other aspects of Italian culture. Cultural journals, main newspapers and CD-ROM databases available for reference
Services: Language courses, cultural events, internet access (under the Librarian's supervision), photocopies, some audiovisual materials loaned to institutions
Availability: Open to the general public for reference; loans available for members
Hours: 10.00-13.00, 14.00-17.00 Monday to Friday
Transport: Tube: Hyde Park Corner, Victoria; Rail: Victoria
Special facilities: Refreshment and toilet facilities available
Publications: Quarterly programme of events available on request

[338]
ITN Archive – Independent Television News
200 Grays Inn Road
London WC1X 8XZ
Borough: Camden
Telephone: 020 7430 4480
Fax: 020 7430 4453
E-mail: sales@itnarchive.com
World Wide Web: www.itnarchive.com
Constitution: Company limited by guarantee; TV news provider and responsible for reporting world news, 20 hours a day in six languages, from the Euronews headquarters in Lyon, France, Radio LNR (London News Radio)
Key staff: Linda Reeve
Stock and subject coverage: ITN Archive is one of the largest commercial archives in the world, consisting of ITN output since 1955 and the entire Reuters library, with historic newsreel footage dating from 1896. The newsreels collection includes Gaumont Graphic, Empire News, Gaumont British and British Paramount News. An ever growing resource, ITN Archive holds over 250,000 hours of news and feature material and an additional 15 hours is added each day. ITN Archive has offices in New York, Tokyo and London and also represents French Pathé in the UK
Services: Free online access to database via website; material supplied on payment of research, copying and licence fees
Availability: Available to professional researchers, by appointment. Material for viewing is available on VHS and charges may be incurred for some services
Hours: 09.00-21.00 every day of the year
Transport: Tube: Chancery Lane, King's Cross; Rail: Farringdon, King's Cross; Bus: 17, 45, 46, 341

Special facilities: Refreshment and toilet facilities available; access for users with disabilities

Linked organisations
The Archive acts as a news provider for ITV and Channel Four

[339]
The Japan Foundation London Language Centre
27 Knightsbridge
London SW1X 7QT
Borough: Kensington and Chelsea
Telephone: 020 7838 9955
Fax: 020 7838 9966
World Wide Web: www.nihongocentre.org.uk
Constitution: Government funded body
Stock and subject coverage: Japanese language related materials for teaching and linguistics. Ca. 5,500 journals, videos, CD-ROMs
Services: Photocopies; loans by post; advisory service
Availability: Loans limited to teachers of Japanese language at educational institutions. Open to all for reference use
Hours: 10.00-13.00, 14.00-17.00 Monday to Friday
Transport: Tube: Hyde Park Corner
Special facilities: Toilet facilities; access for users with disabilities (lift available)
Publications: MADO (2 p.a.)

Linked organisations
Japan Foundation Tokyo headquarters

[340]
Japan Information and Cultural Centre
JICC
(Embassy of Japan)
101-104 Piccadilly
London W1 7JT
Borough: Westminster
Telephone: 020 7465 6500
Fax: 020 7491 9347
E-mail: info@embjapan.org.uk
World Wide Web: www.embjapan.org.uk
Constitution: Government funded body
Stock and subject coverage: Loan collection covering Japanese literature and a wide range of general, educational, historical and cultural topics relating to Japan, in both English and Japanese. Reference books, Japanese government publications and a few magazines available for consultation on the premises. Videos, slides and photographs are also loaned
Services: Enquiry service; book and other loans; provision of information materials; videos on Japan are available to view in the Library
Availability: To the public
Hours: 09.30-12.45 and 14.30-17.00 Monday to Friday
Transport: Tube: Green Park
Special facilities: Toilet facilities available
Publications: 'Japan'; full list available on request

[341]
Jerwood Library of the Performing Arts

Trinity College of Music
King Charles Court
Old Royal Naval College
Greenwich
London SE19 9JF
Borough: Greenwich
Telephone: 020 8305 3950 (general enquiries)
020 8305 3893 (Mander and Mitchenson Theatre
Collection)
020 8691 8009 (Centre for Young Musicians Library)
Fax: 020 8305 3999
E-mail: library@tcm.ac.uk
World Wide Web: www.tcm.ac.uk
Constitution: Registered charity
Key staff: Chief Librarian: Dr Rosemary Williamson;
Director: Mander and Mitchenson Theatre
Collection; Library Assistant, Centre for Young
Musicians Library: Tony Lynes
Stock and subject coverage: Collections on music and the
performing arts and the history of the British theatre.
Books, printed music, audiovisual materials including
the Music Preserved collection of historic live sound
recordings, archives, pictures and portraits
Services: Photocopying; photographic reproductions
from the Mander and Mitchenson Theatre
Collection; online catalogue at sirsi2.tcm.ac.uk/
uhtbin/webcat
Availability: Loan service to Trinity College of Music
students and staff; interlibrary loans; research and
special collections open to external researchers by
appointment
Hours: Term-time: 09.00-19.30 Monday to Thursday;
09.00-18.30 Friday; 10.00-15.00 Saturday;
Vacations: 09.00-17.00 Monday to Friday
Transport: Rail: Greenwich; DLR: Cutty Sark
Special facilities: Access technology for visually impaired
users; wheelchair accessible toilet facilities

[342]
JETRO

Leconfield House
Curzon Street
London W1J 5HZ
Borough: Westminster
Telephone: 020 7470 4700
Fax: 020 7491 7570
World Wide Web: www.jetro.co.uk
Constitution: Japanese government related non-profit
organisation, funded partly from Japanese
government, partly from Japanese companies
Objectives/purposes: To promote harmonious trade
worldwide
Stock and subject coverage: Japanese trade directories,
customs tariffs and publications dealing with
miscellaneous associated trade matters, particularly
import/export statistics; also economic and other
statistical references
Services: General enquiries
Availability: Open to the general public
Hours: 10.00-12.00 and 14.00-16.30 Monday to Friday
Transport: Tube: Green Park; Bus: 2, 2B, 9, 10, 36, 73, 74

[343]
John Squire Library

Northwick Park and St Mark's Hospital North West
London Hospitals NHS Trust
Watford Road
Harrow
Middlesex HA1 3UJ
Borough: Harrow
Telephone: 020 8869 3322
Fax: 020 8869 3332
E-mail: jslib@clara.net
World Wide Web: www.jslib.clara.net
Constitution: NHS Trust hospital
Objectives/purposes: The provision of quality health care
Key staff: Head Librarian: Mike Kendall; Electronic
Information Librarian: Jason Curtis
Stock and subject coverage: Journals and books on clinical
medicine and biomedical sciences
Services: Photocopies and interlibrary loans (charged);
online and CD-ROM searching
Availability: Admission on application to the Head
Librarian. Day visits are accepted. A proportion of
the stock is available for loan to Library members
Hours: 09.00-18.00 Monday to Friday, 10.00-16.00
Saturday (term-time only)
Transport: Tube: Northwick Park
Special facilities: Refreshment and toilet facilities; access
for users with disabilities

Linked organisations
**London Region Library and Information
Services** Part of the Services

[344]
Jones Lang LaSalle

22 Hanover Square
London W1A 2BN
Borough: Westminster
Telephone: 020 7493 6040
Fax: 020 7399 5818
Constitution: Private venture. Jones Lang LaSalle has
offices world wide and UK regional offices
Key staff: Information Centre Manager: Alison Jones
Stock and subject coverage: Collection focusing on
property information and business information.
Stock includes: journals, small book stock, online
databases, annual reports, subject boxes, e.g. EU
Services: Photocopies; online searching; CD-ROM
Availability: For inhouse staff. Library deals with JLL
publication requests and information queries from
the public by post, telephone or e-mail only
Hours: 08.00-18.00 Monday to Friday
Transport: Tube: Oxford Circus
Special facilities: Refreshment and toilet facilities; access
for users with disabilities
Publications: Publications list available on request

[345]
Joseph Conrad Society
JCS

c/o POSK
238-246 King Street
Hammersmith
London W6 0RF

Borough: Hammersmith and Fulham
E-mail: allansimmons@compuserve.com
World Wide Web: www.bathspa.ac.uk/conrad
Constitution: Registered charity and association with
    voluntary subscribing membership
Objectives/purposes: To further research into the works
    and life of Joseph Conrad
Key staff: Secretary: Hugh Epstein; Treasurer and Editor
    of 'The Conradian': Allan Simmons
Stock and subject coverage: About 500 volumes belonging
    to the JCS and a further 400 volumes belonging to
    the Polish Library. Coverage includes: works by
    Joseph Conrad – first and later editions; letters,
    translations, biographical and critical works on
    Conrad; Conradiana, The Conradian and L'Epoque
    Conradienne journals
Availability: Free admission for reference only. Access is
    by authorisation from the Secretary (tel: 020 8892
    5583)
Hours: 10.00–18.00 Monday to Friday; 10.00–13.00
    Saturday (entry via the Polish Library)
Transport: Tube: Ravenscourt Park
Special facilities: Toilet facilities available
Publications: The Conradian – journal of the Joseph
    Conrad Society (2 p.a.)

Linked organisations

Joseph Conrad Societies in the USA, France and
Japan

[346]
The Kennel Club Library

1 Clarges Street
Piccadilly
London W1J 8AB
Borough: Westminster
Telephone: 020 7518 1009
Fax: 020 7518 1058
E-mail: library@the-kennel-club.org uk
World Wide Web: www.the-kennel-club.org.uk
Constitution: Independent non-profit distributing
    organisation; private venture
Objectives/purposes: Provision of a public access reference
    library relating to 'the dog'
Stock and subject coverage: All types of material relating to
    the dog: multimedia, books, journals, pictures and
    audiovisual materials. The collections include the
    Official Kennel Club Archives, show catalogues
    1860- and a complete collection of Crufts Dog Show
    catalogues
Services: Photocopies; research can be carried out for
    researchers who cannot visit the library
Availability: Open to the general public by appointment
    for reference only
Hours: 09.30–16.30 Monday to Friday
Transport: Tube: Green Park; Bus: 8, 9, 14, 19, 22, 38
Special facilities: Toilet facilities available; access for users
    with disabilities
Special features: Only specialist library in the UK dealing
    with dogs

[347]
Kenneth Ritchie Wimbledon Library

Wimbledon Lawn Tennis Museum
Church Road
Wimbledon
London SW19 5AE
Borough: Merton
Telephone: 020 8946 6131
Fax: 020 8944 6497
Constitution: Independent non-profit distributing
    organisation and private venture
Objectives/purposes: To provide research facilities on the
    subject of lawn tennis
Key staff: Honorary Librarian: JA Little; Assistant
    Librarian: Miss Audrey Snell
Stock and subject coverage: Materials from around the
    world on lawn tennis. Stock includes: books, annuals,
    programmes, newspaper cuttings, journals,
    photographs and specialist papers
Services: Photocopies
Availability: Open to the public free of charge, by
    appointment, for reference only
Hours: 10.30–13.00, 14.00–17.00 Tuesday to Friday
Transport: Tube: Southfields, Wimbledon; Rail:
    Wimbledon
Special facilities: Refreshment and toilet facilities available;
    access for users with disabilities with prior notice

Linked organisations

Wimbledon Lawn Tennis Museum
The Library is part of the Museum which is based at
the All England Lawn Tennis Club, Wimbledon

[348]
Kensington and Chelsea (Royal Borough of Kensington and Chelsea)
Kensington and Chelsea Libraries and Arts Service

World Wide Web: www.rbkc.gov.uk
Constitution: Public library service, funded by local
    authority. The Libraries and Arts Service is part of the
    Education and Libraries Business Group of the Royal
    Borough of Kensington and Chelsea
Availability: Borrowing facilities available for members of
    the public who live, work or study in the Borough

[348][a]
Central Library

Phillimore Walk
London W8 7RX
Telephone: 020 7937 2542
Fax: 020 7361 2976
E-mail: information.services@rbkc.gov.uk
Key staff: Head of Libraries and Arts: John McEachen;
    Head of Bibliographical and Technical Services: John
    Swindells

Stock and subject coverage: General public library lending and reference stock; local history relating to Kensington and Chelsea; music; video and DVDs. Major collection of biography, autobiography and genealogy. Folklore and customs collection (up to 1974)

Services: Photocopies (b&w and colour); free internet access; microfilm/fiche reader-printer; telephone; CD-ROMs; input/output centre for computer hire; scanning and fax services

Hours: 09.30-20.00 Monday, Tuesday and Thursday; 09.30-17.00 Wednesday, Friday and Saturday

Transport: Tube: High Street Kensington

Special facilities: Access for users with disabilities (ramp to main door, lift to first floor)

Special features: Kensington Central Library is a Grade II★ listed building

[348][b]
Brompton Library

210 Old Brompton Road
London SW5 0BS

Telephone: 020 7373 3111

Key staff: Area Librarian: Ingrid Lackajis

Stock and subject coverage: General public lending library and small reference collection. 'SPACE' centre – Supporting Parents As Co-Educators – IT area for parents and children to support homework and give access to IT for parents

Hours: 10.00-20.00 Monday, Tuesday and Thursday; 10.00-17.00 Friday and Saturday; 10.00-13.00 Wednesday

Transport: Tube: Earls Court; Bus: C1

Special facilities: Access for users with disabilities (lift to first floor)

[348][c]
Chelsea Library

Chelsea Old Town Hall
Kings Road
Chelsea SW3 5EE

Telephone: 020 7352 6056

Fax: 020 7351 1294

Key staff: Chelsea Area Librarian: Ingrid Lackajis

Stock and subject coverage: General public library lending collection. Separate reference and local history collections (for Chelsea only) costume collection forms part of Chelsea reference library stock. The Library also holds the Borough's fiction reserve collections for authors beginning CAQ-CHD

Services: Photocopies; free internet access; microfilm/fiche reader-printers

Hours: 10.00-20.00 Monday, Tuesday and Thursday; 10.00-17.00 Friday and Saturday; 10.00-13.00 Wednesday

Transport: Tube: Sloane Square, South Kensington; Bus: 11, 19, 22, 49

Transport: Disabled access (access by bell push)

[348][d]
Kensal Library

20 Golborne Road
London W10 5PF

Telephone: 020 8969 7736

Key staff: North Kensington Area Librarian: Cath Anley

Stock and subject coverage: Small community library with adult lending and children's library

Services: Photocopies; free internet access

Hours: 13.00-18.00 Monday, Tuesday and Thursday; 10.00-12.00, 13.00-18.00 Friday; 10.00-13.00, 14.00-17.00 Saturday

Transport: Bus: 52

Special facilities: Access for users with disabilities (ramp provided)

[348][e]
North Kensington Library

108 Ladbroke Grove
London W11 1PZ

Telephone: 020 7727 6583

Key staff: North Kensington Area Librarian: Cath Anley

Stock and subject coverage: General public lending library with small reference collection; Open Learning Centre

Services: Photocopies; free internet access

Hours: 10.00-20.00 Monday, Tuesday and Thursday; 10.00-17.00 Friday and Saturday; 10.00-13.00 Wednesday

Transport: Tube: Ladbroke Grove; Bus: 7, 23, 52, 70

Special facilities: Access for users with disabilities (ramp into library, lift to all floors)

[348][f]
Notting Hill Library

1 Pembridge Square
London W2 4EW

Telephone: 020 7229 8574

E-mail: information.services@rbkc.gov.uk

Key staff: Central Area Librarian: Iseult Pilkington

Stock and subject coverage: Small community library with adult lending stock and children's library

Hours: 10.00-20.00 Monday; 13.00-19.00 Tuesday; 10.00-13.00 Thursday; 10.00-13.00, 14.00-17.00 Friday and Saturday

Transport: Tube: Notting Hill Gate: Bus: 12, 27, 28, 31, 52, 70, 94, 302

Special facilities: Limited access for users with disabilities

[349]
Kew Bridge Engines Trust and Water Supply Museum Ltd

Kew Bridge Steam Museum
Green Dragon Lane
Brentford
Middlesex TW8 0EN

Borough: Hounslow

Telephone: 020 8568 4757

Fax: 020 8569 9978

World Wide Web: www.kbsm.org

Constitution: Registered charity and association with voluntary subscribing membership

Objectives/purposes: Organisation devoted to stationary steam engines, London's water supply

Key staff: Archivist: PR Stokes; B Caller, J Osborn, A Hurley, R Howes (water industry specialist)

Stock and subject coverage: Small library/archive holding materials on steam and steam engines, water supply, miscellaneous steam engineering and pumping

Kew Bridge Steam Museum

Availability: Charges made (for visiting the museum of which the library and archive are a part). Library visits by appointment only
Hours: 11.00–17.00 all week
Transport: Tube: Gunnersbury, Kew Gardens; Rail: Kew Bridge; Bus: 65, 237, 267, 391
Special facilities: Refreshment facilities available at weekends; toilet facilities
Special features: Working museum in early 19th century buildings

[350]
King's College London
Constitution: Department of the University of London
World Wide Web: www.kcl.ac.uk/library
Key staff: Head of Site Services: Vivien Robertson
Availability: Access open to all bona fide researchers for material not available elsewhere. Reference only, unless 'visitor' status granted (cost £60 p.a.). All applications should be made in writing
Hours: Opening hours are different in term and vacation (check website for details at www.kcl.ac.uk/depsta/iss/sites/)

Linked organisations
   University of London Part of the University

[350][a]
Information Services Centre
Franklin–Wilkins Building
150 Stamford Street
London SE1 9NN
Borough: Southwark
Telephone: 020 7848 4378
Fax: 020 7848 4290
E-mail: libraryenquiry@kcl.ac.uk
Stock and subject coverage: The collections include materials on: life sciences, gerontology, nutrition, education, nursing, management and pharmacy
Hours: 09.00–21.00 Monday to Friday
Transport: Tube and Rail: Waterloo
Special facilities: Refreshment and toilet facilities available; access for users with disabilities

[350][b]
Maughan Library and Information Services Centre
Chancery Lane
London WC2A 1LR
Borough: Corporation of London
Telephone: 020 7848 2424
Fax: 020 7848 2277
Stock and subject coverage: Very wide subject coverage with materials relating to all subjects taught in the College. Particularly strong collections include: theology, Portuguese, Modern Greek, war studies. Special collections at the Strand include the Burrows collection on Greek and Byzantine studies and the Enk Classics library of Professor Petrus Johannes Enk.
Wide range of special collections including the libraries of: William Marsden; Miron Grindea; Rev Professor George Herbert Box; Professor Ernst Cohn; Gen Sir Ian Hamilton; Sir Basil Liddell Hart; Prof Reginald Ruggles Gates; Prof Walter Skeat; Dr Frederick J Furnivall and Prof Sir Charles Wheatstone
Services: Photocopies; online searching; inter-library loans
Hours: Term-time: 08.30–22.00 Monday to Friday; vacation hours vary
Transport: Tube: Chancery Lane, Holborn, Temple; Bus: 8, 25, 242, 501, 521 or 4, 11, 15, 23, 26, 76, 172, 341
Special facilities: Refreshment and toilet facilities available
Publications: Information sheets

Denmark Hill Campus
[350][c]
Bethlam Library
Multidisciplinary Library
Bishopsgate Centre
Bethlem Royal Hospital
Monks Orchard Road
Beckenham
Kent BR3 3BX
Borough: Bromley
Telephone: 020 8776 4817
Fax: 020 8776 4818
E-mail: libraryenquiry@kcl.ac.uk
Stock and subject coverage: Psychiatric nursing and related disciplines including clinical psychology, sociology of health and medicine, social policy, health promotion,

health service management and psychiatry. Stock includes ca. 6,000 books and 40 current journal subscriptions
Services: Photocopies, internet access, fax machine, scanner
Availability: Open to bona fide researchers for reference only
Hours: 09.00–17.00 Monday and Friday; 13.00–17.00 Tuesday and Thursday; 09.00–13.00 Wednesday
Transport: Rail: Eden Park; Bus: from Croydon 119, 194, 356; from Bromley: 119, 367
Special facilities: Refreshment and toilet facilities available on site; access and special facilities for users with disabilities

[350][d]
Information Services Centre – Weston Education Centre
Cutcombe Road
London SE5 9JP
Borough: Southwark
Telephone: 020 7848 5541/5542
Fax: 020 7848 5550
E-mail: libraryenquiry@kcl.ac.uk
Stock and subject coverage: Clinical medicine and dentistry with related sciences and health service topics. The stock comprises books, journals, audiovisual and electronic material. There are two special collections: an archive of books about 'King's Men' and a small antiquarian collection of medical texts
Services: Enquiry service; photocopies (on purchase of copy card); database searching facilities; computing facilities with full internet access; multimedia and computer assisted learning software
Hours: 09.00–19.00 Monday to Friday; 10.00–13.30 Saturday
Transport: Rail: Denmark Hill; Bus: 40, 68, 176, 185
Special facilities: Refreshment and toilet facilities available

Guy's Campus
[350][e]
Information Services Centre, New Hunts House
Guys Hospital
St Thomas Street
London SE1 9RT
Borough: Southwark
Telephone: 020 7848 6600
E-mail: libraryenquiry@kcl.ac.uk
Stock and subject coverage: Books and journals on clinical, biomedical and related subjects and physiotherapy
Hours: 09.00–20.45 Monday to Friday
Transport: Tube and Rail: London Bridge
Special facilities: Refreshment and toilet facilities available

[350][f]
FS Warner Library
27th floor
Guy's Tower
King's College London
Guy's Campus
London Bridge
London SE1 9RT
Borough: Southwark

Telephone: 020 7955 4238
Stock and subject coverage: Books and journals relating to dentistry
Hours: 09.00–19.00 Monday to Friday

[350][g]
St Thomas's Hospital Medical Library
Block 9
St Thomas's Hospital
Lambeth Palace Road
London SE1 7EH
Borough: Lambeth
Telephone: 020 7928 9292 ext 2367
Fax: 020 7401 3932
E-mail: libraryenquiry@kcl.ac.uk
Stock and subject coverage: Materials on medicine, dentistry, the history of medicine. Publications by Guy's and St Thomas's staff
Services: Photocopies
Availability: Requests for access to be made in writing to the Librarian. Loans not available to external users
Hours: Check website at www.kcl.ac.uk/depsta/iss/sites/
Transport: Tube: Westminster, Waterloo; Rail: Waterloo
Special facilities: Toilet facilities available
Publications: Catalogue of the Printed Books and Manuscripts (1491–1900) in the Library of St Thomas's Hospital Medical School, by DT Bird, 1984

[351]
King's Fund Library
11–13 Cavendish Square
London W1G 0AN
Borough: Westminster
Telephone: 020 7307 2568/9
Fax: 020 7307 2805
E-mail: library@kehf.org.uk
World Wide Web: www.kingsfund.org.uk
Constitution: Registered charity
Objectives/purposes: To provide a public reference collection and library enquiry service to support the needs of managers working within the field of health and social care, and those training in related management areas
Key staff: Information and Library Service Manager: Lynette Cawthra; Enquiry Services Librarian: Valerie Wildridge
Stock and subject coverage: Management and delivery of health and social care services, primarily in the UK, though some international coverage. Material includes government documents, books, journals and informally published literature. The Library is a WHO Regional Office for Europe Documentation Centre and holds ca. 30,000 books and 300 journals
Services: Photocopies; internet access
Availability: Visits, written and telephone enquiries accepted; charges are made for literature searches requested by phone or in writing. Material is for reference only
Hours: Open to visitors: 09.30–17.30 Monday, Tuesday, Thursday and Friday; 11.00–17.30 Wednesday; 09.30–17.00 Saturday. Telephone enquiry hours: 10.00–18.00 Monday, Tuesday, Thursday, Friday and Saturday; 11.00–15.00 Wednesday
Transport: Tube: Oxford Circus

Special facilities: Refreshment and toilet facilities available; access for users with disabilities
Publications: Current Awareness Bulletin; Annual Report; Periodicals List; reading lists on specific topics

Linked organisations
King Edward's Hospital Fund for London
Parent body

[352]
Kingston Museum and Heritage Service
North Kingston Centre
Richmond Road
Kingston KT2 5PE
Borough: Kingston upon Thames
Telephone: 020 8547 6738
Fax: 020 8547 6747
E-mail: local.history@rbk.kingston.gov.uk
World Wide Web: www.kingston.gov.uk/museum/
Constitution: Local government run (independent operating unit)
Objectives/purposes: Local history library concerned with the history of the Royal Borough of Kingston upon Thames
Key staff: Local History Officer: Tim Everson; Archivist: Jill Lamb
Stock and subject coverage: Ca. 15,000 books and pamphlets, 5,000 photographs, old maps and newspapers, ephemera and some AV material on Kingston – its history, geography, etc.
Services: Photocopies (charges made); microfilm-fiche reader-printer; census database and other relevant CD-ROM databases; limited internet access via staff
Availability: No restriction on access. All material is reference only
Hours: 10.00–13.00, 14.00–17.00 Monday, Thursday and Friday; 10.00–13.00, 14.00–19.00 Tuesday
Transport: Tube: Richmond; Rail: Kingston; Bus: 65
Special facilities: Refreshment and toilet facilities available; disabled users cannot access the Library as it is on the first floor and there is no lift, materials can be provided for them on the ground floor and disabled toilet facilities are available

Linked organisations
Kingston Museum

[353]
Kingston University
Constitution: Department of a university
Borough: Kingston upon Thames
E-mail: library@kingston.ac.uk
World Wide Web: www.king.ac.uk/library-media
Key staff: Head of Library and Media Services: Nik Pollard
Availability: Reference access to all; annual fee-based membership for loan services
Special features: Kingston University Library is located on four sites: , Penrhyn Road (the main library – listed first), Kingston Hill, Knights Park and Roehampton Vale

[353][a]
Penrhyn Road Library

Penrhyn Road
Kingston upon Thames
Surrey KT1 2EE
Telephone: 020 8547 7101
Fax: 020 8547 8115
E-mail: library@kingston.ac.uk
Key staff: Senior Faculty Librarian, Penrhyn Road/Roehampton Vale: Rob James
Stock and subject coverage: Books, journals, CD-ROMs, abstracting journals, audio and video material on: chemistry, physics, life sciences and health studies, mathematics, computing, geological science, geography, economics, languages, social sciences, humanities, electronics, civil engineering and technical information. Special collections of statistics and careers information
Services: Photocopies; microform reader-printer
Hours: Term-time: 08.45-21.00 Monday to Thursday; 10.00-17.30 Friday; 10.15-15.45 Saturday and Sunday
Vacations: telephone site for information
Transport: Rail: Kingston, Surbiton; Bus: K2, K3, 71, 281, 406, 465, 479, 727
Special facilities: Refreshment and toilet facilities; access for users with disabilities – lift on ground floor

[353][b]
Kingston Hill Library

Kingston Hill
Kingston upon Thames
Surrey KT2 7LB
Telephone: 020 8547 7381
Fax: 020 8547 7312
E-mail: srobertson@kingston.ac.uk
Key staff: Senior Faculty Librarian, Kingston Hill: Sue Robertson
Stock and subject coverage: Books, journals, CD-ROMs, abstracting journals, audio and video material on: business, law, education, music and social work. Extensive collection of business and company information
Services: Photocopies; microform reader-printer
Hours: Term-time: 08.45-21.00 Monday to Thursday; 10.00-17.30 Friday; 10.15-15.45 Saturday and Sunday
Vacations: telephone site for information
Transport: Rail: Kingston, Surbiton; Bus: 85

[353][c]
Knights Park Library

Knights Park
Kingston upon Thames
Surrey KT1 2QJ
Telephone: 020 8547 2000
Fax: 020 8547 7011
Key staff: Information Librarians: Susan St Clair, Nicola Bonnick
Stock and subject coverage: Collections on fashion, fine art, foundation studies, graphic design, history of art, three-dimensional design, architecture, urban estate management and quantity surveying. Special collection of antiquarian and fragile material: pop-up books, medical drawings, typography, illustration, fashion, building construction, architecture, world trade fairs, interior design, furniture, painting, literature, prints, textile and wallpaper designs, ornament and decorative wrought iron. Slide collection
Services: Colour photocopies, CD-ROM databases
Hours: Term-time: 09.00-21.00 Monday to Thursday; 10.00-17.30 Friday
Vacations: telephone site for information
Transport: Rail: Kingston, Surbiton; Bus: K2, K3, 71, 281, 406, 465, 479, 727
Special facilities: Refreshment facilities available (term-time only); toilet facilities; limited disabled access – lift to first floor available
Publications: Guides to services and subject areas

[353][d]
Roehampton Vale Library

Roehampton Vale
Friars Avenue
London SW15 3DW
Telephone: 020 8547 7803
Fax: 020 8547 7800
E-mail: downey@kingston.ac.uk
Key staff: Senior Faculty Librarian, Penrhyn Road/Roehampton Vale: Rob James; Information Librarian: Bill Downey
Stock and subject coverage: Books, journals, CD-ROMs, abstracting journals, audio and video material on: mechanical, aeronautical, automotive and production engineering. Collection of technical information
Services: Photocopies; microform readers; CD-ROM; video and audio players
Hours: Term-time: 08.30-18.00 Monday, Tuesday and Thursday; 08.30-18.00 Wednesday; 08.30-17.30 Friday
Vacations: telephone site for information
Transport: Rail: Kingston, Surbiton; Bus: K6, 85, 265
Special facilities: Toilet facilities available; library housed on single level (ground floor) for disabled access

[354]
Kingston upon Thames (Royal Borough of Kingston upon Thames)

World Wide Web: www.kingston.gov.uk/libs/
Constitution: Public library funded by local authority
Availability: Free access to any member of the public. Items can only be borrowed by registered readers (no joining charge for Borough or non-Borough residents); reference items cannot be borrowed; charges levied for borrowing non-book items
Note: Each of the seven branches has a basic information collection including dictionaries and atlases, and a compendium of higher education and council information. The larger branches at Kingston and Surbiton carry a wider range of material including university and college prospectuses, phone directories for the UK and some business information. Internet access is available in all branches offering over 1,000 of the best websites on a wide variety of topics free of charge via Kingston Libraries' Online Reference Service

[354][a]
Hook and Chessington Library

Hook Road
Chessington
Surrey KT9 1EJ
Telephone: 020 8397 4931
Fax: 020 8391 4416
E-mail: hookandchess.library@rbk.kingston.gov.uk
Key staff: Library Manager: Miss Rosalind Fryer
Stock and subject coverage: Small reference collection and children's collection. Books, CDs and cassettes for loan; magazines and newspapers
Services: Fax and photocopying; internet access; hall for hire
Hours: 10.00–20.00 Monday and Friday; 10.00–17.00 Tuesday and Thursday; 09.30–17.00 Saturday
Transport: Rail: Chessington North
Special facilities: Access for users with disabilities; flly accessible for wheelchair users

[354][b]
Kingston Library (Adult Lending)

Fairfield Road
Kingston upon Thames
Surrey KT1 2PS
Telephone: 020 8547 6400
Fax: 020 8547 6401
E-mail: kingston.library@rbk.kingston.gov.uk
Stock and subject coverage: General collection of fiction and non-fiction for adults, youths and children; music scores and play sets; CDs, spoken word cassettes and videos (including Indian videos)
Services: Fax and photocopies; internet access; study area
Hours: 09.30–19.00 Monday; 09.30–17.30 Tuesday and Friday; 09.30–20.00 Thursday; 09.00–17.30 Saturday; 13.30–17.00 Sunday
Transport: Tube: Wimbledon, Richmond; Rail: Kingston; Bus: 65, 85, 131, 281, 371, 406
Special facilities: Access for users with disabilities; wheelchair ramp at front door
Special features: Good example of a Carnegie building
Publications: Annual Report

[354][c]
Kingston Children's Library

Wheatfield Way
Kingston
Surrey KT1 2PS
Telephone: 020 8547 6438
E-mail: kingston.library@rbk.kingston.gov.uk
Stock and subject coverage: Books, videos and cassettes
Services: Photocopies; storytime sessions and craft sessions; class visits for schools
Hours: 10.00–12.00, 14.00–17.30 Monday, Tuesday and Friday; 10.00–12.00, 14.00–19.00 Thursday; 10.00–17.30 Saturday; 13.30–17.00 Sunday
Transport: Rail: Kingston
Special facilities: Access for users with disabilities; wheelchair ramp at front door

[354][d]
New Malden Library

Kingston Road
New Malden
Surrey KT3 3LY

Telephone: 020 8547 6540
Fax: 020 8547 6545
E-mail: newmalden.library@rbk.kingston.gov.uk
Stock and subject coverage: Small reference collection; local information (limited); children's collection; CDs, spoken word cassettes and videos (including Asian videos); current newspapers
Services: Fax and photocopies; internet access; IT Learning Centre (charged); storytime sessions
Hours: 10.00–20.00 Monday and Friday; 10.00–17.30 Tuesday and Thursday; 09.00–17.30 Saturday
Transport: Tube: Wimbledon; Rail: New Malden; Bus: 131, 213
Special facilities: Access for users with disabilities with ramp and handrails to main entrance
Special features: Unique example of late 1930s architecture

[354][e]
Old Malden Library

Church Road
Worcester Park
Surrey KT4 7RD
Telephone: 020 8337 6344
Fax: 020 8330 3118
E-mail: oldmaldenlibrary@rbk.kingston.gov.uk
Key staff: Library Manager: Miss Margaret Vine
Stock and subject coverage: Adult and children's collections; books, CDs, spoken word cassettes and videos for loan; current newspapers
Services: Fax and photocopies; internet access; storytime sessions; class visits for schools
Hours: 10.00–12.30, 13.30–19.00 Monday and Friday; 13.30–17.00 Tuesday; 10.00–12.30, 13.30–19.00 Friday; 09.30–17.00 Saturday
Transport: Rail: Malden Manor; Bus: 213
Special facilities: Access for users with disabilities; wheelchair accessible with ramp to main entrance and no stairs in the building

[354][f]
Surbiton Library

Ewell Road
Surbiton
Surrey KT6 6AG
Telephone: 020 8399 2331
Fax: 020 8539 9805
E-mail: surbiton.library@rbk.kingston.gov.uk
Stock and subject coverage: Reference collection; local information (limited); children's collection; books, CDs, spoken word cassettes and videos (including Indian videos) for loan
Services: Fax and photocopies; internet access; study area; storytime sessions; class visits for schools
Hours: 10.00–20.00 Monday and Friday; 10.00–17.00 Tuesday and Thursday; 09.30–17.00 Saturday
Transport: Rail: Surbiton; Bus: 71, 281, 406, 479
Special facilities: Access for users with disabilities including ramp for wheelchairs and adapted toilet facilities. Access to Surbiton Library hall is via a flight of stairs only

[354][g]
Tolworth Community Library and IT Learning Centre

37–39 The Broadway
Tolworth
Surrey KT6 7DJ
Telephone: 020 8339 6950
Fax: 020 8339 6955
E-mail: tolworth.library@rbk.kingston.gov.uk
Stock and subject coverage: Reference collection; local information (limited); children's collection; books, CDs and spoken word cassettes for loan
Services: Fax and photocopies; internet access; IT Learning Centre (charged); storytime sessions; class visits for schools; weekly homework club
Hours: 10.00–20.00 Monday and Friday; 10.00–18.00 Wednesday and Thursday; 09.30–17.00 Saturday
Special facilities: Access for users with disabilities to library and IT room; adapted toilet facilities

[354][h]
Tudor Drive Library

Tudor Drive
Kingston
Surrey KT2 5QH
Telephone: 020 8546 1198
Fax: 020 8547 2295
E-mail: tudordrive.library@rbk.kingston.gov.uk
Stock and subject coverage: Reference collection; children's collection; books, CDs, spoken word cassettes and videos for loan; current magazines and newspapers
Services: Fax and photocopies; internet access; storytime sessions; class visits for schools
Hours: 10.00–12.30, 13.30–19.00 Monday and Friday; 10.00–12.30, 13.30–17.00 Tuesday; 13.30–17.00 Thursday; 09.00–17.00 Saturday
Transport: Rail: Kingston; Bus: 371
Special facilities: Access for users with disabilities including wheelchair users

[355]
Kurdish Cultural Centre
KCC

14 Stannary Street
London SE11 4AA
Borough: Lambeth
Telephone: 020 7735 0918
Fax: 020 7582 8894
Constitution: Company limited by guarantee; registered charity and association with voluntary subscribing membership
Objectives/purposes: Assisting Kurdish refugees in the UK and abroad, promotion of Kurdish culture and Kurdish studies. Publication of materials on Kurdish affairs in various languages
Key staff: Librarian and Archivist: Sarbest Kirkuky
Stock and subject coverage: Material and publications on all aspects of Kurdish affairs
Services: Photocopies
Availability: Access for all researchers and members of the public
Hours: 09.30–17.30 Fridays only
Transport: Tube: Oval, Kennington; Bus: 36, 109, 133, 159, 185, 355

Special facilities: Photocopies
Special features: Toilet facilities available; access for users with disabilities
Publications: Annual Report

[356]
Laban Centre London

Creekside
London SE8 3DZ
Borough: Lewisham
Telephone: 020 8691 8600
Fax: 020 8691 8400
E-mail: library@laban.co.uk
World Wide Web: www.laban.co.uk
Constitution: Registered charity
Objectives/purposes: All aspects of dance, primarily in the performing arts
Key staff: Head of Media and Information Resource Centre: Ralph Cox ALA
Stock and subject coverage: Materials on dance and movement plus related subjects, e.g. design, anatomy, aesthetics, administration, education, arts therapies, music, psychology, sociology, political science. The collections include: books, journals, videos, CDs, music, theatre programmes, notated dance scores, manuscripts, photographs, slides, pamphlets, ephemera, microfilm and fiche
Services: Photocopies; UK and USA standards video players; microfilm-fiche reader; CD players; CD-ROM; 'Calaban' computer notation software
Availability: Open for reference use for researchers. Charges levied on non-Centre users as follows: £5 per morning or afternoon (max 5 hours), £20 per week, £50 per term, £100 per year. Reduced rates for students: £2.50 per morning or afternoon, £6 per week, £25 per term and £40 per year
Hours: Term-time: 09.00–20.00 Monday, Wednesday and Thursday; 09.00–19.30 Tuesday; 09.00–17.00 Friday; 09.00–13.00 Saturday
Vacations: 09.00–17.00 Monday to Friday
Transport: DLR: Cutty Sark; Rail: Deptford, Greenwich; Bus: 47, 53, 89, 177, 188, 225
Special facilities: Refreshments available (vending machine); toilet facilities available; limited access for users with disabilities (no lift)
Special features: Sited in St James's Church, Hatcham, scene of rioting following the Public Worship Regulation Act of 1874
Publications: List of Theses; Periodicals List, Library Bulletin (3 p.a.)

Linked organisations
City University
Degree courses validated by the University

[357]
The Labour Party

Millbank Tower
Millbank
London SW1P 4GT
Borough: Westminster
Telephone: 08705 900 200
World Wide Web: www.labour.org.uk
Constitution: Political party

Stock and subject coverage: Labour Party pamphlets and
    leaflets from 1900 to present day; Labour Party
    Archives – last ten years on closed access
Availability: Written enquiries only

[358]
Lakeman Library for Electoral Studies

6 Chancel Street
London SE1 0UX
Borough: Southwark
Telephone: 020 7620 1080
Fax: 020 7928 4366
E-mail: admin@mcdougall.org.uk
Objectives/purposes: To advance knowledge of, and
    encourage the study of and research in: political and
    economic science, the functions of government and
    the services provided to the community by public
    and voluntary organisations; and methods of election
    of, and the selection and government of,
    representative organisations whether national, civic,
    commercial, industrial, or social
Key staff: Librarian/Information Officer: Paul Wilder
Stock and subject coverage: Ca. 3,000 books and 2,000
    pamphlets; extensive press cuttings collection. Covers
    elections; voting systems; electoral procedures;
    electoral statistics; electoral reform and related issues.
    Includes archives of the Electoral Reform Society
Services: Photocopier available; catalogue held on
    database (Tinlib) for search purposes
Availability: Open to all bona fide researchers by
    appointment with the Executive Secretary. Loans
    subject to agreement with Librarian/Information
    Officer
Hours: 09.30–17.30 Monday to Friday
Transport: Tube: Southwark, Waterloo, Blackfriars; Rail:
    Waterloo, Blackfriars
Special facilities: Refreshment and toilet facilities available
Publications: Twelve Democracies: Electoral System in
    the European Community, by Enid Lakeman, 1991
    (£5). Representation: the Journal of Representative
    Democracy (quarterly journal – £60 p.a. for UK
    institutions; £25 p.a. for UK individuals. Overseas
    subscription rates available on request)

Linked organisations

McDougall Trust (The Arthur McDougall Fund)
    Electoral Reform Society's associated charity

[359]
Lambeth (London Borough of Lambeth)
Lambeth Environmental Services, Public Library and Archives Services

Library and Archives Headquarters
4th Floor
Blue Star House
234–244 Stockwell Road
Brixton
London SW9 9SP
Telephone: 020 7926 0750
Fax: 020 7926 0751

Constitution: Public library, funded by local government
Note: Lambeth's main reference library is based at
    Brixton

[359][a]
Brixton Central Library

Brixton Oval
London SW2 1JQ
Telephone: 020 7926 1056
    020 7926 1067 (Reference)
Fax: 020 7926 1070
Stock and subject coverage: Reference collection; local
    information and children's collection; government
    and legal publications; special collection on ethnic
    diversity in Britain
Services: Fax and photocopier facilities; study area
Hours: 11.00–20.00 Monday; 10.00–18.00 Tuesday,
    Wednesday and Friday; 10.00–20.00 Friday; 09.00–
    17.00 Saturday: 12.00–17.00 Sunday
Transport: Tube and Rail: Brixton; Bus: 2, 3, P4, P5, 35,
    37, 45, 45A, 109, 118, 133, 159, 189, 196, 250, 322
Special facilities: Access for users with disabilities to
    ground floor only; induction loop and minicom

[359][b]
Carnegie Library

188 Herne Hill Road
London SE24 0AG
Telephone: 020 7926 6050
Fax: 020 7926 6072
Reference facilities: Reference collection; local
    information and children's collection
Hours: 13.00–20.00 Monday; 10.00–13.00 Wednesday;
    14.30–18.00 Friday; 14.30–17.00 Saturday
Transport: Rail: Herne Hill; Bus: P4, P5, 35, 45, 68, 68A,
    189
Special facilities: Access for users with disabilities

[359][c]
Clapham Library

1 Northside
Clapham Common
London SW4 0QW
Telephone: 020 7926 0717
Fax: 020 7926 5804
Reference facilities: Reference collection; local information
    and children's collection
Hours: 12.00–20.00 Monday; 10.00–18.00 Tuesday,
    Wednesday and Friday; 10.00–20.00 Thursday: 09.00–
    17.00 Saturday
Transport: Tube: Clapham Common; Bus: 35, 37, 45A,
    60, 88, 137, 137A, 155, 189, 355
Special facilities: Access for users with disabilities, toilet
    for use by people with disabilities

[359][d]
Durning Library

167 Kennington Lane
London SE11 4HF
Telephone: 020 7926 8682
Fax: 020 7926 8684
Reference facilities: Reference collection; local
    information and children's collection
Services: Photocopier; PC, bookable in advance

Hours: 13.00-18.00 Monday; 10.00-13.00 Tuesday;
   10.00-20.00 Wednesday; 10.00-18.00 Friday; 09.00-
   17.00 Saturday
Transport: Tube: Kennington, Oval; Bus: 3, 109, 159, 322
Special facilities: Access for users with disabilities, toilet
   for use by people with disabilities

[359][e]
Lambeth Archives and Library
Minet Library
52 Knatchbull Road
London SE5 9QY
Telephone: 020 7926 6076
   020 7926 6070 (Library)
Fax: 020 7926 6080
Key staff: Archivist: Jon Newman; Assistant Archivist:
   Pauline Tilbury; Local History Librarian: Beryl
   Barrow
Stock and subject coverage: Collections of local material
   which chart the history and growth of Lambeth and
   its people over five centuries up to the present day.
   The Archive contains: the records of the present
   Lambeth Council and its predecessors back to the
   16th century; deeds, papers and archives of many
   local individuals, organisations and businesses; a map
   collection; illustrations collection; cuttings and
   ephemera collection; small oral history and audiovisual collection; local newspaper library; local
   history library of books, pamphlets and directories;
   and a microfilm collection
Services: Enquiry service; microfilm and microfiche
   readers and printers; photocopies; map copying;
   photographic copying; internet access
Availability: Open to the general public, free of charge.
   Telephone or write to make an appointment
Hours: 13.00-20.00 Monday; 10.00-18.00 Tuesday and
   Thursday; 10.00-13.00 Friday: 09.00-17.00 Saturday
Transport: Bus: 3, P5, 35, 36, 36B, 45, 45A, 59, 109, 133,
   159, 185, 196
Special facilities: Staff can advise on local refreshments;
   toilets; disabled access to building ñ including toilet
   facilities, lift, ramps, visual aids, ample on-street
   parking
Publications: Range of publications for sale and free
   leaflets on the Department and its collections

[359][f]
North Lambeth Library
114-118 Lower Marsh
London SE1 7AG
Telephone: 020 7926 8690
Fax: 020 7926 8684
Reference facilities: Reference collection; local
   information and children's collection
Hours: Temporarily closed, check website for details
Transport: Tube: Waterloo, Lambeth North; Rail:
   Waterloo; Bus: 12, 53, 109
Special facilities: Access for users with disabilities

[359][g]
South Lambeth Library
180 South Lambeth Road
London SW8 1QP
Telephone: 020 7926 0705
Fax: 020 7926 8684

Reference facilities: Reference collection; local
   information and children's collection
Hours: 12.00-18.00 Monday; 14.30-18.00 Tuesday,
   Wednesday and Friday; 10.00-20.00 Thursday: 13.30-
   17.00 Saturday
Transport: Bus: 2, 88
Special facilities: Access for users with disabilities

[359][h]
Streatham Library
63 Streatham High Road
London SW16 1PL
Telephone: 020 7926 6768
Fax: 020 7926 5804
Reference facilities: Reference collection; local
   information and children's collection
Hours: 13.00-20.00 Monday; 10.00-20.00 Tuesday and
   Wednesday; 10.00-18.00 Thursday and Friday; 09.30-
   17.00 Saturday; 12.00-17.00 Sunday
Transport: Bus: G1, 57, 60, 109, 115, 118, 133, 159, 200,
   249, 250, 319
Special facilities: Access for users with disabilities

[359][i]
West Norwood Library
Norwood High Street
London SE27 9JX
Telephone: 020 7926 8092
   020 7926 8034 (Renewals only)
Fax: 020 7926 8032
Reference facilities: Reference collection; local
   information and children's collection
Hours: 12.00-20.00 Monday; 10.00-20.00 Tuesday;
   10.00-18.00 Wednesday to Friday; 09.00-17.00
   Saturday
Transport: Rail: West Norwood; Bus: G1, 2, 68, 68A,
   196, 322
Special facilities: Access for users with disabilities

---

[360]
Lambeth College
Special features: Lambeth College is a multi-site college
   located on four separate sites

[360][a]
Brixton Centre
Brixton Hill
London SW2 1QS
Transport: Tube: Brixton

[360][b]
Clapham Centre
Southside
Clapham Common
London SW4 9ES
Transport: Tube: Clapham Common

[360][c]
Tower Bridge Centre
Tooley Street
London SE1 2JR
Transport: Tube: Tower Hill; Rail: London Bridge

[360][d]
Vauxhall Centre
Wandsworth Road
London SW8 2JY
Transport: Tube: Vauxhall, Stockwell; Rail: Vauxhall
Telephone: 020 7501 5000
Fax: 020 7501 5780
World Wide Web: www.lambethcollege.ac.uk
Constitution: Further education college
Key staff: Head of Library Services: Mary Findlay;
    Systems Librarian: Kay Stopforth: Learning
    Resources Managers: Jane Bramwell, Bruce Hawkins,
    Chloe Watkins
Stock and subject coverage: Ca. 90,000 volumes, 2,000
    videos and 200 journal subscriptions. Materials
    support a wide range of training courses and
    qualifications – including: BTEC, RSA, City and
    Guilds, Access, GNVQ/NVQ – provided by the
    College. Subjects covered include: business studies,
    computing, design, counselling, hair and beauty,
    media, journalism, nursing, social work, recreation,
    sports, construction, a wide range of 'A' level and
    GCSE subjects, and the sciences, e.g. dentistry,
    horticultural and food technology
Services: Photocopies; internet access; CD-ROMs; open
    access computers
Availability: Full access for all students and staff at
    Lambeth College. Open to members of the public,
    free of charge, by appointment and for reference only
Hours: Core hours for all Centres: 09.00-17.00 Monday
    to Thursday; 10.00-16.00 Friday
Special facilities: Refreshment and toilet facilities available
    on sites; access for users with disabilities is good on
    most sites except Tower Bridge, CCTV for visually
    impaired students available on all sites
Publications: Library and ILT Centre guides

[361]
Lambeth Palace Library
Lambeth Palace
London SE1 7JU
Borough: Lambeth
Telephone: 020 7898 1400
Fax: 020 7928 7932
World Wide Web: www.lambethpalacelibrary.org
Constitution: Independent non-profit distributing
    organisation
Objectives/purposes: Principal library and record office for
    the history of the Church of England
Key staff: Librarian and Archivist: Dr RJ Palmer; Deputy
    Librarian and Archivist: Miss M Barber; Senior
    Assistant Librarian (Printed Books): Miss C Mackwell
Stock and subject coverage: Ca. 200,000 printed books
    (20,000 before 1700); 4,000 manuscripts from the 9th
    to 20th centuries; extensive archives of the
    Archbishops and Province of Canterbury Faculty
    Office, Lambeth Conferences, etc.; Tudor and Stuart
    family papers; Carew papers for the history of
    Ireland; ecclesiastical records of Commonwealth
    period; records of Queen Anne's Commisssion for
    Building Fifty New Churches, Incorporated Church
    Building Society and numerous other Church
    societies; correspondence and papers of the Bishops
    of London, churchmen and statesmen. The
    collections are primarily on Church history, but they

also cover the history of art; architecture; local
    history; genealogy; colonial and Commonwealth
    history; English social, political and economic history;
    and many other subjects
Services: Photocopies; microfilm/microfiche reader-
    printer; photography
Availability: Freely available at the discretion of the
    Librarian. Reference only. Applicants should bring
    two passport style photographs, proof of address and a
    letter of introduction
Hours: 10.00-17.00 Monday to Friday; closed on public
    holidays and for ten days at Christmas and Easter
Transport: Tube: Westminster, Lambeth North; Rail:
    Vauxhall, Waterloo; Bus: C10, 3, 344, 507
Special facilities: Refreshment and toilet facilities available
    on site; access for users with disabilities by
    arrangement
Special features: One of England's oldest public libraries,
    founded by Archbishop Bancroft in 1610. Buildings
    include Morton's Tower (15th century), the Great
    Hall (17th century) as well as the modern reading
    room
Publications: Annual Review; extensive series of
    catalogues of manuscripts and archives

Linked organisations
The historic library of the Archbishops of
    Canterbury (founded 1610) and maintained by the
    Church Commissioners

[362]
Lambeth, Southwark and Lewisham Health Authority
LSLHA
1 Lower Marsh
London SE1 7RJ
Borough: Southwark
Telephone: 020 7716 7002
Fax: 020 7716 7039
E-mail: gina.mchale@ob.lslha.sthames.nhs.uk
Constitution: National Health Service commission
Key staff: Librarian: Gina McHale; Assistant Librarian:
    Linda M Kalinda
Stock and subject coverage: Collections on the management
    and delivery of health care; purchasing healthcare in
    the NHS; epidemiology and health economics (very
    little clinical information. Special collection of
    Department of Health Circulars
Services: Photocopying facilities (limited)
Availability: Open to all bona fide researchers for
    reference, by appointment only
Hours: 09.00-17.00 Monday to Friday
Transport: Tube: Lambeth North, Waterloo; Rail:
    Waterloo
Special facilities: Refreshment and toilet facilities available
    on site; access for users with disabilities
Publications: Public Health annual report; various
    consultation documents

Linked organisations
The Health Authority comprises six primary care
    groups: North and South Lambeth; North and South
    Lewisham; and North and South Southwark

[363]
Latin America Bureau
LAB
1 Amwell Street
London EC1R 1UL
Borough: Islington
Telephone: 020 7278 2829
Fax: 020 7278 0165
E-mail: lab@gn.apc.org
World Wide Web: www.lab.org.uk/
Constitution: Independent non-profit distributing organisation and company limited by guarantee
Objectives/purposes: Research, publishing and education on Latin America and the Caribbean
Key staff: Editor: Marcela Lúpez Levy
Stock and subject coverage: Links to news sources and material from and about Latin America and the Caribbean
Services: Website based information services
Publications: Latin America News (3 p.a); contact LAB for a catalogue of publications

[364]
Law Commission
Conquest House
37–38 John Street
Theobald's Road
London WC1N 2BQ
Borough: Camden
Telephone: 020 7453 1241
Fax: 020 7453 1296
E-mail: library.lawcomm@gtnet.gov.uk
World Wide Web: www.lawcom.gov.uk
Key staff: Librarian: Keith Tree BA, tel: 020 7453 1241
Constitution: Government funded body
Objectives/purposes: The Law Commission of the government's law reform body for England and Wales
Stock and subject coverage: Ca. 50,000 items. General coverage of the whole field of law, and more detailed coverage of the areas under investigation by the Commission (see Annual Reports); Law reform publications from other countries, especially the Commonwealth
Services: Loans: To government departments and to other libraries
Hours: 09.00-17.00 Monday to Friday
Transport: Tube: Holborn, Chancery Lane

Linked organisations

Court Service Library and Information Services
The Library operates as part of the Court Service Library and Information Services

[365]
Law Society Library
113 Chancery Lane
London WC2A 1PL
Borough: Westminster
Telephone: 0870 606 2511
Fax: 020 7831 1687
E-mail: lib-enq@lawsociety.org.uk

World Wide Web: www.lawsociety.org.uk
Constitution: Chartered professional body
Key staff: Librarian: Chris Holland; Library Enquiries: 0870 606 2511
Stock and subject coverage: About 65,000 volumes, principally UK and European Communities legal and parliamentary material, for reference use only
Availability: A private library, primarily serving solicitors in England and Wales who are members of the Society. Bona fide researchers should apply in writing if they wish to consult the rare books collection or Law Society archival material. Reference library only
Hours: 09.00-17.00 Monday to Friday
Transport: Tube: Chancery Lane, Holborn, Temple
Special facilities: Refreshment and toilet facilities available; access for users with disabilities (enlarged text from books and VDUs and transfer to audiotape and braille. Minicom phone. Lift access to building and Library)
Special features: Grade II★ listed building

[366]
League of British Muslims UK
Ilford Muslim Community Centre
Eton Road
Ilford
Essex IG1 2UE
Borough: Redbridge
Telephone: 020 8514 0706
Constitution: Registered charity
Objectives/purposes: To provide social, cultural and religious activities for all members. Drop in day centre facilities, free legal advice and immigration counselling
Key staff: Director: BA Chaudhry; Library staff are mainly volunteers
Stock and subject coverage: Materials on Islamic religion, history and Asian culture. Pamphlets on Islamic education and other topics
Services: Photocopies; translation services; fax; office space and hall available for hire
Availability: Available to all free of charge
Hours: 10.00-19.00 Monday to Friday
Transport: Tube: Barking; Rail: Ilford
Special facilities: Refreshment and toilet facilities available; access for users with disabilities including ramp for wheelchairs and toilet facilities
Publications: The League (monthly); Annual Report and various books on Islam

Linked organisations

Disabled Muslim Women's Association, Redbridge

Eton Road Community centre, Ilford

Pakistan Welfare Organisation, Redbridge

[367]
Leo Baeck College – Centre for Jewish Education Library
Sternberg Centre for Judaism
80 East End Road
London N3 2SY
Borough: Barnet

Telephone: 020 8349 5611
Fax: 020 8343 2558
Constitution: Department of a college
Objectives/purposes: Library of Judaica
Key staff: Librarian: Dr César Merchán Hamann
Stock and subject coverage: Materials on all aspects of
    Jewish studies: Bible, Talmud, Midrash, Codes, liturgy,
    education, language, literature, arts, history, Israel and
    Zionism. The collections include journals and
    encyclopaedias, ca. 40,000 books in various
    languages, 3,000 pamphlets, and tapes of lectures.
    They also include the Podro collection of books and
    pamphlets as well as a rare book collection
    comprising some of the books that formed part of
    the library of the Beit Din of the United Synagogue
Services: Photocopies (charges made)
Availability: Access open to all bona fide researchers,
    Library fee £20 per year
Hours: 09.00–17.00 Monday to Thursday; 09.00–13.00
    Friday
Transport: Tube: Finchley Central
Special facilities: Refreshment and toilet facilities available
Publications: Annual Report (published by the Leo Baeck
    College – Centre for Jewish Education)

---

[368]
The Leprosy Mission
TLM
80 Windmill Road
Brentford
Middlesex TW8 0QH
Borough: Hounslow
Telephone: 020 8569 7292
Fax: 020 8569 7808
Constitution: Registered charity
Objectives/purposes: International Christian charity
    committed to the care of leprosy sufferers and the
    eradication of the disease of leprosy
Key staff: General Director: Trevor Durston
Stock and subject coverage: Current literature covering
    medical aspects of leprosy including treatment,
    diagnosis, POD and rehabilitation. Historical library
    with collections from the 1880s to date on medicine,
    the history of the mission, or works by TLM staff.
    Archives include correspondence and documents
    from the 1890s to date
Services: Photocopies (charges made)
Availability: Open to researchers by appointment only.
    Current literature, available to medical staff in need
    of material on leprosy. Library books for reference
    only
Hours: 09.00–17.00 Monday to Friday
Transport: Tube: Northfields then bus E2; Rail: Brentford
Special facilities: Toilet facilities; access for users with
    disabilities – lift, wide doors, ramp at rear of building
Publications: Annual Report; Ask (annual prayer guide,
    includes directory of centres and staff); booklist and
    order form available on request

[369]
Lewisham (London Borough of Lewisham)
Library and Information Service
Town Hall Chambers
Rushey Green
London SE6 4RU
Constitution: Public library funded by local authority,
    part of the Directorate for Education and Culture

[369][a]
Lewisham Central Library
199–201 High Street
London SE13 6LG
Telephone: 020 8297 9677
Fax: 020 8297 8127
Key staff: Operations Manager: John Simmons;
    Reference Librarian: Carol Evans; Librarian: Michelle
    Gammon; Archivist: Jean Wait
Stock and subject coverage: Children's library; adult lending
    (fiction and non-fiction) with special collections for
    lesbians and gay men, black interest, Irish interest,
    women's issues, environmental issues, basic skills,
    European information. Open and flexible learning
    materials: videos, CDs, cassettes and talking books.
    Reference and information services including tourist
    information and European information, local studies
    (see separate entry) and archives collections
Services: Minicom; fax machines; colour and b&w
    photocopiers; CD-ROM; bookshop, coffeeshop
Availability: All lending services free and open to all –
    no charges for audio materials. Services available free
    of charge to researchers, research materials available
    for consultation
Hours: 10.00–17.00 Monday; 09.00–17.00 Wednesday,
    Friday and Saturday; 09.00–20.00 Tuesday and
    Thursday
Transport: Tube: New Cross, New Cross Gate; Rail:
    Lewisham, New Cross and New Cross Gate; Bus: P4,
    47, 54, 75, 122, 136, 180, 181, 185, 284, 298, 484
Special facilities: Refreshment and toilet facilities available
    on site; access for users with disabilities, facilities
    include: robotron reading machine, induction loops at
    enquiry desks and meeting room, CCTV, speaking
    lift and escalator, toilets, car parking spaces and
    minicom
Special features: New central library opened in October
    1994: includes coffeeshop, bookshop, art gallery,
    performance and exhibition space, meeting and
    conference room, Borough information centre,
    tourist information centre and disability information
    area

Linked organisations
Lewisham Local Studies Centre
The local studies centre is located in the same
building

[369][b]
Blackheath Village Library
3–4 Blackheath Grove
London SE3 0DD

Telephone: 020 8852 5309
Key staff: Senior Library Assistant: Greer Codd
Reference facilities: Reference collection; local
   information and children's collection
Hours: 14.30–20.00 Tuesday; 09.30–13.30, 14.30–20.00
   Thursday; 09.30–13.30, 14.30–17.00 Saturday
Transport: Rail: Blackheath; Bus: 54, 89, 108B, 202, 306
Special facilities: Access for users with disabilities

[369][c]
Catford Library
   Laurence House
   Catford
   London SE6 4RU
Telephone: 020 8314 6399
Fax: 020 8314 1110
Key staff: Operations Manager: Kevin Yeates
Reference facilities: Reference collection; local
   information and children's collection
Hours: 09.30–20.00 Tuesday and Thursday; 09.30–17.00
   Monday, Wednesday and Friday
Transport: Rail: Catford Bridge, Catford; Bus: 47, 54,
   124, 136, 160, 172, 185, 208
Special facilities: Access for users with disabilities and
   kurzweil machine

[369][d]
Crofton Park Library
   Brockley Road
   London SE4 2AF
Telephone: 020 8692 1683
Key staff: Senior Library Assistant: Kerry Hart
Reference facilities: Reference collection; local
   information and children's collection
Hours: 09.30–13.00, 14.00–17.00 Monday and Saturday;
   09.30–13.00, 14.00–20.00 Tuesday and Thursday;
   09.30–13.00 Friday
Transport: Rail: Crofton Park; Bus: 171, 172
Special facilities: Access for users with disabilities

[369][e]
Downham Library
   Moorside Road
   Downham
   London SE4 2AF
Telephone: 020 8698 1475
Key staff: Senior Library Assistant: Sue Court
Reference facilities: Reference collection; local
   information and children's collection
Hours: 09.30–13.00, 14.00–17.00 Monday and Saturday;
   09.30–13.00, 14.00–20.00 Tuesday and Thursday;
   09.30–13.00 Friday
Transport: Rail: Grove Park; Bus: 136, 124, 284
Special facilities: Access for users with disabilities

[369][f]
Forest Hill Library
   Dartmouth Road
   London SE23 3HZ
Telephone: 020 8699 2065
Fax: 020 8699 8296
Key staff: Senior Library Assistant: Celia Hart

Reference facilities: Reference collection; local
   information and children's collection
Hours: 09.30–17.00 Monday and Saturday; 09.30–20.00
   Tuesday and Thursday; 09.30–13.00 Friday
Transport: Rail: Forest Hill; Bus: 122, 176, 185, 312
Special facilities: Access for users with disabilities

[369][g]
Grove Park Library
   Somertrees Avenue
   London SE12 0BX
Telephone: 020 8857 5794
Key staff: Senior Library Assistant: Katie Drew
Reference facilities: Reference collection; local
   information and children's collection
Hours: 09.30–13.00 Monday; 14.30–20.00 Tuesday and
   Thursday; 09.30–13.00 Saturday
Transport: Rail: Grove Park; Bus: 124, 136, 160, 202, 284
Special facilities: Access for users with disabilities

[369][h]
Lewisham Local Studies Centre
   Lewisham Library
   199–201 Lewisham High Street
   London SE13 6LG
Telephone: 020 8297 0682
Fax: 020 8297 1169
Objectives/purposes: To collect, list, preserve and make
   available for consultation archives and local history
   material relating to the London Borough of
   Lewisham
Key staff: Archivist: Jean Wait
Stock and subject coverage: Archives of any organisation or
   individual operating in the London Borough of
   Lewisham. Books, pamphlets, maps and other
   publications, visual and audio-visual material relating
   to the past and present of the London Borough of
   Lewisham and of those portions of Deptford and
   Blackheath which are within the Local Borough of
   Greenwich, recognising the multicultural nature of
   the community. Publications concerning the history
   of neighbouring boroughs and of Kent and London,
   and general works on local history, where these are
   relevant to the Borough
Services: Photocopier and microprinter
Availability: Free access for all for reference only
Hours: 10.00–17.00 Monday; 09.00–20.00 Tuesday and
   Thursday; 09.00–17.00 Wednesday, Friday and
   Saturday. (It may not be possible to produce material
   on closed access 12.00–14.00 or 17.00–20.00, such
   material can be ordered)
Transport: Tube: New Cross, New Cross Gate; Rail:
   Lewisham, New Cross and New Cross Gate; Bus: P4,
   47, 54, 75, 122, 136, 180, 181, 185, 284, 298, 484
Special facilities: Refreshment and toilet facilities
   available; fully accessible for disabled users, toilets for
   wheelchair users and facilities for partially sighted
   readers provided
Publications: Various publications on local history
   including: local histories, town trails, books of
   photographs, postcards, greetings cards and mini-
   guide

[369][i]
Manor House Library
Old Road
Lee
London SE12 5SY
Telephone: 020 8852 0357
Key staff: Senior Library Assistant: Bronwen Cobell
Reference facilities: Reference collection; local information and children's collection
Hours: 09.30-13.00, 14.00-17.00 Monday and Saturday; 09.30-13.00, 14.00-20.00 Tuesday and Thursday; 09.30-13.00 Friday
Transport: Rail: Hither Green, Lewisham; Bus: 122, 261

[369][j]
New Cross Library
283-5 New Cross Road
London SE14 6AS
Telephone: 020 8694 2534
Key staff: Senior Library Assistant: Robert Tamplin
Reference facilities: Reference collection; local information and children's collection
Hours: 14.30-20.00 Tuesday; 09.30-13.00, 14.00-20.00 Thursday; 09.30-13.00 Friday; 09.30-13.00, 14.00-17.00 Saturday
Transport: Tube and Rail: New Cross, New Cross Gate; Bus: 21, 36, 53, 136, 171, 172, 177
Special facilities: Access for users with disabilities

[369][k]
Sydenham Library
Sydenham Road
London SE26 5SB
Telephone: 020 8778 7563
Key staff: Senior Library Assistant: Carol Bowen
Reference facilities: Reference collection; local information and children's collection
Hours: 09.30-13.00, 14.00-17.00 Monday and Saturday; 09.30-13.00, 14.00-20.00 Tuesday and Thursday; 09.30-13.00 Friday
Transport: Rail: Sydenham; Bus: 181, 194, 202, 306
Special facilities: Access for users with disabilities

[369][l]
Torridon Road Libary
Torridon Road
London SE6 1RQ
Telephone: 020 8698 1590
Key staff: Senior Library Assistant: David Rees
Reference facilities: Reference collection; local information and children's collection
Hours: 09.30-13.00, 14.00-17.00 Monday and Saturday; 09.30-13.00, 14.00-20.00 Tuesday and Thursday; 09.30-13.00 Friday
Transport: Rail: Hither Green (15 minute walk); Bus: 124, 180, 181, 284
Special facilities: Access for users with disabilities

[369][m]
Wavelengths Library
Giffin Street
Deptford
London SE8 4RJ
Telephone: 020 8694 2535

Fax: 020 8694 9652
Key staff: Senior Library Assistant: Rita Blackabee
Reference facilities: Reference collection; local information and children's collection
Hours: 09.30-17.00 Monday, Wednesday, Friday and Saturday; 09.30-20.00 Tuesday and Thursday
Transport: Tube: New Cross; Rail: Deptford, New Cross; Bus: 47 (stops outside), 53, 199
Special facilities: Access for users with disabilities

[370]
Liberty (National Council for Civil Liberties)
21 Tabard Street
London SE1 4LA
Borough: Southwark
Telephone: 020 7403 3888
Fax: 020 7407 5354
E-mail: info@liberty-human-rights.org.uk
World Wide Web: www.liberty-human-rights.org.uk
Constitution: Association with voluntary subscribing membership
Stock and subject coverage: Ca. 8,000 books, pamphlets, government and other reports; press cuttings and journals on civil liberties and human rights in the UK. Includes collections on policing, public order, privacy, justice and the legal system, discrimination, and some material on human rights in Europe
Services: Photocopies
Availability: By appointment only; small fee charged to non-members
Hours: 10.00-13.00, 14.00-17.30 Monday to Friday
Transport: Tube: Borough; Bus: P3, 21, 35, 40, 133
Special facilities: Toilet facilities available
Publications: List available on request

[371]
The Library of the Worshipful Company of Clockmakers
Guildhall Library
Aldermanbury
London EC2P 2EJ
Borough: Corporation of London
Telephone: 020 7332 1868/1870
Fax: 020 7600 3384
Constitution: Registered charity. The Library belongs to the Worshipful Company of Clockmakers but is loaned to the Company's Museum and Educational Trust
Key staff: The Keeper: Sir George White Bt FSA
Stock and subject coverage: Printed books and manuscripts covering all aspects of horology, especially clock and watchmaking within the City of London. The collection contains the workbooks of several well known London clockmakers and has a particularly fine section devoted to the work of John Harrison of Barrow
Services: Photocopier available (very little copying allowed)
Availability: Available to all researchers on the same terms as other books and manuscripts in Guildhall Library. Entrance is free, but material is for reference only

Hours: 09.30-17.00 Monday to Saturday, except bank holidays (including Bank Holiday Saturdays)
Transport: Tube: Bank, Moorgate, Mansion House, St Paul's; Bus: 8, 22, 22B, 25, 501 to Cheapside, 9, 11, 21, 43, 76, 133, 141 to Moorgate, 141, 279A, 502 to London Wall
Special facilities: Toilet facilities available, access for users with disabilities – via ramps and lifts
Special features: The Library was founded in 1813 and as such is the oldest devoted solely to horology. The Worshipful Company of Clockmakers was granted its charter in 1632. The Library contains all its Minute Books and documents from that period onwards

Linked organisations

Guildhall Library The Library is housed within Guildhall Library

[372]
The Linacre Centre for Health Care Ethics
60 Grove End Road
London NW8 9NH
Borough: Westminster
Telephone: 020 7806 4088
Fax: 020 7266 5424
E-mail: admin@linacre.org
World Wide Web: www.linacre.org
Constitution: Registered charity
Objectives/purposes: Research, study, publications and consultancy work in the field of bioethics
Key staff: Librarian: Donald JA Smith
Stock and subject coverage: Ca. 6,000 titles, 50 current journals on bioethics with some material on medicine, philosophy and theology
Services: Photocopies
Availability: Access to all bona fide students of bioethics (health care ethics) for reference. Only Centre staff are entitled to borrow
Hours: 09.30-17.00 except bank holidays and during Librarian's holidays
Transport: Tube: St John's Wood
Special facilities: Refreshment and toilet facilities available
Publications: Series of monographs in bioethics

Linked organisations

Linacre Centre Library is part of the Centre which has a lay staff and lay governing body; its Trustees are the five Roman Catholic Archbishops of England and Wales

[373]
Lincoln's Inn Library
Lincoln's Inn
London WC2A 3TN
Borough: Camden
Telephone: 020 7242 4371
Fax: 020 7404 1864
E-mail: library@lincolnsinn.org.uk
World Wide Web: www.lincolnsinn.org.uk
Constitution: Unincorporated association for professional and educational purposes

Objectives/purposes: Legal reference library for barristers and bar students; also a repository of rare books and manuscripts for scholarly use
Key staff: Librarian: Guy Holborn; Deputy Librarian: Catherine McArdle; Archivist: Josephine Hutchings
Stock and subject coverage: Modern Collections: English law for practitioners; Commonwealth legislation and law reports, especially Australia, New Zealand, Malaysia, Singapore and Africa; parliamentary papers and debates.
Historical Collections: Over 1,500 volumes of manuscripts (including the Hale collection) and printed items. Legal materials predominate, but there is much material of wider historical interest. Archives of the Inn and legal portraits
Services: Photocopiers; microfiche reader-printer; various online and CD-ROM databases
Availability: Modern Collections: Open to members of the Inn and barristers; open to solicitors (for reference only and by appointment) for material not in other London law libraries. Not available to the general public or litigants in person.
Historical Collections: Bona fide researchers by appointment. Historical and genealogical enquiries preferably in writing
Hours: Term-time: 09.00-20.00 Monday to Friday Vacations: 09.30-17.30
Transport: Tube: Chancery Lane, Holborn
Special facilities: Refreshment and toilet facilities available

Linked organisations

Library is one of the four Inns of Court which are independent bodies but which cooperate closely

[374]
Linnean Society of London
Burlington House
Piccadilly
London W1J 0BF
Borough: Westminster
Telephone: 020 7434 4479/4470
Fax: 020 7287 9364
E-mail: gina@linnean.org
World Wide Web: www.linnean.org
Constitution: Registered charity; association with voluntary subscribing membership; learned society
Key staff: Executive Secretary: Dr John Marsden; Librarian and Archivist: Miss Gina Douglas
Stock and subject coverage: Over 90,000 books and periodical volumes on biology; botany; zoology; with special emphasis on evolution, distribution and taxonomy. Especially strong in 18th and 19th century material; good collection of 16th and 17th century works. Around 400 current journals. Secondary interest – history of biology, especially Linnaeana. Scientific library, manuscripts and specimen collection of Linnaeus. Correspondence of John Ellis, EM Holmes, A and WS M'Leay, R Pulteney, W Swainson, Sir JE Smith, N Winch and others. Numerous bound miscellaneous mss and many hundreds of loose mss and letters. Complete archives of the Society since 1788. Collection of engraved portraits and photographs of many hundreds of naturalists prior to the 20th century
Services: Photocopies; fax machine

Availability: For reference to bona fide researchers on application to the Librarian

Hours: 10.00-17.00 Monday to Friday

Transport: Tube: Piccadilly, Green Park; Bus: 9, 14, 19, 22, 38

Special facilities: Toilet facilities

Special features: Grade II listed building, part of the historic courtyard buildings of Burlington House created by Banks and Barrie

Publications: Biological Journal of the Linnean Society; Botanical Journal of the Linnean Society; Zoological Journal of the Linnean Society; Synopses of the British Fauna; Symposia; Catalogue of Printed Books, etc. (1925); Catalogue of MSS, Parts 1-4; The Linnean; Newsletter; Proceedings of the Linnean Society of London

[375]
Listening Books
Formerly National Listening Library
12 Lant Street
London SE1 1QH

Borough: Southwark

Telephone: 020 7407 7476/9417

Fax: 020 7403 1377

E-mail: info@listening-books.org.uk

World Wide Web: www.listening-books.org.uk

Constitution: Registered charity

Objectives/purposes: To provide a postal audio-book library service to anyone in the UK who cannot read in the usual way due to illness or disability

Key staff: Membership Services Manager: Lisa Knightsbridge; Schools Development Officer: Julie King

Stock and subject coverage: Over 4,000 titles covering adult and children's fiction and non-fiction material, primarily for leisure reading. Can also provide support to the National Curriculum for Key Stages 2, 3 and 4

Services: Members can request specially adapted tape machines for severe disabilities

Availability: Members only

Hours: 09.00-17.00 Monday to Friday

Publications: Monthly catalogues available; Members Newsletter

[376]
Lloyd's of London
1 Lime Street
London EC3M 7HA

Borough: Corporation of London

Telephone: 020 7327 5448

Fax: 020 7327 6400

World Wide Web: www.lloydsoflondon.com

Constitution: Society incorporated by Act of Parliament

Objectives/purposes: Competitive insurance market where individual underwriters accept risks on behalf of syndicates of individual and corporate members

Key staff: Chief Information Officer: Howard Knight; Information Officer: Paul Carter; Information: Caroline Helm

Stock and subject coverage: Ca. 15,000 volumes and 200 journals on insurance, Lloyd's law, some shipping,

general reference and country information. Lloyd's syndicate reports and accounts are available from 1983 onwards. Newspapers are held for two months

Services: Internet access; online databases; CD-ROMs; self-service photocopier; microfiche reader-printer; fax machine; insurance journals index; sale of Lloyds' syndicate report and accounts CD-ROM

Availability: Reference only. Free access to Lloyd's personnel. Outsiders may use the facilities on payment of an entry fee

Hours: 09.30-17.00 Monday to Friday

Transport: Tube: Bank, Monument, Aldgate; Rail: Fenchurch Street, Liverpool Street; Bus: 25, 48

Special facilities: Toilet facilities; access for users with disabilities

Special features: Housed within the award winning Richard Rogers designed building

Publications: Lloyd's Syndicate Annual Report and Accounts CD-ROM; Lloyd's Global Results and Annual Report; statistics relating to Lloyd's

[377]
Lloyd's Register of Shipping Information Services
71 Fenchurch Street
London EC3M 4BS

Borough: Corporation of London

Telephone: 020 7423 2475

Fax: 020 7423 2039

World Wide Web: www.lr.org

Constitution: Registered charity

Objectives/purposes: Provides safety, quality and environmental inspection and certification services to customers at sea and on land throughout the world. The Information Group Library handles shipping information

Key staff: Information Officer and Archivist: Barbara Jones

Stock and subject coverage: Ca. 3,000 books including a complete collection of Lloyd's Register of Ships and associated publications from 1764 to date. Collections of books on shipping history; shipwrecks and company histories. Augustin Creuze Library of 18th and 19th century books on naval architecture

Services: Photocopies (charity donation required); information sheets

Availability: Open to all for reference only

Hours: 09.30-12.00, 13.00-16.30 Monday to Friday

Transport: Tube: Liverpool Street, London Bridge, Cannon Street, Aldgate, Bank, Tower Hill; Rail: Liverpool Street, London Bridge, Cannon Street, Fenchurch Street; Bus: 15, 25, 40, 344

Special facilities: Refreshment and toilet facilities; access for users with disabilities

Special features: Library housed in the acclaimed building designed by Richard Rogers and adjacent to Lloyd's Registers' other building completed in 1901

Publications: World Fleet Statistics; World Casualty Statistics; Register of Ships; List of Shipowners; Maritime Guide

[378]
Local Government Association
LGA

Local Government House
Smith Square
London SW1P 3HZ
Borough: Westminster
Telephone: 020 7664 3131
Fax: 020 7664 3030
E-mail: info@lga.gov.uk
World Wide Web: www.lga.gov.uk
Constitution: Association with voluntary subscribing
    membership
Objectives/purposes: The LGA was formed by the merger
    of the Association of County Councils, the
    Association of District Councils and the Association
    of Metropolitan Authorities. The LGA has just under
    500 members, including all 238 shire district
    councils; 36 metropolitan district councils; 34 county
    councils; 46 new unitary authorities; 33 London
    authorities and 22 Welsh authorities. In addition, the
    LGA represents police authorities, fire authorities and
    passenger transport authorities. The LGA provides
    the national voice for local communities in England
    and Wales
Key staff: Information staff can be contacted on 020
    7664 3131
Stock and subject coverage: Materials on public
    administration and local government issues
Services: Internet access; photocopies; online searching;
    fax machines
Availability: Telephone enquiry service. Library open to
    members of the LGA, others by appointment only
Hours: 09.00–17.30 Monday to Friday
Transport: Tube: Westminster; Rail: Charing Cross; Bus:
    3, 77A, 507
Special facilities: Refreshment and toilet facilities; access
    for users with disabilities including lift to all floors
Publications: First Magazine (weekly); LGA Yearbook
    (annual); various publications on local government
    issues

Linked organisations

**Welsh Local Government Association
Improvement and Development Agency
Employers' Organisation**

[379]
Local Government International Bureau
LGIB
European Information Service

Local Government House
Smith Square
London SW1P 3HZ
Borough: Westminster
Telephone: 020 7664 3100
Fax: 020 7664 3128
E-mail: eis@lgib.gov.uk
World Wide Web: www.lgib.gov.uk
Constitution: Company limited by guarantee;
    international arm of Local Government Association

Key staff: Senior Information Officer: Judith Barton;
    European Information Officers: Simon James, Tracey
    Lazarus; Adminstrative Assistant: Kathy Buckley
Stock and subject coverage: EC official documentation;
    range of journals and publications relating to the
    European Community and local government
Services: Enquiry service for local authorities on the
    European Community; European Information
    Service (EIS); current awareness bulletin; special
    reports; no loans. The EIS online database and
    twinning database are available via the LGIB website
    at www.lgib.gov.uk
Availability: Open to all local government officers and
    members by appointment. Others under special
    circumstances
Hours: 09.00–17.00 Monday to Friday
Transport: Tube: Pimlico, Westminster; Rail: Victoria,
    Waterloo; Bus: 77A, 88, 507
Special facilities: Toilet facilities available; access for users
    with disabilities
Publications: European Information Service Bulletin;
    Members International Newsletter; LG International
    Newsletter; International Reports series

Linked organisations

**Local Government Association for England
and Wales** International Unit of the Association

**Association of Local Authorities of Northern
Ireland (ALANI)** LGIB is supported by ALANI

**Council of European Municipalities and
Regions (CEMR)** British section of CEMR

[380]
London Bible College
LBC

Green Lane
Northwood
Hillingdon HA6 2OW
Borough: Hillingdon
Telephone: 01923 456190
Fax: 01923 456001
E-mail: library@londonbiblecollege.ac.uk
Constitution: Registered charity; private college offering
    first and postgraduate research degrees
Key staff: Librarian: Alan M Linfield BA MCILIP
Stock and subject coverage: Ca. 45,000 volumes and 200
    journals on theology, especially post 1970 biblical
    and systematic theology. Developing collection of
    Islamic material
Services: Photocopies; CD-ROMs
Availability: Open, for reference only, to academic
    researchers or those in Christian ministry or leadship.
    No charge for one-off visits, but a termly charge may
    be levied if regular access is required. Visitors are
    asked to make an appointment before visiting
Hours: 09.00–17.00 Monday to Friday
Transport: Tube: Northwood
Special facilities: Toilet facilities available

Linked organisations

Brunel University LBC is an associated institution
of Brunel University, which is the validating body for
all academic qualifications awarded by the College

[381]
The London Buddhist Vihara
The Avenue
Bedford Park
London W4 1UD
Borough: Ealing
Telephone: 020 8995 9493
Fax: 020 8994 8130
E-mail: london.vihara@virgin.net
World Wide Web: www.londonbuddhistvihara.co.uk
Constitution: Association with voluntary subscribing
  membership
Objectives/purposes: Centre for Buddhist studies
Key staff: Librarian: Ven T Bandula; Co-ordinators: Mr
  Richard Jones, Ms Cleone Rear
Stock and subject coverage: Over 3,000 books on
  Buddhism (covering all sects) and other religions.
  Journals and manuscripts; ola leaf manuscripts;
  Chinese, Burmese, Thai, Sinhalese and English
  Buddhist texts
Services: Photocopies
Availability: Free access for students, researchers and well
  wishers of the organisation
Hours: 09.00–18.00 Monday to Friday
Transport: Tube: Turnham Green; Bus: E3, 27, 94, 237
Special facilities: Refreshment and toilet facilities available
Publications: Samadhi (4 p.a.)

Linked organisations
Maha Bodhi Society of Sri Lanka
Anagarika Dharmapala Trust
Managed by the Trust

[382]
London Business School
LBS
25 Taunton Place
Regent's Park
London NW1 4SA
Borough: Wesminster
Telephone: 020 7724 7875
Fax: 020 7706 1897
E-mail: library@london.edu
World Wide Web: www.london.edu
Constitution: Registered charity; independent non-profit
  organisation; department of the University of London
Key staff: Head of Information Services: Helen Edwards;
  Deputy Head of Library: Gillian Dwyer; Manager,
  Business Information Service: Sue Watt
Stock and subject coverage: 20,000 books; 1,000 current
  journals and statistical serials; working papers; annual
  reports and company directories. wide range of
  electronic resources – news, market research, full-text
  journals and financials
Services: Wide range of electronic resources available to
  members of the School. Commercial document
  delivery and business information services
Availability: Primary purpose to serve present and past
  members of the School. Free admission to current
  academics and PhD students from other institutions
  (proof required); charged access for reference £30
  per day; individual and corporate membership also
  available
Hours: Term-time: 08.30–22.00 Monday to Friday;
  09.00–19.00 Saturday; 11.00–19.00 Sunday

Summer vacation: 09.00–21.00 Monday to Friday;
  09.00–17.00 Saturday
Transport: Tube: Baker Street; Rail: Marylebone
Special facilities: Refreshments (vending machines) and
  toilet facilities available
Publications: List of Accessions; Contents of Current
  Journals (several sections

Linked organisations
University of London Part of the University

[382][a]
LBS Information Service
Telephone: 020 7723 3404
Fax: 020 7706 1897
World Wide Web: www.bestofbiz.com
Key staff: Manager: Sue Watt
Services: Fee-based information service offering fast
  assistance with all business document and
  information needs, including access to a broad
  spectrum of worldwide online computer databases
Publications: Guide to European Market Information;
  Guide to European Company Information; Source
  Guide to Central and East European Information;
  Source Guide to Economic Information

[383]
London Central Mosque Trust and the Islamic Cultural Centre
ICC
146 Park Road
London NW8 7RG
Borough: Westminster
Telephone: 020 7724 3363
Fax: 020 7724 0493
E-mail: islamic200@aol.com
World Wide Web: www.islamicculturalcentre.co.uk
Constitution: Registered charity and company limited by
  guarantee
Key staff: Head of Education Department: Dr Fatima
  Amer
Stock and subject coverage: Ca. 10,000 books on all topics
  related to the religion of Islam, including theology,
  history, culture (main languages Arabic and English).
  Journals from, and related to, the Arab/Muslim
  world; books and journals on interfaith and Muslim
  minorities in Europe. Resource Centre to serve
  schools and researchers
Services: Photocopies (charges made); translation services;
  internet access; online searches; fax machines; lecture
  hall for seminars and conferences
Availability: Reference library open to researchers for
  reference only
Hours: 09.30–16.00 Monday to Friday
Transport: Tube: Baker Street, St John's Wood; Rail:
  Marylebone; Bus: 13, 82, 113, 274
Special facilities: Refreshment and toilet facilities available;
  access for users with disabilities
Publications: The Islamic Quarterly (academic articles on
  Islam)

[384]
London Chamber of Commerce and Industry, Research and Information Centre
LCCI
33 Queen Street
London EC4R 1AP
Borough: Corporation of London
Telephone: 020 7248 4444
Fax: 020 7203 1863
E-mail: info@londonchamber.co.uk
World Wide Web: www.londonchamber.co.uk
Constitution: Association with voluntary subscribing
   membership
Objectives/purposes: The LCCI's mission is to help
   London businesses succeed by promoting their
   interests and expanding their opportunities as
   members of a world-wide business network
Key staff: Acting Chief Executive: Peter Bishop; Head of
   Information: Marita Ewins
Stock and subject coverage: General business library
   specialising in UK and international product
   sourcing; corporate intelligence to include company
   tracing, credit and financial reports; market research
   and mailing lists
Availability: Access to the Information Centre free to
   members of the London Chamber of Commerce and
   Industry and to non-members on payment of a fee;
   selected services free to members; fee based services
   available to non-members
Services: Product sourcing service; online databases and
   mailing lists available
Hours: 09.00-17.30 Monday to Friday
Transport: Tube: Cannon Street, Mansion House; Rail:
   Cannon Street
Special facilities: Toilet facilities available; access for users
   with disabilities
Special features: The Information Centre was established
   in 1888, making it one of the oldest business
   information centres in the country
Publications: London Economic Review (quarterly);
   Business Matters (monthly); International Business
   matters (quarterly); Annual Review Report and
   Accounts (June)

Linked organisations
British Chambers of Commerce The LCCI is a
member of the British Chambers of Commerce

[385]
London Chest Hospital
Education Centre
Bonner Road
London E2 9JX
Borough: Tower Hamlets
Telephone: 020 8980 4433 ext 3203
World Wide Web: www.smd.qmul.ac.uk
Constitution: Part of Queen Mary, University of London
Objectives/purposes: Serving medical staff and students of
   London Chest Hospital
Key staff: Site Librarian: Theresa Dyce
Stock and subject coverage: Materials on cardiac and
   respiratory medicine
Availability: Open to staff and students of Barts and the
   London School of Medicine and Dentistry

Hours: 09.00-17.00 Monday to Friday
Transport: Tube: Bethnal Green; Bus: 8

Linked organisations
Queen Mary, University of London Part of the
university

[386]
London College of Fashion Library
20 John Princes Street
Oxford Circus
London W1G 0BJ
Borough: Westminster
Telephone: 020 7514 7453/7455
Fax: 020 7514 7580
World Wide Web: www.linst.ac.uk/library
Constitution: Higher education corporation
Key staff: Head of Learning Resources: Katherine Baird
Stock and subject coverage: One of the most extensive
   collections of information on fashion in the country.
   Resources include collections of fashion designer and
   illustration files, fashion forecasts, videos, multimedia
   and text CD-ROM, the internet, as well as over 200
   current periodicals. Approximately 48,000 books
   relating to all aspects of the fashion and clothing
   industry, including fashion design, garment
   construction, costume history, fashion styling and
   promotion, make-up and beauty. These collections
   are complemented by books on photography, film,
   media, cultural studies and management. LCF
   recently merged with Cordwainers College with its
   secialist collections of information on footwear,
   leather and accessories.
   Archive collections include the Clothing and
   Footwear Institute Archive of ca. 350 tailoring and
   clothing industry books and journals spanning the
   19th and early 20th centuries. London College of
   Fashion Archive of printed, manuscript and audiovisual materials chronicling the history of the
   College from its origins in several early London
   trade schools, to the present day. LCF Digitised
   Archive of 1,000 digitised black and white images
   and accompanying metadata depicting the history of
   the College from the 1910s to the 1970s
Services: Black and white, acetate and colour
   photocopier; open access reprographics area for
   presentation work
Availability: Open to students of the London Institute
   and by appointment to IMA members (the Institute's
   alumni association). Reference access may be granted
   to users unable to access material elsewhere. Visitors
   must phone in advance to make an appointment to
   use the library (visitors are restricted – currently one
   per day)
Hours: Term-time: 09.30-20.15 Monday to Thursday;
   10.00-17.15 Friday; 11.15-17.00 Saturday
   See website for details of vacation opening hours
Transport: Tube: Oxford Circus; Bus: 7, 8, 12, 16, 25, 73,
   88
Special facilities: Wheelchair access by special
   arrangement

Linked organisations
The London Institute Part of the Institute

[387]
London College of Printing
LCP
The LCP offers information services to the staff and students of the College over two sites: Elephant and Castle and Back Hill
World Wide Web: www.linst.ac.uk/library
Constitution: Department of an educational organisation
Availability: Contact the Reader Services Librarian. Non London Institute members should make a written application to use the Library. Reference access can be granted for agreed periods

Linked organisations
The London Institute Part of the Institute

[387][a]
London College of Printing Library
Elephant and Castle
London SE1 6SB
Borough: Southwark
Telephone: 020 7514 6527
Fax: 020 7514 6597
Key staff: Head of Learning Resources: Elizabeth Davison, ext 6599
Stock and subject coverage: Materials on art and design, fine art, graphic design, advertising, marketing and management, printing and publishing, retail, travel and tourism, typography and visual merchandising. Printing and historical collection
Services: Photocopies (black and white and colour; CD-ROMs; internet access
Hours: 09.30–20.15 Monday to Thursday; 09.30–17.45 Friday; 10.00–15.45 Saturday
Transport: Tube and Rail: Elephant and Castle; Bus: 1, 10, 12, 35, 53, 63, 109, 131
Special facilities: Refreshment and toilet facilities; access for users with disabilities – ramp at College entrance
Publications: New additions booklist and subject guides

[387][b]
Back Hill Site
Back Hill
London EC1R 5EN
Borough: Camden
Telephone: 020 7514 6882
Fax: 020 7514 6866
Stock and subject coverage: Collections on film and video, journalism, media and photography
Availability: As above
Hours: 09.30–19.00 Monday; 09.30–20.00 Tuesday to Thursday; 09.30–18.00 Friday
Transport: Tube and Rail: Farringdon; Bus: 17, 19, 38, 45, 55, 63, 505

[388]
London Contemporary Dance School Library
LCDS
The Place
17 Dukes Road
London WC1H 9AB

Borough: Camden
Telephone: 020 7387 0152 ext 245
Fax: 020 7383 4851
E-mail: lcds@theplace.org
World Wide Web: www.theplace.org
Constitution: Registered charity, independent non-profit distributing organisation, company limited by guarantee
Key staff: Librarian: Matthew McCarthy
Stock and subject coverage: Books, videos, journals, audio CDs and reports on art, contemporary dance, theatre, dance history, music, cultural studies, gender and fiction
Services: Photocopies
Availability: Reference only for outside users
Hours: 10.30–18.00 Monday, Tuesday, Thursday and Friday; 12.00–8.00 Wednesday; by appointment for outside users
Transport: Tube and Rail: Euston; Bus: 68, 73, 188
Special facilities: Cafe and toilet facilities available; access for users with disabilities

Linked organisations
Contemporary Dance Trust, **The Place Theatre**

[389]
London Cycling Campaign
LCC
Unit 228
30 Great Guildford Street
London SE1 0HS
Borough: Southwark
Telephone: 020 7928 7220
Fax: 020 7928 2318
E-mail: office@lcc.org.uk
World Wide Web: www.lcc.org.uk
Constitution: Company limited by guarantee; association with voluntary subscribing membership
Objectives/purposes: To promote cycling and protect the rights of cyclists
Key staff: Administrator: Sue King
Stock and subject coverage: Books, reports, magazines, photographs and other material relating to all aspects of cycling and cycle planning/campaigning, as well as more general transport issues
Services: Photocopies (charges made)
Availability: Adult researchers are admitted to use the collections for reference only. Restricted access to the photograph library
Hours: 10.00–17.00 Monday to Friday
Transport: Tube: Borough
Special facilities: Refreshment and toilet facilities and bike parking available on site
Publications: Central London Cyclist's Route Map (annual); London Cyclist (6 p.a.)

Linked organisations
Cyclists Public Affairs Group (C-PAG)
Cycle Campaign Network (CCN)
The LCC plays a major role on C-PAG and CCN

[390]
London Fire and Emergency Planning Authority
LFEPA

London Fire Brigade
Room 520
Hampton House
20 Albert Embankment
London SE1 7SD
Borough: Lambeth
Telephone: 020 7587 6340 (Main Library); 020 7587 6339 (Photographic Library)
Fax: 020 7587 6086
E-mail: judy.seaborne@london-fire.gov.uk
World Wide Web: www.london-fire.gov.uk
Constitution: Fire and civil defence authority
Key staff: Librarian: Ms Judy Seaborne BA ALA
Stock and subject coverage: Multimedia library. Main collection is of materials on the fire services, firefighting techniques and fire safety. The Library also stocks materials to support related areas such as health and safety and to support the varied training needs of the Authority.
Photographic Library is a large collection of all photographs taken by the Brigade, some of which date from the 1880s
Services: Enquiry service to general public. Loans to other libraries
Availability: Reference facilities available by appointment; Photographic Library – viewing is by appointment only, but telephone and written enquiries are welcome. Photographic reprint ordering service available; charges on application
Hours: 10.00-16.30 Monday to Friday
Transport: Tube and Rail: Vauxhall; Bus: 77, 344
Special facilities: Toilet facilities available; access for users with disabilities

[391]
London Foot Hospital and School of Podiatric Medicine
London Foot Hospital

33 Fitzroy Square
London W1P 6AY
Borough: Camden
Telephone: 020 7530 4509
Fax: 020 7530 4540
Constitution: Department of a university
Key staff: Librarian (part-time)
Stock and subject coverage: Comprehensive and long established stock of books and journals in podiatry/chiropody. There is also a large collection of slides and a collection of books on related medical subjects
Services: Photocopies (charged); Medline and AMED databases
Availability: Acess for all bona fide researchers subject to prior arrangement with the Librarian. Reference facilities only. Visitors should not arrive without prior notice, the Librarian is available only on two days during the week
Hours: By arrangement with the Librarian, normally 09.00-17.00 Tuesday and Wednesday

Transport: Tube: Goodge Street, Warren Street, Great Portland Street, Oxford Circus; Rail: Euston, King's Cross; Bus: 18, 30, 73
Special facilities: Toilet facilities available
Special features: 18th century building

Linked organisations
University of London

[392]
London Hazards Centre

Hampstead Town Hall Centre
213 Haverstock Hill
London NW3 4QP
Borough: Camden
Telephone: 020 7794 5999
Fax: 020 7794 4702
E-mail: mail@lhc.org.uk
World Wide Web: www.lhc.org.uk
Constitution: Independent non-profit distributing organisation; company limited by guarantee; registered charity and association with voluntary subscribing membership
Objectives/purposes: Resource centre on occupational and environmental health and safety serving trade unions and community groups in London
Stock and subject coverage: Books, journals and CD-ROM databases on health and safety with an emphasis on information produced by, or aimed at, trade unionists and community groups
Services: Photocopies
Availability: Restricted to trade union representatives, community groups and others seeking to organise action on health and safety issues. The Centre is not able to serve the needs of students. Reference only
Hours: By appointment only
Transport: Tube: Belsize Park; Rail: Hampstead Heath
Special facilities: Refreshment and toilet facilities available on site; full access and toilet facilities for users with disabilities
Publications: The Daily Hazard newsletter (4 p.a.); website with full text of many publications; Hazards handbook series

The London Institute

The London Institute is Europe's largest centre for education in art and design and includes:
Camberwell College of Arts
Central Saint Martins College of Art and Design
Chelsea College of Art and Design
London College of Fashion
London College of Printing and Distributive Trades
See separate entries for each institution

[393]
The London Library

14 St James's Square
London SW1Y 4LG
Borough: Westminster
Telephone: 020 7930 7705
Fax: 020 7766 4766
E-mail: membership@londonlibrary.co.uk

World Wide Web: www.londonlibrary.co.uk
Constitution: Independent non-profit distributing organisation; registered charity; association with voluntary subscribing membership; private venture
Objectives/purposes: Independent subscription library serving the needs of its members by lending books and providing reference services within the arts and humanities
Key staff: Librarian: Inez Lynn BA ALA
Stock and subject coverage: Growing collection of over 1 million volumes in all European languages, mainly on open access to members. Subject range is mainly within the humanities, with emphasis on literature, history, biography and related subjects; good representation of fine and applied art, architecture, philosophy, religion, topography and travel. Subscriptions to, and historic holdings of, a wide range of periodicals and learned journals
Services: Photocopies; internet access, and postal loans service available to members
Availability: Access to members, and to others by prior application. The Library participates in national interlibrary loan schemes
Hours: 09.30–17.30 Monday, Friday and Saturday; 09.30–19.30 Tuesday, Wednesday and Thursday
Transport: Tube: Green Park, Piccadilly Circus
Special facilities: Toilet facilities available
Special features: The Library was founded in 1841. The present building dates from the 1890s with several extensions
Publications: Annual Report (October) distributed to membership

[394]
London Metropolitan Archives
LMA

40 Northampton Road
Clerkenwell
London EC1R 0HB
Borough: Islington
Telephone: 020 7332 3820
Minicom (text phone): 020 7278 8703
Fax: 020 7833 9136
E-mail: ask.lma@corpoflondon.gov.uk
World Wide Web: www.cityoflondon.gov.uk/lma
Constitution: Local authority funded organisation
Objectives/purposes: Regional record office for Greater London area
Key staff: Head Archivist: Dr Deborah Jenkins; Senior Archivist, Enquiries Section: Rhys Griffith
Stock and subject coverage: 32 miles of archives, maps, plans, prints, photographs and books primarily relating to the history of London. Archives include local government bodies such as the Greater London Council, the London and Middlesex County Councils and the Metropolitan Board of Works (covering 1855–1986). Also includes Middlesex Sessions of the Peace records – judicial and administrative – from 1549 to 1889. Parish, Poor Law, businesses, charities, courts and hospitals all strongly represented. 100,000 volume library focused on history of London.
    Due to essential building work the Keats House collections of manuscripts, letters and books relating to the life of the poet John Keats, his circle and the

English Romantic movement are currently stored at the Archive. For information on access contact Keats House on 020 7435 2062
Services: Free distance enquiry service for information about holdings. Family History Research Service available for basic paid research. Reprographics services including photocopying, digital scanning, photography and microfilming
Availability: Free and open to the general public, no reader's ticket required. Most popular resources available on self-service microfilm. Some material is closed for statutory reasons or at the request of the depositor, some may be too damaged to be produced for research. Copying charges, reproduction charges and research charges only where applicable
Hours: 09.30–16.45 Monday, Wednesday and Friday; 09.30–19.30 Tuesday and Thursday, limited Saturday opening 09.30–16.45, approximately two Saturdays per month – contact the LMA for details
Transport: Tube: Angel, Farringdon; Rail: King's Cross, Farringdon; Bus: 19, 38, 55, 63, 243, 341, 505. Cycle racks are available; some private car parks and meters in the vicinity
Special facilities: Locker room with hot and cold drinks machines. Public rooms on first floor accessible by lift or stairs. Foot pedal for electric microfilm viewers. Induction loops, two blue badge parking spaces available on request

Linked organisations
Corporation of London Owned and funded by the Corporation of London

[395]
London Metropolitan University
World Wide Web: www.londonmet.ac.uk/learning-resources/libraries.cfm
Constitution: University
Availability: Open to London Metropolitan University staff and students; members of UK Libraries Plus; staff and students from other universities; and to individuals for private research
Special features: London Guildhall University and University of North London merged in August 2002 to form London Metropolitan University. Students have access to materials at two campuses: London City and London North

London City Campus
World Wide Web: www.lgu.ac.uk/as/library/

[395][a]
Calcutta House Library
Old Castle Street
London E1 7NT
Borough: Tower Hamlets
Telephone: 020 7320 1185
Fax: 020 7320 1182
Stock and subject coverage: Collections on civil aviation, computing information systems and mathematics, language studies, politics and modern history, psychology and sociology
Hours: 09.00–21.00 Monday; 10.15–21.00 Tuesday; 09.00–17.00 Wednesday to Friday; 11.00–16.00

Saturday. Telephone 020 7320 1183 for details of vacation opening times

Transport: Tube: Aldgate, Aldgate East, Liverpool Street; Rail: Liverpool Street; Bus: 15, 15B, 25, 40, 42, 67, 78, 100, 253

[395][b]
Commercial Road Integrated Learning Resource Centre

41 Commercial Road
London E1 1LA
Borough: Tower Hamlets
Telephone: 020 7320 1869/1892
Stock and subject coverage: Collections on art and design; communications and media studies; computer imaging and animation; design research for disability; film and video; interior design; photography; musical instrument technology; furniture and furnishings and jewellery
Services: Access to online and internet resources; photocopies
Hours: 09.00-20.00 Monday, Wednesday and Thursday; 10.15-20.00 Tuesday; 09.00-17.00 Friday. See website for vacation opening hours
Transport: Tube: Aldgate East; Rail: Liverpool Street

[395][c]
Moorgate Learning Resource Centre

84 Moorgate
London EC2M 6SQ
Borough: Corporation of London
Telephone: 020 7320 1563
Key staff: Learning Resource Manager: Doreen Pinfold
Stock and subject coverage: Collections on business and law; accountancy; economics; insurance; marketing; transport and shipping
Services: Access to online and internet resources; photocopies
Hours: 09.00-21.00 Monday, Wednesday and Thursday; 10.15-21.00 Tuesday; 09.00-17.00 Friday; 11.00-16.00 Saturday. See website for vacation opening hours
Transport: Tube: Moorgate, Liverpool Street; Rail: Liverpool Street; Bus: 43, 76, 133

[395][d]
The Women's Library
(formerly the Fawcett Library)

Old Castle Street
London E1 7NT
Borough: Tower Hamlets
Telephone: 020 7320 2222
Fax: 020 7320 2333
E-mail: enquirydesk@thewomenslibrary.ac.uk
World Wide Web: www.thewomenslibrary.ac.uk
Stock and subject coverage: Materials relating to every aspect of women's lives and dating back to 1745. Ca. 60,000 books and 2,400 periodicals ranging from popular magazines to academic quarterlies. Special collections consist of 350 archival collections, including diverse personal papers, records of societies and associations, and research and oral history projects. There are also rich holdings of photographs, posters, postcards and other visual materials

Services: Readers can use their own laptops in the reading room. Photocopier; digital reader-printers; photographic service; study carrels for hire
Availability: Open to all bona fide researchers. Visitors will need to complete a registration form, provide proof of identity with signature, and a £4.50 deposit for a Reading Room pass
Hours: 09.30-17.00 Tuesday Wednesday and Friday; 09.30-20.00 Thursday; 10.00-16.00 Saturday
Transport: Tube: Aldgate East; Bus: 15, 25, 40, 42, 67, 78, 100, 115, 253
Special facilities: Café facilities; access for users with disabilities

London North Campus
World Wide Web: www.unl.ac.uk
Key staff: Learning Services Manager: Julie Howell

[395][e]
Ladbroke House Library

Ladbroke House
62-66 Highbury Grove
London N5 2AD
Borough: Islington
Telephone: 020 7133 5149
Fax: 020 7753 5100
Key staff: Site Library Manager: Ann Aungle
Stock and subject coverage: Materials on: Social science, law, librarianship, psychology and health
Services: Photocopies
Hours: Term-time: 09.00-20.30 Monday to Thursday; 09.00-18.00 Friday; 11.00-16.00 Saturday
Vacations: 09.30-17.00 Monday to Friday, including one evening until 19.00
Transport: Tube and Rail: Highbury and Islington
Special facilities: Refreshment and toilet facilities; access for users with disabilities

[395][f]
The Learning Centre
LC

236-260 Holloway Road
London N7 6PP
Borough: Islington
Telephone: 020 7133 5170
Fax: 020 7753 7037
Stock and subject coverage: Stock covering the following University of North London faculties: Humanities; Business School; Environmental and Social Studies (including architecture and interior design); Science, Computing and Engineering. Special collections include: TUC Library; Workers Education Authority (WEA) Archive. Access to special collections by appointment only, apply to Christine Coates, TUC Librarian (020 7753 3184, c.coates@unl.ac.uk)
Services: Language learning facilities and learning workshops area
Hours: Term-time: 09.00-21.00; 10.00-17.00 Saturday; 13.00-17.00 Sunday
Vacations: 09.00-19.00 Monday to Friday
Transport: Tube: Holloway Road
Special facilities: Refreshment and toilet facilities; access for users with disabilities – independent study unit for students with disabilities

[396]
London School of Hygiene and Tropical Medicine
Keppel Street
London WC1E 7HT
Borough: Camden
Telephone: 020 7927 2283
Fax: 020 7927 2273
Telex: 8953474
E-mail: library@lshtm.ac.uk
World Wide Web: www.lshtm.ac.uk/as/library
Constitution: Postgraduate medical school
Key staff: Librarian: Brian Furner BA MSc MIInfSc;
    Deputy Librarian: John Eyers BA MLS MIInfSc
Stock and subject coverage: Collection of books, journals
    and other materials on public health and tropical
    medicine, including: health services management;
    health planning and financing; health promotion;
    human nutrition; epidemiology; medical statistics;
    medical demography; public health in developing
    countries; applied molecular biology of infectious
    diseases; medical and clinical parasitology;
    immunology of infectious diseases; medical
    microbiology; and virology. Special collections
    include the Reece collection on vaccination and the
    archives of Sir Ronald Ross
Services: Photocopies; online catalogues; CD-ROM;
    online searches (charges made)
Availability: Open to bona fide researchers for reference.
    External members qualify for limited loan facilities
    (deposit and annual fee payable)
Hours: 08.30–20.25 Monday to Friday (all year); 09.00–
    12.30 Saturday (all year)
Transport: Tube: Russell Square, Goodge Street; Bus: 10,
    14, 24, 29, 73, 134
Special facilities: Refreshment and toilet facilities available
Special features: Contains a sculptural mural by Eric
    Kennington. Reading room designed by Vernor Rees
Publications: Catalogue of the Ross Archives, by M
    Gibson, 1982

Linked organisations
University of London School of the University of
London

[397]
London School of Jewish Studies
The Library
Schaller House
Albert Road
London NW4 2SJ
Borough: Barnet
Telephone: 020 8203 6427
Fax: 020 8203 6420
E-mail: enquiries@lsjs.ac.uk
Constitution: Registered charity and independent non-
    profit organisation
Key staff: Esra Kahn
Stock and subject coverage: Ca. 100,000 volumes. Books,
    manuscripts and pamphlets on Jewish studies
    (Hebraica, Judaica); Hebrew language and literature;
    history and Holocaust studies; Rabbinics – liturgy
Services: Photocopies (charges made)
Availability: Free access to all academics and students for
    reference. Access for members of the public

Hours: 09.00–18.00 Monday, Tuesday and Thursday;
    09.00–21.00 Wednesday; 09.00–13.00 Friday; 09.30–
    12.30 Sunday
Transport: Tube: Golders Green then bus 240 or 185
    (Brent Street, Bell Lane stop)
Special facilities: Refreshment and toilet facilities; access
    for users with disabilities (wheelchair access to all
    parts of library)
Publications: LE'ELA: A Journal of Judaism Today (2 p.a.)

Linked organisations
**School of Oriental and African Studies
(SOAS), University of London**
Associate institution of the University

[398]
The London Society
Mortimer Wheeler House
46 Eagle Wharf Road
London N1 7ED
Borough: Hackney
Telephone: 020 7253 9400
E-mail: londonsociety@hotmail.com
World Wide Web: www.lonsoc.org.uk/lonsoc/
Constitution: Registered charity; association with
    voluntary subscribing membership
Objectives/purposes: To stimulate concern for the beauty
    of London, the preservation of its charms and the
    careful consideration of its development
Key staff: Chairman: Gayne Wells; Secretary: Benita Jones
Stock and subject coverage: Selection of books covering a
    wide range of subjects about London, its history and
    development
Services: Photocopies
Availability: Open to all for research. Only members may
    borrow. No charge for services
Hours: By appointment 10.00–19.00 Monday to Friday;
    10.00–14.00 first and third Saturdays each month
Transport: Tube: Angel, Old Street; Rail: Essex Road;
    Bus: 38, 56, 73, 76, 141, 271, 341
Special facilities: Toilet facilities available
Publications: Journal of the London Society (2 p.a. April
    and October, by subscription £6 p.a.)

[399]
London Subterranean Survey Association
98E Cambridge Gardens
London W10 6HS
Borough: Kensington and Chelsea
Telephone: 020 8361 2097
E-mail: plnfm@rbkc.gov.uk
Constitution: Association with voluntary subscribing
    membership
Objectives/purposes: Study and promotion of
    underground space
Key staff: Dr Roger Morgan
Stock and subject coverage: Books, magazines and articles
    on tunnels, sewers, subways, underground railways,
    cable tunnels and ducts and bunkers
Availability: Open to anyone with a serious interest,
    principally for advice rather than reference. No open
    access, by arrangement only
Hours: By appointment

Linked organisations

Subterranea Britannica The Association is allied to Subterranea Britannica

[400]
London Voluntary Service Council
LVSC

356 Holloway Road
London N7 6PA
Borough: Islington
Telephone: 020 7700 8104
Fax: 020 7700 8108
E-mail: library@lvsc.org.uk
World Wide Web: www.lvsc.org.uk
Constitution: Independent non-profit distributing organisation; company limited by guarantee; registered charity
Key staff: Assistant librarians: Manuda Toporowska, Peter Berry
Stock and subject coverage: Materials on the voluntary sector, social policy, organisational management, personnel management, funding and fundraising
Services: Enquiries; photocopies; FunderFinder for groups in need; online searching from May 2000
Availability: Reference service only for personal visitors; telephone and written enquiry service; photocopies (charges made)
Hours: 10.00-17.00 Monday to Friday
Transport: Tube: Holloway Road, Highbury and Islington; Rail: Highbury and Islington; Bus: 17, 29, 43, 91, 153, 253, 259, 271, 279
Special facilities: Refreshment and toilet facilities; access for users with disabilities
Publications: Voluntary Voice (10 pa); Annual Report; Just About Managing; Voluntary But Not Amateur

[401]
London Weekend Television Information and Research Unit
LWT

London TV Centre
London SE1 9LT
Borough: Lambeth
Telephone: 020 7261 3386
Fax: 020 7737 8561
E-mail: fiona.sanson@granadamedia.com
Constitution: Company limited by guarantee
Key staff: Information Manager: Fiona Sanson
Stock and subject coverage: General reference collection specialising in the media. National newspapers and a broad range of magazine titles are held
Services: Online searching from £35 per search
Availability: Not open to the public but a fee based service is available for independent producers and researchers
Hours: 10.00-18.00 Monday to Friday

[402]
Lord Chancellor's Department

Headquarters Library
Southside
105 Victoria Street
London SW1E 6QT
Borough: Westminster
Telephone: 020 7210 1980/1979
Fax: 020 7210 1981
E-mail: lcd.library@courtservice.gsi.gov.uk
World Wide Web: www.lcd.gov.uk
www.courtservice.gov.uk/
Constitution: Government funded body
Key staff: Librarian: Christine Younger
Stock and subject coverage: Materials on law and public administration
Services: Loans; enquiries; internet access; photocopies; online searches
Availability: Loans and enquiries to staff and other government departments; others at the discretion of the Librarian
Hours: 09.30-17.00 Monday to Friday
Transport: Tube: St James's Park, Victoria; Rail: Victoria

Linked organisations

The Court Service Agency of the Lord Chancellor's Department
Law Commission
Supreme Court Library
Sister libraries

[403]
Low Pay Unit
LPU

9 Arkwright Road
Hampstead
London NW3 6AB
Borough: Camden
Telephone: 020 7435 4268
Fax: 020 7431 9614
World Wide Web: www.lowpayunit.org.uk
Constitution: Independent non-profit distributing organisation; company limited by guarantee; registered charity; association with voluntary subscribing membership
Objectives/purposes: To tackle the problem of in-work poverty through research, campaigning and giving employment rights advice
Key staff: Director: Bharti Patel; Employment Policy Officer: Jeff Masters; Resource Manager: Sakina Ahmed; Online Officer: Lise Smith
Stock and subject coverage: Employment rights advice sheets; labour market data; social security data; news releases on poverty
Availability: Access for employment rights advice free to low-paid workers. Any other research material or data restricted to subscribers only
Hours: 09.30-17.30 Monday to Friday
Transport: Tube: Finchley Road, Hampstead
Publications: The New Review (information on employment and poverty issues) 6 p.a. £6 per issue, available free of charge to subscribers

[404]
MAKE the Organisation for Women in the Arts
(formerly Women's Art Library)
107-109 Charing Cross Road
London WC2H 0DU
Borough: Camden
Telephone: 020 7514 8860
Fax: 020 7514 8864
E-mail: a.greenan@csm.linst.ac.uk (research and
   resource)
   t.nadim@csm.linst.ac.uk (general)
World Wide Web: www.womensart.org.uk
Constitution: Registered charity
Objectives/purposes: To promote the work of women
   artists
Key staff: Director: Katrina Crookall; Programming:
   Tahani Nadim; Research Resource: Althea Greenan
Stock and subject coverage: Over 200, 000 slides and
   transparencies, 5, 000 books, catalogues and artists
   books, 100 audio tapes,100 videotapes, and press-
   cuttings on over 8, 000 women artists. Collected
   from artist-members, publishers, and other supporters
   for over 20 years, MAKE Resource is one of the
   world's most comprehensive information centres on
   contemporary and historical women artists. The
   range of historical periods covered by MAKE is
   comprehensive and covers all fine art including
   installation, artist's books and digital media. The
   published materials of books, journals and catalogues
   are international and many North American women
   artists are also represented in the files. The collection
   began in the late 1970s and includes documentation
   relating to the second wave of the women's
   movement in the UK
Services: Photocopier available
Availability: Reference only
Hours: 10.00-18.00 Tuesday to Friday, closed August
Transport: Tube: Tottenham Court Road; Buses: buses
   serving Tottenham Court Road, Oxford Street and
   Charing Cross Road
Special facilities: Toilet facilities available; access for users
   with disabilities, advise the Library before visiting
Publications: MAKE Magazine (special editions on an
   irregular basis only); Contemporary Arab Women's
   Art: Dialogue of the Present (1999); Private Views:
   Gender and Space in Contemporary Art from Britain
   to Estonia (2000); Bulletin newsletter (quarterly)

[405]
Manorial Society of Great Britain
MSGB
104 Kennington Road
London SE11 6RE
Borough: Lambeth
Telephone: 020 7735 6633
Fax: 020 7582 7022
E-mail: msgb@manor.net
World Wide Web: www.msgb.co.uk
Constitution: Independent non-profit distributing
   organisation
Objectives/purposes: Manorial history, aristocratic and
   manorial genealogy
Key staff: Robert Smith, Debbie Reeves, Stephen Johnson

Stock and subject coverage: Useful collection for local
   historians and topographers. Collections include:
   county directories, county histories, genealogical
   histories (e.g. Burke, Lodge, Websters), over 2,000
   manorial descents and titles in files
Services: Photocopies (charges made)
Availability: Postgraduate students. No charges except for
   photocopying
Hours: 10.00-18.00 Monday to Friday, by appointment
   only
Transport: Tube: Lambeth North; Bus: 3, 109, 159
Special facilities: Toilet facilities available
Publications: Bulletin; The Sudeleys – Lords of
   Toddington; The House of Lords, 1,000 years of
   British Tradition, The House of Commons (a
   history); The Monarchy (a history); Manorial Law,
   Blount's Jocular Tenures (reprint); Blood Royal, a
   Genealogy of the Royal Family (in preparation)

[406]
Marx Memorial Library
37A Clerkenwell Green
London EC1R 0DU
Borough: Islington
Telephone: 020 7253 1485
Fax: 020 7251 6039
E-mail: marx.library@britishlibrary.net
World Wide Web:
   www.marxmemoriallibrary.sageweb.co.uk
Constitution: Independent non-profit distributing
   organisation; registered charity; association with
   voluntary subscribing membership
Objectives/purposes: The advancement of education,
   knowledge and learning by the provision of a library
   of books, journals and manuscripts relating to all
   aspects of the science of Marxism, the history of
   Socialism and the working class movement
Key staff: Librarian: Ms Tish Collins
Stock and subject coverage: Materials on Marxism, the
   history of Socialism and working class movements,
   including: Marx, Engels, Lenin, science, history,
   economics, biographies and literature. Extensive
   journal holdings dating from the 1840s. Specialist
   collections include: the John Williamson American
   Collection, the International Brigade Spanish Civil
   War Archive, the JD Bernal Peace Library and the
   James Klugmann Collection of radical and Chartist
   material
Services: Photocopies
Availability: Membership library, accessible to all who
   join or affiliate
Hours: 13.00-18.00 Monday; 13.00-20.00 Tuesday,
   Wednesday and Thursday; 10.00-13.00 Saturday
Transport: Tube and Rail: Farringdon; Bus: 55, 63, 243,
   259, 505
Special facilities: Toilet facilities; access for users with
   disabilities – ground floor access by ramp, hearing
   loop in meeting hall
Special features: Listed building over 260 years old with
   15th century tunnels in the basement. Lenin worked
   in the building in 1902-3
Publications: Bulletin of the Marx Memorial Library
   (approx. 2 p.a.)

[407]
Marylebone Cricket Club Library
MCC Library
Lord's Ground
London NW8 8QN
Borough: City of Westminster
Telephone: 020 7289 1611
Fax: 020 7432 1062
Constitution: Private club
Objectives/purposes: To record cricket in all its aspects
Key staff: Curator: Stephen EA Green MA; Assistant Curator: Glenys A Williams BA MPhil; Secretary: Michael Wolton B Comm
Stock and subject coverage: Reference library formed in 1893 and specialising in cricket; small section on real tennis and other games
Services: Photocopies; photography
Availability: Mainly intended for MCC members; open to all by appointment only
Hours: Summer: 10.00-17.00 Monday to Thursday; 10.00-16.00 Fridays; open on Saturday and Sunday on match days
Winter: 10.00-17.00 Monday to Thursday; 10.00-16.00 Fridays
Transport: Tube: St John's Wood; Rail: Marylebone; Bus 6, 13, 16, 46, 82, 98, 113, 139, 189, 274
Special facilities: Refreshment and toilet facilities available; access for users with disabilities with prior arrangement
Special features: Library linked by a bridge to Lord's Pavilion
Publications: Annual Report of the MCC; yearbooks, newsletters, etc.

[408]
Mayday Healthcare NHS Trust, Medical Library
Croydon Health Sciences Library
Mayday Healthcare NHS Trust
Mayday Hospital
Mayday Road
Thornton Heath
Surrey CR7 7YE
Borough: Croydon
Telephone: 020 8401 3197
Fax: 020 8401 3883
E-mail: ray.phillips@mayday.nhs.uk
Constitution: NHS library
Key staff: Librarian: Ray Phillips; Deputy Librarians: Arpita Banerjee, David Hayes
Stock and subject coverage: Books and journals on medicine, nursing, midwifery and other health-related subjects
Services: Photocopies, literature searching, internet access, word processing facilities
Availability: Free access to all who work for the NHS in Croydon. Most materials available for loan, some for reference only. Charges for on-site photocopying and for printing from the internet
Hours: 09.00-17.00 Monday to Friday
Transport: Rail: East Croydon, West Croydon; Bus: 109, 198, 250
Special facilities: Refreshment and toilet facilities available on site; access for users with disabilities (lifts and ramps provided)

Linked organisations
London Library and Information Development Unit
Southwest London Workforce Development Confederation

[409]
The Medical Council on Alcohol
MCA
3 St Andrew's Place
London NW1 4LB
Borough: Westminster
Telephone: 020 7487 4445
Fax: 020 7935 4479
E-mail: mca@medicouncilalcol.demon.co.uk
World Wide Web: www.medicouncilalcol.demon.co.uk
Constitution: Independent non-profit distributing organisation; company limited by guarantee; registered charity and association with voluntary subscribing membership
Objectives/purposes: Education of the medical professions about the effects of alcohol on health
Key staff: Executive Director: Dr Guy Ratcliffe
Stock and subject coverage: Small stock of books, pamphlets, leaflets, journals and newsletters covering the medical aspects of alcoholism. The collections include some unpublished material, statistical data, some slides, a few videos and a website
Services: Photocopies, telephone/fax machine
Availability: Library mainly for members but open to bona fide researchers. Material (barring publications) is for reference only. Charges are made for photocopying, purchase of handbooks or slides
Hours: 09.30-16.30 Monday to Friday, by appointment only. Closed on public holidays and over Christmas/New Year and Easter
Transport: Tube: Regent's Park, Great Portland Street; Bus: 3, 18, 27, 30, 53, 137, 176
Special facilities: Toilet facilities available
Publications: Alcohol and Alcoholism journal (6 p.a.); Alcoholis newsletter (6 p.a.); Annual Report; books and leaflets

[410]
Medical Devices Library
MDA
Hannibal House
Elephant and Castle
London SE1 6TQ
Borough: Southwark
Telephone: 020 7972 8341
Fax: 020 7972 8079
E-mail: library@medical-devices.gov.uk
World Wide Web: www.medical-devices.gov.uk
Constitution: Executive Agency of the Department of Health
Key staff: Librarian-in-Charge: Mrs Karen Morgan BSc (Hons) MSc ALA
Stock and subject coverage: About 10,000 books and pamphlets and 140 current journals, concerned with information on medical devices
Services: Enquiry service; loans; bibliography compilation; current awareness and abstracting services; online information retrieval

Availability: To staff; other libraries and health authorities in England for borrowing; research workers and other accredited persons, by appointment, to consult material not readily available elsewhere
Hours: 09.00–17.00 Monday to Friday
Transport: Tube and Rail: Elephant and Castle
Special facilities: Access for users with disabilities

Linked organisations

Department of Health Executive agency of the DoH

[411]
Medicines Control Agency
MCA
Information Centre
10th Floor Market Towers
1 Nine Elms Lane
London SW8 5NQ
Telephone: 020 7273 0000
Fax: 020 7273 0353
E-mail: info@mca.gov.uk
World Wide Web: www.mca.gov.uk
Constitution: Government agency
Key staff: Head of Information Services: Mrs Diane Leakey
Stock and subject coverage: Ca 200 journal titles covering pharmacy, pharmacology and matters relating to medicines production. A small 'intense' collection of books on medicines, pharmacy and related matters. The library specialises in the safety, quality and efficacy of medicines
Services: Photocopies (limited service available)
Availability: The Information Centre exists only to serve the MCA. However it will support postgraduate research in medicines regulation and related matters
Hours: 09.00–17.00 Monday to Friday
Transport: Tube: Vauxhall; Bus: 77, 77A, 88, 327, 344
Special facilities: Refreshment and toilet facilities available; access for users with disabilities
Publications: MCA Annual Report and Accounts; Eurodirect subscription service; MAIL updating newsletter

Linked organisations

Department of Health Executive agency of the DoH

[412]
Menzies Centre for Australian Studies
MCAS
28 Russell Square
London WC1B 5DS
Borough: Camden
Telephone: 020 7862 8854
Fax: 020 7580 9627
E-mail: menzies.centre@kcl.ac.uk
World Wide Web: www.kcl.ac.uk/menzies
Constitution: Department of a university
Objectives/purposes: To promote Australian studies in British and European universities
Key staff: Secretary

Stock and subject coverage: Collections on Australian history, culture, literature, Aboriginal affairs. Collection includes literary periodicals and Australian poetry
Services: Photocopier available at Institute of Commonwealth Studies Library
Availability: Open to all, but users must phone or write ahead for permission. Materials are available for reference only
Hours: 10.00–17.00 Monday to Thursday
Transport: Tube: Russell Square: Rail: Euston, King's Cross; Bus: 7, 68, 91, 168, 188
Special facilities: Refreshment and toilet facilities available

Linked organisations

School of Humanities, King's College London, University of London

[413]
The Mercers' Company
Mercers' Hall
Ironmonger Lane
London EC2V 8HE
Borough: Corporation of London
Telephone: 020 7776 7244
Fax: 020 7600 1158
E-mail: ursulac@mercers.co.uk
World Wide Web: www.mercers.co.uk
Constitution: One of the 12 Great Livery Companies of the City of London. (The order of precedence of livery companies, which places the Mercers Company as the first, was decided by the Lord Mayor in 1515, following years of dispute between the companies.)
Key staff: The Archivist and Curator
Stock and subject coverage: Archives of the Mercers' Company from 1348, documenting every aspect of the history of the Company and its administration. General subjects covered by records in the archives include: City history; Livery Company history; the colonisation of Northern Ireland; charitable works, including the care of the elderly; the development of housing; and the history of the provision of education
Services: Photocopying
Availability: Available to bona fide researchers, for research, at the discretion of the Company. Potential researchers should contact the Archivist in writing in the first instance, with details of their research interest, before telephoning or booking appointments
Hours: 09.30–17.00 Monday to Friday
Transport: Tube: Barbican, St Paul's, Bank, Cannon Street, Mansion House; Rail: Cannon Street, Blackfriars
Publications: General information brochures on Company history; partial bibliography available on website; full bibliography available on request

[414]
Merton (London Borough of Merton)
Merton Libraries and Heritage Services
World Wide Web: www.merton.gov.uk
Constitution: Public library service funded by local authority

Special features: Wimbledon Reference Library (listed first) is the main reference resource for the Borough with specialist information workers staffing the enquiry point at all times. Morden and Mitcham Libraries have satellite reference services with availability of reference staff at core times

[414][a]
Wimbledon Library
Wimbledon Hill Road
London SW19 7NB
Telephone: 020 8946 7979/7432
020 8946 1136 (reference)
Fax: 020 8944 6804
E-mail: wimbledonlibrary@merton.gov.uk
Key staff: Library and Service Manager: Pamela Row
Stock and subject coverage: General lending stock of books, videos, CDs and talking books. Extensive reference collection of journals, books, CD-ROMs. Children's section and Internet Exchange – a commercial centre offering computer facilities and training in Library premises
Services: Charges for audio and video loans, fax and self-service photocopy facilities; limited internet access
Availability: All material is freely available to all on a reference only basis
Hours: 09.30-19.00 Monday, Tuesday, Wednesday and Friday; 09.30-20.00 Thursday; 09.30-17.00 Saturday
Transport: Tube, Rail and Tramlink: Wimbledon; Bus: 57, 93, 131, 163, 164, 200, 219
Special facilities: Toilet facilities; access for users with disabilities – automatic doors, adapted toilet; CCTV for visually impaired users
Special features: Victorian facade locally listed. Interior retains some of the features of a 19th century public library

[414][b]
Donald Hope Library
Cavendish House
High Street
Colliers Wood SW19 2HR
Telephone: 020 8542 1975
Fax: 020 8543 9767
E-mail: donaldhopelibrary@merton.gov.uk
Key staff: Library and Service Manager: Peter Campion
Stock and subject coverage: General lending stock – books, journals, videos, talking books. Open learning Centre – computer learning packs for use in the Library. Small reference and children's collections
Availability: Hire charges for audio and video items; Open Learning Centre available on subscription
Hours: 09.30-18.00 Monday, Tuesday, Thursday and Friday; 09.30-17.00 Saturday
Transport: Tube: Colliers Wood; Bus: 57, 219
Special facilities: Access for users with disabilities

[414][c]
Mitcham Library
London Road
Mitcham CR4 2YR
Telephone: 020 8648 4070/6516
Fax: 020 8646 6360
E-mail: mitcham.library@merton.gov.uk

Key staff: Library and Service Manager: Dabinder Chaudhri
Stock and subject coverage: General lending and reference materials – books, journals, videos, talking books, CDs for loan. Reference and children's collections
Availability: Hire charges for audio and video items
Hours: 09.30-19.00 Monday to Friday; 09.30-17.00 Saturday
Transport: Rail: Mitcham; Bus: 118, 127, 152, 200, 201, 264, 270, 280, 355
Special facilities: Access for users with disabilities

[414][d]
Morden Library
Merton Civic Centre
London Road
Morden SM4 5DX
Telephone: 020 8545 4040
Fax: 020 8545 4037
E-mail: morden.library@merton.gov.uk
Key staff: Library and Service Manager
Stock and subject coverage: General lending and reference materials – books, journals, videos, CDs and talking books. Local Studies Centre covering whole of Merton and comprising books, pictures, maps, ephemera. Special collections on Nelson and William Morris. Internet Exchange – a commercial firm – operates computer facilities from library premises
Availability: Hire charges for audio and video items
Hours: 09.30-19.00 Monday to Friday; 09.30-17.00 Saturday
Transport: Tube: Morden; Rail: Morden South, South Merton; Tramlink: Morden Road; Bus: 86, 93, 118
Special facilities: Access for users with disabilities – lift to other floors, disabled toilets; automatic doors

[414][e]
Pollards Hill Library
South Lodge Avenue
Mitcham CR4 1LT
Telephone: 020 8764 5877
Fax: 020 8765 0925
E-mail: pollardshill.library@merton.gov.uk
Key staff: Library and Service Manager
Stock and subject coverage: General lending and reference books, journals and talking books. Children's collection; Open Learning Centre – computer learning packs for use in Library
Availability: Hire charges for talking books and Open Learning Centre
Hours: 09.30-17.00 Monday, Tuesday, Thursday, Friday and Saturday
Transport: Bus: 60, 152, 255
Special facilities: Access for users with disabilities

[414][f]
Raynes Park Library
Approach Road
London SW20 8BA
Telephone: 020 8542 1893
Fax: 020 8543 6132
Key staff: Library and Service Manager: Patricia Roberts
Stock and subject coverage: General lending and reference books, journals and talking books. Children's section
Availability: Hire charges for audio items

Hours: 09.30-18.00 Monday, Tuesday, Thursday and
    Friday; 09.30-17.00 Saturday
Transport: Rail: Raynes Park; Bus: 57, 131, 152, 163
Special facilities: Access for users with disabilities

[414][g]
West Barnes Library
    Station Road
    New Malden KT3 6JF
Telephone: 020 8942 2635
Fax: 020 8336 0554
E-mail: westbarneslibrary@merton.gov.uk
Key staff: Library and Service Manager: Alison Williams
Stock and subject coverage: General lending collection of
    books, videos and talking books; small reference
    collection and children's section
Availability: Hire charges for videos
Hours: 09.30-18.00 Monday, Tuesday, Thursday and
    Friday; 09.30-17.00 Saturday
Transport: Rail: Motspur Park; Bus: K5
Special facilities: Access for users with disabilities

[415]
The Middle East Association
MEA
    Bury House
    33 Bury Street
    St James's
    London SW1Y 6AX
Borough: Westminster
Telephone: 020 7839 2137
Fax: 020 7839 6121
E-mail: mail@the-mea.co.uk
World Wide Web: www.the-mea.co.uk
Constitution: Association with voluntary subscribing
    membership
Objectives/purposes: Promotion of trade and investment
    between the UK and the Middle East (all Arab States,
    Iran, Turkey, Afghanistan)
Key staff: Director General: Mr Brian Constant;
    Director, Trade Relations: Mr Michael Thomas;
    Director of Information Services: David Lloyd;
    Librarian: Mrs Jennifer Webb
Stock and subject coverage: Materials relating to doing
    business in the Middle East. Ca. 800 books, 94
    journal titles and pamphlets. Coverage includes
    general information, maps, national and economic
    surveys; laws, regulations and decrees; taxation; market
    reports by area and by industry; local company
    reports; trade statistics; budgets, development plans
    and projects; living and working conditions; seminars,
    conferences, exhibitions, trade fairs and trade
    missions; local business, trade and telephone
    directories, yellow pages; newspaper cuttings; items
    issued by British diplomatic missions in the area
Services: Photocopies (charges made), fax, lists of
    translating services, recruitment agencies for Middle
    East
Availability: Access to all bona fide researchers. Material
    mainly for reference but certain duplicates can be
    provided free
Hours: 09.30-17.30 Monday to Friday
Transport: Tube: Green Park, Piccadilly Circus; Bus: 8, 9,
    14, 19, 22, 38

Special facilities: Tea and coffee facilities; toilets available;
    access for users with disabilities – lift to first floor
    library
Publications: Handbook and Classified List of Members
    (annual); Information Digest (fortnightly);
    Opportunity Middle East (quarterly)

[416]
Middle Temple Library
    The Honourable Society of the Middle Temple
    Middle Temple Lane
    London EC4Y 9BT
Telephone: 020 7427 4830
Fax: 020 7427 4831
E-mail: library@middletemple.org.uk
World Wide Web: www.middletemple.org.uk/library.
    htm
Constitution: Registered charity; chartered professional
    body
Objectives/purposes: To provide a library service for
    practising barristers and other members of the Inn
Key staff: Librarian and Keeper of the Records: Vanessa
    Hayward; Deputy Librarian: Angela Knox; Readers'
    Services Librarian: Stuart Adams; European
    Communities Librarian: Ruth Jones; Cataloguer:
    Anne Bailey; Systems Librarian: Julian Reckert;
    Archivist: Lesley Whitelaw
Stock and subject coverage: The Library holds a
    comprehensive collection of British legal material,
    including some Scottish and Irish, as well as
    collections of Commonwealth, International and
    American law. It also houses and administers the Inns
    of Court European Communities library. There are
    approximately 150,000 volumes in the working
    library, consisting of practitioners' texts, law reports,
    journals, loose-leaf works, parliamentary papers,
    statutes, reference works, Hansards, etc. A considerable
    collection of older material includes incunabula,
    manuscripts, tracts and rare books
Services: Photocopies (charges made); newspaper law
    reports cuttings and index; card indexes and
    checklists; CD-ROMs; online catalogue, online access
    to the catalogues of the other Inns; Daily Law
    Reports and Legal Journals Index; supply of
    photocopies (subject to copyright) to Middle Temple
    barristers outside central London
Availability: Open to all members of the Bar and to
    Middle Temple students. Bona fide researchers are
    admitted at the discretion of the Librarian upon
    written application. Mainly reference, with a strictly
    limited loans facility for Middle Temple members
    only
Hours: Legal and student terms: 09.00-20.00 Monday to
    Thursday, 09.00-18.30 Friday
    Vacations: 09.00-17.30
    Closed for the first two weeks in August
Transport: Tube: Temple; Rail: Blackfriars; St Paul's City
    Link; Bus: 4, 11, 15, 23, 26, 76, 171A
Special facilities: Refreshment and toilet facilities available;
    access for users with disabilities – wheelchair users
    should contact the Library in advance
Special features: The library building, designed by Sir
    Edward Maufe and erected in 1958, is sited within a
    conservation area

Publications: Range of guides to the Library and its services; Middle Temple Bench Book; Register of Admissions; Middle Temple Minutes of Parliament, list of publications available on request

Linked organisations

Honourable Society of the Middle Temple
Middle Temple is one of four Inns of Court which have responsibility for the selection, training and regulation of barristers in England and Wales. The other Inns are: Lincoln's Inn, Inner Temple and Gray's Inn. They are equal to, and independent of, each other

[417]
Middlesex University

Bounds Green Road
London N11 2NQ
Borough: Enfield
Telephone: 020 8362 5286
Fax: 020 8362 5613
World Wide Web: www.ilrs.mdx.ac.uk
Key staff: Head of Information and Learning Resource Services(ILRS): William Marsterson; Deputy Head: Gill Madden; Assistant Head: Judith Cattermole; Head of ILRS Language Centres and Audio Visual Services: John Rees-Smith
Middlesex is a multi-campus university with collections spread across 13 locations, but they are all accessible from any campus and operate under the same regulations. One OPAC gives access to all resources
Services: Card-operated photocopiers (at cost)
Availability: By appointment to bona fide researchers for reference only. Visitors must report to campus reception where they will be asked to sign in and collect a visitors badge. Library membership is available for external borrowers at an annual cost of £90. Further information can be supplied on request
Hours: Opening hours are with the range 9.00-22.00 Monday to Friday; 10.00-16.00 weekends and 09.00-17.00 during vacations. Consult the webpages for information on hours and on transport facilities
Special facilities: Access points and lifts for wheelchair users and those with mobility problems are provided. All libraries have a range of equipment that helps students with disabilities to access resources more easily. These include Galileo machines (scan text and read it back) and Alpha Vision machines (enhance text). Advice and assistance is offered at library counters. Refreshments and toilet facilities are available on each Campus

[417][a]
Archway and Hospitals' Campus

Key staff: Sue Hill, Royal Free Hospital Library, 020 7830 2788; Bev Chapman, Archway Healthcare Library, 020 7288 3567; Linda Farley, Chase Healthcare Library, 020 8366 2245; Ann Mason, North Middlesex Library, 020 8887 2223
Learning Resource Manager: Dilys Hall, 020 8363 5424
Stock and subject coverage: Collections at Royal Free Hospital and shared multidisciplinary libraries at Archway Healthcare, Chase Farm and North Middlesex. All libraries have a varied collection of

materials to support nursing and health related provision across the University
Note: Middlesex University manages the hospital libraries at the Archway (Whittington) and Chase Farm on behalf of partners (NHS Trusts and University College, London); MU manages its own library at Royal Free and buys into the Trust's Library at North Middlesex, which uses the MU Library system. MU teaches students on all four sites, and provides computing support and audiovisual support at all four

[417][b]
Cat Hill (including Quicksilver Place)

Cat Hill
Barnet
Herts EN4 8HT
Telephone: 020 8362 5044
Key staff: Campus Library and Information Manager; Learning Resource Manager: Penny Dade
Stock and subject coverage: The Library's main art and design collections, with resources covering the following subjects - architecture, art and design history, ceramics, decorative arts, fashion, film studies and cultural theory, fine art, furniture, graphics, interior design, jewellery and textiles. There is a strong emphasis on visual materials with collections of slides, videos, illustrations and extensive reprographic facilities. The collection also supports the work of fine art and includes books, exhibition catalogues and videos. Special collections include: Hall-Carpenter Newspaper Cuttings Archive; Product Information Collection; History of Fashion Collection. The Sir James Richards Library, on architecture and town planning in the UK and overseas, is housed in the adjacent Museum of Domestic Architecture and Design, accessible via Library OPAC
Hours: 09.30-20.00 Monday to Friday
Transport: Tube: Cockfosters

[417][c]
Enfield

Queensway
Enfield
Middlesex EN3 4SF
Telephone: 020 8362 5546
Key staff: Campus Library and Information Manager: Kathy McGowan; Learning Resource Manager: Diane Coxon
Stock and subject coverage: The main social sciences collections, with resources covering the following subjects - economics, geography, health studies, psychology, social work, sociology and environmental science
Hours: 10.00-21.00 Monday to Thursday; 10.00-18.00 Friday
Transport: Rail: Southbury

[417][d]
Hendon

The Burroughs
London NW4 4BT
Telephone: 020 8362 5851

Key staff: Campus Library and Information Manager:
Hilary Cummings; Learning Resource Manager:
Pauline Hollis
Stock and subject coverage: The main business studies and
management collections, with resources covering the
following subjects – accountancy, computing science,
economics, law, management and mathematics
Hours: 09.00–22.00 Monday to Thursday: 09.00–18.00
Friday
Transport: Tube: Hendon Central

[417][e]
Tottenham

White Hart Lane
London N17 8HR
Telephone: 020 8362 6724
Key staff: Campus Library and Information Manager:
Meg Kirk
Stock and subject coverage: The main humanities
collection, with resources covering the following
subjects – English, history, law, media and
communication studies, modern languages and
philosophy. Special collections include: Brazilian
Embassy Library; Gareth Roberts Collection (literary
criticism and witchcraft)
Hours: 09.00–21.00 Monday to Thursday: 09.00–18.00
Friday
Transport: Rail: White Hart Lane

[417][f]
Trent Park (including Bedford and Ivy House)

Bramley Road
London N14 4YZ
Telephone: 020 8362 6295
Key staff: Campus Library and Information Manager:
Rosie Sinden-Evans, Learning Resources Manager:
Monica Glynn
Stock and subject coverage: The main education collection
as well as computing science and performing arts,
with resources covering the following subjects -
computing, dance, drama, education, humanities, life
sciences and music. There is also a specialist teaching
practice collection and a music and media section
with audio and videotapes, CDs, records and scores.
Special collections: Elizabeth Goodacre Collection
(reading schemes); Folk Tale collection. Bedford
incorporates the specialist collection from the
London College of Dance, while Ivy House has the
drama and theatre studies collection including
playsets
Hours: 09.00–23.00 Monday to Friday
Transport: Tube: Oakwood

---

[418]
Military Survey Library and Information Centre (LIC) Tolworth

Borough: Kingston upon Thames
Military Survey maintains a comprehensive library of
worldwide modern topographic and thematic maps and
also a Book Library which is split between the Tolworth
and Feltham sites. There is an additional book library in
the School of military Survey at Hermitage. This is part
of the Directorate of Geographic Field Support

[418][a]
Book Library (Tolworth)

Directorate of Geographic Information
Government Buildings Block A
Hook Rise South
Tolworth
Surbiton
Surrey KT6 7NB
Telephone: 020 8335 5301
Fax: 020 8335 5387
E-mail: lic@knox1.milsvy.gov.uk
World Wide Web: www.military-survey.mod.uk
Key staff: Assistant Director Geographic Libraries: Mr P
Jones MBE, ext 5300; Mr R Sampson, ext 5301
Stock and subject coverage: A specialist collection of
geographic and related topics to support MOD and
the activities of Military Survey. It includes mapping
and survey reports; boundaries and place name
information; geographic guides; map catalogues and
specified cartographic, geographic and topographic
texts and journals
Services: Photocopies (at cost)
Availability: By appointment to bona fide researchers,
subject to the material not being available elsewhere;
telephone and written enquiries accepted as time
permits
Hours: 08.30–17.00 Monday to Friday
Transport: Rail: Tolworth

[418][b]
Library and Information Centre

Clarke Building
Military Survey
Elmwood Avenue
Feltham
Middlesex TW13 7AH
Telephone: 020 8890 3622
Fax: 020 8818 2574
E-mail: geodetic@clarke1.demon.co.uk
Key staff: Librarians: Mr S Miles, 020 8818 2227; Miss L
Anderson: 020 8818 2226
Stock and subject coverage: Books, reports, journals, etc. on
geodesy; GIS; mathematics; cartography;
photogrammetry; geophysics; and computer science.
Also a collection of survey records
Services: Photocopies (at cost)
Availability: By appointment to bona fide researchers,
subject to the material not being available elsewhere;
telephone and written enquiries accepted as time
permits
Hours: 08.30–17.00 Monday to Friday
Special facilities: Refreshment and toilet facilities available

[418][c]
Map Library

Directorate of Geographic Information
Government Buildings Block A
Hook Rise South
Tolworth
Surbiton
Surrey KT6 7NB
Telephone: 020 8335 5300
Fax: 020 8335 5387
E-mail: maplib@knox1.milsvy.gov.uk
World Wide Web: www.military-survey.mod.uk

Constitution: Government body

Key staff: Assistant Director Geographic Libraries: Mr P Jones MBE; Head of Map Library: Mr P Ayers, ext 5337

Stock and subject coverage: Comprehensive collection of worldwide topographical mapping. Also includes aeronautical charts; town plans; and selected thematic maps to meet MOD and Military Survey needs

Services: Photocopies (at cost)

Availability: By appointment to bona fide researchers subject to the material not being available elsewhere; telephone and written enquiries accepted as time permits

Hours: 08.30-17.00 Monday to Friday

Transport: Rail: Tolworth

[419]
Ministry of Defence
Headquarters Library Services
3-5 Great Scotland Yard
London SW1A 2HW

Borough: Westminster

Constitution: Government department

Telephone: 020 7218 plus extension

Fax: 020 7218 5413

Government Telecommunications Network: 218 plus extension

E-mail: whitehall.lib@dgics.mod.uk

Key staff: Chief Librarian: RH Searle MPhil ALA; Head of Customer Services: MM Chapman MA ALA, ext 5416; Head of Enquiries Team: Miss M Guy BA ALA, ext 0139

Stock and subject coverage: The Library is developing its role as an information resource centre for the MoD. It holds around 250,000 books and reports and around 1,000 journals. Coverage includes current defence policy and defence forces worldwide, politics, economics, public administration, languages, biographies, history, science and technology, computer science, management and parliamentary papers. There are special collections covering histories of the British Army, Royal Air Force and military campaigns

Availability: All staff serving with the Ministry, irrespective of rank, grade, service or location may borrow direct from the stock of the MoD library system. Staff in outstations or establishments should channel their requests through their own library where such a facility exists. Loans are made to libraries outside government service through national interlibrary loan services. The staff of other ministries may borrow from MoD; loans are normally through Ministry or local establishment libraries. An information and enquiry service is maintained and enquiries from members of the public are answered. In general access is normally only possible if the required material is not available from another, more public source. Open to the public by prior arrangement in writing to the Chief Librarian

Hours: 09.00-17.30 Monday to Friday. For outside visitors: 09.30-12.30 and 13.30-16.30

Transport: Tube: Embankment, Charing Cross; Rail: Charing Cross

Special facilities: Toilet facilities, access for users with disabilities

Special features: 3-5 Great Scotland Yard was built around 1908 as the Central London Army Recruiting Depot

[420]
The Model Railway Club
MRC
Keen House
4 Calshot Street
London N1 9DA

Borough: Islington

Telephone: 020 7837 2542

Fax: 020 7833 1840

World Wide Web: www.themodelrailwayclub.org

Constitution: Company limited by guarantee

Objectives/purposes: Club concerned with railways and model railways

Key staff: Chief Librarian: Andrew Jones

Stock and subject coverage: Materials on: railways (limited cover on the USA and Europe); model railways; railway dominated forms of travel, e.g. shipping (limited cover); model and prototype railway magazines (including the USA); related subjects

Availability: Open to members only. Some material available for loan to members, no charge for member's usage. Annual subscription for membership £50

Hours: 19.00-21.00 Thursday only

Transport: Tube and Rail: King's Cross; Bus: 30, 73, 214

Special facilities: Refreshment and toilet facilities available on site

Special features: Probably the most comprehensive railway library in the UK

[421]
Model Yachting Association
MYA
8 Sherard Road
London SE9 6EP

Borough: Greenwich

Telephone: 020 8850 6805

E-mail: rpotts@talk21.com

World Wide Web: www.radiosailing.org

Constitution: Association with voluntary subscribing membership; private venture

Objectives/purposes: National Authority controlling competitive model sailing in the UK

Key staff: Archivist: RR Potts

Stock and subject coverage: The MYA collection includes: manuscript records of the MYA – Council and AGM minutes from 1930 and Yacht Registers from 1925; some other MYA materials, including Rating Rules, Racing Rules, Acquaints newsletter from 1960. The Library includes a comprehensive private collection of published material on model yachting (since 1879) including specialist magazine coverage (from 1884)

Services: Photocopies

Availability: Open to all, charges are made for photocopying

Hours: By appointment

Transport: Rail: Eltham

Special facilities: Toilet facilities available

Publications: MYA Yearbook; MYA Handbook (occasional); A Bibliography of Model Yachting, Potts

and Craxson (London: Curved Air Press, 1999).
Enquiries about MYA publications should be
addressed to the Archivist in the first instance

Linked organisations

Vintage Model Yacht Group (VMYG) Linked
organisation concerned with the history of the sport
and the preservation and sailing of older styles of
model

Royal Yachting Association (UK)

**International Yacht Racing Union (Model Yacht
Racing Division)**
MYA is affiliated to both organisations

[422]
The Moravian Church Archive and Library

Moravian Church House
5–7 Muswell Hill
London N10 3TJ
Borough: Haringey
Telephone: 020 8883 3409
Fax: 020 8365 3371
E-mail: archive@moravianchurch.freeserve.co.uk
World Wide Web: www.moravian.org.uk
Objectives/purposes: To maintain the archives of the
British Province of the Moravian Church
Key staff: Archivist: Paul Blewitt
Stock and subject coverage: Printed material on Moravian
Church history and theology. Collection of hymn
books of various denominations. The Moravian
Church is a Protestant church, and material dates
from before the founding of the first congregation in
Britain in 1742
Services: Photocopies (charged); microfilming and
photography can be arranged on individual
application to the archivist
Availability: Access is free to anyone with an interest in
the Church and its history, by appointment with the
archivist
Hours: 10.00–16.00 Monday and Tuesday by
appointment
Transport: Tube: Finsbury Park then bus W3, W7 to the
bottom of Muswell Hill
Special facilities: Toilet facilities available; users with
special needs should inform the archivist in advance
of visiting

[423]
Mount Vernon Hospital Postgraduate Medical Centre

Les Cannon Memorial Library
Mount Vernon Hospital
Postgraduate Medical Centre
Northwood
Middlesex HA6 2RN
Borough: Hillingdon
Telephone: 01923 844143
Fax: 01923 827216
E-mail: library.mvernon@whht.nhs.uk
Constitution: Company limited by guarantee, registered
charity, part of the NHS

Key staff: Library Development Manager: Richard
Osborn; Assistant Librarian: Jane McFarlane
Stock and subject coverage: Multidisciplinary library
specialising in plastic surgery; oral surgery and
medicine; and cancer research and treatment.
Approximately 150 current journals are received and
there are 3,000 books in stock. At Harefield the
library concentrates particularly on heart surgery,
cardiology, thoracic medicine and surgery and
transplantation. 125 journals are taken and there is a
bookstock of over 750 volumes
Services: Photocopies, CD-ROM for Medline and
CINAHL searching, fax machine, internet access,
other computer applications (eg word processing)
Availability: Free access to all Mount Vernon and
Harefield Hospital staff (material available for loan
and reference), other readers should apply to the
Librarian by letter or telephone
Hours: 09.00–17.00 Monday to Friday
Transport: Tube: Northwood; Bus: R1, R2, H11, 282,
348
Special facilities: Refreshment and toilet facilities on site;
access for users with disabilities (disabled toilet
facilities in Postgraduate Medical Centre)
Publications: Annual report and business plan, Library
Bulletin, journals holdings list

Linked organisations

Harefield Hospital Medical Library (01895
828947)
**London Regional Library and Information
Service**

[424]
Museum and Library of the Order of St John, St John Ambulance

St John's Gate
St John's Lane
Clerkenwell
London EC1M 4DA
Borough: Corporation of London
Telephone: 020 7324 4070
Fax: 020 7336 0587
E-mail: museum@nhq.sja.org.uk
World Wide Web: www.sja.org.uk
Key staff: Librarian (Honorary): Professor Jonathan
Riley-Smith; Curator: Pamela Willis; Museum
Administrator: Caroline Brownhill
Constitution: Royal Order of Chivalry; registered charity
Objectives/purposes: To make the history of the Order of
St John and its foundation available to the widest
possible public
Stock and subject coverage: Specialised reference collection
on the Order of St John, its charities and related
subjects, covered by 20,000 books, pamphlets, maps
and manuscripts dating from the 12th century.
Subject areas covered include: the Crusades and the
military religious Orders – especially the Knights of
St John (Knights Hospitallers) and Knights Templars,
the Order's military, naval and medical history, the
history of the Order in the Latin East, Cyprus,
Rhodes and Malta, and the present day Order and its
work – including the St John Ophthalmic Hospital
in Jerusalem and St John Ambulance
Services: Photocopies

Availability: Reference material available to all by appointment with library staff. No charge, though donations are welcome

Hours: By appointment with library staff during the Museum's weekday opening hours: Monday to Friday 10.00-17.00

Transport: Tube: Farringdon, Barbican; Rail: Farringdon; Bus: 55, 243, 277, 279, 503, 505

Special facilities: Toilet facilities available; limited wheelchair access – advise library before visiting, toilet for disabled people

Special features: Museum and library are housed in St John's Gate, a Grade I listed building. Built in the 16th century the Museum formed the southern entrance to the Priory of Clerkenwell. The Museum displays physical evidence of the subjects covered in the Library and is open Monday to Friday 10.00-17.00 and Saturday 10.00-16.00. Guided tours of St John's Gate, the Grand Priory Church and the 12th century Crypt are available on Tuesdays, Fridays and Saturdays at 11.00 and 14.30. Suggested donation of £5 for a tour

Publications: St John's Gate, illustrated guide book; Brief History of the Order of St John; Silver at St John's Gate; Maps of Malta; Malta Views; Image of a Knight; St John Ambulance in Victorian Britain; Your Good Health, education pack published in association with the London Museums of Health and Medicine

Linked organisations

Order of St John Parent organisation of St John Ophthalmic Hospital in Jerusalem

St John Ambulance Association and Brigade

[425]
Museum of London

London Wall
London EC2Y 5HN
Borough: Corporation of London
Telephone: 020 7600 3699
Fax: 020 7600 1058
World Wide Web: www.museumoflondon.org.uk
Constitution: Jointly funded by central and local government (City of London)
Key staff: Sally Brooks MA ALA
Stock and subject coverage: Ca. 50,000 volumes. Covers London history, topography and archaeology. Special collections on the Plague and Fire of London, 1660s; English Civil War and Inter-regnum; historical maps. Incorporates library of the London and Middlesex Archaeology Society. The museum also has collections of paintings, prints, photographs and printed ephemera held by the Department of Later London History & Collections
Services: Enquiries (telephone or letter); photocopies. General historical enquiries should be directed to the appropriate curatorial department, not to the Library
Availability: By appointment only
Hours: 10.00-17.00 (Museum galleries open 10.00-17.50 Monday to Saturday; 12.00-17.50 Sunday)
Transport: Tube: Barbican, St Paul's; Bus: 4, 172, any bus to City
Special facilities: Refreshment and toilet facilities available; access for users with disabilities

Linked organisations

Museum of London, Information Resources Section The Library is part of the Section
Museum of London Archaeological Service Archaeological Archive
Related bodies
Note: A new Museum of Docklands is to be set up as a separate organisation

[426]
Napoleonic Society of Great Britain

Napoleonic Society
157 Vicarage Road
London E10 5DU
Borough: Waltham Forest
Telephone: 020 8539 3876
Fax: 020 8539 3876
E-mail: napoleon@smartgroups.com
World Wide Web: www.smartgroups.com/vault/napoleon
Constitution: Independent non-profit organisation
Objectives/purposes: To foster research into French history 1756-1945
Key staff: Librarian: Ronald King
Stock and subject coverage: Books, journals, CD-ROMs and newspaper cuttings on the military, political and social history of Napoleonic rule (Napoleon I and III)
Availability: At the discretion of the Secretary
Hours: By appointment only
Transport: Tube: Leyton, Walthamstow Central; Rail: Leyton Midland, Walhamstow Central; Bus: 48, 69, 97, 256
Special facilities: Refreshment and toilet facilities available
Publications: Napoleon - Bulletin of the Napoleonic Society of Great Britain (4 p.a.)

National Archives
see Public Record Office and the Historical Manuscripts Commission

[427]
National Army Museum

Royal Hospital Road
London SW3 4HT
Borough: Kensington and Chelsea
Telephone: 020 7730 0717
Fax: 020 7823 6573
E-mail: info@national-army-museum.ac.uk
World Wide Web: www.national-army-museum.ac.uk
Constitution: Registered charity and government-funded body
Key staff: Director: Ian G Robertson MA FMA; Head of Department of Printed Books: Michael Ball; Head of Archives, Photographs, Film and Sound: Dr Alastair Massie; Head of Fine and Decorative Art: Miss Jenny Spencer-Smith
Stock and subject coverage: Includes printed books, manuscripts, photographs and prints. Covers history of the British Army, from 1485; Indian Army to 1947; Colonial Armies to independence. 44,000 books; 30,000 pamphlets; 1,500 ft run of archives; 40,000 prints; 500,000 photographs

Services: Photographic, photocopying and microfilm services available (charges made)

Availability: Reference library only; no loans. Entry for general public by reader's ticket. Prior application must be made, application form available from the Department of Printed Books

Hours: 10.00–16.30 Tuesday to Saturday

Transport: Tube: Sloane Square; Victoria; Rail: Victoria; Bus: 239

Special facilities: Refreshment and toilet facilities; access for users with disabilities – adapted toilet available

Publications: Publications normally accompany Museum special exhibitions

[428]
National Art Library
NAL
Victoria and Albert Museum

Cromwell Road
South Kensington
London SW7 2RL

Borough: Kensington and Chelsea
Telephone: 020 7942 2400
Fax: 020 7942 2401
E-mail: nal.enquiries@vam.ac.uk
World Wide Web: www.nal.vam.ac.uk
Constitution: Government funded body
Key staff: Keeper of the Library: Susan Lambert
Stock and subject coverage: Largest specialist collection in the UK in its field. Ca. 1 million books on all branches of fine and applied art and design; 19th and 20th century periodicals and exhibition catalogues; 18th–20th century sale catalogues; collections of illuminated and calligraphic manuscripts, fine bookbindings, fine printing and illustrated books, artists' books, comics and graphic novels, and children's books. The Dyce and Forster Libraries of English and foreign literature. Clements collection of armorial bindings. Piot collection of festival books
Services: Enquiry and staffed photocopying services
Availability: Reader registration required. Appointment required for consultation of some rare material and manuscripts
Hours: 10.00–17.00 Tuesday to Saturday (Special Collections material must be requested by 16.00 and General Collection material by 16.30). The Library is closed for annual stocktaking for three weeks beginning with the Saturday before August Bank Holiday Monday
Transport: Tube: South Kensington; Bus: C1, 14, 74
Special facilities: Refreshment and toilet facilities; access for users with disabilities – it is advisable to contact the Museum's Control Room in advance of a visit
Special features: Original library accommodation from the 19th century

[428][a]
Museum Archives

Blythe House
23 Blythe Road
London W14 0QF

Borough: Kensington and Chelsea
Telephone: 020 7942 2400
Fax: 020 7942 2394

E-mail: nal.enquiries@vam.ac.uk
World Wide Web: www.nal.vam.ac.uk
Constitution: The Museum Archives form one section of the National Art Library at the Victoria and Albert Museum. They comprise three units: the Archive of Art and Design; the Beatrix Potter Collections; and the V&A Archive
Objectives: The AAD collects, conserves and makes available for research the archives of individuals, associations, and companies involved in any stage of the art and design process. Particular emphasis is placed on the records of British 20th century design
Key staff: Head of Archives: Serena Kelly; Museum Archivist: Christopher Marsden; Archivist, Archive of Art and Design: Guy Baxter; Archivist V&A Archive and Registry: Lynn Young; Assistant Curator: Eva White
Stock and subject coverage: The Archive of Art and Design holds over 200 separate archive groups which vary in size from a few to several thousand items. The Beatrix Potter collections include the Linder Bequest of Beatrix Potter material (for further information contact the Frederick Warne Curator of Children's Literature, tel: 020 7602 0281, ext 212). The V&A Archive dates from the mid 1840s and includes 60,000 'registered files' many of which record the acquisition, loan and disposal of objects, and the planning of V&A exhibitions, from 1864 to date
Services: Enquiry and staffed photocopying services
Availability: Reader registration required. Appointment required for consultation of some rare material and manuscripts
Hours: 10.00–16.30 Tuesday to Thursday; closed for stocktaking for three weeks during late August and early September
Transport: Tube: Olympia, Barons Court, Hammersmith, Shepherd's Bush, West Kensington; Bus: 9, 10, 27, 28, 209 and 391

[429]
National Association of Goldsmiths
NAG

78A Luke Street
London EC2A 4XG

Borough: Hackney
Telephone: 020 7613 4445
Fax: 020 7613 4450
E-mail: nag@jewellersuk.com
World Wide Web: www.jewellers.org
Constitution: Company limited by guarantee; association with voluntary subscribing membership
Objectives/purposes: Trade association for retail jewellers in the UK and Ireland
Key staff: Librarian and Archivist: Jacqueline Van Bueren
Stock and subject coverage: The Sir James Walton Library: subject coverage includes jewellery, horology, goldsmithing, silversmithing and medals
Services: Photocopies; fax machine
Availability: Open subject to pre-booking for all bona fide researchers. Normally available only for reference, no charge made
Hours: 10.00–16.00 Monday to Friday
Transport: Tube and Rail: Old Street, Liverpool Street
Special facilities: Toilet facilities available

Linked organisations

Gemmological Association The Association holds part of the Sir James Walton Library which was divided in 1990

[430]
National Audit Office
NAO
157-197 Buckingham Palace Road
Victoria
London SW1W 9SP
Borough: Westminster
Telephone: 020 7798 7264
Fax: 020 7828 3774
E-mail: enquiries@nao.gsi.gov.uk
World Wide Web: www.nao.gov.uk
Constitution: Parliamentary body
Key staff: Information Centre Manager: Mandy Dolphin BA(Hons)
Stock and subject coverage: House of Commons and Command Papers, Hansards, Acts and Statutory Instruments. Ca. 3,000 books and 120 periodicals on audit, accountancy and public finance
Services: Loans to government libraries
Availability: Reference services to outside users by arrangement
Hours: 10.00-17.30 Monday; 09.00-17.30 Tuesday; 09.00-17.00 Wednesday to Friday
Transport: Tube: Victoria, Sloane Square; BR and coach: Victoria; Bus: C10, 11, 211, C239

[431]
The National Autistic Society
NAS
393 City Road
London EC1V 1NG
Borough: Islington
Telephone: 020 7833 2299
Fax: 020 7833 9666
E-mail: nas@nas.org.uk
World Wide Web: www.nas.org.uk
Constitution: Registered charity
Objectives/purposes: Working with parents, carers, professionals and people with autism to provide a range of services
Key staff: Information Centre Manager; Information Officer; Information Assistants
Stock and subject coverage: Small, specialised collections of books, files and journals on autism. A research information database is also available
Services: Photocopies
Availability: Open to all as a reference library, by appointment only
Hours: 10.00-16.00 Monday to Friday
Transport: Tube: King's Cross, Euston, Angel; Rail: King's Cross, Euston; Bus: 4, 19, 30, 38, 43, 56, 73, 153, 214, 274, 341
Special facilities: Toilet facilities available; access for users with disabilities - wheelchair access, ramp, lift, disabled toilet
Publications: Catalogue of publications available

Linked organisations:

Network of affiliated local societies

[432]
The National Centre for Volunteering Library
Regent's Wharf
8 All Saints Street
London N1 9RL
Borough: Islington
Telephone: 020 7520 8900
Fax: 020 7520 8910
E-mail: information@thecentre.org.uk
World Wide Web: www.volunteering.org.uk
Constitution: Registered charity and association with voluntary subscribing membership
Objectives/purposes: Aims to extend the quality, quantity, contribution and accessibility of volunteering throughout the UK; anticipate, identify and exert influence upon policies, practices and other external factors likely to affect or be affected by volunteering. Also aims to provide expert information and advice to volunteers and professionals
Key staff: Mark Restall, Kate Bowgett
Stock and subject coverage: Specialist collection of over 30,000 items, the largest of its kind in Europe. Information held includes: research papers, case studies, training material, government circulars, legislation, guides to good practice, books, journals and Volunteer Centre publications all on volunteering and related topics
Services: Reference library; photocopies; searches of own database
Availability: Open access for reference, by appointment only. Written, telephone and email enquiries accepted
Hours: 10.00-17.00 Monday to Friday
Transport: Tube and Rail: King's Cross
Special facilities: Toilet facilities available; access for users with disabilities to building, library access is restricted as too cramped for wheelchairs
Publications: Volunteering magazine (10 p.a. available by subscription); The Good Practice Guide; Safe & Alert good practice guide; National Survey of Volunteering

Linked organisations

Home Office, Active Community Unit
Supported by the Active Community Unit (Home Office, Horseferry House, London SW1P 2AW, tel: 020 7217 8400) and by members from volunteer involving organisations, companies, trusts and foundations

[433]
National Childbirth Trust Library
NCT
Alexandra House
Oldham Terrace
London W3 6NH
Borough: Ealing
Telephone: 020 8992 2616 ext 17
Fax: 0870 770 3237
World Wide Web: www.nctpregnancyandbabycare.com
Constitution: Registered charity
Objectives/purposes: The NCT offers information and support to parents and wants all parents to have an experience of pregnancy, birth and early parenthood

that enriches their lives and gives them confidence in being a parent

Key staff: Information Officer and Librarian

Stock and subject coverage: Material on pregnancy; birth; early parenthood; caesarian; homebirth; breast feeding; disabled parenting; and UK services. Collections are aimed at the interested lay person and include 2,500 books; 120 periodicals; 300 subject files; and surveys

Services: Current awareness and SDI service to members only; enquiry service for members and non-members. Cochrane Database on Pregnancy and Childbirth (on disc)

Availability: To members and others strictly by appointment only. Charge for commercial users

Hours: 09.30-17.00 Monday to Friday

Transport: Tube: Acton Town; Bus: E3, 207, 266, 607

Special facilities: Refreshment and toilet facilities available; access for users with disabilities - toilet facilities available; limited access to library

Publications: New Generation and New Digest journals; Small maternity units resources list; bibliography/resource list on pregnancy, birth and early parenthood; series of leaflets, information sheets and books

[434]
National Children's Bureau

8 Wakley Street
London EC1V 7QE
Borough: Islington
Telephone: 020 7843 6007
Fax: 020 7278 9512
E-mail: library@ncb.org.uk
World Wide Web: www.ncb.org.uk
Constitution: Registered charity
Objectives/purposes: To identify and promote the interests of all children and young people and to improve their status in a diverse society
Key staff: Head of Library and Information Service: Nicola Hilliard
Stock and subject coverage: Ca. 32,000 items including government and statistical publications, journal and grey literature on children and young people, including child health, disability and illness; children's rights; residential care; sex education; children with HIV/AIDS; and substance misuse
Services: Telephone enquiry line: 020 7843 6008, open 10.00-12.00, 14.00-16.00 Monday to Friday
Availability: Reference library open to visitors by appointment only
Hours: Personal visits: 10.00-17.00, by appointment
Transport: Tube: Angel, King's Cross; Rail: King's Cross; Bus: 19, 30, 38
Special facilities: Toilet facilities available; access for users with disabilities
Publications: Key information databases and a range of full text publications are contained on ChildData (CD-ROM/www) available on a subscription basis; Highlights (abstracts of research findings); Childstats (bimonthly digest of statistics); ChildData Abstracts; Children in the News; reading lists; organisations lists

Linked organisations
Children in Scotland
Children in Wales

[435]
National Dairy Council
NDC

5-7 John Princes Street
London W1G 0JN
Borough: Westminster
Telephone: 020 7499 7822
Fax: 020 7408 1353
E-mail: info@dairycouncil.org.uk
World Wide Web: www.milk.co.uk
Constitution: Independent non-profit distributing organisation; funded by the Milk Marketing Board and the Dairy Trade Federation
Key staff: Enquiries to: Head of Information Services
Stock and subject coverage: Information on the dairy industry; milk, cream and cheese products
Transport: Tube: Oxford Circus

Linked organisations
Milk Marketing Board
Dairy Trade Federation

[436]
National Eczema Society

Hill House
Highgate Hill
London N19 5NA
Borough: Islington
Telephone: 0870 241 3604 (helpline)
    020 7281 3553
Fax: 020 7281 6395
World Wide Web: www.eczema.org
Constitution: Registered charity
Key staff: Information Coordinator: Colette Chambers
Stock and subject coverage: Material concerning all aspects of eczema - its treatment and management
Services: Advice and information about eczema; photocopies
Availability: Material available for reference only, telephone enquiry service
Hours: 09.30-17.00 Monday to Friday
Publications: Information packs; members journal; professional booklets; and a wide range of information sheets

Linked organisations
Skin Care Campaign
Long-Term Medical Conditions Alliance
Member of both groups

[437]
National Information Centre for Speech Language Therapy
NICEST

Department of Human Communication Science
University College London
Chandler House
2 Wakefield Street
London WC1N 1PG
Borough: Camden
Telephone: 020 7679 4207
Fax: 020 7713 0861
E-mail: hcs.library@ucl.ac.uk
World Wide Web: http://library.hcs.ucl.ac.uk/

National Maritime Museum, Caird Library

Constitution: Department of a university
Objectives/purposes: The Department of Human
    Communication Science runs undergraduate,
    postgraduate and research programmes in human
    communication and speech sciences
Key staff: Site Librarian: Stevie Russell; Library
    Assistants: Breege Whiten and Sharon James
Stock and subject coverage: Ca. 6,000 books and over 200
    journals on: speech sciences; voice, psychology;
    linguistics; hearing sciences; neurology and special
    education. TEST Collection on voice, speech and
    language; collection of over 100 videos
Services: Photocopies; audiovisual resources room; online
    catalogue
Availability: Free to members of UCL; external
    membership scheme for members of the Royal
    College of Speech and Language Therapists; services
    available to non-members on payment of fees (check
    website for full details)
Hours: Term-time: 09.15-18.00 Monday; 09.15-19.00
    Tuesday, Wednesday and Thursday; 10.00-18.00
    Friday (no access to building after 17.00)
    Vacations: 09.30-17.00. Telephone before visiting the
    Library to check opening hours
Transport: Tube: Russell Square, King's Cross; Rail:
    King's Cross; Bus: 10, C11, 14, 14A, 17, 18, 30, 45,
    46, 63, 73, 77A, 214, 221, 259
Special facilities: Refreshment and toilet facilities available
    on site; access for users with disabilities – including
    lift, ramps and toilet facilities
Publications: Library Guides

Linked organisations
    **Royal College of Speech and Language
    Therapists (RCSLT)**
    University College London Library Services
    The library is a branch of UCL Library Services

[438]
National Institute of Economic and Social Research
NIESR
    2 Dean Trench Street
    Smith Square
    London SW1P 3HE
Borough: Westminster
Telephone: 020 7654 1907
Fax: 020 7654 1900
E-mail: library@niesr.ac.uk
World Wide Web: www.niesr.ac.uk
Constitution: Independent non-profit organisation;
    registered charity
Key staff: Librarian: Claire Schofield BA DipLIS
Stock and subject coverage: Statistics, journals (ca. 300
    titles), monographs and working papers on
    economics, education and training
Services: Photocopies (charges made)
Availability: To bona fide researchers, by appointment,
    for reference only
Hours: 10.00-18.00 Monday to Friday
Transport: Tube: St James's Park, Westminster; Rail:
    Victoria; Bus: C10, 507
Special facilities: Refreshment and toilet facilities available
Publications: Annual Report

[439]
National Maritime Museum
    Caird Library
    Greenwich
    London SE10 9NF
Borough: Greenwich
Telephone: 020 8312 6673
Fax: 020 8312 6599
World Wide Web: www.nmm.ac.uk
Constitution: Registered charity; part government
    funded, part engendered income

Key staff: Head of Library and Manuscripts: Jill Davies
Stock and subject coverage: 100,000 books; 20,000 pamphlets; 25,000 periodicals and serials (equivalent of bound volumes); 200 current periodicals; 2,000 reels of microfilm; CD-ROMs. Covers all aspects of maritime history. Special collections: sea and terrestrial atlases, piracy and privateering; rare books 1474-1850. UDC classification used. Manuscript collection includes Lloyds Surveys, crew lists, lieutenants' logs, personal papers, etc. The library and manuscripts catalogues are computerised and available on OPAC terminals
Services: Photocopying, microfilming, OPAC terminal, enquiries
Availability: By reader's ticket or day pass on application. Material is for reference only. Charges for research and photocopying and microfilming
Hours: 10.00-16.45 Monday to Friday; 10.00-13.00, 14.00-16.45 by appointment only on Saturdays. Closed Bank Holidays and third week in February
Transport: DLR: Cutty Sark for Maritime Greenwich; Rail: Greenwich, Maze Hill; River boats; Bus: 53, 177, 188
Services: Refreshment and toilet facilities on site; access for users with disabilities
Special features: Housed in historical complex at Greenwich, early 19th century buildings, plus 17th century royal palace and Royal Observatory Greenwich. Library itself is a listed interior
Publications: Guide to Manuscripts in the National Maritime Museum. London, Mansell, 1977-80, 2 vols; Library and Manuscripts Collections Guide

---

[440]
National Monuments Record
NMR

55 Blandford Street
London W1U 7HN
Borough: Westminster
Telephone: 020 7208 8200
Fax: 020 7224 5333
E-mail: london@rchme.co.uk
World Wide Web: www.english-heritage.org.uk/nmr
Key staff: Anne Woodward
Stock and subject coverage: Specialist library holding architectural records relating to Greater London. Historic photographs (including 75,000 on open access, browseable by the public) as well as measured drawings and written information. Information for architecture outside London and archaeology for the whole of England. Users include family and local historians, architectural consultants and the media
Services: Photocopies; cover searches
Availability: Open to all. Material is for consultation only. Charges made for photocopying/printing/reproduction of all items
Hours: 10.00-17.00 Tuesday to Friday
Transport: Tube: Oxford Circus, Bond Street, Marble Arch, Baker Street; Bus: 15
Special facilities: Toilet facilities available
Publications: Annual Report; Newsletter (3 p.a.); leaflets and user guides; monographs and general books on the NMR's work of survey and record (published by NMR/The Stationery Office)

Linked organisations
English Heritage

---

[441]
National Philatelic Society
NPS

British Philatelic Centre
107 Charterhouse Street
London EC1M 6PT
Borough: Islington
Telephone: 020 7336 0882
Fax: 020 7490 4253
E-mail: nps@ukphilately.org.uk
World Wide Web: www.ukphilately.org.uk
Constitution: Association with voluntary subscribing membership
Key staff: Librarian: Glenn H Morgan
Stock and subject coverage: Developed since 1916, there is some 1,750 linear feet of shelf space. Holdings consist of handbooks, catalogues, monographs, journals and auction catalogues relating to the hobby of stamp collecting in its many disciplines. Coverage is worldwide
Services: Photocopies, fax, microfilm and fiche readers, CD-ROM player, comb and 'easibind' binding equipment, video playback and meeting room hire
Availability: Reference services to outside users on payment of a Day Library Membership Fee (£2 per visit)
Hours: 11.00-16.45 Tuesday to Thursday; plus most Mondays and Saturdays. Call the day before (020 7336 0882) to check opening hours
Transport: Tube: Farringdon, Barbican; Rail: Farringdon
Special facilities: Tea and coffee available; toilet facilities; limited access for users with disabilities - staff will assist wherever possible
Publications: New acquisitions are listed in the Society's journal, Stamp Lover

---

[442]
National Physical Laboratory
NPL

Queens Road
Teddington
Middlesex TW11 0LW
Borough: Richmond
Telephone: 020 8943 6880
Fax: 020 8943 2155
World Wide Web: www.npl.co.uk
Constitution: Operated on behalf of the Department of Trade and Industry by NPL Management Ltd, a wholly owned subsidiary of Serco Group plc
Key staff: Head of Information Services: Sue Osborne ALA
Stock and subject coverage: 15,000 books; 500 current periodicals. Covers pure and applied physics; physical chemistry; materials science; information technology; radiation science and acoustics
Services: Loan of books and journals not available from the British Library
Availability: Open to staff of NPL and other researchers by appointment

Hours: 09.00-17.00 Monday to Wednesday; 09.00-16.30 Thursday; 09.00-16.00 Friday
Transport: Rail: Teddington
Special facilities: Refreshment and toilet facilities available; access for users with disabilities
Publications: See website for details

[443]
National Portrait Gallery, Heinz Archive and Library
St Martin's Place
London WC2H 0HE
Borough: Westminster
Telephone: 020 7306 0055 ext 257
Fax: 020 7306 0056
World Wide Web: www.npg.org.uk
Constitution: Government funded body
Objectives/purposes: The National Portrait Gallery collects portraits of famous British men and women. The Heinz Archive and Library is the prime centre for research in the field of British portraiture
Key staff: Head of Archive and Library: Robin Francis: Librarian and Study Room Manager: Antonia Leak
Stock and subject coverage: The Archive consists of extensive files of engravings, photographs and reproductions of portraits in collections worldwide. The Library contains more than 35,000 books on portraiture, history, biography, iconography, costume and related subjects and 180 journal titles, 80 of which are current. There are a number of special collections including artists' sitter books, sketch books and autograph letters. The Archive also houses the Gallery's historical records
Services: Photocopies
Availability: Open by appointment to those studying some aspect of British portraiture who cannot readily find their material elsewhere. Material is available for reference to members of the public
Hours: 11.00-17.00 Monday to Friday
Closed on Bank holidays, 24 December-1 January inclusive and for a two week stocktake period mid-August to mid-September
Transport: Tube: Leicester Square, Charing Cross; Rail: Charing Cross
Special facilities: Refreshment and toilet facilities available; access for users with disabilities - including lifts and toilet facilities

[444]
The National Society's Religious Education Centre
Church House
Great Smith Street
London SW1P 3NZ
Borough: Westminster
Telephone: 020 7898 1495/1518
Fax: 020 7898 1493
E-mail: rec@natsoc.c-of-e.org.uk
info@natsoc.c-of-e.org.uk
World Wide Web: www.natsoc.org.uk/recentre
Constitution: Independent non-profit distributing organisation; registered charity and association with voluntary subscribing membership

Objectives/purposes: Resource centre to support everyone involved in Christian and religious education. Provides information and advice for children, students, teachers, school governors, parents, clergy, diocesan and local authority education teams
Key staff: Centre Administrator: Julia Jones; Resources Officer (part-time): Angela Wright
Stock and subject coverage: Comprehensive collection of resources for religious education, Christian education, spirituality, personal and social education and moral education. The resources cover all the major world faiths. Stock includes books, journals, CD-ROMs, audio cassettes, slides and artefact collections
Services: In-service training; consultancy
Availability: Free access for all bona fide visitors. Books are available for reference only
Hours: 09.00-16.30 Monday to Friday, telephone 020 7898 1495 before visiting to make an appointment
Transport: Tube: Westminster, St James's Park; Rail: Victoria; Bus: 11, 24, 211
Special facilities: Toilet facilities; access for users with disabilities
Publications: Annual Report; catalogue of publications available on request; annual lecture series

Linked organisations
The National Society (Church of England) for Promoting Religious Education
The National Society Archive (Church of England Record Centre), 15 Galleywall Road, South Bermondsey, London SE16 3PB. Tel: 020 7222 7010 ext 4155)

[445]
National Sports Medicine Institute
NSMI
32 Devonshire Street
London W1G 6PX
Borough: Westminster
Telephone: 020 7486 3974
Fax: 020 7935 0402
E-mail: enquiry@nsmi.org.uk
World Wide Web: www.nsmi.org.uk
Constitution: Registered charity; government funded body
Key staff: Library/Information Officer: Eva Niewiadomska
Stock and subject coverage: Sports and exercise medicine and science, including exercise physiology, sport nutrition, injury prevention and treatment, biomechanics, sport psychology, use of performance enhancing substances, health and fitness and disease. Also covers different population groups such as children, women and the disabled
Services: Literature searches; photocopies (charges made); SPORTDiscus database; SMART database on sports medicine and related topics
Availability: Open to all for reference only. Membership is available for £18 per year, £12 for students (first visit is free)
Hours: 09.00-17.00 Monday, Tuesday, Thursday and Friday; 09.00-18.00 Wednesday
Transport: Tube: Baker Street
Special facilities: Toilet facilities available

Publications: List of publications available

Linked organisations

Sports Council Funded by the Sports Council

[446]
National Statistics Reference Library
ONS

Drummond Gate
London SW1V 2QQ
Borough: Westminster
Telephone: 020 7533 6266
Fax: 01633 652747
E-mail: info@ons.gov.uk
World Wide Web: www.ons.gov.uk
Key staff: Chief Librarian: John Birch
Stock and subject coverage: Collections based on the former Office of Population Censuses and Surveys in London and the Central Statistical Office in Newport. The London collection is strong in social statistics but now being expanded to include all major government statistical series whether or not they are produced by the ONS. Core collection includes all published census volumes since 1801; reports and publications of all UK Registrar Generals; government social surveys and publications on statistical collection and methodology. An international collection already strong on social statistics is being expanded
Services: Reference service; CD-ROMs including UK Census small area statistics for 1981 and 1991; photocopies (priced); shop selling most ONS and GSS titles
Availability: Open to the public for reference
Hours: 09.00-17.00 Monday to Friday
Transport: Tube: Pimlico

Linked organisations

Newport Library, Newport Gwent The Newport Library is particularly strong in the areas of business and economic statistics and has similar general collections to those in London

[447]
Natural Death Centre

20 Heber Road
London NW2 6AA
Borough: Brent
Telephone: 020 8208 2853
Fax: 020 8452 6434
E-mail: rhino@dial.pipex.com
World Wide Web: www.naturaldeath.org.uk
Key staff: Stephanie Wienrich
Constitution: Registered charity
Objectives/purposes: Provision of information on cheap, green DIY funerals and dying at home
Stock and subject coverage: Books, articles and letters on natural death
Availability: Restricted access. Researchers should apply by telephone or in writing
Hours: 10.30-17.30 Monday to Friday
Transport: Tube: Willesden Green; Rail: Cricklewood; Bus: 260

Special facilities: Toilet facilities available
Publications: Natural Death Handbook edited by N Albery, available from the Centre

Linked organisations

Institute for Social Inventions Parent charity

[448]
Natural History Museum
NHM

Cromwell Road
London SW7 5BD
Borough: Kensington and Chelsea
Telephone: 020 7942 5460
Fax: 020 7942 5559
E-mail: library@nhm.ac.uk
World Wide Web: www.nhm.ac.uk
Constitution: Government funded body
Key staff: Head of Information and Library Systems: Graham Higley, 020 7942 5261
Deputy Head of Information and Library Services and Head of Collections and Readers' Services: Christopher Mills 020 7942 5574
Botany Librarian: Malcolm Beasley, 020 7942 5220
Earth Sciences Librarians: Ann Lum/Nadera Latif-Shaikh, 020 7942 5269
Entomology Librarian: Julie Harvey, 020 7942 5241
Natural History Librarian: Carol Gokce, 020 7942 5027
Zoology Librarian: Ann Datta, 020 7942 5645
Head of IT: Len Nunn, 020 7942 5373
Head of Systems and Central Services: Neil Thomson, 020 7942 5294
Enquiries: 020 7942 5685 (Botany Library)
020 7942 5476 (Earth Sciences Library)
020 7942 5751 (Entomology Library)
020 7942 5460 (General and Zoology Libraries)
Stock and subject coverage: One million volumes. One of the finest and most complete collections of books and periodicals on natural history and allied subjects. 23,000 serial titles, of which 10,000 titles are current
Services: Photocopying services
Availability: For reference only. Reader's ticket required, access by appointment
Hours: 10.00-16.30 Monday to Friday. Closed on public and Civil Service holidays
Transport: Tube: South Kensington
Special facilities: Refreshment and toilet facilities; access for users with disabilities – lifts provide access to all libraries
Special features: To reach all four libraries readers pass through the spectacular Waterhouse Building opened in 1881 with terracotta decor and painted ceilings
Publications: Catalogue of the Books, Manuscripts, Maps and Drawings in the British Museum (Natural History), 5 vols (1903-1915); Supplement, 3 vols (1922-1940); List of Serial Publications in the BM (NH) Library (1985); A Short History of the Libraries and List of MSS and Original Drawings (1971); Compendium of the Biographical Literature on Deceased Entomologists (1977); Bulletin of the British Museum (Natural History) Historical series (1953–1991)

[449]
Netherlands British Chamber of Commerce
NBCC

307 High Holborn
London WC1V 7LS
Borough: Camden
Telephone: 020 7405 1358
Fax: 020 7831 4831
E-mail: nbcc@binternet.com
World Wide Web: www.nbcc.co.uk
Constitution: Association with voluntary subscribing membership
Stock and subject coverage: Dutch and British commercial information
Services: Photocopies, internet access, translating services, online searching, fax machines
Availability: Available to members and non-members for a fee
Hours: 09.00-17.30 Monday to Friday
Transport: Tube: Chancery Lane
Publications: In Touch journal (quarterly)

[450]
Newham (London Borough of Newham)

World Wide Web: www.newham.gov.uk
Constitution: Public library, funded by local authority
Availability:
Special features: The main library for the Borough is Stratford Library (listed first). East Ham is also a major library with lending and reference facilities

[450][a]
Stratford Library

3 The Grove
London E15 1EL
Telephone: 020 8430 6890
World Wide Web: www.newham.gov.uk
Key staff: Area Manager: Katy Hughes; Site Manager: Helen Allsop; Reference Librarian: Helen Dowling; Archivist: Richard Durack
Stock and subject coverage: Materials for loan and reference. Children's library; teenage zone; adult and reference library; archives and local studies collection for the borough
Services: Photocopies, internet services, meeting room for hire, TVs with satellite channels for the public to watch, open learning collection, skills for life collection, drugs information collection; charges for loan of AV material
Hours: 08.00-20.00 Monday and Thursday; 09.30-17.30 Tuesday, Wednesday, Friday and Saturday; 13.00-17.00 Sunday
Transport: Tube: Stratford
Special facilities: Access for users with disabilities - lift to all floors, adapted toilets, public PCs for users with disabilities

[450][b]
Beckton Library

1 Kingsford Way
London E6 5JQ
Telephone: 020 8430 4063
Key staff: Site Manager: Andrew De-Heer; Advisor: Ann Poyton, Zainab Jalil
Reference facilities: Adult and children's libraries; quick reference collection; public internet facilities; open learning collection; charges for loan of AV material
Hours: 09.30-17.30 Monday, Wednesday, Friday and Saturday; 13.00-20.00 Tuesday; 09.30-20.00 Thursday; 14.00-17.00 Sunday
Transport: DLR: Beckton
Special facilities: Access for users with disabilities

[450][c]
Canning Town Library

Barking Road
London E16 4HQ
Telephone: 020 7476 2696
Key staff: Site Manager: Jo Udall; Advisor: Michael Ward
Reference facilities: Adult and children's libraries; quick reference collection; public internet facilities; charges for loan of AV material
Hours: 09.30-17.30 Monday, Thursday, Friday and Saturday; 13.00-20.00 Tuesday
Transport: Rail and Tube: Canning Town
Special facilities: Access for users with disabilities

[450][d]
Custom House Library

Prince Regent Lane
London E16 3JJ
Telephone: 020 7476 1565
Key staff: Site Manager: Catherine Garvey
Reference facilities: Adult and children's libraries; quick reference collection; charges for loan of AV material
Hours: 13.00-20.00 Monday; 09.30-17.30 Wednesday, Friday and Saturday
Transport: BR and DLR: Custom House
Special facilities: Access for users with disabilities

[450][e]
East Ham Library

High Street South
London E6 6EL
Telephone: 020 8430 3647
Fax: 020 8503 5383
Key staff: Site Manager: David Hemmings; Advisor: Jenny Bowen; Reference Librarian: Ann Laskey
Stock and subject coverage: Adult and children's libraries; reference library
Services: Photocopies; fax machine; online search service; internet access; charges for loan of AV material
Hours: 09.30-20.00 Monday and Thursday; 09.30-18.30 Tuesday; 09.30-17.30 Wednesday, Friday and Saturday
Transport: Tube: East Ham
Special facilities: Access for users with disabilities - including disabled toilet facilities; wheelchair lift to reference library

[450][f]
Forest Gate Library

Woodgrange Road
London E7 0QH
Telephone: 020 8534 6952
Key staff: Site Manager: Mandy Newman

Reference facilities: Adult and children's libraries; quick
    reference collection; charges for loan of AV material
Hours: 09.00–17.30 Monday, Thursday, Friday and
    Saturday; 13.00–20.00 Tuesday
Transport: Rail: Forest Gate

[450][g]
Green Street Library

337–41 Green Street
London E13 9AR
Telephone: 020 8472 4101
Fax: 020 8472 0927
Key staff: Site Manager: Gurdip Ahadi
Reference facilities: Adult and children's libraries; quick
    reference collection; charges for loan of AV material
Hours: 09.30–17.30 Monday, Tuesday, Wednesday, Friday
    and Saturday; 13.00–20.00 Thursday; 14.00–17.00
    Sunday
Transport: Tube: Upton Park
Special facilities: Access for users with disabilities

[450][h]
Manor Park Library

Romford Road
London E12 5JY
Telephone: 020 8478 1177
Key staff: Site Manager: Mark Blair; Advisor: Angeli Das
Reference facilities: Adult and children's libraries; quick
    reference collection; public internet facilities
Hours: 09.30–17.30 Monday, Tuesday, Friday and
    Saturday; 13.00–20.00 Thursday
Transport: Rail: Manor Park

[450][i]
North Woolwich Library

(at St John's Centre)
London E16 2JD
Telephone: 020 7511 2387
Key staff: Site Manager: Leslie Pickard
Reference facilities: Adult and children's libraries; quick
    reference collection; charges for loan of AV material
Hours: 09.30–13.30, 14.30–18.30 Monday and Tuesday,
    13.00–17.00, 17.30–20.00 Thursday; 09.30–13.30,
    14.30–17.30 Friday; 09.30–13.30 Saturday
Transport: Rail: North Woolwich
Special facilities: Access for users with disabilities

[450][j]
Plaistow Library

North Street
London E13 9HL
Telephone: 020 8472 0420
Fax: 020 8471 3148
Key staff: Site Manager: Eileen Norris; Advisor: Julie
    Priest; Community Outreach: Pat Lloyd
Reference facilities: Adult and children's libraries; quick
    reference collection; public internet facilities; charges
    for loan of AV material
Hours: 09.30–17.30 Monday, Wednesday, Friday and
    Saturday; 13.00–20.00 Thursday
Transport: Tube: Plaistow
Special facilities: Access for users with disabilities

[451]
Nigeria High Commission Library

Nigeria High Commission
9 Northumberland Avenue
London WC2N 5BX
Telephone: 020 7839 1244
Fax: 020 7839 8746
E-mail: library@nigeriahighcommissionuk.com
World Wide Web: www.nigeriahighcommissionuk.com
Constitution: Diplomatic Mission
Objectives/purposes: Reference library exists primarily to
    support the work of the High Commission
Key staff: Chief Librarian: Anthony Adeloye ALA, MPhil,
    MIInfSc
Stock and subject coverage: Federal Republic of Nigeria
    publications, e.g. government gazettes, trade
    directories and a wide range of general educational
    and cultural materials on Nigeria. Collection of
    monthly and annual reports of a number of key
    parastatals and regulatory bodies in Nigeria
Services: Photocopies
Availability: Admission by appointment only, for
    reference use
Hours: 10.00–17.00 Monday to Friday, by appointment
Transport: Tube: Embankment, Charing Cross; Rail:
    Charing Cross; Bus: any bus stopping at Trafalgar
    Square
Special facilities: Toilet facilities available
Publications: Guide to Library Services (annual);
    Accession List

[452]
North London Postgraduate Medical Centre Library

St Ann's Hospital
St Ann's Road
Tottenham
London N15 3TH
Borough: Haringey
Telephone: 020 8442 4220/4271
Fax: 020 8442 6725
E-mail: nol@claramail.com
Constitution: Department of a university
Key staff: Karen Galber
Stock and subject coverage: Small collection with the main
    emphasis being psychoanalysis and psychotherapy. It
    also has a collection of psychiatric books. Specialist
    areas are eating disorders and transcultural psychiatry
Services: Photocopies; CD-ROM searching: Medline and
    ClinPsyc (charged, contact the Librarian for costs)
Availability: Not open to members of the public. Bona
    fide students may apply to the Librarian for reference
    use. There is a day membership charge
Hours: 09.00–16.00 Monday to Friday; visitors should
    contact the Library before paying a visit
Transport: Tube: Turnpike Lane, Manor House; Bus: 67
    (Turnpike Lane) and 171A (Manor House)
Special facilities: Refreshment and toilet facilities available;
    access for users with disabilities – good wheelchair
    access

Linked organisations

**University of London, British Postgraduate
Medical Federation** Part of the University
Haringey Healthcare NHS Trust Part of the Trust

[453]
Northern Ireland Office
NIO
11 Millbank
London SW1P 4PN
Borough: Westminster
Telephone: 020 7210 0253
Fax: 020 7210 0208
Constitution: Government department
Key staff: Head of Library: Roger Smethurst
Stock and subject coverage: Books, pamphlets, etc. on Northern Ireland matters
Availability: Available to government officers only; no loans
Hours: 09.30-12.30, 13.30-16.30 Monday to Friday
Transport: Tube and Rail: Westminster

[454]
The Novartis Foundation
(formerly The Ciba Foundation)
41 Portland Place
London W1B 1BN
Borough: Westminster
Telephone: 020 7636 9456
Fax: 020 7436 2840
E-mail: dchadwick@novartisfound.org.uk
World Wide Web: www.novartisfound.org.uk
Constitution: Registered charity and independent non-profit organisation
Key staff: Director: Dr DJ Chadwick; Deputy Director: Dr GR Bock
Stock and subject coverage: Ca. 1,000 textbooks and 700 biographies in biomedical science; major journals in biomedicine. All Ciba and Novartis Foundation publications (ca. 450 volumes)
Services: Photocopies
Availability: Open, for reference only, to graduates in science or medicine. Researchers should telephone in advance of visiting
Hours: 09.00-17.00 Monday to Friday
Transport: Tube: Great Portland Street, Oxford Circus, Regent's Park; Bus: C2, 88
Special facilities: Toilet facilities available; access for users with disabilities
Special features: Library housed in Grade II★ Adam-style building constructed in the 18th century
Publications: Annual Report and Handbook; email bulletin; eight Symposium volumes per year

[455]
NSPCC
(National Society for the Prevention of Cruelty to Children)
42 Curtain Road
London EC2A 3NH
Borough: Hackney
Telephone: 020 7825 2706 (Library enquiries)
Fax: 020 7825 2706
E-mail: library@nspcc.org.uk
World Wide Web: www.nspcc.org.uk
Constitution: Registered charity
Key staff: Head of Library and Information Service: Catherine Tite and Karen Childs Smith

Stock and subject coverage: Over 8,000 books, pamphlets and packs on child protection, abuse, therapies and child/social welfare. Over 20,000 articles indexed. 100 journals. NSPCC archive
Services: Reference and enquiry services. Literature searches of in-house database; photocopies and current awareness (charges made)
Availability: Loans to NSPCC staff and via the BL interlending scheme. By appointment to child protection workers, childcare practitioners and researchers
Hours: 09.30-16.30 Monday to Friday, by appointment only
Transport: Tube: Liverpool Street, Moorgate, Old Street; Rail: Liverpool Street, Moorgate
Special facilities: Toilet facilities available; access for users with disabilities
Publications: Statistics, research and practice publications; bibliographies; various publications for sale

[456]
Nuffield Council on Bioethics
28 Bedford Square
London WC1B 3PS
Borough: Camden
Telephone: 020 7681 9619
Fax: 020 7637 1712
Constitution: Independent non-profit distributing organisation
Objectives/purposes: To identify and define ethical questions raised by recent advances in biological and medical research, and to publish reports
Key staff: Director: Dr Sandy Thomas; Assistant Directors: Susan Bull, Tor Lezemore; Research Officer: Yvonne Melia; Public Liaison Officer: Nicola Perrin; PA to the Secretariat: Julia Fox; Secretary: Amanda Jones; Research Assistant: Maria Gonzalez-Nogal
Stock and subject coverage: Includes a library of files on biological and medical topics containing cuttings from the major journals and daily press, with some dating back to 1990 and additionally, a collection of texts and reports relating to bioethics
Availability: Bona fide researchers upon prior appointment. Materials are for reference only
Hours: 10.00-16.00 Monday to Friday
Transport: Tube: Tottenham Court Road, Goodge Street
Publications: Annual Report; Genetic Screening: Ethical Issues; Human Tissue: Ethical and Legal Issues; Animal-to-Human Transplants: the Ethics of Xenotransplantation; Mental Disorders and Genetics: the Ethical Context; Genetically Modified Crops: Ethical and Social Issues; The Ethics of Clinical Research in Developing Countries: A Discussion Paper; Stem Cell Therapy: Ethical Issues: A Discussion Paper

[457]
Oak Hill College Library
Chase Side
Southgate
London N14 4PS
Borough: Barnet
Telephone: 020 8449 0467 ext 253

Fax: 020 8441 5996
E-mail: wendyb@oakhill.ac.uk
World Wide Web: www.oakhill.ac.uk
Constitution: Church of England theological college
Key staff: Librarian: Wendy Bell
Stock and subject coverage: Ca. 30,000 books and 200
    journals on all aspects of theology: world religions,
    church history, biblical studies, doctrine, practical
    theology, plus some philosophy, history, sociology and
    languages
Services: Photocopies; internet access
Availability: Free reference facilities. £50 annual fee for
    borrowing subject to the Librarian's discretion
Hours: 09.00–17.00 Monday to Friday
Transport: Tube: Southgate
Special facilities: Refreshment and toilet facilities; access
    for users with disabilities

[458]
Occupational and Environmental Diseases Association
OEDA

Ground Floor, Rear Office
Mitre House
66 Abbey Road
Bush Hill Park
Enfield
Middlesex EN1 2QH
Borough: Enfield
Telephone: 020 8360 6413
Fax: 020 8360 6413
Constitution: Registered charity
Key staff: Information Officer: Mrs Nancy Tait MBE
    Hon DUniv (Southampton)
Stock and subject coverage: Early papers on the risks of
    asbestos and action taken to control them
Services: Photocopies (charges made); advice service;
    electron microscope unit
Availability: Researchers by appointment
Hours: 09.30–14.30 for telephone enquiries
Transport: Rail: Bush Hill Park
Special facilities: Toilet facilities available

[459]
Office of Fair Trading Library and Information Centre
OFT

Fleetbank House
2-6 Salisbury Square,
London EC4Y 8JX
Borough: Corporation of London
Telephone: 020 7211 8938
Fax: 020 7211 8940
E-mail: enquiries@oft.gov.uk
World Wide Web: www.oft.gov.uk
Constitution: Government department
Key staff: Head of Library and Information Services:
    Martin Shrive, tel 020 7211 8941
Stock and subject coverage: Printed and electronic materials
    in the fields of consumer affairs, consumer credit and
    competition policy
Services: Research and intelligence to OFT staff; loans of
    material to other government departments

Hours: 09.00–17.15 Monday to Friday (closes 17.00 on
    Friday)

[460]
Office of Gas and Electricity Markets
Ofgem

9 Millbank
London SW1P 3GE
Borough: Westminster
Telephone: 020 7901 7000 (switchboard)
    020 7901 7332/7119 (Library public enquiry lines)
Fax: 020 7901 7066
E-mail: library@ofgem.gov.uk
World Wide Web: www.ofgem.gov.uk
Constitution: Government funded body
Key staff: Librarian: Beryl Scott; Assistant Librarian:
    Michael Pudham; Library Assistant: Paul Dunneen
Stock and subject coverage: Books and serials on UK gas
    and electricity industries, economies, regulation,
    energy use and efficiency, renewables. Growing
    collection of European and other countries gas and
    electricity industries. Public register of all gas and
    electricity licences
Services: Photocopies (charges made); loans through the
    British Library Document Supply Centre
Availability: Other Government departments and bona
    fide researchers
Hours: Open to visitors 14.00–16.30 Monday to Friday
    (24 hours notice required); public enquiry telephone
    lines: 14.00–16.30
Transport: Tube: Westminster: Bus: 3, 77a, 88
Special facilities: Toilet facilities available; access for users
    with disabilities
Publications: Annual Report; consultation and decision
    documents, Ofgem plan and budget, publications list

Linked organisations
Ofgem was formed from the amalgamation of Ofgas
(Office of Gas Supply) and Offer (Office for
Electricity Regulation)

[461]
Office of Health Economics
OHE

12 Whitehall
London SW1A 2DY
Borough: Westminster
Telephone: 020 7930 3477
Fax: 020 7747 1447
E-mail: ccoomber@abpi.org.uk
World Wide Web: www.abpi.org.uk
Key staff: Librarian: Caroline Coomber
Constitution: Research organisation
Stock and subject coverage: Joint library between OHE and
    the Association of the British Pharmaceutical
    Industry. Ca. 600 books and 200 journals covering
    economics, health, general medicine and pharmacy
Services: Interlibrary loans and photocopies
Availability: Not usually open to external users.
    Enquiries from other libraries welcome. Loans only
    through libraries
Hours: 10.00–16.00 Monday to Friday

Transport: Tube and Rail: Charing Cross; Bus: 3, 11, 12, 24, 53, X53, 77A, 88, 91, 109, 139, 159
Special facilities: Toilet facilities available
Publications: Details of OHE publications available from the OHE Secretary (not the Library)

Linked organisations

Association of the British Pharmaceutical Industry (ABPI) Funded by ABPI

[462]
Office of Telecommunications
Oftel

Export House
50 Ludgate Hill
London EC4M 7JJ
Borough: Corporation of London
Telephone: 020 7634 8761 (Enquiries, loans, publications)
Fax: 020 7634 8946
Government Telecommunications Network: 3828
World Wide Web: www.oftel.gov.uk
Constitution: Government department
Key staff: Head of Research and Information: Anne Cameron
Stock and subject coverage: A specialised collection of books, serials and standards in the fields of telecommunications, information technology, competition and consumer protection. The Library also houses the Public Registers of licences and approvals and acts as a sales point for priced publications
Services: Loans usually through the British Library; photocopying facilities
Availability: Other government departments; the Public Register is open to the public during office hours, by appointment only
Hours: 09.30-12.00, 14.00-16.00 Monday to Friday
Transport: Tube: St Pauls, Blackfriars; Rail: Blackfriars; Bus: 4, 11, 23, 26, 76, 172
Special facilities: Toilet facilities available; access for users with disabilities – disabled toilet close to library
Publications: List of Telecommunications Licences; Monthly Publication list; Oftel News (4 p.a.); consultations and statements all available via the web

Linked organisations

Department of Trade and Industry Information and Library Services The Library operates as part of the DTI Information and Library Services

[463]
Office of the Deputy Prime Minister and Department for Transport
ODPM-DFT

Constitution: Government department
Borough: Westminster
World Wide Web: www.dft.gov.uk
www.odpm.gov.uk

[463][a]
Ashdown House (Victoria) Library and Information Centre

Zone 2/H24
Ashdown House
London SW1E 6DE
Telephone: 020 7944 3039
Fax: 020 7944 6098
Key staff: Information Sources and Services Chief Librarian: Sue Westcott MA DipLib ALA; Library and Information Centres Manager: Clare Gibson BA MA; ISS Communication Registry and LIC Support Services: Ann Layton BA
Stock and subject coverage: All aspects of the work of the Department are covered
Availability: Open to staff, and by appointment to other government departments and to researchers needing to consult materials not available elsewhere
Hours: 09.00-17.00 Monday to Friday
Transport: Tube: Victoria; St James's Park; Rail: Victoria

[463][b]
Eland House Library and Information Centre

Zone 1/F8
Eland House
Bressenden Place
London SW1E 5DU
Telephone: 020 7944 3199
Fax: 020 7944 3189
Stock and subject coverage: All aspects of the work of the Department are covered, including housing, regeneration, local and regional government and planning
Availability: As Headquarters Information Centre
Hours: 09.00-17.00 Monday to Friday
Transport: Tube: Victoria, St James's Park; Rail: Victoria

[463][c]
Great Minster Library and Information Centre

Zone 1/10
Great Minster House
76 Marsham Street
London SW1P 4DR
Telephone: 020 7944 2002
Fax: 020 7944 4716
Stock and subject coverage: All aspects of the work of the Department are covered, including integrated transport, roads and local transport, railways, aviation, logistics and maritime
Availability: As headquarters Information Centre
Hours: 09.00-17.00 Monday to Friday
Transport: Tube: Victoria, St James's Park; Rail: Victoria

[464]
One Plus One Marriage and Partnership Research

The Wells
7-15 Rosebery Avenue
London EC1R 4SP
Telephone: 020 7841 3660
Fax: 020 7841 3670
E-mail: info@oneplusone.org.uk

World Wide Web: www.oneplusone.org.uk
Constitution: Marriage and parnership research charity
Key staff: Information Officer: Fiona Hovsepian
Stock and subject coverage: The information resource includes 1,500 books and pamphlets, 500 offprints and reference materials detailing statistical trends in the UK and Europe. Key journals include: Journal of Social and Personal Relationships, Journal of Marriage and the family, Journal of Family Issues, Family Relations, Journal of Family Psychology, Personal Relationships, Family Matters. The collection is international, but with a concentration on trends within the UK
Services: Photocopies (5p per sheet)
Availability: Visitors are charged at a basic rate of £5 per half day.
Hours: 10.00–16.00 Monday to Friday by prior appointment
Special facilities: Refreshment and toilet facilities available
Publications: Annual reports, information packs and research publications, quarterly research magazine
Note: One plus One was set up in 1971 as the Marriage Research Centre

[465]
Open University Validation Services
OUVS
344-54 Gray's Inn Road
London WC1X 8BP
Borough: Camden
Telephone: 020 7278 4411
Fax: 020 7833 1012
E-mail: s.j.cooksey@open.ac.uk
Constitution: Department of a university
Objectives/purposes: To maintain and make available certain of the records and publications of the former Council for National Academic Awards (CNAA)
Key staff: Stephen Cooksey
Stock and subject coverage: OUVS holds awards records of the former CNAA and records of approved CNAA courses and institutions (1964-1992), including the structure and curriculum content of courses. These records are on microfilm. OUVS holds a hard copy reference set of all CNAA publications (but not research degree theses) including annual reports, course directories, subject review and research project publications
Services: Photocopies, fax machine
Availability: Free access on application only. Material is available for reference on site but not for loan. Printed pages from microfilms charged at cost per page
Hours: 09.00–17.00 Monday to Friday, by appointment only
Transport: Tube: King's Cross; Rail: King's Cross, St Pancras
Special facilities: Refreshment and toilet facilities; access for users with disabilities

[466]
Orleans House Gallery
Riverside
Twickenham
Middlesex TW1 3DJ
Borough: Richmond upon Thames
Telephone: 020 8892 0221
Fax: 020 8744 0501
E-mail: galleryinfo@richmond.gov.uk
 m.denovelis@richmond.gov.uk
World Wide Web: www.richmond.gov.uk/depts/opps/ leisure/arts/orleanshouse
Constitution: Local authority funded
Objectives/purposes: To promote knowledge, understanding and enjoyment of the Gallery's collections to visitors and residents of the Borough
Key staff: Acting Curator: Rachel Tranter; Assistant Curator: Mark De Novellis
Stock and subject coverage: Extensive collection of resource material including: topographical prints, oils and watercolours of scenes and images from Richmond upon Thames, ephemera and collections relating to Twickenham
Services: Photocopies; fax machine
Availability: Facilities available on request; visits free of charge
Hours: 13.00–17.30 Tuesday to Saturday; 13.00–16.30 Sundays and bank holidays
 October to March: 13.00–16.30 Tuesday to Saturday; 14.00–16.30 Sundays and bank holidays
Transport: Tube: Richmond; Rail: St Margarets, Twickenham; Bus: H22, R68, R70, 33, 90, 290 (buses from Richmond); car parking space within grounds
Special facilities: Refreshment facilities; toilet and baby changing facilities; partial access for users with disabilities - includes ramp access and toilet facilities, guide dogs welcome
Special features: Octagon room designed by James Gibbs ca. 1720, for Queen Caroline wife of George II, with stunning Baroque interior (hall available for hire)
 Stables Gallery (behind the Orleans House Gallery) open April-November with same opening hours as main gallery
Publications: Exhibition catalogues; lists of works and catalogue of permanent collection (photocopied)

Linked organisations
London Borough of Richmond upon Thames
The Gallery is part of the Borough's Education, Arts and Leisure Department

[467]
Overseas Development Institute
ODI
111 Westminster Bridge Road
London SE1 7JD
Borough: Lambeth
Telephone: 020 7922 0343
Fax: 020 7922 0399
E-mail: library@odi.org.uk
World Wide Web: www.odi.org.uk
Constitution: Registered charity
Key staff: Librarian: Kate Kwafo-Akoto MA DipLib FLA
Stock and subject coverage: The ODI's Library is transforming from being a predominantly document based library into a largely electronically based information centre. About 16,000 documents including, books, CD-ROMs, electronic journals, periodicals and research working and discussion papers. Subject coverage includes macroeconomics,

Orleans House Gallery, Octagon Room

trade, finance, aid, humanitarian policy, poverty, politics and rural resource management (including water resources, pastoral development, rural development forestry and agricultural research and extension). Rural resource management holdings are supplemented by a special collection of grey literature, around 2,000 items, assembled by the agriculture and forestry networks supported by ODI. The Library also holds a substantial collection of materials on Non Governmental Organisations

Services: Limited photocopying facilities available

Availability: A limited research facility maintained primarily for staff. Open to bona fide researchers for reference only. Access for visitors is by prior appointment only and they must be able to specify the material they plan to use

Hours: 10.00–17.00 Monday to Friday

Transport: Tube: Waterloo, Lambeth North; Rail: Waterloo

Special facilities: Toilet facilities; access for users with disabilities

---

[468]
Paint Research Association
Waldegrave Road
Teddington
Middlesex TW11 8LD

Borough: Richmond upon Thames
Telephone: 020 8614 4800
Fax: 020 8943 4705
E-mail: library@pra.org.uk
World Wide Web: www.pra.org.uk
Constitution: Independent non-profit organisation
Key staff: Librarian: Miss SC Haworth BSc MA ALA, ext 818
Stock and subject coverage: 7,000 books, 350 current periodicals; also patents, standards, specifications, reports, conference proceedings, preprints and trade literature. Covers science and technology of surface coatings, pigments, oils, resins and polymers; paint application; health and safety; hazards and toxicity; legislation and regulations; pollution problems; paint defects; corrosion and fouling; protection and preservation of building materials such as concrete, masonry and wood; chemistry, spectroscopy, rheology; colour science and colorimetry; physical testing methods; microbiology; biodeterioration; techno-commercial information
Services: Enquiry service; photocopies; SDI profiles; literature searches generally available; and loans to members only
Availability: Intended primarily for members of the Association, but services also available to non-members by arrangement, usually for a fee
Hours: 08.45–17.15 Monday to Friday

Transport: Rail: Teddington; Bus: 33, 68A, 281, 285
Publications: World Surface Coatings Abstracts (monthly);
   SDI profiles and computerised literature searches on
   demand; Paint Titles (weekly current awareness
   bulletin); Emulsion Polymerisation and Polymer
   Emulsions (monthly); Recent Advances in
   Crosslinking and Curing (6 p.a.); Coatings COMET
   (monthly); CORE - Coatings, Regulations and the
   Environment (monthly); SHE Alert (monthly);
   Coatings COMET - Coatings Markets and
   Economic Trends (monthly). Special publications and
   business information online for the coatings industry.
   Latest list available on request

[469]
Parkinson's Disease Society of the United Kingdom
PDS
   215 Vauxhall Bridge Road
   London SW1V 1EJ
Borough: Westminster
Telephone: 020 7931 8080
   0808 800 0303 (Freephone helpline, available 09.30-
   17.30 Monday to Friday)
Fax: 020 7233 9908
E-mail: enquiries@parkinsons.org.uk
World Wide Web: www.parkinsons.org.uk
Constitution: Independent non-profit organisation,
   registered charity and association with voluntary
   subscribing membership
Key staff: Information Officer: Helen Barber
Stock and subject coverage: Books, journals and other
   material on Parkinson's, neurology, some material on
   caring, ageing and disability
Availability: Open to anyone with an interest in
   Parkinson's, for reference only
Hours: 09.00-17.00 Monday to Friday
Transport: Tube and Rail: Victoria
Special facilities: Toilet facilities; access for users with
   disabilities - small lift available
Publications: Publications lists available

[470]
Partnership House Mission Studies Library
   World Mission Association Ltd
   Partnership House
   157 Waterloo Road
   London SE1 8XA
Borough: Southwark
Telephone: 020 7803 3215
Fax: 020 7928 3627
E-mail: phmslib@FreeNet.co.uk
World Wide Web: http:///phmsl.soutron.com
Constitution: Registered charity
Objectives/purposes: To provide a library service for the
   member societies of the Partnership for World
   Mission
Key staff: Librarian: Colin Rowe; Assistant Librarian:
   Elizabeth Williams
Stock and subject coverage: The Library was formed in
   1988 by bringing together the post-1945 collections
   of USPG and CMS. CMS' pre-1945 collection (Max
   Warren Collection) is also in the Library. The

collections contain about 25,000 books and more
than 300 current journals. Subjects covered include
the work of the church worldwide, particularly areas
of USPG and CMS involvement. It includes church
history, biographies, social and economic concerns,
history and theology of mission, and other religions.
There is also a wide-ranging reference collection
Services: Photocopies
Availability: Open to all interested in Christian mission.
   Loan of books free to staff, missionaries and council
   members of PWM societies. Members of the public
   may borrow books on payment of an annual
   subscription fee
Hours: 09.30-17.00 Monday to Friday
Transport: Tube: Waterloo, Lambeth North; Rail:
   Waterloo, Waterloo East; Bus: 1, 4, 5, 68, 70, 76, 149,
   155, 171, 176, 177, 188, 199, 501, 502, 505, 507, 511,
   513, 555
Special facilities: Drinks machine available, staff canteen
   can be used by prior arrangement; toilet facilities
   available; access for users with disabilities
Publications: Library Guide; Library Bulletin (monthly)
   giving news, list of new books and journal abstracts

Linked organisations
   **Birmingham University Library (CMS -
   Church Missionary Society - Archives)**
   **Rhodes House Library, Oxford University
   (USPG - United Society for the Propagation
   of the Gospel - Archives)**
   USPG's pre-1945 book collection is housed at
   Rhodes House Library

[471]
Paul Mellon Centre for Studies in British Art
   16 Bedford Square
   London WC1B 3JA
Borough: Camden
Telephone: 020 7580 0311
Fax: 020 7636 6730
E-mail: library@paul-mellon-centre.ac.uk
World Wide Web: www.paul-mellon-centre.ac.uk
Constitution: Educational charity
Objectives/purposes: Established to promote and support
   the study of British history of art and architecture,
   the Centre provides a reference library and a
   photographic archive
Key staff: Librarian: Emma Floyd; Photo Archivist:
   Emma Lauze
Stock and subject coverage: The library covers British
   painting, sculpture, drawing and architecture from the
   16th to the mid 20th century. Ca. 12,000 books,
   pamphlets and exhibition catalogues and 120
   periodicals (50 current) on art, architecture and
   garden history. There are a large number of books on
   British painters, sculptors, illustrators, architects and
   landscape gardeners as well as many general books on
   the art and architecture of the period. The collection
   also includes major reference sources; multi-volume
   sets of 17th-19th century letters, diaries and collected
   works; collection catalogues of British arts; auction
   catalogues; and guides to British country houses and
   notable historic gardens

The Centre also houses the working papers of some distinguished historians of British art and architecture, including Dr Robert Raines' papers relating to foreign artists working in England in the 18th century and Sir Brinsley Ford's archive relating to British and Irish visitors to Italy in the 18th century

Photographic Archive of over 80,000 black and white reference photographs of British paintings, decorative painting, sculpture, drawings and prints covering the period 1500-1900 with particular emphasis on the 18th century

Services: Photocopies; computer catalogue; readers can use their own laptop computers in the main library

Availability: Open to scholars and research students for reference only

Hours: Library and Photographic Archive open 09.30-17.30 Monday to Friday

Transport: Tube: Tottenham Court Road, Russell Square, Goodge Street

Linked organisations

Yale Center for British Art, New Haven, Connecticut, USA Affiliated to the Centre

[472]
Percival David Foundation of Chinese Art

53 Gordon Square
London WC1H 0PD
Borough: Camden
Telephone: 020 7387 3909
Fax: 020 7383 5163
E-mail: sp17@soas.ac.uk
Constitution: Collection of Chinese ceramics administered for London University by the School of Oriental and African Studies
Key staff: Curator: Stacy Pierson; Administrator: Elizabeth Jackson
Stock and subject coverage: Important reference library on Chinese ceramics
Availability: Use of Library chargeable. Permission to use the library should be sought in advance by writing to the curator
Hours: 10.30-13.00, 14.00-16.45 Monday to Friday
Transport: Tube: Euston Square, Russell Square
Special facilities: Cloakroom
Publications: Full list of publications available

Linked organisations

School of Oriental and African Studies, University of London Administered by SOAS

[473]
Peter Warlock Society

32A Chipperfield House
Cale Street
London SW3 3SA
Borough: Kensington and Chelsea
Telephone: 020 7589 9595
Fax: 020 7589 9595
E-mail: mrudland@talk21.com
Constitution: Registered charity

Objectives/purposes: To widen interest in the music and life of Peter Warlock
Key staff: Malcolm Rudland
Stock and subject coverage: Central Office of Information for the Peter Warlock Society. Much material is stocked at other private residences so visitors should telephone in advance
Services: Photocopies
Availability: Open to all, materials available for photocopying, some charges for hire of material
Hours: By appointment
Transport: Tube: South Kensington; Bus: 11, 14, 49
Special facilities: Refreshment and toilet facilities available
Publications: Newsletter (2 p.a.)

[474]
The Poetry Library

Royal Festival Hall
South Bank Centre
London SE1 8XX
Borough: Lambeth
Telephone: 020 7921 0943/0664
Fax: 020 7921 0939
E-mail: info@poetrylibrary.org.uk
World Wide Web: www.poetrylibrary.org.uk
Constitution: Independent non-profit reference and loan library; registered charity. Founded by the Arts Council
Key staff: Librarian: Mary Enright
Stock and subject coverage: Unique library of 20th Century poetry in the English language. Ca. 60,000 volumes (including translations into English); comprehensive collection of all poetry published in the UK since 1912; also a large stock of international poetry; poetry on cassette, record and video; magazines; a children's section; poster and card poems; and press cuttings
Services: Loans; reference facilities; interlibrary loans; telephone and postal enquiries; information service; computerised catalogue and index; CD-ROMs on poetry on public access; special database on 20th century poetry
Availability: Available to all; membership free to UK residents. To join visitors should bring proof of identity and of permanent home address
Hours: 11.00-20.00 Tuesday to Sunday, closed Mondays
Transport: Tube: Waterloo, Embankment; Rail: Waterloo; Bus: buses to Waterloo Station/Bridge
Special facilities: Refreshment and toilet facilities; access for users with disabilities; audiotapes for the blind, available by post or to personal callers
Publications: Library guides; teacher's information file; current awareness lists

[475]
Policy Studies Institute
PSI

100 Park Village East
Camden
London NW1 3SR
Borough: Camden
Telephone: 020 7468 0468
Fax: 020 7388 0914

E-mail: library@psi.org.uk
World Wide Web: www.psi.org.uk
Constitution: Non-profit research institute. A wholly owned subsidiary of the University of Westminster
Key staff: Librarian: post vacant
Stock and subject coverage: Small book stock covering all aspects of social policy. Some foreign material. Statistics collection
Services: Interlibrary loans only. Photocopying facilities
Availability: Open to all, but please contact the Librarian before visiting
Hours: 09.30-17.30 (approximately), Monday to Friday
Transport: Tube: Euston, Euston Square, Mornington Crescent, Camden, Warren Street, Great Portland Street; Rail: Euston; Bus: 24, 27, 29, 134, 135
Special facilities: Cold drinks machine; toilet facilities; access for users with disabilities – including ramped entrance, lift to the Library floor, disabled toilet on ground floor (access to stack area difficult)

[476]
Polish Cultural Institute
34 Portland Place
London W1N 4HQ
Borough: Westminster
Telephone: 020 7636 6032/3/4
Fax: 020 7637 2190
E-mail: pci@polishculture.org.uk
World Wide Web: www.polishculture.org.uk
Constitution: Government funded body
Objectives/purposes: To promote cultural activities
Key staff: Director: Joanna Stachyro
Stock and subject coverage: Minimal reference library, small lending library, videocassettes, newspapers, CD, tapes and records and photographs
Services: Photocopies
Availability: Free access to all
Hours: 12.00-16.00 Monday to Wednesday; 16.00-20.00 Thursday; 12.00-16.00 Friday
Transport: Tube: Oxford Circus, Regent's Park
Special facilities: Toilet facilities available

[477]
Polish Institute and Sikorski Museum
PISM
20 Princes Gate
London SW7 1PT
Borough: Kensington and Chelsea
Telephone: 020 7589 9249
Constitution: Registered charity
Objectives/purposes: Collecting and making available for research archive materials on Poland in WW2. Educational and cultural role promoted through public museum
Key staff: Chairman: Ryszard Dembinski; Hon Curator: Krzysztof Barbarski; Keeper of Archives: Andrzej Suchcitz; Keeper of Photographic Library: Elzbieta Barbarska; Head of Film/Video Library: Jerzy Ciaglinski; Sound Archive: Waclaw J Fiedler
Stock and subject coverage: Archives: covering mainly WW2. Materials include Polish Government in exile papers, as well as those of the Polish Armed Forces

1939-1947. Over 470 collections of private papers belonging to: politicians, military personnel, diplomats, writers, scientists, Polish exiled activists. Photographic Library: Over 200,000 photographs, primarily concerning Poland during WW2. Film Library: Over 1,000 films illustrating Poland's role in WW2
Services: Photocopies
Availability: Access to all bona fide researchers with restrictions on certain groups. Materials are for reference use only
Hours: Archives: 10.30-16.00 Tuesday to Friday
Transport: Tube: South Kensington, Knightsbridge; Bus: 9, 10, 52
Special facilities: Toilet facilities available
Publications: Annual Report (in Polish and English); ten books of documents from the Archive in the Materialy series; Guide to the Archives of the Polish Institute and Sikorski Museum, 1985 vol. 1 by W Milewski, A Suchcitz and A Gorczycki; photographic albums about General Sikorski, General Anders, General Maczek and General Sosabowski

Linked organisations
Polish Historical Institution Limited
Polish Underground Movement (1939-1945) Study Trust
Polish Armed Forces Historical Commission (Ealing Branch) The Commission publishes books and a journal and has a small library collection (19 Woodville Gardens, London W5 2LL, tel: 020 8997 7965)
All amalgamated with the Polish Institute and Sikorski Museum

[477][a]
Polish Institute and Sikorski Museum Library
11 Leopold Road
London W5 3PB
Borough: Ealing
Telephone: 020 8992 6057
Key staff: Aleksander J Szkuta
Stock and subject coverage: Collection of ca. 23,000 books in Polish on history and politics
Hours: 12.00-16.00 Tuesday to Thursday
Transport: Tube: Ealing Common
Special facilities: Toilet facilities available

[477][b]
Polish Underground Movement (1939-45) Study Trust
11 Leopold Road
London W5 3PB
Borough: Ealing
Telephone: 020 8992 6057
Key staff: Keeper of Archives: Andrzej Suchcitz
Stock and subject coverage: Archive relating to the activities of the Armia Krajowa (Polish Home Army), including the Warsaw Uprising of 1944
Hours: 10.00-15.30 Monday to Thursday
Transport: Tube: Ealing Common
Special facilities: Toilet facilities available

[478]
The Polish Library
238-246 King Street
London W6 0RF
Borough: Hammersmith and Fulham
Telephone: 020 8741 0474
Fax: 020 8741 7724
E-mail: bibliotekapolska@posklibrary.fsnet.co.uk
Constitution: Association with voluntary subscribing
  membership
Objectives/purposes: To provide information about
  various aspects of Polish affairs
Key staff: Librarian: Jadwiga Szmidt
Stock and subject coverage: Collection of books and other
  publications on Polish culture, history, literature,
  language, economics, law, sociology, politics,
  geography, arts, folklore, music, philosophy, etc.
  Special collections of Conradiana, Polish
  underground samizdat publications, Anglo-Polonica,
  maps, bookplates and manuscripts. The collection has
  ca. 150,000 books and pamphlets and over 3,000
  journal titles
Services: Photocopies
Availability: Free access to all scholars, researchers and
  readers. Most holdings available at the Reading
  Room only. Members on paying an annual fee are
  entitled to borrow books from the Lending Library
Hours: 10.00-20.00 Monday and Wednesday; 10.00-
  17.00 Friday; 10.00-13.00 Saturday
Transport: Tube: Ravenscourt Park; Bus: 27, H91, 190,
  267, 390
Special facilities: Refreshment and toilet facilities available
Publications: Books in Polish or Relating to Poland
  Added to the Collection of the Polish Library (4
  p.a.); Bibliography of Books in Polish or Relating to
  Poland Published Outside Poland Since September 1,
  1939, published 8 vols (others in preparation); The
  Polish Library 1942-1979 guide; other publications
  in Polish

Linked organisations
  Polish Social and Cultural Association The
  Library is owned by the Association
  Library Commission The Library is supervised by
  the Library Commission

[479]
Pollock's Toy Museum
Scala Street
London W1P 1LT
Borough: Camden
Telephone: 020 7636 3452
E-mail: toymuseum@hotmail.com
World Wide Web: www.pollocks.cwc.net
Constitution: Registered charity
Objectives/purposes: Archive information on toys
Key staff: Managing Director: John Fawdry; Curator:
  Veronica Sheppard; Assistant: Barry Clarke
Stock and subject coverage: Toys, games, children' books,
  materials on folklore, customes, social history, etc.,
  museum catalogues
Availability: Open for research only; book in advance,
  small charge
Hours: 10.00-17.00 Monday to Saturday

Transport: Tube: Goodge Street; Bus: 10, 14, 24, 29, 73
Special facilities: Toilet facilities available

[480]
Portuguese Chamber
The Portuguese UK Business Network
1st floor
22/25A Sackville Street
London W1S 1DR
Borough: Westminster
Telephone: 020 7494 1844
Fax: 020 7494 1822
E-mail: info@portuguese-chamber.org.uk
World Wide Web: www.portuguese-chamber.org.uk
Constitution: Independent non-profit organisation,
  company limited by guarantee and association with
  voluntary subscribing membership
Stock and subject coverage: Directories, newsletters, special
  reports, brochures and videos on the Portuguese
  economy and business
Availability: Not open to the public; special reports
  prepared for members free or discounted, all others
  charged
Hours: 09.30-17.30 Monday to Friday
Publications: Tradewinds newsletter; annual directory and
  yearbook; e-Tradewindows online newsletter

Linked organisations:
  ICEP (official government agency for investment,
  trade and tourism)
  Madeira Development Company
  Portuguese Stock Exchange
  Portuguese Industrial Association
  The Network has protocols with these bodies

[481]
Press Association
P A NewsCentre
Denison House
292 Vauxhall Bridge Rd
London SW1V 1AE
Borough: Lambeth
Constitution: Company limited by guarantee
Objectives/purposes: PA News is the national news
  agency for the UK and the Republic of Ireland
World Wide Web: www.pa.press.net

[481][a]
PA News Library
Telephone: 020 7963 7011
  PA Customer Services
  (HelpDesk) 08701 202095
Fax: 020 7936 7065
E-mail: newslibrary@pa.press.net
Key staff: Librarian: Eugene Weber
Stock and subject coverage: Editorial news library. More
  than 14 million cuttings from British national
  newspapers dating back, in some cases, to 1920.
  Updated daily
Services: Photocopies
Availability: Access to the general public, visitors
  welcome. Commissioned research available. Special
  student rates

Hours: 08.00–20.00; 08.00–18.00 Saturday; 09.00–18.00 Sunday (commissioned research 08.00–18.00 weekdays)
Special facilities: Refreshment and toilet facilities available

[481][b]
PA Photos
Telephone: 020 7963 7990
E-mail: paphotos.research@pa.press.net
Key staff: Picture Library Manager: Milica Timotic
Stock and subject coverage: The Library includes all work from PA photographers dating from the turn of the century, plus bought in collections. It is a UK agent for several European agencies. The collection includes ca. 6 million pictures covering news, sport, royalty and showbusiness
Services: PA Photos has three dedicated websites: PA Photos, PA PicSelect and PA SportsPhotos
Availability: Access to the general public
Hours: 09.00–17.00

[482]
Primary and Community Health Information Services Library
PCHIS
Medical Sciences Building
Queen Mary and Westfield College
Mile End Road
London E1 4NS
Borough: Tower Hamlets
Telephone: 020 7982 6347
Fax: 020 7982 6396
E-mail: pchis@qmw.ac.uk
World Wide Web: www.smd.qmul.ac.uk/library/sites
Constitution: Part of Queen Mary, University of London
Key staff: Shabbir Ahmed, Damian Hippisley (both part-time)
Stock and subject coverage: Clinical library specialising in general practice and care of the elderly
Services: Loans, photocopy facilities, inter-library loans, enquiries, information skills training
Availability: Available to staff and students of Queen Mary and Westfield College; staff of Barts and the London NHS Trust; staff of Tower Hamlets Primary Care Trust; staff of East London and the City Mental Health Trust; academic staff and research students from the M25 Consortium by arrangement
Hours: 09.00–12.00 Monday; 09.00–17.00 Tuesday to Friday
Transport: Tube: Mile End; Bus: 25
Special facilities: Access for users with disabilities via lift to first floor of Medical Sciences Building; cafes on campus
Publications: Library guide

Linked organisations
Queen Mary, University of London Part of the university

North East London Workforce Development Confederation Participant in library services network

[483]
Prime Minister's Office Library
10 Downing Street
London SW1A 2AA
Borough: Westminster
Telephone: 020 7968 3154
Fax: 020 798 1350
E-mail: mlee@no10.x.gsi.gov.uk
World Wide Web: www.number-10.gov.uk
Key staff: Michael L Lee BA MSc
Stock and subject coverage: Small collection of policy and politically related texts, statistical publications and biographies
Availability: Not open to public; available to No 10 staff and other government libraries
Hours: 09.30–17.30 Monday to Friday

[484]
Psychiatric Rehabilitation Association
PRA
Bayford Mews
Bayford Street
London E8 3SF
Borough: Hackney
Telephone: 020 8985 3570
Fax: 020 8986 1334
Email: ppra528898@aol.com
World Wide Web: www.cityhack.dircon.co.uk
Constitution: Registered charity
Objectives/purposes: Rehabilitation and community care of the mentally ill
Key staff: Director: John Wilder
Stock and subject coverage: Basic books on psychiatry, some sociology, copies of PRA research
Services: Photocopies; fax machine
Availability: Materials available for reference and purchase, by arrangement
Hours: 09.30–17.30 Monday to Friday, answerphone out of hours
Transport: Tube: Bethnal Green; Bus: 106, 253
Special facilities: Toilet facilities available
Publications: Annual Report; publications list

Linked organisations
PRA Aids for the Handicapped Ltd
PRA Plastics (and Developments) Ltd
Linked rehabilitation workshops

[485]
Public Health Laboratory Service – Communicable Disease Surveillance Centre
PHLS – CDSC
61 Colindale Avenue
London NW9 5EQ
Borough: Barnet
Telephone: 020 8200 6868
Fax: 020 8200 7868
E-mail: eyusef@phls.org.uk
World Wide Web: www.phls.co.uk

Constitution: Government funded organisation

Objectives/purposes: To support the diagnosis, treatment and control of infectious and communicable diseases

Key staff: Erol Yusuf

Stock and subject coverage: Medical books, journals and internal databases covering all aspects of infection and communicable diseases, microbiology and infectious diseases

Services: Photocopies and online searches (charged); Medline on CD-ROM; OPAC version of library database on microbiological literature; internet access

Availability: Written and telephone enquiries accepted from bona fide researchers

Hours: 09.00-17.00 Monday to Friday

Transport: Tube: Colindale; Bus: 32, 142, 204, 303

Special facilities: Toilet facilities available; access for users with disabilities

Publications: CDR Weekly (available on the PHLS website)

[486]
Public Record Office
The National Archives (PRO)
Ruskin Ave
Kew
Richmond
Surrey TW9 4DU

Borough: Richmond upon Thames

Telephone: 020 8392 5200 (records enquiries)

Fax: 020 8878 8905

E-mail: enquiry@pro.gov.uk

World Wide Web: www.pro.gov.uk

Constitution: Government funded body

Key staff: Keeper: Mrs S Tyacke

Stock and subject coverage: The Office is the national repository for records of the central government of the United Kingdom and the law courts of England and Wales, which extend in time from the eleventh to the twenty-first century. They form an accumulation occupying over 167 km of shelving. Under the Public Records Acts records are normally opened to inspection when they are 30 years old. Please telephone in advance of a visit. The Family Record Centre, 1 Myddelton Street, Islington, London EC1R 1UW (telephone: 020 8392 5300; fax: 020 8392 5307) holds microfilms of the decennial census returns, 1841-1891, Prerogative Court of Canterbury wills to 1858 and nonconformist registers to 1840

Availability: Readers' tickets are issued free of charge upon completion of a simple application procedure and production of documentary proof of identity. No reader's ticket is required to use the Family Record Centre

Hours: 09.00-17.00 (last orders for documents 16.00) Monday, Wednesday and Friday; 10.00-19.00 Tuesday; 09.00-19.00 Thursday; 09.30-17.00 Saturday (document orders on Saturday from 09.30-12.00, 13.30-15.00)

Transport: Tube: Kew Gardens; Rail: Kew Bridge, Kew Gardens: Bus: 65, 391

Special facilities: Refreshment and toilet facilities available on site; access for users with disabilities – ramps, lifts, toilet facilities

[486][a]
Public Record Office Resource Centre and Library
Contact details as for Public Record Office above

Key staff: Head of Resource Centre and Library: Helen Pye-Smith

Stock and subject coverage: Ca. 15,000 books, 300 current periodicals. Specialises in all aspects of British history, law, topography and archives, administrative history and their auxiliary studies

Services: Self-service photocopying available

Availability: Open to the public under the same conditions as the document reading rooms and same opening hours

Linked organisations

The National Archives Launched in April 2003, The National Archives brings together the Historical Manuscripts Commission and the PRO. The two organisations will merge more fully by Spring 2004.

[487]
Pugin Guild
157 Vicarage Road
London E10 5DU

Borough: Waltham Forest

Telephone: 020 8539 3876

Fax: 020 8539 3876

E-mail: pugin@smartgroups.com

World Wide Web: www.smartgroups.com/vault/pugin

Constitution: Independent non-profit organisation

Objectives/purposes: Pugin, Gothic architecture, the gild system and traditional crafts

Key staff: Librarian: Ronald King

Stock and subject coverage: Books, journals and newspaper cuttings, prints and photographs on Pugin and Gothic architecture

Availability: At the discretion of the Librarian

Hours: By appointment

Transport: Tube: Leyton, Walthamstow; Rail: Leyton Midland, Walthamstow; Bus: 48, 69, 97, 256

Special facilities: Refreshment and toilet facilities available

Publications: Contrasts – Bulletin of the Pugin Gild (2 p.a.)

Linked organisations

Christian Social Order

[488]
The Puppet Centre Trust
BAC
Lavender Hill
London SW11 5TN

Borough: Wandsworth

Telephone: 020 7228 5335

E-mail: pct@puppetcentre.demon.co.uk

World Wide Web: www.puppetcentre.com

Constitution: Registered charity

Objectives/purposes: To promote and further the arts of puppetry and animation in all their forms

Key staff: Katie Richardson

Stock and subject coverage: Library, archive and videos relating to the art of puppetry. Large collection of puppets and puppetry and related ephemera

Services: Photocopies, puppet hire (charges made), internet access
Availability: Materials are for reference only, although some videos may be loaned
Hours: 14.00–18.00 Monday, Wednesday and Saturday; other times by appointment
Transport: Rail: Clapham Junction
Special facilities: Refreshment and toilet facilities available; access for users with disabilities
Special features: Integral part of major resource centre for puppetry in the UK

Linked organisations

British Puppet and Model Theatre Guild
British UNIMA
Punch and Judy Fellowship
Puppeteers UK

[489]
Queen Elizabeth Hospital NHS Trust

Healthcare Library
Queen Elizabeth Hospital
Stadium Road
Woolwich
London SE18 4QH
Borough: Greenwich
Telephone: 020 8836 6741
Fax: 020 8836 6744
Constitution: NHS Acute Hospital
Key staff: Knowledge Services Manager: Andy Richardson; Deputy Librarian: Imrana Ghumra
Stock and subject coverage: Over 100 medical and nursing related journals currently received. Around 1,500 books and videos. Subject coverage includes: medicine, dentistry, clinical audit, health management and nursing
Services: Photocopies; networked medical databases, such as Medline, Cochrane, AMED, CINAHL and online journals
Availability: Open to all Queen Elizabeth Hospital NHS Trust employees
Hours: 09.00–17.00; plus two late nights until 19.00 depending on education/training department commitments
Transport: Tube: North Greenwich, then 161 or 486 bus; Rail: Woolwich Arsenal; Bus: 161, 291, 386, 469
Special facilities: Toilet facilities available on site; access for users with disabilities
Publications: List of serial holdings, library guide, newsletter

Linked organisations

London Regional Library Service (NHS) The Library is part of the Service

[490]
Queen Elizabeth's Hunting Lodge

Rangers Road
Chingford
London E4 7QH
Borough: Waltham Forest
Telephone: 020 8529 6681
Fax: 020 8529 8209

Constitution: Part of the Epping Forest Department of the Corporation of London
Objectives/purposes: Maintaining records on the history of Epping Forest
Key staff: Information Services Manager: Tricia Moxey
Stock and subject coverage: Archives pertaining to the Epping Forest department of the Corporation of London. A small number of documents pertaining to the period when Epping Forest was a royal forest
Availability: Access difficult but researchers can apply for an appointment
Hours: By appointment
Transport: Rail: Chingford; Bus: 69, 97, 179, 212
Special facilities: Toilet facilities available

Linked organisations

Epping Forest Information Centre

[491]
Queen Mary and Westfield College
QMW

Main Library, Queen Mary
University of London
Mile End Road
London E1 4NS
Borough: Tower Hamlets
Telephone: 020 7882 5555
Fax: 020 7882 5500
E-mail: library@qmw.ac.uk
World Wide Web: www.library.qmw.ac.uk
Constitution: Department of a university
Key staff: Library Manager: Neil Entwistle; Assistant Library Manager: June Hayles
Stock and subject coverage: The stock includes ca. 450,000 volumes of books, journals and other materials. Subject coverage includes: arts (drama, English, French, German, history, Russian, Spanish and linguistics); social sciences (economics, geography and politics); computer science; mathematics; engineering (aeronautical, civil, electronic and mechanical); natural sciences (biology, chemistry and physics); and basic medical sciences. Special collections include the European Documentation Centre and archive collections relating to the history of the college including Constance Maynard Archive and People's Palace Archive
Services: Photocopies; CD-ROM and online searching; video viewing facilities and computer workstations (some of these available only to members of the College)
Availability: Access to members of the University of London during normal opening times. For others access is normally available only after 17.00 on weekdays in term time, on Saturdays during term time and at any time during vacations
Hours: During term time (telephone or see website for details), admission for most visitors is restricted to weekday evenings and Saturdays (17.00–21.00 Monday to Friday, 10.00–16.00 Saturday). Visitors are normally admitted at any time during vacations
Transport: Tube: Mile End, Stepney Green; Bus: 25
Special facilities: Refreshment and toilet facilities available; access for users with disabilities
Special features: Awarded the SCONUL Building Design Award in 1993

Linked organisations

University of London College of the University. Medical libraries that are part of, or linked to Queen Mary's are located on several sites, see separate entries for: Whitechapel, West Smithfield, The London Chest Hospital, the Wolfson Institute of Preventive Medicine and the Primary and Community Health Information Servcies Library (PCHIS)

[492]
Queen Mary's Hospital Library

Postgraduate Centre, Queen Mary's Hospital
South West London Community Trust
Roehampton Lane
London SW15 5PN
Borough: Wandsworth
Telephone: 020 8355 2093
Fax: 020 8355 2856
E-mail: marber@sghms.ac.uk
Constitution: Hospital
Objectives/purposes: The library provides a service to all local NHS staff
Key staff: Librarian: Mick Arber
Stock and subject coverage: Ca. 69 journal titles (20 current); 1,500 books. Special interest on rehabilitation
Services: Photocopies (charged); internet access, and through internet: Medline, Cinahl, BNI, HMIC, Amed
Availability: Access to NHS staff
Hours: 09.00-17.00 Tuesday and Wednesday
Note: The South West London Community NHS Trust came into being on 1 April 1999 following the merger of Merton & Sutton Community NHS Trust, Richmond, Twickenham & Roehampton Healthcare NHS Trust and Wandsworth Community Health Trust

Linked organisations

St George's Hospital Medical School Library
The Library is managed from St George's

[493]
Radio Authority
RA

Public Reading Room
Holbrook House
14 Great Queen Street
London WC2B 5DG
Borough: Westminster
Telephone: 020 7430 2724
Fax: 020 7405 7064
E-mail: info@radioauthority.org.uk
World Wide Web: www.radioauthority.org.uk
Constitution: Independent non-profit distributing organisation
Key staff: Press and Information Officer: Kerry Curtis
Stock and subject coverage: By appointment, applications for eight year local radio and digital licences may be read
Services: General enquiries about the development of Independent Radio and the Authority's existing licensees. Reading room in which applications for local licenses may be viewed
Availability: Reference use only, by appointment

Hours: 09.00-17.30 Monday to Friday
Transport: Tube: Holborn
Special facilities: Toilet facilities available
Publications: Pocket Book; Annual Report; News and Current Affairs Code and Programme Code; Local Analogue Licence Engineering Code; Advertising and Sponsorship Code

[494]
Radiocommunications Agency Library
RA

Information and Library Service
9th Floor
Wyndham House
189 Marsh Wall
London E14 9SX
Borough: Tower Hamlets
Telephone: 020 7211 0502/0505
Fax: 020 7211 0507
E-mail: library@ra.gsi.gov.uk
World Wide Web: www.radio.gov.uk
Constitution: Executive agency of the Department of Trade and Industry (DTI)
Key staff: Information and Publicity Manager: Julia Fraser; Librarian: Jenny Cann
Stock and subject coverage: Specialises in information covering the use and management of the UK radio frequency spectrum
Services: Loans usually through the British Library. Acts as the distribution point for RA publications
Availability: By appointment with Library Manager
Hours: 09.00-17.00 Monday to Friday
Transport: Tube: Canary Wharf; Docklands Light Railway: South Quay
Special facilities: Refreshment and toilet facilities available; access for users with disabilities
Publications: RA information sheets; RA annual report; MPT specifications; press notices

[495]
The Railway Club

Room 208
25 Marylebone Road
London NW1 5JS
Borough: Westminster
Telephone: 020 8536 0864
Constitution: Association with voluntary subscribing membership
Objectives/purposes: Study of railway history and operation
Key staff: Honorary Librarian: Mr G Waterer
Stock and subject coverage: Large lending library available to members. Extensive reference library including: files of magazines and journals; collection of standard reference books; maps and diagrams; official reports (including BoT/MoT accident reports); Bradshaw and Company/BR timetables; railway rule books and appendices; historic guide books and pamphlets
Availability: Open to members and to other genuine researchers on application to the Honorary Librarian
Hours: Available to visitors by appointment
Transport: Tube: Baker Street; Bus: 18, 30

Special facilities: Toilet facilities available
Special features: One of the best collections of railway historical material in the country
Publications: Quarterly Bulletin of Club Activities

[496]
The Railway Correspondence and Travel Society
RCTS

23 Hillingdon Road
Uxbridge
Middlesex
Borough: Hillingdon

Correspondence address
17 Raisins Hill
Pinner
Middlesex HA5 2BU
Fax: 0870 1318711 (temporarily inaccessible)
E-mail: librarian@rcts.org.uk
E-mail listserver: rctslibrary@yahoogroups.com
World Wide Web: www.rcts.org.uk
Objectives/purposes: Leading international society for anyone interested in railway operation and history. Holds regular meetings at 29 centres throughout the country and organises visits to railway installations
Key staff: The Librarian
Stock and subject coverage: Extensive collections of more than 3,500 books and pamphlets and 1,500 bound volumes of magazines on railway history and operations in the UK and overseas. Large collection of accident reports (UK and USA) and historic working and public timetables
Services: Library e-mail list server to keep members up-to-date with additions to the Library's loan and sales stock of duplicated items. The list server is also for the posing and answering of members' queries. Digital catalogue files and other useful data is downloadable from the associated groups area at yahoogroups.com
Availability: Library is for members only (membership £18 per annum for 2002, current information available on website)
Hours: Weekday evenings or Saturday afternoons, normally open about 33 times per year at dates and times announced in the Society's magazine, The Railway Observer
Transport: Tube: Uxbridge; Buses from Uxbridge and West Drayton stations
Publications: Railway Observer (monthly); numerous books on railway and locomotive history since 1935 (see website)

[497]
The Raymond Mander and Joe Mitchenson Theatre Collection
Mander and Mitchenson

The Mansion
Beckenham Place Park
Beckenham
Kent BR3 2BP
Borough: Lewisham
Telephone: 020 8658 7725

E-mail: richard@mander-and-mitchenson.co.uk
World Wide Web: www.mander-and-mitchenson.co.uk
Constitution: Registered charity
Objectives/purposes: To promote and advance education for the study of the history of drama, music and the arts
Key staff: Administrator: Richard Mangan; Assistant: Donna Percival
Stock and subject coverage: 1,500 boxes containing programmes, playbills, photographs, engravings, cuttings, etc. These cover mainly London theatres, actors, actresses, directors, designers, music hall, opera, dance, etc. Ca. 7,000 books on theatre and allied arts
Services: Photocopies
Availability: Open only to researchers by appointment. Pictures and other material for reproduction are loaned at commercial rates. Other material can be loaned for exhibition, etc.
Hours: 10.30–16.30 Monday to Friday
Transport: Rail: Beckenham Junction; Bus: 54
Special facilities: Refreshment and toilet facilities available

[498]
RDS (formerly Research Defence Society)

58 Great Marlborough Street
London W1F 7JY
Borough: Westminster
Telephone: 020 7287 2818
Fax: 020 7287 2627
E-mail: info@rds-online.org.uk
World Wide Web: www.rds-online.org.uk
Constitution: RDS is funded by its members, most of whom are medical researchers, doctors and vets. Membership is open to individuals and to organisations
Objectives: RDS is the UK organisation representing medical researchers in the public debate about the use of animals in medical research and testing. It provides information about the need for animal research, the controls under which this research is carried out, and the benefits to medicine which have resulted. It also helps government and animal welfare groups to promote best practice in laboratory animal welfare and develop non-animal techniques.
Key staff: Executive Director: Dr Mark Matfield; Communications Director: Barbara Davies
Stock and subject coverage: Extensive library of books, animal rights literature, press cuttings, radio/TV tapes and videos
Availability: RDS welcomes approaches from bona fide researchers and from the media – to encourage balanced reporting on the issue of animal research
Hours: By prior arrangement only
Transport: Tube: Oxford Circus

[499]
Redbridge (London Borough of Redbridge)

World Wide Web: www.redbridge.gov.uk
Constitution: Public library funded by local authority
Availability: Open to anyone living in Redbridge (proof of identity and address required to join lending

libraries). Persons holding valid tickets from other public libraries may also use the service

Special features: There is one main library, the Central Library, and a number of smaller branch libraries. Redbridge libraries also has three mobile libraries visiting over 40 sites a week

[499][a]
Central Library

Clements Road
Ilford
Essex IG1 1EA
Telephone: 020 8478 7145
Fax: 020 8553 3299
E-mail: centrallibrary@redbridge.gov.uk
Key staff: Chief Librarian: Martin Timms; Central Library Manager: Peter Ledger; Local Studies Librarian: Ian Dowling; Lending Librarian: Bob Terry; Archivist: Tudor Allen; Reference Librarian: Rebecca Naismith
Stock and subject coverage: Main stock of reference and information sources for the Borough. Audio material, videos, DVDs, CD-ROMs for loan. The Local Studies and Archives Service is based at the Central Library
Services: Free internet access (charge for printing). Charges for photocopies, audio material, videos, DVDs CD-ROMs, fax. Public telephones, meeting rooms and exhibition space for hire. Local access Point (i.e. free telephone to all Council Services)
Hours: Adult library: 09.30-20.00 Monday to Friday; 09.30-16.00 Saturday
Children's library: 09.30-18.30 Monday to Friday; 09.30-16.00 Saturday
Transport: Rail: Ilford: Bus: 25, N25, 86, 123, 128, 129, 147, 150, 167, 169, 296, 364, 366, 369, 462, 551, 645, 920, 947, 948, 955, 958, 959
Special facilities: Toilet facilities; access for users with disabilities - including adapted toilet, automatic doors, lifts, free audio loans to disabled Redbridge residents, free large print reservations

[499][b]
Aldersbrook Library

2A Park Road
London E12 5HQ
Telephone: 020 8989 9319
Fax: 020 8496 0001
E-mail: bob.luxmore@redbridge.gov.uk
Key staff: Branch Librarian: Robert Luxmore
Reference facilities: General adult lending stock, small reference collection, small local history section, children's collection, CDs, videos, talking books
Services: Internet access free of charge (charge for printing); charges for photocopying and fax; loan charges for audio material and videos; Local Access Point (i.e. free telephone to all Council Services)
Hours: 14.30-17.00, 17.30-20.00 Monday, Tuesday and Thursday; 14.30-17.00 Friday; 09.30-13.00, 14.00-16.00 Saturday
Transport: Tube: Wanstead; Bus: 101
Special facilities: Access for users with disabilities - automatic doors, free audio loans and large print

[499][c]
Gants Hill Library

490 Cranbrook Road
Gants Hill
Ilford
Essex IG2 6LA
Telephone: 020 8554 5211
Fax: 020 8708 9015
E-mail: john.hayward@redbridge.gov.uk
Key staff: Branch Librarian: John Hayward
Reference facilities: General adult lending stock, small reference collection, small local history section, children's collection, CDs, videos, talking books
Services: Internet access free of charge (charge for printing); charges for photocopying and fax; loan charges for audio material and videos; Local Access Point (i.e. free telephone to all Council Services)
Hours: Adult library: 09.30-20.00 Monday, Tuesday and Thursday; 09.30-17.00 Friday; 09.30-16.00 Saturday
Children's library: 13.00-18.30 Monday, Tuesday and Thursday; 13.00-17.00 Friday; 09.30-16.00 Saturday
Transport: Tube: Gants Hill; Bus: N8, N25, 66, 123, 129, 150, 167, 179, 251, 296, 396, 462
Special facilities: Access for users with disabilities - ramp and automatic doors, free audio loans and large print

[499][d]
Goodmayes Library

76 Goodmayes Lane
Goodmayes
Ilford IG3 9QB
Telephone: 020 8590 8362
Fax: 020 8708 7756
E-mail: bill.george@redbridge.gov.uk
Key staff: Branch Librarian: Bill George
Reference facilities: General adult lending stock, small reference collection, small local history section, children's collection, CDs, videos and talking books
Services: Internet access free of charge (charge for printing); charges for photocopying and fax; loan charges for audio material and videos; Local Access Point (i.e. free telephone to all Council Services)
Hours: 09.30-20.00 Monday, Tuesday and Thursday; 09.30-17.00 Friday; 09.30-16.00 Saturday
Transport: Rail: Goodmayes; Bus: 387
Special facilities: Access for users with disabilities - level access to automatic doors, adapted toilet, free audio loans and large print reservations for users with disabilities

[499][e]
Hainault Library

100 Manford Way
Chigwell
Essex IG7 4DD
Telephone: 020 8500 1204
Fax: 020 8708 9025
E-mail: evelyn.reid@redbridge.gov.uk
Key staff: Branch Librarian: Evelyn Reid
Reference facilities: General adult lending stock, small reference collection, small local history section, children's collection, CDs, videos, talking books
Services: Internet access free of charge (charge for printing); charges for photocopying and fax; loan charges for audio material and videos; Local Access Point (i.e. free telephone to all Council Services)

Hours: 09.30-20.00 Monday, Tuesday and Thursday;
    09.30-17.00; 09.30-16.00 Saturday
Transport: Tube: Hainault, Grange Hill; Bus: 150, 247,
    362
Special facilities: Access for users with disabilities - level
    access to automatic doors, free audio loans and large
    print reservations for users with disabilities

[499][f]
South Woodford Library
116 High Road
London E18 2QS
Telephone: 020 8504 1407
Fax: 020 8559 2476
E-mail: geraldine.pote@redbridge.gov.uk
Key staff: Branch Librarian: Geraldine Pote
Reference facilities: General adult lending stock, small
    reference collection, small local history section,
    children's collection, CD-ROMs, CDs, videos, talking
    books
Services: Internet access free of charge (charge for
    printing); charges for photocopying and fax; loan
    charges for audio material and videos; Local Access
    Point (i.e. free telephone to all Council Services);
    photobooth; PC with Microsoft Office available for
    hire
Hours: Adult library: 09.30-20.00 Monday, Tuesday and
    Thursday; 09.30-17.00 Friday; 09.30-16.00 Saturday
    Children's library: 13.00-18.30 Monday, Tuesday and
    Thursday; 13.00-17.00 Friday; 09.30-16.00 Saturday
Transport: Tube: South Woodford (10 mins); Bus: W13,
    123, 179, 645; cycle rack
Special facilities: Access for users with disabilities - ramp,
    automatic doors, lift with braille keys, adapted toilet,
    loop system at enquiries desk, free audio loans and
    large print reservations for users with disabilities

[499][g]
Wanstead Library
Spratt Hall Road
Wanstead
London E11 2RQ
Telephone: 020 8989 9462
Fax: 020 8708 7405
E-mail: bob.luxmore@redbridge.gov.uk
Key staff: Branch Librarian: Robert Luxmore
Reference facilities: General adult lending stock, small
    reference collection, small local history section,
    children's collection, CDs, videos, talking books
Services: Internet access free of charge (charge for
    printing); charges for photocopying and fax; loan
    charges for audio material and videos; Local Access
    Point (i.e. free telephone to all Council Services)
Hours: 09.30-20.00 Monday, Tuesday and Thursday;
    09.30-17.00 Friday; 09.30-16.00 Saturday
Transport: Tube: Wanstead; Bus: W12, W13, W14, 66, 101,
    145, 308
Special facilities: Access for users with disabilities - level
    access to automatic doors, free audio loans and large
    print reservations for users with disabilities

[499][h]
Woodford Green Library
Snakes Lane
Woodford Green
Essex IG8 0DX

Telephone: 020 8504 4642
Fax: 020 8502 9034
E-mail: jill.fellerman@redbridge.gov.uk
Key staff: Branch Librarian: Jill Fellerman
Reference facilities: General adult lending stock, small
    reference collection, small local history section,
    children's collection, CDs, videos, talking books
Services: Internet access free of charge (charge for
    printing); charges for photocopying and fax; loan
    charges for audio material and videos; Local Access
    Point (i.e. free telephone to all Council Services); PC
    with Microsoft Office available for hire
Hours: 09.30-20.00 Monday, Tuesday and Thursday;
    09.30-17.00 Friday; 09.30-16.00 Saturday
Transport: Tube: Woodford; Bus: 387
Special facilities: Access for users with disabilities - level
    access to automatic doors, free audio loans and large
    print reservations for users with disabilities

[500]
Regent's College Library
Inner Circle
Regent's Park
London NW1 4NS
Borough: Westminster
Telephone: 020 7487 7449
Fax: 0171 487 7545
E-mail: collinsm@regents.ac.uk
World Wide Web: www.regents.ac.uk
Constitution: Independent non-profit organisation;
    registered charity, part of Regent's College
Key staff: Head Librarian: Mary Collins
Stock and subject coverage: Stock related to Regent's
    College courses: business, the arts and humanities,
    psychotherapy and counselling
Services: Photocopies
Availability: Lending facilities for students, open for
    reference only to others
Hours: 09.00-17.00 weekdays; extended hours in term-
    time to include evenings and weekends
Transport: Tube: Baker Street; Rail: Marylebone
Special facilities: Refreshment and toilet facilities available;
    limited access for users with disabilities
Publications: Readers guides and booklists

Linked organisations

International Planned Parenthood Federation
Located on the Regent's College site

[501]
The Religious Drama Society of Great Britain
RADIUS
Christ Church and Upton Chapel
1a Kennington Road
London SE1 7QP
Borough: Lambeth
Telephone: 020 7401 2422
Constitution: Independent non-profit organisation;
    registered charity; association with voluntary
    subscribing membership
Objectives/purposes: To offer training, advice and library
    facilities in the encouragement of drama which
    illuminates the human condition and communicates
    Christian understanding

Key staff: Doris Whistler, Rosemary Stephens

Stock and subject coverage: Stage scripts of all types and for all ages. Books on all aspects of drama. Biographies, work and lives of authors. Technical, historic, religious material (seasonal and general). Helpful reference sources for these

Services: Photocopies

Availability: Loans to members only; non-members welcome to use library for small fee

Hours: 11.00-15.30 Tuesday and Thursday

Transport: Tube: Lambeth North; Rail: Waterloo; Bus: 12, 53, 109, 149

Special facilities: Toilet facilities available

Publications: Radius (quarterly magazine)

[502]
Religious Society of Friends (Quakers)

Library
Friends House
Euston Road
London NW1 2BJ

Borough: Camden

Telephone: 020 7663 1135

Fax: 020 7663 1001

E-mail: library@quaker.org.uk

World Wide Web: www.quaker.org.uk

Constitution: Registered charity; religious organisation

Key staff: Librarian: Heather Rowland

Stock and subject coverage: Archives, manuscripts, printed books and pamphlets, periodicals, and pictures, all relating to Quaker history, thought and interests, including peace and anti-slavery

Services: Photocopies; microfilm reader-printer

Availability: To members of the Religious Society of Friends and other bona fide researchers on letter of introduction (see website for details). Charges made for use of genealogical resources

Hours: 13.00-17.00 Monday, Tuesday, Thursday and Friday; 10.00-17.00 Wednesday

Transport: Tube and Rail: Euston; Bus: 10, 18, 30, 68, 73, 91, 168, 188, 253

Special facilities: Refreshment and toilet facilities available; access for users with disabilities – most parts of library accessible, ramp up to Friends House entrance

Publications: Introductory leaflets

[503]
Richmond Adult And Community College

On two sites:
Clifden Road
Twickenham TW1 4LT

Parkshot
Richmond TW9 2RE

Borough: Richmond

Telephone: 020 8891 5907 ext 7983 (Clifden); ext 4008 (Parkshot)

World Wide Web: www.racc.org.uk

Constitution: Adult education college funded under the LSC

Objectives/purposes: The Learning Centres provide a library service to all students and staff in the college as well as providing learning opportunities in the IT centre

Key staff: Head of Learning Centres: Cristina Llewellyn; Deputy Head/College Librarian: Renee Anderson

Stock and subject coverage: Ca. 12,000 titles (books, videos, audio cassettes and CDs) across two sites on subjects relating to the courses taught. The Richmond site has a strong art and design collection

Services: Photocopies; access to reference materials on CD-ROM; free computer access for members

Availability: Material available for reference only. Materials may be borrowed by current students, staff and members of community groups affiliated with NIACE). Charge of £3.50 to join the Learning Centre

Hours: Clifden site (term-time): 09.30-19.30 Monday to Thursday; 09.00-13.00 Friday; 09.30-13.00 Saturday
Parkshot site (term-time): 09.30-19.30 Monday to Thursday; 09.30-16.00 Friday
Outside term-time contact the Learning Centre for opening hours

Transport: Clifden site: Rail: Twickenham
Parkshot site: Tube and rail: Richmond

Special facilities: Refreshment facilities available in term-time; toilet facilities available; access for users with disabilities (lift to mezzanine level at Clifden)

[504]
Richmond: The American International University in London
RIC

Constitution: Private venture

On two sites:

Taylor Library, Richmond Campus
Queen's Road
Richmond
Surrey TW10 6JP

Telephone: 020 8332 8210

Fax: 020 8332 3050

Borough: Richmond on Thames

Transport: Tube: Richmond; Rail: Richmond; Bus: 371

Library, Kensington Campus
1 St Albans Grove
Kensington
London W8 5PN

Borough: Kensington and Chelsea

Telephone: 020 7368 8410

Transport: Tube: High Street Kensington, Gloucester Road

Key staff: Director of Information Resources and Libraries: David Nutty; Librarians: Frank Trew, Sandra Tury, Val Boyle

Stock and subject coverage: Ca. 60,000 books and 225 journal titles. Subject coverage includes: business administration, economics, international business, history of art, studio art, British studies, English literature, mathematical sciences, computer science, anthropology/sociology, political science, psychology, women's studies, communications and management

Services: Internet access and online searching by arrangment; self-service photocopies (charged)

Availability: Free access by arrangement with the Library, for reference only

Hours: Term-time: 09.00-23.00 Monday to Thursday; 09.00-17.00 Friday; 13.00-17.00 Saturday; 13.00-23.00 Sunday

Vacations: 09.00-17.00 Monday to Friday

Special facilities: Toilet facilities available; access for users with disabilities to Richmond campus

---

[505]
Richmond upon Thames (London Borough of Richmond upon Thames)

Constitution: Public library, funded by local authority
Special features: The Libraries and Arts Division has two administrative offices:

Bibliographical and Computer Services and Young People's Services (based at: The Cottage, Little Green, Richmond, Surrey TW9 1QL

Stock Manager: MJ Johnson; Principal Librarian, Young People's Services: Sharon Kirkpatrick; Assistant Chief Librarian (Information Services): Kate Davenport

Libraries and Arts Headquarters (based at Langholm Lodge, 142 Petersham Road, Richmond TW10 6UX)
Telephone: 020 8940 0031
Fax: 020 8940 7568
Key staff: Chief Librarian: Jane Battye; Assistant Chief Librarian (Lending Services and Promotions): Sheila Harden

[505][a]
Richmond Central Reference Library

Old Town Hall
Whittaker Avenue
Richmond
Surrey TW9 1TP
Telephone: 020 8940 5529
Fax: 020 8940 6899
E-mail: reference.services@richmond.gov.uk
World Wide Web: www.richmond.gov.uk
Key staff: Central Reference Librarian: Julie Hall; Local Studies Librarian: Jane Baxter
Stock and subject coverage: General reference library for the Borough. Local studies collection covering Richmond upon Thames (Barnes, Mortlake and East Sheen, Kew, Ham and Petersham). Vancouver Collection relating to the navigator George Vancouver. Sladen Collection of the correspondence of Douglas Sladen (early 20th century). Burton Collection of books by and relating to Sir Richard Burton, explorer and author
Services: Photocopies; microfilm and microfiche reader printers; Tourist Information Centre (ETB networked) 10.00-17.00 Monday to Friday
Availability: Open to all as a reference library. Charges for reservations, photocopies, etc.
Hours: Reference Library: 10.00-18.00 Monday, Thursday and Friday; 10.00-13.00 Tuesday; 10.00-20.00 Wednesday; 10.00-17.00 Saturday
Local Studies: closed Monday; 13.00-17.00 Tuesday; 13.00-20.00 Wednesday; 10.00-12.00, 13.00-18.00 Thursday and Friday; 10.00-12.00, 13.00-17.00 Saturday

Transport: Tube and Rail: Richmond
Special facilities: Refreshment and toilet facilities available; access for users with disabilities – lift from disabled entrance to ground floor levels, lift from ground floor to 1st and 2nd floors, special arrangements for access to Local Studies material housed on 3rd floor, disabled toilets on ground and 1st floors
Special features: Victorian building (Architect: WJ Ancell) on the Riverside Development by Quinlan Terry (1987)
Publications: Official Guide to Richmond upon Thames; Official Street Plan of Richmond upon Thames; Official Business Directory of Richmond upon Thames; Catalogue of the Works of Alexander Pope in the Twickenham Local Studies Collection; Catalogues of Maps in the Richmond and Twickenham Local Studies Collections; Union List of Periodicals held in the Public Reference Libraries of Richmond upon Thames (public libraries and colleges)

[505][b]
Castelnau Library (serving Barnes)

75 Castelnau
London SW13 9RT
Telephone: 020 8748 3837
E-mail: castelnau.library@richmond.gov.uk
World Wide Web: www.richmond.gov.uk
Key staff: Team Manager (Sheen, Castelnau and Kew libraries): Leslie Cranfield; Library Administrator: Bernadette Lawrence
Reference facilities: Adult and children's lending collections; reference collection; audiovisual services (videos, talking books, CDs); free internet access
Services: Photocopies; charges for audiovisual services and internet printouts
Hours: 10.00-13.00 Tuesday; 14.00-18.00 Wednesday and Friday; 10.00-13.00, 14.00-17.00 Saturday
Transport: Rail: Barnes
Special facilities: Access for users with disabilities

[505][c]
East Sheen Library

Sheen Lane Centre
Sheen Lane
London SW14 8LP
Telephone: 020 8876 8801
E-mail: eastsheen.library@richmond.gov.uk
World Wide Web: www.richmond.gov.uk
Key staff: Library Administrator: Jeremy Preston; Team Manager (Sheen, Kew and Castelnau Libraries): Leslie Cranfield
Reference facilities: Adult and children's lending collections; reference collection; audio-visual services (videos, talking books, CDs); free internet access
Services: Photocopies; charges for audiovisual services and internet printouts
Hours: 10.00-18.00 Tuesday; 10.00-20.00 Wednesday; 10.00-18.00 Thursday and Friday; 10.00-17.00 Saturday
Transport: Rail: Mortlake
Special facilities: Access for users with disabilities

[505][d]
Ham Library
Ham Street
Ham TW10 7HR
Telephone: 020 8940 8703
E-mail: ham.library@richmond.gov.uk
World Wide Web: www.richmond.gov.uk
Key staff: Library Administrator: Gail Sharif; Team
   Manager (Richmond and Ham): Carole Thompson
   and Hazel Rutledge
Reference facilities: Adult and children's lending
   collections; reference collection; audio-visual services
   (videos, talking books, CDs); free internet access
Services: Photocopies; charges for audiovisual services
   and internet printouts
Hours: 10.00-13.00, 14.00-18.00 Tuesday, Thursday and
   Friday; 10.00-13.00, 14.00-20.00 Wednesday; 10.00-
   13.00, 14.00-17.00 Saturday
Transport: Rail: Richmond then bus 371
Special facilities: Access for users with disabilities

[505][e]
Hampton Hill Library
Windmill Road
Hampton Hill TW12 1RF
Telephone: 020 8979 3705
E-mail: hamptonhill.library@richmond.gov.uk
World Wide Web: www.richmond.gov.uk
Key staff: Library Adminstrator: Sheila Bligh; Team
   Manager (Teddington and the Hamptons): Paul
   Donaghy
Reference facilities: Adult and children's lending
   collections; reference collection; audiovisual services
   (videos, CDs); free internet access
Services: Photocopies; charges for audio-visual services
   and internet printouts
Hours: 10.00-13.00 Tuesday; 14.00-18.00 Wednesday;
   14.00-18.00 Friday; 10.00-13.00, 14.00-17.00
   Saturday
Transport: Rail: Hampton, Fulwell
Special facilities: Access for users with disabilities

[505][f]
Hampton Library
Rosehill
Hampton TW12 2AB
Telephone: 020 8979 5110
E-mail: hampton.library@richmond.gov.uk
World Wide Web: www.richmond.gov.uk
Key staff: Library Administrator: Annie Turner; Team
   Manager (Teddington and the Hamptons): Paul
   Donaghy
Reference facilities: Adult and children's lending
   collections; reference collection; audio-visual services
   (videos, talking books, CDs); free internet access
Services: Photocopies; charges for audiovisual services
   and internet printouts
Hours: 10.00-18.00 Monday, Thursday and Friday;
   10.00-20.00 Wednesday; 10.00-17.00 Saturday
Transport: Rail: Hampton
Special facilities: Access for users with disabilities
Special features: The home of William Ewart, the
   promoter of the public library Acts, between 1838
   and 1842

[505][g]
Hampton Wick Library
Bennet Close
Hampton Wick KT1 4AT
Telephone: 020 8977 1559
E-mail: hamptonwick.library@richmond.gov.uk
World Wide Web: www.richmond.gov.uk
Key staff: Library Administrator: Linda Brignall; Team
   Manager (Teddington and the Hamptons): Paul
   Donaghy
Reference facilities: Adult and children's lending
   collections; reference collection; audiovisual services
   (videos, CDs); free internet access
Services: Photocopies; charges for audiovisual services
   and internet printouts
Hours: 10.00-13.00 Tuesday; 14.00-18.00 Wednesday
   and Friday; 10.00-13.00, 14.00-17.00 Saturday
Transport: Rail: Hampton Wick
Special facilities: Access for users with disabilities

[505][h]
Heathfield Library
Percy Road
Whitton TW2 6JL
Telephone: 020 8894 1017
E-mail: heathfield.library@richmond.gov.uk
World Wide Web: www.richmond.gov.uk
Key staff: Library Administrator: Claire Thompson; Team
   Manager (Twickenham, Whitton and Heathfield):
   Stephen Ashby
Reference facilities: Adult and children's lending
   collections; reference collections; audiovisual services
   (videos, CDs, talking books); free internet access
Services: Photocopies; audiovisual services and internet
   printouts
Hours: 10.00-13.00 Tuesday; 14.00-18.00 Wednesday
   and Friday; 10.00-13.00, 14.00-17.00 Saturday
Transport: Rail: Whitton
Special facilities: Access for users with disabilities

[505][i]
Kew Library
106 North Road
Kew TW10 6UX
Telephone: 020 8876 8654
E-mail: kew.library@richmond.gov.uk
World Wide Web: www.richmond.gov.uk
Key staff: Library Administrator: Kim Hacker; Team
   Manager (East Sheen, Kew and Castelnau) Leslie
   Cranfield
Reference facilities: Adult and children's lending
   collections; reference collection; audiovisual services
   (videos, CDs); free internet access
Services: Photocopies; charges for audiovisual services
   and internet printouts
Hours: 10.00-13.00 Tuesday; 14.00-18.00 Wednesday
   and Friday; 10.00-13.00, 14.00-17.00 Saturday
Transport: Tube and Rail: Kew Gardens
Special facilities: Access for users with disabilities

[505][j]
Richmond Central Lending Library
Little Green
Richmond
Surrey TW9 1QL
Telephone: 020 8940 0981
E-mail: richmond.library@richmond.gov.uk
World Wide Web: www.richmond.gov.uk
Key staff: Library Administrator: Sarah Alderson; Team Manager (Richmond and Ham): Carole Thompson, Hazel Rutledge
Reference facilities: Adult and children's lending collections; audiovisual services (videos, CDs, talking books, DVDs); free internet access
Services: Photocopies; charges for audiovisual services; internet printouts
Hours: 10.00–18.00 Tuesday, Thursday and Friday; 10.00–18.00 Wednesday; 10.00–20.00 Saturday; 13.00–17.00 Sunday
Transport: Tube and Rail: Richmond
Special facilities: Access for users with disabilities

[505][k]
Teddington Library
Waldegrave Road
Teddington
Middlesex TW11 8LG
Telephone: 020 8977 1284
E-mail: teddington.library@richmond.gov.uk
World Wide Web: www.richmond.gov.uk
Key staff: Library Administrator: Alison Painter; Team Manager (Teddington and the Hamptons): Paul Donaghy
Reference facilities: Reference collection; local information and children's collection
Services: Photocopies; charges for audiovisual services and internet printouts
Hours: 10.00–18.00 Tuesday, Thursday and Friday; 10.00–20.00 Wednesday; 10.00–17.00 Saturday
Transport: Rail: Teddington
Special facilities: Access for users with disabilities

[505][l]
Twickenham Library
Garfield Road
Twickenham TW1 3JS
Telephone: 020 8892 8091
E-mail: twickenham.library@richmond.gov.uk
World Wide Web: www.richmond.gov.uk
Key staff: Library Administrator: Sharon Matthews; Team Manager (Twickenham, Whitton and Heathfield): Stephen Ashby
Reference facilities: Adult and children's lending collection; audiovisual services (videos, CDs, talking books); reference collection; free internet access
Services: Photocopies; charges for audiovisual services and internet printouts
Hours: 10.00–18.00 Tuesday, Thursday and Friday; 10.00–20.00 Wednesday; 10.00–17.00 Saturday
Transport: Rail: Twickenham
Special facilities: Access for users with disabilities to the General Library on the ground floor, special arrangements available for those needing access to the reference and lending stock on the first floor

[505][m]
Whitton Library
Nelson Road
Whitton TW2 7BB
Telephone: 020 8894 9828
E-mail: whitton.library@richmond.gov.uk
World Wide Web: www.richmond.gov.uk
Key staff: Library Administrator: Derek McCullagh; Team Manager (Twickenham, Whitton, Heathfield): Stephen Ashby
Reference facilities: Adult and children's lending collections; reference collection; audiovisual services (videos, CDs, talking books); free internet access
Services: Photocopies; charges for audiovisual services and internet printouts
Hours: 10.00–18.00 Tuesday, Thursday and Friday; 10.00–20.00 Wednesday; 10.00–17.00 Saturday
Transport: Rail: Whitton
Special facilities: Access for users with disabilities

[506]
Royal Academy of Arts
Burlington House
Piccadilly
London W1J 0BD
Borough: Westminster
Telephone: 020 7300 5737
Fax: 020 7300 5765
E-mail: library@royalacademy.org.uk
World Wide Web: www.royalacademy.org.uk
Constitution: Specialist art library
Key staff: Head of Library Services: Adam Waterton; Assistant Librarian: Linda Weston
Stock and subject coverage: Ca 40,000 books; 15,000 prints and drawings; photography library. Covers British arts and artists 1750 to date; life and work of Royal Academicians, 1769 to date; artists' papers; the Royal Academy of Arts archives; special collection of pre-1871 books on the Fine Arts
Services: Free information relating to the Royal Academy; photocopies
Availability: Visits for bona fide researchers by appointment; telephone, written and e-mail enquiries accepted
Hours: 10.00–13.00, 14.00–17.00 Tuesday to Friday
Transport: Tube: Piccadilly Circus, Green Park
Special facilities: Refreshment and toilet facilities on site

[507]
Royal Academy of Dance Library
RAD Library
36 Battersea Square
London SW11 3RA
Borough: Wandsworth
Telephone: 020 7326 8010 / 8032
Fax: 020 7585 0640
E-mail: library@rad–org.uk
World Wide Web: www.rad.org.uk
Constitution: Registered charity and department of an educational establishment
Objectives/purposes: History and aesthetics of all forms of dancing, classical ballet teaching, etc.
Key staff: Senior Librarian: Eleanor Jack

Stock and subject coverage: The collection of dance materials held in the Library of the Royal Academy of Dancing provides a comprehensive reference resource on dance. The collections include books, journals, videos, programmes and souvenir brochures, covering all aspects of ballet and dance from history and biography to movement notation and technique. The Photographic Archive of the late GBL Wilson is also housed in the Library along with the personal collections of Dame Adeline Genée and Phyllis Bedells. Since the amalgamation of the Benesh Institute with the RAD in 1997, the Library is also the home of over 1,000 Benesh Movement notation scores

Services: Photocopies; viewing and listening facilities; literature searches for a fee and by arrangement

Availability: Access to the Library is free of charge for RAD members and members of the Society for Dance Research. Access, for a fee, to all bona fide researchers. Half day: organisations £10, individuals £5, students £2; full day: organisations £20, individuals £10, students £4. Access is for reference only and it is essential to make an appointment

Hours: Open Monday to Friday, phone for details

Transport: Train: Clapham Junction; Tube: South Kensington; Bus: 19, 49, 239, 319, 345

Special facilities: Refreshment and toilet facilities available on site; access for users with disabilities, lift provided

Publications: Dance Gazette - RAD (3 p.a.); Annual Report

[508]
Royal Academy of Dramatic Art
RADA
18 Chenies Street
London WC1E 7PA
Borough: Camden
Telephone: 020 7908 4878
Fax: 020 7323 3865
E-mail: library@rada.ac.uk
World Wide Web: www.rada.org
Objectives/purposes: Academy for professional theatre training, acting and stage management
Stock and subject coverage: Books, journals and playtexts. Subject coverage includes dramatic theatre; theatre criticism, theatre crafts; acting and stage management
Special collections include: the Currell Bequest (450 books and 40 albums of press cuttings by and about George Bernard Shaw) and the RADA archives 1904-
Availability: Access for reference use only; written application required in advance of visiting
Hours: 11.00-14.00, 15.00-19.00 Monday to Friday
Transport: Tube: Goodge Street
Special features: The Academy was opened in 1906 and the library in 1968

[509]
Royal Academy of Music Library
RAM
Marylebone Road
London NW1 5HT
Borough: Westminster
Telephone: 020 7873 7323
Fax: 020 7873 7322
E-mail: library@ram.ac.uk
World Wide Web: www.ram.ac.uk
Constitution: Registered charity
Key staff: Librarian: Kathryn Adamson; Assistant Librarians: Rosalind Cyphus, Bridget Palmer, Ruth Harris
Stock and subject coverage: 200,000 items, including sheet music, books, sound recordings, microforms, manuscripts and early printed music
Services: Photocopies; microfilm reader-printer; audio facilities
Availability: RAM students and staff. Visitors should telephone in advance to make an appointment.
Hours: Term-time: 09.00-18.00 Monday to Friday; 09.00-12.00 Saturday. Vacation hours vary, please enquire
Transport: Tube: Regents Park; Baker Street; Rail: Marylebone
Special facilities: Refreshment and toilet facilities

[510]
Royal Aeronautical Society
RAeS
4 Hamilton Place
London W1J 7BQ
Borough: Westminster
Telephone: 020 7670 4362
Fax: 020 7670 4359
E-mail: brian.riddle@raes.org.uk
World Wide Web: www.aerosociety.com
Constitution: Registered charity and chartered professional body
Key staff: Librarian: BL Riddle
Stock and subject coverage: Holdings include 27,000 books, 1,000 periodicals (300 current), 20,000 technical reports and 100,000 photographs. Extensive collection of material relating to the development and recent technical advances in aeronautics, aviation and aerospace technology. Collection of various government reports related to aviation and the aircraft industry. Major holdings of Air Ministry Air Publications (APs), accident reports issued by the Air Accidents Investigations Branch (AAIB) and of the Reports and Memoranda (R&Ms) and Current Papers (CPs) issued by the Advisory Committee for Aeronautics/Aeronautical Research Council (ARC). Special collections include: the Cuthbert-Hodgson, Poynton and Maitland collections of early ballooning, airships and other early aeronautical material. Extensive collections of pioneers' letters, papers and manuscripts, including those of Sir George Cayley (1773-1857), John Stringfellow (1799-1883), Wilbur Wright (1867-1912), Orville Wright (1871-1948), Katherine Wright (1874-1929), Lawrence Hargrave (1850-1915), Major BFS Baden-Powell (1860-1937), CG Grey (1875-1953) and the design notebooks of FS Barnwell (1880-1938). Files of papers relating to the history of the Society. Extensive photographic/glass lantern slide/lithographic collection of aviation images (over 100,000) from the early days of ballooning and airships to civil and military aircraft, space technology and modern aircraft plus portrait photographs of aviation personalities

Services: Photocopying; photographic services; web-based catalogue available at www.aerosociety.com

Availability: Library open by appointment to non-members of Engineering Council institutions on a daily fee-paying basis

Hours: 10.00–17.00 Monday to Friday

Transport: Tube: Green Park, Hyde Park Corner; Bus: 2, 8, 9, 10, 12, 14, 19, 22, 26, 36, 38, 73, 74, 82, 137

Special facilities: Refreshment and toilet facilities available; access for users with disabilities

Publications: Royal Aeronautical Society Archive series of CD-ROMs including: Early Aviation: the Pioneering Years Through to the First World War, ISBN 1-903129-22-2 (including over 400 photographs and illustrations of early aircraft, airships and gliders); Aeronautical Classics, ISBN 1-903129-23-0 (recording the early writings on aeronautics); Imperial Airways, ISBN 1-903129-30-3 (tracing the development of Imperial Airways, its routes and aircraft); Aircraft of the 1920s, ISBN 1-903129-51-6 (tracing the development of aircraft during the decade). CD-ROMs can be ordered (price £11.44 each) direct from Archive Britain, Suite 407, Victory House, Somers Road North, Portsmouth PO1 1PJ (tel: 023 9275 6275; fax: 023 9275 6283; e-mail: raes@archivebritain.com)

[511]
Royal Air Force Museum
RAF Museum

Grahame Park Way
Hendon
London NW9 5LL

Borough: Barnet
Telephone: 020 8205 2266 (4 lines)
Fax: 020 8200 1751
E-mail: info@rafmuseum.com
World Wide Web: www.rafmuseum.com
Constitution: Registered charity; national museum
Key staff: Keeper of Research and Information Services: PJV Elliott BSc MIInfSc, ext 4850; Enquiries: ext 4873

Stock and subject coverage: The literature of aviation history and aerospace developments. Stock of about 100,000 volumes, comprising 65,000 air publications, 20,000 books and 15,000 periodical volumes. About 100 current periodicals are taken. 5,000 microfiche; 8,000 air diagrams; 3,000 aeronautical maps. Smaller collections of air display programmes, aircraft recognition cards and charts, miscellaneous pamphlets and cigarette and tea cards are kept

Services: Enquiries; photocopies; microform copies

Availability: Reading room open (by prior appointment) for reference purposes only

Hours: 10.00–17.00 Monday to Friday

Transport: Tube: Colindale; Rail: Mill Hill Broadway; Bus: 303

Special facilities: Refreshment and toilet facilities available; access for users with disabilities – lift to reading room

Publications: Annual Report; information sheets on RAF related research

[512]
Royal Anthropological Institute of Great Britain and Ireland
RAI

50 Fitzroy Street
London W1T 5BT

Borough: Camden
Telephone: 020 7387 0455
Fax: 020 7383 4235
E-mail: photo@therai.org.uk
World Wide Web: www.rai.anthropology.org.uk
Constitution: Independent non-profit distributing organisation; company limited by guarantee; registered charity and association with voluntary subscribing membership
Key staff: Director: Jonathan Benthall; Photo Archivist: Chris Wright; Film Officer: Gail Baker

Stock and subject coverage: The Institute's Photographic Collection is an archive of over 40,000 photographs from the period 1865–1960 covering most areas of the world. They depict a variety of cultural practices as wide as their geographical range, and are a unique historical record of the diversity of the world's cultures. The Film Library contains over 190 carefully selected anthropological films and videos, one of the largest collections of this type of visual material in the UK. The coverage of the collection is worldwide, and contains a number of popular and award-winning documentaries

Services: Copy prints are available from photographs in the RAI's Photographic Collection on payment of the appropriate fee. Photocopies of index cards from the catalogue are also available

Availability: The Photographic Collection is for reference only and is intended for the use of serious researchers and publishers. Prints are available on payment of the appropriate fee. The Film Library hires out films and videos for educational purposes, within the UK only (managed by the Concord Video and Film Council, Norwich). An increasing number of video cassettes are offered for international sale

Hours: 09.30–17.30 usually on Monday and Tuesday, by appointment only

Transport: Tube: Warren Street

Special facilities: Toilet facilities available

Special facilities: The Photographic Collection is one of the main historical archives of its kind in the UK

Publications: The Journal of the Royal Anthropological Institute; Anthropology Today (journal); Anthropological Index Online (online bibliographic index to periodicals in the Museum of Mankind Library) www.lucy.ukc.ac.uk/AIO.html

Linked organisations

Museum of Mankind In 1976 the RAI's extensive library of anthropological books was merged with the library of the Museum of Mankind

[513]
Royal Armouries Library
HM Tower of London
London EC3
Borough: Tower Hamlets
Telephone: 020 7480 6358, ext 30
Fax: 020 7481 2922
World Wide Web: www.armouries.org.uk
Key staff: Librarian: Mrs Bridget Clifford
Stock and subject coverage: Part of one of the world's most important libraries on arms and armour; Tower history
Services: Photocopies
Availability: By appointment
Hours: 10.00–12.30 and 14.00–17.00 Monday to Friday
Transport: Tube: Tower Hill; Rail: Fenchurch Street; DLR: Tower Gateway
Special facilities: Refreshment and toilet facilities; limited access for users with disabilities
Special features: Located in the Tower of London

Linked organisations
Royal Armouries Museum, Armouries Drive, Leeds LS10 1LT

Fort Nelson Down End Road, Fareham PO17 6AN

[514]
Royal Artillery Institution Library
RA Institution Library
James Clavell Library
Royal Arsenal (West)
Warren Lane
Woolwich
London SE18 6ST
Borough: Greenwich
Telephone: 020 8312 7125
E-mail: paule@firepower.org.uk
Constitution: Independent non-profit distributing organisation and registered charity
Objectives/purposes: To record and promote research into the history of the Royal Artillery and related subjects
Key staff: Historical Secretary: Lieutenant Colonel WAH Townend; Librarian: Maurice Paul Evans; Researcher: Matthew Buck; Administrative Officer: Jill Lindsey
Stock and subject coverage: Coverage includes materials on Royal Artillery regimental history; artillery equipment; armed forces; warfare; tactics; training; fortification; military history; military geography; and biography. The stock includes books, journals, pamphlets, manuscripts, diaries, maps, plans, drawings, photographs, film and microfiche
Services: Photocopying, photographic reproduction and enquiry/research service available (charges apply throughout)
Availability: David Evans Reading Room open for readers 10.00–16.00 Tuesday to Thursday, by prior appointment with librarian
Hours: 09.30–13.00, 14.00–17.00 Monday to Friday
Transport: Rail: Woolwich Arsenal; Bus: 53, 54, 161, 180, 380, 422, 472

Special facilities: Part of Firepower! Museum complex with access to the History Gallery, Gunnery Hall, Medal Gallery and the Field of Fire audiovisual experience with gift shop and cafe on site
Publications: History of the Royal Regiment of Artillery (vols i–v available, vi for release in 2002, vii in production)

Linked organisations
Royal Regiment of Artillery The Library is part of the Regimental HQ of the Royal Artillery, part of the Royal Regiment of Artillery

Firepower! Museum

[515]
Royal Asiatic Society
60 Queen's Gardens
London W2 3AF
Borough: Westminster
Telephone: 020 7724 4741
Fax: 020 7706 4008
E-mail: royalasiaticsociety@btinternet.com
World Wide Web: www.royalasiaticsociety.co.uk
Constitution: Registered charity
Key staff: Librarian: MJ Pollock MA ALA
Stock and subject coverage: 100,000 books; 2,000 oriental manuscripts; 165 current journals; over 2,000 prints, drawings and paintings. Covers the history, language and culture of Asia
Services: Book loan service for Fellows; no postal interlibrary loans; staff-operated Xerox machine; microfiche and microfilm readers
Availability: Primarily for Fellows, but visitors welcome (please telephone in advance)
Hours: 11.00–17.00 (open until 20.00 on Tuesday; closed on Monday and Friday)
Transport: Tube: Bayswater, Lancaster Gate, Paddington
Special facilities: Toilet facilities available

[516]
Royal Automobile Club
RAC
89 Pall Mall
London SW1Y 5HS
Borough: Westminster
Telephone: 020 7747 3398
Fax: 020 7451 9980
E-mail: library@royalautomobileclub.co.uk
World Wide Web: www.royalautomobileclub.co.nk
Constitution: Company limited by guarantee, association with voluntary subscribing membership
Key staff: Clubhouse Librarian: Mr TG Dunmore
Stock and subject coverage: Stock covers history of motoring and motor sport. Selections of material on veteran, vintage and classic cars. Biographies of motoring personalities. Coverage of motor racing and rallying. Complete runs of motoring magazines, including Autosport, Autocar, Motor Sport, etc. Collection totals ca. 10,000 items. Large collection of RAC memorabilia including badges, models, photographs, programmes, yearbooks, etc. dating from the Club's inauguration in 1897
Services: Photocopies (charges made)

Availability: Open to members (gentlemen's club); and bona fide researchers upon application. Most material is for reference only. Charges are made for photocopying, faxing and online services
Hours: 09.00–17.00 Monday to Friday
Transport: Tube: Charing Cross, Piccadilly, Green Park; Rail: Charing Cross
Special facilities: Toilet facilities available; access for users with disabilities – lifts available but users with disabilities should advise the Library in advance
Special facilities: The Clubhouse occupies the extensive site of the old War Office
Publications: Badges of the RAC; The Motoring Century: the Story of the Royal Automobile Club

Linked organisations

Royal Automobile Club Motoring Services
Many contacts with RAC Motoring Services, but since the de-merger in 1999 reverted to a gentlemen's club

---

[517]
Royal Ballet School
RBS

[517][a]
Lower School, Ballet Museum, Ballet Library and Archives
The Royal Ballet School
White Lodge
Richmond Park
Surrey
Borough: Richmond upon Thames
Telephone: 020 8392 8021 (Lower School)
E-mail: trbs@aol.com
World Wide Web: www.royal-ballet-school.org.uk

[517][b]
Upper School, Ballet Library
Michael Wood Reading Room
155 Talgarth Road
Barons Court
London W14 9DE
Borough: Hammersmith
Telephone: 020 8748 6335 (Upper School)
Fax: 020 8563 0649 (Upper School)
Constitution: Company limited by guarantee; registered charity
Objectives/purposes: Ballet library, museum and archives
Key staff: Archivist/Ballet Librarian: Anna Meadmore MA ARAD
Stock and subject coverage: History of the Royal Ballet Organisation (i.e. School and Companies). Rare books and other books on the history of ballet. Books on ballet notation - Benesh, Stepanov, Laban, notated items, etc. Three collections of 19th century ballet prints and lithographs. Books on ballet biographies, ballet technique, etc.
Archives include photographs, Academy of Choreographic Art, early photographs of Vic-Wells Ballet, Camargo Society, Diaghilev Ballet, Pavlova, Harold Turner Collection, Vera Vaganova Collection. Programmes from the Vic-Wells/Sadlers Wells Ballet, Diaghilev Ballet, Pavlova Company, etc. Some press

cuttings including albums concerning Camargo Society, Vic-Wells Ballet
Museum collections, sculpture collections, ballet shoes, paintings, etc. Most of the items have been donated to RBS. Donations of archive material such as photographs, letters, etc. as gifts greatly appreciated
Services: Photocopies; prints of photographs by special request; sale of mounted photographs of lithographs and prints in RBS Archives, greetings cards and some framed photographs of prints
Availability: Primarily for use of RBS staff, pupils and students and members of the Royal Ballet, Birmingham Royal Ballet, etc. Under special circumstances only, available for reference to outsiders. Open to outsiders by written application
Hours: By appointment
Transport: Lower School: BR to Richmond Station then taxi
Upper School: Tube: Barons Court
Special facilities: Refreshment and toilet facilities available on site

Linked organisations

Royal Opera House, **Archives** Exists independently of RBS

---

[518]
Royal Botanic Gardens, Kew
Kew
Richmond
Surrey TW9 3AE
Borough: Richmond upon Thames
Telephone: 020 8332 5414 (Enquiries Desk)
Fax: 020 8332 5430
E-mail: library@rbgkew.org.uk
World Wide Web: www.rbgkew.org.uk
Constitution: Registered charity; government funded body; research institute
Key staff: Acting Head of Library and Archives: John Flanagan ALA
Stock and subject coverage: Over 140,000 monographs; 4,000 periodical titles (1,600 current); 140,000 pamphlets; 175,000 plant illustrations; 11,000 sheet maps; 250,000 mss and letters. One of the finest and most complete botanical libraries, with special emphasis on taxonomy; conservation; horticulture; biochemistry; anatomy; genetics; and economic botany. Branch libraries in the Jodrell Laboratory, Banks Centre for Economic Botany, Living Collections Department and at Wakehurst Place. Statutory place of deposit under the Public Record Acts
Services: Enquiry service. Microfilm and microfiche readers available. Photocopying service, subject to Copyright Regulations
Availability: For reference only, to bona fide research workers who should write in the first instance
Hours: 09.00–17.00 Monday to Friday. Closes on public holidays
Transport: Tube: Kew Gardens; Rail: Kew Bridge; Bus: 65, 391
Special facilities: Refreshment and toilet facilities; access for users with disabilities – ramp access to building, disabled parking outside entrance (book in advance), adapted toilet facilities

Note: The Library and Archives form part of RBG Kew's Information Services Department and support the work of the Herbarium, the Jodrell Laboratory, the Seed Conservation Department and the Living Collections Department. RBG Kew holds large reference collections of living and preserved plants, and artefacts made from plant materials, and carries out research and conservation work especially on tropical plants. The results of this work are disseminated through publications, conferences, tours and lectures

[519]
Royal College of Art Library
RCA
Kensington Gore
London SW7 2EU
Borough: Westminster
Telephone: 020 7590 4224
Fax: 020 7590 4500
E-mail: p.rae@rca.ac.uk
Constitution: Postgraduate school of art design and communication
Key staff: Librarian and Head of Information and Learning Services: Peter Hassell; Library Manager: Pauline Rae; Slide Curator: Jan Murton
Stock and subject coverage: Ca. 70,000 books on art, design and communication, together with support material on topics such as philosophy and psychology. Special collection on all aspects of colour. Slide collection with 140,000 slides on art and design. Product information collection with commercial literature, directories and samples
Services: Photocopies; video and CD-ROM facilities not available to visitors
Availability: Open to bona fide researchers for reference. Researchers admitted by appointment only
Hours: Term-time: 09.00-21.00 Monday to Friday; 12.00-17.00 Saturday
Vacations: 10.00-17.00 Monday to Friday
Transport: Tube: Kensington High Street, South Kensington; Rail: Victoria; Bus: 9, 10, 52
Special facilities: Refreshment and toilet facilities available; access for users with disabilities – ramp from road to street door entrance and lift to 1st floor library entrance, toilet on same floor as library

[520]
Royal College of Defence Studies
RCDS
Seaford House
37 Belgrave Square
London SW1X 8NS
Borough: Westminster
Telephone: 020 7915 4836/4814
Fax: 020 7915 4999
Constitution: Government funded body
Key staff: Librarian: Mrs AP Brady BA DipLib ALA; Assistant Librarian: Mr Paul Chandler BA; Library Clerk: Miss J Miller
Stock and subject coverage: Ca. 15,000 books and pamphlets; 200 current periodicals; small collection of videos and CD-ROMs. Subjects covered include:

international affairs, military studies, politics, economics and history
Services: Photocopying, internet access and online services
Availability: Open to MoD and government bodies only
Hours: 09.00-17.30 Monday to Friday
Transport: Tube: Hyde Park Corner, Victoria; Rail: Victoria
Publications: Seaford House Papers (annual)

Linked organisations
Ministry of Defence

[521]
Royal College of General Practitioners
Information Services Section
RCGP
The Geoffrey Evans Reference Library
14 Princes Gate
Hyde Park
London SW7 1PU
Borough: Westminster
Telephone: 020 7581 3232, ext 254
Fax: 020 7225 3047
E-mail: library@rcgp.org.uk
World Wide Web: www.rcgp.org.uk
Constitution: Independent non-profit distributing organisation; registered charity; royal medical college with membership by examination and subscription
Objectives/purposes: Providing information services in support of the work of the College and its members in its objective of improved quality of patient care in British general practice and in raising the profile of the profession of general practice within the field of medical care
Key staff: Senior Information Manager: Mr GM Richardson; Information Officer (Enquiries): Ms V Whelan; Information Librarian (Library): Ms B Berry; College Archivist: Ms P Baker
Stock and subject coverage: 6,000 books and 250 current journal titles covering general practice and primary health care in the UK and abroad. Special collection on general practice including collection of 200 theses from general practice
Services: Photocopies; literature searches on internal database; online and CD-ROM; enquiry service. All services are provided on a fee paying basis
Availability: Available to members, by appointment only to non-members. Reference only, loans of College publications only. Enquiries are accepted by telephone, fax and letter, priority being given to members
Hours: 09.00-17.00 Monday to Friday
Transport: Tube: Knightsbridge, South Kensington; Bus: 9, 10, 52
Special facilities: Refreshment and toilet facilities available; access for users with disabilities including toilet facilities
Special features: In American ownership for the first 100 years by the Morgan and Kennedy families. Chronicled in *14 Princes Gate* by John Horder and Stephen Pasmore

Publications: RCGP Occasional Papers; Clinical Series; Members reference book (includes Annual Report); Reports from General Practice; British Journal of General Practice

[522]
Royal College of Midwives Library
RCM
15 Mansfield Street
London W1G 9NH
Borough: Westminster
Telephone: 020 7291 9220/9221
Fax: 020 7312 3536
E-mail: library@rcm.org.uk
Constitution: Registered charity; association with voluntary subscribing membership
Objectives/purposes: To promote the art and science of midwifery
Key staff: Librarian: Mrs J Ayres; Senior Library Assistant: Miss J Ions
Stock and subject coverage: Over 6,500 books, 1,700 reports and 50 current journal titles on midwifery and related subjects plus growing thesis collection and the Marion Rabl Collection of paediatric textbooks.
Separate RCM archive collection spanning over 120 years and including committee minutes, reports, photographs, correspondence, accounts, press cuttings and scrap books. Enquiries should be addressed to the Archivist on 020 7291 9204, fax: 020 7312 3536
Services: Photocopies (charged); bibliographies (charged)
Availability: Library open to all RCM members as a lending library. The RCM has corporate membership of the Royal College of Nursing and the British Medical Association libraries and RCM members can request books or journal articles held by these libraries (contact the library for details of availability and charges). The Library is open as a reference library to non-members (telephone at least one day in advance to make an appointment). First time visitors to the Library should ask the Reception desk at 15 Mansfield Street for directions
Hours: 09.15–16.45 Monday to Friday
Transport: Tube: Oxford Circus, Bond Street, Great Portland Street; Bus: C2, 7, 8, 10, 13, 15, 25, 73, 159
Special facilities: Toilet facilities available

[523]
Royal College of Music Library
RCM Library
Prince Consort Road
London SW7 2BS
Borough: Kensington and Chelsea
Telephone: 020 7591 4325
Fax: 020 7589 7740
World Wide Web: www.rcm.ac.uk
Constitution: Registered charity; department of an educational organisation
Key staff: Chief Librarian: Pamela Thompson BA RCM, 020 7591 4323
Stock and subject coverage: Ca. 250,000 music scores, manuscripts, books on music and recordings, dating from ca. 1500 to the present day. Special collections include: Library of the Sacred Harmonic Society,

Library of the Concerts of Ancient Music, Heron-Allen Collection, Maurice Frost Collection
Services: Hire of orchestral parts and vocal sets; photocopies; microfilm/microfiche reader-printer; photographs; audiovisual facilities
Availability: Open to the public for reference, but no loans to non-members
Hours: Term-time: 9.30–18.15 Monday to Thursday; 09.30–17.30 Friday
Vacations: hours vary
Transport: Tube: South Kensington; Bus: 9, 10, 52
Special facilities: Refreshment facilities (in term-time); toilet facilities
Publications: Catalogue of the Manuscripts of Herbert Howells in the RCM Library; Joseph Doane: A Musical Directory for the Year 1794

[524]
Royal College of Nursing Library and Information Services
RCN UK Library
20 Cavendish Square
London W1G 0RN
Borough: Westminster
Telephone: 020 7647 3610
Fax: 020 7647 3420
E-mail: rcn.library@rcn.org.uk
World Wide Web: www.rcn.org.uk
Constitution: Registered charity; association with voluntary subscribing membership; independent trade union
Key staff: Head of Library and Information Services: Ms J Lord, ext 3616; Library Operations Manager: Ms C Banks, ext 3856; Librarians: Miss Thomas, ext 3618, Mrs Clark, ext 3617, Mrs Atlass, ext 3606, Mrs Lalani, ext 3906, Mrs Everitt, ext 3908, Mrs S Cull, ext 3908; Ms E Connolly, ext 3807
Stock and subject coverage: 65,000 volumes covering nursing and related subjects. 400 current journals. Steinberg Collection of Nursing Research: a collection of UK theses on nursing submitted for higher degrees
Services: Loans (including postal loans) for RCN members and RCN Institute students; photocopying service; information service; literature searches for full RCN members
Availability: External researchers are able to use the Library for a fee of £5 per day (advance booking required). A corporate membership scheme is available offering document supply and loans
Hours: 08.30–19.00 Monday, Tuesday, Thursday and Friday; 10.00–19.00 Wednesday; 09.00–17.00 Saturday
During August: 09.00–18.00 Monday to Friday
Transport: Tube: Oxford Circus
Special facilities: Refreshment and toilet facilities; access for users with disabilities (lifts to Library)
Publications: BNI plus and BNI available on subscription; RCN Thesaurus of Nursing Terms; RCN Library Classification Scheme; RCN Library Guide to the Subject Index

Linked organisations
RCN Institute

[525]
Royal College of Obstetricians and Gynaecologists
RCOG
27 Sussex Place
Regents Park
London NW1 4RG
Borough: Westminster
Telephone: 020 7772 6309
Fax: 020 7262 8331
E-mail: library@rcog.org.uk
World Wide Web: www.rcog.org.uk
Constitution: Registered charity
Key staff: Head of Information Services: Alice Breton
Stock and subject coverage: Comprehensive collection of books and journals in obstetrics and gynaecology, including an important collection of historical material

Separate Archive collection relating to the history of obstetrics and gynaecology open Monday, Wednesday and Friday (contact Clare Cowling, the College Archivist, on 020 7772 6277, e-mail: ccowling@rcog.org.uk)
Services: Access to the internet, Medline and Cochrane databases; photocopies
Availability: Loans to members only; serious outside enquiries accepted in special circumstances; bona fide researchers, normally with a medical qualification, may use reference facilities if they are introduced by a Fellow of the College
Hours: 09.00–18.00 Monday to Friday
Transport: Tube: Baker Street; Rail: Marylebone; Bus: 13, 27A, 82, 113
Special facilities: Access for users with disabilities – ramp available if required
Publications: List of journal holdings and early printed books available on website

[526]
Royal College of Physicians
RCP
11 St Andrew's Place
London NW1 4LE
Borough: Camden
Telephone: 020 7935 1174 ext 312
Fax: 020 7486 3729
E-mail: info@rcplondon.ac.uk
World Wide Web: www.rcplondon.ac.uk
Constitution: Registered charity; association with voluntary subscribing membership; professional association
Objectives/purposes: To sustain standards of medical practice by promoting medical education and research
Key staff: Manager: C Moss-Gibbons; Information Officers: J Beckwith, D Leach; Information Scientist: H Shaikh; Archivist: Susan Em; Curator: B Kelly
Stock and subject coverage: About 50,000 books; 20,000 manuscript/archive items; ca. 100 current journals; 210 sets of medical/scientific journals mainly from the 18th and 19th centuries; 13,000 engraved portraits and photographs. Also collections of slides,

videos and bookplates. Primarily covers the history of medicine with smaller collection covering UK health policy. The Library does not cover clinical medicine. Special collections: Dorchester Library (13,400 volumes bequeathed in 1688), Evan Bedford Library of Cardiology (donated in 1971)
Services: Photocopies; enquiry service (charges for non-Fellows and Members); internet available to Fellows and Members only
Availability: Open to Fellows and Members of the College and its facilities and to bona fide researchers. Loan service available to Fellows and Members. Charges for some services including research for non-Fellows and Members
Hours: 09.00–17.00 Monday to Friday
Transport: Tube: Regent's Park, Great Portland Street; Bus: C2, 18, 27, 30, 135
Special facilities: Refreshment facilities for Fellows and Members. Toilet facilities available; access for users with disabilities – including toilet facilities
Special features: College and library date from 1518. The current building, designed by Sir Denys Lasdun, opened in 1964 and now has Grade 1 listing
Publications: Evan Bedford Library of Cardiology: Catalogue (1977); Lives of the Fellows of the Royal College of Physicians; The Royal College of Physicians and its Collections - an Illustrated History (2001)

[527]
Royal College of Psychiatrists Information Service
RCPsych
17 Belgrave Square
London SW1X 8PG
Borough: Westminster
Telephone: 020 7259 6303
Fax: 020 7245 1231
E-mail: infoservices@rcpsych.ac.uk
World Wide Web: www.rcpsych.ac.uk
Constitution: Registered charity; part of a professional body
Key staff: Librarian: Ms M Davis
Stock and subject coverage: Psychiatry and related medical fields; 40 journals and a reference collection of around 2,000 books. Historical/antiquarian collection of psychiatry
Services: Photocopying; internet access; online databases
Availability: To Fellows, Affiliates and Members of the College. Chargeable limited service to external health professionals and bona fide researchers, by appointment only
Hours: 09.30–16.30 Monday to Friday
Transport: Tube: Knightsbridge, Hyde Park Corner, Victoria; Rail: Victoria
Special facilities: Refreshment and toilet facilities available
Publications: Reading lists for trainees in basic sciences; Index to Statement; Guidelines and College policy documents

[528]
The Royal College of Surgeons of England
RCS Eng

Library and Lumley Study Centre
35–43 Lincoln's Inn Fields
London WC2A 3PE
Borough: Camden
Telephone: 020 7869 6555 (Library)
  020 7869 6556 (Lumley Study Centre)
  020 7405 3473 (College)
Fax: 020 7405 4438
E-mail: library@rcseng.ac.uk
  lumley@rcseng.ac.uk
World Wide Web: www.rcseng.ac.uk
Constitution: Registered charity; part of a professional body
Objectives/purposes: The RCSEng is an independent professional body committed to promoting and advancing the highest standards of surgical care for patients
Key staff: Librarian: Mrs T Knight; Deputy Librarian: Mrs T Craig
Stock and subject coverage: Holdings include ca. 60,000 books and 3,000 journals (400 current) on all aspects of clinical surgery including surgical specialities and dental surgery; also surgical anatomy, physiology and pathology. Medical biography and the history of medicine are widely collected. The large historical collection includes 57 items of incunabula. Special collections, which consist of printed books, manuscripts and autograph letters include the Hunter–Baillie collection (1,500 items); John Hunter – his contemporaries and pupils (1,100); Lord Lister (250); Richard Owen (750); and Arthur Keith (300). Added to this are ca. 3,000 engraved portraits, 2,000 bookplates and 150 medals. The Library provides a photographic service based on the College's paintings and sculptures and its own holdings. Computer assisted learning and multimedia programs. Audiovisual programs illustrating basic sciences and techniques in surgical practice.
The Lumley Study Centre is a facility for multimedia teaching and educational resources in surgery and dentistry encompassing current books and journals as well as audiovisual material and computer assisted learning programmes. The Lumley Study Centre is available to Diplomates of the College, including the Faculty of Dental Surgery and the Faculty of General Dental Practitioners and participants registered on RCSEng courses. Those undertaking independent self-directed study in surgery and dentistry, as well as researchers with professional interest requiring information in surgery and dentistry, should preferably contact the Deputy Librarian (Current Services) in advance of any visit. A temporary membership charge may apply
Services: Library catalogue of holdings from 1850 – on Unicorn Library Management System available via website (www.webcat.rcseng.ac.uk); Medline, Cochrane and other online/CD-ROM resources; interlibrary loans; literature searches; historical enquiries. Full details and scale of charges on website
Availability: Open to bona fide researchers provided a prior appointment is made. A charge is made for temporary membership. Materials are for reference use only. Charges are made for photocopies and faxes and there is a scale of charges for genealogical enquiries and the photographic services
Hours: 09.00–18.00 Monday, Tuesday, Thursday and Friday; 10.00–18.00 Wednesday. See website for holiday closures
Transport: Tube: Holborn, Chancery Lane, Temple; Bus: all routes along High Holborn, Kingsway and Aldwych
Special facilities: Refreshment and toilet facilities; access for users with disabilities
Special features: Neo-classical Reading Room by Charles Barry, 1835
Publications: English books before 1701 in the Library of the RCS; Lives of the Fellows of the Royal College of Surgeons; audiovisual catalogue; multimedia catalogue

[529]
Royal College of Veterinary Surgeons

RCVS Library and Information Service
Belgravia House
62–64 Horseferry Road
London SW1P 2AF
Borough: Westminster
Telephone: 020 7222 2021
Fax: 020 7222 2004
E-mail: library@rcvs.org.uk
World Wide Web: www.rcvs.org.uk
Constitution: Chartered professional body
Key staff: Head of Library and Information Service: Tom Roper BA DipLib MIInfSc ALA
Stock and subject coverage: 25,000 volumes; 250 current periodicals. Covers veterinary science and its history. Historical collection of books from 1514. Ernest Grey collection on late 19th to early 20th century ornithology
Services: Online searches; enquiry service; loans (UK only; photocopies. CD-ROMs available for use in the library
Availability: To College members and others working in animal health. Non-members admitted by appointment
Hours: 09.15–17.00 Monday to Friday
Transport: Tube: Westminster, St James Park, Pimlico, Victoria; Bus: 507
Special facilities: Access for people with disabilities, including toilet facilities

[530]
Royal Entomological Society

41 Queen's Gate
London SW7 5HR
Borough: Kensington and Chelsea
Telephone: 020 7584 8361
Fax: 020 7581 8505
E-mail: lib@royensoc.co.uk
World Wide Web: www.royensoc.co.uk
Constitution: Registered charity and association with voluntary subscribing membership
Objectives/purposes: The improvement and diffusion of entomological science

Key staff: Librarian: Berit Pedersen

Stock and subject coverage: Ca. 11,000 books, 750 journal titles (250 current) on insect taxonomy and general biology, with particular reference to the Western Palaearctic Region

Services: Photocopies; CD-ROM

Availability: Access is open to Fellows and Members of the Society and to bona fide researchers on written application to the Registrar. Charges are made for photocopies and research time

Hours: 09.30-17.00 Monday to Friday

Transport: Tube: Gloucester Road, South Kensington; Bus: C1, 49

Special facilities: Refreshment and toilet facilities available

Publications: Ecological Entomology; Systematic Entomology; Medical and Veterinary Entomology; Physiological Entomology; Insect Molecular Biology; Bi-annual Symposia

---

[531]
Royal Free and University College Medical School Medical Library

Medical Library
Royal Free Hospital
Rowland Hill Street
London NW3 2PF

Borough: Camden

Telephone: 020 7794 0500 ext 3203

Fax: 020 7794 3534

E-Mail: library@rfc.ucl.ac.uk

World Wide Web: www.rfc.ucl.ac.uk

Constitution: Independent non-profit distributing organisation; registered charity; medical School of the University of London

Objectives/purposes: To support undergraduate and postgraduate continuing medical education, medical research and clinical practice

Key staff: Librarian: Betsy Anagnostelis

Stock and subject coverage: Ca. 20,000 books and 400 current journals covering general medicine. Friern Collection of psychology and psychiatry materials

Services: Photocopies; online searching; current awareness services - weekly and monthly; bibliographic database advice; training in the use of networked information sources, including internet-based resources

Availability: The Medical Library offers services to all staff and students based at the Royal Free and University College Medical School of UCL, all staff at the Royal Free Hampstead NHS Trust, including doctors in training based at the Royal Free, local Primary Care Groups and other professionals employed by the local Health Authority

Hours: 09.00-22.00 Monday to Friday: 09.00-17.00 Saturday (except August)

Transport: Tube: Belsize Park; Rail: Hampstead Heath; Bus: C11, 24, 46, 168

Special facilities: Access for users with disabilities

Publications: Annual Report and Prospectus (published by Medical School). Library publications include: guides to services, newsletters, journals holdings lists, etc.

Linked organisations

> **University College London** Member of the College
> **Royal Free Hampstead NHS Trust**
> **Royal Free and University College Medical School** The Royal Free campus of the School is one of the main teaching and research sites. Other School sites are the Gower Street campus and the Archway campus

---

[532]
Royal Geographical Society (with The Institute of British Geographers)
RGS-IBG

1 Kensington Gore
London SW7 2AR

Borough: Westminster

Telephone: 020 7591 3040

Fax: 020 7591 3001

E-mail: library@rgs.org

World Wide Web: www.rgs.org

Constitution: Registered charity and learned society

Key staff: Director and Secretary: Dr Rita Gardner; Keeper: Dr AF Tatham; Librarian: Eugene Rae MA; Curator of Maps: Francis Herbert; Archives Assistant: Sarah Strong; Picture Library Manager: Joanna Wright

Stock and subject coverage: About 170,000 volumes containing works on geography, topography, cartography, and voyages and travels. Extensive series of geographical periodicals. An extensive author and subject card catalogue is maintained, with analytical entries of periodical articles as well as book entries

Map room: Contains ca. 1 million map and chart sheets and 4,000 atlases, as well as ca. 2,000 indexed expedition reports. Also an enquiry service and photocopies

Expedition Advisory Centre: Provides an information and training service to those planning an expedition. An expedition report library, a list of expedition consultants, a register of planned expeditions, information on lecturers, a register of members available for expeditions, broadsheets on expedition topics, and an information library are also available

Hours: 11.00-17.00 Monday to Friday

Availability: The Library and Reading Room will be closed until the end of 2003. Archives and Picture Library are open by appointment (access fees are charged)

Transport: Tube: South Kensington; Bus: 9, 10, 52

Special facilities: Refreshment and toilet facilities available; access for users with disabilities – limited wheelchair access

Publications: Geographical Journal (3 p.a.); Transactions of the Institute of British Geographers; Area (4 p.a.); Maps; Geographical Magazine (12 p.a. – part owner); Directory of University Geography Courses (every other year)
Geographical Journal (3 p.a.); Maps; Pamphlets; Geographical (monthly - part owner)

[533]
Royal Holloway, University of London
Egham
Surrey TW20 0EX
Borough: Richmond upon Thames
Telephone: 01784 443334
Fax: 01784 477670
E-mail: library@rhul.ac.uk
Constitution: Department of a university
Key staff: Librarian and Deputy Director of Information
   Services: Ms SE Gerrard, BA hons DipLib, ALA;
   Academic Services Manager: Mr D Ward
Stock and subject coverage: There are three libraries:
   Founder's Library – subject coverage includes:
   modern languages and literature in English, French,
   German, Italian and Spanish; classics including Greek
   and Latin language and literature and ancient history;
   and fine arts. Others are the Music Library and the
   Bedford Library – subject coverage includes: general
   science; modern history; and the social sciences
Services: Photocopies
Availability: Open to all. Reference facilities only for
   non-members of the College. Membership at £60
   p.a. allows limited borrowing rights
Hours: Founder's Library. Term-time: 09.00–21.00
   Monday to Thursday; 09.00–19.00 Friday; 11.00–
   17.00 Saturday; 13.00–18.00 Sunday
   Vacations: 09.00–17.00 Monday to Friday
   Music Library. Term-time: 09.00–17.00 Monday to
   Friday
   Vacations: 09.00–17.00 Monday to Friday
   Bedford Library. Term-time: 09.00–21.00, 11.00–
   17.00 Saturday; 13.00–18.00 Sunday
   Vacations: 09.00–17.00 Monday to Friday
Transport: Rail: Egham
Special facilities: Refreshment and toilet facilities available;
   access for users with disabilities
Special features: The Bedford Library was opened in
   1993. The Founder's Library is located in a grade I
   listed building
Publications: Royal Holloway University of London
   Annual Report

Linked organisations
   University of London Part of the University

---

[534]
Royal Horticultural Society
RHS
Lindley Library
80 Vincent Square
London SW1P 2PE
Borough: Wesminster
Telephone: 020 7821 3050
Fax: 020 7630 6060
E-mail: library_enquiries@rhs.org.uk
World Wide Web: www.rhs.org.uk/libraries
Constitution: Registered charity and association with
   voluntary subscribing membership
Objectives/purposes: To promote horticulture in all its
   branches
Key staff: Librarian and Archivist: Dr Brent Elliott;
   Assistant Librarians: Barbara Collecott, Gillian
   Goudge, Jennifer Vine

Stock and subject coverage: World's foremost horticultural
   library. Subject coverage mainly horticulture,
   including fruit and vegetable growing and garden
   design. Other subjects covered include: history of
   gardens and gardening; flower arrangement; botanical
   art and subsidiary collections on botany, agriculture,
   forestry and cookery. The stock includes ca. 50,000
   books from 1514 to present day; ca. 18,000 drawings;
   ca. 1,500 journal titles (over 300 current titles) and
   the largest collection of horticultural trade catalogues
   in the UK
Services: Photocopies (charges made)
Availability: Accessible to the public, for reference only,
   by appointment. Members of the RHS have
   borrowing privileges
Hours: 09.30–17.30 Monday to Friday
Transport: Tube: Victoria, St James's Park, Pimlico; Rail:
   Victoria; Bus: 11, 24
Special facilities: Toilet facilities available; no special access
   for users with disabilities but staff assistance provided
Special features: The Society's original library was sold in
   1859. The library of John Lindley (1799–1865),
   botanist and Secretary of the Society, was purchased
   to form the nucleus of the new library, which
   became the Lindley Library in 1868 (independent
   trust, to ensure against any future sale)
Publications: Journal, yearbooks, etc. published by the
   RHS

Linked organisations
   **National Council for the Conservation of
   Plants and Gardens (NCCPG)
   Institute of Horticulture**
   Both organisations were set up under the RHS's
   auspices

   The Wisley Garden Library, **Hyde Hall Garden
   Library**, **Harlow Carr Garden Library** The three
   Garden Libraries are small informal libraries aimed at
   the amateur gardener with reference collections,
   journals and a wide range of horticultural books. A
   Rosemoor Garden Library is in development. The
   Garden Libraries are an integral part of the Lindley
   Library

   Wisley Laboratory Library Support library for
   the RHS scientific, advisory, horticultural and
   educational staff. Part of the Lindley Library (contact
   RHS Garden Wisley, Woking, Surrey GU 23 6QB,
   tel: 01483 212428, e-mail: library@rhs.org.uk)

---

[535]
Royal Institute of British Architects
RIBA
British Architectural Library
BAL
66 Portland Place
London W1B 1AD
Borough: Westminster
Telephone: 020 7580 5533
   0906 302 0400 (Public Information Line, cost 50p
   per minute)
Fax: 020 7631 1802
E-mail: bal@inst.riba.org
World Wide Web: www.architecture.com
Constitution: Registered charity; chartered professional

body and association with voluntary subscribing membership

Key staff: Director: Ruth Kamen; Special Collections: Charles Hind; Information Services: Jane Oldfield; Books and Periodicals: Julian Osley

Stock and subject coverage: The largest and most comprehensive resource for research on all aspects of architecture in Britain. About 135,000 volumes. Unique collection of at least 600,000 drawings. About 2,000 periodicals from many countries. Card index of journal articles. Some 700 linear metres of mss, predominantly relating to 19th century and early 20th century architectural practice. Collection of over 650,000 photographs

Services: Enquiry service; loans library; photocopy service and coin-operated colour and black and white photocopiers available; photography service. Library catalogue available via website for material catalogued since the early 1980s

Availability: Admission to the public by day ticket (reference only) or annual membership of the RIBA. Contact library for current charges

Hours: 13.30-17.00 Monday; 10.00-20.00 Tuesday; 10.00-17.00 Wednesday to Friday; 10.00-13.30 Saturday. Drawings collection by appointment only. Closed for part of August

Transport: Tube: Oxford Circus, Great Portland Street, Regent's Park; Bus: C1, 135

Special facilities: Refreshment and toilet facilities available; access for users with disabilities

Publications: Architectural Publications Index (quarterly); Architectural Publications Index on Disc (quarterly); RIBA List of Recommended Books (annual); Royal Institute of British Architects: A Guide to its Archive and History (Mansell); 20 volume Catalogue of the Drawings Collection of the RIBA (Gregg) (also available on microfiche and microfilm from World Microfilms Ltd); 5 volume RIBA Drawings Series (Trefoil Books); RIBA Nomination Papers 1834-1900 (Emmett Publishing); Directory of British Architects 1834-1914 (Continuum); Early Printed Books 1478-1840: A Catalogue of the British Architectural Library Early Imprints Collection (Bowker Saur); microfilm collections of original drawings, manuscripts and early printed books (World Microfilms Ltd); Guide to the British Architectural Library (a series of information sheets); list of the Library's publications

[536]
Royal Institute of International Affairs
RIIA

Chatham House
10 St James's Square
London SW1Y 4LE
Borough: Westminster
Telephone: 020 7957 5723
Fax: 020 7957 5710
E-mail: libenquire@riia.org
World Wide Web: www.riia.org
Constitution: Independent non-profit distributing organisation; registered charity; association with voluntary subscribing membership; private research institute/learned society

Key staff: Librarian: Mrs Catherine Hume

Stock and subject coverage: Specialist library of ca. 150,000 books and pamphlets on most aspects of international affairs, focusing particularly on foreign policy, politics, economics, security and the environment, covering approximately 30 years for books and 15 years for periodicals. Approximately 300 periodicals, of which 70 are currently indexed. Large collection of press cuttings on international affairs 1924-1997, 30 current newspapers. Archive collection also available. Visitors wanting to consult the archives must apply in advance, in writing, to the Librarian

Availability: Open to members. Also open to bona fide researchers, upon payment of a fee. Applications must be made in advance. Lending stock is available via interlibrary loan. Newspapers, cuttings, periodicals and reference material are not available for loan

Services: Photocopies; microform reader-printer; film and fiche readers, free internet access and online searching available on request

Hours: Library: 11.00-17.30 Monday to Friday. Closed part of August and extra days at some Bank Holidays

Transport: Tube: Green Park, Piccadilly Circus, Leicester Square

Special facilities: Refreshment and toilet facilities available; limited access for users with disabilities – wheelchair access from the street is awkward, once in the building a lift gives access to the library and to toilet for disabled people

Publications: International Affairs (quarterly); World Today (monthly). Library Publications: Monthly List of Articles in Periodicals; Monthly List of Books and Pamphlets added to the Library; The Royal Institute of International Affairs Library Resources, Vol I: Classification Schedules, Vol II: Alphabetical Thesaurus (1992)

[537]
Royal Institute of Navigation
RIN

1 Kensington Gore
London SW7 2AT
Borough: Kensington and Chelsea
Telephone: 020 7591 3130
Fax: 020 7591 3131
E-mail: info@rin.org.uk
World Wide Web: www.rin.org.uk
Constitution: Registered charity
Objectives/purposes: To promote the art and science of navigation
Key staff: Mrs Rebecca Dudley
Stock and subject coverage: Books, journals and papers on all areas of navigation: land, sea, air, animal, satellite and space
Availability: Open to all for reference only. Loan facilities for RIN members only
Hours: 09.30-16.30 Monday to Friday
Transport: Tube: South Kensington, Kensington High Street; Bus: 9, 10, 52
Special facilities: Refreshment and toilet facilities available; access for users with disabilities – lift provided
Publications: Navigation News (6 p.a.) published by Mercator Media Ltd

[538]
Royal Institution of Chartered Surveyors
RICS

12 Great George Street
London SW1P 3AD
Borough: Westminster
Telephone: 0870 333 1600
Fax: 020 7334 3784
E-mail: library@rics.org.uk
World Wide Web: www.rics.org
Constitution: Chartered professional body
Objectives/purposes: To promote the highest standards of professionalism, skills and integrity in all matters relating to the economics and management of land, property and construction and the associated environmental issues
Key staff: Head of Library and Information Services: Pauline Lane-Gilbert; Information Officer: Annette Howard; Team Leader, User Services: Hilary Oakley
Stock and subject coverage: Ca. 32,000 volumes on statistics; law; photogrammetry; land surveying; minerals; agriculture; estate management; building and construction; quantity surveying; housing and property management; landlord and tenant; planning and development; rating; valuation; estate agency. Special collections: historical collections on land surveying, building economics, fine arts, Board of Agriculture Reports (19th century); Royal Commission Reports on land use (19th century); Topographical collections; legal serials
Services: Photocopying. Books available on loan to members and on interlibrary loan. Some services are chargeable. Internet access available to RICS members only
Availability: Library book collection available for consultation by non-members by prior appointment only. Daily, five-day and annual passes available. Details of charges available on request
Hours: 09.30-17.30 Monday to Friday
Transport: Tube: Westminster; Rail: Charing Cross, Waterloo, Victoria; Bus: 3, 11, 12, 24, 53, 77, 109, 159
Services: Toilet facilities available; access for users with disabilities – toilet facilities for wheelchair users; induction loop
Publications: RICS Library Information Service (Subscriber Service); Weekly Briefing; RICS Abstracts and Reviews; reading lists on property and construction topics

[539]
Royal Institution of Great Britain Library
The Royal Institution

21 Albemarle Street
London W15 4BS
Borough: Westminster
Telephone: 020 7409 2992
Fax: 020 7629 3569
E-mail: ril@ri.ac.uk
World Wide Web: www.ri.ac.uk
Constitution: Registered charity and association with voluntary subscribing membership

Key staff: Dr Frank James
Stock and subject coverage: Ca. 60,000 volumes and several hundred journals. Collections on: science and technology mainly for the non-specialist; science in relation to art, government and religion; science education; history of science; research literature mainly in solid state chemistry; catalysis and computational methods in chemistry. Scientific archives of H Davy, M Faraday and other personalities connected with the Royal Institution
Services: Photocopies (charges made); information service; conducted tours of the RI building, including the Faraday Museum, for parties by appointment (there is a charge). Faraday Museum open to the public 09.00-17.00 (£1 admission charge)
Availability: Information service available to all – non-members by appointment; loan service for members only
Hours: Non-members: 10.00-17.00. Members: 09.00-18.00 Monday to Friday
Transport: Tube: Green Park, Piccadilly
Special facilities: Toilet facilities available; access for users with disabilities – lift available
Special features: Library is housed in a beautiful 18th century building, the headquarters of the Royal Institution since its foundation in 1799
Publications: Proceedings of the Royal Institution (annual, published by Oxford University Press); Annual Report; lecture lists (3 p.a.); wide range of publications (list available on request)

[540]
The Royal London Hospital Archives and Museum

The Royal London Hospital
Whitechapel
London E1 1BB
Borough: Tower Hamlets
Telephone: 020 7377 7608
Fax: 020 7377 7413
E-mail: jonathan.evans@bartsandthelondon.nhs.uk
World Wide Web: www.bartsandthelondon.org
www.medicalmuseums.org
Constitution: Government funded body
Objectives/purposes: Archives and museum of the Royal London Hospital and affiliated institutions
Key staff: Archivist: Mr Jonathan Evans; Modern Records Manager: Mrs Penelope Baker
Stock and subject coverage: The Archives collection includes records of the London (now Royal London) Hospital from its foundation in 1740 and the London Hospital Medical College from 1785. Records of affiliated bodies such as the Samaritan Society (founded 1791) and School of Nursing (founded 1783) are also held. Records of 12 other hospitals in Tower Hamlets, Newham and Hackney (from 1840s). Special collections of the London Hospital Medical College include medical texts from ca. 1500, alumini collection and reference works on orthodontics and forensic medicine. The Archive holds a library of nursing texts ca. 1850 to present, approximately 100,000 photographs, 200 films and 20,000 newspaper cuttings

Services: In Medical College library: photocopies; microfiche reader; MPEG viewer; slide transparency viewer

Availability: Usual restrictions on hospital (i.e. public) records, but bona fide researchers may apply for access. Free access to all `open' records. Administrative fee for loan of copy film or photographic material

Hours: 10.00–16.30 Monday to Friday, subject to staff availability

Transport: Tube: Whitechapel; Rail: Bethnal Green, Liverpool Street

Special facilities: Access for users with disabilities – ramped access

Special features: Archives located in basement of St Augustine with St Philip's Church, now used as the London Hospital Medical College Library. Readers have use of the reading room facilities in this Early English style Victorian listed building. The Archives and Museum has an exhibition on the history of the Hospital

Publications: Royal London Trust annual report (now discontinued); Royal Hospitals Trust Prospectus 1994; The London Hospital Gazette (annual); The Link (monthly staff newspaper)

Linked organisations

St Bartholemew's and the Royal London School of Medicine and Dentistry, Queen Mary, University of London Part of the University

Barts and the London NHS Trust The Archives and Museum are part of the Trust and linked thereby to St Bartholemew's Hospital Archives Department

London Hospital Medical College The Royal London's Archives are held together with those of the London Hospital Medical College and are located in the College Library building

St Bartholemews and the Royal London Charitable Foundation

[541]
Royal Mail Heritage Services

Freeling House
Phoenix Place
London WC1X 0DL
Borough: Camden
Telephone: 020 7239 2570
Fax: 020 7239 2576
E-mail: heritage@royalmail.com
World Wide Web: www.royalmail.com
Objectives/purposes: To collect historic operational records of the British Post Office dating from 1635; to curate the collections of the former National Postal Museum; and to make all material available for public access

Key staff: Head of Heritage; Archives Manager: Martin Rush; Collections Manager: Christine Jones

Stock and subject coverage: Material on all aspects of Post Office operations including: old operational files and papers; internal publications; published material; posters, philatelic artwork and extensive collection of British stamps; and other items relating to the history and people associated with the British postal history

Services: Photocopies; microfiche readers; photography can be arranged

Availability: Free access for all for reference only. Philatelic collections viewed by appointment only. Proof of identity required

Hours: 09.00–16.15 (except Bank Holidays and Christmas week). Occasional closure for staff training, so please phone prior to visit

Transport: Tube: King's Cross, Farringdon, Chancery Lane; Rail: King's Cross, Euston, Farringdon; Bus: 17, 19, 38, 45, 46, 55, 63, 243 and 341

Special facilities: Refreshment point; toilets; access for users with disabilities

[542]
Royal Mencap Society

MENCAP National Centre
123 Golden Lane
London EC1Y 0RT
Borough: Corporation of London
Telephone: 020 7454 0454
Fax: 020 7608 3254
E-mail: information@mencap.org.uk
World Wide Web: www.mencap.org.uk
Constitution: Registered charity
Objectives/purposes: Mencap is the leading charity working with children and adults with learning disabilities in England, Wales and Northern Ireland. Through its regional network and more than 500 affiliated local societies, Mencap is able to offer local services, support and advice to people with learning disability and their parents/carers

Key staff: Information Services: Christine Thomas
Stock and subject coverage: Information available through the National Learning Disability Helpline (freephone: 0808 808 1111, minicom: 0808 808 8181, fax: 020 7608 3254, e-mail: help@mencap.org.uk) and Information Service

Services: Enquiry service; reading lists. No loan service. Bookshop stocking titles on all aspects of learning disabilities. Booklist available on request

Availability: Available to all professional and public enquiries

Hours: 09.30–17.30 Monday to Friday
Publications: Range of information leaflets available from the Information Service National Centre; Viewpoint: the Newspaper of Mencap and Gateway (contact Helen Ketton, National Centre)

Linked organisations

Seven divisional offices, district offices and network of 550 local societies

[543]
Royal National Institute for the Blind
RNIB

[543][a]
Research Library

105 Judd Street
London WC1H 9NF
Borough: Camden

Telephone: 020 7391 2052
Fax: 020 7388 0891
E-mail: library@rnib.org.uk
World Wide Web: www.rnib.org.uk/library/research
Constitution: Registered charity
Key staff: Librarian: Fiona Bell MA
Stock and subject coverage: Largest collection of material on blindness and partial sight in the UK. Books, journals, pamphlets, annual reports and government papers (mostly in print) on all aspects of visual impairment. Subject coverage includes: the medical and administrative aspects of visual impairment; psychology; education; daily living; recreation and leisure; vocational rehabilitation; literature; technology; biography; and special groups (deaf blind, older blind people, learning disabilities and blindness). Special collection of early embossed literature: braille, Moon, etc.
Services: Enquiry and reference service; bibliographies; some loans; photocopies (charged). Access technology for visually impaired users includes: scanner, CCTV, braille embosser
Availability: Open to all, with facilities for access by visually impaired users
Hours: 09.00-17.00 (preferably by appointment)
Transport: Tube and Rail: King's Cross
Special facilities: Toilet facilities available; access for users with disabilities (see services)
Publications: New Literature on Visual Impairment (bi-monthly, subscription on request); reading lists

[543][b]
Royal National Institute for the Blind – Falcon Park
Talking Book Service

Neasden Lane
London NW10 1TB
Borough: Brent
Telephone: 0845 7626843
Fax: 01733 371555
Key staff: Local Authority Relationship Manager: Joyce Bis; Customer Services Manager: Jan Kerr
Stock and subject coverage: A large collection of popular fiction (romance, children's stories, etc.) and non-fiction material
Services: Enquiry and loan service; bibliographies; catalogues
Availability: Open to blind and partially sighted people. There is an annual membership subscription, often paid by the Local Authority. Information on subscription rates may be obtained from RNIB Talking Book Customer Services (telephone: 0845 7626843, e-mail: services@rnib.org.uk, post: RNIB Talking Book Service, PO Box 173, Peterborough PE2 6WS)
Hours: 08.00-18.00 Monday, Tuesday, Thursday and Friday; 10.00-18.00 Wednesday; 09.00-16.00 Saturday

Linked organisations
Royal National Institute for the Blind

[544]
Royal Opera House Archives

Royal Opera House
Covent Garden
London WC2E 9DD
Borough: Westminster
Telephone: 020 7212 9353
Fax: 020 7212 9489
E-mail: archives@roh.org.uk
World Wide Web: www.royalopera.org
Constitution: Department of a performing arts organisation
Objectives/purposes: Archives for the Royal Opera House and its performing companies. Records of the three theatres to have stood on the Covent Garden site since 1732
Key staff: Archivist: Francesca Franchi; Assistant Archivist: Jane Jackson
Stock and subject coverage: The Archives were established to record the history of the Royal Opera House and its companies since the first Theatre Royal, Covent Garden opened in 1732. The Archives record the work of the ROH's three companies – The Royal Ballet; The Birmingham Royal Ballet and the Royal Opera – at Covent Garden and on tour, as well as information on companies visiting the ROH and associated ballet, opera and general music and theatre material. Visual material includes: 18th and 19th century prints and song sheet covers, photographs, costume and set designs and posters. Written material includes: playbills, programmes, press-cuttings, play-texts, libretti, 19th and early 20th century music and administrative records
Services: Photocopies and copy photography (charges made)
Availability: Access to all bona fide researchers by prior appointment. Research fees are charged. There is a hire fee for copy photographs and colour transparencies. Original material is loaned for exhibition to approved venues
Hours: 10.30-13.00, 14.30-17.00 Tuesday, Thursday and Friday
Transport: Tube: Covent Garden
Special facilities: Refreshment and toilet facilities available; access for users with disabilities
Special facilities: The Archives mount regular exhibitions in the public areas of the theatre. These are open, free of charge, 10.00-15.30 Monday to Saturday

[545]
Royal Pharmaceutical Society of Great Britain
RPSGB

1 Lambeth High Street
London SE1 7JN
Borough: Lambeth
Telephone: 020 7572 2300 (Library)
020 7572 2302 (Technical information)
Fax: 020 7572 2499
E-mail: library@rpsgb.org.uk
World Wide Web: www.rpsgb.org.uk

Constitution: Department of a professional body

Key staff: Head of Information: Roy Allcorn; Librarian: Roddy Morrison; Assistant Librarian: Anne Walker

Stock and subject coverage: 66,000 books and pamphlets; 500 current periodicals on the pharmaceutical sciences. Historical collection of pharmacopoeias, herbals and illustrated botanical works

Services: Loans; photocopies; enquiry service, CD-ROMs, internet access

Availability: To members for borrowing and reference; to non-members for reference only, on payment of a fee

Hours: 09.00-17.00 Monday to Wednesday, Friday; 10.00-17.45 Thursday

Transport: Tube: Waterloo, Vauxhall, Lambeth North; Rail: Waterloo, Vauxhall; Bus: 3, 344, 507

Special facilities: Toilet facilities available; access for users with disabilities by prior arrangement

Publications: List of current journals

Linked organisations

RPSGB Scottish Department (36 York Place, Edinburgh EH1 3HY)

[546]
Royal Society

6 Carlton House Terrace
London SW1Y 5AG

Borough: Westminster

Telephone: 020 7451 2606

Fax: 020 7930 2170

E-mail: library@royalsoc.ac.uk

World Wide Web: www.royalsoc.ac.uk

Constitution: Registered charity

Key staff: Head of Library and Information Services: Karen Peters; Library Manager: Rupert Baker; Archivist: Joanna Corden

Stock and subject coverage: Over 40,000 books on all branches of science, history of science and scientific biography. Recent science policy reports and publications of International Council of Scientific Unions (ICSU). 80,000 volumes of journals, chiefly publications of national academies worldwide. Manuscript archives of the Society and papers of some Fellows

Services: Photocopies; photographic service

Availability: Library for Fellows and staff of the Society. Open to other bona fide researchers on production of photographic identification

Hours: 10.00-17.00 Monday to Friday

Transport: Tube: Piccadilly Circus, Charing Cross; Rail: Charing Cross

Special facilities: Refreshment and toilet facilities available; access for users with disabilities – including ramp to front door, adapted toilet

Special features: Built by John Nash; home of the Prussian, and later, German, Embassy until 1939

Publications: Science Policy Information; List of Fellows of the Royal Society 1660-2000; Obituaries and Biographical Memoirs of Fellows of the Royal Society 1830-2000

[547]
The Royal Society for Asian Affairs (formerly Royal Central Asian Society)
RSAA

2 Belgrave Square
London SW1X 8PJ

Borough: Westminster

Telephone: 020 7235 5122

Fax: 020 7259 6771

E-mail: info@rsaa.org.uk

World Wide Web: www.rsaa.org.uk

Constitution: Registered charity

Objectives/purposes: The Library provides information on Asia mostly from the 19th and 20th centuries, mainly, but not exclusively, for the benefit of the members of the Society. Subject range is described below – it excludes law, science and technology, commerce and economics

Key staff: Secretary: Mr Norman Camerson MA BA

Stock and subject coverage: Ca. 7,000 books, no journals (other than the Society's journal – Asian Affairs), small collections of private papers and photographs (mainly slides). Subject coverage includes geography, history, travel, politics and biographies. The collection covers the 19th and 20th centuries, with a limited amount of 18th century material

Availability: Open to members of the Society and others by appointment. Most books are available for loan to members of the Society

Hours: 10.00-13.00, 14.00-16.00 Monday to Thursday; 10.00-13.00 Friday (check by telephone before visiting)

Transport: Tube: Hyde Park; Bus: all routes via Hyde Park Corner

Special facilities: Lift to Library floor; toilet facilities available

Publications: Asian Affairs - a continuation of the Journal of the Royal Central Asian Society (3 p.a.)

[548]
The Royal Society for the Promotion of Health

38A St George's Drive
London SW1V 4BH

Borough: Westminster

Telephone: 020 7630 0121

Fax: 020 7976 6847

E-mail: rshealth@rshealth.org.uk

Constitution: Registered charity

Objectives/purposes: Promotion of health and hygiene

Key staff: Chief Executive: Hugh Lowson; Executive Assistant: Nils Kendall

Stock and subject coverage: Coverage of a broad area of health issues; back issues of RSPH Journal containing research papers, book review, current topics and membership details

Availability: For use by members of the Society. Researchers admitted on request

Hours: 09.00-17.00, by appointment

Transport: Tube and Rail: Victoria

Special facilities: Toilet facilities available

Publications: Journal of the Royal Society for the Promotion of Health (quarterly); annual review, newsletter for members

[549]
Royal Society of Chemistry Library and Information Centre
RSC LIC
Burlington House
Piccadilly
London W1J 0BA
Borough: Westminster
Telephone: 020 7437 8656
Fax: 020 7287 9798
E-mail: library@rsc.org
World Wide Web: www.rsc.org/library
Constitution: Registered charity; association with voluntary subscribing membership and professional society
Objectives/purposes: To provide a comprehensive chemical information service to members and the chemical community at large
Key staff: Librarian: Nigel Lees; Information Officers: Ron Hudson; Susan Kelly; Senior Library Assistant: Nicola Best
Stock and subject coverage: The largest collection of publications in the UK specifically devoted to the subject of chemistry. The LIC holds 2,000 journals (over 630 current) on all aspects of chemistry and over 25,000 text and reference books. The LIC has one of the best collections in the UK on historical chemical books (from the 16th to the 19th century) including the Nathan and Roscoe collections. The portrait collection (over 8,000 items) features the collected works of Cecil Howard Cribb (433 prints and portraits). The LIC is an important source of information on chemical hazards data, physical property data and the effect of chemicals on humans, animals and the environment. The LIC also holds techno-commercial information, e.g. chemical suppliers, trade names, price trends, company data and market report identification
Services: Photocopy service for both remote and onsite users (preferential rates apply for members and subscribers, rates on application); CD-ROMs on chemistry, environment and business; online service (STN) including structure searching; microfiche-microfilm reader printers
Availability: Free access to Members of the RSC and Corporate members of the LIC. Other bona fide researchers and users need a letter of introduction from a member or university head of department. A day charge may apply. Loans available only to members or corporate members
Hours: 09.30–17.30 Monday to Friday
Transport: Tube: Piccadilly Circus, Green Park; Bus: 9, 14, 19, 22, 38
Special features: The LIC is located in Burlington House built by the Earl of Burlington (Robert Boyle's brother) between 1664–1667. Burlington House (a Grade 1 listed building) forms part of a quadrangle with other learned societies. The RSC (formerly the Chemical Society) moved there in 1857
Publications: List of new accessions (4 p.a.); journal holdings list (annual)

Linked organisations
Royal Society of Chemistry Publishing Department The LIC is part of the RSC's Publishing Department

[550]
Royal Society of Medicine
RSM
1 Wimpole Street
London W1G 0AE
Borough: Westminster
Telephone: 020 7290 2940
Fax: 020 7290 2939
E-mail: library@rsm.ac.uk
World Wide Web: www.rsmlibrary.ac.uk
Constitution: Registered charity
Objectives/purposes: Postgraduate research library in biomedicine
Key staff: Director of Information Services: Ian Snowley
Stock and subject coverage: Ca. 500,000 books; 10,000 journals (2,000 current) on postgraduate level biomedicine. Historical collection dating from 1474 and large portrait collection
Services: Loans (within Europe only); photocopying (worldwide); fax; databases
Availability: Access to members only but there is provision for temporary library membership for which a fee is payable on a daily, weekly or monthly basis
Hours: 09.00–20.30 Monday to Friday; 10.00–17.00 Saturday
Transport: Tube: Oxford Circus, Bond Street
Special facilities: Restaurant and buttery; toilet facilities; access for users with disabilities
Special Features: Library, on first floor, has traditional library gallery
Publications: The Society's publications include: Journal of the Royal Society of Medicine (monthly); The AIDS Letter (6 p.a.); International Journal of STD & AIDS (6 p.a.); Journal of Tropical and Geographical Neurology (4 p.a.); Tropical Doctor (quarterly); Round Table series (irregular); International Congress and Symposium Series (irregular); Current Medical Literature Series (over 20 subject titles, frequency varies by subject); Journal of Medical Biography

[551]
Royal Town Planning Institute
41 Botolph Lane
London EC3R 8DL
Borough: Corporation of London
Telephone: 020 7929 9452
Fax: 020 7929 9490
E-mail: library@rtpi.org.uk
World Wide Web: www.rtpi.org.uk
Constitution: Registered charity; department of a professional body
Key staff: Librarian: Pam Dobby BA ALA
Stock and subject coverage: Ca. 3,000 monographs and local plans; good collection of post-1990 periodicals (100 titles). Subject coverage includes: town planning; local government; housing; landscape; transport; conservation. Library catalogue available via website at www.rtpi.org.uk

Services: Photocopier; internet access

Availability: To members, and public for reference and loan. Phone in advance, as there may not always be a member of staff available to help

Hours: 09.00-17.00 Monday to Thursday; 09.00-16.00 Friday

Transport: Tube: Monument, Bank; Rail: Cannon Street; Bus: buses via Eastcheap (Eastbound only), Bank or London Bridge

Special facilities: Toilet facilities available; access for users with disabilities to the Library and meeting rooms

Publications: Planning (weekly); Planning Theory and Practice (3 p.a.); RTPI Library Series (published by Routledge). See website for details

[552]
Royal United Services Institute for Defence Studies
RUSI

Whitehall
London SW1A 2ET

Borough: Westminster
Telephone: 020 7747 2604
Fax: 020 7321 0943
E-mail: library@rusi.org
World Wide Web: www.rusi.org
Constitution: Independent non-profit distributing organisation; registered charity and association with voluntary subscribing membership
Objectives/purposes: The study of defence and international security
Key staff: Librarian: John Montgomery
Stock and subject coverage: The RUSI Library contains approximately 14,000 volumes and receives over 100 journal titles (most retained for five years only). Among the Library's holdings are books on British military history, military related biographies and books of personal experience of war, as well as contemporary defence/security issues, defence economics and international relations. There are special collections of British regimental histories and works on subjects such as the Napoleonic Wars, World Wars I and II, the Ruso-Japanese War and the American Civil War. The Library contains, in addition, The RUSI Journals (1857 – present) and The United Service Magazine (1829-1923)
Services: Access to the Library's catalogue will be available via the website. The Lancaster Index to Defence and International Security Literature and the Air University Library to Military Periodicals are both available electronically to Library users
Availability: Primarily for use by members of the RUSI and to non-members upon application to the librarian. Journals are not lent, but the majority of books can be borrowed by members or by non-members through inter-library lending. Photocopies of journal articles may be obtained from the librarian in many cases
Hours: 09.30-17.30 Monday to Friday
Transport: Tube: Westminster, Charing Cross, Embankment; Rail: Charing Cross; Bus: 3, 11, 12, 24, 53, 77, 88, 159
Special facilities: Toilet facilities available; access for users with disabilities – lift available to the main floor and

gallery level of the Library. Cloakroom facilities for users with disabilities are present on the ground floor
Special features: The RUSI was founded in 1831 and is housed in a Grade II listed building designed by Aston Webb and Ingres Bell in 1890. It adjoins the 17th century Banqueting House, site of the execution of Charles I in 1642
Publications: The RUSI Journal (6 p.a.); Newsbrief (monthly); International Security Review (annual); Whitehall Papers (6 p.a.); occasional books

[553]
The Royal Veterinary College
RVC

Royal College Street
London NW1 0TU

Borough: Camden
Telephone: 020 7468 5162
E-mail: library@rvc.ac.uk
World Wide Web: www.rvc.ac.uk
Constitution: Department of a university
Key staff: College Librarian: Simon Jackson; Deputy Librarian: Deborah Walker; Historical Collections: Deborah Walker
Stock and subject coverage: Split site library (collections of material on the clinical side of veterinary science are held in the Hawkshead site library in Hertfordshire). The London site has a comprehensive undergraduate collection of pre-clinical material with a journal bias towards research interests. It has the best collection of historical veterinary literature in the world with ca. 5,000 volumes of books and journals dating from the early 16th century until 1900; College Archives and a museum
Services: Photocopies, CD-ROM and AV facilities
Availability: Open to all members of the University of London and the general public for reference only. Visitors must telephone 24 hours in advance to make an appointment to visit
Hours: 09.00-18.00 Monday to Friday
Transport: Tube: King's Cross, Camden Town; Rail: King's Cross
Special facilities: Refreshment and toilet facilities available; limited wheelchair access to the library – please advise before visiting (no disabled access to Museum)

Linked organisations

University of London The College is part of the University
Hawkshead Site Library, Hawkshead Lane, North Mymms, Hatfield, Hertfordshire AL9 7TA (tel: 01707 666214)

[554]
Royal Watercolour Society/Royal Society of Painter-Printmakers
RWS/RE

Bankside Gallery
48 Hopton Street
London SE1 9JH

Borough: Southwark
Telephone: 020 7928 7521

Fax: 020 7928 2820
E-mail: info@banksidegallery.com
Constitution: Company limited by guarantee and
   registered charity
Objectives/purposes: The RWS is the oldest society of its
   kind in the world. It exists to further the practice and
   appreciation of watercolour painting. The RE exists
   to promote the practice and appreciation of all forms
   of original printmaking
Key staff: Director: Judy Dixey; Archivist: Simon
   Fenwick; Honorary Curators: Trevor Frankland, Vikki
   Slowe
Stock and subject coverage: Primary source literature,
   documents and photographs relating to the Societies
Services: Photocopies and faxing at cost by arrangement
Availability: Materials available for reference, by
   appointment
Hours: 10.00–17.00 Monday to Friday
Transport: Tube: Blackfriars, Waterloo, Southwark; Rail:
   Blackfriars, Waterloo; Bus: D1, P11, 45, 63, 149, 172
Special facilities: Refreshment and toilet facilities available;
   access for users with disabilities – ramps for
   wheelchairs, magnifiers
Special features: The RWS, founded in 1804, and the RE,
   founded in 1880, are the oldest and foremost
   associations of their kind in the world
Publications: Bi-annual catalogues of Society shows;
   Bankside Bulletin journal shared with the Royal
   Society of Painter-Printmakers (4 p.a.)

Linked organisations

Royal Society of Painter-Printmakers The RWS
has shared facilities with the Society for more than
100 years

[555]
RSA
(Royal Society for the Encouragement of Arts, Manufactures and Commerce)

8 John Adam Street
London WC2N 6EZ
Borough: Westminster
Telephone: 020 7930 5115
Fax: 020 7839 5805
E-mail: julie.cranage@rsa.org.uk
   chris.denvir@rsa.org.uk
Constitution: Registered charity and learned society
Key staff: Library Coordinator: Julie Cranage; Archivist:
   Christopher Denvir
Stock and subject coverage: About 10,000 volumes. Special
   collections: archives (from 1754 to date); early library
   (books predating 1830)
Services: Loans: To Fellows and bona fide researchers and
   other libraries through the British Library
Availability: To Fellows and bona fide researchers
Hours: By appointment to non-Fellows. Library is
   normally open 08.30–20.00 Monday to Friday
Transport: Tube: Charing Cross, Embankment; Rail:
   Charing Cross
Special facilities: Refreshment and toilet facilities; access
   for users with disabilities – lift and toilet
Special features: Headquarters building designed by the
   Adam brothers and in occupation since 1774. Library
   in adjoining private house (incorporated into main
   property) with Adam features

Publications: Journal (bi-monthly); electronic publications
   via www.rsa.org.uk

[556]
Rudolf Steiner House Library

Library of the Anthroposophical Society in Great
Britain
Rudolf Steiner House
35 Park Road
London NW1 6XT
Borough: Camden
Telephone: 020 7224 8398
Fax: 020 7224 8398
E-mail: rsh-library@anth.org.uk
World Wide Web: www.anth.org.uk
Constitution: Registered charity; part of a philanthropic,
   charitable and educational association
Objectives/purposes: Organisation devoted to the ideas
   and work of Rudolf Steiner and the practical
   activities arising out of this
Key staff: Librarian and Archivist: Margaret Jonas
Stock and subject coverage: Published and unpublished
   lectures and books by Rudolf Steiner in English and
   German; all available anthroposophical works in
   English, some in German, on Waldorf education,
   health, bio-dynamic agriculture, social studies, the
   arts, science and technology; journals and news sheets
   in English and German from around the world on
   aspects of anthroposophical work, many complete
   runs; archive material on the history of the
   Anthroposophical Society, the Goetheanum in
   Dornach, Switzerland, institutions developing from
   Steiner's work, photographs, press cuttings, prints,
   videos. General books on esotericism, religion,
   mythology, biography, history, cultural and artistic
   themes
Services: Photocopies
Availability: Free to members of the Anthroposophical
   Society in Great Britain. Loans to all others on
   payment of a subscription. Discretionary loans of
   photographic and archive material on payment of a
   fee or deposit
Hours: Term-time: 11.00–13.00, 14.00–17.00 Wednesday,
   Thursday; 11.00–13,00, 14.00–19.30 Tuesday; 13.00–
   18.00 Friday; 12.00–17.00 Saturday. Vacations – no
   late evenings, some Saturdays
Transport: Tube: Baker Street; Bus: 13, 18, 27, 30, 82, 113,
   139, 274
Special facilities: Limited refreshment facilities available
   Tuesday evenings and Saturdays in term-time; toilet
   facilities available; limited wheelchair access in Steiner
   House (Library door widths limit access) lift service
   to Library and other floors
Special features: Rudolf Steiner House is a listed building
   dating from 1926 with many architectural features
   based on Steiner's work. It has a small theatre and
   meeting rooms for hire
Publications: Duplicated stock and subject lists on request

Linked organisations

Anthroposophical Society in Great Britain Part
of the Society

[557]
St Bartholomew's Hospital

West Smithfield
London EC1A 7BA
Borough: Corporation of London
Telephone: 020 7601 7837
Fax: 020 7601 7853
E-mail: m.b.montague@qmul.ac.uk
World Wide Web: www.smd.qmul.ac.uk/library/home/
Constitution: Part of Queen Mary, University of London
Key staff: Marie Montague
Stock and subject coverage: Clinical medicine
Services: Loans; photocopy facilities; inter-library loans; enquiries; information skills training
Availability: Open to staff and students of Queen Mary and Westfield Collee, staff of Barts and the London NHS Trust, staff of East London and the City Mental Health Trust, academic staff and research students from M25 consortium by arrangement
Hours: Term-time: 10.00-21.00 Monday; 09.00-21.00 Tuesday to Thursday; 09.00-18.00 Friday Christmas, July and August opening hours: 10.00-18.00 Monday; 09.00-18.00 Tuesday to Friday
Transport: Tube: St Paul's, Barbican, Farringdon; Bus: 8, 22B, 25, 56, 501, 521
Special facilities: Unsuitable for users with mobility disability at present. Adjacent to cafe facilities in Robin Brook Centre at St Bartholomew's Hospital
Publications: Library guide

Linked organisations

Queen Mary, University of London Part of the university

North East London Workforce Development Confederation Participant in library services network

[558]
St Christopher's Hospice, Halley Stewart Library

51-59 Lawrie Park Road
Sydenham
London SE26 6DZ
Borough: Bromley
Telephone: 020 8768 4660
Fax: 020 8776 9345
E-mail: d.brady@stchristophers.org.uk
Constitution: Independent non-profit organisation
Objectives: Medical foundation caring for patients with advanced disease, supporting their families and advancing palliative education and research
Key staff: Librarian
Stock and subject coverage: Specialised library dealing with hospice and palliative care - symptom control, psychosocial issues and policy, death and dying and bereavement. Includes books, journals and pamphlet collections
Services: Photocopies, use of specialist in-house database
Availability: Available for reference only by appointment. Queries accepted by telephone, email, and letter
Hours: 09.00-17.00 Monday to Friday
Transport: Rail: Sydenham, Penge East

Special facilities: Refreshment and toilet facilities available on site; access for users with disabilities
Special features: One of the first modern hospices founded in 1967. The collection spans about 15 years with some older material going back to 1967. Site includes a small bookshop specialising in palliative care
Publications: Catalogue of titles available from the Hospice bookshop

[559]
St George's Hospital Medical School

St George's Library
Hunter Wing
Cranmer Terrace
London SW17 0RE
Borough: Wandsworth
Telephone: 020 8725 5466
Fax: 020 8767 4696
E-mail: s.gove@sghms.ac.uk
World Wide Web: www.sghms.ac.uk/depts/is
Constitution: Department of a university
Key staff: Librarian and Director of Information Services: Susan Gove
Stock and subject coverage: Multidisciplinary health care library serving the Medical School, Faculty of Health and Social Care Sciences and Hospital trusts of Wandsworth, Merton and Sutton Health Authority. Ca.800 current journals and 50,000 books including archives and small rare book collection of hospital founded in 1733
Services: Photocopies; online searching; fax machine; scanner
Availability: Access to bona fide researchers for reference. A fee is payable by commercial users or by external users for regular access for reference/borrowing
Hours: Term-time: 08.00-22.00 Monday and Thursday; 08.00-21.00 Friday; 09.00-17.00 Saturday Vacations: 08.00-21.00 Monday to Friday
Transport: Tube: Tooting Broadway; Bus: 44, 57, 77, 127, 133, 155, 264, 280, 355
Special facilities: Refreshment and toilet facilities; access for users with disabilities – wheelchair access
Special features: 'Blossom's skin' cowskin on wall of the Library dates from Edward Jenner's time when he developed a vaccine to protect against smallpox (1795); artefacts associated with John Hunter – father of scientific medical research
Publications: Annual Report; School newsletter; library newsletter; periodicals guide; library guide and various guide sheets

Linked organisations

University of London Part of the University
South West London Workforce Development Confederation
Queen Mary's Hospital Library Library is managed from St George's

[560]
St Mary's College
Waldegrave Road
Strawberry Hill
Twickenham
Middlesex TW1 4SX
Borough: Richmond upon Thames
Telephone: 020 8240 4097
Fax: 020 8240 4270
World Wide Web: www.smuc.ac.uk
Constitution: Department of a university
Key staff: Director Information Services and Systems:
    Máire Lanigan; Assistant Director Library Operations:
    Nyla Prieg; Academic Services Manager: Martin
    Scarrott
Stock and subject coverage: Ca. 150,000 volumes; 500
    journals with strong collections in education,
    theology, Irish studies, history and sports science
Services: Photocopiers. All other services restricted to
    registered students (including: microfiche reader
    printer; microfilm reader printer; CD-ROM and
    word processors)
Availability: Open to the public for reference purposes
    only – no access to electronic materials. Reciprocal
    arrangements with UK Plus, M25 and SWEZTEC
Hours: Term-time: 09.00-21.00 Monday to Friday
    Vacations: 09.00-17.00 Monday to Friday
Transport: Tube: Richmond; Rail: Strawberry Hill; Bus:
    33 from Richmond tube
Special facilities: Refreshment and toilet facilities available;
    access for users with disabilities
Special features: Located on the site of Horace Walpole's
    gothic villa
Publications: Guide to the Library; various bibliographies

Linked organisations
   University of Surrey College of the University

[561]
St Paul's Cathedral Library
London EC4M 8AE
Borough: Corporation of London
Telephone: 020 7246 8345
Fax: 020 7248 3104
E-mail: librarian@stpaulscathedral.org.uk
World Wide Web: www.stpauls.co.uk
Constitution: Cathedral library, library of the Dean and
    Chapter of St Paul's
Key staff: Librarian: JJ Wisdom
Stock and subject coverage: Ca. 21,000 bibliographical
    items on theology, ecclesiastical history, bibles and
    liturgy, the history of St Paul's Cathedral and people
    connected with it
Services: Photocopying available, subject to conservation
    requirements
Availability: Open to bona fide researchers by
    appointment, for reference only
Hours: By appointment, opening hours currently all day
    Monday and Tuesday, Friday morning
Transport: Tube: St Paul's; Rail: Cannon Street
Special facilities: Refreshment and toilet facilities available;
    access for users with disabilities – access to Triforium
    level by lift, six steps, but every assistance will be
    afforded
Special features: Library designed by Wren

Linked organisations
   Guildhall Library The archives of Dean and
   Chapter are deposited at Guildhall Library
   Manuscripts Section

[562]
St Paul's School
Lonsdale Road
London SW13 9JT
Borough: Richmond upon Thames
Telephone: 020 8748 9162
Fax: 020 8748 9557
E-mail: librarian@stpaulsschool.org.uk
World Wide Web: www.stpaulsschool.org.uk
Constitution: School and independent non-profit
    distributing organisation
Key staff: Librarian: Mrs AM Aslett BA ALA
Stock and subject coverage: General range of subjects,
    particularly strong in history. Rare books collection
    of works from the 16th century onwards, largely
    concerned with the history of the school and the
    lives and careers of Old Paulines. Small general
    journal, video, audio and CD-ROM collections
Services: Internet access, photocopiers
Availability: Access for reference only to all bona fide
    researchers, by prior appointment only
Hours: Term-time: 08.00-16.30 Monday to Friday
    Vacations: Access by appointment only in school
    holidays
Special facilities: Toilet facilities available; limited access
    for users with disabilities – lift at some distance from
    the library which is on the first floor
Publications: Introduction to the Walker Library, subject
    guides to research

Linked organisations
   St Paul's Girls School

[563]
St Thomas's Hospital Medical School Library
North Wing
St Thomas' Hospital
London SE1 7EH
Borough: Lambeth
Telephone: 020 7928 9292 ext 2507
Fax: 020 7922 8251
World Wide Web: www.hospital.org.uk
Constitution: Hospital
Key staff: Librarian: vacant
Stock and subject coverage: Popular fiction and non-fiction.
    Special collection on NHS management and
    information and consumer health information
Services: Photocopies; online searching; CD-ROM
    databases – MDX Healthcare, Healthplan; Help for
    Health database
Availability: Availability to all inpatients and staff at St
    Thomas' Hospital; reference service for the general
    public
Hours: 08.30-17.00 Monday to Friday
Transport: Tube: Waterloo, Westminster; Rail: Waterloo;
    Bus: 12, 53, 77, 109, 507, 511
Special facilities: Refreshment and toilet facilities; access
    for users with disabilities
Publications: Booklists (quarterly)

The Library of the Dean and Chapter, St Paul's Cathedral

[564]
Saintpaulia and Houseplant Society

33 Church Road
Newbury Park
Ilford
Essex IG2 7ET
Borough: Redbridge
Telephone: 020 8590 3710
Constitution: Association with voluntary subscribing
membership
Objectives/purposes: To encourage more people to grow
houseplants in their homes
Key staff: Secretary and Treasurer
Stock and subject coverage: Books and journals on
Saintpaulias (African Violets) and all types of indoor
plants
Availability: Books available to members only at
meetings or by post
Hours: Meetings held from 18.00–20.00. Ten meetings
per year at the RHS Lawrence Hall on Tuesdays, on
the same day as an RHS Westminster Show
Special facilities: Toilet facilities available at RHS Hall
Publications: Bulletins (4 p.a.); Success with Houseplants
pamphlets

Linked organisations

Royal Horticultural Society
African Violet Society of America
Saintpaulia International
The Society is affiliated to all three organisations

[565]
The Salvation Army
Schools and Colleges Department

101 Newington Causeway
London SE1 6BN
Borough: Southwark
Telephone: 020 7367 4706
Fax: 020 7367 4711
E-mail: schools@salvationarmy.org.uk
Constitution: Registered charity
Key staff: Captain Christine Clement
Stock and subject coverage: Materials for students in both
primary and secondary schools. University project
material; social services; statements on moral and
social issues
Hours: 08.00–15.30 Monday to Friday
Services: Photocopies; fax machines; online searching;
student pack (£3 including p&p); teacher pack (£5
including p&p); videos for hire; fact sheets
Availability: To all bona fide researchers
Transport: Tube and Rail: Elephant and Castle
Special facilities: Canteen available
Publications: Annual Reports and Year Books

[566]
The Salvation Army International Heritage Centre

101 Queen Victoria Street
London EC4P 4EP
Borough: Corporation of London
Telephone: 020 7332 0101, ext 8704
Fax: 020 7332 8099

E-mail: heritage@salvationarmy.org
World Wide Web: www.salvationarmy.org
Constitution: Registered charity; part of the Christian
Church
Objectives/purposes: International archives and research
centre for all aspects of Salvation Army work
Key staff: Director: Major Jim Bryden; Archivist: Gordon
Taylor
Stock and subject coverage: Books, journals, pamphlets and
programmes of events relating to the history and
work of the Christian Mission (1865–78), renamed
the Salvation Army (from 1878). Archives also
comprise Salvation Army journals, diaries, memoirs,
administrative records and journals, including The
War Cry (on microfilm). Letters of William and
Catherine Booth, other members of the Booth
family and prominent Salvationists over the years
form part of the collection. The photographic library
contains many rare and unusual prints that may be
copied or loaned by arrangement
Services: Photocopies; fax machine; card index
Availability: Open to researchers by appointment
(charges are made). Material available for reference
only
Hours: 09.30–15.30 Monday to Friday (telephone 020
7332 0101, ext 8704 for an appointment).
Transport: Tube: Blackfriars, Cannon Street, Mansion
House; Rail: Blackfriars, Cannon Street
Special facilities: Refreshment and toilet facilities available;
access for users with disabilities
Publications: Annual Reports and Year Books

[567]
The Salvation Army, William Booth Memorial College

Champion Park
Denmark Hill
London SE5 8BQ
Borough: Southwark
Telephone: 020 7326 2747
Fax: 020 7326 2750
E-mail: maurice.foley@salvationarmy.org.uk
Constitution: Christian church and registered charity
Objectives/purposes: The College exists to train men and
women to make the world a better place
Key staff: Librarian: Maurice Foley
Stock and subject coverage: Books, journals, newspapers
and software. Materials on theology and spirituality,
including Christian scriptures, doctrine, history,
counselling, hermeneutics, missiology, biography.
Specialist Salvation Army history and biography
Services: Photocopies; fax; online catalogue
Availability: Access can be granted by prior arrangement
with the Librarian
Hours: 08.30–16.30 Monday to Friday
Transport: Rail: Denmark Hill; Bus: 68, 176, 184, 185

[568]
Save the Children
SC

Mary Datchelor House
17 Grove Lane
Camberwell
London SE5 8RD

Borough: Southwark
Telephone: 020 7716 2263
Fax: 020 7703 2278
E-mail: j.lane@scfuk.org.uk
World Wide Web: www.scfuk.org.uk
Constitution: Registered charity
Save the Children has two libraries. One provides materials on marketing, market research, fundraising, voluntary sector trends, childcare issues, etc; the other services SC's Programmes Department and covers development issues, fieldwork, etc.
Key staff: Research and Information Manager (Marketing): Michelle Madden
Stock and subject coverage: Save the Children publications; reference library of ca. 300 publications on general development and childcare issues, marketing, voluntary sector trends, fundraising and market research; ca. 60 periodicals on the same subjects and archives
Services: Archive and current information service on Save the Children work
Availability: By appointment
Hours: 09.30–17.30 Monday to Friday
Transport: Tube: Elephant and Castle, Oval, then bus; Rail: Denmark Hill; Bus: 12, 35, 36, 36A, 36B, 40, 45, 68, 171, 176, 184, 185
Special facilities: Toilet facilities available; access for users with disabilities
Publications: Bookshelf (current awareness service); journals list; library guide

[568][a]
Programmes Resource Centre

66 South Lambeth Road
London SW8 1RH
Borough: Lambeth
Telephone: 020 7703 5400 ext 2505
E-mail: prc@scfuk.org.uk
Stock and subject coverage: Books, reports and 'grey literature' on development issues relating to children
Availability: By appointment only
Hours: 09.00–17.00 Monday to Friday
Transport: Tube and rail: Vauxhall

[569]
School of Oriental and African Studies
SOAS

Thornhaugh Street
Russell Square
London WC1H 0XG
Borough: Camden
Telephone: 020 7898 4163
Fax: 020 7898 4159
E-mail: libenquiry@soas.ac.uk
World Wide Web: www.soas.ac.uk
Constitution: Department of a university
Key staff: Librarian: Keith Webster; Deputy Librarian, Specialist Information Services and Collection Development: Helen Cordell; Deputy Librarian, Central Information Services and Document Supply: Wallace Batchelor

Stock and subject coverage: The Library aims to acquire the important contributions to Asian and African scholarship published anywhere in the world in the humanities and social sciences as well as representative collections of literature written in Asian and African languages. Stock of over 850,000 volumes and 5,000 current journals. In addition there are thousands of microforms, 45,000 sheet maps and an Art Section with 25,000 photographs and a collection of prints and drawings. Sound and video recordings are also held. Special collections include: the library and archives of the Council for World Mission (formerly the London Missionary Society) deposited in 1973, and the papers of the Conference of British Missionary Societies, the Methodist Missionary Society, John Swire & Son Ltd, the China Association, the Movement for Colonial Freedom and Christian Aid
Services: Photocopies; internet access (restricted); CD-ROM databases; audiovisual facilities
Availability: Available to students and permanent members of the School. Academic related staff of other institutions in the University of London are admitted without charge (under certain conditions in accordance with the principles of the University of London access agreement). Other researchers and students may be admitted under certain conditions. Members of UK higher education institutions may apply for a total of five free day passes per academic year. Other researchers will be charged for each day pass required (£6 for private researchers, £12 for corporate users)
Archive users may make up to 20 free visits in a year. Academic staff of other FE institutions may be granted reference access on production of a letter of recommendation from their institution, while students from institutions with reciprocal agreements may be admitted during vacations on proof of identify. Other researchers may be admitted upon production of a letter of recommendation and payment of the appropriate fee (see the Library's webpages for more information)
Hours: Term-time, Christmas and Easter vacations: 09.00–20.45 Monday to Thursday; 09.00–19.00 Friday; 09.30–17.00 Saturday
Summer vacation: Visitors are advised to check opening hours in advance, 09.00–17.00 Monday to Friday; 09.30–17.00 Saturday
Transport: Tube: Holborn, Goodge Street, Russell Square
Special facilities: Refreshment facilities (Monday to Friday); toilet facilities; access for users with disabilities
Special features: Building designed by the architect Sir Denys Lasdun
Publications: Annual Report, Guide to the Archive and Manuscript Collections

Linked organisations

University of London SOAS is part of the University

[570]
School of Pharmacy

29–39 Brunswick Square
London WC1N 1AX

Borough: Camden
Telephone: 020 7753 5833
Fax: 020 7278 0622
Constitution: Part of a university
Key staff: Librarian: Mrs L Lisgarten BA ALA MIInfSc
Stock and subject coverage: Materials on pharmacy, pharmacology, biochemistry and toxicology
Services: Special services not generally available to outside visitors
Availability: Borrowing restricted to School of Pharmacy members only. Other categories of reader, with appropriate identification, admitted for reference only at the discretion of the Librarian. Telephone in advance before visiting
Hours: Term-time: 08.45-21.00 Monday to Friday
Vacations: 09.00-17.00 Monday to Friday
Transport: Tube: Russell Square, King's Cross: Rail: King's Cross
Special facilities: Toilet facilities available

Linked organisations

University of London   Part of the University

---

[571]
School of Slavonic and East European Studies Library
SSEES

North Wing
Senate House
Malet Street
London WC1E 7HU
Borough: Camden
Telephone: 020 7862 8523
Fax: 020 7862 8644
E-mail: ssees_library@ssees.ac.uk
World Wide Web: www.ssees.ac.uk
Constitution: Department of a university
Key staff: Librarian: Lesley Pitman
Stock and subject coverage: The collection comprises some 357,000 volumes on the history, languages, literature, politics, economics, geography and bibliography of Russia and the western Republics of the former USSR, Finland, Poland, the Czech Republic, Slovakia, former Yugoslavia, Hungary, Romania, Bulgaria, Albania, Estonia, Latvia and Lithuania. Extensive collection of over 1,200 video cassettes of feature films and documentaries from most countries studied by the School. Manuscript collections relating particularly to Russia, Hungary and Czechoslovakia
Services: Self-service photocopies; microform reader-printers; computer rooms with word-processing facilities
Availability: Bona fide researchers may apply to use the Library for reference or borrowing. A fee may be charged
Hours: Term-time: 09.00-21.00 Monday to Friday; 10.00-17.00 Saturday
Christmas and Easter vacations: 10.00-19.00 Monday to Thursday: 10.00-18.00 Friday
Summer vacation and last two weeks of summer term: 10.00-18.00 Monday to Friday
Transport: Tube: Russell Square, Tottenham Court Road, Goodge Street; Bus: 7, 68, 168, 188 to Russell Square, 10, 24, 29, 73 to Goodge Street/Gower Street
Special facilities: Toilet facilities available

Publications: Short Guide to the Library (1994)

Linked organisations

University College London Member of the College

---

[572]
Science Photo Library
SPL

327-329 Harrow Road
London W9 3RB
Borough: Westminster
Telephone: 020 7432 1100
Fax: 020 7286 8668
E-mail: info@sciencephoto.com
World Wide Web: www.sciencephoto.com
Constitution: Company limited by guarantee
Key staff: Managing Director: Giancarlo Zuccotto; Director of Photography: Rose Taylor; Research Manager: Justin Hobson
Stock and subject coverage: The Library is the leading provider of science imagery. The whole collection of over 100,000 images is available online at www.sciencephoto.com. Subjects covered include images of the human body, health and medicine, research, genetics, technology and industry, space exploration and astronomy, earth science, satellite imagery, environment, nature and wildlife and the history of science
Services: Internet access and email; photocopies; fax
Availability: Researchers may visit by appointment only
Hours: 09.30-18.00 Monday to Friday
Transport: Tube: Westbourne Park
Publications: Catalogue of selected images produced every two years

---

[573]
SCOPE for People With Cerebral Palsy
(formerly The Spastics Society)

Library and Information Unit
6 Market Road
London N7 9PW
Borough: Islington
Telephone: 020 7619 7342
0808 800 3333 (Helpline for all external enquiries)
Fax: 020 7619 7360
World Wide Web: www.scope.org.uk
Constitution: Registered charity; company limited by guarantee
Objectives/purposes: To provide a range of services for people with Cerebral Palsy, their families and carers, including schools, college, residential care, information and careers advice
Key staff: Information Officer: Jonathan Clarke
Stock and subject coverage: Information about cerebral palsy and related disabilities. Information about the work of the Society including schools, units, employment schemes, etc. Library/Information Unit covers a range of subjects including: equipment, transport, personal care, feeding, education, etc
Services: Photocopies (charged). SCOPE publications list available by post (UK only). Large part of the service is referral to other relevant bodies/contacts

Availability: Access by appointment, for reference only; charges for photocopies

Hours: 09.00-17.00 Monday to Friday

Transport: Tube: Caledonian Road; Rail: King's Cross, Caledonian and Barnsbury; Bus: 17, 91

Special features: Refreshment and toilet facilities; access for users with disabilities, including toilet facilities, CCTV personal reader for people with visual impairments

Publications: Annual Report and Accounts; Disability Now (monthly); Left Out (2000); Focusing on CP (2001)

[574]
Shelter: The National Campaign for Homeless People
Shelter
88 Old Street
London EC1V 9HU

Borough: Islington
Telephone: 020 7505 2000
Fax: 020 7505 2169
World Wide Web: www.shelter.org.uk
Constitution: Company limited by guarantee and registered charity
Objectives/purposes: To campaign nationally on housing and homelessness issues and to run a network of housing advice centres
Key staff: Information Officer: Rita Diaz; Information Assistant: Carolyn Baker
Stock and subject coverage: Materials on housing and homelessness and related social issues such as poverty, housing and benefits-related law
Services: Photocopies; publications available for sale
Availability: Library primarily for the use of Shelter staff. Library access is limited due to lack of space so appointments are essential. Materials are for reference only
Hours: 09.30-13.00, 14.00-17.30 Monday to Friday
Transport: Tube and Rail: Old Street; Bus: 55, 273
Special facilities: Refreshment and toilet facilities available; access for users with disabilities – including wheelchair access and disabled toilets

[575]
Sir John Soane's Museum
13 Lincoln's Inn Fields
London WC2A 3BP

Borough: Camden
Telephone: 020 7440 4251 (library direct line)
Fax: 020 7831 3957
E-mail: library.soane1@ukgateway.net
World Wide Web: www.soane.org
Constitution: Registered charity
Objectives/purposes: To preserve the house, collection and library of Sir John Soane (1753-1837) intact. Main field of interest – architecture ca. 1500-1837
Key staff: Archivist: Susan Palmer; Assistant Curator (Drawings): Stephen Astley
Stock and subject coverage: Sir John Soane's book collection gathered before his death in 1837. The main emphasis is on architecture, travel, topography and the arts but it also includes general books

appropriate to a gentleman's library of the period. Also an interesting collection of Sale Catalogues for works of art and books, and of pamphlets on miscellaneous topics, ca. 8,000 volumes. The collection also has ca. 30,000 original architectural drawings by British, Italian and French architects ca. 1500-1837 and also an Archive of Soane's personal and business papers. There is a small reference library of modern books and journals and articles on architecture and related subjects

Services: Photocopying of modern books, restricted copying of older books and archive material. Print-outs from microfilm of architectural drawings

Availability: Open for research by appointment. Only the modern books are on open access. No loans

Hours: 10.00-13.00, 14.00-15.00 Tuesdays to Fridays; 10.00-13.00 Saturday

Transport: Tube: Holborn; Bus: 1, 8, 19, 22A, 25, 38, 55, 68, 91, 168, 171, 188

Special facilities: Toilet facilities available

Special features: Important centre for research into British architecture ca. 1600-1837, and Italian architecture ca. 1500-1750

[576]
Ski Club of Great Britain Ltd
The White House
57-63 Church Road
Wimbledon
London SW19 5SB

Borough: Merton
Telephone: 020 8410 2000
Fax: 020 8410 2001
E-mail: skiers@skiclub.co.uk
World Wide Web: www.skiclub.co.uk
Constitution: Company limited by guarantee
Objectives/purposes: Recreational skiing
Key staff: Sebastian Bowen, Olivia Freeman
Stock and subject coverage: Skiing records and skiing history
Services: Photocopies
Availability: Open to non-members for reference only
Hours: By prior arrangement
Transport: Tube and Rail: Wimbledon
Special facilities: Toilet facilities available; access for wheelchair users
Publications: Ski and Board (4 p.a.)

[577]
Society for Co-operation in Russian and Soviet Studies
SCRSS
(formerly Society for Cultural Relations with the USSR)
320 Brixton Road
London SW9 6AB

Borough: Lambeth
Telephone: 020 7274 2282
Fax: 020 7274 3230
E-mail: ruslibrary@scrss.co.uk
World Wide Web: scrss.fsnet.co.uk
Constitution: Association with voluntary subscribing membership; independent non-profit organisation

Objectives/purposes: Founded in 1924 as the Society for Cultural Relations With the USSR by a group of leading intellectuals, including EM Forster, Maynard Keynes, Bertrand Russell and Virginia Woolf. Its aim is to bring together people from the UK and the former Soviet Union through a range of cultural, scientific and professional contacts

Key staff: Librarian: Jane Rosen

Stock and subject coverage: 30,000 volumes on all subjects, in Russian and English. Photo-Library

Services: General information service; loans in certain circumstances; photocopies (charged)

Availability: Research fees are charged for use of reference library and information service. Membership is required for borrowing

Hours: 10.00-13.00, 14.00-18.00 Monday to Friday

Transport: Tube and Rail: Brixton; Bus: 3, 59, 133, 159

Special facilities: Toilet facilities available; access for users with disabilities – telephone to arrange help for access; loan library is not accessible, but help will be given to locate items

Publications: Annual Reports; SCR Newsletter (3 p.a.); SCR Information Digest

Special features: Founded in 1924. Founders include: GDH Coke, EM Forster, Bertrand Russell, Sybil Thorndike, Sidney Webb and Virginia and Leonard Woolf

[578]
The Society for Psychical Research
SPR
49 Marloes Road
Kensington
London W8 6LA

Borough: Kensington and Chelsea

Telephone: 020 7937 8984

Fax: 020 7937 8984

World Wide Web: www.spr.ac.uk

Constitution: Company limited by guarantee; registered charity

Objectives/purposes: Research into those faculties of man commonly called psychic; psychical research; parapsychology

Key staff: Librarian: Mrs MW Poynton; Secretary: Mr P Johnson

Stock and subject coverage: About 6,000 volumes on mediumship, out of the body experiences, apparitions, clairvoyance and telepathy, survival after death, poltergeists and psychokinesis, precognition and extrasensory perception, psychic healing

Services: Photocopies

Availability: Open to members of the SPR and others by prior arrangement

Hours: 13.00-17.00 Tuesday, Wednesday and Thursday

Transport: Tube: Kensington High Street, Earls Court; Bus: 9, 10, 27, 28, 49, 74

Special facilities: Toilet facilities available

Special features: The oldest psychical research organisation in the world, founded in 1882

Publications: Journal of the Society for Psychical Research (4 p.a.); Proceedings of the Society for Psychical Research (occasional); Paranormal Review (4 p.a.)

Linked organisations

Cambridge University Library, West Road, Cambridge. The Society's old books and archives are held by Cambridge Library

[579]
Society for the Protection of Ancient Buildings
SPAB
37 Spital Square
London E1 6DY

Borough: Tower Hamlets

Telephone: 020 7377 1644

Fax: 020 7247 5296

E-mail: info@spab.org.uk

World Wide Web: www.spab.org.uk

Constitution: Registered charity

Objectives/purposes: To promote the conservative repair of historic buildings, as stated in manifesto of 1877

Key staff: Archivist: Miss Cecily Greenhill

Stock and subject coverage: No library but extensive archives, about 13,000 files relate principally to cases considered by the Society, most of them pre-Georgian buildings and many churches

Services: Photocopies (charges made)

Availability: Open to bona fide researchers free of charge by appointment. Limited space for visitors. Reference facilities only, materials cannot be ordered

Hours: By appointment

Transport: Tube and Rail: Liverpool Street

Special facilities: Toilet facilities available

Special features: Oldest conservation body in Britain funded by William Morris in 1877. The Society's headquarters are in an early 18th century house in Spitalfields

Publications: Various pamphlets on historic building repair methods, quarterly magazine and Annual Report

[580]
Society of Antiquaries of London
Burlington House
Piccadilly
London W1J 0BE

Borough: Westminster

Telephone: 020 7479 7084

Fax: 020 7287 6967

E-mail: library@sal.org.uk

World Wide Web: www.sal.org.uk

Constitution: Registered charity; learned society governed by royal charter

Key staff: Librarian: Bernard Nurse MA ALA

Stock and subject coverage: Ca. 80,000 books; 500 current periodicals; large collection of topographical prints and drawings and brass rubbings. Subjects covered include archaeology (especially British and European); architectural history; the decorative arts (especially mediaeval); heraldry; and British local history

Services: Enquiries; photocopies; microfilm reader; reference services; interlibrary loans

Availability: To Fellows and members of the Royal Archaeological Institute, the British Archaeological

Association and members of the Heraldry Society. Others by prior arrangement

Hours: 10.00-17.00 Monday to Friday. Closed in August

Transport: Tube: Piccadilly Circus, Green Park; Bus: 9, 14, 19, 22, 38

Special facilities: Toilet facilities available; access for users with disabilities – lift available

Special features: Founded in 1707; historic building (1875)

Publications: Antiquaries Journal; Archaeologia

[581]
Society of Chiropodists and Podiatrists

1 Fellmonger's Path
Tower Bridge Road
London SE1 3LY

Borough: Southwark
Telephone: 020 7234 8620
Fax: 020 7935 6359
World Wide Web: www.feetforlife.org
Constitution: Professional body/trade union
Stock and subject coverage: Material on chiropody; podiatry; podology; and related subjects
Services: Professional body representing State Registered Chiropodists/Podiatrists
Availability: By appointment
Hours: 09.30-16.30 Monday to Friday
Transport: Tube and rail: London Bridge

[582]
Society of Genealogists
SoG

14 Charterhouse Buildings
Goswell Road
London EC1M 7BA

Borough: Islington
Telephone: 020 7251 8799 (switchboard)
020 7702 5485 (library)
Fax: 020 7250 1800
E-mail: library@sog.org.uk
World Wide Web: www.sog.org.uk
Constitution: Company limited by guarantee; registered charity and learned society
Objectives/purposes: To promote and encourage the study of genealogy and heraldry
Key staff: Librarian: Sue Gibbons; Genealogy Officer: Else Churchill
Stock and subject coverage: Materials on family history; genealogy; heraldry; history – national, local, social and economic; and topography. Coverage focuses on the British Isles and former colonies and the Commonwealth but the collections include materials on most countries. Materials held include: Parish register copies and transcripts; monumental inscriptions; Census transcripts and indexes; directories; poll books; will and marriage licence indexes and abstracts, family histories, topographical works, civil registration indexes, etc.
Services: Photocopiers; fiche and film printers; bookshop selling microfiche, computer disks, archival repair sundries, maps, magazines, etc. available to personal visitors, online and by post. Internet suite available

for use of genealogical websites, e.g. 1901 census site, Familysearch, Commonwealth War Graves, etc. The Society runs lectures, courses and meetings throughout the year on genealogy and related subjects
Availability: The Library is open free to members and available, for a fee, to non-members. Some materials available for loan to members, reference only for non-members. Charges made for use of photocopiers, fiche and film printers. Donations encouraged for use of electricity by portable computers
Hours: 10.00-18.00 Tuesday, Wednesday, Friday and Saturday; 10.00-20.00 Thursday. Closed for stocktaking in the week of the first Monday in February
Transport: Tube: Barbican; Rail: Farringdon; Bus: 4, 55, 243, 505
Special facilities: Drinks machine and toilet facilities available; lift to all floors and toilet for users with disabilities
Special features: The largest genealogical library in the country; one of the largest online genealogical bookshops on the web with secure credit card payment facility
Publications: Genealogists Magazine (4 p.a.); Computers in Genealogy (4 p.a.); wide variety of publications of interest to the family historian, list available on request

Linked organisations

Federation of Family History Societies
Nominating member of the Federation

[583]
The Society of Operations Engineers
SOE

22 Greencoat Place
London SW1P 1PR

Borough: Westminster
Telephone: 020 7630 1111
Fax: 020 7630 6677
E-mail: soe@soe.org.uk
Constitution: Professional institution; registered charity with voluntary subscribing membership; company limited by guarantee
Objectives/purposes: Professional body of engineers and technicians devoted to the operation and maintenance of road vehicles, plant and facilities and to the education of entrants to the industry
Key staff: Chief Executive: Philip Corp; Engineering Executive: Clive Price
Stock and subject coverage: The Institute keeps a small library mainly comprising back copies of the house magazines Transport Engineer and The Plant Engineer and other journals with a road transport engineering content. It also has a small number of reference books on vehicle engineering, workshop management and allied topics and is developing a collection of papers on automotive topics presented at various British and international conferences, seminars and colloquia
Availability: The Library is primarily provided for the use of permanent staff, Council members of the

Institute and visiting ordinary members. Outside researchers admitted by prior appointment for reference use only

Hours: 09.00–17.00 Monday to Friday; not normally open at weekends

Transport: Tube: Victoria, St James's Park, Pimlico; Rail: Victoria; Bus: C1, C10, 2, 8, 11, 16, 24, 36, 36B, 38, 52, 73, 82, 88, 185, 211, 239, 507

Special facilities: Toilet facilities available

Publications: Annual Report of the Society; Transport Engineer and Bulletin (monthly). Codes of practice and guides are published from time to time on vehicle engineering matters

Linked organisations

The Society of Operations Engineers was formed on 1 September 2000 by the merger of The Institute of Road Transport Engineers (IRTE) and The Institution of Plant Engineers (IPlantE)

[584]
Sonic Arts Network

The Jerwood Space
171 Union Street
London SE1 0LN
Borough: Southwark
Telephone: 020 7928 7337
Fax: 020 7928 7338
E-mail: sonicart@demon.co.uk
World Wide Web: www.sonicartsnetwork.org
Constitution: Company limited by guarantee; registered charity
Objectives/purposes: The promotion of electroacoustic music and other creative types of music technology
Key staff: Executive Director: Phil Hallett
Stock and subject coverage: Listening library containing CDs, DATs and cassettes of electroacoustic music, both British and international
Availability: Access open to all for reference only; free facilities
Hours: 09.30–17.30 Monday to Friday by appointment
Transport: Tube and Rail: London Bridge
Special facilities: Refreshment and toilet facilities
Publications: Sonic Arts Network Diffusion (11 p.a.); Sonic Arts Network Journal of Electroacoustic Music (annual)

[585]
South Africa House Reference Library

South Africa House
Trafalgar Square
London WC2N 5DP
Borough: Westminster
Telephone: 020 7451 7299 (general switchboard)
Fax: 020 7451 7283 (mark faxes for: 'attention of Reference Library')
World Wide Web: www.southafricahouse.com
Constitution: Government funded body
Key staff: Miss Y Baker
Stock and subject coverage: Very limited general reference collection of books of South African interest
Availability: Written enquiries only (by letter or fax). Stock not on open access. A Resource Centre is

under refurbishment to provide touch screens for basic information. Please telephone before visiting to check whether the Centre is open and for opening times, which are under review
Hours: 11.00–13.00, 14.00–16.00 Monday, Wednesday and Friday
Transport: Tube: Charing Cross; Rail: Charing Cross; Bus: all buses through Trafalgar Square

[586]
South Bank University, Learning and Information Services

World Wide Web: www.lisa.sbu.ac.uk
Constitution: Department of a university
Key staff: Head of Learning and Information Resources: John Akeroyd
The University's library services are located on four sites

[586][a]
East London Campus Library

Whipps Cross Education Centre
Whipps Cross Hospital
Leytonstone
London E11 1NR
Borough: Waltham Forest
Telephone: 020 7815 4728
Fax: 020 7815 4732
Key staff: Director: Diane Watmough
Hours: Term-time: 08.30–19.30 Monday to Thursday; 08.30–17.00 Friday; 10.00–16.00 Saturday Vacations: 08.30–17.00 Monday to Friday; 10.00–16.00 Saturday
Stock and subject coverage:
Services: Photocopies, CD-ROM services, online services, internet access
Availability: Access to bona fide researchers, reciprocal agreements with other organisations. Reference only
Transport: Tube: Leytonstone; Rail: Wood Street; Bus: W12, W15, 20, 97, 230, 257

[586][b]
Essex Campus Library

Harold Wood Education Centre
Harold Wood Hospital
Gubbins Lane
Harold Wood
Romford
Essex RM3 0BE
Telephone: 020 7815 5981
Fax: 020 7815 5906
E-mail: meadt@sbu.ac.uk
World Wide Web: www.lisa.sbu.ac.uk
Key staff: Director: Matthew Lawson
Hours: Term-time: 08.30–19.30 Monday to Thursday; 08.30–17.00 Friday; 10.00–16.00 Saturday Vacations: 08.30–17.00 Monday to Friday; 10.00–16.00 Saturday
Stock and subject coverage:
Services: Photocopies, CD-ROM services, online services, internet access
Availability: Access to bona fide researchers, reciprocal agreements with other organisations. Reference only
Transport: Rail: Harold Wood; Bus: 246, 256, 294, 296

[586][c]
Perry Library
250 Southwark Bridge Road
London SE1 6NJ
Borough: Southwark
Telephone: 020 7815 6604
Fax: 020 7815 6699
Key staff: Director: John Akeroyd; Deputy Head:
Christine Muller; Academic Services Librarian: Peter
Godwin; User Services Managers: Sally Brock, Tricia
Noble
Stock and subject coverage: Ca. 300,000 books, 1,850
journal subscriptions and 10,500 audiovisual items.
All major academic disciplines held, plus historical
collections (as a result of amalgamation of libraries
from Brixton School of Building; National Bakery
School; National College of Heating, Ventilating and
Fan Engineering; Battersea College of Education;
and Rachel Macmillan College of Education). Main
strengths are computing, health subjects,
management, law, biotechnology and engineering
Services: Photocopies; word processing facilities; CD-
ROMs (some networked); access to main university
computers; document publishing/design service
(staff); audiovisual collection and online searches
(students and staff)
Availability: Unrestricted access to all South Bank
students and staff. Reference usage on application to
Managers - valid for evenings, weekends and
vacations only. Former staff/students may gain access
on application to Alumni Association (contact:
Marketing Services). Member of M25 and UK plus
schemes
Hours: Term-time: 08.30-21.00 Monday to Wednesday;
08.30-21.30 Thursday; 08.30-19.00 Friday; 10.30-
16.30 Saturday and Sunday
Vacations: 09.00-17.00 Monday to Friday
Transport: Tube: Elephant and Castle; Bus: 1, 12, 53, 68,
133, 188, 501
Special facilities: Toilet facilities available; access for users
with disabilities - no disabled parking, special adapted
toilets on every floor, magnifying equipment,
designated librarian to help, braille printer and
scanner
Publications: Annual Report; Library Guide (annual);
Study Skills Guide (annual); Services to Staff and
Researchers (annual); subject related help sheets; lists
of journals; indexes/abstracts etc. and guides to
services

[586][d]
Wandsworth Road Library
2nd Floor
Wandsworth Road
London SW8 2JZ
Borough: Lambeth
Telephone: 020 7815 8320
Key staff: Site Manager: P Noble
Stock and subject coverage: Materials on the built
environment: architecture; civil engineering; town
planning; housing; construction; construction
economics; estate management, etc. Collection of
18th and 19th century architectural and building
books
Services: Photocopies (self-service)

Availability: Members of UK universities (with
appropriate identification). Others should enquire in
writing to the Learning Resources Manager
Hours: Term-time: 08.30-21.00 Monday, Tuesday and
Thursday; 08.30-19.00 Wednesday and Friday;
Saturday (check for details); 10.30-16.30 Sunday
Vacations: 09.00-17.00 Monday to Friday
Transport: Tube: Stockwell; Bus: 77, 77A, 322
Special facilities: Refreshment and toilet facilities available

[587]
South London Botanical Institute
SLBI
323 Norwood Road
London SE24 9AQ
Borough: Lambeth
Telephone: 020 8674 5787
Fax: 020 8674 5787
Constitution: Company limited by guarantee and
registered charity
Objectives/purposes: The encouragement of the study of
plants
Key staff: Chair: Judy Marshall; Librarian: Ewart Thomas
Stock and subject coverage: Ca. 3,000 volumes plus slide
collection and journals. Subject coverage includes:
British floras, current and historical; foreign floras,
mainly European; various works on aspects of botany,
mycology, and horticulture (including arboriculture)
both current and historical. Index Kirwensis etc.
Herbarium (mainly British, some foreign) including:
pteridophytes and bryophytes, some marine algae, in
addition to flowering plants
Services: Photocopying can be arranged
Availability: Access to members and bona fide
researchers for reference only
Hours: 10.00-16.00 Monday and Thursday, other times
by arrangement
Transport: Rail: Tulse Hill, Herne Hill; Bus: P13, 2, 68,
68A, 196, 201
Special facilities: Toilet facilities available
Publications: Annual Report; Understanding Lichens by
George Baron, 1999 (published by SLBI and
Richmond Publishing Co. Ltd.)

[588]
South Place Ethical Society
SPES
Conway Hall Humanist Centre
25 Red Lion Square
London WC1R 4RL
Borough: Camden
Telephone: 020 7242 8037/4
Fax: 020 7242 8036
E-mail: library@ethicalsoc.org.uk
World Wide Web: www.ethicalsoc.org.uk
Constitution: Independent non-profit distributing
organisation; registered charity; association with
voluntary subscribing membership
Objectives/purposes: The study of ethics and the
cultivation of a humane and rational way of life
based on Humanism via an Educational Programme,
Journal and Reference Library
Key staff: Librarian: Jennifer Jeynes, MSc; Editor:
Norman Bacrac

Stock and subject coverage: The book collection comprises around 10,000 volumes combining those of the South Place Ethical Society, the Rationalist Press Association Library and the Coit Memorial Library. The Library specialises in subjects relating to ethics, humanism, rationalism and philosophy. Particular areas of interest include history of science and religion, cosmology, evolution and consciousness, history of ideas and the autobiographies of eminent freethinkers and the history of ethical and humanist societies. Conway Hall also houses the almost complete run of The Freethinker

Services: Photocopies by arrangement

Availability: Access to bona fide researchers for reference only; no fixed charges

Hours: 14.00-18.00 by appointment with the Librarian

Transport: Tube: Holborn; Bus: 19, 59, 68, 168, 188

Special facilities: Refreshment and toilet facilities available; no lift to 1st floor library, books can be brought to the ground floor for users with disabilities

Special features: The Library was built in 1929, the oak panelled room includes portraits of important figures in the Society's history hung on the walls, these include Moncure Conway, WJ Fox, C Bradlaugh, B Russell, William Morris, HG Wells, GB Shaw, EM Forster, etc

Publications: Ethical Record (10 p.a.); Conway Memorial Lecture (annual, beginning 1910); Annual Report; occasional books and pamphlets

Linked organisations

British Humanist Association (BHA)
Rationalist Press Association (NSS)
National Secular Society (RPA)
The Ethical Society is housed in the same building as these organisations and shares the same aims. The Library houses the extensive RPA collection and SPES Library acts as the Humanist Reference Library

---

[589]
Southwark (London Borough of Southwark)
Southwark Libraries and Information Service

Office Headquarters
15 Spa Road
Bermondsey
London SE16 3QW
Telephone: 020 7525 3445/3719
Fax: 020 7525 1568
E-mail: southwarklibraries@southwark.gov.uk
World Wide Web: www.southwark.gov.uk
Constitution: Public library funded by local authority
Key staff: Southwark Arts, Libraries and Museums Manager: Adrian Olsen; Strategy, Commissioning and Development Unit Manager: Gill Butler
Stock and subject coverage: Southwark Libraries stock and subject coverage includes: adult and children's fiction and non-fiction; large print; talking books; records; cassettes; videos; CDs; reference material; local studies material and educational (National Curriculum) materials.
LASER Joint Fiction Reserve: BAJ-BEL (plus BOS-CAP, RVA-RZ to 1988). Sound recordings (mainly records): Berlioz, Messiaen, Jazz JOD-LED, music of

South-East Asia (GLASS collections). Finnish and Swedish fiction

Services: Bookbus and home library service for the elderly and disabled

Availability: Loan of books freely available to those who live, work and study full-time in the borough. Free public access for book borrowing, reference and information services and the internet. Charges for audiovisual loans, photocopies, fax, etc

Publications: Local history publications (irregular); Annual Report

Special features: Southwark's flagship Peckham Library won the prestigious Stirling Award in 2000 – the top European award for architecture

[589][a]
Blue Anchor Library

Market Place
Southwark Park Road
London SE16 3UQ
Telephone: 020 7231 0475
Key staff: Area Librarian: Kathy Anstey; Library Manager: Anne Wayte
Stock and subject coverage: Reference collection; local information; music collections and children's collections
Services: Fax and photocopier. Homework clubs and Under 5 sessions; access to a local community information database – SCAN; CD-ROM facilities
Hours: 09.00-19.00 Monday, Tuesday and Thursday; 10.00-18.00 Friday; 09.00-17.00 Saturday
Transport: Bus: 1, P13, 381
Special facilities: Access for users with disabilities – library entrance is 50 yards from street (no dedicated parking). Short ramp to entrance, level internal access, Horizon CCTV magnifier for the visually impaired

[589][b]
Brandon Library

Maddock Way
Cooks Road
London SE17 3NH
Telephone: 020 7735 3430
Key staff: Area Librarian: Christine Brown; Library Manager: Sonja Williams
Stock and subject coverage: Community library with book and video collections and talking books
Services: Fax and photocopier. Under 5 sessions; access to a local community information database – SCAN; CD-ROM facilities
Hours: 10.00-12.30, 13.30-19.00 Monday and Tuesday; 09.00-12.30, 13.30-19.00 Thursday; 10.00-12.30, 13.30-17.00 Saturday
Transport: Tube: Kennington; Bus: P5
Special facilities: Access for users with disabilities – library entrance is 50 yards from street (no dedicated parking); slight incline to entrance but no steps and level access

[589][c]
Camberwell Library

17-19 Camberwell Church Street
London SE5 8JR
Telephone: 020 7703 3763

Key staff: Area Librarian: Christine Brown; Library Manager: Pam Wiles

Stock and subject coverage: Town centre library with book, music and talking book collections

Services: Fax and photocopier. Homework clubs, Under 5 sessions and Teenage Reading Group; access to a local community information database – SCAN; CD-ROM facilities

Hours: 09.00-20.00 Monday, Tuesday and Thursday; 10.00-18.00 Friday: 09.00-17.00 Saturday

Transport: Bus: 12, 36, 345

Special facilities: Access for users with disabilities – no dedicated parking (red route parking bay adjacent to library allows three hour disabled parking between 10.00-13.00). Level approach, adult library on level; junior library in basement with 13 steps (no lift)

[589][d]
Dulwich Library and Reference Library

368 Lordship Lane
London SE22 8NB

Telephone: 020 8693 5171
020 8693 8312 (Reference Library)

Key staff: Area Librarian: Steve Collins; Library Manager: Margaret Sparks
Reference Library: Reference Librarian: Sue Highley; Library Manager: Musharraf Chaudhury

Stock and subject coverage: Book, music and video collections; talking books; Hindi books section

Services: Fax and photocopier. Homework clubs and Under 5 sessions; access to a local community information database – SCAN; CD-ROM facilities

Hours: 09.00-20.00 Monday, Thursday and Friday; 10.00-20.00 Tuesday; 09.00-17.00 Saturday; 12.00-16.00 Sunday (study only, no reference library facilities)

Transport: Bus: 12, 40, 176, 185, 312

Special facilities: Access for users with disabilities – no dedicated parking but single yellow lines in Eynella and Woodwarde Roads. Three steps to entrance with ramp; level access in library; accessible automated public toilet immediately outside library. Kurzweil reading machine and Horizon CCTV magnifier; subtitled videos for hearing impaired users; audio-described videos for the visually impaired.
Reference Library situated on first floor above lending library (28 steps, no lift). Staff will bring reference materials downstairs for use in the lending library for users unable to climb stairs. Information and reference enquiries can also be answered by telephone

[589][e]
East Street Library

168-170 Old Kent Road
London SE1 5TY

Telephone. 020 7703 0395

Key staff: Area Librarian: Kathy Anstey; Branch Manager: Jean Pearce

Stock and subject coverage: Community library with book and talking book collections

Services: Fax and photocopier. Homework clubs and Under 5 sessions; access to a local community information database – SCAN; CD-ROM facilities

Hours: 10.00-19.00 Monday and Thursday; 10.00-18.00 Tuesday; 10.00-17.00 Saturday

Transport: Bus: 21, 42, 53, 63, 172

Special facilities: Access for users with disabilities – no dedicated parking (red route on Old Kent Road); level approach and level internal access; induction loop at counter

[589][f]
Education Resource Centre

Cator Street
London SE15 6AA

Telephone: 020 7525 2830

Fax: 020 7525 2837

Key staff: Education Library Service Manager: Elvena Brumant

Services: Provides library and education resourcing to primary, secondary and special schools in the borough

Availability: Open to teachers and similar educational staff only

Hours: 13.00-17.00 Monday to Wednesday, Friday; 13.00-18.00 Thursday

Transport: Bus: P11, 63, 78

Special facilities: Access for users with disabilities

[589][g]
Grove Vale Library

368 Lordship Lane
London SE22

Telephone: 020 8693 5734
Fax: 020 8693 0755

Key staff: Area Librarian: Steve Collins; Library Manager: Christine Mullett

Stock and subject coverage: Community library with book and talking book collections

Services: Fax and photocopier. Homework clubs and Under 5 sessions; access to a local community information database – SCAN; CD-ROM facilities

Hours: 10.00-19.00 Monday and Thursday; 10.00-18.00 Tuesday; 10.00-17.00 Saturday

Transport: Bus: P13, 40, 176, 185, 484

Special facilities: Access for users with disabilities – no dedicated parking; level approach and level internal access but restricted circulation; induction loop for hearing impaired users

[589][h]
John Harvard Library

211 Borough High Street
London SE1 1JA

Telephone: 020 7407 0807

Key staff: Area Librarian: Christine Brown; Library Manager: Joseph Cabey

Stock and subject coverage: Town centre library with book, video and talking book collections; Bengali collection

Services: Fax and photocopier. Homework clubs, Under 5 sessions and Family Reading Group; access to a local community information database – SCAN; CD-ROM facilities

Hours: 10.00-19.00 Monday, Tuesday and Thursday; 10.00-18.00 Wednesday and Friday; 10.00-14.00 Saturday

Transport: Tube: Borough, London Bridge; Rail: London
Bridge; Bus: P3, 21, 35, 40, 133
Special facilities: Access for users with disabilities and
adapted toilet. No dedicated parking (red route in
Borough High Street, metered bays in Tabard Street,
100 yards from Library); level approach and level
internal access; induction loop at counter and in
library hall

[589][i]
Kingswood Library
Seeley Drive
London SE21 8QR
Telephone: 020 8670 4803
Key staff: Area Librarian: Steve Collins; Library Manager:
Andrew Bodnar
Stock and subject coverage: Community library with book,
video and talking book collections
Services: Fax and photocopier. Homework clubs and
Under 5 sessions; access to a local community
information database – SCAN; CD-ROM facilities
Hours: 10.00-14.00 Monday and Thursday; 14.00-18.00
Tuesday and Friday; 13.00-17.00 Saturday
Transport: Rail: Sydenham Hill; Bus: 3, 450
Special facilities: Access for users with disabilities –
entrance is 300 yards from bus stop; dedicated
parking area immediately outside library; two steps to
entrance (temporary ramp available on request); level
access apart from teenage area; adapted toilet facilities

[589][j]
Local Studies Library
211 Borough High Street
London SE1 1JA
Telephone: 020 7403 3507
Fax: 020 7403 833
E-mail: local.studies@southwark.gov.uk
Objectives/purposes: To collect and make available
materials on the London Borough of Southwark area
past and present
Key staff: Local Studies Librarian: Len Reilly
Stock and subject coverage: The Library collects and makes
available materials on the London Borough of
Southwark area. Collections include books and
pamphlets, press cuttings, illustrations (prints and
photographs), maps and plans, microforms, archives,
film, video, audiotapes and computer programmes
Services: Photocopies; microfilm reader-printer; research
service for census returns and electoral registers
Availability: Free access to all users for reference only
Hours: 09.30-20.00 Monday and Thursday; 09.30-17.00
Tuesday and Friday; 09.30-13.00 Saturday
Transport: Tube: Borough, London Bridge; Bus: P3, 21,
35, 40, 133
Special facilities: Toilet facilities available; access for users
with disabilities. No dedicated parking available (red
route on Borough High Street, metered bays in
Tabard Street, 100 yards from library). Level approach
and level internal access; restricted circulation. No
large print material available, but staff can enlarge
material on photocopier

[589][k]
Newington Library and Reference Library
155-7 Walworth Road
London SE17 1RS
Telephone: 020 7703 3324
020 7708 0516 (reference library)
Key staff: Area Librarian: Christine Brown; Library
Manager: Fred Haynes
Reference Library: Reference Librarian: Sue Highley;
Library Manager: Musharraf Chaudhury
Stock and subject coverage: Book, music and video
collections. Turkish and Chinese collections; talking
books
Services: Fax and photocopier. Under 5 sessions; access
to a local community information database – SCAN;
CD-ROM facilities; word processors and internet
access
Hours: 09.00-20.00 Monday, Tuesday, and Friday; 10.00-
20.00 Thursday; 09.00-17.00 Saturday: 10.00-14.00
Sunday
Transport: Tube and Rail: Elephant and Castle; Bus: P3,
P5, 12, 35, 40, 45, 68, 171, 468
Special facilities: Access for users with disabilities. Three
disabled parking bays in Wansey Street (30 yards from
entrance); three steps to entrance with ramp. Lending
library on the level with restricted circulation.
Internal steps and ramp to audiovisual library. Large
print children's books and Clearvision Brailled books
for children available in junior library

Reference Library is situated on the first floor above
the lending library (29 steps, no lift). Restricted
circulation; staff will bring reference materials
downstairs for use in the lending library for users
unable to climb stairs. Information and reference
enquiries can also be answered by telephone

[589][l]
Nunhead Library
Gordon Road
London SE15 3RW
Telephone: 020 7639 0264
Key staff: Area Librarian: Steve Collins; Library Manager:
Christine White
Stock and subject coverage: Town centre library with book,
music, video and talking book collections
Services: Fax and photocopier. Under 5 sessions, Family
Reading Group and Teenage Reading Group; access
to a local community information database – SCAN;
CD-ROM facilities
Hours: 10.00-19.00 Monday, Tuesday and Thursday;
10.00-18.00 Friday; 10.00-17.00 Saturday
Transport: Bus: P12, 78
Special facilities: Access for users with disabilities – level
access internally and induction loop at counter. No
dedicated parking but two disabled parking bays
opposite library

[589][m]
Peckham Library
167 Peckham Hill Street
London SE15 5JZ
Telephone: 020 7525 0200

Key staff: Area Librarian: Kathy Anstey; Library Manager: Janice Phillips

Stock and subject coverage: Major library with book and talking book collections

Services: Fax and photocopier. Homework clubs, Under 5 sessions, Read Around the Family Group; Family Reading Group and Teenage Reading Group; access to a local community information database – SCAN; CD-ROM facilities and internet access.

One Stop Shop offers direct access to Council services and information.

Learning Centre on second floor; Library on fourth floor; activity and meeting 'pods' on 5th floor

Hours: 09.00-20.00 Monday to Friday (10.00 Wednesday); 09.00-17.00 Saturday; 12.00-16.00 Sunday

Transport: Bus: P12, P13, 12, 36, 63, 78, 171, 312, 381

Special facilities: Full access to all floors for users with disabilities (lift access). Two disabled parking bays; adapted toilets on all public floors; induction loops in reception areas; Kurzweil Reading Edge machine, Dolphin CCTV magnifier and access technology for the visually impaired; sub-titled videos for the deaf and hard of hearing

[589][n]
Rotherhithe Library

Albion Street
London SE16 1JA

Telephone: 020 7237 2010

Key staff: Area Librarian: Kathy Anstey; Library Manager: Jafer Sharif

Stock and subject coverage: Book and talking book collections. Finnish collection

Services: Fax and photocopier. Homework clubs and Under 5 sessions; access to a local community information database – SCAN; CD-ROM facilities

Hours: 10.00-19.00 Monday and Thursday; 10.00-18.00 Tuesday; 10.00-17.00 Saturday

Transport: Tube: Rotherhithe; Bus: P13, 47, 188, 225, 381

Special facilities: Access for users with disabilities – disabled parking bay outside library. Five steps to entrance with ramp; level internal access

[590]
Spanish Chamber of Commerce in Great Britain

5 Cavendish Square
London W1G 0LH

Borough: Westminster

Telephone: 020 7637 9061

Fax: 020 7436 7188

E-mail: spanishchamber@compuserve.com

World Wide Web: www.spanishchamber.co.uk

Key staff: Information department

Stock and subject coverage: Materials on Spanish trade and industry

Services: Telephone and written enquiries accepted from members. The Information Department compiles a list of UK and Spanish sources of commerce and trade information

Availability: Primarily members only. Enquiries from non-members are redirected to appropriate sources

Hours: 09.00-17.30 Monday to Friday

Transport: Tube: Oxford Circus, Bond Street

Publications: Range of publications, including the Anglo Spanish Trade Directory; El Comerico Hispano Britanico (magazine); Trade Opportunities Bulletin

[591]
Spelthorne Museum

Old Fire Station
Market Square
Staines
Middlesex TW18 4RH

Borough: Hounslow

Telephone: 01784 461804

E-mail: staff@spelthorne.free-online.co.uk

Key staff: Honorary Curator: Ralph Parsons; Chairman: Nick Pollard

Stock and subject coverage: Local history of Spelthorne Borough, particularly Staines. Records of former Staines Linoleum Company

Availability: Open to bona fide researchers on completion of an application form and by appointment only. Material is for reference only, no charges but donations appreciated

Hours: 14.00-16.00 Wednesday and Friday; 13.30-16.30 Saturday; other times by appointment

Transport: Rail: Staines

Special features: The Museum is housed in a former fire station dating from 1882

Linked organisations

Spelthorne Archaeological Field Group
Registered charity

Friends of Spelthorne Museum
The Museum is run by these groups

[592]
Spinal Injuries Association
SIA

76 St James's Lane
Muswell Hill
London N10 3DF

Borough: Haringey

Telephone: 020 8444 2121
0800 980 0501 (Freephone information line)

Fax: 020 8444 3761

E-mail: sia@spinal.co.uk

World Wide Web: www.spinal.co.uk

Constitution: Registered charity and association with voluntary subscribing membership

Objectives/purposes: Self help and support group for people with spinal cord injury and their families

Key staff: Executive Director: Paul Smith

Stock and subject coverage: Books, reports, etc. on: access, aids and equipment, benefits, education and employment, housing, legislation, medicine and health, sexuality, transport and welfare

Services: Photocopies (charges made)

Availability: Open to all, by appointment, for reference only

Hours: 09.30-17.30 Monday to Friday

Transport: Tube: Highgate then bus 43, 134 or 234 to Muswell Hill

Special facilities: Refreshment and toilet facilities available; access for users with disabilities – completely wheelchair accessible

Publications: Annual Review; Newsletter (6 p.a.); Moving Forward – A Guide to Living With Spinal Cord Injury, 2002 (and CD-ROM); range of fact sheets and books

Linked organisations

Spinal Injuries, Scotland Sister organisation

[593]
Sport England
16 Upper Woburn Place
London WC1H 0QP
Borough: Camden
Telephone: 020 7273 1500 (Switchboard)
020 7273 1700 (Information Centre)
Fax: 020 7383 5740
E-mail: info@sportengland.org
World Wide Web: www.sportengland.org
Constitution: Government funded body
Key staff: Senior Information Manager: Sally Hall; Manager: Melina Greensmith
Stock and subject coverage: 33,000 items on all aspects of sport and physical recreation
Services: Internet access; photocopies
Availability: Open to those working in sport, specialist researchers and postgraduate students; by appointment for reference only
Hours: 13.30-16.30 Monday to Friday for visitors; 14.00-16.00 for telephone enquiries
Transport: Tube: Euston, Euston Square, Russell Square; Rail: Euston
Special facilities: Toilet facilities available; access for users with disabilities

[594]
Spurgeon's College
189 South Norwood Hill
London SE25 6DJ
Borough: Croydon
Telephone: 020 8653 0850
Fax: 020 8771 0959
E-mail: enquiries@spurgeons.ac.uk
World Wide Web: www.spurgeons.ac.uk
Constitution: Registered charity
Key staff: Librarian: Mrs Judith Powles
Stock and subject coverage: Ca. 45,000 volumes and 90 current journals mainly on theology (including ethics, church history, world religions, sociology, etc.) As a Baptist Theological college, the Library has large holdings relating to Baptist theory and doctrine. The College also has a special archive collection relating to the life and work of its founder, the Rev. Charles Haddon Spurgeon. This includes manuscript letters, newspaper cuttings, portraits, etc.
Services: Photocopies
Availability: Open access to all bona fide researchers for reference only. (A written application should be made to the Librarian in advance of a first visit.) No charge for a 'one-off' visit. A small charge is levied for regular usage
Hours: 09.00-16.15 Tuesday to Friday

Transport: Tube: Brixton, then bus 196; Rail: Norwood Junction; Bus: 196, 468
Special facilities: Refreshment and toilet facilities available

Linked organisations

University of Wales The College offers BD and MTh courses validated by the University

[595]
Subterranea Britannica
98E Cambridge Gardens
London W10 6HS
Borough: Kensington and Chelsea
Telephone: 020 7361 2097
Constitution: Association with voluntary subscribing membership
Objectives/purposes: Study and promotion of artificial underground space
Key staff: Dr Roger Morgan
Stock and subject coverage: Subject coverage of anything artificial and underground, i.e. tunnels, crypts, services, mines, follies and bunkers. Materials include: books, journals, pamphlets, ephemera, maps and surveys
Availability: Open to anyone with a serious research interest, principally for advice rather than reference. No open access
Hours: By appointment only
Publications: Newsletter (4 p.a.); Bulletin (annual); introductory leaflet

Linked organisations

London Subterranean Survey Association Allied to the Association

[596]
Supreme Court Library
Royal Courts of Justice
Queen's Building
Strand
London WC2A 2LL
Borough: Westminster
Telephone: 020 7947 6587/6607/7758
Fax: 020 7947 6661
Constitution: Government funded body
Stock and subject coverage: Ca. 200,000 volumes on English law, with some coverage of Commonwealth and EC law; older editions of legal textbooks; typescripts of judgments of the Immigration Appeal Tribunals. Special collection: Transcripts of the judgments of the Court of Appeal (Civil Division) 1951 to date
Services: Loans to other libraries and legal branches of government departments only; enquiries
Availability: Although primarily for the use of the Judges and Officials of the High Court and Court of Appeal, the Library may be used by others for reference to material not readily available to them in other libraries
Hours: Law terms: 09.30-17.00 Monday to Friday; Vacations: 09.30-16.30 Monday to Friday
Transport: Tube: Temple, Holborn; Bus: 4, 6, 9, 11, 13, 15, 23, 26, 68, 77A, 88, 168, 171, 171A, 176
Special facilities: Refreshment and toilet facilities

Linked organisations
> Library operates as part of the Court Service Library and Information Services

---

[597]
Sutton Libraries (London Borough of Sutton)
World Wide Web: www.sutton.gov.uk
Constitution: Public library funded by local authority
Key staff: Head of Libraries and Heritage: Trevor Knight; Commissioning Managers: Cathy McDonough and Angela Fletcher
Special features: Sutton Libraries is part of the Learning for Life Group in the Borough

[597][a]
Sutton Central Library
> St Nicholas Way
> Sutton
> Surrey SM1 1EA

Telephone: 020 8770 4700
Fax: 020 8770 4777
Key staff: Resource and Development Manager: David Bundy; Information Managers and Specialists: Olwyn Peers and Leigh Allen; Heritage Manager: John Phillips
Stock and subject coverage: Comprehensive reference and loan collections in all subjects and in the following media: books, audio, video, pictures – for both adults and children. Special collections on heraldry; astronomy and allied science. Borough's archives and extensive local studies collection
Services: Enquiry, loan and photocopying services; CD-ROM databases; International Genealogical Index; study carrell; internet and wordprocessor hire; Kurzweil reading machine; CCTV; LearnIT Centre
Availability: Free public access for reference and borrowing books. Charges are made for borrowing other materials and for some specialist services
Hours: 09.30-20.00 Tuesday to Friday; 09.30-17.00 Saturday; 14.00-17.00 Sunday
Transport: Rail: Sutton; Bus: S1, 80, 151, 164, 213, 280, 408, 413, 420, 422, 520, 726
Special facilities: Refreshment and toilet facilities; access for users with disabilities – wheelchair access and lifts
Special features: Opened in 1975, Sutton Central Library was an innovation in library design. It incorporates the Europa Gallery – a popular exhibition space
Publications: Various guides to library services in the Borough and local history publications

[597][b]
Beddington Library
> 18 The Broadway
> Plough Lane
> Beddington
> Surrey CR0 4QR

Telephone: 020 8688 5093
Reference facilities: Reference collection and children's collection
Hours: 14.00-18.00 Tuesday and Friday; 09.00-13.00 Thursday; 09.30-13.00, 14.00-17.00 Saturday

Transport: Bus: 255, 407, 408, 726
Special facilities: Access for users with disabilities – wheelchair access

[597][c]
Carshalton Library
> The Square
> Carshalton
> Surrey SM5 3BN

Telephone: 020 8647 1151
Reference facilities: Reference collection and children's collection
Hours: 09.30-20.00 Tuesday; 09.30-17.00 Wednesday and Saturday; 09.30-13.00 Thursday; 09.30-18.00 Friday
Transport: Rail: Carshalton; Bus: 127, 157, 408, 726
Special facilities: Access for users with disabilities – limited wheelchair access

[597][d]
Cheam Library
> Church Road
> Cheam
> Surrey SM1 1SE

Telephone: 020 8644 9377
Reference facilities: Reference collection and children's collection
Hours: 09.30-20.00 Tuesday, Wednesday and Friday; 09.30-13.00 Thursday; 09.30-17.00 Saturday
Transport: Rail: Cheam; Bus: 151, 213, 408, 726
Special facilities: Access for users with disabilities – wheelchair access

[597][e]
Middleton Circle Library
> Green Wrythe Lane
> Carshalton
> Surrey SM5 1JJ

Telephone: 020 8648 6608
Reference facilities: Reference collection and children's collection
Hours: 09.30-18.00 Tuesday; 09.30-17.00 Wednesday, Friday and Saturday; 09.30-13.00 Thursday
Transport: Bus: S1, 151, 393
Special facilities: Access for users with disabilities – wheelchair access

[597][f]
Ridge Road Library
> Ridge Road
> Sutton
> Surrey SM3 9LY

Telephone: 020 8644 9696
Reference facilities: Reference collection and children's collection
Hours: 09.30-20.00 Tuesday; 09.30-17.00 Wednesday and Saturday; 09.30-13.00 Thursday; 09.30-18.00 Friday
Transport: Bus: 93, 293, 413
Special facilities: Access for users with disabilities – wheelchair access

[597][g]
Roundshaw Library
Mollison Drive
Roundshaw
Wallington
Surrey SM6 9HG
Telephone: 020 8770 4901
Reference facilities: Reference collection and children's
collection
Hours: 09.30–18.00 Tuesday; 09.30–17.00 Wednesday,
Friday and Saturday; 09.30–13.00 Thursday
Transport: Bus: 154, 255
Special facilities: Access for users with disabilities –
wheelchair access

[597][h]
Wallington Library
Shotfield
Wallington
Surrey SM6 0HY
Telephone: 020 8770 4900
Fax: 020 8770 4884
Reference facilities: Reference collection; local information
and children's collection
Hours: 09.30–20.00 Tuesday, Wednesday and Friday;
09.30–17.00 Saturday and Thursday
Transport: Rail: Wallington; Bus: 127, 151, 154, 157, 255,
301, 407, 412
Special facilities: Access for users with disabilities –
wheelchair access and lift

[597][i]
Worcester Park Library
Windsor Road
Worcester Park
Surrey KT4 8ES
Telephone: 020 8337 1609
Reference facilities: Reference collection and children's
collection
Hours: 09.30–20.00 Tuesday, Wednesday and Friday;
09.30–17.00 Thursday and Saturday
Transport: Rail: Worcester Park; Bus: K10, 151, 213, 726
Special facilities: Access for users with disabilities –
wheelchair access

[598]
The Swedenborg Society
20-21 Bloomsbury Way
London WC1A 2TH
Borough: Camden
Telephone: 020 7405 7986
Fax: 020 7831 5848
E-mail: swed.soc@netmatters.co.uk
World Wide Web: www.swedenborg.org.uk
Constitution: Independent non-profit distributing
organisation; company limited by guarantee;
registered charity and association with voluntary
subscribing membership
Objectives/purposes: To publish, translate and distribute
the works of Emanuel Swedenborg. To maintain a
library containing biographies of him, all known
editions of his works and collateral and archival items
related to his life, works and followers

Key staff: Society Secretary: Madeline G Waters;
Librarian and Archivist: Nancy S Dawson;
Publications Manager: Stephen McNeilly; Property
Manager: Eoin McMahon
Stock and subject coverage: The Swedenborg Collection of
ca. 4,500 items: books in 35 languages, including 55
volumes of photo-facsimile manuscripts.
Swedenborgiana: including original letters,
photographs, slides and archival items. Printed
collateral literature: ca. 7,000 items including journals
from 1790 to present day. Miscellaneous archival
items relating to the Society and followers of
Swedenborg's teachings: including correspondence,
mss typescripts, photographs, etc.
Services: Photocopies (charges made). Updating of
catalogue to database with cross-reference facilities
currently in progress
Availability: Open to all bona fide researchers. Materials
are for reference only, although a few duplicate items
are also available for loan
Hours: 09.30–17.00 Monday to Friday
Transport: Tube: Holborn, Tottenham Court Road; Bus:
8, 9, 22B, 25, 30, 38, 55, 168, 171, 188, 196, 501, 505
Special facilities: Reading room; toilet facilities available
Special features: Library housed in Grade II listed
Georgian building in Bloomsbury
Publications: Swedenborg Society Report (annual);
Supplement to Annual report (annual); annual
Journal; quarterly Newsletter; occasional new editions
or reprints of Swedenborg Society sales catalogue and
works of Emanuel Swedenborg in Latin and English

[599]
Swedish Chamber of Commerce
Sweden House
5 Upper Montagu Street
London SW19 4DT
Borough: Westminster
Telephone: 020 7224 8001
Fax: 020 7224 8884
E-mail: link@swedish-chamber.org.uk
World Wide Web: www.swedish-chamber.org.uk
Constitution: Independent non-profit member
organisation
Stock and subject coverage: Annual reports on some
Swedish companies; general information on Sweden
Services: Photocopies (charged); simple enquiries free;
complex enquiries charged
Availability: Freely available
Hours: 10.00–15.00 Monday to Friday
Transport: Tube: Baker Street or Edgware Road
Special facilities: Toilet facilities available
Publications: Link magazine (members only); Trade
Directory (£35 p.a.)

[600]
Tate Library and Archive
Hyman Kreitman Research Centre
Tate Britain
Millbank
London SW1P 4RG
Borough: Westminster
Telephone: 020 7887 8838
Fax: 020 7887 8901

E-mail: library@tate.org.uk
Constitution: National museum
Key staff: Librarian: Meg Duff
Stock and subject coverage: Over 45,000 books; 120,000 exhibition catalogues; 400 current journals. Covers subjects reflecting the Tate Gallery's collections – historic British painting from the Renaissance onwards; modern art from ca. 1870
Services: Coin-operated photocopier; written and telephone enquiries; PCs with Internet access; online databases
Availability: Open by appointment, for reference use only, to readers wishing to consult material not readily available elsewhere; no loans
Hours: 10.00-17.00 Monday to Friday
Transport: Tube: Pimlico; Bus: 77A, 88
Special facilities: Refreshment and toilet facilities

[601]
Tavistock and Portman NHS Library

120 Belsize Lane
London NW3 5BA
Borough: Camden
Telephone: 020 7447 3868
Fax: 020 7447 3734
E-mail: adouglas@tavi-port.org
World Wide Web: www.tavi-port.org
Constitution: Part of the Tavistock and Portman NHS Trust
Objectives/purposes: To provide library and information services to support the training, research and clinical work of the Tavistock and Portman Clinics
Key staff: Librarian: Angela Douglas: Deputy Librarian: Angela Haselton
Stock and subject coverage: Ca. 29,000 books and pamphlets, 300 current journals and 500 items of audiovisual material. Covers psychology; psychiatry; psychoanalysis; social work; sociology; management; some medicine
Services: Interlibrary loans; circulation of accessions list (on request); internet access; full-text journal access; web-based catalogue; bibliographic databases available via the internet; electronic resources. Brief replies to information enquiries, as staff time permits
Availability: Open to staff and students of the Tavistock Clinic, Portman Clinic and Tavistock Marital Studies Institute. For research purposes a day ticket is obtainable on application to the Librarian, outside researchers are charged a fee
Hours: 09.30-17.30 Monday to Friday. Extended evening opening until 21.00 Monday to Thursday in term-time
Transport: Tube: Swiss Cottage, Finchley Road; Bus: 113
Special facilities: Refreshment and toilet facilities available; easy access for users to library on ground floor
Publications: Annotated List of Publications (i.e. publications of the Tavistock Clinic); Accessions List (each term); List of Periodical Holdings; Guide to the Library
Special features: National resource for mental health and physiotherapy

[602]
Thames Police Museum

Wapping Police Station
98 Wapping High Street
London E1W 2NE
Borough: Tower Hamlets
Telephone: 020 7275 4421
Fax: 020 7275 4490
E-mail: thames.metpol@gtnet.gov.uk
Constitution: Private collection on police premises
Key staff: Honorary Curator: Bob Jeffries
Stock and subject coverage: Collections on marine police matters. Books written by founders and early written records from 1798
Availability: Access to bona fide researchers by appointment only
Hours: By appointment
Transport: Tube: Wapping; Bus: 100
Publications: Bi-annual journal

Linked organisations

Metropolitan Police Museum

[603]
Thames Valley University
TVU

St Marys Road
Ealing
London W5 5RF
Borough: Ealing
Telephone: 020 8579 5000
Fax: 020 8231 2631
E-mail: lrs@tvu.ac.uk
World Wide Web: www.tvu.ac.uk
Constitution: Department of a university
Key staff: Head of Learning Resources: John Wolstenholme; Learning Resource Centre Managers: Peter Hassell (St Mary's Road LRC); Brent Evans (Westel House LRC); Simon Whitby (Paul Hamlyn LRC, Slough)
Stock and subject coverage: Three health science libraries. The two main libraries (in Ealing and Slough) cover: law, hospitality, humanities, sociology and politics, creative arts, accountancy, business, management and psychology
Services: Open access PCs with internet access, electronic datasets and journals; photocopying; Open Access language facility; media services loans
Availability: Open to TVU students and staff and to members of the UK Plus and M25 schemes (on application)
Hours: Term-time: 08.30-22.00 Monday to Friday (vacation opening times vary)
Transport: Tube: South Ealing and Ealing Broadway; Rail: Slough (Paul Hamlyn LRC)
Special facilities: Refreshment facilities (Ealing only); toilet facilities; access for users with disabilities
Special features: Slough building designed by Sir Richard Rogers
Publications: Annual Report, various guides and handouts

Linked organisations

Wolfson Institute (Health Sciences)
London College of Music and Media
Also a part of TVU

[604]
Theatre Museum

1E Tavistock Street
London WC2E 7PA
Borough: Westminster
Fax: 020 7943 4777
E-mail: tmenquiries@vam.ac.uk
World Wide Web: www.theatremuseum.org
Constitution: Government funded body
Objectives/purposes: National museum and archive of the Performing Arts
Key staff: Head of Museum: Margaret Benton; Head of Information Services and Collections Management: Claire Hudson
Stock and subject coverage: The Theatre Museum covers all aspects of the live performing arts, including drama, dance, opera, musical theatre, circus, music hall and puppetry. Its research collections include books (ca. 100,000), playbills, programmes and reviews (over 1 million), photographs (over 2 million), prints (25,000) and designs (6,000). The National Video Archive of Performance, established in 1992, houses current British stage productions – a collection of other performance videos is also being developed. In addition to the collections housed at the Museum, over 250 special collections are housed at an archival store in Olympia
Services: Enquiry, photographic and photocopying services; video playback facilities
Availability: Public study room available for reference use, by appointment only, two weeks notice normally required (telephone: 020 7943 4727, fax: 020 7943 4777, e-mail: tmenquiries@vam.ac.uk)
Hours: 10.30–16.30 Tuesday to Friday (note: Library opening hours differ from the Museum)
Transport: Tube: Covent Garden, Charing Cross; Rail: Charing Cross
Special facilities: Toilet facilities; access for users with disabilities

Linked organisations

Victoria and Albert Museum Branch of the Museum
SIBMAS (the International Association of Libraries and Museums of the Performing Arts) The Theatre Museum is the UK headquarters of SIBMAS

[605]
Theatres Trust

22 Charing Cross Road
London WC2H 0QL
Borough: Westminster
Telephone: 020 7836 8591
Fax: 020 7836 3302
E-mail: info@theatrestrust.org.uk
World Wide Web: www.theatrestrust.org.uk
Objectives/purposes: Established by Acts of Parliament to promote the better protection of theatres
Key staff: Administrator: Paul Connolly
Stock and subject coverage: Some books and journals, but mainly files. Covers theatre buildings in England, Northern Ireland, Scotland and Wales (mainly since 1976) with materials on their architecture and design;

planning; and history. Also holds correspondence relating to planning applications, etc.
Services: Photocopies (charged); bibliography compilation; information source guidance
Availability: Telephone and written enquiries accepted; bona fide researchers, by appointment only, for reference use
Hours: 09.30–17.30 Monday to Friday
Transport: Tube: Leicester Square, Tottenham Court Road

[606]
The Theosophical Society in England

50 Gloucester Place
London W1U 8EA
Borough: Westminster
Telephone: 020 7935 9261
Fax: 020 7935 9543
Constitution: Registered charity; association with voluntary subscribing membership
Objectives/purposes: The Society aims to: form a nucleus of the Universal Brotherhood of humanity without distinction of race, creed, sex, caste or colour; to encourage the study of comparative religion, philosophy and science; to investigate unexplained laws of nature and the powers latent in man
Key staff: Miss J Grayson
Stock and subject coverage: Ca. 12,500 volumes on: theosophy, the psychic world, religion, philosophy, mysticism, science, modern civilisation and culture, literature and fiction, health and healing, folklore and mythology, arts, yoga, ancient civilisations, western occultism, psychology and para-psychology, astrology and allied arts, sociology and unexplained phenomena
Services: Photocopies
Availability: Restricted to members or subscribers (rates on request)
Hours: 14.00–18.30 Tuesdays to Fridays
Transport: Tube: Baker Street, Marble Arch; Rail: Marylebone; Bus: 2, 13, 30, 74, 82, 113, 139, 159, 274
Special facilities: Refreshment and toilet facilities; access for users with disabilities – lift to library
Special features: The Theosophical Society is an international, non-sectarian organisation. Founded in 1875 it is active in 50 countries. The library is housed in a listed building
Publications: Insight journal (6 p.a.)

Linked organisations

International headquarters located at Adyar, near Madras, India

[607]
Tower Hamlets Libraries (London Borough of Tower Hamlets)

World Wide Web: www.ideastore.co.uk
Constitution: Public library funded by local authority
Availability: Lending services are for those living, working or studying in Tower Hamlets. Reference services are unrestricted
Note: Tower Hamlets plans to open purpose-built 'Idea Stores' in local shopping areas, combining lifelong

learning and cultural attractions with the services normally associated with libraries. Seven Idea Stores are planned over the next five years: the first in Bow is currently open, with others planned for Bethnal Green, Whitechapel (summer 2004), Watney market, Chrisp Street (late 2003), Canary Wharf and Isle of Dogs

[607][a]
Bancroft Library
277 Bancroft Road
London E1 4DQ
Telephone: 020 8980 4366
Fax: 020 8983 4510
E-mail: bancroftlibrary@towerhamlets.gov.uk
Key staff: Local History Librarian: Chris Lloyd; Archivist: Malcolm Barr-Hamilton
Reference facilities: General adult and children's lending collections; local studies and archives collections
Services: Photocopies (b&w); fax; PC for hire; microfilm reader/printers
Hours: 09.00-20.00 Monday, Tuesday and Thursday; closed on Wednesdays; 09.00-18.00 Friday; 09.00-17.00 Saturday
Local History and Archives closed Mondays, otherwise as above
Transport: Tube: Stepney Green; Bus: D6, 25, 277, 309
Special facilities: Access for users with disabilities (lift available)

[607][b]
Bethnal Green Library
Cambridge Heath Road
London E2 0HL
Telephone: 020 8980 3902/6274
Fax: 020 8981 6129
E-mail: bethnalgreenlibrary@towerhamlets.gov.uk
Key staff: Principal Information Librarian: John Jasinski
Stock and subject coverage: General mid-level reference library; music and children's collections. Bethnal Green library houses a reference and information service, e-mail: referencelibrary@towerhamlets.gov.uk
Services: Photocopies (b&w); fax; PC for hire; CD-ROMs; microfilm reader/printer
Hours: 09.00-20.00 Monday, Tuesday and Thursday; closed on Wednesdays; 09.00-18.00 Friday; 09.00-17.00 Saturday
Transport: Tube: Bethnal Green; Bus: D6, 8, 106, 253
Special facilities: Access for users with disabilities

[607][c]
Cubitt Town Library
Strattondale Street
London E14 3HG
Telephone: 020 7987 3152
Fax: 020 7538 2795
E-mail: cubittownlibrary@towerhamlets.gov.uk
Reference facilities: Small collection of material on Isle of Dogs history; reference collection, local information and children's collection
Services: Photocopier and fax; study facilities for 8 people
Hours: 09.00-20.00 Monday, Tuesday and Thursday; 09.00-17.00 Friday; 09.00-12.30, 13.30-17.00 Saturday

Transport: DLR: Crossharbour
Special facilities: Access for users with disabilities

[607][d]
Dorset Library
Ravenscroft Street
London E2 7QX
Telephone: 020 7739 9489
Fax: 020 7729 2548
Reference facilities: Reference collection, local information and children's collection
Services: Photocopier
Hours: 09.00-12.30, 13.30-18.00 Tuesday and Friday; 09.00-12.00 Saturday
Transport: Tube: Bethnal Green, Liverpool Street; Rail: Liverpool Street

[607][e]
Idea Store Bow
1 Gladstone Place
Roman Road
London E3 5ES
Telephone: 020 7364 4332
Fax: 020 7364 5773
E-mail: bowideastore@towerhamlets.gov.uk
Key staff: Sergio Dogliani
Reference facilities: Reference collection, local information and children's collection
Services: Photocopier and fax, internet access, adult education classes, events
Hours: 09.00-21.00 Monday to Thursday; 09.00-18.00 Friday; 09.00-17.00 Saturday; 10.00-16.00 Sunday
Transport: Tube: Bow Road
Special facilities: Cafe, access for users with disabilities
Special features: Opened in May 2002, piloting the borough's Idea service and philosophy

[607][f]
Lansbury Library
23-27 Market Walk
London E14 7HS
Telephone: 020 7987 3573
Fax: 020 7538 5520
E-mail: lansburylibrary@towerhamlets.gov.uk
Reference facilities: Reference collection; general adult and children's collections
Services: Photocopies
Hours: 09.00-18.00 Monday, Tuesday, Thursday and Friday; closed Wednesday; 09.00-17.00 Saturday
Transport: Tube: Poplar, All Saints
Special facilities: Wheelchair accessible

[607][g]
Limehouse Library
638 Commercial Road
London E14 7HS
Telephone: 020 7364 2527
Fax: 020 7364 2502
Key staff: Library Resources Co-ordinator: David Hancock
Reference facilities: General lending and children's services. French, German, Portuguese, Chinese and Vietnamese language collections

Services: Photocopies (b&w) and fax
Hours: 09.00-20.00 Monday; 09.00-18.00 Friday; 09.00-12.00 Saturday
Transport: DLR: Limehouse; Bus: 5, D9, D14, 15, 15B, 40

[607][h]
Stepney Library
Lindley Street
London E1 3AX
Telephone: 020 7790 5616
Fax: 020 7264 9873
Reference facilities: General lending and children's services
Services: Photocopies
Hours: 09.00-12.30, 13.30-18.00 Monday and Thursday; closed Tuesday, Wednesday and Friday; 14.00-17.00 Saturday
Transport: Tube: Whitechapel; Bus: 25

[607][i]
Wapping Library
St Peter's Centre
Reardon Street
London E1 9QN
Telephone: 020 7488 3535
Reference facilities: General lending and children's services
Services: Photocopies
Hours: 14.30-18.00 Monday, Tuesday and Thursday; closed rest of the week
Transport: Tube: Wapping, Shadwell

[607][j]
Watney Market Library
30-32 Watney Market
London E1 2PR
Telephone: 020 7790 4039
Fax: 020 7265 9401
E-mail: watneymarketlibrary@towerhamlets.gov.uk
Reference facilities: General lending and children's services
Services: Photocopies
Hours: 09.00-20.00 Monday and Thursday; 09.00-17.00 Tuesday and Friday; closed on Wednesdays; 09.00-12.30, 13.30-17.00 Saturday
Transport: Tube: Shadwell

[607][k]
Whitechapel Library
77 Whitechapel High Street
London E1 7QX
Telephone: 020 7247 5272
Fax: 020 7247 5731
E-mail: whitechapellibrary@towerhamlets.gov.uk
Key staff: Community Librarian: Caroline Algar
Reference facilities: General lending and children's services; music services. Indic languages collection
Services: Photocopies (b&w) and fax
Hours: 09.00-20.00 Monday, Tuesday and Thursday; closed on Wednesdays; 09.00-18.00 Friday; 09.00-17.00 Saturday
Transport: Tube: Aldgate East; Bus: 5, 15, 15B, 25, 40, 67, 253

Trade Partners UK Information Centre
(formerly Export Market Information Centre)
Kingsgate House
67-74 Victoria Street
London SW1E 6SW
Borough: Westminster
Telephone: 020 7215 5444/5
Fax: 020 7215 4231
E-mail: via website at www.tradepartners.gov.uk
World Wide Web: www.tradepartners.gov.uk
Government Telecommunications Network: 215
Constitution: Government funded body for the promotion of exports
Key staff: Manager: Duncan Packer; Enquiry Services Manager: Cass Johnson
Stock and subject coverage: The Centre is provided by the DTI to enable British exporters, or their representatives, to research into overseas markets and to bring commercial opportunities, arising from the lending programmes of the multilateral development agencies, to the attention of UK companies. The collection includes overseas statistical compilations; statistics of trade, production, price, employment, population and other economic topics; current editions of foreign trade directories; overseas market surveys; information on multilateral aid funded projects throughout the world; development plans; economic reports; sector analyses; tender notices; and overseas mail order catalogues. A range of statistical, marketing and company information is available on CD-ROM and online services, via free Information Centre internet terminals. Access to export market information websites via Trade Partners UK Information Centre website
Services: Statistical material, directories, information on multilateral funded aid projects, development plans and mail order catalogues are available for reference only. Photocopying and microfiche reader-printers are available subject to copyright regulations. There are internet and CD-ROM workstations, fax and a payphone. Workshops are available for new or inexperienced users (prior booking required)
Availability: Open to British exporters and their representatives without appointment. Please note that students must make an appointment in advance, as space is limited. It is advisable to book CD-ROM and internet workstations in advance
Hours: 09.00-20.00 Monday to Thursday, last admissions at 19.30; 09.00-17.30 on Friday, last admission at 17.00
Transport: Tube: St James's Park, Victoria; Rail: Victoria; Bus: 11, 24, 29, 70
Special facilities: Toilet facilities available; access for users with disabilities

[608][a]
World Aid Section
Telephone: 020 7215 4165
Fax: 020 7215 4535
Key staff: Librarian: Ms Terri Lewis

Stock and subject coverage: 6,000 items on projects financed by the multilateral aid agencies
Availability: Serious researchers and UK exporters only
Hours: 09.30–16.45 Monday to Friday by appointment only
Transport: Tube: St James's Park, Victoria; Rail: Victoria; Bus: 11, 24, 29, 70

Linked organisations
Department of Trade and Industry
Project Export Promotion Directorate
Part of the Directorate

[609]
Trades Union Congress Library Collections
TUC
University of North London Learning Centre
236 Holloway Road
London N7 6PP
Borough: Islington
Telephone: 020 7753 3184
Fax: 020 7753 3191
E-mail: tuclib@unl.ac.uk
World Wide Web: www.unl.ac.uk/library/tuc
Key staff: Librarian: Christine Coates MA ALA (c.coates@unl.ac.uk)
Stock and subject coverage: Industrial relations; wages and conditions of employment; trade unions; economics; industrial health; international trade union activities; and other areas covered by TUC policy
Services: Telephone enquiry service
Availability: Open for research by appointment only
Hours: 09.15–17.15 Monday to Friday
Transport: Tube: Holloway Road
Special facilities: Refreshment and toilet facilities available; access for users with disabilities

[610]
Transport 2000
The Impact Centre
12-18 Hoxton Street
London N1 6NG
Borough: Hackney
Telephone: 020 7613 0743
Fax: 020 7613 5280
Constitution: Company limited by guarantee and registered charity
Objectives/purposes: Environmental transport group
Stock and subject coverage: Materials on transport policy, environmental issues, sustainable cities, road building and rail
Services: Photocopies; fax machine
Availability: Open to all for reference only, free of charge (by appointment)
Hours: 09.30–16.30 Monday to Friday
Transport: Tube: Old Street: Rail: Liverpool Street; Bus: 35, 48, 149
Special facilities: Toilet facilities available
Publications: Transport Report (4 p.a.); Annual Review; publications catalogue

[611]
Treasury and Cabinet Office
Treasury Chambers
London SW1P 3AG
Borough: Westminster
Telephone: 020 7270 5290 (Enquiries)
020 7270 5299 (Loans)
Fax: 020 7270 5681
E-mail: library@hm-treasury.x.gsi.gov.uk
Constitution: Government department. Serves the Treasury and Cabinet Office government departments
Key staff: Chief Librarian: Miss Jean Clayton BA ALA
Stock and subject coverage: About 40,000 books and 3,000 serials taken. Main subjects are economics, all aspects of management and public administration. Current and retrospective material on the Civil Service. Large collections of parliamentary papers, statistical series and working papers on economics and related subjects
Services: Loans: To government libraries direct; current material loaned to libraries outside government in exceptional circumstances. There is a Public Enquiry Unit (020 7270 4558) which handles requests for Treasury publications (not published by TSO) from outside organisations and other government departments
Hours: 09.00–18.00 Monday to Friday
Transport: Tube: Westminster, Charing Cross; Rail: Charing Cross; Bus: 12, 53, 77A, 88

[612]
Treasury Solicitor's Library Information Centre
Queen Anne's Chambers
28 Broadway
London SW1H 9JS
Borough: Westminster
Telephone: 020 7210 3044/3045
Fax: 020 7210 3058
E-mail: tsol-library@treasury-solicitor.gsi.gov.uk
World Wide Web: www.treasury-solicitor.gov.uk
Constitution: Government funded body
Key staff: Senior Librarian: Mrs Evelyn Stevens BA ALA; Deputy Librarian: Mrs Alberta Charles
Stock and subject coverage: Ca. 25,000 volumes, principally English legal material, but also some coverage of Scotland, Northern Ireland and EC law
Services: Loans (to government departments and other reciprocating libraries); enquiry service; internet access; photocopies
Availability: To departmental staff, and to government departments and agencies
Hours: 08.45–17.30 Monday to Friday
Transport: Tube: St James's Park
Publications: Current Awareness Bulletin

[613]
The Turner Library, Whitefield Schools and Centre

Macdonald Road
Walthamstow
London E17 4AZ
Borough: Waltham Forest
Telephone: 020 8531 3426/8703
Fax: 020 8527 0907
E-mail: lib@whitefield.org.uk
World Wide Web: www.whitefield.org.uk
Objectives/purposes: Special educational needs resource centre
Key staff: Librarian: Gillian Goodchild; Library Assistant: Maureen May
Stock and subject coverage: Books, journals and curriculum documents on the topics of curriculum, policy, legislation and educational management. Regularly updated collection of articles and pamphlets on specific special education topics, including a section on syndromes and disorders. The Library's collection reflects the needs of parents, educators, support services, health services and administrators
Services: Computerised catalogue; photocopies; searches and select bibliographies of library materials prepared (charges to non-members)
Availability: Open to all. Charges made for book loan membership, Current Awareness Bulletin and photocopying
Hours: Term-time: 09.00-18.30 Monday and Wednesday; 09.00-17.00 Tuesday and Thursday; 09.00-16.30 Friday
Holidays: 09.00-16.30 Monday to Friday (closed Christmas and New Year)
Transport: Tube and Rail: Walthamstow Central; Bus: 212, 275
Special facilities: Toilet facilities available; access for users with disabilities (including wheelchair accessible toilet)
Publications: Current Awareness Bulletin (6 p.a.), subscription year starts September with backcopies sent to anyone starting a subscription mid-year

[614]
Union of Muslim Organisations of UK and Eire
UMO

109 Camden Hill Road
London W8 7TL
Borough: Kensington and Chelsea
Telephone: 020 7229 0538
 020 7221 6608
Fax: 020 7792 2130
Constitution: Independent non-profit distributing organisation; association with voluntary subscribing membership
Objectives/purposes: Coordinating the activities of Muslim organisations in the UK and Ireland. Representative body of 2.5 million British muslims
Key staff: General Secretary (Honorary), voluntary help from members
Stock and subject coverage: Books on Islam and Islamic culture
Availability: Reference only, by appointment

Hours: 10.00-17.30 Monday to Friday
Transport: Tube: Notting Hill Gate; Bus: 12, 27, 31, 52, 70, 94
Special facilities: Toilet facilities available

[615]
United Lodge of Theosophists
ULT

62 Queens Gardens
London W2 3AH
Borough: Westminster
Telephone: 020 7723 0688
Fax: 020 7262 8639
E-mail: ult@ultlon.freeserve.co.uk
World Wide Web: www.ultlon.freeserve.co.uk
Constitution: Independent non-profit distributing organisation; company limited by guarantee; association with voluntary subscribing membership
Objectives/purposes: Three objects: to form a nucleus of Universal Brotherhood; study of comparative religions; investigations of the paranormal
Key staff: Miss O Rouget
Stock and subject coverage: Original Theosophical magazines from 1875 onwards, i.e. The Theosophist, Lucifer, The Path (New York), and others published by the various Theosophical organisations. Photographic editions of the main original books relating to Theosophy, also translated scriptures such as the Bhagavad Gita, the Dhammapada, the Tao Te King; of special interest are The Secret Doctrine, Isis Unveiled – The Key to Theosophy, Theosophical articles by HP Blavatsky and WQ Judge the original founders of the Theosophical Movement in 1875
Services: Photocopies
Availability: Available to all enquirers by appointment. Rare books not available for loan. Charges are made. Some books may be purchased
Hours: By appointment only
Transport: Tube: Paddington, Lancaster Gate; Rail: Paddington; Bus: 7, 15, 23, 27, 36
Special facilities: Toilet facilities available
Special features: The ULT holds classes on Theosophy and lectures every Sunday; Study group 19.00-20.00 Wednesdays – Open to all, no need to register; Public lectures: 19.00-20.00 Sundays - free and open to all
Publications: Theosophy (quarterly, published by Los Angeles ULT); The Theosophical Movement (monthly, published by the Bombay ULT); Theosophy (Los Angeles, 4 p.a.). Complimentary copies available on request. Programme and booklist available (send SAE)

Linked organisations

Mother Lodge at Los Angeles, New York, Bombay, and Paris lodges

[616]
United Nations Association – UK
UNA – UK

3 Whitehall Court
London SW1A 2EL
Borough: Westminster
Telephone: 020 7930 2931
Fax: 020 7930 5893

E-mail: info@una-uk.org
World Wide Web: www.una-uk.org
Constitution: Company limited by guarantee; association with voluntary subscribing membership
Objectives/purposes: Support and lobbying on behalf of the UN system
Key staff: Sustainable Development: Felix Dodds; Human Rights: Suzanne Long; UN and Conflict: Alexander Ramsbotham
Stock and subject coverage: Mainly UN documents relating to environment and development, human rights and refugees, UN and conflict, UN reform. Also material from many sources relating to these topics
Services: Photocopies
Availability: Materials can be used by outsiders by arrangement, but there is limited space available. Resources are mainly used by staff and UNA members. Membership is open to all £20 p.a. (£10 low income; £5 under 26)
Hours: 09.30-17.30 Monday to Friday, telephone to make arrangements
Transport: Tube: Embankment, Charing Cross; Rail: Charing Cross; Bus: buses along Whitehall and Trafalgar Square
Special facilities: Toilet facilities; access for users with disabilities
Publications: New World (4 p.a.)

Linked organisations
Branches throughout the UK

[617]
United Nations Information Centre
UNIC

Millbank Tower (21st Floor)
21-24 Millbank
London SW1P 4QH
Borough: Westminster
Telephone: 020 7630 1981
Fax: 020 7976 6478
E-mail: kdavies@uniclondon.org
World Wide Web: www.unitednations.org.uk
Key staff: Karen Davies
Stock and subject coverage: Holds the official publications of the United Nations and some materials from the specialised agencies (e.g. UNDP, UNEP, UNCTAD, etc.)
Services: Photocopies and internet access
Availability: Open to the public for reference purposes by appointment only
Hours: 09.30-13.00, 14.00-17.00 Monday to Thursday
Transport: Tube: Pimlico, Westminster
Special facilities: Toilet facilities, access for users with disabilities

Linked organisations
United Nations (UN) Part of the UN

[618]
The United Society for the Propagation of the Gospel
USPG

Partnership House
157 Waterloo Road
London SE1 8XA
Borough: Lambeth
Telephone: 020 7928 8681
Fax: 020 7928 2371
E-mail: archive@uspg.org.uk
World Wide Web: www.uspg.org.uk
Constitution: Registered charity
Objectives/purposes: Anglican mission agency working in partnership with the world church
Key staff: Archivist: Catherine Wakeling
Stock and subject coverage: The USPG archives date back to 1701 and include those of its predecessors, the Society for the Propagation of the Gospel (SPG), the Universities' Mission to Central Africa (UMCA) and the Cambridge Mission to Delhi (CMD), which merged in 1965 to form the United Society. In addition to the Society's own records, the archive contains the deposited papers of people associated with the Society. The majority of the earlier records are held on deposit at Rhodes House Library in Oxford, where they are available for consultation by researchers. The more recent records and all personal files are at Partnership House in London
Services: Photocopies
Availability: The archive is subject to a 30 year closure rule, but otherwise access is open to bona fide researchers. Personal files are closed for 50 years from date of death
Hours: 10.00-16.00 Monday to Thursday, by appointment only
Transport: Tube: Waterloo, Elephant and Castle; Rail: Waterloo, Waterloo East; Bus: 1, 4, 12, 26, 45, 53, 63, 68, 76, 168, 171, 171A, 172, 188, 344, 501, 505
Special facilities: Refreshment and toilet facilities available; access for users with disabilities – advise of any requirements before visiting
Publications: USPG Yearbook; Transmission (quarterly); Thinking Mission (quarterly); The Christ we Share resource pack; Three Centuries of Mission: the United Society for the Propagation of the Gospel, 1701-2000 by Daniel O'Connor and others (London, Continuum, 2000)

[619]
University College London Library

Gower Street
London WC1E 6BT
Borough: Camden
Telephone: 020 7679 7700
        020 7679 7793 (enquiries)
        020 7679 7789 (science enquiries)
Fax: 020 7679 7373
E-mail: library@ucl.ac.uk
World Wide Web: www.ucl.ac.uk/library
Constitution: Department of a university

Key staff: Director of Library Services: Paul Ayris MA
PhD ALA

Stock and subject coverage: Over one million bound
volumes and pamphlets, 160 collections of
manuscripts and 8,000 current journals. Subject
coverage includes: American history; anthropology;
archaeology; architecture; history of art; classical
studies; clinical sciences; computer science; Dutch;
economics; Egyptology; engineering; English; fine art;
geography; German; Hebrew; history; Jewish studies;
Latin American studies; law; librarianship; life
sciences; linguistics; London history; mathematical
sciences; medical sciences; natural sciences; phonetics;
physical sciences; planning; Romance languages;
Scandinavian studies and history of science.

Special collections include: Barlow Library (Dante);
Carswell Drawings (medicine); Graves Early Science
Library; James Joyce Collection; Johnston Lavis
Library (vulcanology); Little Magazines Collection;
CK Ogden Library; George Orwell Archive; Sir John
Rotton Library; Whitley Stokes Celtic Library.
Manuscript Collections of: Jeremy Bentham, Edwin
Chadwick, Sir Francis Galton, Moses Gaster, Latin-
American Business Archives, Karl Pearson, Sir
William Ramsay, Routledge and Kegan Paul
Archives, Society for the Diffusion of Useful
Knowledge, Hugh Gaitskell papers, Lord Brougham,
Henry Balfour, Alex Helm, George Greenough,
Lionel Penrose, Richard Rees, Sharpe Family, William
Townsend.

Libraries of learned societies housed in the College
Library are:

British Chess Problem Society; British Society of
Franciscan Studies; Filtration Society; Folklore
Society; Gaelic Society; Geologists Association;
Hertfordshire Natural History and Field Club;
Huguenot Society; Jewish Historical Society of
England; London Mathematical Society;
Malacological Society; Mocatta Library of Anglo-
Judaica; Philological Society; Royal Historical
Society; Royal Statistical Society; Viking Society for
Northern Research (now incorporated with the
Scandinavian Library)

Services: Photocopies; the Library's online catalogue is
accessible via the web at www.ucl.ac.uk/library

Availability: By arrangement, write to the Librarian

Hours: Main Library and Science Library: Term-time
(main sites): 09.30-19.00, 09.30-16.30 Saturday, issue
desks close 15 minutes before closing time. (Reading
rooms are open for reference use 08.45-22.30
Monday to Thursday; 08.45-19.00 Friday.)
Summer Vacation (main sites): 09.30-17.00 Monday
to Friday
Manuscripts and Rare Books Room (in the Science
Library): 10.00-17.00 Monday, Thursday and Friday;
10.00-19.00 Tuesday and Wednesday

Transport: Tube: Euston Square; Euston, Warren Street;
Rail: Euston

Special facilities: Refreshment and toilet facilities available;
limited disabled access – by arrangement

Publications: Library guide

Linked organisations

University of London Part of the University

[620]
University of East London
UEL
World Wide Web: www.uel.ac.uk/lss
Constitution: University
Availability: Access for UEL students, researchers and
staff. Students from other London universities
participating in the UK Plus scheme may use the
UEL Learning Resource Centres (LRCs). External
users may have access to certain library facilities
subject to a sliding scale of fees
Publications: Annual Report for UEL; Library News
(produced approx. once a semester)

[620][a]
Barking Campus Learning Resource Centre
Longbridge Road
Dagenham
Essex RM8 2AS
Borough: Barking
Telephone: 020 8223 2610
Fax: 020 8223 2804
Key staff: University Librarian and Head of Learning
Support Services: Dr Mary Davies; Deputy Head of
Learning Support Services: Liz Jolly (e-mail
e.jolly@uel.ac.uk)
Stock and subject coverage: The stock reflects the subjects
taught (at undergraduate and postgraduate levels):
computing, civil engineering, estates management,
land surveying, law, business studies; finance and
accountancy, education, sociology, social work, social
sciences, languages/linguistics
Services: Photocopies; microform reader-printer;
Reading Edge, Dragon Dictate, and Texthelp for
dyslexic/visually impaired students. 95 PCs available
for student use with access to the internet, electronic
databases and Microsoft Office software
Hours: Term-time (full service): 09.00-21.00 Monday to
Friday; 10.00-17.00 Saturday and Sunday
Term-time (overnight service): 21.00-09.00 Monday
to Thursday
Vacations: 09.00-17.00 Monday to Friday
Transport: Tube and Rail: Barking; Bus: 5, 87, 145, 387
Special facilities: Refreshment and toilet facilities available;
access for users with disabilities – lift to all floors

[620][b]
Docklands Campus Learning Resource Centre
Royal Albert Way
London E16 2QJ
Borough: Newham
Telephone: 020 8223 3434
Fax: 020 8223 7497
Key staff: Docklands Campus Manager: Judith Preece
Stock and subject coverage: Caters for undergraduates and
postgraduates in the fields of art and design;
communication studies; cultural studies; electrical and
manufacturing systems engineering; media studies;
and new technology
Services: Photocopies; CD-ROM workstations. Reading
Edge, Read and Write software for dyslexic/visually
impaired students. 83 PCs available for student use

with access to the internet, electronic databases and Microsoft Office software. Slides, videos and video-viewing facilities

Hours: Term-time (full service): 09.00-21.00 Monday to Friday; 10.00-17.00 Saturday and Sunday
Term-time (overnight service): 21.00-09.00 Monday to Thursday
Vacations: 09.00-17.00 Monday to Friday

Transport: DLR: Cyprus

Special facilities: Toilet facilities available; access for users with disabilities – lift to all floors

[620][c]
Duncan House Site Learning Resource Centre

High Street
Stratford
London E15 2JB

Borough: Newham
Telephone: 020 8223 3346
Fax: 020 8223 3377
E-mail: h.campbell@uel.ac.uk
Key staff: Site Manager: Helena Campbell
Stock and subject coverage: Site LRC for the East London Business School. All stock is postgraduate level and above. Subjects covered include: management, business studies, IT related to business, marketing, accounting and finance, human resource management, management in education
Hours: Term-time: 09.00-21.00 Monday to Friday; 10.00-17.00 Saturday
Vacations: 09.00-17.00 Monday to Friday
Transport: Tube and Rail: Stratford; Bus: 25, 86, 108 any bus going to Stratford
Special facilities: Refreshment and toilet facilities available; access for users with disabilities

[620][d]
Holbrook Learning Resource Centre

Holbrook Road
Stratford
London E15 3EA

Borough: Newham
Telephone: 020 8223 3251
E-mail: s.p.lyes@uel.ac.uk
Key staff: Site Manager: Simon Lyes
Stock and subject coverage: Materials on architecture and related subjects. Collections of trade literature and large scale O/S maps
Services: Photocopies; PCs available for student use with access to the internet, electronic databases and Microsoft Office software; binding facilities
Hours: Term-time: 10.00-19.00 Monday to Thursday; 10.00-17.00 Friday
Vacations: 10.00-17.00 Monday to Friday
Transport: Tube: Plaistow, Stratford; Rail: Stratford; Bus: 69, 147, 173
Special facilities: Refreshment and toilet facilities; wheelchair access to the LRC on ground floor

[620][e]
Maryland House Learning Resource Centre

Manbey Park Road
Stratford
London E15 1EY

Borough: Newham
Telephone: 020 8223 4224
Fax: 020 8849 4273
Key staff: Campus Manager: Paul Chopra
Stock and subject coverage: Books, journals, abstracts, CD-ROMs, IT facilities. Subject coverage includes: psychology, life sciences, environmental sciences, biological sciences, physiotherapy, and health studies
Services: Photocopies; PCs available for student use with access to the internet, electronic databases and Microsoft Office software; screen enlarger and text scanner for visually impaired students
Hours: Term-time: 09.00-21.00 Monday to Friday; 10.00-17.00 Saturday and Sunday
Vacations: 09.00-17.00 Monday to Friday
Transport: Tube: Stratford; Rail: Stratford, Maryland
Special facilities: Refreshment and toilet facilities, access for users with disabilities – hoist and a lift for wheelchair users

[621]
University of Greenwich

Library and Information Services
Woolwich Campus
Riverside House
Beresford Street
London SE18 6BU

Borough: Greenwich
Telephone: 020 8331 8192
Fax: 020 8331 9084
Constitution: Part of a university
Key staff: University Librarian: D Heathcote MA ALA; Head of Information Services: Ms A Murphy BA DipLib
Availability: Open to members of the M25 Consortium and UK Libraries Plus
Special features: The library facilities are divided between a number of campus libraries

[621][a]
Avery Hill Campus Library

Mansion Site
Bexley Road
Eltham
London SE9 2PQ

Borough: Greenwich
Telephone: 020 8331 8484
Fax: 020 8331 9645
Key staff: Avery Hill Campus Librarians: Chris Hogg, Rosemary Moon
Stock and subject coverage: Books, journals, CD-ROM, online datasets and multimedia. Collections on education, health, social sciences and sports science
Services: Access to the internet or electronic information resources restricted to Greenwich staff and students; photocopies

Hours: Term-time: 08.30-21.00 Monday to Thursday;
08.30-17.00 Friday; 10.00-17.00 Saturday

Transport: Rail: Eltham, New Eltham, Falconwood; Bus:
132 (from Eltham), B13 (from New Eltham)

Special facilities: Refreshment and toilet facilities available
(refreshment facilities limited during vacations); access
for users with disabilities (lift available)

Special features: The Library is located in the Avery Hill
mansion (grade II listed) created in 1894 by the
'Nitrate King', Colonel John North

[621][b]
Dreadnought Library

Maritime Greenwich Campus
30 Park Row
London SE10 9LS

Borough: Greenwich
Telephone: 020 8331 7551
Fax: 020 8331 7775

Key staff: Maritime Greenwich Campus Librarians: Tim
Cullen, Virginia Malone

Stock and subject coverage: Computing and mathematical
sciences; post compulsory education and training,
maritime studies, law, humanities, business and
management

Services: Access to internet or electronic information
resources restricted to Greenwich staff and students;
photocopies

Hours: 09.00-21.00 Monday to Thursday; 09.00-17.00
Friday; 10.00-17.00 Saturday

Transport: DLR: Cutty Sark; Rail: Greenwich

Special facilities: Refreshment facilities (term-time only);
toilet facilities; access for users with disabilities – lift
and wheelchair adapted toilet facilities

Special features: The Library, together with 200 PCs for
student use, is housed in the refurbished
Dreadnought Seaman's Hospital (Grade I listed),
originally built in the 1760s as the Infirmary to the
Royal Naval Hospital, Greenwich

Linked organisations

The University has two other libraries: **King's Hill
Institute Resource Centre** (6 Alexander Grove,
West Malling, Kent ME19 4GR, tel: 020 8331 9201)
and **Medway Campus Library** (Nelson Building,
Central Avenue, Chatham Maritime, Kent ME4 4AW,
tel: 020 8331 9617)

University of London

There are too many libraries within the University of
London to list under one heading. Check individual
entries for details. Libraries within the University of
London include:

Archway Healthcare Library
Birkbeck College Library
Boldero Library
British Library of Political and Economic Science
(London School of Economics)
Charing Cross and Westminster Medical School
Courtauld Institute of Art
Cruciform Library
Eastman Dental Institute for Oral Health Care Sciences
Goldsmiths' College
Heythrop College
Imperial College of Science, Technology and Medicine
Institute of Advanced Legal Studies

Institute of Archaeology
Institute of Cancer Research
Institute of Child Health
Institute of Classical Studies
Institute of Commonwealth Studies
Institute of Education
Institute of Germanic Studies
Institute of Historical Research
Institute of Latin American Studies
Institute of Neurology
Institute of Opthalmology
Institute of Orthopaedics
Institute of Psychiatry
King's College London
London Business School
London Chest Hospital
London Foot Hospital
London School of Hygiene and Tropical Medicine
London School of Jewish Studies Library
Menzies Centre for Australian Studies
National Information Centre for Speech Language
Therapy
Primary and Community Health Information Services
Queen Mary and Westfield College
Royal Academy of Music
Royal Free and University College Medical School
Medical Library
Royal Holloway
The Royal London Hospital Archives and Museum
Royal Postgraduate Medical School
Royal Veterinary College
St Bartholomew's Hospital Medical Library
St George's Hospital Medical School
School of Advanced Legal Studies (School of Advanced
Study)
School of Oriental and African Studies
School of Pharmacy
School of Slavonic and East European Studies
University College London
Warburg Institute (School of Advanced Study)
West Smithfield Library
Whitechapel
Wolfson Institute of Preventive Medicine

[622]
University of London Library
ULL

Senate House
Malet Street
London WC1E 7HU

Borough: Camden
Telephone: 020 7862 8461/8462
Fax: 020 7862 8480
E-mail: ull@ull.ac.uk
World Wide Web: www.ull.ac.uk

Constitution: Central library of the federal University of
London

Key staff: Librarian: Emma Robinson; Sub-Librarian,
User Services: Paul McLaughlin; Sub-Librarian,
Administration and Resources: Gail Duggett: Sub-
Librarian, Information Strategy: Steve Clews; Head of
Historic Collections Services: Dr Julia Walworth

Stock and subject coverage: Ca. 2 million titles; 5,500
current serials. Concentrated primarily in the arts,
humanities and social sciences. The ULL's most

important research strengths include: English (major special collections include the Durning-Lawrence and Sterling libraries); economics and social history (the Goldsmith's Library of Economic Literature is the world's greatest collection in its field); history (where collections complement those of the Institute of Historic Research); modern languages (primarily Romance and Germanic); geography (including an extensive map collection); music; philosophy (the collection acts as the library for the Royal Institute of Philosophy) and psychology (the collection includes the Library of the British Psychological Society).

Area studies collections include Latin American (including Caribbean), US and Commonwealth studies (both the Canadian and Australian High Commission libraries are held). The Palaeography Room houses the greatest open-access collection in Europe. The collections also include a leading collection of British Government publications, over 50 significant Special Collections, plus extensive archives, all University of London theses and federal archives.

There is a close, complementary relationship between the ULL and the School of Advanced Study and, in a number of cases, the ULL also functions as an Institute library.

Services: Access to the internet and a wide range of databases; photocopies; digital scanners and online searching; Kurzweil machine and PC based magnification aids

Availability: Those who are not included under the terms of the University of London or other institutional access arrangements will usually be required to pay a fee (UK Higher Education Institution researchers are granted free access for reference use). Enquiries, telephone: 020 7862 8439/40

Hours: Term-time: 09.00-21.00 Monday to Thursday; 09.00-18.30 Friday; 09.30-17.30 Saturday
Special collections: 09.30-20.45 Monday; 09.30-18.00 Tuesday to Friday: 09.30-13,00, 14.00-17.15 Saturday
Vacations: 09.30-18.00 Monday to Friday: 09.30-17.30 Saturday
Special collections: 09.30-13.00, 14.00-17.15

Transport: Tube: Russell Square, Goodge Street; Rail: Euston, King's Cross, St Pancras; Bus: 10, 14, 24, 29, 68, 73, 77, 188

Special facilities: Refreshment and toilet facilities available on site; access for users with disabilities – lifts

Special features: The Senate House building is perhaps the best known example of Sir Charles Holden's work. It is a grade II listed building

Publications: Annual Report; newsletters; Fullview (Friends' newsletter); Catalogue of the Goldsmiths' Library, vol. 1-5, 1970-95; wide range of guides

Linked organisations

University of London The ULL is a federal academic service of the University of London. It is one of the most prestigious academic libraries in the UK and for general Humanities research
Depository Library located at Spring Rise, Egham, Surrey TW20 9PP, tel: 01784 434560

[623]
University of Surrey Roehampton

Constitution: Collegiate institution with over 7,000 students following a range of undergraduate, Master's and Research programmes across the three faculties of Arts and Humanities, Education, and Social and Life Sciences

Key staff: Director of Information Services: Sue Clegg, tel: 020 8392 3051; Assistant Directors: John Hill, tel: 020 8392 3446; and Paul Scarsbrook, tel: 020 8392 3052

Stock and subject coverage: Information Services provides materials to support teaching and research. There is a bookstock of approximately 370,000 volumes, 8,500 videos and 1,500 current journal subscriptions. RL LRC houses the Children's Literature Centre, a collection of ca. 2,000 volumes of children's literature and related critical and biographical material, chiefly 20th century, but including some 8th and 19th century materials. Whitelands College and Froebel Institute College both have separate college archives. Whitelands College, tel: 020 8392 3038. Froebel Institute College, includes the Early Childhood Collection, Archivist: Jane Read, tel: 020 8392 3323

Services: Photocopies (cards purchased at Shop and Media Counter at RL LRC and Issue Desk at W LRC)

Availability: Applicants to use the LRCs for reference should be made in writing to the Customer Services Co-ordinator at RL LRC. Charges made for borrowing rights, photocopies, etc

Hours: 08.30-21.00 Monday to Thursday; 08.30-19.00 Friday; 12.00-17.00 Saturday and Sunday. Vacations: 09.00-17.00 Monday to Friday. Visitors should contact the LRC they wish to visit beforehand to check holiday times, term-times, etc

Linked organisations:

University of Surrey Federated with the University

[623][a]
Roehampton Lane Learning Resources Centre
RL LRC

Digby Stuart College
Roehampton Lane
London SW15 5SZ
Borough: Wandsworth
Telephone: 020 8392 3770
Fax: 020 8392 3259
E-mail: enquiry.desk@roehampton.ac.uk
World Wide Web: www.roehampton.ac.uk
Key staff: Faculty Information Officers: Arts and Humanities: Felicity Lander, tel: 020 8392 3761; Education, Julie Harrison, tel: 020 8392 3771; Customer Services Co-ordinator and Site Manager, Helen Cocker, tel: 020 8392 3351
Transport: Rail: Barnes
Special facilities: Refreshment facilities; customer lift to all floors and easy access toilet

[623][b]
Whitelands Learning Resources Centre
W LRC

Whitelands College
West Hill
London SW15 5SN
Borough: Wandsworth
Telephone: 020 8392 3354
Fax: 020 8392 3359
Key staff: Faculty Information Officer for Social and Life Sciences and Site Manager: Andrea Peace, tel: 020 8392 3551
Transport: Tube: East Putney
Special facilities: Refreshment and toilet facilities

---

[624]
University of Westminster
Borough: Westminster
World Wide Web: www.wmin.ac.uk/library
Availability: Access to members of the University. UK Libraries Plus membership. Bona fide researchers admitted by appointment for research and reference. External membership considered

[624][a]
Cavendish Campus Library
115 New Cavendish Street
London W1W 6UW
Borough: Westminster
Telephone: 020 7911 5000 ext 3627/3613
Fax: 020 7911 5871
E-mail: a.sainsbury@wmin.ac.uk
Key staff: Library Manager: Ann Sainsbury BA ALA; Deputy Library Manager: Glynis Browning BA DipLib ALA
Stock and subject coverage: The Library supports the School of Biosciences, the School of Integrated Health and the Cavendish School of Computer Science. Ca. 60,000 books and 420 current journal subscriptions covering: biomedical and biological sciences, biotechnology, community care, food nutrition, public health, complementary therapies, computing, information and database systems engineering, mathematical and decision sciences, electronic systems, digital technology, mechanical engineering and product design. The Library also includes a collection of British standards on microfiche
Hours: 09.30-21.00 Monday to Thursday; 09.30-19.00 Friday. 11.00-17.00 Saturday and Sunday during term-time only
Transport: Tube: Goodge Street, Warren Street
Special facilities: Refreshment facilities available (during the day in term-time only); toilet facilities; limited access for users with disabilities, no wheelchair access to Level 4, limited wheelchair access to Level 3

[624][b]
Harrow Learning Resources Centre (LRC)
Watford Rd
Northwick Park
Harrow

Middlesex HA1 3TP
Borough: Harrow
Telephone: 020 7911 5885
Fax: 020 7911 5952
E-mail: c.symes@wmin.ac.uk
Constitution: Department of a university
Key staff: Library Manager: Carole Symes
Stock and subject coverage: The Harrow Learning Resources Centre (LRC) supports the Harrow Business School, the School of Communication and Creative Industries, and the School of Computer Science. There are some 90,000 books in the Centre, plus a wide range of supporting materials: company reports, electronic databases, music, periodicals, pictures, prospectuses, slides, statistics, theses, trade literature and videos. The Centre also houses the library of the International Institute of Communications (IIC), and the Panchayat Archive, a valuable resource on contemporary artists, with a particular focus on cultural identity
Services: Photocopies, electronic databases (registered readers only), online and CD-ROM searching facilities
Availability: Occasional access, by appointment, to members of the podiatry profession for reference only
Hours: Term-time: 08.30-21.00 Monday to Thursday; 09.30-19.00 Friday; 10.00-17.00 Saturday and Sunday
Vacations: 09.00-17.00 Monday to Friday
Transport: Tube: Northwick Park
Special facilities: Refreshment and toilet facilities available

[624][c]
Marylebone Road Library
35 Marylebone Road
London NW1 5LS
Borough: Westminster
Telephone: 020 7911 5000
Fax: 020 7911 5058
E-mail: jharrington@westminster.ac.uk
Constitution: Department of a university
Key staff: Library Manager: Ms J Harrington
Stock and subject coverage: Collection of ca. 100,000 volumes (including approximately 700 current subscriptions) covering built environment and management
Services: Photocopiers; electronic databases (available to registered readers only); computing facilities (registered readers only)
Hours: Term: 09.15-21.00 Monday to Thursday; 09.15-19.00 Friday; 11.00-17.00 Saturday and Sunday
Vacations: 09.15-17.00
Transport: Tube: Baker Street; Rail: Marylebone; Bus: 13, 74, 159
Special facilities: Refreshment and toilet facilities available

[624][d]
Regent Campus Library
4-12 Little Titchfield Street
London W1W 7UW
Borough: Westminster
Telephone: 020 7911 5000 ext 2537
Fax: 020 711 5894
E-mail: saltere@westminster.ac.uk

World Wide Web: www.wmin.ac.uk

Key staff: Library Manager: Elaine Salter BA MLib ALA; Deputy Library Manager: Nikki Trigg BA ALA

Stock and subject coverage: The Library supports the School of Law and the School of Social Sciences, Humanities and Languages. Subject coverage: area studies, civil and human rights, computers and the law, criminology, English as a foreign language, English law, entertainment and media law, European Union law, geography, history, intellectual property law, languages, legal reasoning, linguistics, literature – English and foreign language, politics and international relations, public international law, psychology, social law, sociology, translation and interpreting, women and the law.

Services: Photocopies

Hours: Term-time: 09.15-21.00 Monday to Thursday; 09.15-19.00 Friday; 11.00-17.00 Saturday and Sunday

Transport: Tube: Oxford Circus

Special facilities: Refreshment and toilet facilities available; access for users with disabilities – wheelchair access and adapted toilet

---

[625]
US Educational Advisory Service
EAS

The Fulbright Commission
Fulbright House
62 Doughty Street
London WC1N 2JZ

Borough: Camden

Telephone: 020 7404 6994

Fax: 020 7404 6874

E-mail: education@fulbright.co.uk

World Wide Web: www.fulbright.co.uk

Constitution: Independent non-profit distributing organisation

Objectives/purposes: Provide information and advice to individuals interested in studying in the United States

Key staff: Director: Josephine Metcalf; Educational Advisors: Lise Ingarfield, Natasa Blecic

Stock and subject coverage: EAS provides information and advice on the US education system, including studying in the US. The EAS maintains a reference library with guides and directories, university prospectuses and test preparation materials. Group and individual advising sessions are also offered, and seminars and a college fair are organised annually

Services: Photocopies; internet access; college search software; test preparation software, books and US university guides for sale

Availability: Free access to the public

Hours: 13.30-19.00 Monday; 13.30-17.00 Tuesday to Friday; closed during UK and some US public holidays

Transport: Tube: Chancery Lane, Russell Square, King's Cross: Rail: King's Cross; Bus: 17, 19, 38, 45, 46, 55, 505

Special facilities: Toilet facilities available; visitors with disabilities should contact the Library before visiting

Publications: Postgraduate Study in the USA; Undergraduate Study in the USA; A Few Things You Should Know Before You Go

Linked organisations

US Department of State – Bureau of Educational and Cultural Affairs

---

[626]
Verification Research, Training and Information Centre
VERTIC

Baird House
15-17 St Cross Street
London EC1N 8UW

Borough: Camden

Telephone: 020 7440 6960

Fax: 020 7242 3266

E-mail: info@vertic.org

World Wide Web: www.vertic.org

Constitution: Independent non-profit research organisation, company limited by guarantee and registered charity

Objectives/purposes: Non-governmental organisation which promotes effective and efficient verification as a means of ensuring confidence in the implementation of treaties or other agreements which have international or national security implications

Key staff: Administrator: Ben Handley

Stock and subject coverage: Books, journals and other materials on arms control, disarmament, environment and peace agreements

Services: Photocopies (charges made)

Availability: Access by appointment only, for reference only. Available to other NGOs, governments, academics, journalists, etc

Hours: 09.30-17.30 Monday to Friday

Transport: Tube: Farringdon, Chancery Lane

Special facilities: Refreshment and toilet facilities available; access for users with disabilities

Publications: Trust and Verify (6 p.a.); Verification Matters (series); VERTIC Briefing Papers (series); Verification: the VERTIC Yearbook; Verification Organisations Directory (annual)

---

[627]
The Vintage Wireless Museum

23 Rosendale Road
West Dulwich
London SE21 8DS

Borough: Lambeth

Telephone: 020 8670 3667

Constitution: Independent non-profit distributing organisation and private venture

Objectives/purposes: Restoration and preservation of domestic wireless equipment, service data, history and association ephemera

Key staff: Secretary: Tina Sandell

Stock and subject coverage: Materials from the first days of radio up to the 1950s. Information on wireless, some early 405-line televisions and valves, service manuals and sheets, blueprints and related data

Services: Photocopying

Availability: Genuine enthusiasts welcome. Small parties preferred. Material available for reference only. A small donation is appreciated for use of the Library.

Charges are made for repair and restoration of visitors' wireless sets
Hours: By appointment
Transport: Tube: Brixton; Rail: West Dulwich, Tulse Hill; Road: South end of Rosendale Road which crosses the South Circular (A205); Bus: 322 (from Brixton); parking easy during the day
Special facilities: Refreshment and toilet facilities available; access for users with disabilities

[628]
Voluntary Euthanasia Society
VES
13 Prince of Wales Terrace
London W8 5PG
Borough: Kensington and Chelsea
Telephone: 020 7937 7770
Fax: 020 7376 2648
E-mail: info@ves.org.uk
World Wide Web: www.ves.org.uk
Constitution: Association with voluntary subscribing membership
Objectives/purposes: Campaigning society to legalise voluntary euthanasia. VES also provides living wills, forms for refusing unwanted life and against prolonging medical treatment. Living wills are legally enforceable
Key staff: Research Officer: Will Frost
Stock and subject coverage: Multi-media library with indexed press cuttings. Subjects covered include: voluntary euthanasia, assisted suicide and advance refusal of medical treatment (living wills)
Services: Photocopies, fax facilities
Availability: Free access to students by appointment. Reference library only
Hours: 10.00-16.00 Monday to Friday
Transport: Tube: High Street Kensington; Bus: 9, 10, 49, 52, 70
Special facilities: Toilet facilities available
Publications: VE News - The Campaign Journal of the Voluntary Euthanasia Society (3 p.a.); Voluntary Euthanasia - the Facts, video for schools; information pack

[629]
The Wallace Collection Library
Hertford House
Manchester Square
London W1M 6BN
Borough: Westminster
Telephone: 020 7563 9515
Fax: 020 7224 2155
E-mail: admin@the-wallace-collection.org.uk
Constitution: Government funded body - national museum
Objectives/purposes: Primarily a curatorial tool for the research and explanation of the collection and its founders
Key staff: Librarian and Archivist: Andrea Gilbert
Stock and subject coverage: Books and articles on all areas of the collection itself as well as on the founders and other collectors. It is particularly strong on the arts of 18th century France (painting, furniture, porcelain, gold boxes and sculpture), also old master and 19th century French painting, and arms and armour. There is also an extensive collection of early and rare French and English sale catalogues. The Archives contain manuscripts and printed material on the founders and their possessions. Numerous primary Sevres porcelain factory documents on microfilm
Services: Photocopies (charges made); microfiche/film reader
Availability: Free access to bona fide researchers
Hours: 10.00-17.00 Monday to Friday
Transport: Tube: Bond Street; Bus: any bus along Oxford Street
Special facilities: Refreshment and toilet facilities available; access for users with disabilities – ramps, lifts and toilets
Publications: The Founders of the Wallace Collection by P Hughes, 1992; The Wallace Collection: Guide, 1992

[630]
Waltham Forest (London Borough of Waltham Forest)
Constitution: Public library, funded by local authority
World Wide Web: www.lbwf.gov.uk/lib/index.stm

[630][a]
Central Library
High Street
Walthamstow
London E17 7JN
Telephone: 020 8520 3031
Fax: 020 8509 0649
Key staff: Neighbourhood Manager: Mr Chris Prince; Central Neighbourhood Supervisor: Mrs Ann Hart
Stock and subject coverage: Main library stock. Audio collections of CDs, cassettes and spoken word recordings. Video collections including: feature films, educational materials and subtitled videos for people with hearing disabilities
Services: Photocopies
Hours: 10.00-20.00 Monday; 09.30-20.00 Tuesday, Thursday and Friday; 09.30-17.00 Saturday
Transport: Tube and Rail: Walthamstow
Special facilities: Access for users with disabilities to the ground floor only

[630][b]
Hale End Library
Castle Avenue
Highams Park
London E4 9QD
Telephone: 020 8531 6423
Key staff: Principal Library Assistant: Helen Bowden-Pickstock
Stock and subject coverage: Reference collection and local information
Hours: 10.00-13.00, 14.00-20.00 Monday; 09.30-13.00, 14.00-18.00 Tuesday, Thursday and Friday; 09.30-13.00, 14.00-17.00 Saturday
Transport: Rail: Highams Park; Bus: 275
Special facilities: Access for users with disabilities

[630][c]
Harrow Green Library
Cathall Road
Leytonstone
London E11 4LF

Telephone: 020 8539 5997
Key staff: Principal Library Assistant: Noreen Taylor;
Southern Neighbourhood Supervisor: Carol Jeffery;
Southern Neighbourhood Area Manager: Jan
Dorkings
Stock and subject coverage: Reference collection; local
information and children's collection
Hours: 10.00-13.00, 14.00-18.00 Monday; 09.30-13.00,
14.00-18.00 Tuesday, Thursday and Friday; 09.30-
13.00, 14.00-17.00 Saturday
Transport: Tube and Rail: Leytonstone: Bus: 257
Special facilities: Full wheelchair access

[630][d]
Higham Hill Library
Countess Road
Walthamstow
London E17 5HF
Telephone: 020 8531 6424
Key staff: Principal Library Assistants: Ms M Phelan and
Ms L Konrad
Stock and subject coverage: Reference collection and local
information
Hours: 10.00-13.00, 14.00-18.00 Monday; 09.30-13.00,
14.00-18.00 Tuesday, Thursday and Friday; 09.30-
13.00, 14.00-17.00 Saturday
Transport: Bus: W11
Special facilities: Access for users with disabilities

[630][e]
Information and Reference Services
6 Central Parade
Hoe Street
Walthamstow
London E17 4RT
Telephone: 020 8509 9815
Fax: 020 8509 9654
Stock and subject coverage: Reference materials,
newspapers and magazines. First stop information
and reference service for the Central Library and for
facilitating the provision of information at other
borough libraries
Services: Free access to the internet and Microsoft
Office; CD-ROM network access to over 60
databases; photocopier and fax
Hours: 10.00-20.00 Monday; 09.30-20.00 Tuesday,
Thursday and Friday; 09.30-17.00 Saturday
Transport: Tube and Rail: Walthamstow
Special facilities: Full wheelchair access

[630][f]
Lea Bridge Library
Lea Bridge Road
Leyton
London E10 7HU
Telephone: 020 8539 5652
Key staff: Principal Library Assistants: Jan Gosling and
Rosie Massey; Southern Neighbourhood Area
Supervisor: Carol Jeffery; Southern Neighbourhood
Area Manager: Jan Dorkings
Stock and subject coverage: Reference collection; local
information and children's collection
Hours: 10.00-13.00, 14.00-18.00 Monday; 09.30-13.00,
14.00-18.00 Tuesday, Thursday and Friday; 09.30-
13.00, 14.00-17.00 Saturday
Transport: Bus: 48, 56, 58, 158

[630][g]
Leyton Library
High Road
Leyton
London E10 5QH
Telephone: 020 8539 1223
Key staff: Principal Library Assistant: Andy Green;
Southern Neighbourhood Area Supervisor: Carol
Jeffery; Southern Neighbourhood Area Manager –
Libraries: Jan Dorkings
Stock and subject coverage: Reference collection; local
information and children's collection
Hours: 10.00-13.00, 14.00-18.00 Monday; 09.30-13.00,
14.00-18.00 Tuesday, Thursday and Friday; 09.30-
13.00, 14.00-17.00 Saturday
Transport: Tube: Leyton; Rail: Leyton Midland Road;
Bus: W15, 58, 69, 97, 158
Special facilities: Access for users with disabilities

[630][h]
Leytonstone Library
6 Church Lane
Leytonstone
London E11 1HG
Telephone: 020 8539 2730
Fax: 020 8556 1026
Key staff: Southern Neighbourhood Area Manager: Jan
Dorkings; Southern Neighbourhood Area
Supervisor: Carol Jeffery
Stock and subject coverage: Reference collection; local
information and children's collection
Hours: 10.00-20.00 Monday; 09.30-20.00 Tuesday and
Thursday; 09.30-18.00 Friday; 09.30-17.00 Saturday
Transport: Tube: Leytonstone: Bus: W13, W14, W15,
W16, 235, 257
Special facilities: Access for users with disabilities – lift
facilities

[630][i]
North Chingford Library
The Green
Station Road
Chingford
London E4 7EN
Telephone: 020 8529 2993
Key staff: Principal Library Assistants: Sue Reason and
Barbara Curry
Stock and subject coverage: Reference collection and local
information
Hours: 10.00-20.00 Monday; 10.00-20.00 Tuesday and
Thursday; 09.30-18.00 Friday; 09.30-17.00 Saturday
Transport: Rail: Chingford; Bus: 97, 97A, 179, 212
Special facilities: Access for users with disabilities

[630][j]
St James Street Library
Coppermill Lane
Walthamstow
London E17 7HA
Telephone: 020 8520 1292
Key staff: Principal Library Assistants: Ms R Ishaq and
Ms J Randle
Stock and subject coverage: Reference collection and local
information
Hours: 10.00-13.00, 14.00-18.00 Monday; 09.30-13.00,
14.00-18.00 Tuesday, Thursday and Friday; 09.30-
13.00, 14.00-17.00 Saturday

Transport: Rail: St James Street: Bus: W12, 58, 158, 230
Special facilities: Full wheelchair access

[630][k]
South Chingford Library

Hall Lane
Chingford
London E4 8EU
Telephone: 020 852 2332
Fax: 020 8559 4113
Key staff: Neighbourhood Libraries Supervisor: Julie Oven
Stock and subject coverage: Reference collection and local information
Hours: 10.00-20.00 Monday, Tuesday and Thursday; 10.00-17.30 Friday; 10.00-17.00 Saturday
Transport: Bus: 97, 97A, 215, 444
Special facilities: Access for users with disabilities

[630][l]
Vestry House Museum

Vestry Road
London E17 9NH
Telephone: 020 8509 1917
Key staff: Librarian: Jo Parker
Stock and subject coverage: Manorial, tithe, parish and Methodist records covering the London Borough of Waltham Forest; former boroughs of Chingford, Leyton and Walthamstow (Essex)
Hours: 10.00-13.00, 14.00-17.30 Tuesday, Wednesday and Friday; 10.00-13.00, 14.00-17.00 Saturday. By appointment only
Transport: Tube and Rail: Walthamstow Central
Special facilities: Access for users with disabilities

[630][m]
Wood Street Library

Forest Road
Walthamstow
London E17 4AA
Telephone: 020 8521 1070
Key staff: Principal Library Assistant: Ms D Clark
Stock and subject coverage: Reference collection and local information
Hours: 10.00-13.00, 14.00-18.00 Monday; 09.30-13.00, 14.00-18.00 Tuesday to Friday; 09.30-13.00, 14.00-17.00 Saturday
Transport: Rail: Wood Street; Bus: W16, 123, 212, 275
Special facilities: Access for users with disabilities and wheelchair adapted toilet facilities; baby changing facilities

---

[631]
Wandsworth Libraries (London Borough of Wandsworth)

Department of Leisure and Amenity Services
Wandsworth Town Hall
London SW18 2PU
Borough: Wandsworth
Telephone: 020 8871 6364
Fax: 020 8871 7630
E-mail: libraries@wandsworth.gov.uk
World Wide Web: www.wandsworth.gov.uk
Constitution: Public library, funded by local authority
Key staff: Head of Libraries, Museum and Arts: Jane Allen BA DMS ALA

[631][a]
Alvering Library

Allfarthing Lane
London SW18 2PQ
Telephone: 020 8871 6398
Stock and subject coverage: Reference collection; local information and children's collection
Services: Free internet access
Hours: 09.30-19.00 Monday, Tuesday and Thursday; 09.30-17.00 Friday; 09.00-17.00 Saturday
Transport: Bus: G1, 37, 39, 77A, 77C, 156, 170, 219, 337
Special facilities: Access for users with disabilities
Special features: Mobile and housebound library service based at Alvering Library

[631][b]
Balham Library

Ramsden Road
London SW12 8QY
Telephone: 020 8871 7195
Fax: 020 8675 4015
Stock and subject coverage: Reference collection; local information and children's collection
Services: Free internet access
Hours: 10.00-20.00 Monday, Tuesday, Thursday and Friday; 10.00-18.00 Saturday; 13.00-17.00 Sunday
Transport: Tube and Rail: Balham; Bus: 115, 155, 355
Special facilities: Access for users with disabilities – lift access to music and children's libraries on 1st floor, wheelchair accessible toilet, minicom

[631][c]
Battersea Lending Library

Lavender Hill
London SW11 1JB
Telephone: 020 8871 7466
Stock and subject coverage: Reference collection; local information and children's collection. African Caribbean Community Library with multi-cultural children's books (tel: 020 8871 7456)
Services: Free internet access
Hours: 10.00-20.00 Monday to Wednesday, Friday; 09.00-17.00 Saturday; 13.00-17.00 Sunday
Local History Service (tel: 020 8871 7753): 10.00-20.00 Tuesday and Wednesday; 10.00-17.00 Friday; 09.00-13.00 Saturday
Transport: Rail: Clapham Junction; Bus: C3, 35, 37, 39, 45A, 49, 77, 77A, 77C, 156, 170, 219, 239, 249, 295, 337, 344, 349
Special facilities: Access for users with disabilities to ground floor only (via separate entrance in Lavender Walk), wheelchair accessible toilet

[631][d]
Battersea Park Library

Battersea Park Road
London SW11 4NF
Telephone: 020 8871 7468
Stock and subject coverage: Reference collection; local information and children's collection
Services: Free internet access
Hours: 09.30-19.00 Monday to Wednesday; 09.30-17.00 Friday, 09.00-17.00 Saturday
Transport: Rail: Battersea Park, Queenstown Road; Bus: 44, 137, 137A, 144
Special facilities: Access for users with disabilities to ground floor

[631][e]
Battersea Reference Library
Altenburg Gardens
London SW11 1JQ
Telephone: 020 8871 7467
Fax: 020 7978 4376
Key staff: Information, Lifelong Learning and Reference
  Librarian: Pauline Hunt
Stock and subject coverage: Reference collection; local
  information and children's collection
Hours: 09.00-21.00 Monday to Friday; 09.00-17.00
  Saturday; 13.00-17.00 Sunday
Transport: Rail: Clapham Junction; Bus: C3, 35, 37, 39,
  45A, 49, 77, 77A, 77C, 129, 156, 170, 239, 249, 295,
  337, 344, 349
Special facilities: Access for users with disabilities via
  lending library (via entrance in Lavender Walk);
  wheelchair accessible toilet

[631][f]
Earlsfield Library*
Magdalen Road
London SW18 3NY
Telephone: 020 8871 6389
Stock and subject coverage: Reference collection; local
  information and children's collection
Services: Free internet access
Hours: 09.30-19.00 Monday, Tuesday and Thursday;
  09.30-17.00 Friday; 09.00-17.00 Saturday
Transport: Rail: Earlsfield; Bus: 44, 77, 270
Special facilities: Access for users with disabilities;
  wheelchair accessible toilet
*Closed September 2003 for refurbishment. See website
for details of temporary service

[631][g]
Northcote Library
Northcote Road
London SW11 6QB
Telephone: 020 8871 7469
Stock and subject coverage: Reference collection; local
  information and children's collection
Services: Free internet access
Hours: 09.30-19.00 Monday, Tuesday and Thursday;
  09.30-17.00 Friday; 09.00-17.00 Saturday
Transport: Bus: 115, 249, 319
Special facilities: Access for users with disabilities – lift
  access to all floors

[631][h]
Putney Library
Disraeli Road
London SW15 2DR
Telephone: 020 8871 7090
Fax: 020 8789 6175
Stock and subject coverage: Reference collection; local
  information and children's collection. Special
  collection of 5,000 early children's books (access by
  appointment only)
Services: Free internet access
Hours: 10.00-20.00 Monday to Wednesday, Friday;
  09.00-17.00 Saturday; 13.00-17.00 Sunday
Transport: Tube: Putney East; Rail: Putney; Bus: C4, 14,
  22, 37, 39, 74, 85, 93, 220, 265, 270, 337

Special facilities: Access for users with disabilities,
  wheelchair accessible toilet, lift to all floors, hearing
  loop

[631][i]
Roehampton Library
Danebury Avenue
London SW15 4HD
Telephone: 020 8871 7091
Stock and subject coverage: Reference collection; local
  information and children's collection
Services: Free internet access
Hours: 09.30-19.00 Monday to Wednesday; 09.30-17.00
  Friday; 09.00-17.00 Saturday
Transport: Bus: 72, 74, 85, 170, 265, 510, 741
Special facilities: Access for users with disabilities,
  wheelchair accessible toilet

[631][j]
Southfields Library
Wimbledon Park Road
London SW19 6NL
Telephone: 020 8871 6388
Stock and subject coverage: Reference collection; local
  information and children's collection
Services: Free internet access
Hours: 09.30-19.00 Monday to Wednesday; 09.30-17.00
  Friday; 09.00-17.00 Saturday
Transport: Rail: Southfields; Bus: 39
Special facilities: Access for users with disabilities, disabled
  parking space, wheelchair accessible toilet

[631][k]
Tooting Library
Mitcham Road
London SW17 9PD
Telephone: 020 8871 7175
  020 8871 7174 (Asian Community Library)
Stock and subject coverage: Reference collection; local
  information and children's collection
Services: Free internet access
Hours: 09.30-19.00 Monday, Tuesday and Thursday;
  09.30-17.00 Friday; 09.00-17.00 Saturday; 13.00-
  17.00 Sunday
Transport: Tube: Tooting Broadway; Bus: 44, 57, 77, 127,
  133, 264, 270, 280
Special facilities: Access for users with disabilities – no lift
  access to 1st floor children's library and Asian
  Community Library

[631][l]
West Hill Library
West Hill
London SW18 1RZ
Telephone: 020 8871 6386
  020 8871 6387 (Reference Library)
Fax: 020 8877 3476 (Reference Library)
Stock and subject coverage: Reference collection; local
  information and children's collection. Special
  collections on European history and travel and on
  the World War I and II
Services: Free internet access
Hours: 09.30-19.00 Monday to Wednesday; 09.30-17.00
  Friday; 09.00-17.00 Saturday

Transport: Tube: East Putney; Rail: Wandsworth Town; Bus: 37, 77A, 77C, 170, 270, 337
Special facilities: Access for users with disabilities, wheelchair accessible toilet

[631][m]
York Gardens Library and Community Centre
Lavender Road
London SW11 2UG
Telephone: 020 8871 7471
Stock and subject coverage: Reference collection; local information and children's collection
Services: Free internet access
Hours: 12.00-19.00 Monday to Friday; 12.00-17.00 Saturday
Transport: Rail: Clapham Junction; Bus: 19, 44, 45A, 49, 219, 344
Special facilities: Access for users with disabilities

[632]
Warburg Institute
Woburn Square
London WC1H 0AB
Borough: Camden
Telephone: 020 7862 8935/6
Fax: 020 7862 8939
E-mail: warburg.library@sas.ac.uk
World Wide Web: www.sas.ac.uk/warburg/
Constitution: Department of a university
Key staff: Librarian: Dr Jill Kraye; Deputy Librarian: John Perkins
Stock and subject coverage: Ca. 330,000 volumes, 3,000 journal titles (1,500 current titles), some manuscripts and incunables, over 1,000 16th and 17th century books with approximately 25% of stock not held in the British Library. The collections cover the history of European culture and the classical tradition plus the history of art, science, magic, religion and culture in general. Strong collections on Humanism, Reformation, Renaissance art and Italian history. The Library is complemented by a photographic collection of over 300,000 items
Services: Photocopies; reader-printer; CD-ROM
Availability: Open to all postgraduate students – letter of recommendation required. Others are admitted on written application to the Librarian. The collections are available for reference only. Commercial firms and media researchers are charged a fee
Hours: 10.00-18.00 Monday and Friday; 10.00-20.00 Tuesday, Wednesday and Thursday (during term-time); 10.00-16.00 Saturday (except August and September)
Transport: Tube: Russell Square, Euston; Rail: Euston
Special facilities: Refreshment and toilet facilities available; no special facilities for users with disabilities but all floors are served by lifts
Special features: The Library was originally sited in Hamburg and came to Britain in 1933 to escape the Nazi Regime

Linked organisations:

University of London, School of Advanced Study The Institute is a member of the School of Advanced Study

[633]
Waste Watch
Europa House
13-17 Ironmonger Row
London EC1V 3QG
Borough: Islington
Telephone: 020 7253 0266
Fax: 020 7253 5962
E-mail: info@wastewatch.org.uk
World Wide Web: www.wastewatch.org.uk
Constitution: Company limited by guarantee and registered charity
Objectives/purposes: National agency for the promotion of waste reduction and recycling
Key staff: Information Assistants: Stephen Webb, Terence Hoad
Stock and subject coverage: Materials on waste reduction and recycling, mainly of household, but increasingly of commercial waste. Collections include: books, reports, government publications, journals, directories and subject box-files. Major items are catalogued and can be searched via a database
Services: Photocopying; wasteline telephone and postal enquiry service 0870 243 0136
Availability: Open to all for reference only. Appointment necessary, telephone Wasteline 0870 243 0136 in advance
Hours: 10.00-17.00 Monday to Friday, by appointment only
Transport: Tube: Old Street: Rail: Liverpool Street
Special facilities: Refreshment and toilet facilities available
Publications: Annual Report; National Recycling Directory (every 2 years); Recycled Products Guide; free information sheets; publication list available on request

Linked organisations:

National Recycling Forum Waste Watch administers the Forum, a 'think-tank' on waste issues

[634]
Wellcome Library for the History and Understanding of Medicine
Borough: Camden
Telephone: 020 7611 8386
Fax: 020 7611 8369
World Wide Web: www.wellcome.ac.uk/library
Constitution: Registered charity; research organisation
Key staff: Head of Public Services
Transport: Tube: Euston, Euston Square; Rail: Euston; Bus: 10, 18, 30, 73
Special facilities: Contact 020 7611 8582, or visit the website, for information about access

[634][a]
History of Medicine Collections
183 Euston Road
London NW1 2BE
Telephone: 020 7611 8582 (enquiry line)
020 7611 7211 (recorded information line)
Fax: 020 7611 8369
E-mail: library@wellcome.ac.uk
World Wide Web: www.wellcome.ac.uk/library
http://library.wellcome.ac.uk (library catalogue)

Stock and subject coverage: Material on medical history and related sciences. Includes history of surgery, military and naval medicine, nursing, psychology and psychiatry, pharmacy and pharmacology, dentistry, sexuality, and veterinary medicine plus social history and anthropology. Stock includes over 600,000 books and journals (ca. 500 current journal titles).
Rare materials include ca. 66,000 pre- 1851 printed books, including over 600 incunables (books printed before 1501) and ca. 5,000 books from the 16th century. The Archives and Manuscripts collections include the papers of eminent figures such as Edward Jenner and ca. 13,000 original and facsimile letters by Florence Nightingale, Lord Lister and Melanie Klein. Holdings include the records of numerous organisations and bodies involved in medical science and health care. The Oriental collections include over 11,000 manuscripts in 43 eastern languages, including Sanskrit, Arabic, Persian, Hebrew, Chinese and Japanese, plus ca. 3,000 items printed in Oriental scripts. The American collection contains materials from the Hispanic and Portuguese American Empires and the British colonies plus material relating to Amerindian medicine. The iconographic collections house over 100,000 prints, drawings, paintings, photographs and moving films, ranging in date from the Middle Ages to today and geographically from the Orient to the Americas. (The Archives and Manuscripts collection and images from the visual resources collections are also available via the web catalogue.)
Services: Photocopy service and enquiry service (020 7611 8582; library@wellcome.ac.uk); photography service; wide range of electronic resources
Availability: Open to the public free of charge for reference and research. Proof of identity is required. Visitors wishing to use contemporary medical archives are advised to make an appointment
Hours: 09.45-17.15 Monday, Wednesday and Friday; 09.45-19.15 Tuesday and Thursday; 09.45-13.00 Saturday
Publications: Current work in the History of Medicine, list available

[634][b]
Information Service
183 Euston Road
London NW1 2BE
Telephone: 020 7611 8722 (enquiry line)
020 7611 7211 (recorded information line)
Fax: 020 7611 8726
E-mail: infoserv@wellcome.ac.uk
World Wide Web catalogue: http://library.wellcome.ac.uk
Stock and subject coverage: Current biomedical collections on biomedical science (including genetics and the human genome), popular science writing, consumer health, science policy, medical research funding, research ethics, public engagement with science and science education. Stock includes over 13,000 volumes and ca. 300 current journal titles
Services: Photocopies; enquiry service (020 7611 8722 or infoserv@wellcome.ac.uk); online searching; bibliography compilation; wide range of electronic resources
Availability: Open to the public free of charge; proof of identity required for use of databases

Hours: 09.00-17.00 Monday to Friday; 09.00-13.00 Saturday
Publications: SPIN database; Labnotes; Wellcome News; Science Policy Information News (SPIN) weekly

[634][c]
Medical Film and Audio Collections
210 Euston Road
London NW1 2BE
Telephone: 020 7611 8596/7
Fax: 020 7611 8765
E-mail: mfac@wellcome.ac.uk
World Wide Web catalogue: http://library.wellcome.ac.uk
Stock and subject coverage: Over 1,300 films, videos, TV programmes, CD-ROMs and audiotapes on current biomedical science and the history of medicine
Services: Information service (020 7611 8596/7 or mfac@wellcome.ac.uk); loans
Availability: Open to the public, free of charge, by appointment only
Hours: 09.15-17.30 Monday to Friday by appointment only

[634][d]
Medical Photographic Library
210 Euston Road
London NW1 2BE
Telephone: 020 7611 8348
Fax: 020 7611 8577
E-mail: photolib@wellcome.ac.uk
World Wide Web catalogue: http://library.wellcome.ac.uk
Stock and subject coverage: Over 160,000 images of medical and social history; 17,000 photographs of modern clinical medicine and biomedical sciences
Services: Information service; photography service
Availability: Open to the public, free of charge, by appointment only
Hours: 09.30-17.30 Monday to Friday

[635]
West Middlesex University Hospital NHS Trust
WES
Library and Information Service
Twickenham Road
Isleworth
Middlesex TW7 6AF
Borough: Hounslow
Telephone: 020 8565 5968
Fax: 020 8565 5408
E-mail: library@wmuh-tr.nthames.nhs.uk
World Wide Web: www.wmuhnhst.demon.co.uk
Constitution: Department of a hospital
Objectives/purposes: Provides a service to West Middlesex NHS Trust and Hounslow and Spelthorne Community and Mental Health Service Trust as well as students from Imperial College School of Medicine
Key staff: Library Services Manager: Mrs P Bowen
Stock and subject coverage: Books, journals, audiovisual material on medicine, nursing, allied health, general health care information
Services: Photocopies; CD-ROMs, fax machine, word processing, internet NHS Net

Availability: Open to NHS Staff and students from
Imperial College School of Medicine and from
Bucks College

Hours: 09.30-19.00 Tuesday and Thursday; 09.30-17.00
Monday, Wednesday and Friday

Transport: Tube: Hounslow East; Rail: Syon Lane; Bus:
H37, 117, 235, 237, 267

Special facilities: Access for users with disabilities,
including ramp

Linked organisations

**North Thames (West) Library and Information
Development Unit**
Thames Postgraduate Medical and Dental Education

[636]
West Thames College

London Road
Isleworth
Middlesex
TW7 4HS

Borough: Hounslow
Telephone: 020 8326 2308
Fax: 020 8569 7787
E-mail: karenk@west-thames.ac.uk
World Wide Web:
Constitution: College of Further Education
Key staff: Head of Library Services: Karen Bewen-
Chappell; Deputy Librarian: Karen Kelly; Assistant
Librarians: James mullan, Victoria MacFarlane
Stock and subject coverage: Books and journals on the
following subjects: art and design; hair and beauty;
media; business and leisure; catering; information
technology; science; care and community studies. The
collections include: CD-ROM, video, slides, cassettes
and illustrations. Special collection on Joseph Banks
Services: Photocopies; personal computing; audio-visual
facilities
Availability: Access only to bona fide researchers on
application. Reference only
Hours: Term-time only: 09.00-21.00 Monday to
Thursday; 09.00-16.00 Friday
Transport: Tube: Osterley, Hounslow East; Rail:
Isleworth; Bus: H37, 116, 117, 203, 237
Special facilities: Refreshment and toilet facilities available;
access for users with disabilities - wheelchair access
to reference library only

Linked organisations

Kingston University Associate college

[637]
Westminster (City of Westminster)
Department of Education, Library Services

World Wide Web: www.westminster.gov.uk/el/libarch
Constitution: Public library funded by local authority
Key staff: Assistant Director: David Ruse ALA MIPM
MILAM
Special features: Part of the Department of Education.
The three largest libraries are Marylebone Library,
Victoria Library and Westminster Reference Library,
all listed first

[637][a]
Marylebone Library

109-117 Marylebone Road
London NW1 5PS

Telephone: 020 7798 1037 (adult lending)
020 7641 1037 (information service)
Fax: 020 7641 1028
Stock and subject coverage: Large adult lending, children's
and general libraries. Sherlock Holmes Collection
Services: Fax machine; microform reader-printers; colour
and b&w photocoping; PCs for hire and computer
training (run by a commercial organisation); CD-
ROMs; telephone for the deaf (for Westminster
residents only); Council information point; internet
access
Availability: Loan service for members only
(membership open to those who live, work or study
in Westminster and on a reciprocal basis with other
local authorities). Information collections open to all
Hours: 09.30-20.00 Monday, Tuesday, Thursday and
Friday; 10.00-20.00 Wednesday; 09.30-17.00
Saturday; 13.30-17.00 Sunday
Children's Library: 09.30-17.30 Monday, Tuesday,
Thursday and Friday; 10.00-17.30 Wednesday; 09.30-
13.00, 14.00-17.00 Saturday
Transport: Tube: Marylebone, Baker Street: Rail:
Marylebone; Bus: 2, 13, 18, 27, 74, 82, 113, 139, 159,
274
Special facilities: Access for users with disabilities,
telephone before visiting

[637][b]
Victoria Library

160 Buckingham Palace Road
London SW1W 9UD

Telephone: 020 7641 4287 (lending)
020 7641 4292 (music library)
Fax: 020 7641 4281
Stock and subject coverage: Large lending library.
Audiovisual and children's library. Westminster Music
Library: extensive collection of books and printed
music, orchestral sets for hire
Services: Colour and b&w photocoping; fax machine;
CD-ROMs; internet access
Availability: Available to all for reference use. Loan
service available to members (those who live, work or
study in Westminster and on a reciprocal basis with
other local authorities).
Hours: 09.30-19.00 Monday, Tuesday, Thursday and
Friday; Westminster Music Library: 11.00-19.00;
10.00-17.00 Saturday
Transport: Tube: Victoria; Rail: Victoria; Coach: Victoria
Coach Station
Special facilities: Access for users with disabilities to the
ground floor only; CCTV magnifier

[637][c]
Westminster Reference Library

35 St Martin's Street
London WC2H 7HP

Telephone: 020 7641 4636
020 7641 4634 (Business and official publications)
020 7641 4638 (Art and design)
Fax: 020 7641 4606

Stock and subject coverage: Performing arts; business; art and design; British official publications and European Union publications
Services: CD-ROMs; photocopying; microfilm reader-printer and internet access
Availability: Available to all for reference use
Hours: 10.00-20.00; 10.00-17.00 Saturday
Transport: Tube: Leicester Square, Charing Cross, Piccadilly Circus; Rail: Charing Cross
Publications: Westminster Union List of Periodicals

[637][d]
Charing Cross Library
4 Charing Cross Road
London WC2H 0HG
Telephone: 020 7641 4628
Fax: 020 7641 4629
Stock and subject coverage: Small reference collection; local information and children's collection. Extensive collection of Chinese materials for loan
Services: Internet access
Hours: 09.30-19.00 Monday to Friday; 10.30-14.00 Saturday; 11.00-17.00 Sunday
Transport: Tube: Leicester Square; Bus: 24, 29

[637][e]
Church Street Library
Church Street
London NW8 8EU
Telephone: 020 7641 5479
Fax: 020 7641 5482
Stock and subject coverage: Reference collection; small local information collection and children's collection
Services: Internet access
Hours: 09.30-19.00 Monday, Tuesday, Thursday and Friday; 10.00-19.00 Wednesday; 09.30-17.00 Saturday
Children's Library: 09.30-18.00 Monday, Tuesday, Thursday and Friday; 10.00-18.00 Wednesday; 09.30-17.00 Saturday
Transport: Tube: Edgware Road; Bus: 16
Special facilities: Access for users with disabilities – wheelchair access

[637][f]
Maida Vale Library
Sutherland Avenue
London W9 2QT
Telephone: 020 7641 3659
Stock and subject coverage: Small general reference collection; local information and children's collection
Services: Internet access
Hours: 09.30-19.00 Monday, Tuesday, Thursday and Friday; 10.00-19.00 Wednesday; 09.30-17.00 Saturday
Transport: Tube: Maida Vale, Warwick Avenue

[637][g]
Mayfair Library
25 South Audley Street
London W1Y 5DJ
Telephone: 020 7798 1391
Stock and subject coverage: Small general reference collection; local information and children's collection

Services: Internet access
Hours: 11.00-19.00 Monday to Friday; 09.30-13.00 Saturday
Transport: Tube: Bond Street; Bus: 8, 25

[637][h]
Paddington Library
Porchester Road
London W2 5DU
Telephone: 020 7641 4475
Fax: 020 7641 4471
Stock and subject coverage: General reference collection; local information; separate children's collection
Services: Internet access; CD-ROMs
Hours: 09.30-22.00 Monday and Friday; 09.30-21.00 Tuesday and Thursday; 10.00-21.00 Wednesday; 09.30-17.00 Saturday; 13.30-17.00 Sunday
Children's Library: 09.30-12.00, 13.00-17.30 Monday, Tuesday, Thursday and Friday; 10.00-12.00, 13.00-17.30 Wednesday; 09.30-12.00, 13.00-17.00 Saturday
Transport: Tube: Royal Oak, Bayswater; Bus: 18

[637][i]
Pimlico Library
Rampayne Street
London SW1V 2PU
Telephone: 020 7641 2983
Fax: 020 7641 2980
Stock and subject coverage: Small reference collection; children's collection
Services: Internet access
Hours: 09.30-19.00 Monday, Tuesday, Thursday and Friday; 10.00-19.00 Wednesday; 09.30-17.00 Saturday; 13.30-17.00 Sunday
Children's Library: 09.30-17.30 Monday, Tuesday, Thursday and Friday; 10.00-17.30 Wednesday; 09.30-13.00, 14.00-17.00 Saturday; 13.30-17.00 Sunday
Transport: Tube: Pimlico; Bus: 2, 24, 82

[637][j]
Queen's Park Library
666 Harrow Road
London NW10 4NE
Telephone: 020 7641 4375
Fax: 020 7641 4576
Stock and subject coverage: Small reference collection; open learning centre
Services: Internet access
Hours: 09.30-19.00 Monday, Tuesday, Thursday and Friday; 10.00-19.00 Wednesday; 09.30-17.00 Saturday
Open Learning: 09.30-12.00 Monday and Thursday; 13.00-15.30 Tuesday, Wednesday and Friday; 09.30-17.00 Saturday
Transport: Tube: Kensal Green, Queen's Park

[637][k]
St John's Wood Library
20 Circus Road
London NW8 6PD
Telephone: 020 7641 5087
Fax: 020 7641 5089

Stock and subject coverage: Small reference and children's collections; local information
Services: Internet access
Hours: 09.30–19.00 Monday, Tuesday, Thursday and Friday; 10.00–19.00 Wednesday; 09.30–17.00 Saturday; 10.30–14.00 Sunday
Transport: Tube: St John's Wood
Special facilities: Access for users with disabilities – wheelchair access; magnifiers available for users with visual impairments

[637] [l]
Westminster City Archives

City of Westminster Archives Centre
10 St Ann's Street
London SW1P 2XR
Telephone: 020 7641 5180
Fax: 020 7641 5179
Stock and subject coverage: Extensive archives and local studies collection for City of Westminster
Services: B&w photocopies; microform printers; fax machine; internet access
Availability: Open to the general public for reference use only
Hours: 09.30–19.00 Tuesday, Thursday and Friday; 10.00–19.00 Wednesday; 09.30–17.00 Saturday
Transport: Tube: St James's Park, Westminster; Rail: Victoria
Special facilities: Toilet facilities available; access for users with disabilities; meeting room available for hire

[638]
Westminster Abbey Library and Muniment Room

The Cloisters
Westminster Abbey
London SW1P 3PA
Borough: Westminster
Telephone: 020 7222 5152
Fax: 020 7654 4827
E-mail: library@westminster-abbey.org
World Wide Web: www.westminster-abbey.org
Constitution: Ecclesiastical library, registered charity
Objectives/purposes: To maintain the historic printed and manuscript collections of the Dean and Chapter of Westminster, and to collect material on the history of Westminster Abbey and related subjects
Key staff: Librarian: Tony Trowles; Keeper of the Muniments: Richard Mortimer; Assistant Keeper: Christine Reynolds
Stock and subject coverage: The 14,000 printed books (including 60 incunabula) form a general collection of the period to 1775 with particular strengths in the scriptures, theology, history and classical literature. There are ca. 40 library manuscripts and an important collecton of 16th and 17th century manuscripts and printed music. Special collections include the pamphlets of the antiquary William Camden and the Oldaker Collection of English decorated bindings. The Westminster Abbey Collection (ca. 1,000 volumes) covers the history of the Abbey, Westminster School, St Margaret's and related topics such as coronations. There is a photographic collection of ca. 5,000 negatives. The Muniment Collection (ca. 70,000 documents) contains the archives of the monastery and its estates and of the post reformation Collegiate Church
Services: Photocopies; photographic service
Availability: Access by appointment only. Students are asked to provide a letter of introduction. All material is for reference only
Hours: 10.00–13.00, 14.00–16.45 Monday to Friday
Transport: Tube: St James's Park; Rail: Victoria, Charing Cross, Waterloo; Bus: 3, 3B, 11, 12, 24, 53, X53, 77A, 88, 109, 159, 184, 511
Special facilities: Limited refreshment facilities; users with disabilities should advise the Library when making an appointment
Special features: The Library is housed in the former dormitory of the Benedictine monastery. The book presses date from 1623 when the Library was founded by John Williams, Dean of Westminster
Publications: Westminster Abbey Record Series: vols 1 and 2; Acts of the Dean and Chapter of Westminster 1543-1609, edited by CS Knighton (1997, 1999)

Linked organisations

St Margaret's Church, Westminster

[639]
Whipps Cross University Hospital Trust, Multidisciplinary Library
MEC

Whipps Cross Hospital
Whipps Cross Road
Leytonstone
London E11 1NR
Borough: Waltham Forest
Telephone: 020 8535 6973
Fax: 020 8504 6973
E-mail: library@fhcare.demon.co.uk
World Wide Web: www.libnel.nhs.uk
Constitution: NHS Confederation
Key staff: Senior Librarian: Anne Weist; Librarian: Susan Kerslake: Clinical Support Librarian: Julie Ann Watson; Library Assistants: Sue Threadwell, Pam Durrant and Ros Treadway
Stock and subject coverage: Health collections with a clinical emphasis. Ca. 160 journals and 5,000 books and reports
Services: Photocopies; internet access to a range of databases with full text links to 163 journals; CD-ROM databases including Medline 1966 to date, CINAHL, AMED and HMIC
Availability: Available to all NELHC NHS staff. Others must apply to the Librarian
Hours: Staffed 09.00–18.00 Monday to Friday
Transport: Tube: Leytonstone, Walthamstow Central; Bus: W15 (from Leytonstone or Walthamstow Central tube stations)
Special facilities: Refreshment and toilet facilities available on site; access for users with disabilities

Linked organisations

LibNEL, North East London Workforce Development Confederation

London Library and Information Development Unit (LLIDU)

The Muniment Room and Library, Westminster Abbey

[640]
Whitechapel Art Gallery
Whitechapel High Street
London E1 7QX
Borough: Tower Hamlets
Telephone: 020 7522 7888
Fax: 020 7377 1685
World Wide Web: www.whitechapel.org
Constitution: Registered charity
Objectives/purposes: Internationally recognised tradition of presenting major exhibitions of British and international art
Key staff: The Archivist
Stock and subject coverage: Materials on 20th century British and international art. Archive resources date back to the foundation of the Gallery in 1901 and include exhibition catalogues and guides, press cuttings and photographs
Services: Photocopies (subject to copyright law, charges made)
Availability: Access to bona fide researchers strictly by appointment only. Charges are made for photocopying and for any extensive research carried out by gallery staff on researchers' behalf
Hours: By appointment

Transport: Tube: Aldgate East, Aldgate, Liverpool Street; Rail: Liverpool Street
Special facilities: Refreshment and toilet facilities available; access for users with disabilities

[641]
Whitechapel Library
The Church of St Augustine with St Philip
Turner Street
London E1 2AD
Borough: Tower Hamlets
Telephone: 020 7882 7110
Fax: 020 7882 7113
E-mail: j.h.thomas@qmul.ac.uk
World Wide Web: www.smd.qmul.ac.uk
Constitution: Part of Queen Mary, University of London
Key staff: Site Librarian: Jacquelyn Thomas; Information Skills: Alain Besson
Stock and subject coverage: Medicine, dentistry and subjects allied to medicine
Services: Photocopier
Availability: Open to staff and students of Queen Mary and Westfield College, academic staff and research students from M25 consortium by arrangement

273

Hours: Term-time: 09.00-22.00 Monday to Thursday; 09.00-20.00 Friday: 10.00-17.00 Saturday
Vacations: 09.00-18.00 Monday to Friday
Transport: Tube: Whitechapel; Bus: 25, 106, 253

Linked organisations

Queen Mary, University of London Part of the University

[642]
William Morris Gallery

Lloyd Park
Forest Road
Walthamstow
London E17 4PP
Borough: Waltham Forest
Telephone: 020 8527 3782
World Wide Web: www.lbwf.gov.uk/wmg
Constitution: Government funded body
Objectives/purposes: Display of life, work and ideas of William Morris and his associates in Morris & Co., and groups associated in the Arts and Crafts Movement. Also 19th and early 20th century fine art
Key staff: Keeper, William Morris Gallery: Norah C Gillow; Deputy Keeper: Peter Cormack; Assistant Keeper: Amy Clarke
Stock and subject coverage: Extensive collection of books, articles, exhibition catalogues on William Morris (1834-96) – the designer, craftsman, poet, writer and socialist – on the Morris firm, and the Arts and Crafts Movement. Books, catalogues and articles on the Pre-Raphaelites and Victorian art and design. Complete set of Morris's works as a writer and poet and full set of editions printed at his famous press, the Kelmscott Press. Archive material includes letters, manuscripts, etc. by Morris or correspondence from others to him. Contemporary late 19th century periodicals including The Studio, The Century Guild 'Hobby Horse' and the Yellow Book
Services: Photocopy service by staff
Availability: Open to all bona fide researchers and students by prior appointment only. Researchers are required to give at least three days notice. Reference library only
Hours: 10.00-13.00, 14.00-17.00 Tuesday to Saturday
Transport: Tube: Walthamstow Central; Bus: buses from terminus C opposite station exit
Special facilities: Toilet facilities available; no disabled access to library on top floor but books can be made available by prior arrangement
Publications: Exhibition catalogues

Linked organisations

London Borough of Waltham Forest, Arts and Leisure Department The Gallery is part of the Department

[643]
William Morris Society

Kelmscott House
26 Upper Mall
Hammersmith
London W6 9TA
Borough: Hammersmith and Fulham
Telephone: 020 8748 5207

Fax: 020 8741 3735
E-mail: william.morris@care4free.net
World Wide Web: www.morrissociety.org
Constitution: Registered charity
Objectives/purposes: To make as widely known as possible the life, work and ideas of William Morris and his circle
Key staff: Curator: Helen Elletson
Stock and subject coverage: Books, theses and designs, materials on the life, work and ideas of William Morris and his circle
Availability: Access open to all for reference only, no charges. The Society welcomes new members, whatever their interests and has an extensive programme of events, lectures and visits
Hours: 14.00-17.00 Thursday and Saturday, no appointment needed; 11.00-14.00 Thursday and Saturday, by appointment only
Transport: Tube: Ravenscourt Park; Bus: 27, 91, 267, 290 to King Street
Special facilities: Wheelchair adapted toilet facilities available; access for users with disabilities
Special features: Number of Kelmscott Press books including the Kelmscott Chaucer
Publications: Journal (2 p.a.); Newsletter (4 p.a.) both available to members only

[644]
Wimbledon School of Art
WSA

Merton Hall Road
London SW19 3QA
Borough: Merton
Telephone: 020 8408 5027
Fax: 020 8408 5050
E-mail: p.harrison@wimbledon.ac.uk
World Wide Web: www.wimbledon.ac.uk
Constitution: Specialist art school; independent non-profit distributing organisation
Key staff: Librarian: Patricia A Harrison
Stock and subject coverage: Materials on: art and design; costume history; theatre design and scenography; dramatic literature
Services: Photocopies; library catalogue available via website; internet access for enrolled students and staff only
Availability: Reference only, on written application to the Head of Learning Resources or the Librarian
Hours: 10.00-19.30 Monday to Friday, term-time only
Transport: Tube: Wimbledon, South Wimbledon; Rail: Wimbledon; Tramline: Dundonald Road; Bus: 157, 163, 164
Special facilities: Access for wheelchair users to first floor only; toilet facilities available

Linked organisations

University of Surrey Degree awarding body

[645]
Wimbledon Society Museum of Local History

22 Ridgway
Wimbledon SW19 4QN
Borough: Merton

Telephone: 020 8296 9914

Constitution: Registered charity and association with voluntary subscribing membership

Objectives/purposes: To collect material relating to the history of the former Borough of Wimbledon and some adjoining areas

Key staff: Chairman, Museum Committee: Charles Toase

Stock and subject coverage: Books and manuscripts, prints, drawings, photographs, artefacts, ephemera, maps, press-cuttings and archaeological and natural history specimens. Materials cover the history of Wimbledon and its inhabitants and include items relating to women's suffrage in Wimbledon and to Merton Place (home of Nelson and the Hamiltons). The collections also include material relating to SCAPA (Society for the Control of Advertising in Public Places) and the diaries of Henry C Forde, Victorian engineer, for years 1858-82, 1889, 1890, 1896

Availability: Free access to material on request, preferably in writing. For reference only

Hours: 14.30-17.00 Saturdays and Sundays; open for researchers at other times by appointment

Transport: Tube and Rail: Wimbledon; Bus: 93, 200

Special facilities: Toilet facilities available; users with disabilities should notify staff in advance

Publications: Publications on local history available

Linked organisations

Wimbledon Society

---

[646]
Wolfson Institute of Preventive Medicine
St Bartholemew's and The Royal London School of Medicine and Dentistry

QMUL

Charterhouse Square

London EC1M 6BQ

Borough: Islington

Telephone: 020 7882 6297

Fax: 020 7882 6270

E-mail: wolfson@qmw.ac.uk

World Wide Web: www.smd.qmul.ac.uk

Constitution: Part of Queen Mary, University of London

Objectives/purposes: Support for medical education and research

Key staff: Site Librarian: Luba Munford

Stock and subject coverage: Clinical library with reference collections on epidemiology and medical screening

Services: Photocopying facilities

Availability: Open to staff and students of Queen Mary, University of London, to academic staff and research students from M25 consortium by arrangement

Hours: 09.00-17.00 Monday to Friday, contact the Institute to make an appointment before visiting

Transport: Tube: Barbican, Farringdon; Bus: 4, 55, 56, 243, 505

Special facilities: Access for users with disabilities

Linked organisations

Queen Mary, University of London Part of the university

---

[647]
Women and Manual Trades

52-4 Featherstone Street

London EC1Y 8RT

Borough: Islington

Telephone: 020 7251 9192

Fax: 020 7251 9193

E-mail: info@wamt.org

World Wide Web: www.wamt.org

Constitution: Company limited by guarantee, association with voluntary subscribing membership, and registered charity

Key staff: Development Worker: Bim Balogun

Stock and subject coverage: Resource library with information on: how to get insurance; estimating and tendering; insurance relating to the building trades; health and safety at work; hazardous building materials and methods; environment friendly building methods and materials; trades federation and other topics

Availability: Free access to tradeswomen, trainees and researchers by appointment. Fees are charged for library materials, Newsletter and for the Workers Register

Hours: 10.00-17.00 Monday to Friday

Transport: Tube: Old Street; Bus: 55, 76, 143, 214, 271, 505

Special facilities: Toilet facilities available; access for wheelchair users

Publications: Annual Report, Women and Manual Trades Newsletter (3 p.a.), occasional European newsletter, Crossing the Border video and schools pack, 'Work Register' of self employed tradeswomen; Tradeswomen's Direction (£5.00); Training Directory (free); A Fair Days Work (£7.00); Staying Power (£7.00)

---

[648]
Women's Health

52 Featherstone Street

London EC1Y 8RT

Borough: Islington

Telephone: 020 7251 6333

Fax: 020 7250 4152

E-mail: womenshealth@pop3.poptel.org.uk

Constitution: Independent non-profit distributing organisation; company limited by guarantee; registered charity; association with voluntary subscribing membership

Objectives/purposes: Providing information in a supportive manner, helping women to make informed decisions about their own health

Key staff: Librarian: Ingrid Smit

Stock and subject coverage: The Library specialises in gynaecological and reproductive information such as hysterectomy, fibroids, menopause, HRT, ovarian problems, abortion, PID, etc. Stock includes 100 journals, 1,500 books and over 1,200 subject dossiers containing information on these women's health subjects

Services: Photocopies

Availability: Free access to the public, material for reference only

Hours: 09.30-16.30 Monday to Friday. Telephone before visiting as space is limited

Transport: Tube: Old Street; Bus: 43, 43X, 55, 76, 141, 214, 243, 271
Special facilities: Toilet facilities available; access for users with disabilities
Publications: Annual Report; Newsletter (4 p.a.); women's health leaflets (send SAE for publications list)

[649]
Women's Resource Centre
76 Wentworth Street
London E1 7SE
Borough: Tower Hamlets
Telephone: 020 7377 0088
Fax: 020 7377 5544
Email: info@wrc.org.uk
Constitution: Registered charity
Objectives/purposes: The WRC is a co-ordinating and support organisation for voluntary and community projects that work for and with women. WRC is a national organisation with a London focus, providing information, training, development support, networking opportunities and policy consultation in the non-profit sector
Stock and subject coverage: Main focus of the library is on organisational development including funding, management and ICT. Where possible the WRC stocks publications relevant to the women's voluntary sector
Services: Laminating, ring-binding, internet access, photocopying (all attract a small fee)
Availability: Open to WRC members organisations. Reference material for use at the Centre only
Hours: Contact the Information Officer for an appointment, no drop in service available
Transport: Tube: Aldgate East
Publications: The Source newsletter (bimonthly), free to members of the WRC; guidelines and publications on topics relevant to the women's voluntary and community sector

[650]
Working Men's Club and Institute Union Ltd
CIU
253-4 Upper Street
London N1 1RY
Borough: Islington
Telephone: 020 7226 0221
Fax: 020 7354 1847
E-mail: information@wmciu.org
World Wide Web: www.wmciu.org
Constitution: Independent non-profit making organisation; company limited by guarantee; club with subscribing membership
Objectives/purposes: Services to bona fide clubs
Key staff: General Secretary: Kevin Smyth
Stock and subject coverage: Annual reports and monthly journals from 1885 plus history of the organisation, some individual club histories and memorabilia
Services: Photocopies; fax machine; website
Availability: Free access to all bona fide researchers for reference only

Hours: 09.00-18.00 Monday to Friday
Transport: Tube: Highbury and Islington
Special facilities: Toilet facilities available; access for users with disabilities
Publications: Annual Report; Club Journal (monthly)

Linked organisations
CIU has 28 branches
Ruskin College
Workers Educational Association
Committee of Registered Clubs Association (CORCA)
Related organisations

[651]
Working Men's College for Men and Women, Library
44 Crowndale Road
Camden Town
London NW1 1TL
Borough: Camden
Telephone: 020 7387 2037
Fax: 020 7383 5561
Constitution: Company limited by guarantee; registered charity
Key staff: Librarian: Gordon John Fox; Assistant Librarian: George Tindall
Stock and subject coverage: Book stock of ca. 21,000 volumes. In particular books, letters and pamphlets by and about the College founders, who include: Rev FD Maurice, John Malcolm Ludlow, Thomas Hughes, FJ Furnivall, Rev J Llewelyn Davies, John Ruskin, Lowes Dickinson, Prof J Westlake, RB Litchfield and Rev Charles Kingsley. The collection includes material on: early 19th century Socialism, Christian Socialism, religious and political history, the Labour Party and the early women's movement; extensive London collection from the early 19th century to date and wide classical history section
Services: Photocopies
Availability: Free access for students and members of the staff of the Working Men's College. Open to research students on application. The Working Men's College is an evening college and special arrangements have to be made for research students wishing to use the Library out of College hours
Hours: Open for four terms during the year, 17.30-21.00 Monday to Thursday. Visitors, especially from abroad, should contact the College beforehand to make arrangements
Transport: Tube: Camden Town, Mornington Crescent: Rail: Euston; Bus: 24, 253
Special facilities: Refreshment and toilet facilities available; access for users with disabilities – easy access for wheelchairs at side entrance, chair lift, wide lift, toilet facilities
Special features: Handsome, specially designed library in a Grade II listed building
Publications: Annual Report (details the Library's activities)

[652]
World Nuclear Association WNA
(formerly the Uranium Institute)

12th Floor
Bowater House West
114 Knightsbridge
London SW1X 7LJ
Borough: Kensington and Chelsea
Telephone: 020 7225 0303
Fax: 020 7225 0308
E-mail: wna@world-nuclear.org
World Wide Web: www.world-nuclear.org
Constitution: International industrial association with voluntary subscribing membership
Key staff: Head of Communications: Mr Ian Hore-Lacy; Information Officer: Mr Warwick Pipe
Stock and subject coverage: Library catalogue lists over 30,000 indexed items. Subject coverage includes materials relevant to the nuclear fuel cycle and the international nuclear energy industry
Services: Photocopies (charged)
Availability: Freely available to member organisations. Others by prior appointment with the Librarian
Hours: 09.30-17.00 Monday to Friday; visits only between 10.00-16.00
Transport: Tube: Knightsbridge; Bus: 9, 10, 19, 22, 52
Special facilities: Refreshments and toilet facilities available; access for users with disabilities
Publications: Weekly news briefing and news digest; bimonthly newsletter; annual symposium proceedings; information papers (all published on website, free of charge); biennial uranium market report (price on application)

[653]
The Worshipful Company of Glaziers and Painters of Glass
The Glaziers Company

Glaziers Hall
9 Montague Close
London Bridge
London SE1 9DD
Borough: Southwark
Telephone: 020 7403 3300
Fax: 020 7403 6652
Constitution: London City Livery Company; registered charity; association with voluntary subscribing membership
Objectives/purposes: The furtherance of interest and education in the craft of stained and painted glass
Key staff: The Clerk: DW Eking; Assistant Clerk: Mrs P Goodwin
Stock and subject coverage: Materials on the history and practice of the craft of stained and painted glass
Availability: Open to anyone interested in the craft of stained glass. Books available only for study on the premises and not for loan. No charges made
Hours: Office hours, by appointment only
Transport: Tube and Rail: London Bridge
Special facilities: Wheelchair accessible toilet facilities available

[654]
The Worshipful Company of Goldsmiths

Goldsmiths' Company or Goldsmiths' Hall
Goldsmiths' Hall
Foster Lane
London EC2V 6BN
Borough: Corporation of London
Telephone: 020 7606 7010
Fax: 020 7606 1511
E-mail: the.library@thegoldsmiths.co.uk
World Wide Web: www.thegoldsmiths.co.uk
Constitution: City Livery Company
Objectives/purposes: To continue to maintain the Company's historic involvement with its craft, and its educational and charitable interests
Stock and subject coverage: Collection of printed books, designs and drawings, maps and plans, photographs, 35mm colour slides, films and archival material. Subject coverage includes: gold and silver – plate and jewellery; assaying and hallmarking – including Trial of the Pyx; and regalia. Archives of the Worshipful Company of Goldsmiths including the London Assay Office. Special emphasis on the goldsmiths' trade and the history of Goldsmiths' Hall
Services: Photocopies (limited, charges made)
Availability: Reference library, visits by appointment
Hours: 10.00-16.45 Monday to Friday
Transport: Tube: St Paul's
Special facilities: Wheelchair accessible toilet facilities available
Publications: Goldsmiths' Review (annual, published in June, subscription £5); range of books, booklets and catalogues (list available on request)

Linked organisations
London Assay Office

[655]
The Worshipful Company of Pewterers
Pewterers' Company

Pewterers Hall
Oat Lane
London EC2V 7DC
Borough: Corporation of London
Telephone: 020 7606 9363
Fax: 020 7600 3896
E-mail: clerk@pewterers.org.uk
World Wide Web: www.pewterers.org.uk
Constitution: Independent non-profit distributing organisation
Objectives/purposes: Livery company concerned with the support and promotion of the pewter industry in the UK and EU. Maintains the historical archives of pewtersmithing and sponsors future work through scholarships, apprenticeships, competitions and trade shows. Charitable activities include medical research, pewter research, and donations to pewter-related and other charitable institutions
Key staff: Archivist: Dr RF Homer PhD FSA
Stock and subject coverage: Historic records of the Company from the 14th century onwards. Books relating to antique and modern pewter, its makers

and marks. Books and journals relating to the City of London and some other City Livery Companies

Services: Internet access; photocopying and fax facilities

Availability: Open to bona fide researchers. Books are generally available for reference only. Some catalogues and other books available for sale

Hours: By appointment only with the Clerk

Transport: Tube: St Pauls, Barbican, Mansion House, Bank

Special facilities: Toilet facilities available; limited access for users with disabilities

Publications: Pewter Review – journal on the pewter trade and the activities of the Livery Company (2 p.a.)

Linked organisations

Association of British Pewter Craftsmen (ABPC) Secretary Mrs GT Steele (tel: 0114 266 3084, fax: 0114 267 0910)

European Pewter Union (EPU) Headquarters of both organisations

The Pewter Society Secretary Mr Peter Hayward (tel: 01600 712864, e-mail: hayw@clara.net)

[656]
Worshipful Company of Stationers and Newspaper Makers

Library and Archive
Stationers' Hall
London EC4M 7DD

Borough: Corporation of London

Telephone: 020 7248 2934

Fax: 020 7489 1975

E-mail: admin@stationers.org
archivist@stationers.org

Constitution: The Library and Archives is a registered charity administered by Trustee appointed by the Court

Objectives/purposes: The Worshipful Company of Stationers is a London livery company, dating from 1403. Its first royal charter was granted in 1557. It continues to have close links with the book and allied trades. In addition to the traditional trades of printing, publishing, bookselling and papermaking its current members include those working in the modern visual and graphic communication industries as well as librarians and archivists

Key staff: Honorary Librarian, Honorary Archivist

Stock and subject coverage: Books and periodicals relating to the history of the book and paper trades and to the Corporation of London and its livery companies. Special collection of almanacks published by the Company (1620-1948). The Library also houses the library of the Bibliographical Society, which contains many works on the history of the Stationers' Company and of the book trade.
The Archive is the single most complete source for the history of the London book trade, almost unbroken from 1554 to the present day, containing its membership records from 1554, copyright and entry book registers (1556-1842), lists of pensioners and ledgers relating to its charities from 1606, material relating to its English Stock publishing enterprise (1644 to 1961). 14,000 miscellaneous documents and a small collection of personal papers

Availability and hours: Honorary Librarian and Archivist usually in attendance Monday mornings and all day Tuesdays. Access by appointment. For use of the archive a written reference may be required

Transport: Tube: Bank

Publications: The Stationers' Company, a History (1403-1959) by C Blagden; The Stationers' Company (1800-2000) by R Myers, 2001; The Stationers' Company Archive 1554-1984 by R Myers, 1990; microfilm of the archive (1554-1920s) available in 75 libraries worldwide, 115 reels, produced by Chadwyck-Healey, 1986

[657]
Xenophon
98E Cambridge Gardens
London W10 6HS

Borough: Kensington and Chelsea

Telephone: 020 8968 1360

E-mail: plnrm@rbkc.gov.uk

Constitution: Association with voluntary subscribing membership

Objectives/purposes: Recreational and historical study of codes and cyphers

Key staff: Regor J Nagrom

Stock and subject coverage: Books, pamphlets, cuttings and grey literature on codes, cyphers, cryptanalysis, and cryptography

Availability: Open to all bona fide researchers principally for advice rather than reference. Access by appointment only

Hours: By appointment only

Publications: Crypt (occasional)

[658]
YMCA George Williams College
199 Freemasons Road
Canning Town
London E16 3PY

Borough: Newham

Telephone: 020 7540 4910

Fax: 020 7511 4900

E-mail: gwclibrary@lycos.co.uk

World Wide Web: www.ymca.ac.uk

Constitution: Registered charity

Objectives/purposes: To produce reflective, professional practitioners of informal and community education. This aim is informed by the College's Christian base and commitment to social justice

Key staff: Librarian

Stock and subject coverage: Over 19,000 volumes and 70 current journals related to informal and community education. The Library is particularly strong in the history of the youth work movement with special reference to the YMCA – the earliest youth organisation dating from the 1840s.
Archives of the YMCA movement are housed in the special collections unit of the University of Birmingham

Services: Photocopies; internet access; word processing facilities

Availability: Open to bona fide researchers, former students and staff of the YMCA movement for reference only, no charges at present

Hours: Term-time: 09.00–17.30 Monday to Friday.
During vacations visitors should telephone to check
opening hours

Transport: Tube: Canning Town (15 minute walk),
Custom House (8 minute walk)

Special facilities: Drinks machine available; access for users
with disabilities and wheelchair adapted toilet

Linked organisations

Canterbury Christ Church University College
YMCA George Williams College is a constituent
College

---

[659]
Zoological Society of London
ZSL

Regent's Park
London NW1 4RY

Borough: Camden
Telephone: 020 7449 6293
Fax: 020 7586 5743
E-mail: library@zsl.org
World Wide Web: www.zsl.org
Constitution: Registered charity, association with
voluntary subscribing membership

Key staff: Librarian: Ann Sylph BSc MSc MIInfSc;
Archivist: Michael Palmer MA

Stock and subject coverage: Ca. 200,000 volumes; 1,300
current journals on all aspects of zoology. Particularly
rich in illustrated animal books of the 19th century.
The Archives of the Zoological Society of London
are also held

Availability: To members and staff of the Society, and to
others on application, with proof of address and
upon payment of a fee

Hours: 09.30–17.30 Monday to Friday (open until 18.15
on Tuesday Talk evenings)

Transport: Tube: Camden Town; Bus: 274

Special facilities: Toilet facilities available

Publications: Journal of Zoology; Animal Conservation;
Symposia; Conservation Biology series (edited by
ZSL and published by Cambridge University Press);
Zoological Record (published in association with
BIOSIS); International Zoo Yearbook

Linked organisations

Institute of Zoology
Whipsnade Wild Animal Park
London Zoo

LIBRARIES LISTED BY BOROUGH

London Boroughs

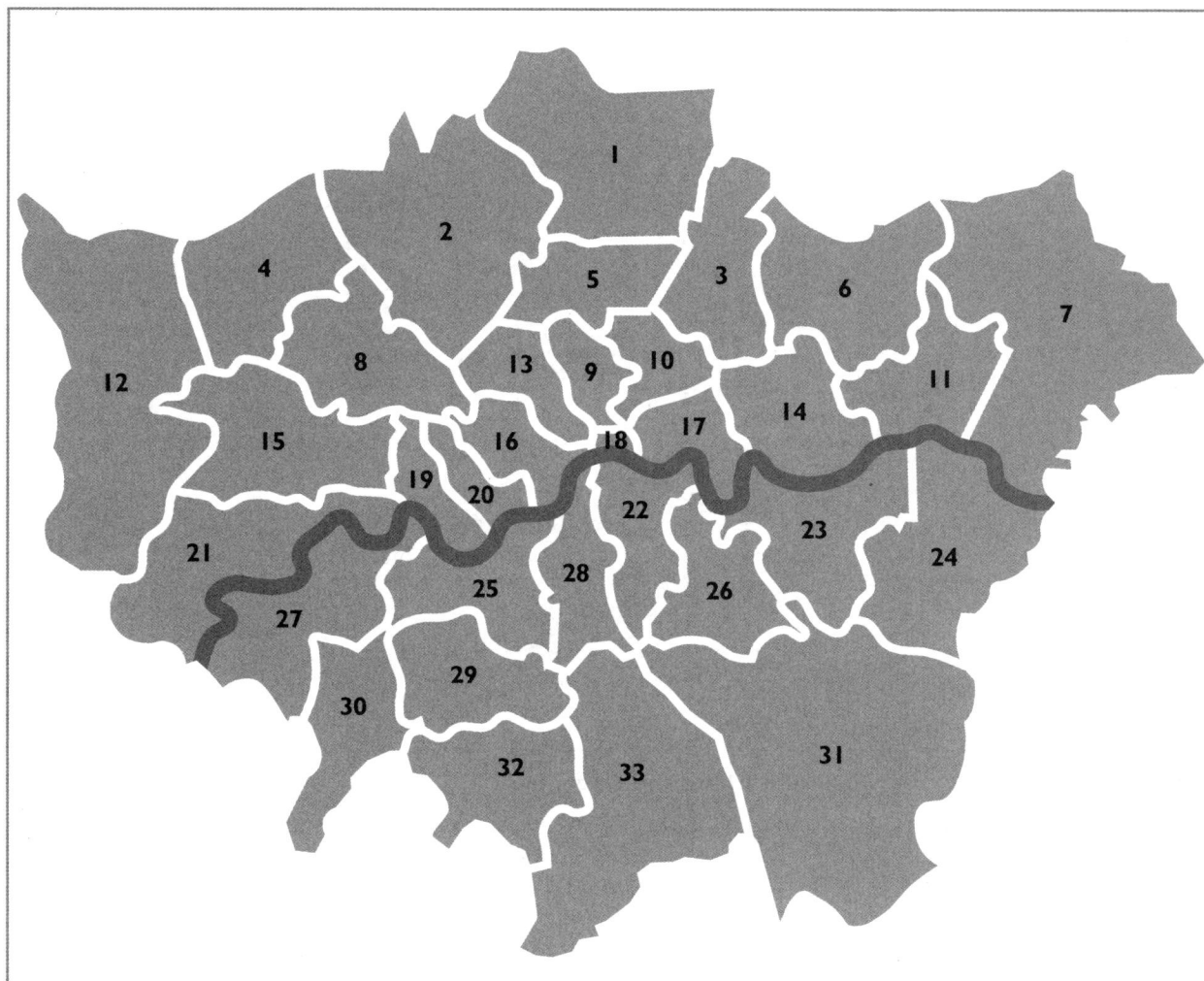

1	Enfield	**18**	Corporation of London
2	Barnet	**19**	Hammersmith & Fulham
3	Waltham Forest	**20**	Kensington & Chelsea
4	Harrow	**21**	Hounslow
5	Haringey	**22**	Southwark
6	Redbridge	**23**	Greenwich
7	Havering	**24**	Bexley
8	Brent	**25**	Wandsworth
9	Islington	**26**	Lewisham
10	Hackney	**27**	Richmond upon Thames
11	Barking & Dagenham	**28**	Lambeth
12	Hillingdon	**29**	Merton
13	Camden	**30**	Kingston upon Thames
14	Newham	**31**	Bromley
15	Ealing	**32**	Sutton
16	City of Westminster	**33**	Croydon
17	Tower Hamlets		

Barking

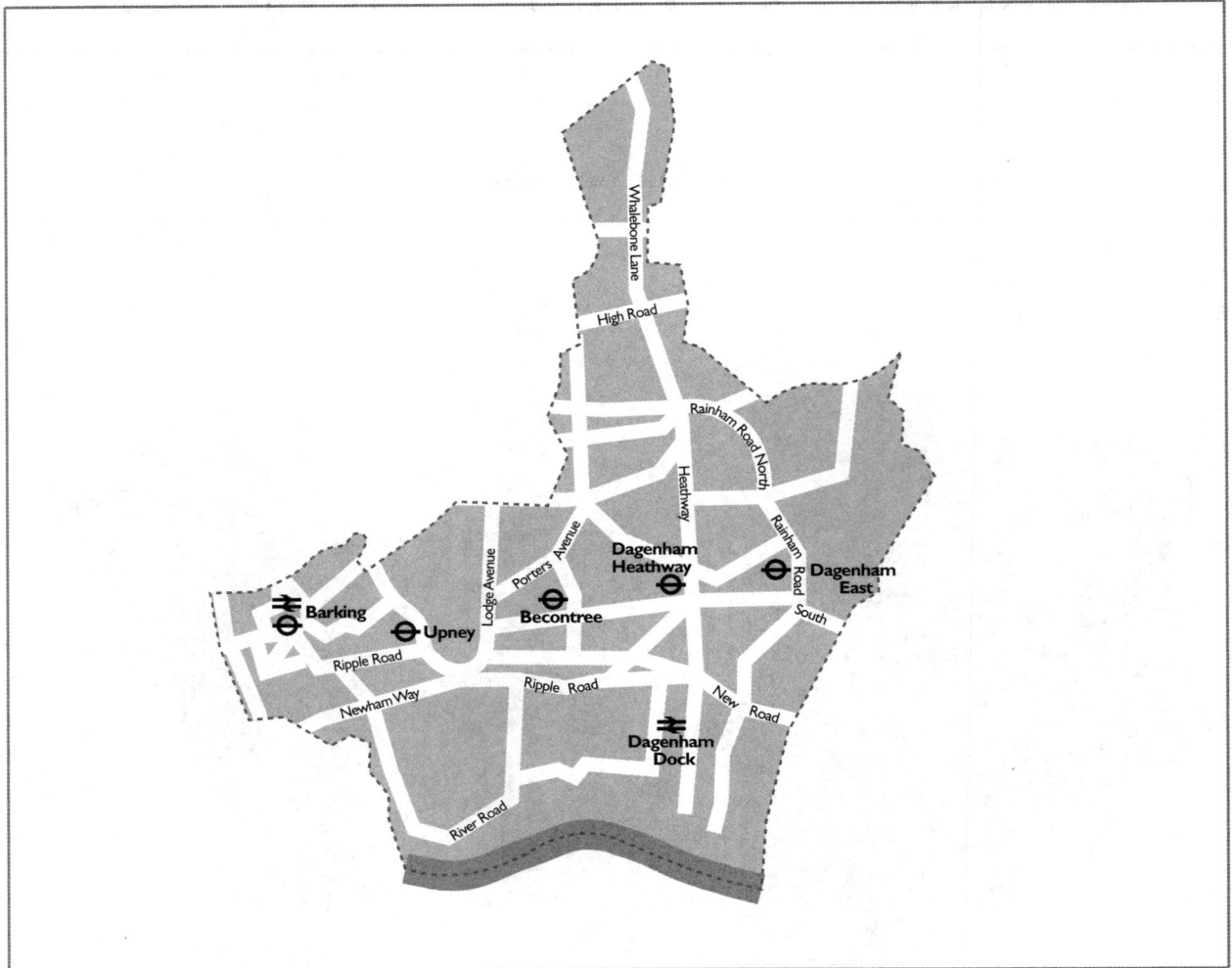

Libraries in the London Borough of Barking and Dagenham

- Barking and Dagenham Libraries (London Borough of Barking and Dagenham)
  Barking Central Library
  Fanshawe Library
  Marks Gate Library
  Markyate Library
  Rectory Library
  Rush Green Library

  Thames View Library
  Valence Library
  Wantz Library
  Whalebone Library
  Woodward Library
- University of East London
  Barking Campus Learning Centre

Barnet

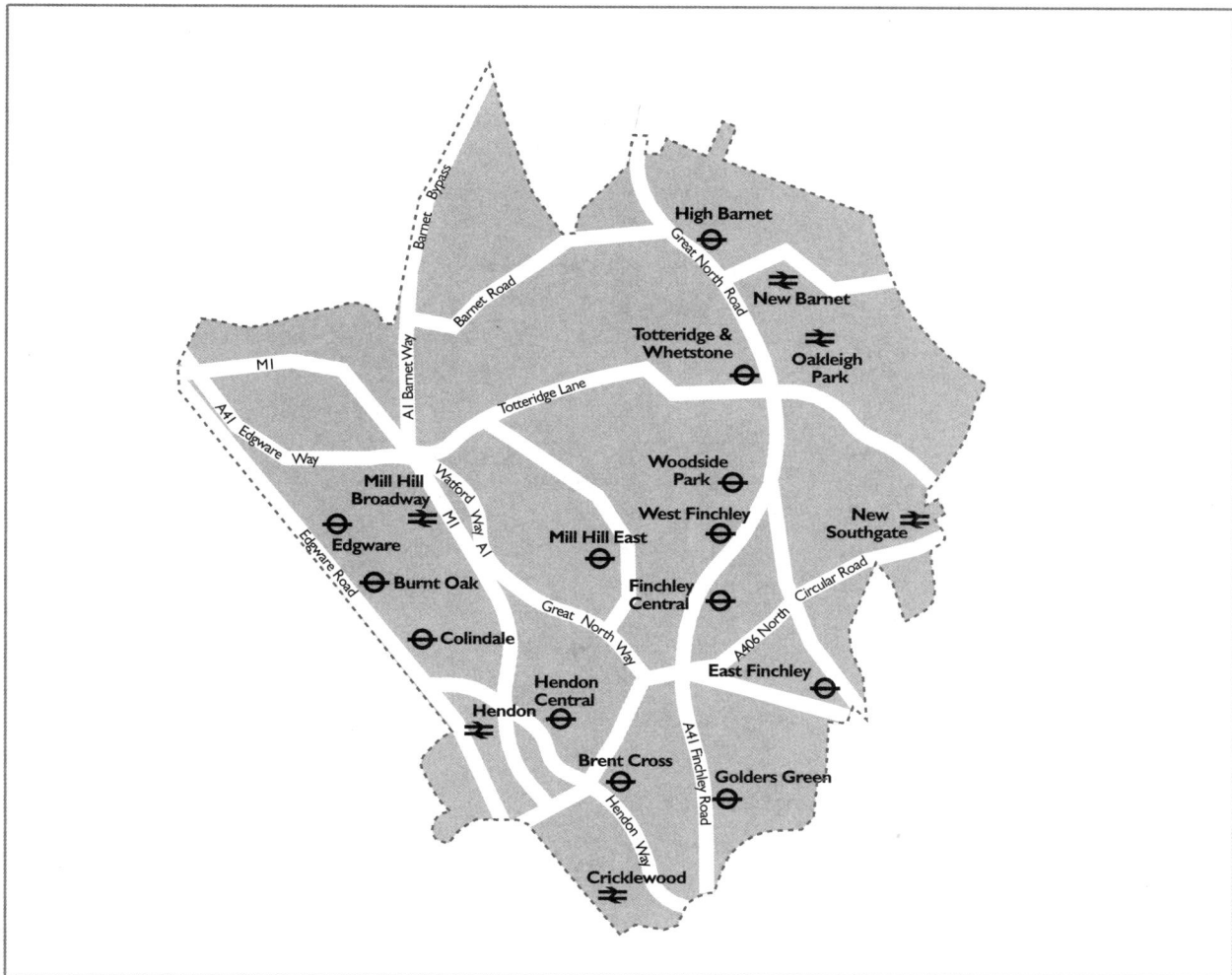

Libraries in the London Borough of Barnet

- Barnet Libraries (London Borough of Barnet)
  Barnet Local Studies and Archives Centre
  Burnt Oak Library
  Childs Hill Library
  Chipping Barnet Library
  Church End Library
  East Barnet Library
  East Finchley Library
  Edgware Library
  Friern Barnet Library
  Golders Green Library
  Grahame Park Library
  Hampstead Garden Suburb Library
  Hendon Library
  Mill Hill Library
  North Finchley Library
  Osidge Library
  South Friern Library
  Totteridge Library

- Barnet Hospital Library
- Barnet Museum
- The British Library
  Newspaper Library
- Edgware Community Hospital Information and
  Knowledge Services
- Leo Baeck College – Centre for Jewish Education
  Library
- London School of Jewish Studies
- Middlesex University
  Cat Hill (including Quicksilver Place)
  Hendon
- Oak Hill College Library
- Public Health Laboratory Service – Communicable
  Disease Surveillance Centre
- Royal Air Force Museum

Bexley

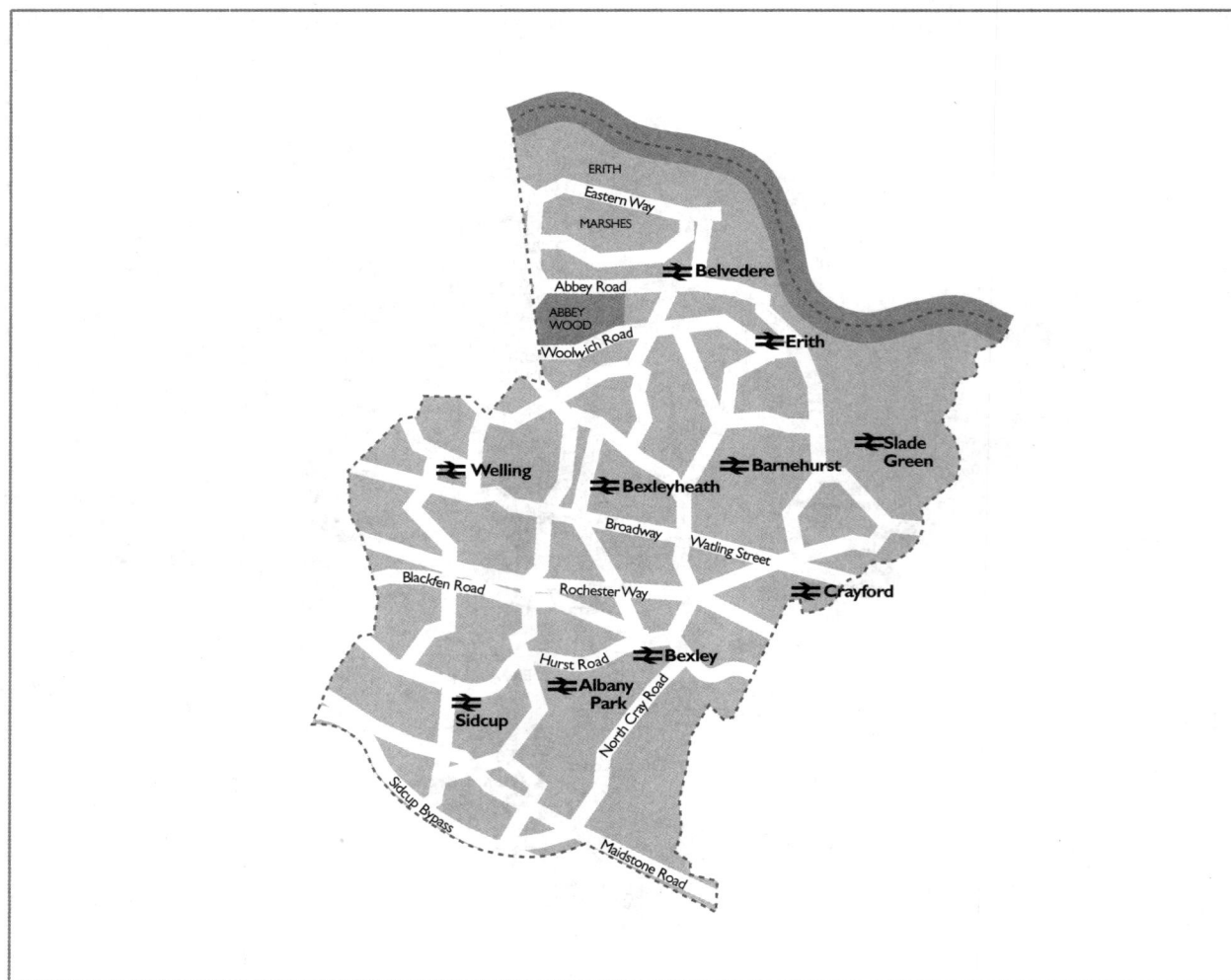

Libraries in the London Borough of Bexley

- Bexley (London Borough of Bexley)
    Barnehurst Library
    Bexley Village Library
    Blackfen Library
    Bostall Library
    Central Library
    Crayford Library

Erith Library
North Heath Library
Sidcup Library
Slade Green Library
Thamesmead Library
Upper Belvedere Library
Welling Library

Brent

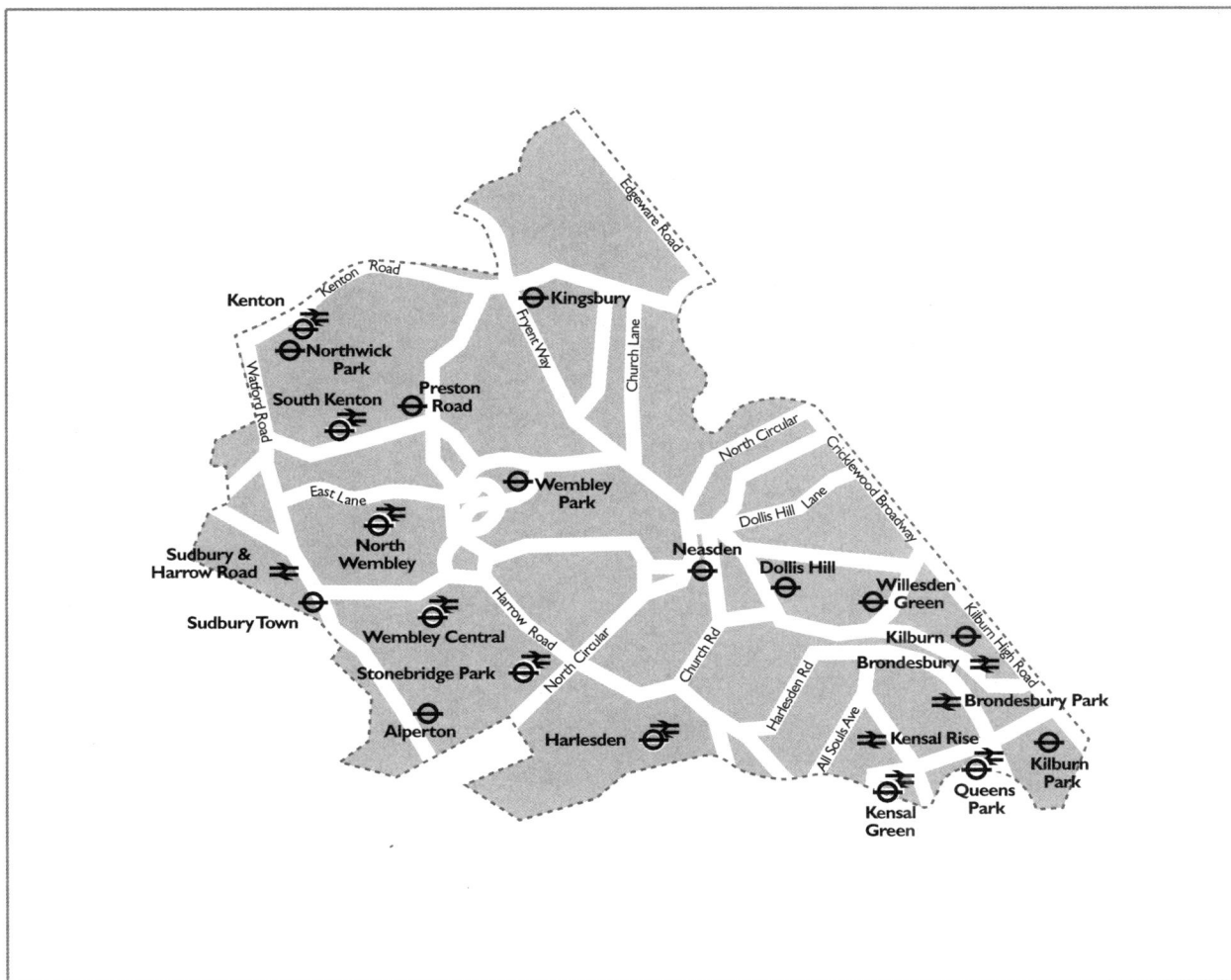

Libraries in the London Borough of Brent

- Brent Libraries (London Borough of Brent)
  Barham Park Library
  Brent Library Service (Administrative Headquarters)
  Cricklewood Library and Archive
  Ealing Road Library
  Harlesden Library
  Kensal Rise Library
  Kilburn Library
  Kingsbury Library
  Neasden Library
  Preston Library
  Tokyngton Library
  Town Hall Library
  Willesden Green Library
- British Association of Psychotherapists
- Central Middlesex Hospital Library
- Institute for Social Inventions
- International Rubber Study Group
- Natural Death Centre
- Royal National Institute for the Blind – Falcon Park Talking Book Service

Bromley

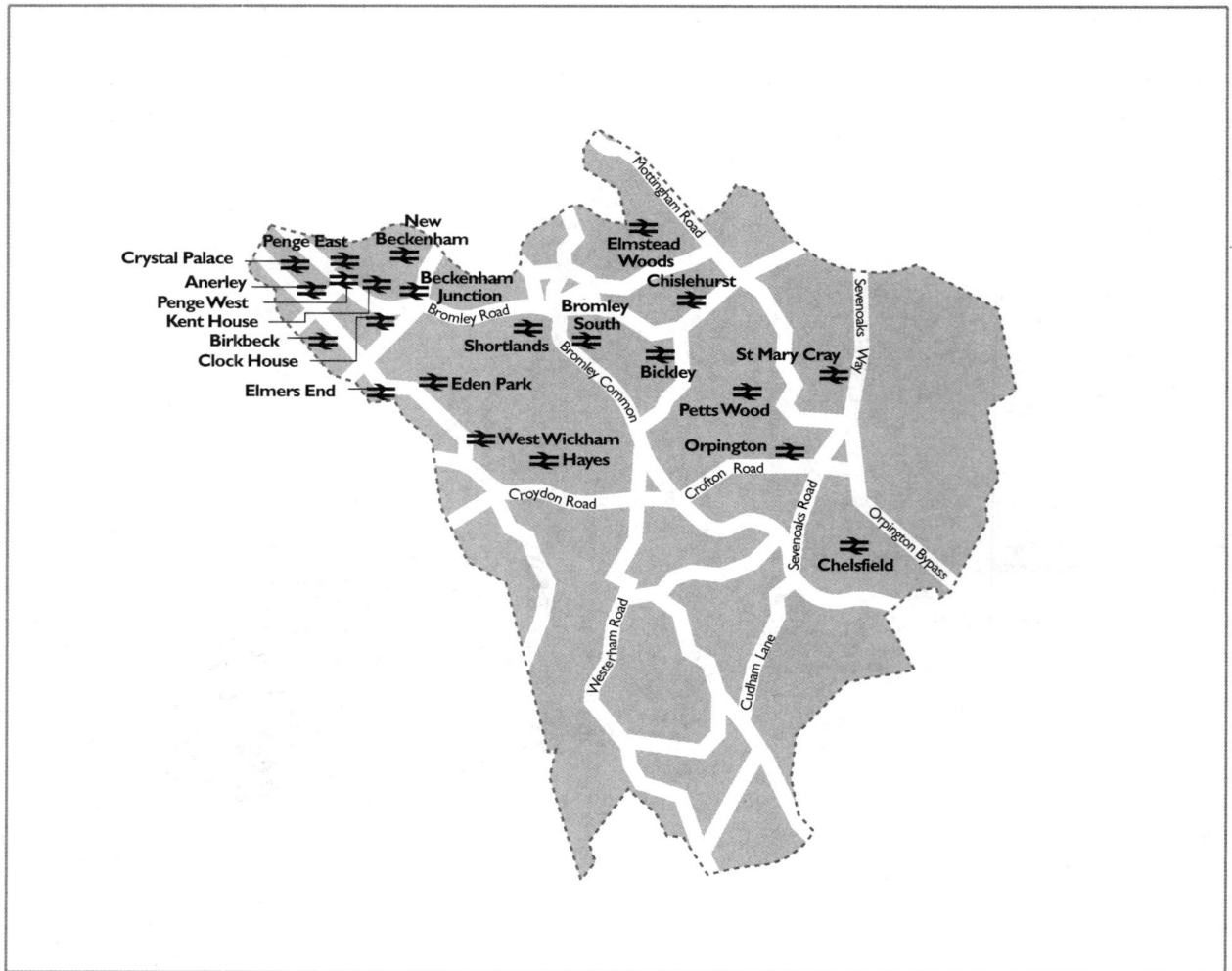

Libraries in the London Borough of Bromley

- Bromley Libraries (London Borough of Bromley)
  Anerley Branch Library
  Beckenham Branch Library
  Biggin Hill Branch Library
  Bromley Central Library
  Burnt Ash Branch Library
  Chislehurst Branch Library
  Hayes Branch Library
  Mottingham Branch Library
  Orpington Branch Library
  Penge Branch Library

  Petts Wood Branch Library
  St Pauls Cray Branch Library
  Shortlands Branch Library
  Southborough Branch Library
  West Wickham Branch Library
- Cystic Fibrosis Trust
- The Hospice Information Service
- King's College London
  Denmark Hill Campus, Bethlam Library
- St Christopher's Hospice, Halley Stewart Library

Camden

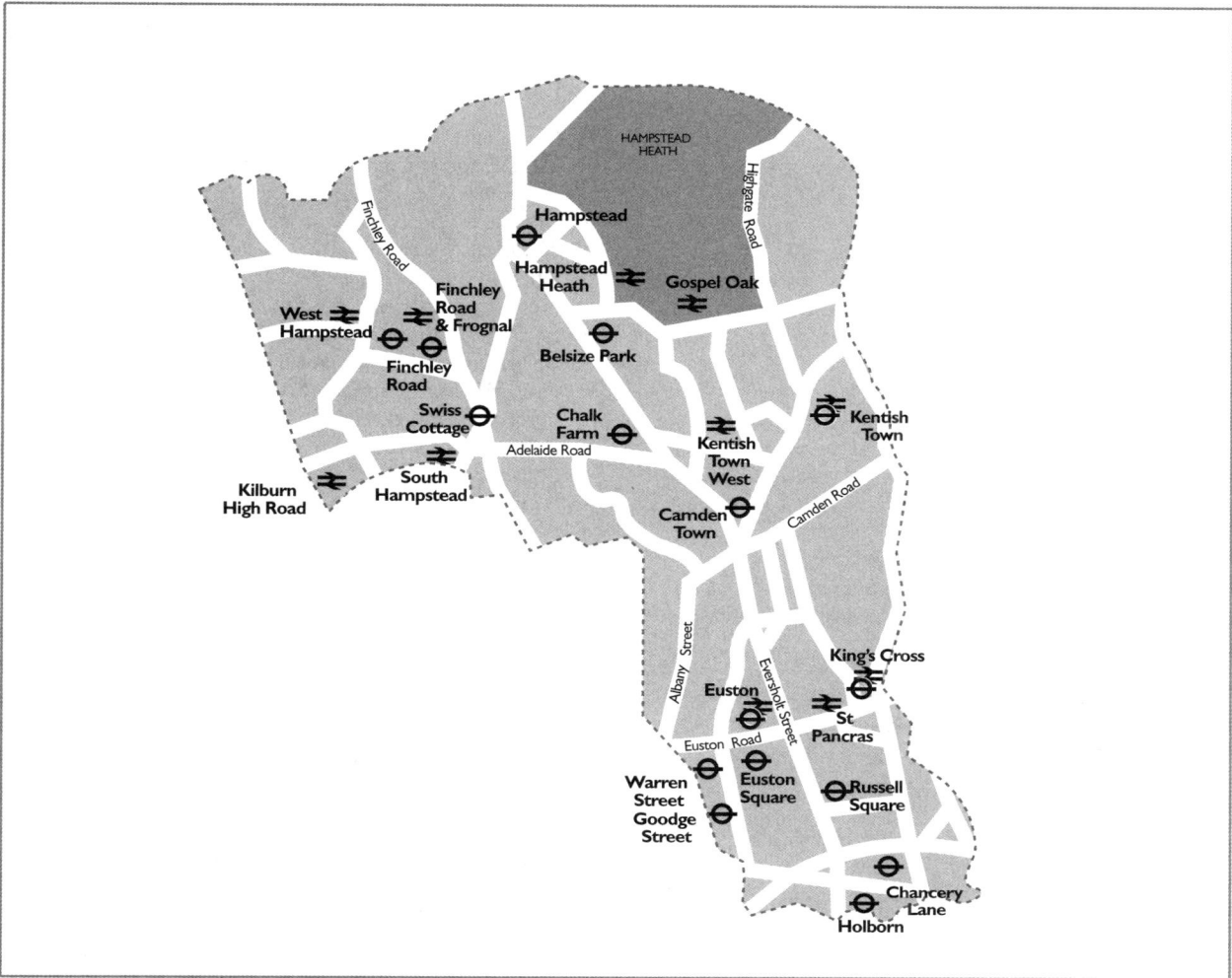

Libraries in the London Borough of Camden

- Advertising Standards Authority
- Architectural Association
  - Architectural Association Library
  - Architectural Association Photo Library
- Association of Anaesthetists of Great Britain and Ireland
- Association of Commonwealth Universities Reference Library
- The Basic Skills Agency Resource Centre
- Birkbeck College Library
- Bloomsbury Healthcare Library
- Boldero Library
- The British Autogenic Society
- The British College of Naturopathy and Osteopathy
- British Film Institute National Library
- British Institute of International and Comparative Law
- The British Library
  - National Bibliographic Service
  - National Preservation Office
  - Press and Public Relations
  - Reader Admissions Office
  - Visitor Services
  - Humanities Reading Rooms
  - Librarian and Information Sciences Service
  - Manuscripts Reading Room

    Maps Reading Room
    Oriental and India Office Collections Reading Room
    Philatelic Collections
    Rare Books and Music Reading Room
    Sound Archive
    Science, Technology and Business Reading Rooms
- British Medical Association
- The British Museum
  - Anthropology Library, British Museum Department of Ethnography
  - Central Library, The British Museum
  - Department of Prints and Drawings
  - The Paul Hamlyn Library
- British Nutrition Foundation
- British Psychological Society
- BT Archives
- Camden (London Borough of Camden)
- Camden Libraries and Information Service
  - Belsize Library
  - Camden Town Library
  - Chalk Farm Library
  - Heath Library
  - Highgate Library
  - Holborn Library
  - Kentish Town Library

Kilburn Library
Queen's Crescent Library
Regent's Park Library
St Pancras Library
Swiss Cottage Central Library
West Hampstead Library
- Cancer Research UK
- Catholic Central Library
- Central Saint Martins College of Art and Design
  Drama Centre London
  Southampton Row Library
- Central School of Speech and Drama
- Chartered Institute of Taxation
- Chartered Institution of Water and Environmental Management
- The Congregational Library
- Cruciform Library
- The Dickens House Museum
- Dr William's Library
- Eastman Dental Institute for Oral Health Care Services
- Edexcel Foundation
- The Egyptian Exploration Society
- English Folk Dance and Song Society
- English National Board for Nursing, Midwifery and Health Visiting
- The Environment Council
- Environmental Studies Library
- Federation of Master Builders
- German Historical Institute Library/Deutsches Historisches Institut
- Gray's Inn Library
- Highgate Literary and Scientific Institution
- HM Land Registry
- Human Communication Science Library, National Information Centre for Speech and Language Therapy
- Independent Healthcare Association
- Institute of Advanced Legal Studies
- Institute of Archaeology Library
- Institute of Child Health
  The Friends of the Children of Great Ormond Street Library
  The SOURCE Collection (housed within the ICH Library)
- Institute of Classical Studies Library and Joint Library of the Hellenic and Roman Societies
- Institute of Commonwealth Studies
- Institute of Education, Information Services
- Institute of Laryngology and Otology Library
- Institute of Latin American Studies Library
- Institute of Neurology, Rockefeller Medical Library
- Institute of Race Relations
- ITN Archive – Independent Television News
- Law Commission
- Lincoln's Inn Library
- Linnean Society of London

- London College of Printing
  Back Hill Site
- London Contemporary Dance School Library
- London Foot Hospital and School of Podiatric Medicine
- London Hazards Centre
- London School of Hygiene and Tropical Medicine
- Low Pay Unit
- MAKE the Organisation for Women in the Arts (formerly Women's Art Library)
- Menzies Centre for Australian Studies
- National Information Centre for Speech Language Therapy
- Netherlands British Chamber of Commerce
- Nuffield Council on Bioethics
- Open University Validation Services
- Paul Mellon Centre for Studies in British Art
- Percival David Foundation of Chinese Art
- Policy Studies Institute
- Pollock's Toy Museum
- Religious Society of Friends (Quakers)
- Royal Academy of Dramatic Art
- Royal Anthropological Institute of Great Britain and Ireland
- Royal College of Physicians
- The Royal College of Surgeons of England
- Royal Free and University College Medical School Medical Library
- Royal Mail Heritage Services
- Royal National Institute for the Blind
  Research Library, Judd Street
- The Royal Veterinary College
- Rudolf Steiner House Library
- School of Oriental and African Studies
- School of Pharmacy
- School of Slavonic and East European Studies Library
- Sir John Soane's Museum
- South Place Ethical Society
- Sport England
- The Swedenborg Society
- Tavistock and Portman NHS Library
- University College London Library
- University of London Library
- US Educational Advisory Service
- Verification Research, Training and Information Centre
- Warburg Institute
- Wellcome Library for the History and Understanding of Medicine
  History of Medicine Collections
  Information Service
  Medical Photographic Library
  Medical Film and Audio Collections
- Working Men's College for Men and Women, Library
- Zoological Society of London

Corporation of London

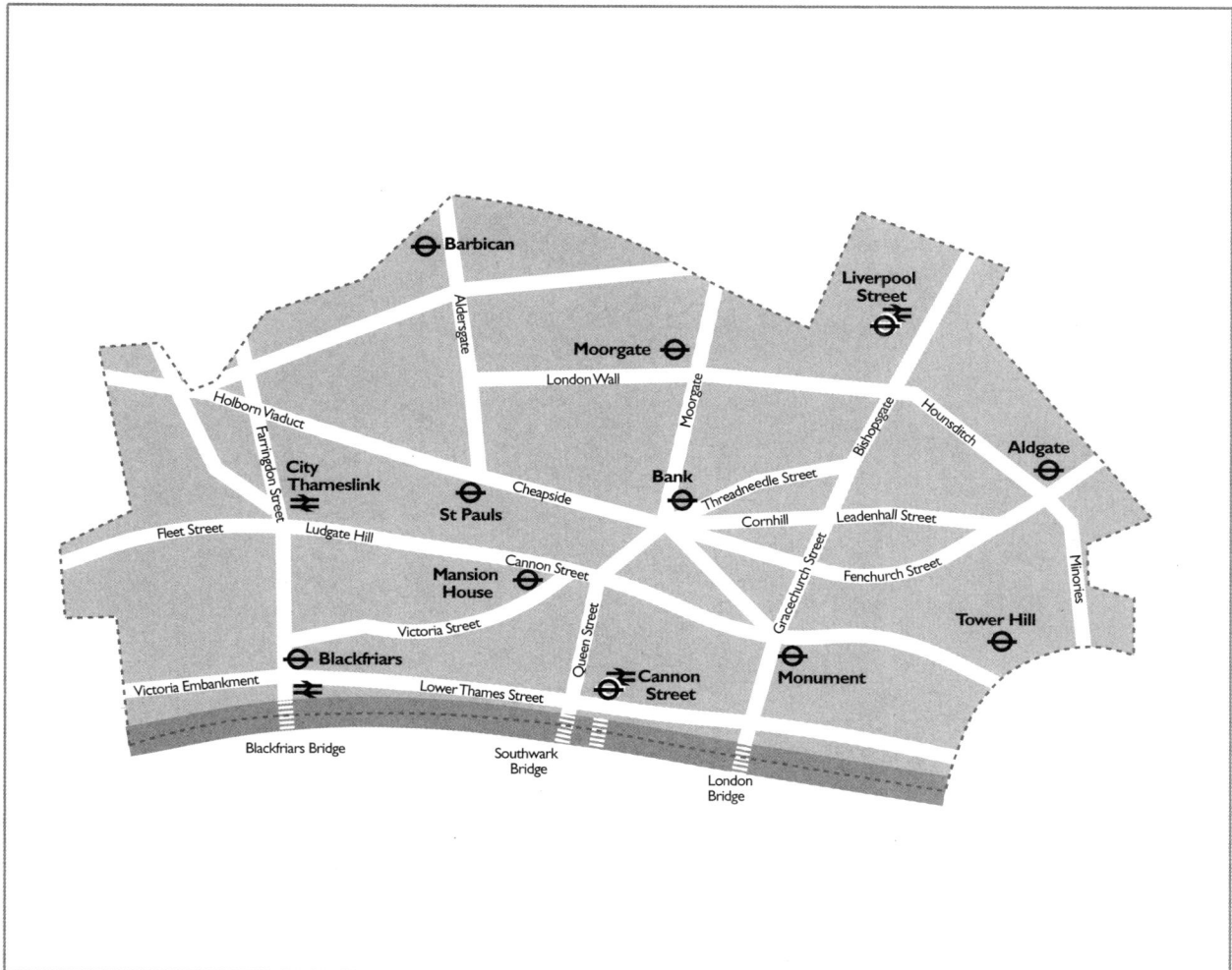

Libraries in the Corporation of London

- Aviation Environment Federation
- Bank of England Archive
- Bank of England Information Centre
- Bishopsgate Institute
- Centre of Medical Law and Ethics Library Collection
- Charity Commission
- Chartered Insurance Institute
- City University
  Arts Policy Resource Centre
  Department of Radiography Library
  West Smithfield Library, City University
- College of Arms
- Copyright Tribunal
- Corporation of London Library Services
  Barbican Library
  Camomile Street Library
  City Business Library
  Corporation of London Records Office
  Guildhall Library
  St Bride Printing Library
  Shoe Lane Library
- Council for Education in World Citizenship
- Crown Prosecution Service
- Dr Johnson's House
- The Drapers' Company
- European Bank for Reconstruction and Development, Business Information Centre

- The Goldsmiths' Company
- Historical Manuscripts Commission
- Inner Temple Library
- Institute of Chartered Accountants in England and Wales
- Institute of Financial Services Information Service
- Institute of Germanic Studies
- Institute of Historical Research
- Institute of Marine Engineering, Science and Technology
- King's College London
  Maughan Library and Information Services Centre
- The Library of The Worshipful Company of Clockmakers
- Lloyd's of London
- Lloyd's Register of Shipping Information Services
- London Chamber of Commerce and Industry, Research and Information Centre
- London Metropolitan University
  Moorgate Learning Resource Centre
- The Mercers' Company
- Museum and Library of the Order of St John, St John Ambulance
- Museum of London
- Office of Fair Trading Library and Information Centre
- Office of Telecommunications

- Royal Mencap Society
- Royal Town Planning Institute
- St Bartholomew's Hospital
- St Paul's Cathedral Library
- The Salvation Army International Heritage Centre

- The Worshipful Company of Goldsmiths
- The Worshipful Company of Pewterers
- Worshipful Company of Stationers and Newspaper Makers

Croydon

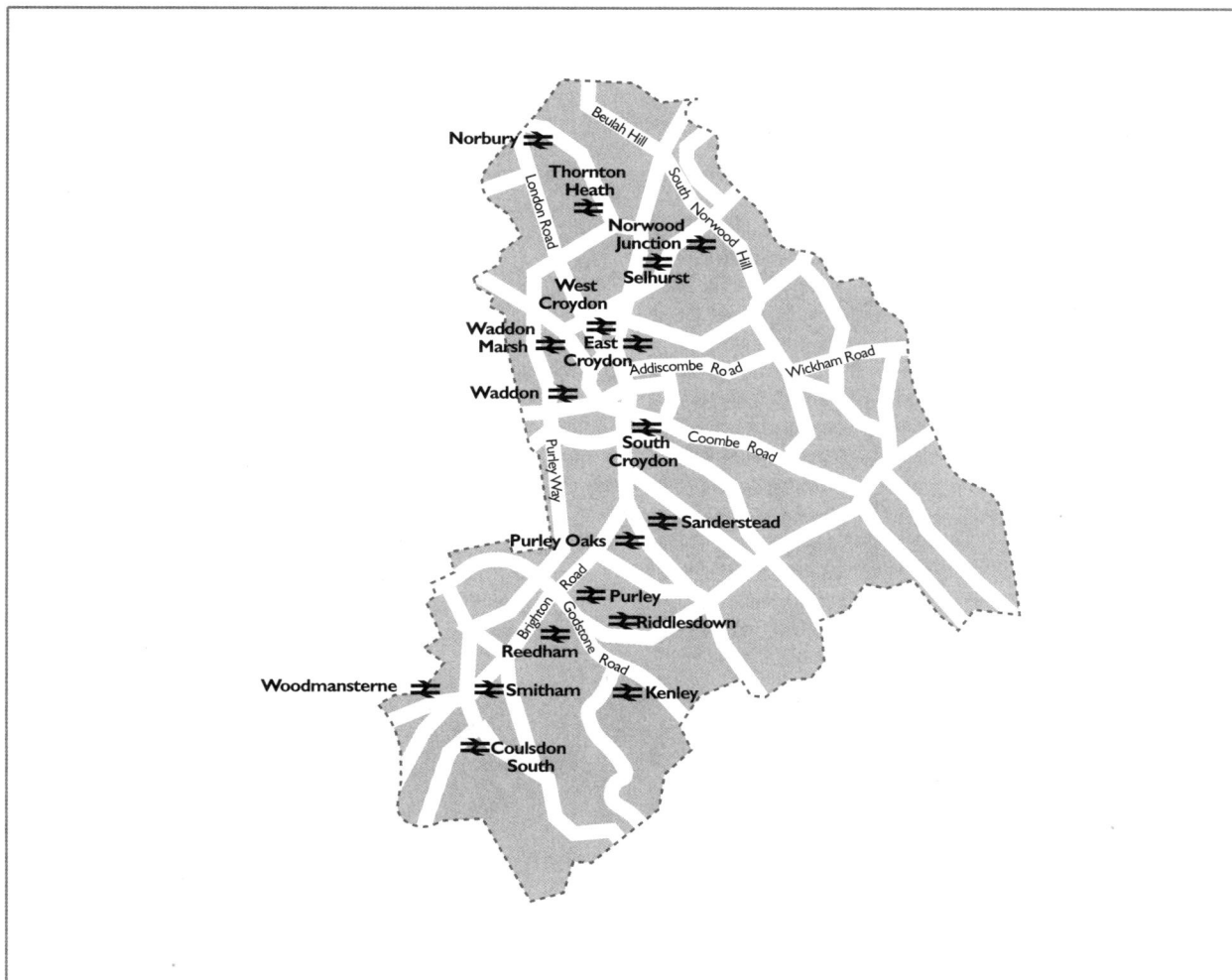

Libraries in the London Borough of Croydon

- Age Concern England
- Croydon (London Borough of Croydon)
- Croydon Libraries, Museum and Arts
    Ashburton Library
    Bradmore Green Library
    Broad Green Library
    Coulsdon Library
    Croydon Central Library
    New Addington Library
    Norbury Library

- Purley Library
- Sanderstead Library
- Selsdon Library
- Shirley Library
- South Norwood Library
- Thornton Heath Library
- Croydon College Library
- Croydon Natural History and Scientific Society Ltd
- Mayday Healthcare NHS Trust, Medical Library
- Spurgeon's College

Ealing

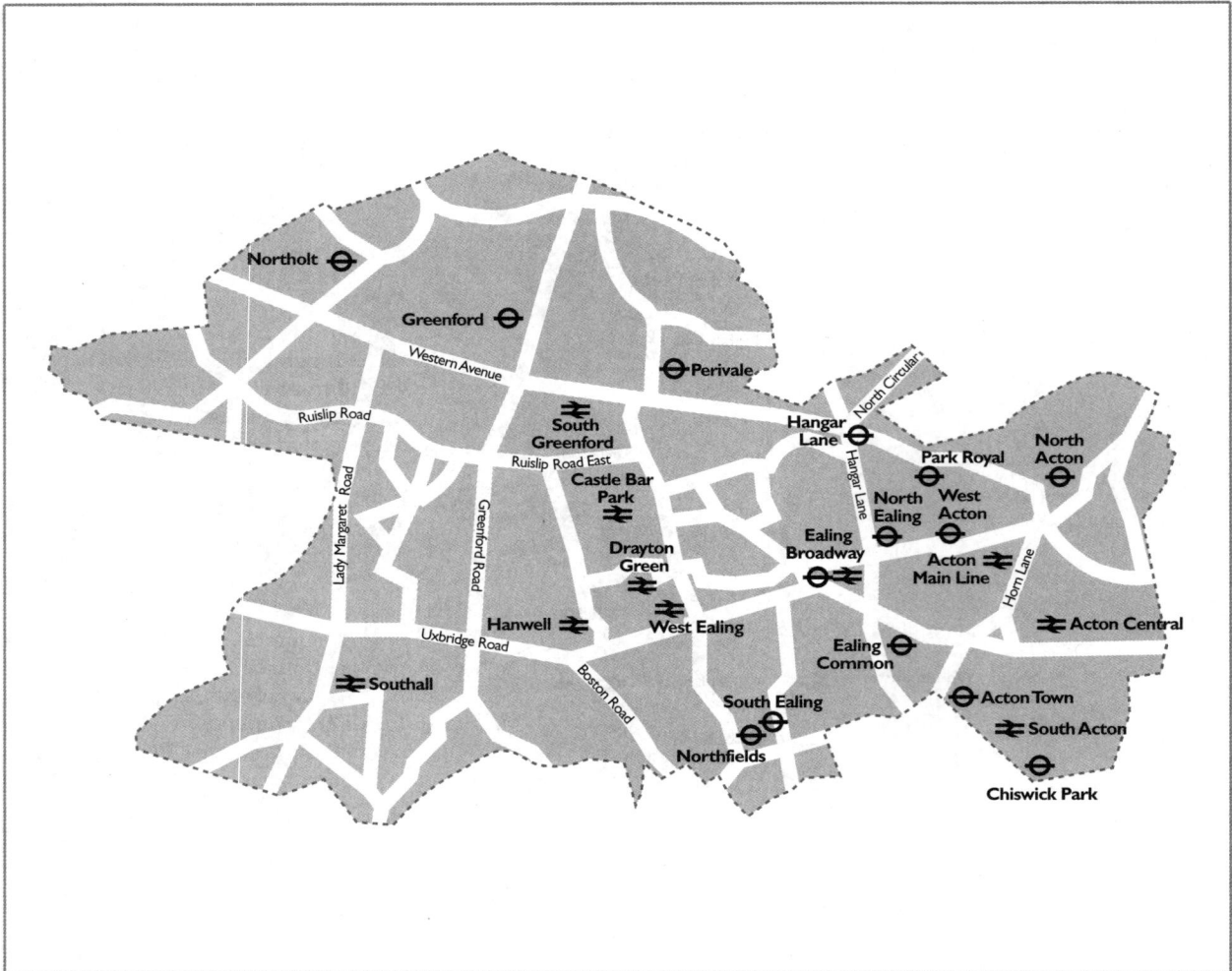

Libraries in the London Borough of Ealing

- Centre for Armenian Information and Advice
- Ealing (London Borough of Ealing)
- Ealing Library and Information Service
  Acton Library
  Ealing Central Library
  Greenford Library
  Hanwell Library
  Jubilee Gardens Library
  Northfields Library
  Northolt Library
  Perivale Library
  Pitshanger Library
  Southall Library
  West Ealing
  Wood End Library
- Ealing, Hammersmith and West London College
  Acton and West London College
  Ealing and West London College
  Southall and West London College
- The London Buddhist Vihara
- National Childbirth Trust Library
- Polish Institute and Sikorski Museum
  Polish Underground Movement (1939-45) Study
  Trust
- Thames Valley University

Enfield

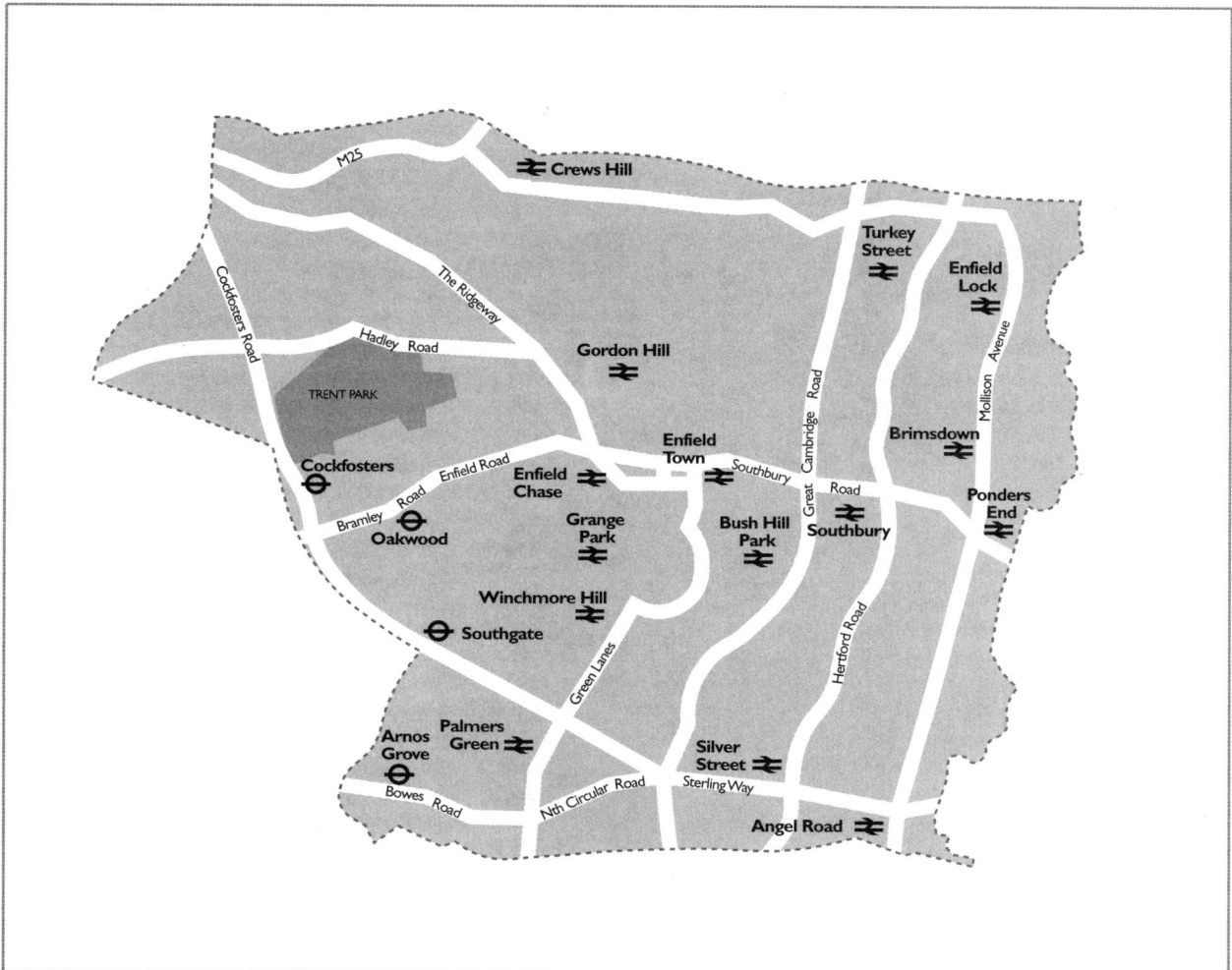

Libraries in the London Borough of Enfield

- Chase Healthcare Information Centre
- Enfield (London Borough of Enfield)
  Enfield Libraries
    Bowes Road Library
    Bullsmoor Library
    Bush Hill Park Library
    Central Library
    Edmonton Green Library
    Enfield Business Library
    Enfield Highway Library
    Enfield Local History Unit
    Merryhills Library
    Ordance Road Library
    Palmers Green Library
    Ponders End Library
    Ridge Avenue Library
    Southgate Circus Library
    Weir Hall Library
    Winchmore Hill Library
- Middlesex University
  Archway and Hospitals' Campus
  Enfield
  Trent Park (including Bedford and Ivy House)
- Occupational and Environmental Diseases Association

Greenwich

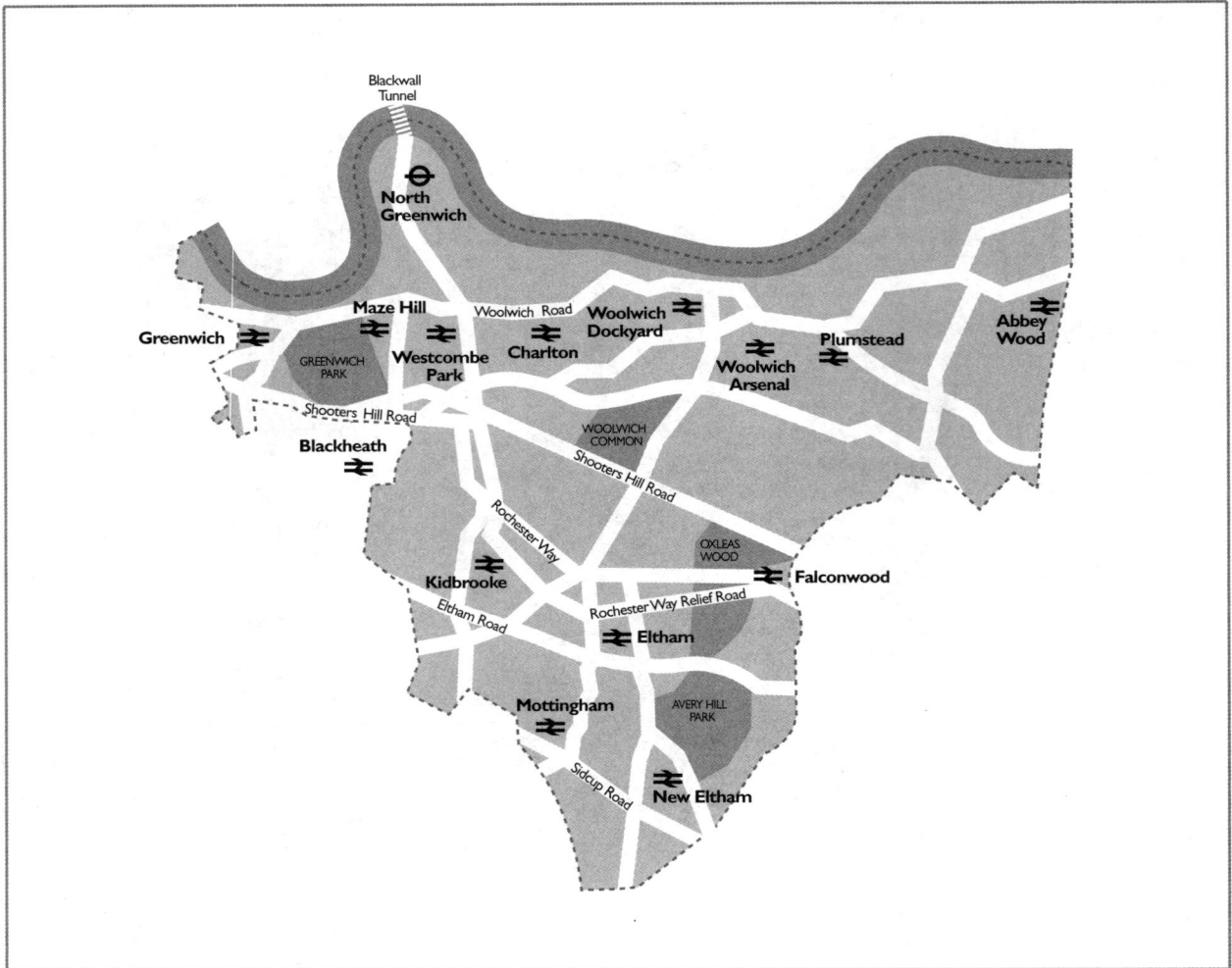

Libraries in the London Borough of Greenwich

- Centre for Micro-Assisted Communication
- The Fan Museum
- Greenwich (London Borough of Greenwich)
  Greenwich Library and Information Service
    Abbey Wood Library
    Blackheath Library
    Charlton Library
    Claude Ramsey Library
    Coldharbour Library
    East Greenwich Library
    Eltham Library
    Ferrier Library
    Greenwich Local History Library

    New Eltham Library
    Plumstead Library
    Slade Library
    West Greenwich Library
    Woolwich Library and Woolwich Reference Library
- Jerwood Library of the Performing Arts
- Model Yachting Association
- National Maritime Museum
- Queen Elizabeth Hospital NHS Trust
- Royal Artillery Institution Library
- University of Greenwich
    Avery Hill Campus Library
    Dreadnought Library

Hackney

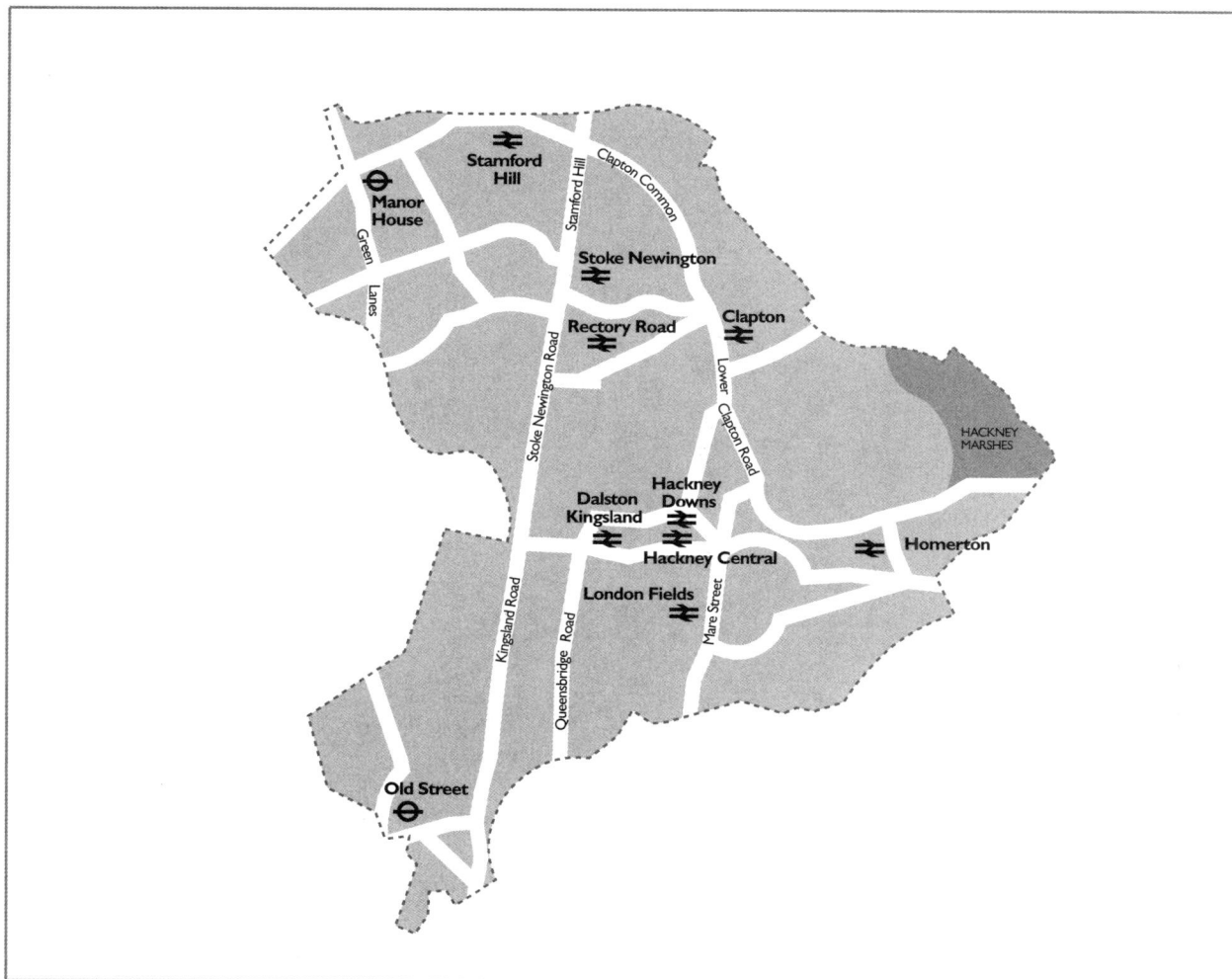

Libraries in the London Borough of Hackney

- Action on Smoking and Health
- Alpine Club Library
- Cancer BACUP
- The Centre for Independent Transport Research in London
- Centre for Policy on Ageing
- City University
  Cass Business School Learning Resource Centre
- Geffrye Museum
- Hackney (London Borough of Hackney)
- Hackney Library Services
  Clapton Library
  Clr James Library
  Hackney Central Library and Reference Library
  Homerton Library

  Shoreditch Library
  Stamford Hill Library
  Stoke Newington Library
- Hackney Archives Department, London Borough of Hackney
- Homerton Hospital NHS Trust
- Howard League for Penal Reform
- Institute of International Visual Arts Library
- The London Society
- National Association of Goldsmiths
- NSPCC (National Society for the Prevention of Cruelty to Children)
- Psychiatric Rehabilitation Association
- Transport 2000

Hammersmith and Fulham

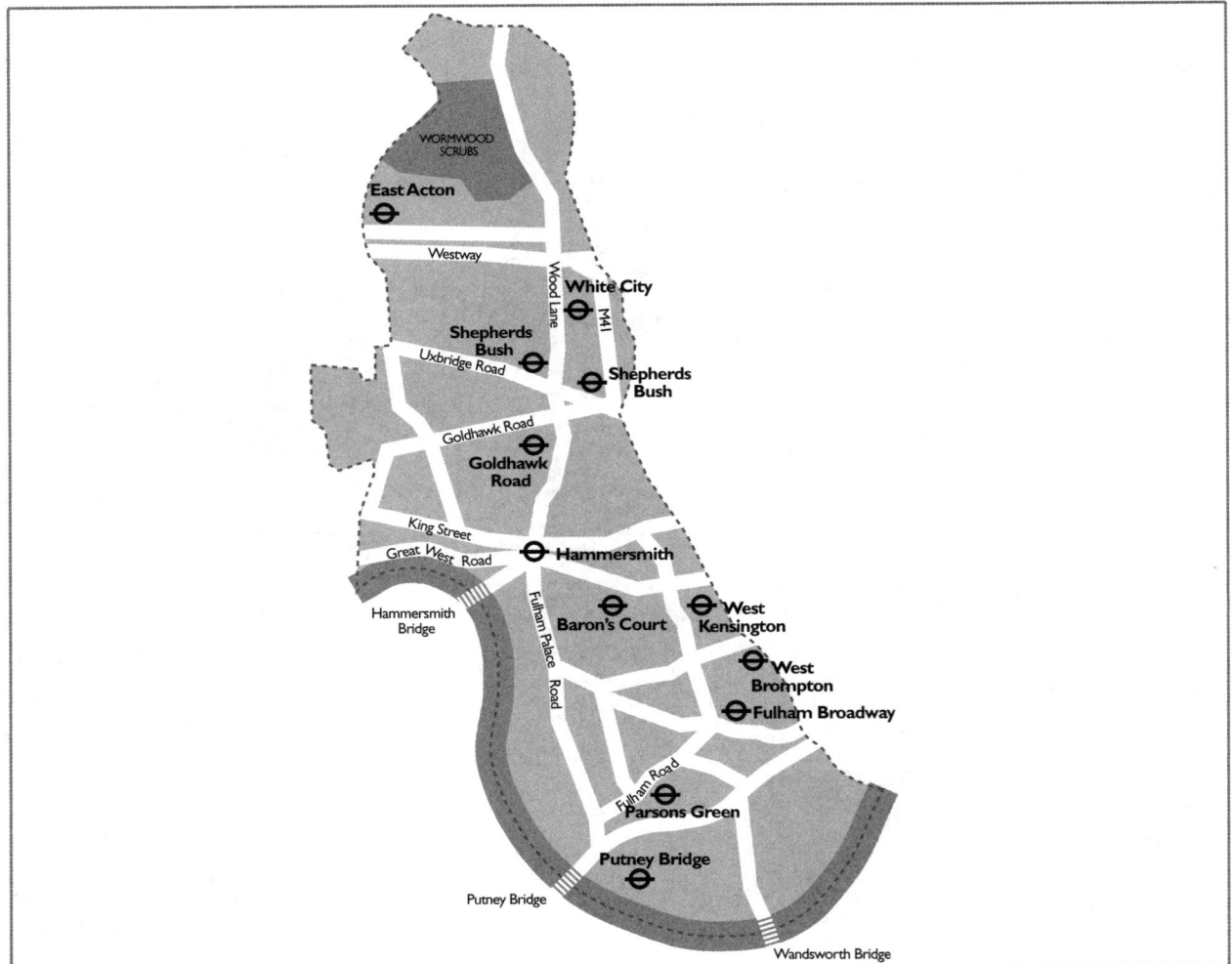

Libraries in the London Borough of Hammersmith and Fulham

- Amateur Rowing Association
- Association of Certified Book-Keepers
- Bharatiya Vidya Bhavan (Institute of Indian Art and Culture), The Bhavan Centre
- British Tourist Authority
- Chelsea College of Art and Design
  Hugon Road Library
  Lime Grove Library
- Ealing, Hammersmith and West London College
  Hammersmith and West London College, Gliddon Road
- Hammersmith and Fulham (London Borough of Hammersmith and Fulham)
- Hammersmith and Fulham Libraries
  Askew Road Library
  Barons Court Library
  Fulham Library
  Hammersmith Library
  Sands End Library
  Shepherd's Bush Library
- Hammersmith and Fulham Archives and Local History Centre
- Imperial College Library, Faculty of Medicine
  Charing Cross Campus
  Chelsea and Westminster Campus
  The Hammersmith Campus (Wellcome Library)
- Institute of Cost and Executive Accountants
- Joseph Conrad Society
- The Polish Library
- Royal Ballet School
  Upper School, Ballet Library
- William Morris Society

Haringey

Libraries in the London Borough of Haringey

- Haringey (London Borough of Haringey)
- Haringey Library Services
  Alexandra Park Library
  Central Library
  Coombes Croft Library
  Highgate Library
  Hornsey Library
  Marcus Garvey Library
  Muswell Hill Library
  St Anns Library
  Stroud Green Library
- Haringey Archive Service
- Middlesex University
  Tottenham
- The Moravian Church Archive and Library
- North London Postgraduate Medical Centre Library
- Spinal Injuries Association

Harrow

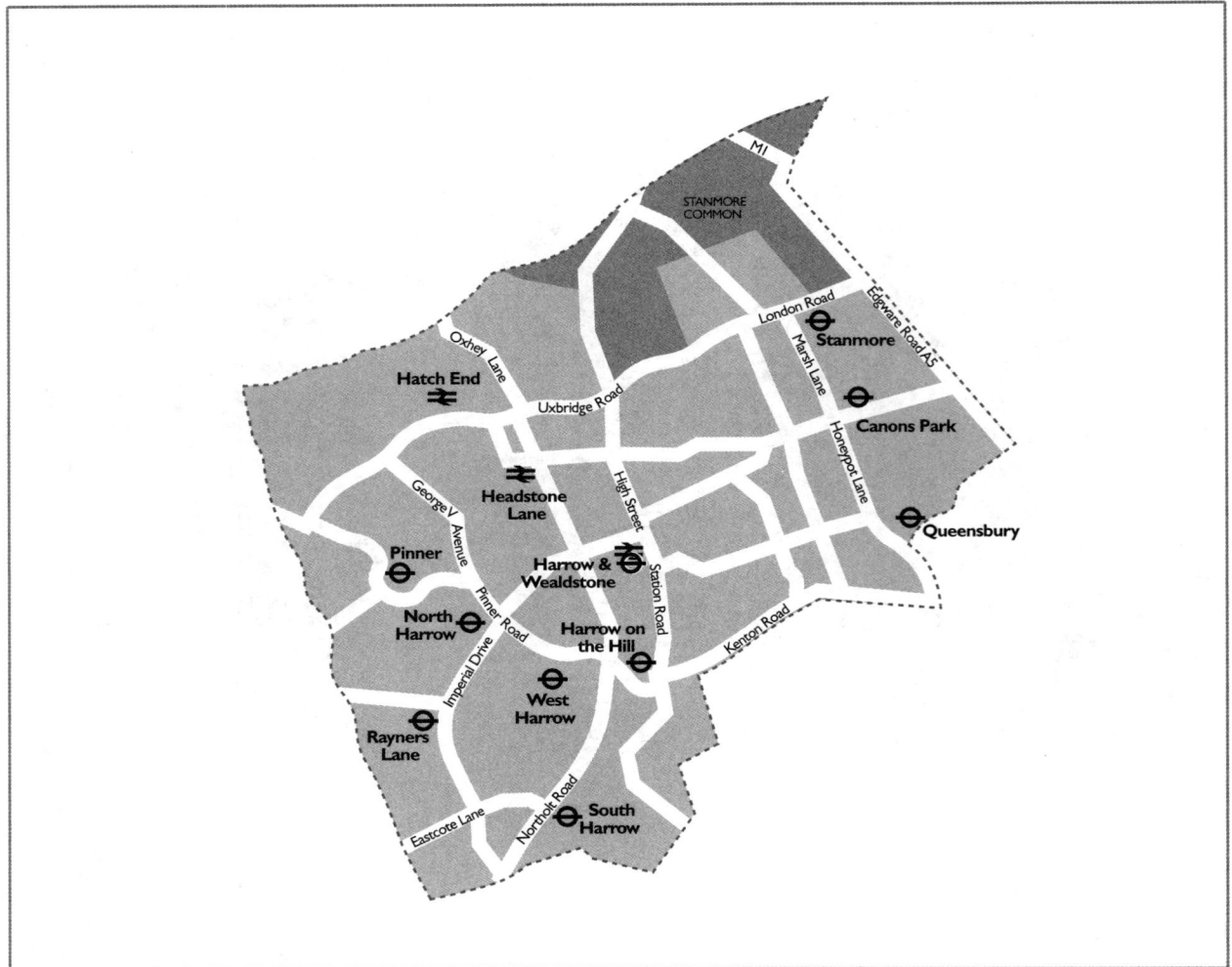

Libraries in the London Borough of Harrow

- Harrow (London Borough of Harrow)
- Harrow Library Services
  Bob Lawrence Library
  Civic Centre Library (Harrow Central Reference Library)
  Gayton Library (Central Lending Library)
  Hatch End Library
  Kenton Library
  North Harrow Library
  Pinner Library

  Rayners Lane Library
  Roxeth Library
  Stanmore Library
  Wealdstone Library
- Harrow School Vaughan Library
- Institute of Orthopaedics Library
- John Squire Library
- University of Westminster
  Harrow Learning Resources Centre

Havering

Libraries in the London Borough of Havering

- Havering Libraries (London Borough of Havering)
  - Central Library
  - Collier Row Library
  - Elm Park Library
  - Gidea Park Library
  - Harold Hill Library
  - Harold Wood Library

  Hornchurch Library
  Rainham Library
  South Hornchurch Library
  Upminster Library
- International Cargo Handling Co-Ordination Association

Hillingdon

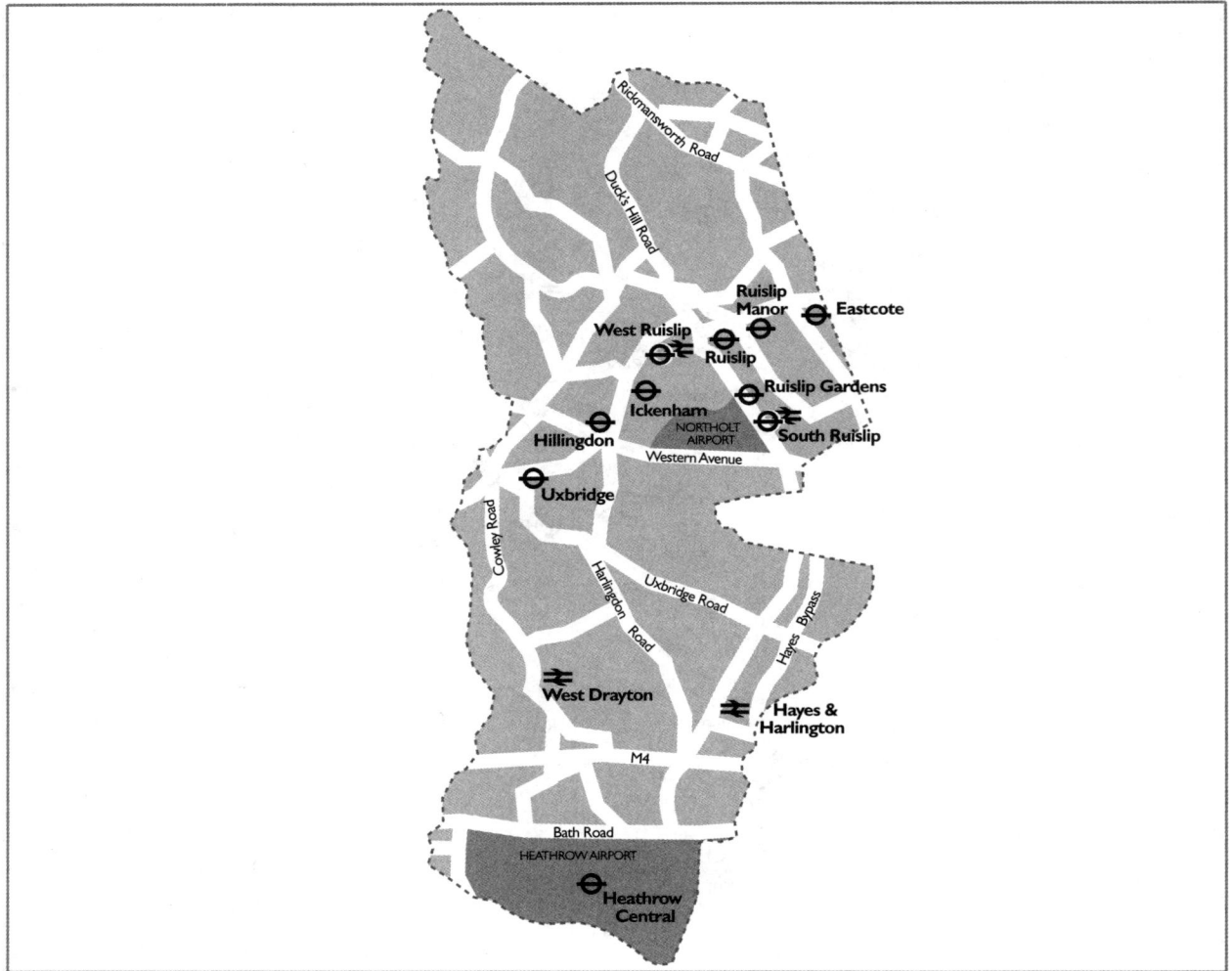

Libraries in the London Borough of Hillingdon

- Brunel University Library
  Osterley Campus Library
- Hillingdon (London Borough of Hillingdon)
  Hillingdon Libraries
    Eastcote Library
    Harefield Library
    Harlington Library
    Hayes End Library
    Hayes Library
    Ickenham Library
    Kingshill Library
    Manor Farm Library
    Northwood Hills Library

    Oak Farm Library
    Oaklands Gate Library
    Ruislip Manor Library
    South Ruislip Library
    West Drayton Library
    Yeading Library
    Yiewsley Library
    Uxbridge Library (Central Library)
- Hillingdon Hospital Medical Library
- London Bible College
- Mount Vernon Hospital Postgraduate Medical Centre
- The Railway Correspondence and Travel Society

Hounslow

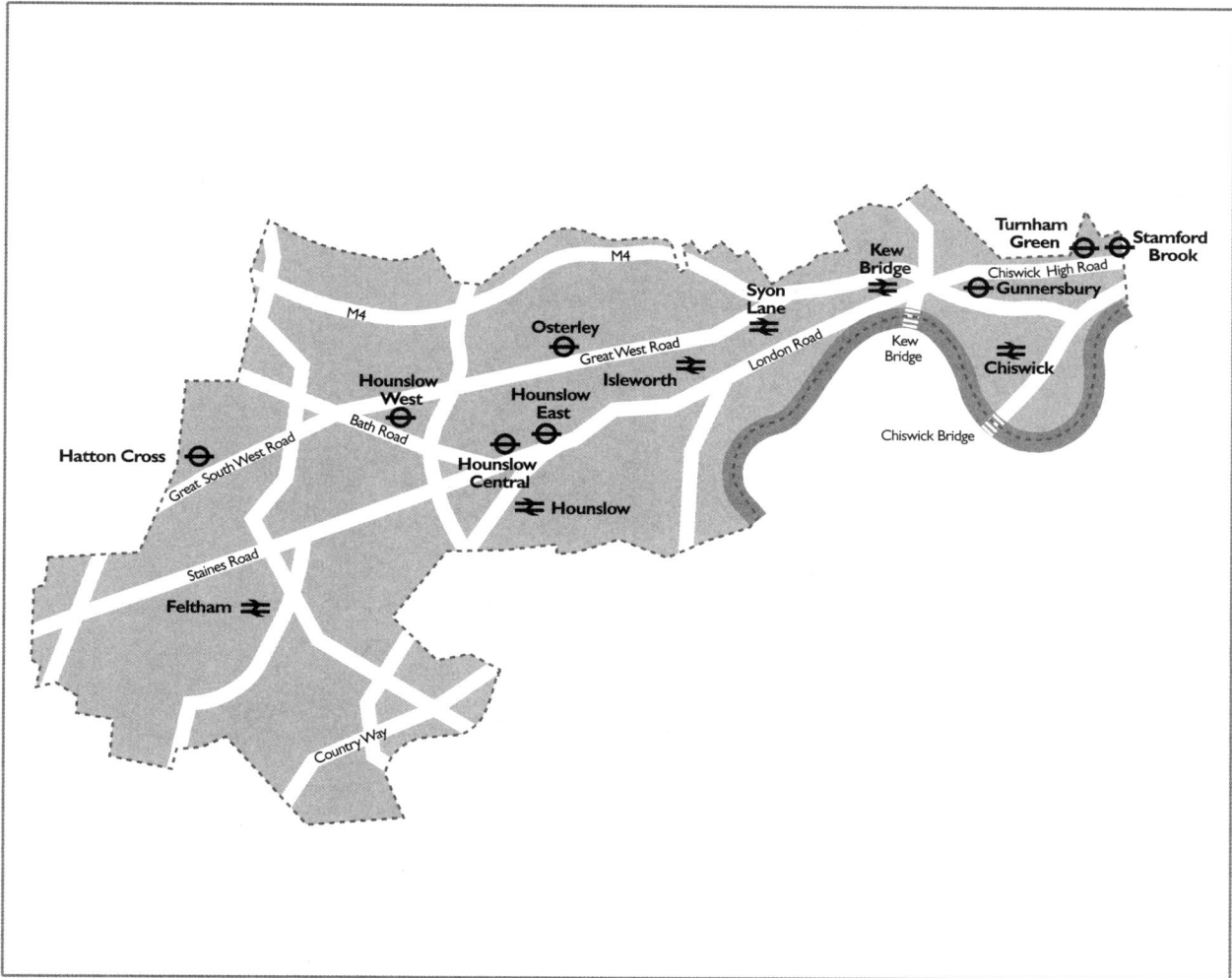

Libraries in the London Borough of Hounslow

- Arthur Sanderson and Sons Ltd, Archive
- British Standards Institution
- Brunel University Library
  Twickenham Campus Library
- Hounslow (London Borough of Hounslow)
- Hounslow Library Network (Community Initiative Partnerships)
  Beavers Library
  Bedfont Library
  Brentford Library
  Chiswick Library
  Cranford Library
  Feltham Library
  Hanworth Library
  Heston Library
  Hounslow Library
  Isleworth Library
  Osterley Library
- Kew Bridge Engines Trust and Water Supply Museum Ltd
- The Leprosy Mission
- Spelthorne Museum
- West Middlesex University Hospital NHS Trust
- West Thames College

Islington

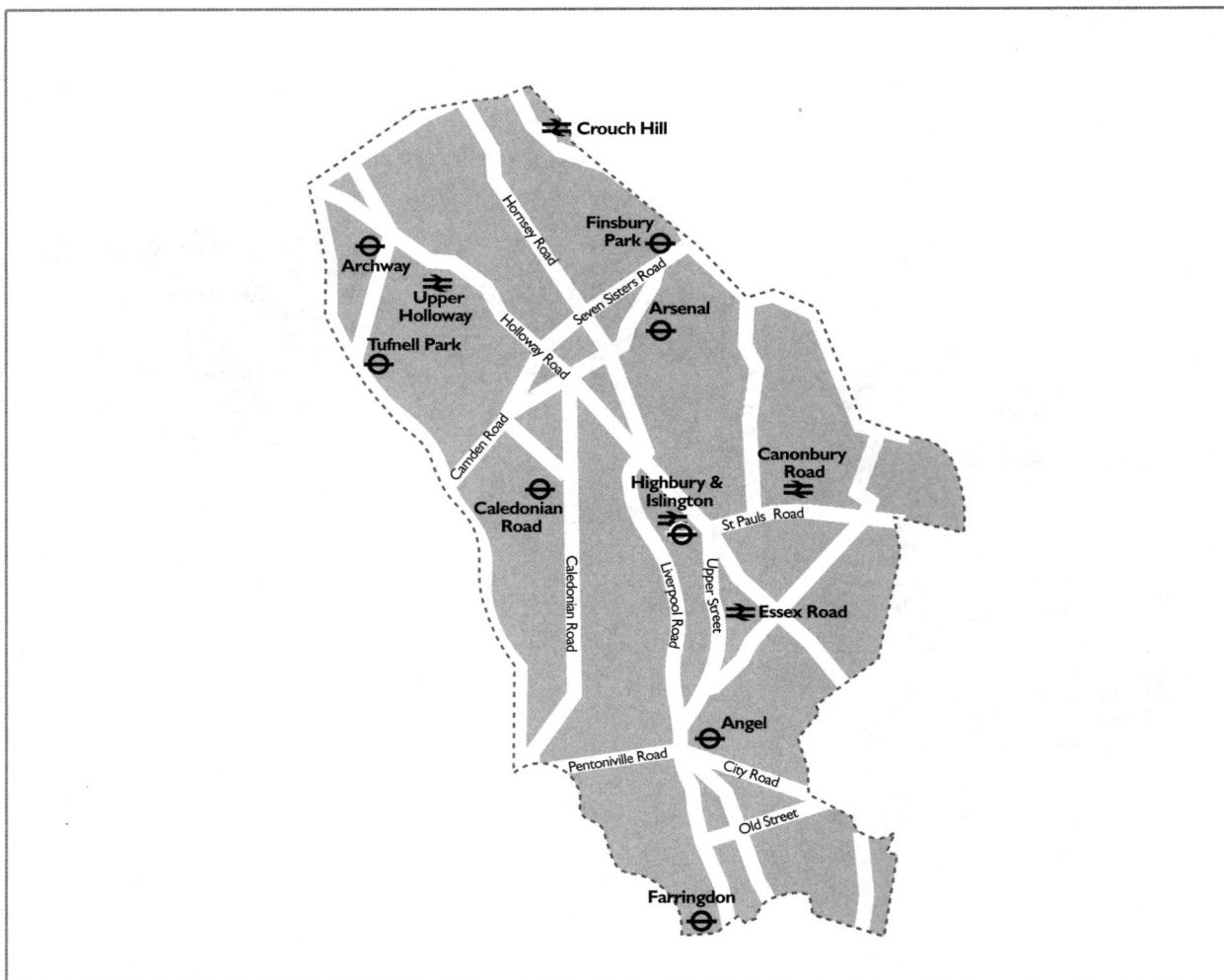

Libraries in the London Borough of Islington

- Active Birth Centre
- Akina Mama wa Afrika
- Archway Healthcare Library
- Association of Financial Controllers and Administrators
- British Water Ski Federation
- Campaign Against Arms Trade
- Centre for Accessible Environments
- Child Accident Prevention Trust
- The Children's Society
- City University
  University Library
- Crafts Council
  Photostore
  Reference Library
- DIALOG, Diversity in Action in Local Government
- Educational and Television Films Ltd
- Family Records Centre
- The Food Commission
- FPA (formerly Family Planning Association)
- Index on Censorship
- Institute of Biomedical Science Library
- Institute of Opthalmology and Moorfields Eye Hospital
- The Institute of Public Relations
- International Resource Centre/ International Centre for Eye Health

- Islington (London Borough of Islington)
  Archway Library
  Arthur Simpson Library
  Central Library
  Finsbury Reference Library
  John Barnes Library
  Lewis Carroll Children's Library
  Mildmay Library
  North Library
  South Library
  West Library
- Latin American Bureau
- London Metropolitan Archives
- London Metropolitan University
  North London Campus, Ladbroke House Library
  North London Campus, The Learning Centre
- London Voluntary Service Council
- Marx Memorial Library
- The Model Railway Club
- The National Autistic Society
- The National Centre for Volunteering Library
- National Childrens' Bureau
- National Eczema Society
- National Philatelic Society
- SCOPE for People with Cerebral Palsy (formerly The Spastics Society)

- Shelter: The National Campaign for Homeless People
- Society of Genealogists
- Trades Union Congress Library Collections
- Waste Watch
- Wolfson Institute of Preventive Medicine, St Bartholemew's and The Royal London School of Medicine and Dentistry

- Women and Manual Trades
- Women's Health
- Working Men's Club and Institute Union Ltd

Kensington and Chelsea

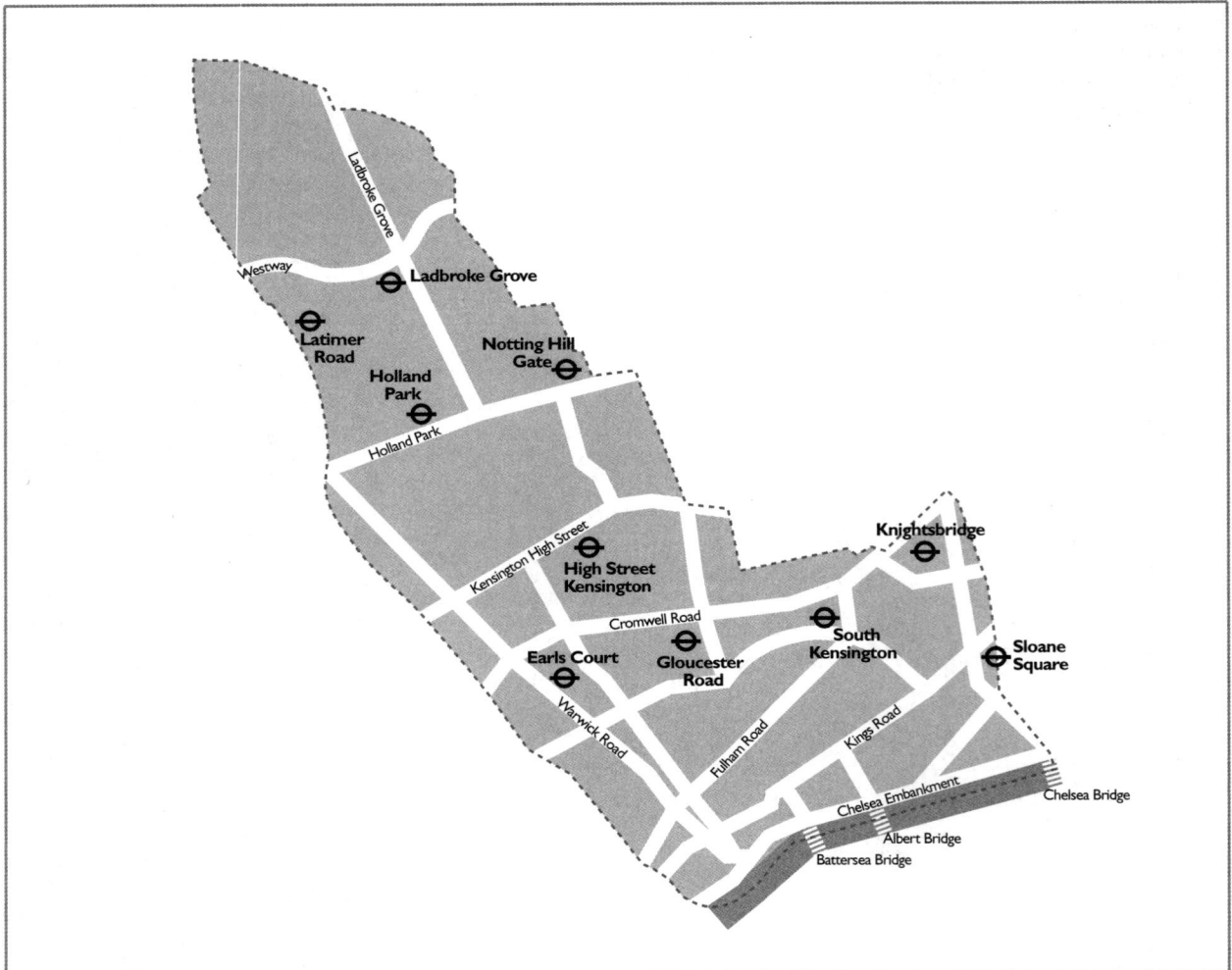

Libraries in the Royal Borough of Kensington and Chelsea

- Arab-British Centre
- British Geological Survey, London Information Office
- British Schools Exploration Society
- Chelsea College of Art and Design
  Manresa Road Library
- Chelsea Physic Garden
- Commonwealth Institute, Commonwealth Resource Centre
- Council for the Advancement of Arab-British Understanding
- Heythrop College Library
- Imperial College Library
  Aeronautics Department Library
  Chemical Engineering and Chemical Technology Department Library
  Chemistry Department Library
  Civil and Environmental Engineering Department Library
  Electrical and Electronic Engineering Department Library
  Imperial College and Science Museum Libraries
  Materials Department Library
  Mathematics Department Library
  Mechanical Engineering Department Library
  Physics Department Library

  Royal Brompton Campus
  St Mary's Campus
- India Welfare Society
- Institut Français du Royaume Uni
- Institute of Cancer Research
- The Japan Foundation London Language Centre
- Kensington and Chelsea (Royal Borough of Kensington and Chelsea)
- Kensington and Chelsea Libraries and Arts Services
  Brompton Library
  Central Library
  Chelsea Library
  Kensal Library
  North Kensington Library
  Notting Hill Library
- London Subterranean Survey
- National Army Museum
- National Art Library, Victoria and Albert Museum
  Museum Archives
- Natural History Museum
- Peter Warlock Society
- Polish Institute and Sikorski Museum
- Richmond: The American International University in London
  Library, Kensington Campus
- Royal College of Music Library

- Royal Entomological Society
- Royal Institute of Navigation
- The Society for Psychical Research
- Subterranea Britannica
- Union of Muslim Organisations of UK and Eire

- Voluntary Euthanasia Society
- World Nuclear Association (formerly the Uranium Institute)
- Xenophon

Kingston upon Thames

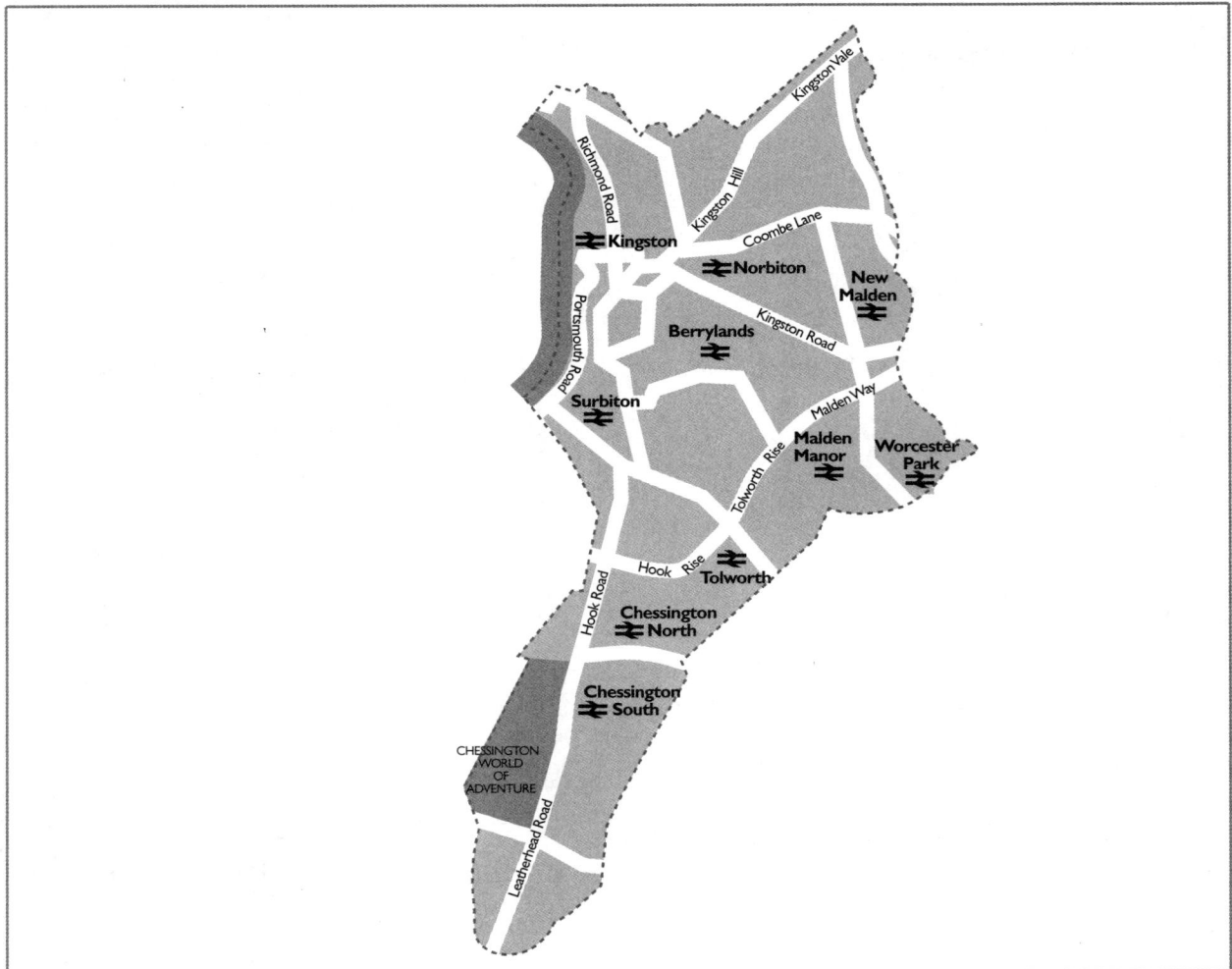

Libraries in the London Borough of Kingston upon Thames

- Kingston upon Thames (Royal Borough of Kingston upon Thames)
  Hook and Chessington Library
  Kingston Library (Adult Lending)
  Kingston Children's Library
  New Malden Library
  Old Malden Library
  Surbiton Library
  Tolworth Community Library and IT Learning Centre
  Tudor Drive Library
- Kingston Museum and Heritage Centre
- Kingston University
  Kingston Hill Library
  Knights Park Library
  Penrhyn Road Library
  Roehampton Vale Library
- Military Survey Library and Information Centre (LIC) Tolworth
  Book Library (Tolworth)
  Library and Information Centre
  Map Library

Lambeth

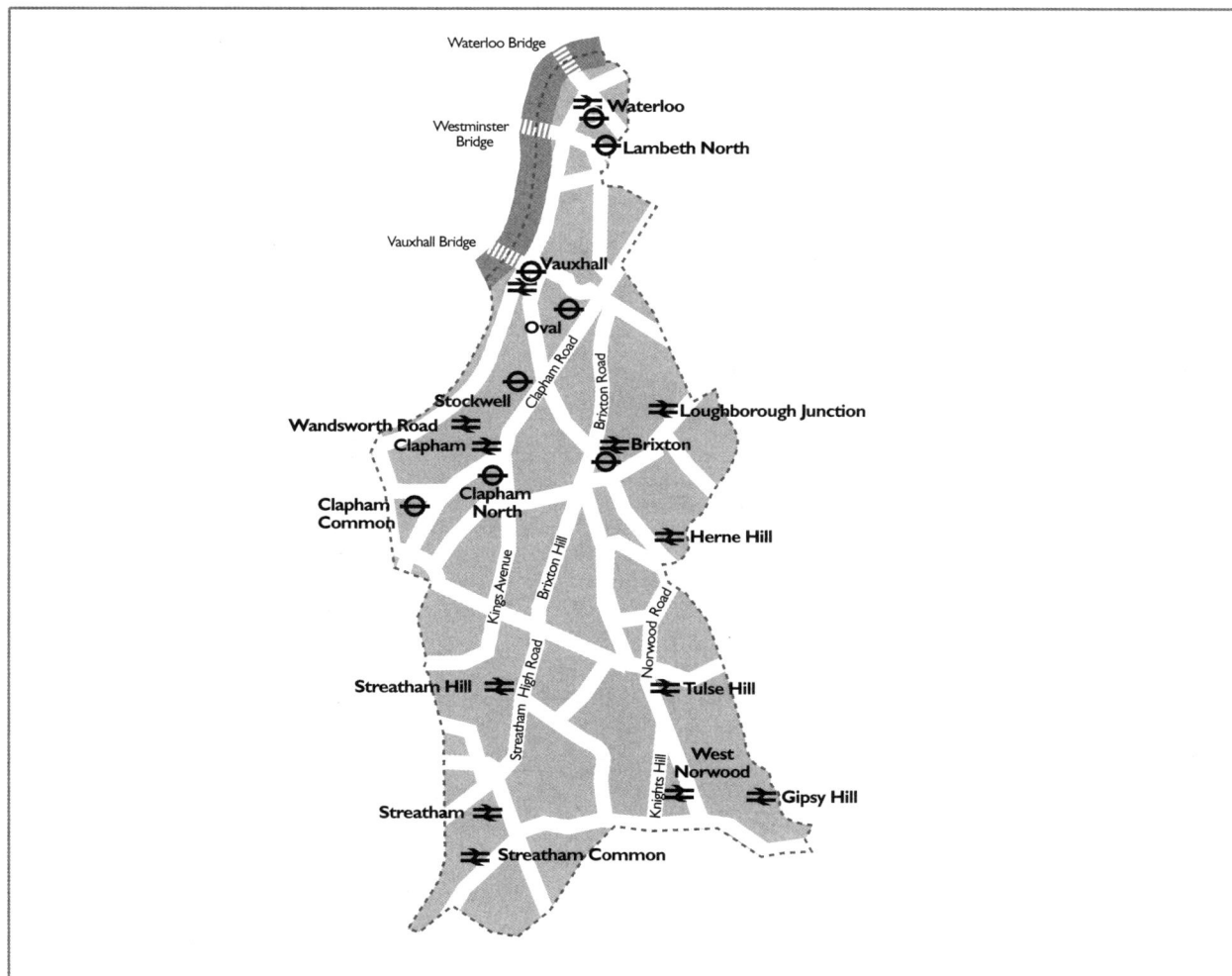

Libraries in the London Borough of Lambeth

- Anti-Slavery International
- The (British) Refugee Council
- The Calnan Library, St John's Institute of Dermatology
- Catholic Fund for Overseas Development
- Christian Aid Information Resources Centre
- Clarinet Heritage Society
- The Florence Nightingale Museum
- Forensic Science Service
- Greater London Association of Disabled People
- International Maritime Organisation
- King's College London
  St Thomas's Hospital Medical Library
- Kurdish Cultural Centre
- Lambeth (London Borough of Lambeth)
- Lambeth Environmental Services, Public Library and Archives Services
  Brixton Central Library
  Carnegie Library
  Clapham Library
  Durning Library
  Lambeth Archives and Library
  North Lambeth Library
  South Lambeth Library
  Streatham Library
  West Norwood Library
- Lambeth College
  Brixton Centre

  Clapham Centre
  Tower Bridge Centre
  Vauxhall Centre
- Lambeth Palace Library
- London Fire and Emergency Planning Authority
- London Weekend Television Information and Research Centre
- Manorial Society of Great Britain
- Overseas Development Institute
- The Poetry Library
- Press Association
  PA News Library
  PA Photos
- The Religious Drama Society of Great Britain
- Royal Pharmaceutical Society of Great Britain
- St Thomas' Hospital Medical School Library
- Save the Children
  Programmes Resource Centre
- Society for Co-operation in Russian and Soviet Studies
- South Bank University, Learning and Information Services
  Wandsworth Road Library
- South London Botanical Institute
- The United Society for the Propagation of the Gospel
- The Vintage Wireless Museum

Lewisham

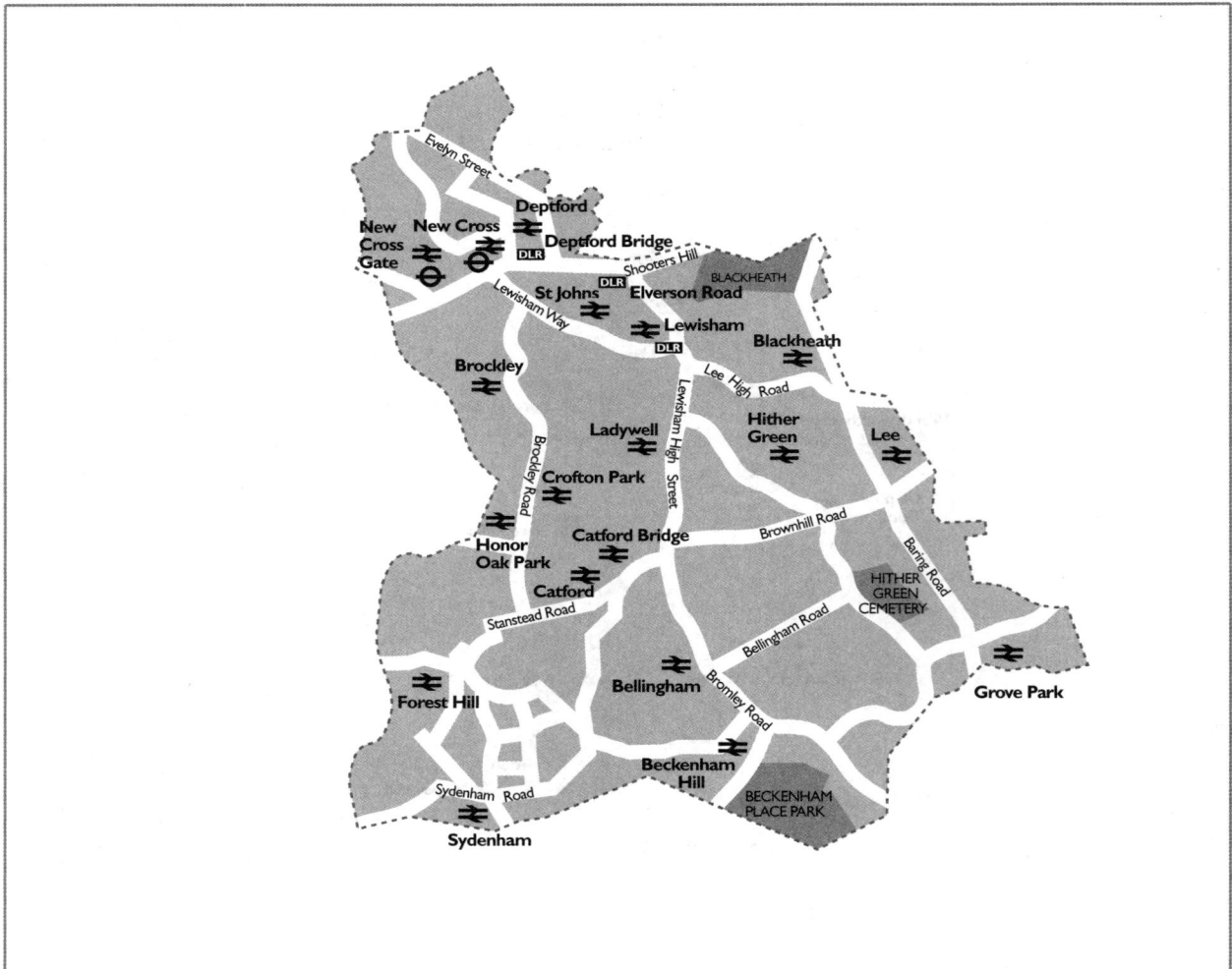

Libraries in the London Borough of Lewisham

- Elimination of Leukaemia Fund
- Goldsmiths College Library
- Guy's and St Thomas' NHS Trust, Medical Toxicology Unit
- The Horniman Library
- Laban Centre London
- Lewisham (London Borough of Lewisham)
- Library and Information Service
  Blackheath Village Library
  Catford Library
  Crofton Park Library
  Downham Library

Forest Hill Library
Grove Park Library
Lewisham Central Library
Lewisham Local Studies Centre
Manor House Library
New Cross Library
Sydenham Library
Torridon Road Library
Wavelengths Library
- The Raymond Mander and Joe Mitchenson Theatre Collection

Merton

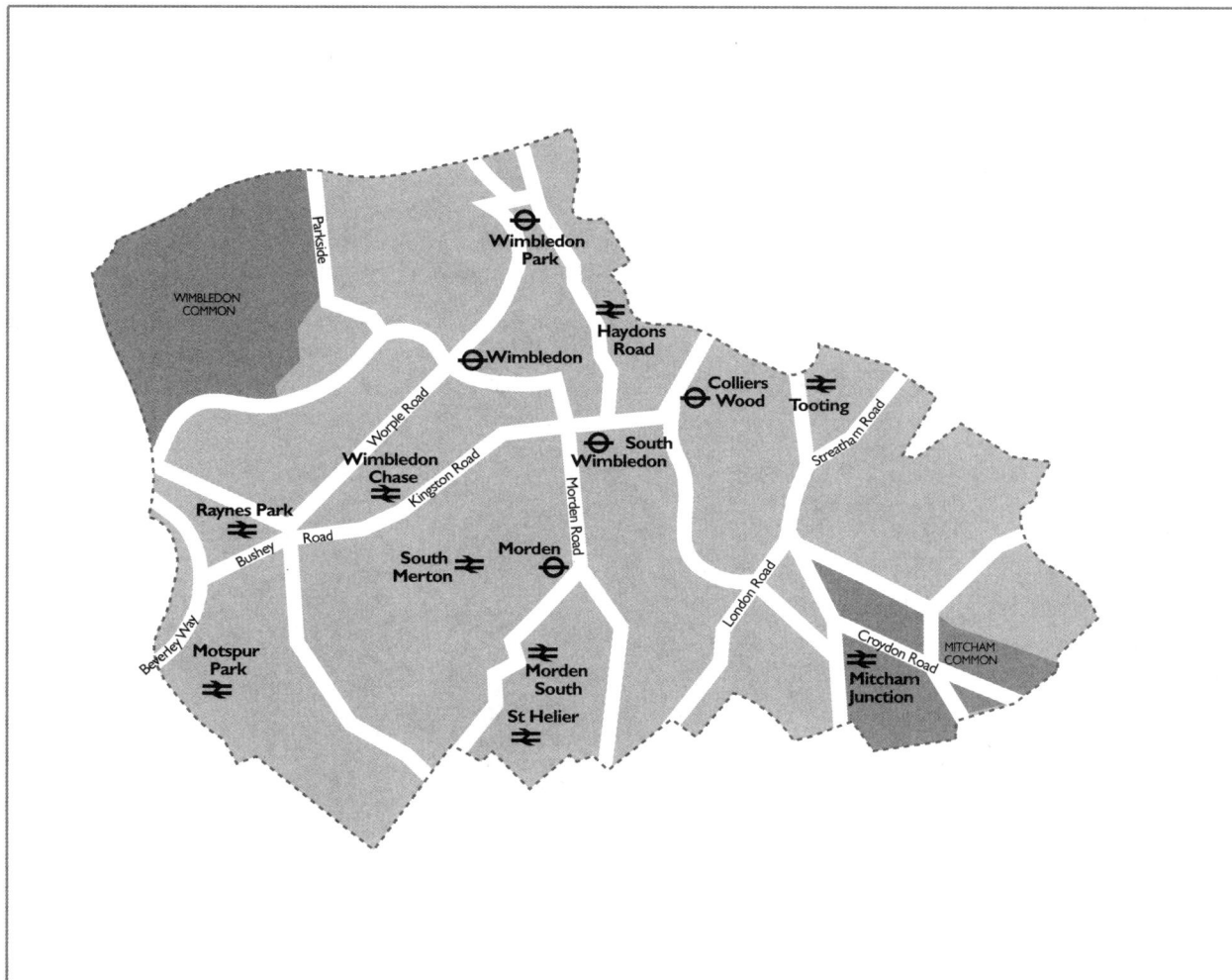

Libraries in the London Borough of Merton

- Action for Sick People
- Chartered Institute of Personnel and Development
- Communications Workers Union
- Kenneth Ritchie Wimbledon Library
- Merton (London Borough of Merton)
- Merton Libraries and Heritage Services
    Donald Hope Library
    Mitcham Library

    Morden Library
    Pollards Hill Library
    Raynes Park Library
    West Barnes Library
    Wimbledon Library
- Ski Club of Great Britain
- Wimbledon School of Art
- Wimbledon Society Museum of Local History

Newham

Libraries in the London Borough of Newham

- Newham (London Borough of Newham)
  - Beckton Library
  - Canning Town Library
  - Custom House Library
  - East Ham Library
  - Forest Gate Library
  - Green Street Library
  - Manor Park Library
  - North Woolwich Library
  - Plaistow Library
  - Stratford Library
- University of East London
  - Docklands Campus Learning Resource Centre
  - Duncan House Site Learning Resource Centre
  - Holbrook Learning Resource Centre
  - Maryland House Learning Resource Centre
- YMCA George Williams College

Redbridge

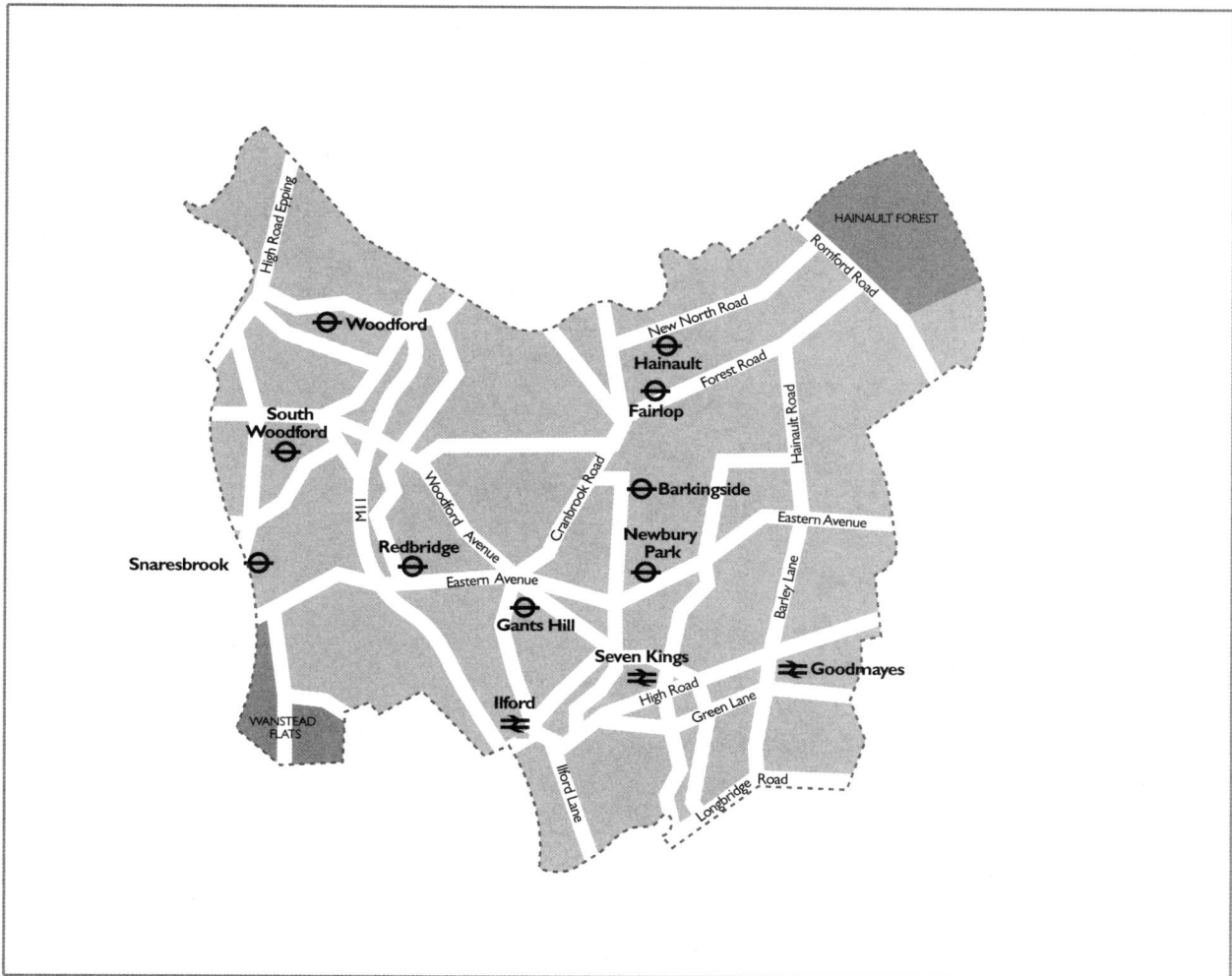

Libraries in the London Borough of Redbridge

- Barnado's
- League of British Muslims UK
- Redbridge (London Borough of Redbridge)
  - Aldersbrook Library
  - Central Library
  - Gants Hill Library
  - Goodmayes Library
  - Hainault Library
  - South Woodford Library
  - Wanstead Library
  - Woodford Green Library
- Saintpaulia and Houseplant Society

Richmond upon Thames

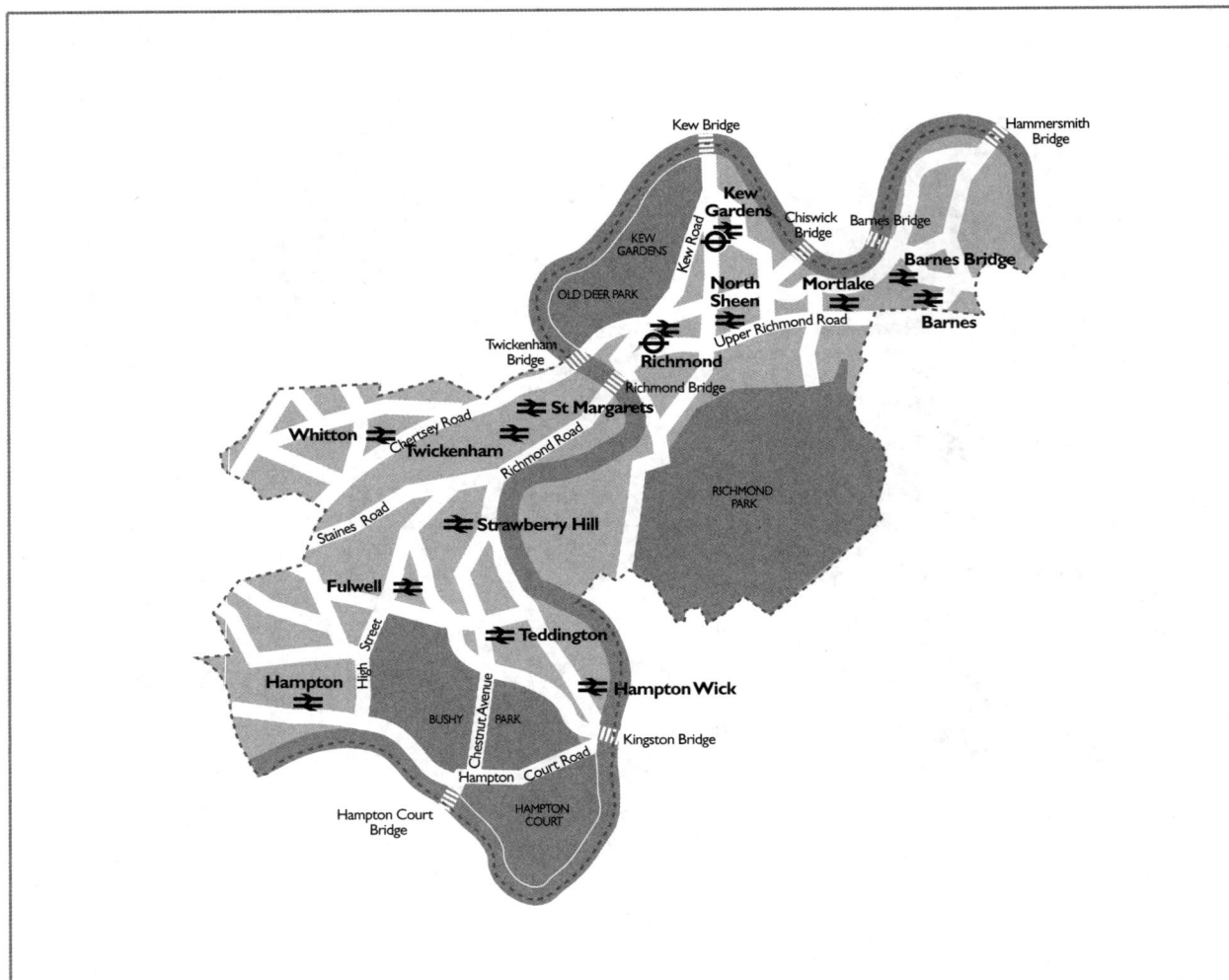

Libraries in the London Borough of Richmond upon Thames

- British Maritime Technology
- National Physical Laboratory
- Orleans House Gallery
- Paint Research Association
- Public Record Office/The National Archives (PRO)
    Public Record Office Resource Centre and Library
- Richmond Adult and Community College
- Richmond: The American International University in London
    Taylor Library, Richmond Campus
- Richmond upon Thames Libraries (London Borough of Richmond upon Thames)
    Castelnau Library (serving Barnes)
    East Sheen Library
    Ham Library
    Hampton Hill Library

- Hampton Library
- Hampton Wick Library
- Heathfield Library
- Kew Library
- Richmond Central Lending Library
- Richmond Central Reference Library
- Teddington Library
- Twickenham Library
- Whitton Library
- Royal Ballet School
    Lower School, Ballet Museum, Ballet Library and Archives
- Royal Botanic Gardens, Kew
- Royal Holloway, University of London
- St Mary's College
- St Paul's School

Southwark

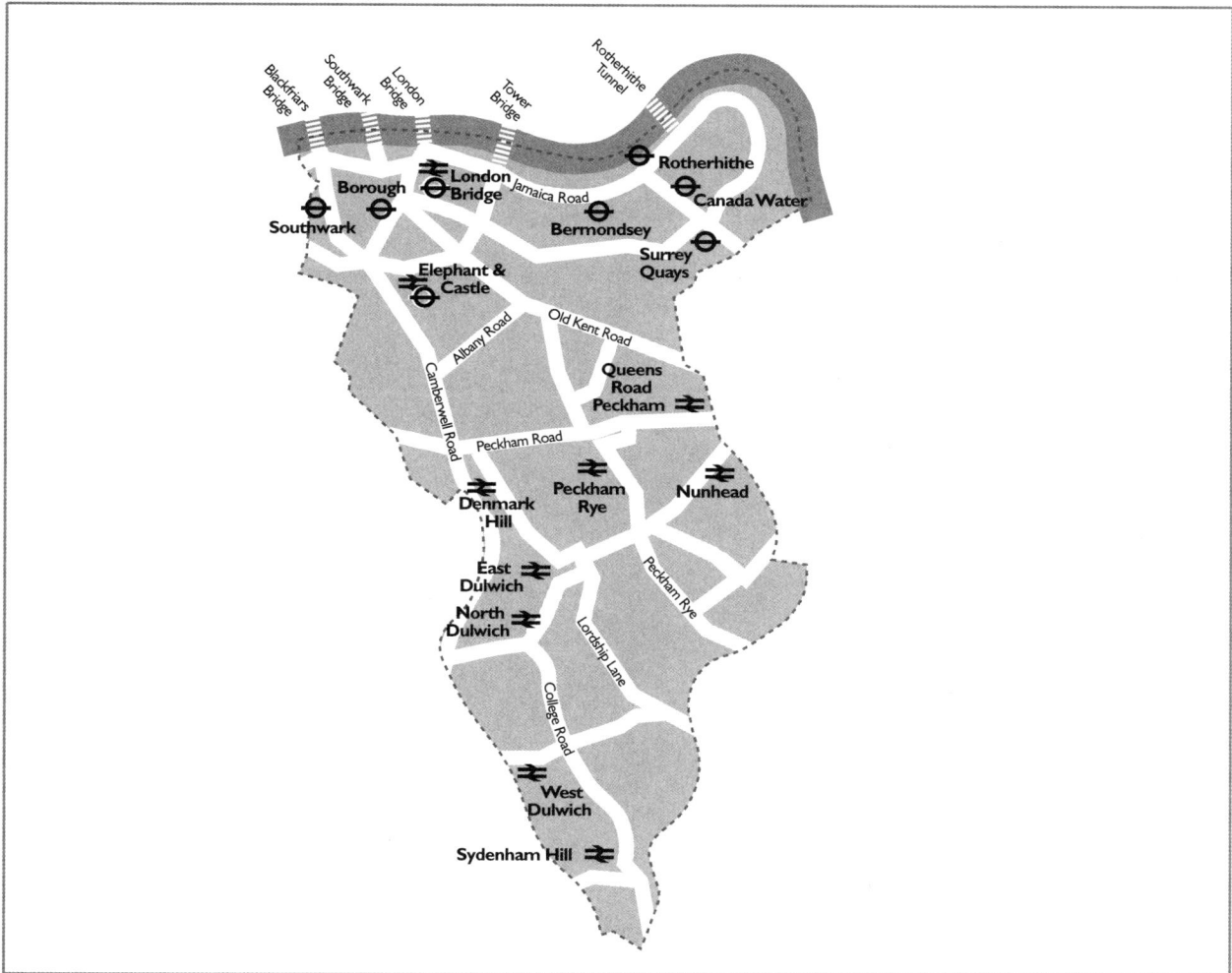

Libraries in the London Borough of Southwark

- Action for Blind People
- Advisory, Conciliation and Arbitration Service
- Al-Anon Family Groups UK & Eire
- Alcohol Concern
- British School of Osteopathy
- Bureau Veritas
- Camberwell College of Arts
- Chartered Society of Designers
- Church of England Record Centre
- College of Occupational Therapists Library
- Commission for Racial Equality
- Confraternity of St James, Stephen Badger Library of Pilgrimage
- Daycare Trust/National Childcare Campaign
- Department of Health
   Skipton House Library
- Drugscope (formerly Institute for the Study of Drug Dependence)
- Dulwich College, Wodehouse Library
- Feminist Library and Information Centre
- Fire Protection Association
- Fostering Network (formerly National Foster Care Association)
- Glass and Glazing Federation
- Greater London Authority
- Health and Safety Executive
- Highways Agency

- HM Customs and Excise Library, London
- Imperial War Museum
   Department of Art
   Department of Documents
   Department of Exhibits and Firearms
   Department of Printed Books
   Film and Video Archive
   Photographic Archive
   Sound Archive
- Institute of Psychiatry
- King's College London
   Information Services Centre
   Information Services Centre, Weston Education Centre
   Information Services Centre, New Hunts House
   FS Warner Library
- Lakeman Library for Electoral Studies
- Lambeth, Southwark and Lewisham Health Authority
- Liberty (National Council for Civil Liberties)
- Listening Books (formerly National Listening Library)
- London College of Printing Library
- London Cycling Campaign
- Medical Devices Library
- Partnership House Mission Studies Library
- Royal Watercolour Society/Royal Society of Painter-Printmakers

- The Salvation Army, Schools and Colleges
Department
- The Salvation Army, William Booth Memorial
College
- Save the Children
- Society of Chiropodists and Podiatrists
- Sonic Arts Network
- South Bank University, Learning and Information
Services
  Perry Library
- Southwark (London Borough of Southwark)
- Southwark Libraries and Information Service
  Blue Anchor Library
  Brandon Library

Camberwell Library
Dulwich Library and Reference Library
East Street Library
Education Resource Centre
Grove Vale Library
John Harvard Library
Kingswood Library
Local Studies Library
Newington Library and Reference Library
Nunhead Library
Peckham Library
Rotherhithe Library
- The Worshipful Company of Glaziers and Painters of
Glass

Sutton

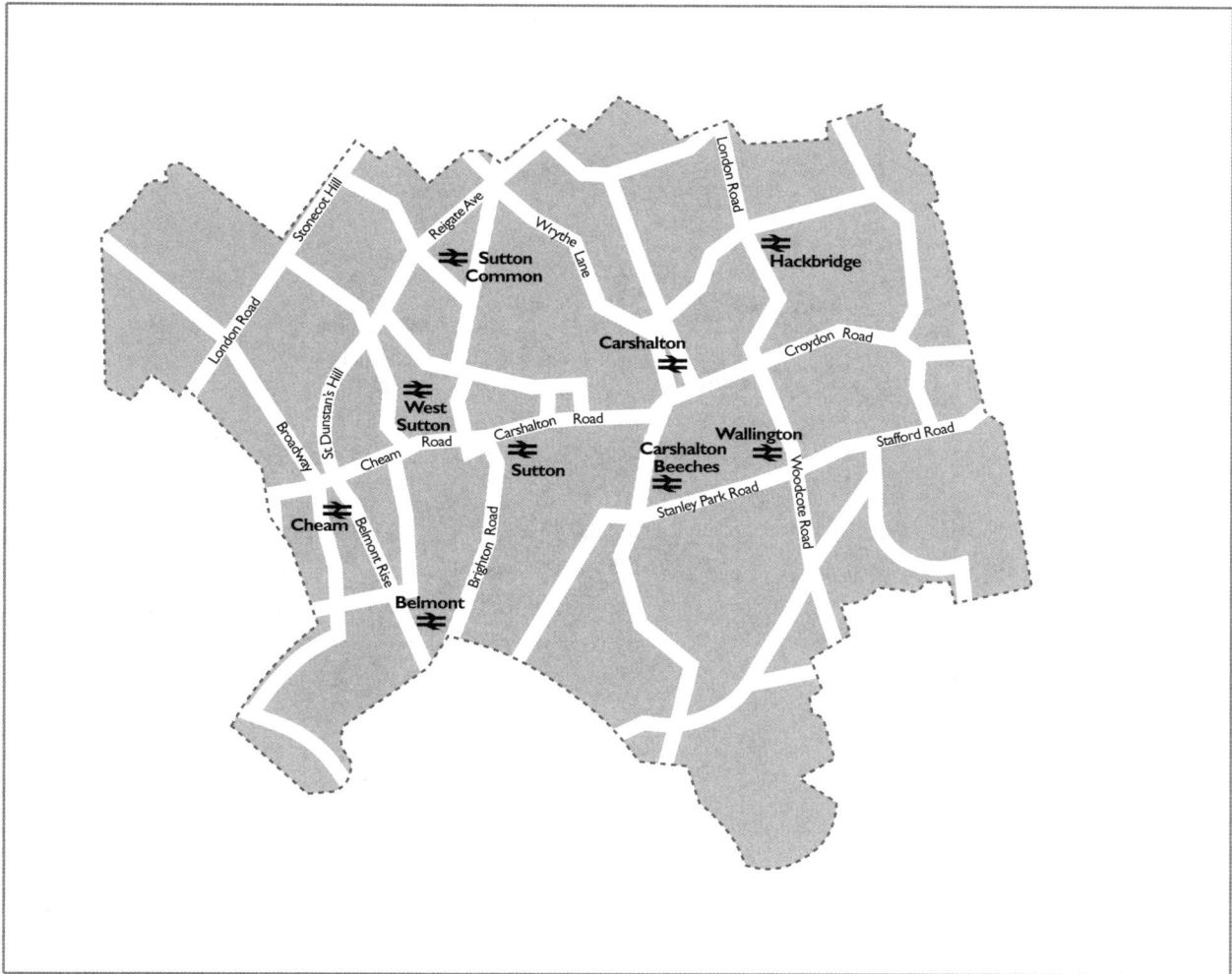

Libraries in the London Borough of Sutton

- Sutton Libraries (London Borough of Sutton)
  Beddington Library
  Carshalton Library
  Cheam Library
  Middleton Circle Library

  Ridge Road Library
  Roundshaw Library
  Sutton Central Library
  Wallington Library
  Worcester Park Library

Tower Hamlets

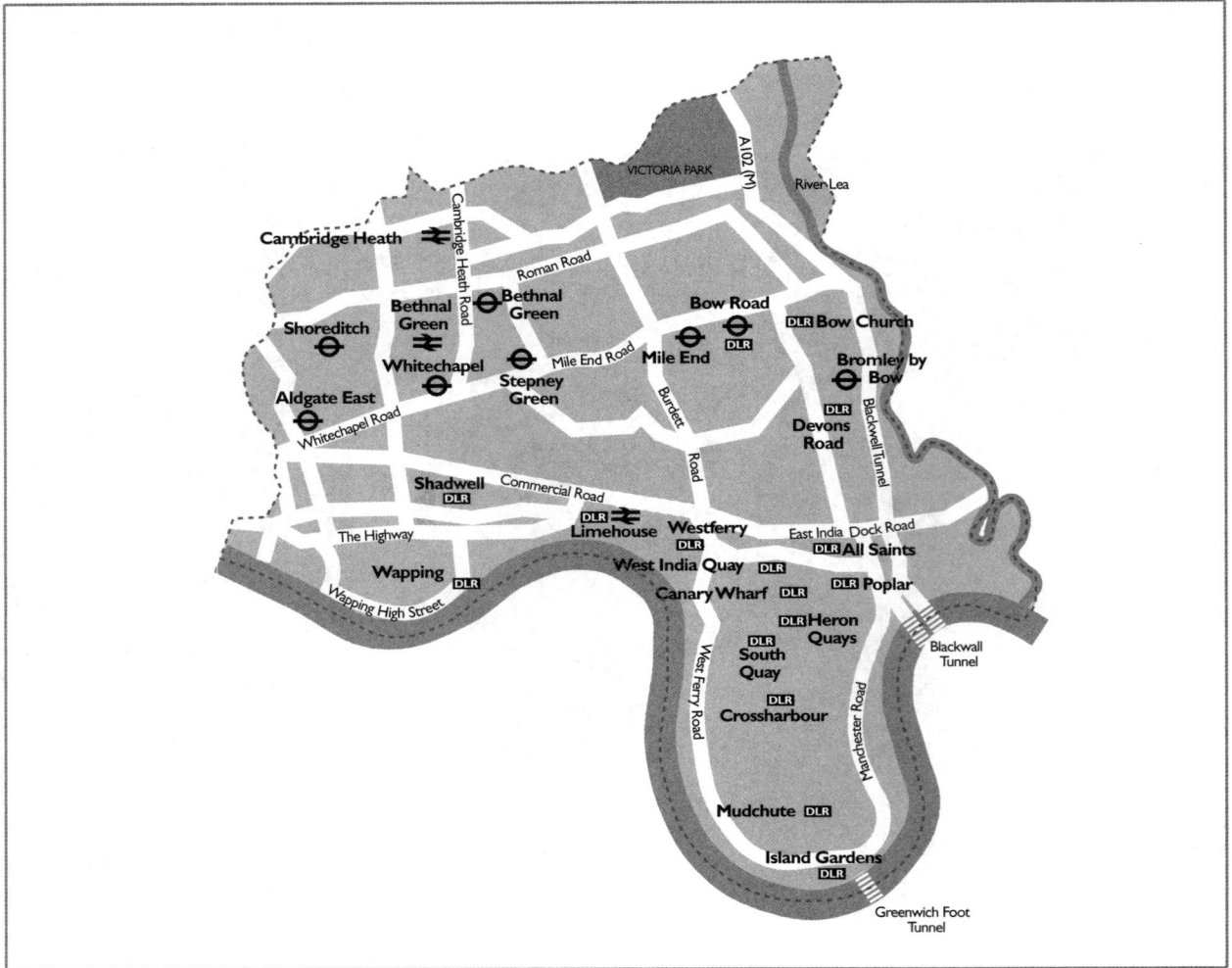

Libraries in the London Borough of Tower Hamlets

- British Records Association
- British Stammering Association
- Business Archives Council
- City University
    Whitechapel Library, City University
- The Corporation of Trinity House
- Docklands Library and Archive
- Export Credits Guarantee Department
- London Chest Hospital
- London Metropolitan University
    Calcutta House Library
    Commercial Road Integrated Learning Resource
    Centre
    The Women's Library (formerly the Fawcett
    Library)
- Primary and Community Health Information
  Services Library
- Queen Mary and Westfield College
- Radiocommunications Agency Library
- Royal Armouries Library
- The Royal London Hospital Archives and Museum
- Society for the Protection of Ancient Buildings
- Thames Police Museum
- Tower Hamlets (London Borough of Tower Hamlets)
- Tower Hamlets Libraries
    Bancroft Library
    Bethnal Green Library
    Cubitt Town Library
    Dorset Library
    Idea Store Bow
    Lansbury Library
    Limehouse Library
    Stepney Library
    Wapping Library
    Watney Market Library
    Whitechapel Library
- Whitechapel Art Gallery
- Whitechapel Library
- Women's Resource Centre

Waltham Forest

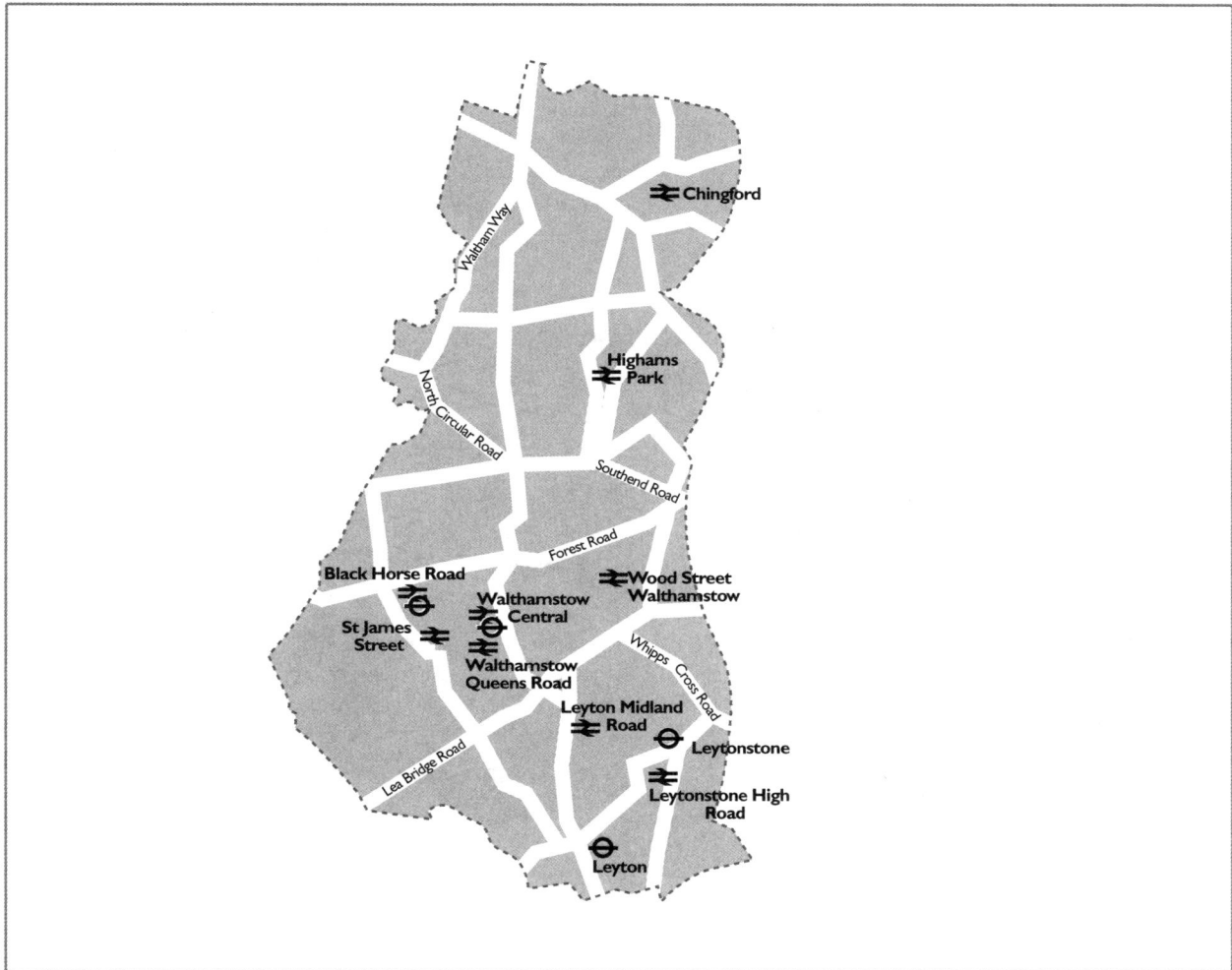

Libraries in the London Borough of Waltham Forest

- Christian Social Order
- Cinema Theatre Association
- Napoleonic Society of Great Britain
- Pugin Guild
- Queen Elizabeth's Hunting Lodge
- South Bank University, Learning and Information Services
  East London Campus Library
- The Turner Library, Whitefield Schools and Centre
- Waltham Forest (London Borough of Waltham Forest)
  Central Library
  Hale End Library
  Harrow Green Library

  Higham Hill Library
  Information and Reference Services
  Lea Bridge Library
  Leyton Library
  Leytonstone Library
  North Chingford Library
  St James Street Library
  South Chingford Library
  Vestry House Museum
  Wood Street Library
- Whipps Cross University Hospital Trust, Multidisciplinary Library
- William Morris Gallery

Wandsworth

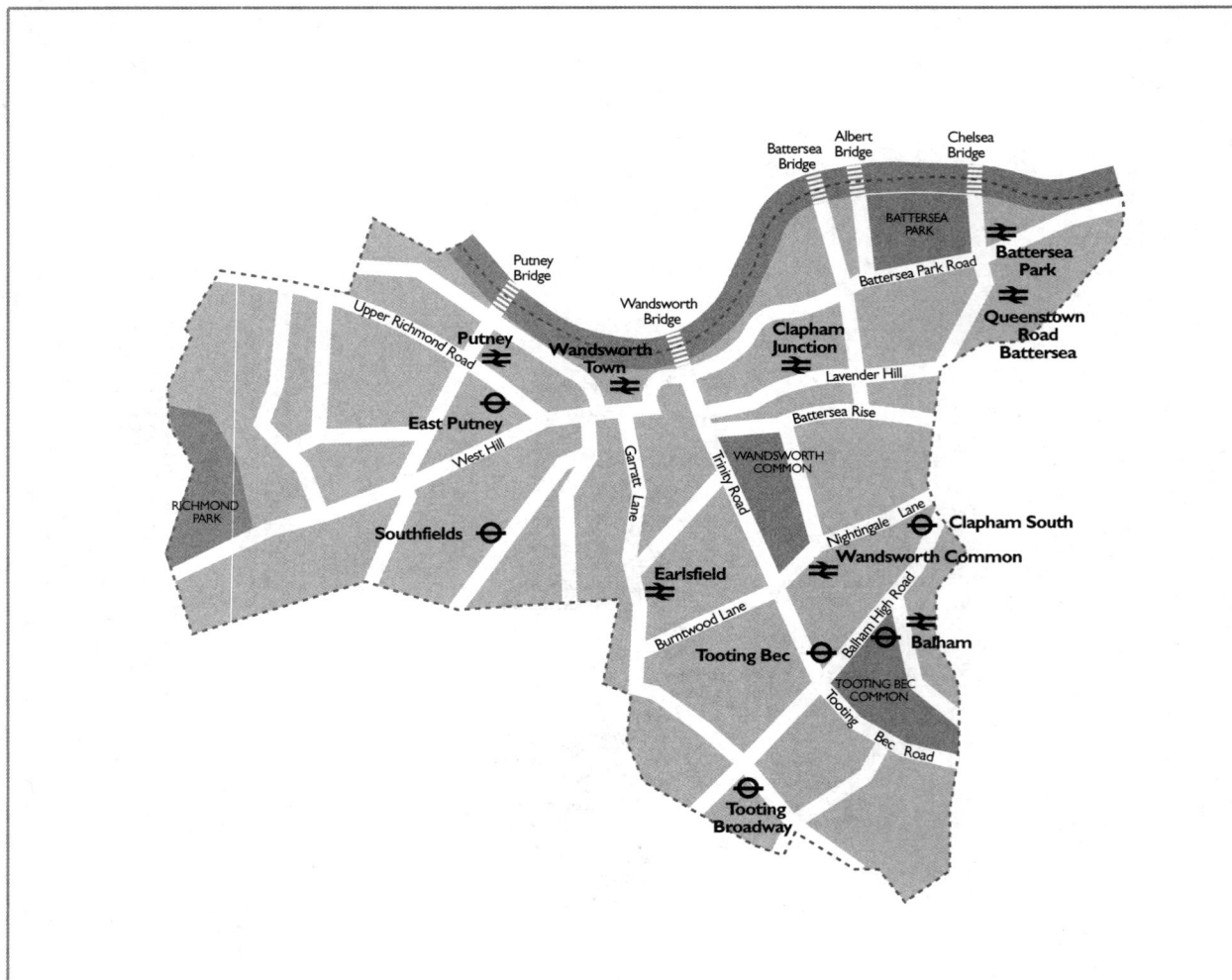

Libraries in the London Borough of Wandsworth

- The Benesh Institute
- Booktrust (formerly Young Book Trust)
- British Olympic Association
- Down's Syndrome Association
- The Institute for Optimum Nutrition
- The Puppet Centre Trust
- Queen Mary's Hospital Library
- Royal Academy of Dance Library
- St George's Hospital Medical School
- University of Surrey Roehampton
    Roehampton Lane Learning Resources Centre
    Whitelands Learning Resources Centre

- Wandsworth Libraries (London Borough of Wandsworth)
    Alvering Library
    Balham Library
    Battersea Lending Library
    Battersea Park Library
    Battersea Reference Library
    Earlsfield Library
    Northcote Library
    Putney Library
    Roehampton Library
    Southfields Library
    Tooting Library
    West Hill Library
    York Gardens Library and Community Centre

Westminster

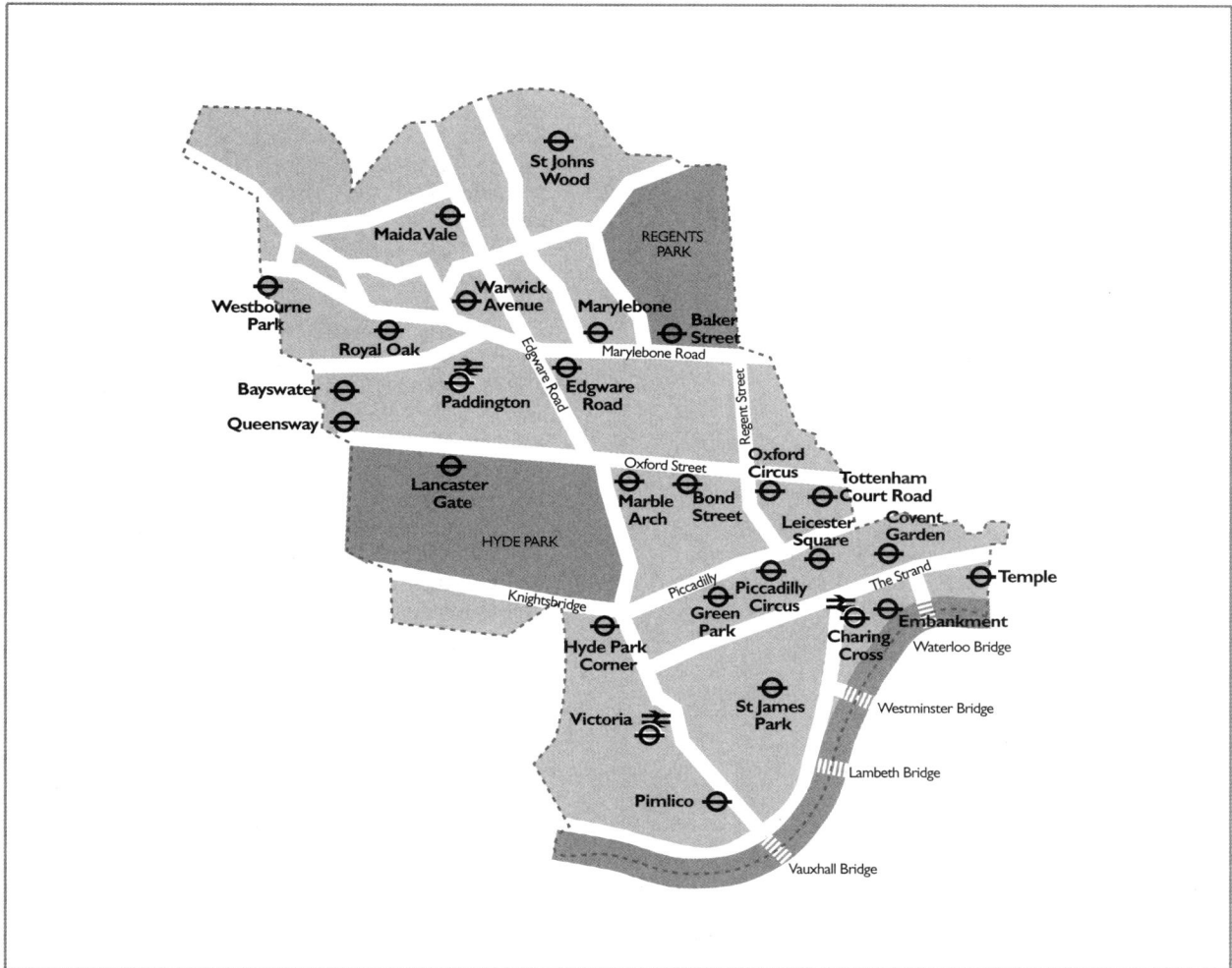

Libraries in the London Borough of Westminster

- Advertising Association Information Centre
- Africa Centre
- Alzheimer's Society, Ann Brown Memorial Library
- American Embassy, The Information Resource Center
- Arts Council of England Library and Enquiry Service
- Aslib, The Association for Information Management
- Association of the British Pharmaceutical Industry
- Astrological Lodge of London
- The Athenaeum
- Australia and New Zealand Chamber of Commerce UK
- BMI Health Services
- The Bridgeman Art Library
- British Association for the Advancement of Science
- British Clothing Industry Association
- British Council Education Information Service
- British Dental Association Information Centre
- British Energy Association
- British Homeopathic Association
- British Institute of Radiology
- The British Knitting and Clothing Export Council
- British Library of Political and Economic Science
- British Music Information Centre
- British National Space Centre Library

- British Psychoanalytical Society
- British Red Cross
- British Retail Consortium
- British Universities Film and Video Council
- British Wind Energy Association
- Building Societies Association
- Central Saint Martins College of Art and Design Charing Cross Road Library
- Centre for Information on Language Teaching and Research, Resources Library
- Centre of Construction Law and Management
- Charles Williams Society Reference Library
- Chartered Institute of Management Accountants
- Chartered Institute of Public Finance and Accountancy
- The Civic Trust
- College of Optometrists
- Commission for Local Administration in England (Local Government Ombudsmen)
- Committee on Standards in Public Life
- Commonwealth Secretariat
- Competition Commission
- Confederation of British Industry
- Conservative and Unionist Central Office
- Consumers in Europe Group
- Council for Science and Technology

- Council for the Care of Churches
- Courtauld Institute of Art
- CPRE (Council for the Protection of Rural England)
- The Cricket Society
- The Dairy Council
- Daiwa Anglo-Japanese Foundation, Library and Information Centre
- Department for Culture, Media and Sport
- Department for Education and Skills
- Department for Environment, Food and Rural Affairs
  Whitehall Place Library
  Nobel House Library
- Department for International Development
- Department for Work and Pensions Information Services
- Diabetes UK
- Duchy of Cornwall Library and Archives
- Ecclesiological Society
- Electricity Association, Business Information Centre
- Employment Appeal Tribunal Library
- Engineering Employers' Federation
- English-Speaking Union of the Commonwealth
- European Commission Representation in the UK
- European Documentation Centre
- The Evangelical Society
- Foreign and Commonwealth Office
  Foreign and Commonwealth Office Library
  Legal Library
  United Nations Information Resources
- Garrick Club
- General Optical Council
- The Geological Society of London
- German-British Chamber of Commerce
- Goethe-Institut Library
- Great Britain-China Centre
- The Guide Association
- Harry Simpson Memorial Library
- Health Development Agency
- Hispanic and Luso-Brazilian Council
- HM Treasury and Cabinet Office Library and Information Service
  Treasury Public Enquiry Unit
- Home Office Commission for Racial Equality
- Home Office Information Services Group
  Main Library
  Prison Service Headquarters Library
- The Honourable Company of Master Mariners
- House of Commons
  House of Commons Library
- House of Lords Library
- Imperial College Library
- Independent Housing Ombudsman
- Independent Schools Council Information Service
- Independent Television Commission
- The Industrial Society
- Information Network Focus on Religious Movements
- Inland Revenue Library
- Institute and Guild of Brewing
- Institute of Alcohol Studies
- Institute of Chartered Secretaries and Administrators
- Institute of Directors
- Institute of Logistics and Transport
- Institute of Materials
- Institute of Petroleum

- Institute of Psycho-Analysis
- Institution of Civil Engineers
- Institution of Contemporary History and Wiener Library
- Institution of Electrical Engineers
- Institution of Gas Engineers
- Institution of Mining and Metallurgy
- Institution of Structural Engineers
- Instituto Cervantes
- International Coffee Organization
- International Institute for Strategic Studies
- International Labour Office
- International Planned Parenthood Federation
- Invest UK
- Italian Cultural Institute
- Japan Information and Cultural Centre
- JETRO
- Jones Lang LaSalle
- The Kennel Club Library
- King's Fund Library
- The Labour Party
- Law Society Library
- The Linacre Centre for Health Care Ethics
- Local Government Association
- Local Government International Bureau
- London Business School
  LBS Information Service
- London Central Mosque Trust and The Islamic Cultural Centre
- London College of Fashion Library
- The London Library
- Lord Chancellor's Department
- Marylebone Cricket Club Library
- The Medical Council on Alcohol
- The Middle East Association
- Ministry of Defence, Headquarters Library Services
- National Audit Office
- National Dairy Council
- National Institute of Economic and Social Research
- National Monuments Record
- National Portrait Gallery, Heinz Archive and Library
- The National Society's Religious Education Centre
- National Sports Medicine Institute
- National Statistics Reference Library
- Nigeria High Commission Library
- Northern Ireland Office
- The Novartis Foundation (formerly The Ciba Foundation)
- Office of the Deputy Prime Minister and Department for Transport
  Ashdown House (Victoria) Library and Information Centre
  Eland House Library and Information Centre
  Great Minster Library and Information Centre
- Office of Gas and Electricity Markets
- Office of Health Economics
- Parkinson's Disease Society of the United Kingdom
- Polish Cultural Institute
- Portuguese Chamber, The Portuguese UK Business Network
- Prime Minister's Office Library
- Radio Authority
- The Railway Club
- RDS (formerly Research Defence Society)
- Regent's College Library
- Royal Academy of Arts

- Royal Academy of Music Library
- Royal Aeronautical Society
- Royal Asiatic Society
- Royal Automobile Club
- Royal College of Art Library
- Royal College of Defence Studies
- Royal College of General Practitioners, Information Services Section
- Royal College of Midwives Library
- Royal College of Nursing Library and Information Services
- Royal College of Obstetricians and Gynaecologists
- Royal College of Psychiatrists Information Service
- Royal College of Veterinary Surgeons
- Royal Geographical Society (with The Institute of British Geographers)
- Royal Horticultural Society
- Royal Institute of British Architects, British Architectural Library
- Royal Institute of International Affairs
- Royal Institution of Chartered Surveyors
- Royal Institution of Great Britain Library
- Royal Opera House Archives
- Royal Society
- The Royal Society for Asian Affairs (formerly Royal Central Asian Society)
- The Royal Society for the Promotion of Health
- Royal Society of Chemistry Library and Information Centre
- Royal Society of Medicine
- Royal United Services Institute for Defence Studies
- RSA (Royal Society for the Encouragement of Arts, Manufactures and Commerce)
- Science Photo Library
- Society of Antiquaries of London
- The Society of Operations Engineers

- South Africa House Reference Library
- Spanish Chamber of Commerce in Great Britain
- Supreme Court Library
- Swedish Chamber of Commerce
- Tate Library and Archive
- Theatre Museum
- Theatres Trust
- The Theosophical Society in England
- Trade Partners UK Information Centre (formerly Export Market Information Centre) World Aid Section
- Treasury and Cabinet Office
- Treasury Solicitor's Library Information Centre
- United Lodge of Theosophists
- United Nations Association – UK
- United Nations Information Centre
- University of Westminster
  Cavendish Campus Library
  Marylebone Road Library
  Regent Campus Library
- The Wallace Collection Library
- Westminster (City of Westminster)
- Dept of Education, Library Services
  Charing Cross Library
  Church Street Library
  Maida Vale Library
  Marylebone Library
  Mayfair Library
  Paddington Library
  Pimlico Library
  Queen's Park Library
  St John's Wood Library
  Victoria Library
  Westminster City Archives
  Westminster Reference Library
- Westminster Abbey Library and Muniment Room

ORGANISATION INDEX

SUBJECT INDEX

Notes to the Index:

1. The numbers given in the index refer to entry numbers and **not** to page numbers;

2. Index entries are **not** made for the holdings of the large, multidisciplinary general and national libraries, except for those collections in which there is a clear specialisation. Otherwise, the collections in these libraries are assumed to cover all subject fields;

3. It should be noted that most libraries and information units listed in this guide are highly specialised. Accordingly, when entries are indexed under a broad subject heading such as 'economics', 'management', 'statistics', etc., account must be taken of the nature of the organisation, as this will invariably indicate the specialised context of the holdings of that organisation (e.g. where an agricultural research institute is indexed under 'economics' it should be assumed that the holdings are primarily concerned with agricultural economics).

M

N

UNDERGROUND

Reg. user No. 04/E/1369

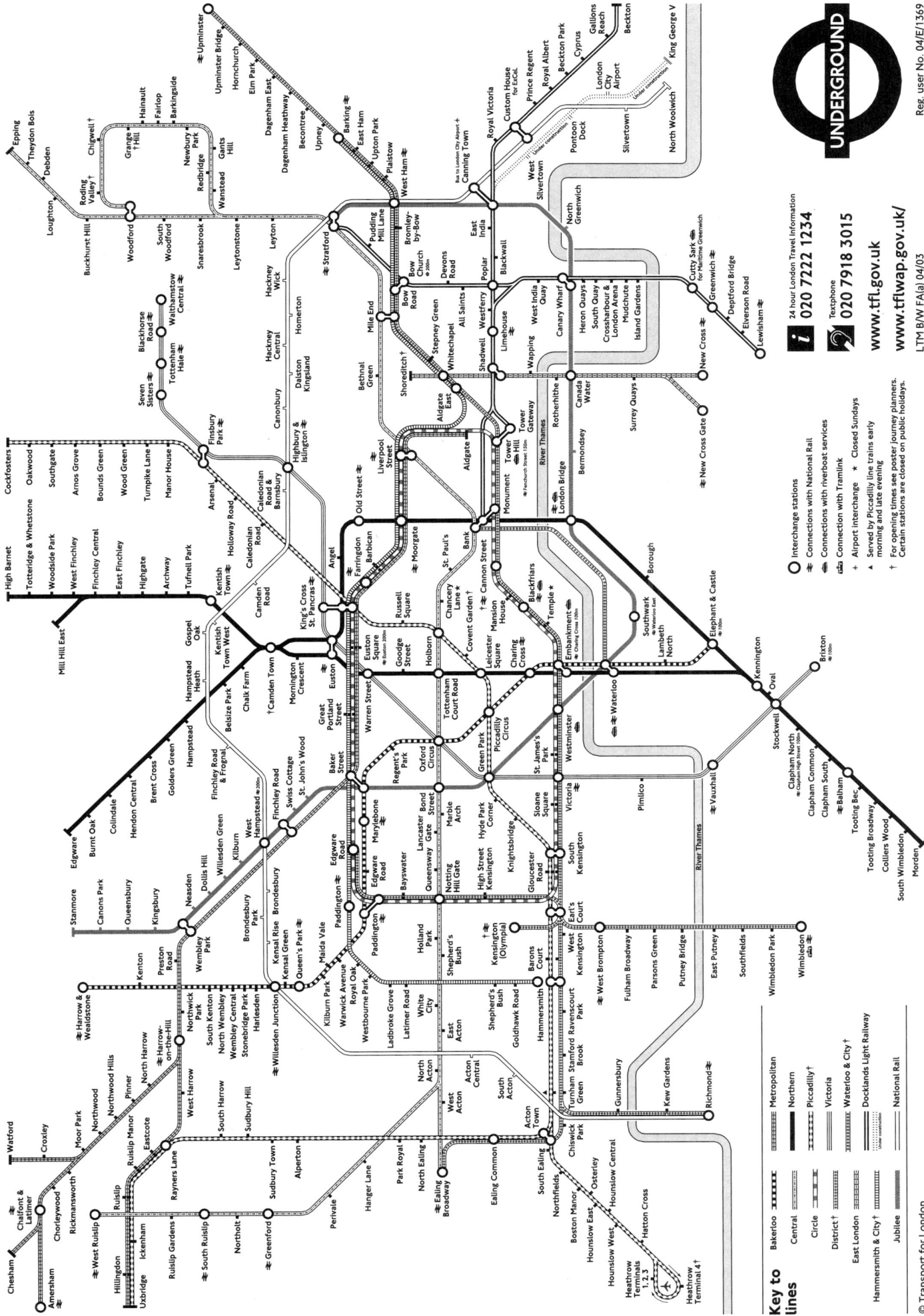

i 24 hour London Travel Information
020 7222 1234

Textphone
020 7918 3015

www.tfl.gov.uk
www.tflwap.gov.uk/

LTM B/W FA(a) 04/03

○ Interchange stations
⇌ Connections with National Rail
⇌ Connections with riverboat services
⇌ Connection with Tramlink

† Served by Piccadilly line trains early
morning and late evening
★ Closed Sundays
▲ Airport interchange

† For opening times see poster journey planners.
Certain stations are closed on public holidays.

Key to lines

- Bakerloo
- Central
- Circle
- District †
- East London
- Hammersmith & City †
- Metropolitan
- Northern
- Piccadilly †
- Victoria
- Waterloo & City †
- Docklands Light Railway
- Jubilee
- Under construction
- National Rail

© Transport for London